Level 3

4th Edition

BTEC NATIONAL SPORT AND EXERCISE SCIENCE

Jennifer Stafford-Brown,
Simon Rea and Tim Eldridge

In order to ensure that this resource offers high-quality support for the associated Pearson qualification, it has been through a review process by the awarding body. This process confirms that this resource fully covers the teaching and learning content of the specification or part of a specification at which it is aimed. It also confirms that it demonstrates an appropriate balance between the development of subject skills, knowledge and understanding, in addition to preparation for assessment.

Endorsement does not cover any guidance on assessment activities or processes (e.g. practice questions or advice on how to answer assessment questions), included in the resource nor does it prescribe any particular approach to the teaching or delivery of a related course.

While the publishers have made every attempt to ensure that advice on the qualification and its assessment is accurate, the official specification and associated assessment guidance materials are the only authoritative source of information and should always be referred to for definitive guidance.

Pearson examiners have not contributed to any sections in this resource relevant to examination papers for which they have responsibility. Examiners will not use endorsed resources as a source of material for any assessment set by Pearson.

Endorsement of a resource does not mean that the resource is required to achieve this Pearson qualification, nor does it mean that it is the only suitable material available to support the qualification, and any resource lists produced by the awarding body shall include this and other appropriate resources.

Although every effort has been made to ensure that website addresses are correct at time of going to press, Hodder Education cannot be held responsible for the content of any website mentioned in this book. It is sometimes possible to find a relocated web page by typing in the address of the home page for a website in the URL window of your browser.

Hachette UK's policy is to use papers that are natural, renewable and recyclable products and made from wood grown in sustainable forests. The logging and manufacturing processes are expected to conform to the environmental regulations of the country of origin.

Orders: please contact Bookpoint Ltd, 130 Park Drive, Milton Park, Abingdon, Oxon OX14 4SE. Telephone: (44) 01235 827720. Fax: (44) 01235 400454. Email education@bookpoint.co.uk Lines are open from 9 a.m. to 5 p.m., Monday to Saturday, with a 24-hour message answering service. You can also order through our website: www.hoddereducation.co.uk

ISBN: 978 1 4718 7863 3

© Jennifer Stafford-Brown, Simon Rea and Tim Eldridge 2016

First published in 2016 by
Hodder Education,
An Hachette UK Company
Carmelite House

50 Victoria Embankment
London EC4Y 0DZ

www.hoddereducation.co.uk

Impression number   10 9 8 7 6 5 4 3 2 1

Year   2020 2019 2018 2017 2016

Cover photo © ostill/123RF.COM

Illustrations by Integra Software Services Pvt. Ltd

Typeset in Integra Software Services Pvt. Ltd., Pondicherry, India

Printed in Slovenia

A catalogue record for this title is available from the British Library.

Contents

Units available online at http://www.hoddereducation.co.uk/BTECSportLevel3

Acknowledgements and photo credits

Jennifer Stafford-Brown

I would like to thank a number of people who have provided me with help in various different ways in researching and writing this book.

First of all, my thanks go out to my husband Matt and children Ellie and Alex for their patience and encouragement throughout the writing process, and to my parents, Ann and Brian, for all of their continued support and help over the years.

I would also like to say a big 'thank you!' to my friend and co-author, Simon, for all of his hard work, expertise and enthusiasm.

I would also like to thank Tim Eldridge for joining the writing team and all his hard work with his contribution to the book.

Finally, I would also like to thank all of the people at Hodder Education who have helped with the publication of this book.

Simon Rea

I would like to thank Stephen Halder for making this book possible and Ana Arêde and Chloé Harmsworth for their editing work.

A huge thank you to my co-authors, Jenny and Tim, who worked exceptionally hard in a short space of time to produce a quality resource for students.

Above all to my wife, Tarya, and our beautiful boys for the love and happiness that they bring this sometimes difficult writer.

Tim Eldridge

Many thanks to all those who have made this book possible.

Most important of all, I would like to thank my parents, Reg and Jackie, for all their kind support and encouragement over the years, and throughout the writing of this book. I owe you everything and words could never describe my gratitude.

I would also like to thank David Waite for the support he has given me throughout my professional career. As a former colleague and trusted friend, your hard work and patience has been gratefully appreciated.

Finally, I would like to thank both my co-authors, Jenny and Simon, who have given me the opportunity to work on the publication of this book. It's been a very long journey, a lot of hard work but we finally got there.

Photo credits

Please see page 400.

Walkthrough

This book contains all the units you need to master the skills and knowledge for the new BTEC National for Sport and Exercise Science.

Key features of the book

About this unit

About this unit: an introduction to the unit briefly explaining the topic, its importance and what will be covered in the unit. Including the learning aims and the ways in which you'll be assessed.

How will I be graded?

How will I be graded: Feature showing the criteria that you need to achieve a Pass, Merit, Distinction.

Key terms

Key terms: To clarify any difficult terms, or to highlight any important terms relevant to the study of the unit.

Activity

Activity: These appear throughout the unit to support the learning of topics and to link them to the assessment criteria.

Distinction Activity

Meeting distinction criteria and distinction activities: Guidance which is directly linked to Distinction criteria and which will help you to prepare for assignments.

Exam practice

Exam practice: Enhance your understanding of the assessment criteria and test yourself with these exam-style questions.

Check your understanding

Check your understanding: Test your knowledge of each unit.

Case studies

Case studies and Think about it: See how concepts are applied in settings with real life scenarios and reflect on what you've learned.

Further reading

Further reading and Useful websites: Includes references to websites, books and other various sources for further reading and research.

Introduction

BTEC National Sport and Exercise Science for the Edexcel examination boards is a subject that helps to prepare you for work in the sports industry or for higher education within the fields of sport science and sport.

BTEC Level 3 National Sport and Exercise Science Fourth Edition is a comprehensive textbook that covers all mandatory units in the BTEC National Sport and Exercise Sciences qualifications for all sizes of the qualification up to the Extended Diploma.

To ensure that you are following the correct pathway for your chosen qualification, please see the table in 'Pathways for BTEC National Sport and Exercise Science Qualifications'.

As well as all mandatory units, *BTEC Level 3 National Sport and Exercise Science Fourth Edition* contains many of the more popular optional units that you can take. Some optional units have been provided as PDFs for you to read online or download via Dynamic Learning. For details of these, look for the Dynamic Learning icon on the Contents page. For details about Dynamic Learning and how to access these online units, see the inside front cover of this book.

The BTEC National Sport and Exercise Science qualifications are assessed through coursework and external assessment in the form of exams and task-based written assessments. You will be given support on how to approach the assignments and how you can approach all of the grading criteria for each unit. *BTEC Level 3 National Sport and Exercise Science Fourth Edition* will help to show you where you can find the information related to the grading criteria that you are working on, which will help to ensure that you are including the appropriate subject content in your coursework.

Success in this qualification is a combination of your teacher's expertise, your own motivation and ability as a student, and accessibility to the appropriate resources – including a relevant textbook! Written by experienced BTEC Sport and Exercise Science teachers, *BTEC Level 3 National Sport and Exercise Science Fourth Edition* is highly relevant to your qualification and provides you with resources that will not only support and help you prepare for your assessments, but which will also stretch and challenge you.

BTEC Level 3 National Sport and Exercise Science Fourth Edition is written in a clear, highly readable way that will help you to understand and learn about Sport and Exercise Science and prepare you and provide information for your assessments in this course.

Pathways for BTEC National Sport and Exercise Science Qualifications

To ensure that you are following the correct pathway for the **Diploma** or **Extended Diploma in BTEC Sport and Exercise Science**, please see the table below.

Unit (number and title)	Unit size (GLH)	Diploma (720 GLH)	Extended Diploma (1080 GLH)
1 Sport and Exercise Physiology	120	M	M
2 Functional Anatomy	90	M	M
3 Applied Sport and Exercise Psychology	120	M	M
4 Field and Laboratory-based Fitness Testing	90	M	M
5 Applied Research Methods in Sport and Exercise Science	90	M	M
6 Coaching for Performance and Fitness	90	M	M
7 Biomechanics in Sport and Exercise Science	60	O	O
8 Specialised Fitness Training	60	O	O
9 Research Project in Sport and Exercise Science	60	O	O
10 Physical Activity for Individual and Group- based Exercise	60	O	O
11 Sports Massage	60	O	O
12 Sociocultural Issues in Sport and Exercise	60	O	O
13 Nutrition for Sport and Exercise Performance	120		M
14 Technology in Sport and Exercise Science	60		O
15 Sports Injury and Assessment	60		O

Optional units 11, 12, 14 and 15 have been provided online via the Hodder Education website.

Command words meanings

In your external assessment, each question will start with one of the following command words or terms, so it is important that you know what each means so that you know how to answer each question.

Command or term	Definition
Analyse	Learners examine in detail in order to discover the meaning or essential features of a theme, topic or situation, or break something down into its components or examining factors methodically and in detail. To identify separate factors, say how they are related and explain how each one contributes to the topic.
Assess	Learners present a careful consideration of varied factors or events that apply to a specific situation or identy those which are the most important or relevant to arrive at a conclusion.
Describe	Learners give an account, or details, of 'something' or give an account of a 'process'.
Discuss	Learners identify the issue/situation/problem/argument that is being assessed in the question given, exploring all aspects and investigating fully.
Evaluate	Learners review information before bringing it together to form a conclusion or come to a supported judgement of a subject's qualities in relation to its context, drawing on evidence: strengths, weaknesses, alternative actions, relevant data or information.
Explain	Learners convey understanding by making a point/statement or by linking the point/statement with a justification/expansion.
Give	Learners can provide examples, justifications and/or reasons to a context.
Identify	Learners assess factual information that may require a single word answer, although sometimes a few words or a maximum of a single sentence are required.
State/Name	Learners give a definition or example.
To what extent	Learners review information then bring it together to form a judgement or conclusion, following the provision of a balanced and reasoned argument.

Table A Definitions of commands/terms

1 Sport and exercise physiology

About this unit

Physiology is the study of how the body systems function and work together to keep us alive! Sport and exercise physiology includes how the body systems work together to allow us to take part in different forms of sport and exercise and provide the energy we need to exercise for very short periods to many hours. In this unit you will explore how each of the body systems, including the skeletal, muscular, cardiovascular, respiratory, energy and endocrine systems, respond to short- and long-term exercise, the causes and effects of fatigue and the effects of the environment on each of these body systems.

How will I be assessed?

External assessment

This unit will be assessed externally, meaning that at the end of the unit you will complete a written examination that has been set by Pearson and will be marked by Pearson examiners.

The paper contains short- and long-answer questions and covers the exercise physiology in normal conditions and in different environmental conditions.

You will be given 1 hour and 30 minutes to sit the exam and the number of marks available is 80.

The exam will be available twice a year from May/June 2017.

How will I be graded?

The assessment outcomes show you the knowledge and skills that you are expected to be able to demonstrate in the exam. It is important when you are covering the unit content that you keep these objectives in mind, as they show what you need to be able to do with the information you are learning about. In this case, the words demonstrate, apply and analyse are particularly important, as they tell you the skills that you will need to show in the external assessment.

Assessment outcomes

The exam is split into four different assessment outcomes (AOs) and each will be covered in varying amounts within the paper. The command words that will be used for each assessment outcome are also provided, to help you to gain an understanding of the depth and breadth that you will need to include in your responses for each AO.

AO1 Demonstrate knowledge and understanding of body systems and how they respond and adapt to exercise in different environments.

Command words: identify, describe, give, state, name, explain

Marks: range from 1 to 5 marks

AO2 Apply knowledge and understanding of body systems and how they respond and adapt to exercise in different environments in context.

Command words: describe, explain

Marks: range from 1 to 5 marks

AO3 Analyse sports performance data to interpret the body's responses and adaptations to exercise and evaluate their impact on sport and exercise performance.

Command words: analyse, assess, evaluate, discuss

Marks: 10 marks

How will I be graded?

AO4 Make connections between how the body systems work together in response to the demands of sport and exercise and to enhance performance.

Command words: analyse, assess, evaluate, discuss

Marks: 10 marks

Grade descriptors

Grade descriptors are provided by Pearson to give an idea of what sorts of skills and knowledge need to be shown to achieve a pass or a distinction grade. However, further grades are available including:

U – Unclassified

Level 3 Pass

Learners are able to demonstrate knowledge of sport and exercise physiology and apply it to sport and exercise performance. They have a sound understanding of how the body's systems respond to exercise in the short term and adapt to regular strength and conditioning training programmes in the long term. They have an understanding of how the body's systems work together during exercise and the impact different environmental conditions and fatigue have on the body's systems.

Level 3 Distinction

Learners are able to demonstrate thorough knowledge and comprehensive understanding of sport and exercise physiology and apply it to performance in a range of exercise and sports contexts. They can analyse how the body's systems respond to exercise in the short term and adapt to regular strength and conditioning training programmes in the long term. They are able to make connections between the body's systems and assess how they work together during exercise to supply and utilise energy. They can analyse the impact that different environmental conditions and fatigue have on the body's systems and the performance of athletes.

Command words meanings

In your external assessment, each question will start with one of the possible command words or terms, so it is important that you know what each means so that you know how to answer each question. Look at page 8 for a table of these.

A Responses of the body systems to a single sport or exercise session

For this learning aim you will need to be able to understand how each body system responds to a single sport or exercise session for a range of activities and the interrelationships between the body systems during this single session.

A1 Skeletal system

Osteoclast activity

Osteoclasts are the bone cells that are responsible for destroying or cleaning away old bone tissue.

Weight-bearing exercises stimulate these cells to destroy old bone tissue which then acts to stimulate the osteoblasts to build new bone tissue which is called remodelling. The effect of this process helps to build stronger bones.

Weight-bearing exercises are exercises that involve holding a person's body weight, therefore activities such as walking and jogging would be classed as weight-bearing. However, activities such as cycling and swimming would not be classed as weight-bearing as neither of these types of exercise require a person to hold their body weight.

Synovial fluid

Synovial fluid is the fluid in synovial joints that helps to lubricate the joint. Taking part in a single bout of exercise will increase the amount of synovial fluid released into the joint and reduce the viscosity of the fluid. This helps the synovial joints that are involved in the exercise to move more freely, so helps with mobilisation of the joints.

A2 Muscular system

Muscle fibre recruitment (Type I, Type IIa, Type IIx)

Depending on the type of exercise intensity, different muscle fibres will be recruited to complete the activity. Each type of muscle fibre is stimulated at different intensities – this process is called muscle fibre recruitment. When the muscles need to produce a large force such as lifting a very heavy weight, the type IIx muscle fibres will be recruited in order to produce these large amounts requiring a lot of force. However, when a person is walking, slow contractions and low forces are required so type I muscle fibres will be recruited.

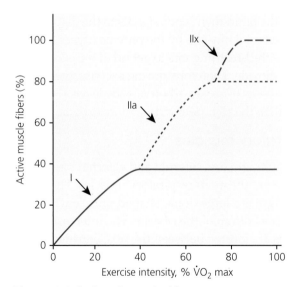

Figure 1.1 Order of muscle fibre type recruitment

Blood flow to working muscles

Blood flows through the body through arteries, arterioles, capillaries, veins and venules.

However, not every one of these blood vessels are in use at the same time. When a person is exercising or taking part in a sport, blood is directed to the muscles that are working through vasodilation of the blood vessels leading to the muscles and vasoconstriction of the blood vessels leading to areas of the body to reduce the blood flow to areas of the body where blood is not required (such as the gut and kidneys). When a person is exercising or taking part in a sport, blood is directed to the muscles that are working – so, if a person is running, more blood will be directed to flow around the leg muscles so that oxygen and nutrients can be delivered to these muscles so that they can function. If a person is playing tennis, more blood will be directed to the arm that is holding the racket compared to the other arm, as the racket arm is doing more work.

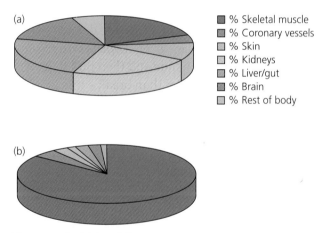

Figure 1.2 a) blood flow at rest;
b) blood flow during exercise

During exercise or sports participation, blood is also directed to flow through blood vessels that are close to the skin surface to help to cool the body down. You will have no doubt experienced the colour change in your face when you are taking part in an energetic sport – it will turn from a paler colour to a pink or red colour.

Micro-tears

When taking part in resistance exercises such as lifting weights, the process is actually designed to break some muscle fibres. These 'breaks' are called 'micro-tears' as the damage is usually very minimal. However, this 'damage' has to occur in order for the muscle to have the stimulation to rebuild itself so that over time it will become bigger and stronger.

Temperature

During a warm-up we usually increase the heart rate and carry out mobilisation activities. By increasing our heart rate, we are pumping our blood around our body at a faster rate which then has the effect of warming up our muscles. When muscles become warmer they become more pliable.

> **Key term**
>
> **Pliable** means able to change shape more easily.

If you imagine a piece of plasticine, when it is cold and you pull it, it is likely to break and split into two pieces. However, if you warm the plasticine up in your hands and then pull it, it will start to stretch rather than break – this is because it has become more pliable. This same principle applies to muscles – if a muscle is cold and then suddenly stretched it is more likely to tear, whereas if it is warmed up, it is more likely to stretch and not tear.

A1 and A2 Check your understanding

1 Identify which cells are responsible for destroying old bone cells.
2 State three types of weight-bearing exercise.
3 State three types of exercise that are not weight-bearing.
4 Describe what synovial fluid is and why it is produced during exercise.
5 Describe what muscle fibre recruitment means.
6 Explain how the body redistributes blood flow when a person is running.
7 Explain what a micro-tear is.

A3 Respiratory system

The respiratory system is responsible for getting oxygen into the body and getting carbon dioxide out of the body. (It is described in detail in Unit 2.) The oxygen is used to help produce energy which is used while we take part in sporting activities. The process of creating energy also produces a waste produce called carbon dioxide which needs to be removed from the body.

Control of breathing rate

Breathing rate is controlled by both neural and chemical mechanisms.

The neural control is from the respiratory centre in the brain which is located in medulla oblongata. During exercise, when the body needs to produce more energy, the amount of carbon dioxide increases and dissolves in the blood stream to produce a weak acid. As levels of carbon dioxide in the blood rise, this increases the acidity of the blood. This increase in acidity of the blood is sensed by chemoreceptors which are specialised cells within the arteries that detect chemical changes in the blood. As the body does not like the acidity of the blood, the chemoreceptors signal the medulla oblongata. This area of the brain then sends signals to the diaphragm and intercostal muscles by the phrenic nerves to increase the breathing rate to get rid of the excess carbon dioxide. Therefore, during exercise, breathing rate increases because carbon dioxide levels rise rather than the cells demanding more oxygen.

Respiratory muscles

The diaphragm and internal and external intercostal muscles are the main respiratory muscles. The diaphragm is a large dome-shaped muscle which covers the bottom of the ribcage. The intercostal muscles are located between the ribs. During rest, the diaphragm contracts and flattens and pushes the two sides of the ribcage away from each other, which results in an increase in the size of the thoracic cavity, forcing air into the lungs. The external intercostal muscles also contract during inspiration to push the ribs upwards and outwards to increase the size of the chest cavity, drawing more air in than just the diaphragm contracting alone.

During expiration at rest, the process does not require any contraction of muscles.

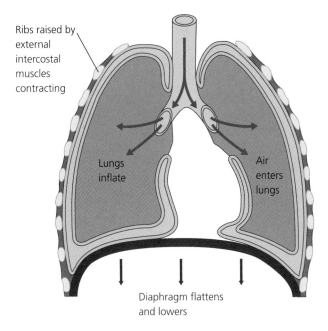

Ribs raised by external intercostal muscles contracting

Lungs inflate

Air enters lungs

Diaphragm flattens and lowers

Figure 1.3 The diaphragm and intercostal muscles

Additional skeletal muscles that aid breathing

During sport and exercise, additional skeletal muscles aid with the process of breathing. During inspiration, the sternocleidomastoid muscle aids the process by contracting to raise the upper half of the chest.

During expiration, the internal intercostal muscles, rectus abdominis, transverse abdominis and the oblique muscles all contract to force air more quickly and more fully out of the lungs, ready for the next inspiration of air.

Minute volume and tidal volume

The amount of air we breathe in and out per minute is called Minute volume and is given the symbol VE.

Minute volume can be worked out using the following equation:

$$VE = Frequency \times Tidal\ volume$$

Frequency is the number of breaths per minute.

Tidal volume is the volume of air breathed in and out during one breath.

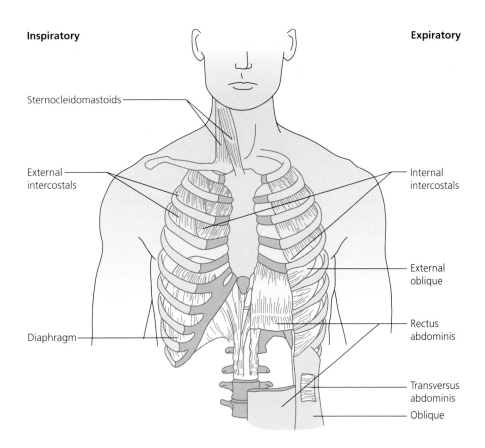

Inspiratory

Expiratory

Sternocleidomastoids

External intercostals

Diaphragm

Internal intercostals

External oblique

Rectus abdominis

Transversus abdominis

Oblique

Figure 1.4 The breathing pump muscles

To calculate VE at rest:

The average breathing rate is around 12 breaths per minute. The average tidal volume is 0.5 l (this will vary depending upon age, gender and size of a person).

Therefore, the Minute volume at rest is:

$$VE = 12 \times 0.5 = 6 \text{ litres}$$

Activity: Minute volume

1 While sitting or lying down, count the number of breaths you breathe in during one minute – try to breathe as normally as possible.
2 Write this number down and then work out your pulmonary ventilation using the equation given above.
3 Compare your pulmonary ventilation with the rest of the class.

When you start to exercise, you need to take more oxygen into your body in order for it to be used to help produce energy. At the start of exercise, this increased oxygen demand occurs by breathing at a faster rate and breathing in more air and breathing out more air during each breath. This means that tidal volume increases.

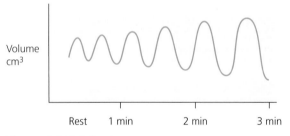

Figure 1.5 Tidal volume increasing

Oxygen dissociation curve

The majority of oxygen is transported in blood by haemoglobin with just 1.5% carried in the plasma. Oxygen reacts with haemoglobin to make oxyhaemoglobin. The reaction of oxygen with haemoglobin is temporary and completely reversible, which means that oxygen can be unloaded from haemoglobin. The binding of oxygen to haemoglobin is dependent on the partial pressure of oxygen. Oxygen combines with haemoglobin in oxygen-rich situations, such as in the lungs.

Oxygen is released by haemoglobin in places where there is little oxygen, such as in exercising muscle.

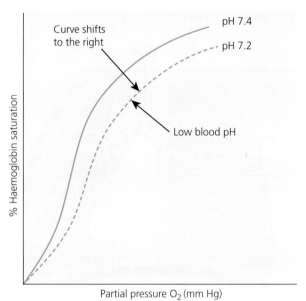

Figure 1.6 Oxygen dissociation curve in response to blood pH changes

The oxygen dissociation curve is an S-shaped curve (see Figure 1.7) that represents the ease with which haemoglobin will release oxygen when it is exposed to tissues of different concentrations of oxygen. The curve starts with a steep rise because haemoglobin has a high affinity for oxygen. This means that when there is a small rise in the partial pressure of oxygen, haemoglobin will pick up and bind oxygen to it easily. Thus, in the lungs the blood is rapidly saturated with oxygen. However, only a small drop in the partial pressure of oxygen will result in a large drop in the percentage saturation of haemoglobin. Thus, in exercising muscles, where there is a low partial pressure of oxygen, the haemoglobin will readily unload the oxygen for use by the tissues.

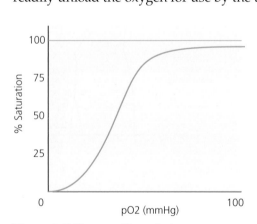

Figure 1.7 Oxygen dissociation curve

Effects of pH and temperature on the oxygen dissociation curve

Changes in blood carbon dioxide level and hydrogen ion concentration (pH) cause shifts in the oxygen dissociation curve. These shifts enhance oxygen release in tissues and increase oxygen uptake in the lungs. This is known as the Bohr Effect, named after the Danish physiologist Christian Bohr who discovered it. During exercise, the blood becomes more acidic because of the increased production of carbon dioxide.

This increase in carbon dioxide and decrease in pH shifts the dissociation curve to the right for a given partial pressure of oxygen, releasing more oxygen to the tissues (see Figure 1.6).

In the lungs there is a low partial pressure of carbon dioxide and low hydrogen ion concentration which shifts the dissociation curve to the left for a given partial pressure of oxygen, and therefore enhances oxygen uptake.

As muscles exercise, they also increase in temperature. This has the effect of shifting the curve to the right, which means oxygen is released much more readily. Conversely, a decreased temperature will shift the curve to the left, which increases oxygen uptake.

A3 Check your understanding

1   Identify the centre in the brain responsible for the neural control of breathing.
2   Identify the three main respiratory muscles involved in breathing.
3   Describe the role of the sternocleidomastoid in breathing.
4   Describe how to work out Minute volume (VE).
5   Describe how oxygen is transported in the body.
6   Explain why taking part in exercise increases the release of oxygen from haemoglobin.

A4 Cardiovascular system

The cardiovascular system consists of the heart and the blood vessels through which the heart pumps blood around the body. During exercise, a number of changes take place to the cardiovascular system to ensure that the muscles receive the required amounts of oxygen and nutrients. The structure of the cardiovascular system is discussed in more detail in Unit 2.

Anticipatory increase in heart rate

During exercise the heart rate needs to be increased in order to ensure that the working muscles receive adequate amounts of nutrients and oxygen, and that the waste products that are produced are removed. Before you even start exercising there is an increase in your heart rate, called the anticipatory rise. This increase in heart rate occurs because when you think about exercising it causes the sympathetic nervous system to release adrenaline.

Key term

Adrenaline (also called Epinephrine in the USA) is a hormone released during times of stress which gets the body ready for action, known as the fight-or-flight response, so that if a person is in danger they are ready to run away quickly or are able to fight in response to the dangerous situation.

One of the effects of adrenaline is to make the heart beat faster. Once exercise has started, there is an increase in carbon dioxide and lactic acid in the body which is detected by chemoreceptors.

Key term

Chemoreceptors are a group of cells that detect changes in the chemical environment around them and transmit this message to the brain so that the body can respond accordingly.

The chemoreceptors trigger the sympathetic nervous system to increase the release of adrenaline, which further increases heart rate. In a trained athlete, heart rate can increase by up to three times within one minute of starting exercise. As exercise continues, the body becomes warmer, which also helps to increase the heart rate because it increases the speed of the conduction of nerve impulses across the heart.

Activity: Heart rate and exercise

Aim

The aim of this activity is to examine what happens to heart rate before and during the onset of exercise.

Equipment

Stopwatch or heart rate monitor

Sports clothes

Pen and paper

Bench

Skipping rope

Method

1   If you have a heart rate monitor, place it around your chest. If not, find your pulse point either on your neck or at your wrist.

2   Sit quietly for five minutes, then take your resting heart rate. If you have a heart rate monitor, write down the heart rate that appears on the monitor. If not, feel for your pulse point, then count your heart rate for 30 seconds. Double this figure and write it down to give you the beats per minute (bpm).

3   Think about what exercise you are about to perform for 1 minute.

4   Record your heart rate after having thought about your exercise.

5   Perform step-ups onto a bench for 2 minutes or skip for 2 minutes with a skipping rope.

6   Immediately after you have finished your exercise, record your heart rate.

Results

Resting heart rate (bpm)	Pre-exercise heart rate (bpm)	Post-exercise heart rate (bpm)

Copy and complete the results table above.

Conclusion

Try to answer the following questions:

1   What happened to your heart rate immediately before you started exercising?

2   What caused this change in your heart rate and why is it necessary?

3   Try to explain why there is a difference between your resting heart rate and your post-exercise heart rate.

Cardiac output and calculation of cardiac output

Cardiac output is the amount of blood pumped from the heart every minute and is the product of heart rate and stroke volume.

Cardiac output (litres per minute) = heart rate (bpm) x stroke volume (litres)

The shorthand for this equation is:

$Q = HR \times SV$

The stroke volume is around 70–90 millilitres, however, it varies depending on a variety of factors. Generally, the fitter you are, the larger your stroke volume is and males tend to have larger stroke volumes than females because they have a larger heart. At rest, a person's cardiac output is approximately 5 litres per minute, while during exercise it can increase to as much as 30 litres per minute.

Activity: Estimate your stroke volume

1   Take your resting heart rate by finding a pulse point and recording your heart rate for 30 seconds. Double this figure to give you beats per minute (bpm).

2   Work out your SV. The average cardiac output for a person is 5 litres per minute. By rearranging the equation we can estimate a person's SV:

   $Q / HR = SV$

   E.g. if your heart rate was 70 bpm:

   5 / 70

   $SV = 0.071$ litre = 71 ml

3   Note down the rest of the class's stroke volumes and then take an average.

4   Separate your class stroke volumes into males and females and then calculate an average stroke volume for the males and another for the females. Is there a difference between the two? If so, try to explain why.

5   What conclusion can you draw about the fitness of your class?

Starling's Law

While exercising, the amount of blood that returns to the heart increases. Blood returning to the heart is given the term venous return.

> **Key term**
>
> **Venous return** is the amount of blood returned to the heart after circulating around the body.

This increased volume of blood has the effect of stretching the cardiac muscle to a greater degree than normal. This stretching has the effect of making the heart contract much more forcibly and thereby pumping out more blood during each contraction, so stroke volume is increased during exercise. This effect is known as 'Starling's Law'.

Blood pressure

Blood pressure is necessary in order for blood to flow around the body. The pressure is a result of the heart contracting and forcing blood into the blood vessels. Two values are given when a person has their blood pressure taken; a typical blood pressure for the average adult male is 120/80. The two values correspond to the systolic value (when the heart is contracting) and the diastolic value (when the heart is relaxing). The higher value is the systolic value (when the heart is contracting) and the lower is the diastolic value (when the heart is not contracting). Blood pressure is measured in milligrams of mercury, mmHg.

The value for a person's blood pressure is determined by the cardiac output (Q), which is a product of stroke volume and heart rate, and the resistance the blood encounters as it flows around the body. This can be put into an equation:

Blood pressure = Q x R

Where Q = cardiac output (stroke volume x heart rate)

R = resistance to flow

Resistance to blood flow is caused both by the size of the blood vessels through which it travels (the smaller the blood vessel, the greater the resistance) and by the thickness of the blood (the thicker the blood the greater the resistance).

Changing the resistance to blood flow can alter blood pressure. This is done by involuntary smooth muscles in the arterioles relaxing or contracting in order to alter the diameter of the arterioles. As the smooth muscle contracts, the diameter of the blood vessel gets smaller, so blood pressure is increased; as the smooth muscle relaxes, the diameter of the blood vessel is increased, which decreases the pressure of the blood flowing through it. The same principle can be applied to altering the diameter of water flow through a hose. If you place your finger over part of the opening of the hose, making the diameter smaller, the water will flow out quite forcibly because it is under higher pressure. However, if the water is left to flow unhindered through the end of the hose it is under lower pressure, and will therefore not 'spurt' so far because there is less resistance.

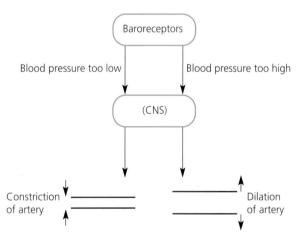

Figure 1.8 How baroreceptors initiate response to high blood pressure and low blood pressure

A reduction in blood pressure is detected by baroreceptors in the aorta and the carotid artery.

> **Key term**
>
> **Baroreceptors** are a collection of cells that detect a change in blood pressure. They send signals to the brain so that the body can respond appropriately.

This detection is passed to the central nervous system, which then sends a nervous impulse signal to the arterioles to constrict. This increases the pressure of the blood and also has the effect of increasing the heart rate.

When blood pressure is increased, the baroreceptors detect this and signal the central nervous system, which makes the arterioles dilate, and reduces blood pressure.

Changes to blood pressure in response to aerobic exercise

Exercise has the effect of increasing heart rate, which will result in an increased cardiac output that will have the effect of increasing blood pressure. This can be seen from the equation:

$$BP = Q \times R$$

This shows that if cardiac output is increased and the resistance to blood flow does not change, then blood pressure will also automatically increase. Systolic blood pressure increases in line with exercise intensity – the higher the exercise intensity, the greater the increase in blood pressure. However, there is very little change in diastolic blood pressure as exercise intensity increases.

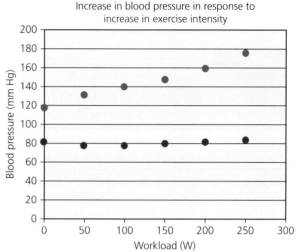

Key
- Systolic BP
- Diastolic BP

Figure 1.9 Effects of incremental exercise on BP

Activity: Blood pressure and exercise

Aim
The aim of this activity is to explore what happens to blood pressure during exercise.

Equipment
Electrical sphygmomanometer

Pen and paper

Sports clothes

Treadmill or cycle ergometer

Free or fixed weights

Method
1. Choose a continuous exercise such as jogging on a treadmill or cycling on an ergometer.
2. Attach the sphygmomanometer to the exercising person and record their resting blood pressure.
3. Your subject should perform 20 minutes of aerobic exercise (try to ensure that they are exercising at the same intensity throughout duration of the exercise).
4. After about 2 minutes of exercise take their blood pressure (ensure that your subject continues to exercise throughout).
5. After about 20 minutes of exercise take their blood pressure (ensure that your subject continues to exercise throughout).
6. After a break of at least 15 minutes, record your subject's blood pressure.

Results

Resting blood pressure (mmHg)	
After 2 minutes of exercise (mmHg)	
After 20 minutes of exercise (mmHg)	
After 15 minutes of recovery (mmHg)	

Copy and complete the table above.

Conclusion
Try to answer the following questions:

1. What happened to the blood pressure after 2 minutes of continuous exercise?
2. What happened to the blood pressure after 20 minutes of continuous exercise?
3. Why did blood pressure increase during exercise?
4. Why was there a difference between the blood pressure readings at 2 minutes and 20 minutes?

Immediately after exercise there is a fall in systolic pressure as the skeletal muscular pump is no longer pumping blood from the muscles to the heart. This can lead to blood pooling in the muscles and cause the athlete to faint as not enough blood is being pumped to the brain.

During aerobic exercise, systolic blood pressure can increase to around 180 mmHg. However, lower intensity exercise will not increase heart rate to the same degree, which in turn means blood pressure values will not reach higher values.

Changes to blood pressure in response to strength training

When taking part in strength training, blood pressure can increase to very high levels, which means it can be a dangerous activity for any person that already has high blood pressure. The higher blood pressure that occurs in strength training is due to the fact that the muscles are contracting very forcibly. This force has the effect of constricting the blood vessels of the working muscles, which means that the heart has to work even harder to push blood through these blood vessels. There is also an increase in blood flow to the thoracic cavity when a person lifting a heavy weight performs the Valsalva Manoeuvre.

Key term

Thoracic cavity is the part of the body that is enclosed by the ribcage and the diaphragm and contains the heart and lungs.

This is the process whereby the person lifting the weight breathes out against a closed glottis or against a closed mouth and nose. The process of performing the Valsalva Manoeuvre while lifting heavy weights helps to stabilise the shoulder girdle and torso, which helps the lifter to move the weight more efficiently. The increase in systolic pressure that a person experiences when weight training is proportional to the load being lifted. Therefore, the greater the weights lifted, the higher the blood pressure will be.

Activity: Valsalva Manoeuvre

You can experience the Valsalva Manoeuvre by performing the following exercise. However, if you have high blood pressure, you are advised not to take part in this activity.

1 Stand up then link both hands together in front of your chest. Take a deep breath and hold that breath while trying to pull your hands apart without letting go. Pull as hard as you can.
2 Try to explain what is happening to your muscles in your chest and how your throat feels while you are carrying out this exercise.

Cardiac cycle

The cardiac cycle is all of the events that occur in one heartbeat. As it is a cycle, there is no beginning and no end. One heart beat usually takes 0.8 seconds and consists of two phases, systole and diastole.

Systole
When the heart contracts it lasts 0.3 seconds. The ventricles contract and blood flows out in the aorta and pulmonary artery.

Diastole
When the heart relaxes it lasts 0.5 seconds. During this phase blood flows from the atria and into the ventricles.

Redistribution of blood flow

As stated previously, the average cardiac output is around 5 litres per minute. When this blood is circulated around the body, some organs receive more blood than others. This is because as blood flows through the body through arteries, arterioles, capillaries, veins and venules, not every one of these blood vessels are in use at the same time. The body is able to redistribute blood flow by constricting the blood vessels leading to organs that do not require such a large blood flow, and dilating the blood vessels feeding the muscles that do. The process of blood vessels constricting is called 'vasoconstriction' and the process of blood vessels dilating is called 'vasodilation'.

Key terms

Vasoconstriction means blood vessels becoming smaller.

Vasodilation means blood vessels becoming larger.

This process of vasoconstriction and vasodilation allows blood to be directed to where it is needed. For example, after we have eaten some food, more blood is directed to the stomach to help us to digest it. When a person is exercising or taking part in a sport, blood is directed to the muscles that are working, delivering oxygen and nutrients so that these muscles can function. See Figure 1.2 on page 11.

During exercise or sports participation, blood is also directed to flow through blood vessels that are close to the skin surface to help to cool the body down. This is why the colour of your face changes when you are taking part in an energetic sport – it will turn from a paler colour to a pink or red colour.

Changes in blood pH

Blood has a pH of 7 at rest which is neutral. This means it is neither acidic nor alkaline. However, during exercise or sports participation, blood pH can be reduced, which means it becomes more acidic (a pH of less than 7 is classed as acidic).

The increase in acidity is due to two main factors: an increase in lactate and an increase in carbon dioxide. As lactic acid is produced during anaerobic exercise, it is converted quickly into lactate which is still acidic. Lactate is carried in the blood stream which makes the blood become more acidic.

Extra carbon dioxide is also produced during exercise, and this is carried in the blood stream too. Carbon dioxide is converted to carbonic acid and carried in the blood which again acts to increase the acidity of the blood.

Diffusion rate

Diffusion is the passage of gas from a high concentration to a low concentration. The main gases we are concerned with in sport and exercise is getting oxygen into the body and getting carbon dioxide out of the body. Both of these gases are transported by the blood stream. Therefore, the faster that oxygen is diffused into the blood stream so that it can be transported to the working muscles and the faster that carbon dioxide is transported away from the working muscles and out of the body, the longer a person can exercise for, and at a higher intensity.

Diffusion rate is affected by the surface area available for diffusion to take place. The larger the surface area, the greater the diffusion rate. Diffusion of gases into the blood stream occurs in the capillaries. Therefore, the greater the number of capillaries, the greater the diffusion rate will be.

Arteriovenous oxygen difference (a-VO$_2$ diff)

This is the difference in oxygen content of arterial blood and venous blood. This gives an indication as to how much oxygen has been removed at the capillaries from the arterial blood before it passes into the veins. The more efficient a person is at extracting oxygen, the greater their arteriovenous oxygen difference will be. The higher the arteriovenous oxygen difference, the better the body is able to extract oxygen from the blood stream. This improved difference is due to increased number of capillaries that occur as the body adapts to endurance exercise – with more capillaries, there is a greater diffusion rate for oxygen to travel from the blood and into the muscles.

a-VO$_2$ difference is usually measured in millilitres of oxygen per 100 millilitres of blood (mL/100 mL). At rest, a-VO$_2$ difference is usually around 5 mL/100 mL but this can increase to up to 16 mL/100 mL during high intensity exercise.

A4 Check your understanding

1 Explain how the heart rate increases before a person even starts taking part in exercise.
2 Describe how to calculate cardiac output.
3 Describe Starling's Law.
4 Explain how resistance affects a person's blood pressure.
5 Describe how weight training can increase a person's blood pressure.
6 Describe how a person's blood pH can change during exercise.
7 State the equation used to work out arteriovenous oxygen difference.

A5 Nervous system

Motor unit

Muscle contracts in response to stimulation from the nervous system. The central nervous system includes the brain and spinal cord and is responsible for stimulating the nervous system to carry nervous impulses to the required muscle in order to produce movement. The nerve that connects with the muscle fibre is called a motor neurone. The motor neurone only stimulates a part of that muscle, which is called the motor unit.

> **Key term**
>
> **Motor unit** is the part of a muscle stimulated by a motor neurone.

The number of muscle fibres that a motor neurone stimulates varies between different muscles. For example, muscles that produce large movements such as the quadriceps will have more muscle fibres per motor unit, whereas muscles that need to produce fine movements such as moving the eye will have less muscle fibres per motor unit. Each motor unit will consist of the same muscle fibre type.

Different muscle fibres and different numbers of muscle fibres will be stimulated at different intensities. When the muscles are working at a high intensity, a larger number of motor units are stimulated to produce these large amounts of force. However, when a person is working at a lower intensity, less motor units are recruited.

Muscle spindles and Golgi tendon organs

The muscles need to be able to report back to the central nervous system (CNS) what they are doing and how they are responding to the stimulation that they are receiving. They are able to do this through two forms or proprioceptors: muscle spindles and Golgi tendon organs.

> **Key term**
>
> **Proprioception** is the body's ability to sense where its body parts are without having to look at them.

Muscle spindles

A muscle spindle is an organ placed within the muscle which communicates with the CNS. The purpose of the muscle spindle is to detect when the muscle is being stretched to prevent over-stretching, which could damage the muscle. The muscle spindles signal to the CNS if the muscle is being stretched too far to stop stretching. This is also known as the stretch reflex.

Golgi tendon organs (GTOs)

These organs are placed in the muscle tendons that attach the muscle to the bone. These organs detect tension within the muscle. When a muscle is contracted, it changes the tension on the GTOs; this is relayed to the CNS which deals with this information accordingly – by either increasing the contraction of the muscle or relaxing the muscle.

Chemoreceptors, thermoreceptors, baroreceptors

Other receptors are located within the body to report back to the CNS what is happening so that the CNS can respond accordingly.

Chemoreceptors – these receptors detect chemical changes in the body. Usually these changes take place in the blood stream. They are located in the medulla in the CNS and in the periphery they are mainly located in the carotid body which is located close the carotid artery.

Thermoreceptors – these receptors detect a change in temperature of the body and report back to the CNS if the body is too hot or too cold. They are located in the hypothalamus in the CNS and also close to the skin's surface and other areas such as the bladder and eye.

Baroreceptors – these receptors detect a change in blood pressure and are located in the main blood vessels, including the aorta and carotid artery.

A6 Endocrine system

The endocrine system consists of a number of glands that release hormones. These hormones allow the glands to send signals to parts of the body to inform it how it to respond in order to regulate metabolism, temperature, growth, etc. The glands that release the hormones have target organs that respond in specific ways when they are in contact with the hormone. This system is similar in some ways to the nervous system. However, rather than sending electric nerve impulses which allow for very quick messages to be sent in the nervous system, the endocrine system is much slower at producing reactions as the hormones are released into the blood stream and carried to the target organ via the blood, which takes longer than nervous impulses.

The main hormones that are going to be examined are:

- adrenaline
- noradrenaline
- cortisol
- testosterone
- human growth hormone (HGH)
- oestrogen.

Adrenaline and noradrenaline

These hormones are also known as epinephrine and norepinephrine in the USA. Both hormones are produced by the adrenal glands and adrenaline is produced from breaking down noradrenaline. These hormones, but primarily adrenaline, are responsible for the fight-or-flight response – getting the body ready to be able to run away quickly or to fight, both of which require the muscles to contract quickly, so energy must be supplied quickly. The target organs and reactions of each are shown in Table 1.1.

Target organ	Effect of adrenaline	Purpose
Heart	Increases heart rate.	Pumps more blood around the body to supply the muscles with oxygen and glucose for energy production.
Liver	Increase rate of conversion of glycogen to glucose.	Increases blood sugar levels so more energy is available for muscle contraction.
Blood vessels	Vasodilatation of blood vessels leading to the skeletal muscle. Vasoconstriction of blood vessels to the gut, kidney and skin.	Redistributes blood flow to the skeletal muscle.
Eye	Pupil dilates.	Allows more light into the eye so vision is improved.
Lungs	Bronchioles relax.	Increases amount of air that can be inhaled and exhaled during inspiration and expiration.

Table 1.1 The effect of adrenalines of the organs and the purpose of this

Cortisol

This hormone is also known as hydrocortisone and is sometimes called the 'stress' hormone as more of it is produced when a person is stressed. It is also released in response to emotional or physical threat in the same way that adrenaline and noradrenalin are released in order to prepare the body to respond to a perceived danger.

Cortisol increases the release of glucose into the blood stream to help to supply energy for muscular contraction. It is released in the morning to help us to wake up and get out of bed and then function for the day ahead. However, if a person is regularly experiencing stress, then more cortisol is produced which can have negative implications for a person as too much glucose in the blood stream is not good. Excessive cortisol production can also lead to a lowering of a person's immune system so they are more prone to being ill. Cortisol also has the effect of stopping the body from taking amino acids into the muscle cells which are required for muscle growth. It also stops the bone remodelling stage so will stop bone growth and repair as well as inhibiting calcium absorption from the diet.

Sleep deprivation, excessive intake of caffeinated drinks and excess alcohol intake all increase cortisol production.

Testosterone and its effect on the muscular system

Testosterone is produced by the testes in males and the ovaries in females, and some is also produced by the adrenal glands in both males and females. Males have higher levels of testosterone than females. In males, testosterone is responsible for many of the changes that happen during puberty such as deepening of the voice, growth of body hair and production of sperm. In both males and females however, testosterone increases muscle growth by increasing muscle protein synthesis.

Human growth hormone

Human growth hormone is also known as human chorionic gonadotropin (hCG). It is produced by the pituitary gland and is important for normal human growth and development, especially in children and teenagers. Low hCG levels in children and teenagers result in dwarfism. Growth hormone stimulates the development of natural male and female sex hormones.

In males, growth hormone acts to increase testosterone levels and results in increased muscle development. Excessive growth hormone levels increase muscle mass by stimulating protein synthesis, strengthen bones by stimulating bone remodelling, and reduce body fat by stimulating the breakdown of fat cells.

Oestrogen and it effect on the skeletal system

Oestrogen is produced by the ovaries in females and the testes in males. In females it is responsible for regulating the menstrual cycle. In both males and females it plays a major role in regulating the process of bone remodelling. Bone remodelling is the process of bones being constantly subject to simultaneous formation and re-absorption. Oestrogen has the effect of regulating osteoclast activity. Osteoclasts are cells that destroy or clean away old bone. In females there is less oestrogen produced by the body after the menopause which results in osteoclasts living longer, resulting in greater re-absorption of bone. This greater re-absorption of bone can lead to a decrease in bone mass which is a condition known as osteoporosis and leaves bones weaker and less able to withstand impacts, so they are more likely to fracture.

A5 and A6 Check your understanding

1 Define proprioception.
2 Explain the difference between the role of the muscle spindles and the role of the Golgi tendon organs.
3 Identify which receptors detect changes in blood pressure.
4 Explain the function of adrenaline.
5 Describe why excess cortisol production is not good for a person trying to increase their muscle strength.
6 Explain why women over the age of 60 are more likely to fracture a bone compared to women who are 25 years old.

A7 Energy systems

The function of energy systems is to produce adenosine triphosphate (ATP). ATP is used to make our muscles contract and therefore allows us to take part in exercise.

ATP is basically a protein (adenosine) with three (tri) phosphates attached to it.

Figure 1.10 Adenosine triphosphate (ATP)

When chemical bonds are broken, energy is released. Therefore, when a phosphate is broken off the ATP to make ADP (adenosine diphosphate (di = two)) energy is released which is used to make the muscles contract (see Figure 1.11).

Figure 1.11 Release of energy from ATP

Energy sources

ATP is not stored in large amounts in skeletal muscle and there is only enough to supply the energy for the first few seconds of exercise. Therefore, ATP has to be continually made from ADP in order for our muscles to continue contracting.

ATP can be produced from a variety of energy sources including phosphocreatine, blood glucose, glycogen and fatty acids. There are three energy systems that the body uses to make ATP and, depending on which one is recruited, will determine which energy course is used to produce ATP. Each energy system differs in the rate at which they make ATP. At the onset of exercise we will want ATP supplied very quickly. However, if we are on a long walk we don't need such a fast production of ATP, so the body uses a different energy system to make it.

Figure 1.12 Phosphocreatine energy system

ATP–PC system

At the onset of exercise, the energy system that supplies the majority of ATP is the ATP–PC system, also known as the phosphocreatine system or creatine phosphate system. It supplies ATP much quicker than any other energy system. It produces ATP in the absence of oxygen, and is therefore an anaerobic energy system.

Phosphocreatine (PC) is made up of a phosphate and a creatine molecule. When the bond between the phosphate and the creatine is broken, energy is released which is then used to make the bond between ADP and a phosphate.

PC stores are used for rapid, high intensity contractions, such as in sprinting or jumping; however, these stores only last for about 10 seconds.

Lactate system

Once our PC stores have run out, we then use the lactic acid system. This is also known as anaerobic glycolysis, which literally means the breakdown of glucose in the absence of oxygen. When glucose is broken down it is converted into a substance called pyruvate. When there is no oxygen present, the pyruvate is converted into lactic acid. This lactic acid is then quickly converted into lactate. This system produces ATP very quickly, but not as quickly as the PC system.

Figure 1.13 How lactic acid is produced

The lactate energy system is the one that is producing the majority of the ATP during high intensity exercise lasting between 30 seconds and 3 minutes, such as an 800 m race.

Aerobic energy system

The aerobic energy system provides ATP at a slower rate than the previous two energy systems discussed. However, it is responsible for producing the majority of our energy while our bodies are at rest or taking part in low intensity exercise such as jogging. This system uses a series of reactions, the first being aerobic glycolysis, as it occurs when oxygen is available to break down glucose. As in the anaerobic energy system, glucose is broken down into pyruvate. However, because oxygen is present, pyruvate is not turned into lactic acid, but continues to be broken down through a series of chemical reactions which include the Krebs cycle and the Electron transport chain.

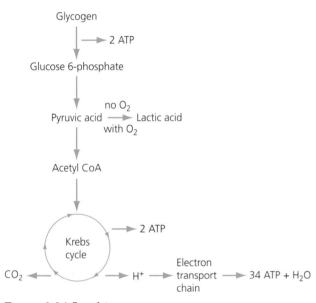

Figure 1.14 Aerobic energy system

Krebs cycle

Pyruvate from aerobic glycolysis combines with Coenzyme A (CoA) to form acetyl CoA. Acetyl CoA enters the Krebs cycle, which combines and reacts with a number of different compounds to produce ATP, hydrogen and carbon dioxide.

Electron transport chain

The hydrogen atoms produced from the Krebs cycle enter the Electron transport chain. The hydrogen atoms are passed along a chain of electron carriers and eventually combine with oxygen to form ATP and water.

Mitochondria

Both the Krebs cycle and the Electron transport chain take place in organelles called mitochondria.

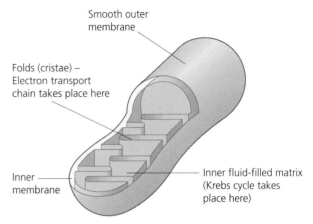

Figure 1.15 Mitochondria

The majority of ATP produced by the aerobic energy system is produced in these organelles, so they are very important for energy production. They are rod-shaped, and have an inner and an outer membrane. The inner membrane is arranged in many folds that project inward. These folds are called 'cristae' and give a large surface area for energy production to take place.

The energy continuum

The energy systems all work together to produce energy. However, what we are doing determines which energy system supplies the majority of the ATP.

The energy continuum highlights which energy systems are producing the most amount of energy at different stages of an activity.

At rest, nearly all of our energy is provided by the aerobic energy system. If we suddenly start to exercise, we need more ATP than the aerobic energy system can supply, so the phosphocreatine (PC) and lactic acid energy system supply the ATP.

In some sport and exercise activities, the energy supply comes from all three energy systems at different points. For example, in football, when you are jogging slowly, the aerobic energy system is

Energy system	Yield of ATP	Speed of energy production	Energy source	Duration of energy production	Production of waste products
ATP–PC	1	Very fast	Creatine and phosphate	8–10 seconds	None
Lactate	2	Fast	Glucose and glycogen	1–3 minutes	Lactic acid
Aerobic	38 2 from glycolysis. 2 from the Krebs cycle. 34 from the Electron transport chain.	Slow	Glycogen and fatty acids	Up to 2 hours	Carbon dioxide and water

Table 1.2 ATP yield for each system

used; for a short sprint to get to the ball, the ATP–PC system is used; running back down the pitch and running quickly to defend will mainly use the lactate energy system.

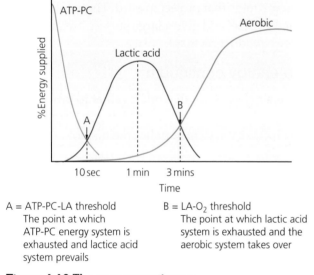

A = ATP-PC-LA threshold
The point at which ATP-PC energy system is exhausted and lactice acid system prevails

B = LA-O₂ threshold
The point at which lactic acid system is exhausted and the aerobic system takes over

Figure 1.16 The energy continuum

Onset blood lactate accumulation (OBLA)

OBLA is also known as the anaerobic threshold. OBLA is the point at which lactate begins to accumulate in the blood. A blood measurement

of 4 mmol/litre of blood is usually the point at which OBLA occurs which is usually when a person is working at an intensity of exercise that is somewhere between 85% and 90% of their maximum heart rate.

Lactate starts to accumulate in the blood when the body is not able to remove it, as it is being produced at a faster rate than it can be removed. As the person continues to exercise at a high intensity, lactate will continue to accumulate and eventually it will stop a person from exercising as their muscles will start to feel very sore.

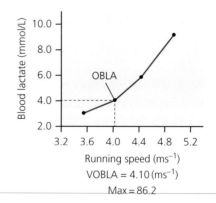

VOBLA = 4.10 (ms⁻¹)

Max = 86.2

Figure 1.17 Increase in blood lactate in relation to running speed

Recovery time for each system

When a person is taking part in training it is important to consider the recovery time for each energy system.

Energy system	Recovery time
ATP-PC	30 seconds to 4 minutes
Lactate	20 minutes to 2 hours
Aerobic	2 to 48 hours.

Table 1.3 Recovery time for each system

The recovery time varies for each energy system depending upon how high an intensity a person has been exercising and for how long. For example, if a person had been running 30 m sprints, then they would require a shorter recovery time compared to if they had been running 100 m sprints, as they would have used up more ATP–PC in the longer distance sprints.

Equally, with the aerobic energy system, if a person has been on a 5 K run, then it would only take around 2 hours to fully recover from the activity. However, if they had taken part in a marathon, a 48-hour recovery period would usually be required.

A7 Check your understanding

1 Explain which energy system a 100 m sprinter would mainly use in their race.
2 Describe which energy system includes anaerobic glycolysis.
3 Explain why the aerobic energy system supplies ATP for walking.
4 Identify where the Electron transport chain takes place.
5 Identify how much ATP is produced during glycolysis.
6 Identify which part of the aerobic energy system produces the most ATP.
7 Describe why OBLA occurs.

B Fatigue and how the body recovers from exercise

B1 Fatigue

We cannot continue to exercise indefinitely because we will eventually fatigue.

Key term

Fatigue means tiredness from physical exertion.

Fatigue occurs as a result of a number of factors including:

- depletion of energy sources
- accumulation of waste products
- depletion of acetylcholine.

As a result, it is necessary to rest in order to recover and return the body to its pre-exercise state.

Depletion of energy sources

In order to exercise we must break down the energy stored in our body and turn it into ATP. Sources of energy include phosphocreatine, glucose and glycogen. We have only enough phosphocreatine to last us for 10 seconds of maximal exercise. We then switch to glucose for energy production. We have around 15–20 g of glucose in our blood stream, around 345 g glycogen in our muscles and 90–110 glycogen stored in our liver. When our blood sugar levels are low, the liver converts either its store of glycogen into glucose or the skeletal muscles store of glycogen into glucose. However, we have only enough glycogen stores to last us for around 2 hours. Once the body's stores of glucose and glycogen are used up, we become fatigued and/or have to exercise at a lower intensity.

Accumulation of waste products

Lactate is the main by-product of anaerobic glycolysis. Blood always contains a small amount of lactate; however, during high-intensity exercise this increases greatly. The increased production of lactate results in the pH of the blood decreasing. A blood pH of 6.4 or lower affects muscle and neural function and eventually prevents continued exercise. Carbon dioxide is also produced as a waste product of the aerobic energy system. This is converted into carbonic acid as it is carried in the blood back to the lungs ready to be exhaled. However, when blood is carrying carbon dioxide in the form of carbonic acid it does lower the pH of the blood as carbonic acid is acidic.

Depletion of acetylcholine

The effect of the depletion of acetylcholine results in neuromuscular fatigue, this means that the muscles are either not able to receive signals from the CNS that stimulate the muscle to contract, or that the muscle tissue is unable to function properly.

High-intensity exercise or exercise for long periods of time can eventually interfere with the availability of acetylcholine. Acetylcholine is required to transmit nervous impulses between the nerves and the muscle fibres. If this neurotransmitter is not available, then this prevents the nervous stimulation from the CNS reaching the muscle tissue/motor unit, so the muscle is not able to contract.

B2 Recovery of energy systems

After taking part in any type of exercise, the body has to recover and return the energy systems back to their pre-exercise state.

Excess post-exercise oxygen consumption (EPOC)

Excess post-exercise oxygen consumption (EPOC) is also referred to as Oxygen debt. EPOC is the total oxygen consumed after exercise in excess of a pre-exercise levels. It occurs when the exercise performed is totally or partially anaerobic. As a result, energy is supplied by the anaerobic energy system, which results in lactate production. When the person stops exercising, their breathing rate remains elevated so that extra oxygen is breathed in to break down lactic acid into carbon dioxide and water, to replenish ATP, phosphocreatine and glycogen, and to pay back any oxygen that has been borrowed from haemoglobin and myoglobin.

After a bout of vigorous exercise, five events must happen before the muscle can operate again:

1   ATP must be replaced.
2   Phosphagen stores must be replenished.
3   Lactate must be removed.
4   Myoglobin must be replenished with oxygen.
5   Glycogen stores must be replenished.

Replacement of muscle ATP and phosphagen

The replacement of ATP and phosphagen takes around 3 minutes. The aerobic energy system is used to produce the ATP required to replenish the PC stores and ATP stores in the body:

$$ADP + P + oxygen = ATP$$

$$ATP + C + P = PC + ADP$$

Around 50% of the replenishment occurs during the first 30 seconds, while full recovery occurs at about 3 minutes.

The amount of oxygen required during this process ranges between 2 to 3.5 litres of oxygen. The fitter you are, the greater the debt, because training increases the PC content within the muscle cells. However, the recovery time of a fitter person is reduced because they have enhanced methods of oxygen delivery, such as increased capilliarisation and an improved cardio-respiratory system, which will increase the rate of ATP production from the aerobic energy system.

Removal of lactate

The removal of lactate takes around 20 minutes to 2 hours after stopping exercises, depending on the intensity of the exercise. The process involves oxygen, which is required to break down the lactate produced during anaerobic glycolysis into pyruvate. Pyruvate can then enter the aerobic energy system and eventually be broken down into carbon dioxide and water.

$$Lactate + oxygen = pyruvate$$

Lactate can also be converted in the liver to glycogen and stored either in the liver or in muscle tissue. Research has shown that an active recovery increases the rate of removal of lactate, so walking or slow jogging after a bout of exercise will help to decrease the time it takes to rid the body of lactic acid. An active recovery keeps the heart rate and breathing rate up, which has the effect of increasing the rate of delivery of oxygen to the working muscles, which will then help to rid the body of the lactate. Therefore, a cool-down is very important after any form of activity in order to maximise recovery.

Replacement of glycogen stores and resaturation of myoglobin

The oxygen replenishment of myoglobin and refilling the glycogen stores take between 2 and 48 hours. If the exercise bout was of a very high intensity then it will take longer to recover; however, the higher the aerobic fitness of a person the faster they will recover. Muscle glycogen stores must also be restored through a high carbohydrate diet and rest, and can take several days to recover, depending on the intensity of the exercise. Myoglobin is used to store oxygen in muscle tissues which is used up during long periods of aerobic exercise. The oxygen intake after exercise is used to replenish these stores of oxygen.

Appropriate nutritional strategy

Nutritional intake is important to help a person to recover from exercise as how long the person has exercised for will determine what sort of nutritional strategy will be best in order to help with recovery from the exercise.

Carbohydrate intake

A person who takes part in sports that are of a relatively high intensity and last longer than around 30 minutes would be classed as an endurance athlete. Examples of these sports include jogging, cycling, swimming, aerobics, football, rugby and netball. An endurance athlete needs to have the energy in order to compete and train. Carbohydrate is the body's preferred source of fuel; however, carbohydrate stores in the body are relatively small so it is vital that these athletes are taking in sufficient quantities of this nutrient every day in order to meet their energy demands.

The amount of carbohydrate a person should consume is based upon the activity level of the individual in terms of length and intensity. If you only take part in low levels of activity you will need less energy and consequently need to consume lower levels of carbohydrate. This would place you in category A in Table 1.4. However, an endurance

athlete would be training or competing for longer periods of time and therefore require greater amounts of carbohydrate and fall into category E in Table 1.4.

Activity: Recovery from exercise

Aim

The aim of this activity is to see how quickly a person's heart rate returns to resting levels after taking part in exercise.

Equipment

Stopwatch

Running track/gym

Sports clothes

Method and results

1 Copy the table below.

Resting pulse rate	
Immediately after exercise	
1 minute after exercise	
2 minutes after exercise	
3 minutes after exercise	
4 minutes after exercise	
5 minutes after exercise	

2 Take your resting pulse rate and make a note of it in your results table.

3 Take part in some form of intensity exercise that lasts at least 5 minutes.

4 Find your pulse, then record your pulse for a 10-second count every minute after the exercise until your heart rate returns to its original level.

5 Convert your heart rate into beats per minute by multiplying by 6.

Conclusion

Try to answer the following questions:

1 Explain why your heart rate was different from resting levels immediately after exercise has stopped.

2 Explain why your heart rate remained elevated after 3 minutes of rest.

Activity level/ Category	Recommended amount of carbohydrate in grams per kilogram of body weight
A Light (less than 1 hour a day/3–5 hours per week)	5 g
B Light to moderate (1 hour a day)	6 g
C Moderate (1–2 hours a day)	7 g
D Moderate to heavy (2–3 hours a day)	8 g
E Heavy (4 hours a day)	10 g

Table 1.4 (Adapted from ACSM, 2000)

Activity: How much carbohydrate should you have?

In order to work out the quantity of carbohydrate you need, you will need to know your body weight in kg and multiply this by the values given related to the relevant category.

For example, if you weighed 70 kg and fell into category D, your required amount of carbohydrate per day would be:

70 x 8 = 560 g

Using Table 1.4, work out the quantity of carbohydrate you would require if you fell into:

1 Category A   4 Category D
2 Category B   5 Category E
3 Category C

During the 2 hours immediately after exercise or competition, your body is able to convert carbohydrate into glycogen at a very fast rate. Therefore, in order to help maximise your body's store of carbohydrate, you should eat foods high in carbohydrate as soon as possible post-exercise. You should aim to eat around 1–1.2 g of carbohydrate per kg of your body weight. However, most people do not feel like eating a large carbohydrate meal after exercise, so many prefer to eat a series of carbohydrate snacks and sports drinks instead – for example, isotonic sports drinks and a current bun or carbohydrate bar. Energy gels are also a popular choice.

Protein intake
Athletes that require high levels of protein during recovery take part in sports that last for a very short period of time and require strength and sometimes speed. Examples of these sports include weightlifting, sprinting, shot put throwing, javelin throwing and the long jump. In order for an athlete to perform well in power sports, they usually need to increase their muscle size, as larger muscles are able to produce more force which makes the athlete stronger and therefore more powerful.

In order for the muscle tissue to heal and grow, the athlete must rest and supply the body with sufficient quantities of protein. The amount of protein recommended depends upon how much activity a person takes part in. The more exercise a person does, the more they break down muscle tissue and consequently the more protein they need in order to repair the muscle tissue. Table 1.5 gives estimated recommended amounts:

Activity level/ Category	Recommended grams of protein per kg of body weight
A Sedentary adult	0.8 g
B Recreational exerciser	0.8–1.5 g
C Endurance athlete	1.2–1.6 g
D Speed/Power athlete	1.7–1.8 g
E Adult building muscle (hypertrophy)	2.0 g

Table 1.5 (Adapted from ACSM, 2000)

Activity: How much protein do you need?

In order to work out the quantity of protein you need, you will need to know your body weight in kg and multiply this by the values given related to the relevant category.

For example, if you weighed 70 kg and fell into category D, your required amount of protein per day would be:

70 x 1.7 = 119 g

Using Table 1.5, work out the quantity of protein you would require if you fell into:

1 Category A   4 Category D
2 Category B   5 Category E
3 Category C

Research has found that protein is best utilised if it is taken in amounts of 30–35 g at a time. If a person was to eat more than this then the excess would be excreted or converted to fat and stored in the body. Therefore, athletes should aim to spread out their consumption of protein into a number of different meals and snacks. For example, an athlete that needs to eat 180 g of protein should consume six snacks and meals with 30 g of protein as opposed to three large protein meals.

Some athletes may find it difficult to consume all their protein requirements from their daily food. Therefore, a range of protein supplements have been devised that deliver high concentrations of protein. These supplements are usually made out of powdered milk, eggs and/or soya. Protein shakes are a popular choice with many power athletes as they contain plentiful supplies of amino acids and are quick and convenient to use. Protein bars are also available which deliver high concentrations of protein and low levels of carbohydrate with very little fat.

Rehydration

Dehydration causes a significant loss of performance. This is because dehydration will cause a loss of blood plasma affecting blood flow and the ability to sweat. Thus temperature starts to increase steadily. When we sweat it is predominantly blood plasma that is lost and so cardiac output (the amount of the blood leaving the heart per minute) is reduced. Therefore, rehydration is important to improve the circulation of the blood and the body's ability to control temperature.

While plain water is a good drink for an athlete to consume, there are now a huge array of sports drinks available that help to quench thirst and supply the body with carbohydrate. Some also supply the body with the electrolytes lost in sweat (such as sodium).

Isotonic

These drinks are the most popular type of sports drink. They are used to help the body rehydrate and also contain some carbohydrate. The drink is termed 'isotonic' because they have a similar concentration of dissolved solids as our blood, which results in the drink being absorbed very quickly into the body so that we can rehydrate at a much faster rate than if we were to drink water alone. The drinks contain 6 mg of carbohydrate per 100 ml of fluid, which provides energy which is beneficial to endurance athletes.

Hypotonic

The main aim of these sports drinks is to hydrate the athlete after exercising. These types of sports drinks are low calorie drinks and have a lower concentration of dissolved solids than blood. They are absorbed by the body at a faster rate than isotonic drinks. They contain no more than 2 g of carbohydrate per 100 ml of fluid, so they provide little energy to the athlete during exercise. They are a relatively poor source of energy.

Hypertonic

The main purpose of these drinks is to supply the body with energy after exercise or during endurance events that last longer than 90 minutes. These drinks have a higher concentration of dissolved solids than blood and are absorbed relatively slowly. They contain 10 g of carbohydrate per 100 ml of fluid and are a very good source of energy but are relatively poor for hydration.

These drinks will also contain the correct amounts of the electrolytes which ensure optimum speed of absorption. However, on the negative side, they often contain additives such as sweeteners and colourings which have a negative effect on health. They are also relatively expensive when compared with water.

B1 and B2 Check your understanding

1. Calculate how much glycogen an average person has stored in their body.
2. Identify waste products from energy production that can cause fatigue.
3. Describe why depletion of acetylcholine can produce fatigue.
4. Describe what is meant by EPOC.
5. Identify three sports that would be classed as endurance sports.

B3 Recovery of musculoskeletal system

Replacement of collagen in tendons and ligaments

Collagen is present in tendons and ligaments to provide them with the strength they need to withstand forces and also stiffness to ensure they hold the joints and muscles in place. Participation in sport and exercise that stresses the tendons and ligaments increases collagen synthesis which results in more collagen being present in these structures. Foods that help to build collagen should be eaten after exercise and include foods high in vitamin C as well as a range of different fruits and vegetables.

Replacement of calcium in bones

Calcium is one of the main minerals in bones which makes them hard and strong. Resistance exercise stimulates bone remodelling so it is important that enough calcium is consumed in the diet after exercise so that it can be taken up by the bones during this remodelling process.

Repair to micro-tears in muscles

Resistance exercise results in micro-tears in muscles which stimulate the muscle to rebuild itself so that it is bigger than before – this is called muscle hypertrophy. This means it is important to have sufficient protein in the diet during recovery so that this can be used for muscle repair.

Delayed onset of muscle soreness (DOMS)

Failure to cool-down adequately means that the levels of lactate will remain elevated. It is thought that this acidity level affects the pain receptors and together with the micro-tears in the muscle fibres contributes to muscle soreness which people may feel some time after having exercise. This muscle soreness, termed 'delayed onset of muscle soreness' (DOMS), is at its most uncomfortable 36–48 hours after exercise has ceased.

B4 Overtraining

Overtraining is a process whereby an athlete is taking part in too much training and is not having sufficient time for their body to recover and adapt, which leads to a decrease in performance and a decrease in fitness levels.

Causes of overtraining

Exercise addiction

Some people can become addicted to taking part in exercise, which means they find it very difficult or not possible to have rest days – they feel the need to exercise every day or even more than once a day. People that are addicted to exercise will also often exercise when they are not well.

There are many reasons why a person may be addicted to exercise, but one of the main reasons is due to the release of endorphins and serotonin. These hormones are released as the body's natural painkillers when a person takes part in exercise, and some people become addicted to how these hormones make them feel, so have to take part in exercise every day in order to produce this feeling.

Imbalanced training programme

All training programmes should have rest and recovery time included in them which usually means at least one day off a week or one day when training is at very low levels so that the body has time to recover. For strength training athletes, they will usually train their upper body on one day then their lower body on the next day so that their upper body has time to repair itself before the next training session. If a training programme does not contain rest periods or alternate body parts to train, then this can lead to overtraining.

Physiological effects

Overtraining will lead to imbalances in the endocrine system which includes excess adrenaline and cortisol production. This results in a higher resting heart rate, elevated basal metabolic rate, anxiousness, feeling tired and reduced enthusiasm to train. As the body has not had time to repair after each exercise bout, it will mean that the muscle tissue does not adapt and get stronger, nor does the skeletal tissues.

Impact on performance and body systems

The impact of overtraining produces a decrement in performance level as the body does not fully recover from each training session. Overtraining leads to increased levels of cortisol in the body which leads to a decreased immune function which means the person is more likely to be unwell and suffer from frequent colds. Increased cortisol in the body is also linked to decreased protein synthesis in the body which is required for muscle hypertrophy. This means that a person's muscles will not repair after having exercised. As their muscles and skeletal tissues have not been able to repair fully after each training session, they will become weaker and are therefore more susceptible to becoming injured. Lastly, a person that is overtraining will also be more susceptible to having an overuse injury.

Inadequate amounts of sleep and rest

One of the main reasons a person suffers from overtraining is due to them not having enough sleep or rest. However, overtraining itself can disturb a person's sleep patterns so that they are actually not able to get to sleep very easily or do not have a high quality of sleep.

B3 and B4 Check your understanding

1 Describe why a person taking part in strength training should eat foods high in vitamin C after their training session.
2 Explain why it is good practice for an endurance athlete to eat a banana soon after completing a training session.
3 Describe how resistance training helps to produce muscle hypertrophy.
4 Explain why a person may have sore muscles 36 hours after a heavy weight-training session.
5 Describe one reason why a person may become addicted to exercise.
6 Describe how overtraining can lead to imbalances in the endocrine system.

C Adaptations of the body systems to exercise

Taking part in regular exercise for long periods of time (a minimum of 8 weeks) affects the body in

a number of ways that makes it more able to cope with the stresses of the exercise. This results in the person being able to exercise at higher intensities and/or for longer periods of time – this process is called adaptation.

The type of training will have a significant impact on what types of adaptations will occur to the body. Aerobic training involves exercising at moderate intensity for long periods of time, 30 minutes or more. This type of training will also train for muscular endurance for the muscles that are working during the exercise, so in running, the muscles of the lower limb will mainly be trained for muscular endurance. Muscular endurance is the ability for a muscle group to keep contracting at moderate forces for prolonged periods of time which is usually classed as 30 minutes or longer.

Resistance training is where a person exercises using resistance which could be in the form of weights, resistance bands, body weight (as in a press-up) – this type of training will increase a person's strength or muscular endurance depending upon the intensity of exercise. If the person uses high loads and low reps then it will increase their strength; if, however, they use light loads and do high reps then it will increase their muscular endurance.

Anaerobic training is where the person carries out short bursts of high intensity exercise followed by rest periods, such as hollow sprints or circuit training.

C1 Skeletal system

Our skeletal system adapts in response to resistance or weight-bearing exercise. The response is primarily to become stronger and more able to withstand impact which means you are less likely to break a bone if you fall over.

Key term

Weight-bearing exercise is where we are using our body weight as a form of resistance, e.g. walking and running.

Osteoblast, osteoclast and osteocyte activity, bone remodelling and bone mineral content

Resistance or weight-bearing exercise has the effect of increasing the strength of our bones. This occurs because the stimulation of exercise means the bone remodelling stages are stimulated. The process of remodelling starts by osteoclasts destroying areas of older bone and the tissue is then reabsorbed by the body. This process by the osteoclasts activates the osteoblasts to start to lay down collagen and minerals in the area that was destroyed and start the process of remodelling. The osteoblasts turn into osteocytes which are bone cells and form the new bone. There is an increased uptake of minerals, mainly calcium and phosphorus, by the bone during this process if they are available in the body, which makes the bones harder and stronger.

Collagen content

Exercise also has an effect on joints by increasing the collagen content of the cartilage, tendons and ligaments. This increase in collagen increases the thickness of the cartilage at the ends of the bones. This will have the effect of making joints stronger and less prone to injury.

The increase in collagen content of the muscle tendons will make them stronger and less prone to injury. Lastly, the increase in collagen content in the ligaments which hold our bones together makes them stronger and therefore able to withstand stretching forces to a greater degree; this again will help to prevent injuries such as joint strains.

C2 Muscular system

Hypertrophy

If you exercise with some sort of resistance, e.g. weights, dyna band or body weight (as in press-ups), it will stress the skeletal muscle. This actually results in parts of the muscle breaking which is called a micro-tear. The more you stress the muscle with heavier weights, the more the muscle breaks down. After having rested and eaten the right foods, the body then starts to repair itself and will actually mend the muscle tissue and make it bigger and better than before. If you continue this process, the muscle tissue will keep getting bigger, which will result in an increase in your muscle size – this is called hypertrophy.

> **Key term**
>
> Hypertrophy is an increase in the size of skeletal muscle.

Muscular strength

The amount of force a muscle can produce is related to its size: the larger the muscle, the more force it can produce. Force is another way of measuring strength. Therefore, the larger the muscle, the more strength it can produce. In order to increase a person's strength, they will need to undergo muscle hypertrophy which can only occur from resistance training. The area in which an increase in muscle strength is required will determine which muscles are included in a strength training programme. For example, a speed cyclist will mainly be concerned with increasing the strength in their legs, so most of their strength training will focus on their lower body.

Figure 1.18 Speed cyclist, Chris Hoy

Muscular endurance (myoglobin, mitochondria, glycogen and triglyceride stores)

Aerobic endurance training will also increase muscular endurance for the muscles that are utilised in the training. Therefore, if a person does swimming, then muscles in their trunk, upper body and lower body muscles would all go through muscular endurance training as all of these groups of muscles are used in the sport. However, in cycling, just the muscular endurance in the lower body muscles will occur. Alternatively, a person could use resistance training with high reps and low loads to increase their muscular endurance of specific muscles that are used in the resistance training. The adaptations on the body from this type of training are to help the muscles to contract for long periods of time, which means the aerobic energy system will need be the main form of energy provision. Therefore, adaptations to improve the efficiency of this system will improve muscular endurance.

Much of the adaptations that occur to the muscle tissues from muscular endurance training are to help to increase the amount of oxygen available to the working muscles and also increase the amount of energy that can be supplied by the aerobic energy system to the muscles, as the aerobic energy system supplies most of the energy during muscular endurance exercises.

Myoglobin is used to store oxygen in muscle tissues. Myoglobin combines with oxygen to form oxymyoglobin. Oxymyoglobin is used as an oxygen storage site for when the body is in oxygen deprivation. When a person is exercising and the oxygen supplied by the blood is not sufficient, this storage of oxygen in myoglobin in the muscle tissue will help to meet the oxygen requirement to produce energy. Through muscular endurance training, these stores of myoglobin are increased, which means there is more oxygen available for the aerobic energy system to use to produce energy for muscle contraction.

The muscles will also increase their stores of glycogen and triglycerides – both of these are sources of energy for the aerobic energy system. This means that more energy is readily available in the muscle tissues to produce ATP. Lastly, there is a significant increase in the number of mitochondria in muscle tissue from muscular endurance training. The energy production from the aerobic energy system takes place mainly in these organelles, so having more mitochondria in muscle tissues means even more energy can be produced by the aerobic energy system.

Muscle tone

Muscle tone is the contraction of muscles while a person is at rest: the more toned the muscles, the firmer they feel when the muscles are relaxed. From regular participation in exercise, muscle tone increases. Increased muscle tone helps a person to maintain their posture so that they have an upright stance, with shoulders back and stomach drawn in. Muscle tone also helps a person to maintain their balance. High levels of muscle tone also help a person to generate heat, which is why a person with more muscle tissue will have a higher metabolic rate compared to a person with less muscle tissue.

Hyperplasia

Hyperplasia is the increase in number of muscle fibres. There is some debate as to whether adaption to exercise does actually lead to an increase in muscle fibres themselves or whether it is just an increase in the muscle fibre size that results in muscle hypertrophy. There has been a lot of research in animals on this topic but very little on humans to date, and the research on humans is not conclusive.

Adaptation of muscle fibre types

Muscle fibre types will adapt to training by increasing in size – high intensity training results in hypertrophy of fast twitch fibres whereas low intensity training will lead to hypertrophy of slow twitch muscle fibres. However, the type of training carried out will determine how type IIx muscle fibres adapt. In response to low intensity endurance training, type IIx fibres will convert so that they are more like type I muscle fibres which have a slow contraction speed and produce low intensity contractions. However, in response to high intensity training, they convert to become more like type IIa fibres which contract with high force for short periods of time.

Capillarisation

Aerobic endurance training has the effect of increasing the number of capillaries in the muscle fibres, which helps to increase the diffusion rate of gas exchange in the muscles. This therefore increases the amount of oxygen entering the muscles from the blood stream, as well as the amount of carbon dioxide leaving the muscles into the blood stream.

C1 and C2 Check your understanding

1 Describe how resistance training increases the strength of bones.
2 Identify an exercise that would increase the strength of the bones of the arms.
3 Describe why resistance exercise can result in a person being less likely to sprain their ankle.
4 Explain why a person with larger muscles is stronger than a person with smaller muscles.
5 Explain how the muscles adapt to endurance training.

C3 Respiratory system

The respiratory system deals with taking oxygen into the body and also with helping to remove waste products associated with muscle metabolism. Aerobic exercise training will result in the main adaptations of the respiratory system, as this type of exercise stresses the respiratory system in order to help it to take in more oxygen to improve aerobic exercise-related performance.

Aerobic training leads to adaption of the following areas in the respiratory system:

- **Respiratory muscles** – training leads to an increase in strength of the respiratory muscles which allows the lungs to take in more air per breath and also more forcibly exhale air. Although aerobic exercise is primarily concerned with producing adaptions in the respiratory system, relatively new research has shown that there a device that can be used to train the inspiratory muscles of the respiratory system. POWERbreathe uses resistance training methodology to train the inspiratory muscles including the diaphragm and external intercostal muscles to help a person to take in more air during inspiration.
- **Lung volumes and respiratory rate** – aerobic training reduces the VE rate during sub-maximal exercise. Endurance training can also provide a small increase in lung volumes: vital capacity increases slightly, as does tidal volume during maximal exercise. Residual volume is the amount of air left in the lungs after full exhalation.

- **Respiratory rate** – as the respiratory muscles respond to training, they are able to contract at a faster rate to allow for an increase in breathing rate, which helps to get more oxygen into the body and more carbon dioxide out of the body.

C4 Cardiovascular system

The main adaptations that occur to the cardiovascular system through endurance training are concerned with increasing the delivery of oxygen to the working muscles.

Cardiac hypertrophy and cardiac output

If you were to examine the heart of a top endurance athlete, you would find that the size of the walls of the left ventricle are markedly thicker than those of a person who did not perform aerobic exercise training. This adaptation is called cardiac hypertrophy.

Key term

Cardiac hypertrophy is where the size of the heart wall becomes thicker and stronger.

It occurs in the same way that we increase the size of our skeletal muscles – the more we exercise our muscles, the larger or more toned they become. In the same way, the more we exercise our heart through aerobic training, the larger it will become. This will then have the effect of increasing the stroke volume, which is the amount of blood that the heart can pump out per beat. As the heart wall becomes bigger, it can pump more blood per beat as the thicker wall can contract more forcibly. As the stroke volume is increased, the heart no longer needs to beat as often to get the same amount of blood around the body. This results in a decrease in heart rate which is known as bradycardia.

Key term

Bradycardia means a decreased resting heart rate.

An average male adult's heart rate is 70 bpm, however, Chris Froome, who was a Tour de France cyclist, has had a resting heart rate recorded at 29 bpm! As stroke volume increases, cardiac output also increases, so an endurance athlete's heart can pump more blood per minute than a non-trained person's. However, resting values of cardiac output do not change.

Sinoatrial node and cardiac cycle

Bradycardia also occurs as a result of aerobic training due to a decrease in firing from the sinoatrial node (SAN). The cardiac cycle is controlled by the SAN as this is the pacemaker of the heart. The faster the SAN fires, the faster the heart beats and the slower the SAN fires, the slower the heart beats. The decrease in firing from the SAN is a result of an increase in vagal tone which is controlled by the parasympathetic nervous system. The parasympathetic nervous system is responsible for calming a person down, and it is also known as the rest and digest response, which is increased from aerobic training.

Key term

Vagal tone is the amount of activity from the parasympathetic nervous system which affects the heart rate. An increase in vagal tone decreases heart rate.

Blood pressure

Aerobic exercise training will reduce a person's resting blood pressure. This is because exercise reduces the resistance of blood flow in the arteries.

However, blood pressure during maximal or sub-maximal exercise will remain unchanged from training.

Blood composition

The composition of blood will also adapt in response to aerobic exercise training. This type of training will increase the amount of haemoglobin in the blood due to an increase in the number of red blood cells (which contain the haemoglobin) which has the effect of further aiding the diffusion rate of oxygen into the blood stream.

Though haemoglobin content rises, there is also an increase in blood plasma which means that the blood haematocrit (ratio of red blood cell volume to total blood volume) is reduced, which lowers viscosity (thickness) and enables the blood to flow more easily.

Diffusion rate

The diffusion rate of oxygen into the blood stream increases as a result of aerobic exercise training. This occurs due to a variety of factors including:

- Capillaries become bigger, allowing more blood to travel through them.
- New capillaries develop (capillarisation) which aids in the extraction of oxygen.
- There is an increase in the oxygen-carrying capacity of the blood due to an increase in haemoglobin concentration.

C3 and C4 Check your understanding

1 Describe how aerobic exercise training will help a person to take in and exhale more air per breath.
2 Describe how aerobic exercise training increases the diffusion rate of oxygen in the lungs.
3 Define what is meant by bradycardia.
4 Describe how bradycardia occurs from aerobic exercise training.
5 Explain how the composition of blood helps to increase the oxygen-carrying capacity of blood.

C5 Nervous system

The main adaptations that occur to the nervous system are from resistance training types of exercise.

When a person starts a weight training programme they will see a noticeable increase in the ability to lift heavier weights before there is significant hypertrophy of the muscle fibres which is partly to do with the adaptations of the nervous system.

Motor units

Resistance training helps the nervous system adapt by increasing the recruitment of additional motor units in response to neural stimulation – these increased numbers of motor units that are stimulated means that more force can be produced as more muscle fibres are activated to contract and produce more force.

Neural pathway transmission efficiency

The neural pathways linking to motor units become more efficient at transmitting the stimulus which results in the target muscles being able to contract more quickly in response to the stimulation.

Nervous inhibition

The antagonistic muscle in the antagonistic pair are inhibited from contracting to a greater degree after resistance training due to adaptations of the nervous system. This allows the agonist and any synergist muscles to continue to contract more forcibly.

C6 Endocrine system

The endocrine system also adapts to aerobic and resistance training.

Adrenaline and noradrenalin

The gland that secretes adrenaline and noradrenaline has an increased capacity to secrete these hormones. This results in increased reaction from the organs targeted by these hormones to enable the body to be ready for exercise and sports participation at a faster rate.

Cortisol

Endurance exercise has the effect of lowering the release of cortisol in the body which helps to reduce the levels of stress a person may be suffering from. However, resistance training will actually increase resting levels of cortisol levels in the body.

Testosterone

Resistance training results in higher resting levels of testosterone and human growth hormone (HGH) which both help to increase protein synthesis for muscle hypertrophy.

C7 Energy systems

Stores of adenosine triphosphate (ATP), phosphocreatine (PC), glycogen and triglyceride

There are increased levels of ATP and PC in the muscle and an increased capacity to generate ATP by the ATP–PC energy system. This is partly due to the increased activity of the enzymes which break down PC. ATP production by anaerobic glycolysis is increased as a result of enhanced activity of the glycolytic enzymes. There is also an increased ability to break down glycogen in the absence of oxygen.

When glucose is stored it is in the form of glycogen which is bound to water (1 g of glucose needs 2.7 g of water) for storage. However, the glycogen molecule is bulky and difficult to store in large amounts. The body can store around 1600 kcals of glycogen, which would enable us to run for around 2 hours.

Triglycerides are dietary fats in that they are how the fats we ingest are packaged. A triglyceride is defined as 'three fatty acids attached to a glycerol backbone'. Glycerol is actually a carbohydrate which the fatty acids attach to; during digestion the fatty acids will be broken off from the glycerol backbone to be used by the body as required. The glycerol will be used as all carbohydrate are used to produce energy.

Number and size of mitochondria

Aerobic endurance exercise leads to the increase in number of mitochondria in the muscles that are used in the exercise. There is also an increase in the numbers of enzymes required in the process for ATP production in the mitochondria which results in the mitochondria being able to produce ATP more quickly.

Onset of blood lactate accumulation (OBLA)

As lactate accumulates it decreases the pH levels of the blood, making it more acidic. This increased level of hydrogen ions will eventually prevent the glycolytic enzyme functioning. However, anaerobic training increases the buffering capacity of the body and enables the body to work for longer in periods of high acidity so OBLA will increase.

Aerobic and anaerobic enzymes

The enzymes required to produce ATP during anaerobic and aerobic exercise increase which means the energy systems can produce ATP much more quickly after appropriate exercise training – i.e. anaerobic training to train the anaerobic energy systems and aerobic training to train the aerobic energy system.

Lactate buffering

Anaerobic training increases the buffering capacity of the body and enables the body to work for longer in periods of high intensity.

Respiratory exchange ratio (RER)

The RER is the ratio of carbon dioxide produced in relation to the amount of oxygen consumed by a person in each breath and is used to work out which fuels a person is using when they exercise.

RER = Volume carbon dioxide produced / volume of oxygen consumed

This is also known as the Respiratory Quotient (RQ). The fuel used to supply energy during exercise will determine the RER value.

The following shows the RER for different fuel sources:

Carbohydrate = 1

Fat = 0.7

Protein = 0.8

An RER of greater than 1 shows that the person is working anaerobically, as more carbon dioxide is being produced compared to oxygen being consumed.

Through aerobic endurance training, the RER will be lowered as a person can exercise at higher intensities before working anaerobically.

C8 Measurement of body systems and their contribution to sport and exercise performance

There are a number of fitness tests that can be carried out to determine how efficient the body systems are when taking part in sport and exercise. The results from these tests can help an athlete determine if they need to change their training programme or use different training methods to improve the efficiency of a targeted body system in order to enhance their sport and exercise performance.

Maximal oxygen consumption

Maximal oxygen consumption is a measure of a person's aerobic capacity, which is their ability to uptake and use oxygen. The higher a person's maximal oxygen consumption, the better they will be at performing aerobic exercise so that they are able to work at higher intensity and for longer periods of time compared to a person with a lower maximal oxygen consumption. A way to test for maximal oxygen consumption is to carry out a VO_2 max test. An untrained male will have an average absolute VO_2 max of 3.5 litres per minute, an untrained female will have an average absolute VO_2 max of 2 litres per minute. The main reasons for this difference are that males are usually bigger than females, as well as the difference in body composition between the genders. Females have approximately 10% more body fat than males, which will reduce their VO_2 max because fat mass hinders performance. Aerobic exercise training increases a person's maximal oxygen consumption due to the fact they are able to take up more oxygen in the lungs from increased depth of breathing and increased diffusion rate of oxygen into the blood from the lungs. Then there is also an increased extraction of oxygen and use of oxygen to produce energy by the muscles due to increased capillarisation and increased numbers of mitochondria and aerobic system enzymes in the mitochondria.

Anaerobic threshold (% of VO_2 Max)

This is the point at which most of the energy supplied is from the anaerobic energy system, so that more lactate is produced than is removed. To test for this, the person will take part in exercise with incremental intensity and blood is taken from their ear lobe or fingers to test for lactate levels in the blood.

Anaerobic power

There are different tests available to work out the power of specific parts of the body such as the Wingate test, Sergeant Jump and Vertical Jump. These tests provide an estimate of the person's anaerobic power which is required for explosive sports such as throwing events (e.g. shot put throwing) or jumping events (e.g. the high jump).

Strength (1RM)

The 1RM is a strength test that aims to measure the maximal weight an individual can lift. The test is frequently used in weight training programmes to measure training progression. A variety of muscle groups can be tested in this way depending on the type of lift that is used in the test.

Muscular endurance

Muscular endurance is the ability of muscles to keep contracting at moderate intensity for prolonged periods of time. Tests for this will target specific muscle groups and count how many repetitions can be completed in a specified timeframe, or how long a person can continue to carry out the exercise until exhaustion.

C5, C6, C7 and C8 Check your understanding

1 Explain why a person can lift heavier weights after the first few weeks of resistance training before muscle hypertrophy occurs.
2 Describe how the endocrine system responds to strength training.
3 Describe how aerobic training affects the amount of ATP that can be produced from the aerobic energy system.
4 Describe why anaerobic training helps a person to tolerate higher levels of lactate in their blood.
5 Identify an RER value that would show a person is working anaerobically.
6 Identify a test that can be used to assess a person's ability to uptake and use oxygen.
7 Identify a test that can be used to assess a person's strength of their quadriceps muscles.

D Environmental factors and sport and exercise performance

For this learning aim, you will need to be able to understand the responses and adaptations of the body systems to differing environmental factors during sport and exercise performance.

D1 High altitude

Anywhere more than 2400 m above sea level is considered to be at high altitude, which affects a person's sporting performance mainly due to the fact that there is a lower partial pressure of oxygen at altitude compared to being at sea level.

Partial pressure of oxygen at altitude compared with sea level

The further above sea level you travel, the lower the barometric pressure becomes. This means that the higher up you go, the 'thinner' the air becomes as there are fewer air molecules in the atmosphere. Therefore, although the percentage of oxygen, carbon dioxide and nitrogen within the air remains the same (20.93%, 0.03% and 79.04% respectively), every breath of air you take contains fewer and fewer molecules of oxygen (and carbon dioxide and nitrogen). As a result, a person must work harder to obtain the same quantities of oxygen compared with when they are at low altitudes. This means that an athlete who exercises or competes at high altitude will have to breathe much faster to take in enough oxygen for their energy systems to work normally than when they exercise at lower altitude.

In 1968 the Olympic Games were held in Mexico City, which stands at an elevation of 2300 m and is therefore classed as being at high altitude. In order to try to overcome the effects of 'thinner air', the athletes went through a period of acclimatisation, during which they trained at high altitude for a number of weeks. (The body responds physiologically by adapting to cope with the decreased levels of oxygen in the air.)

D2 Responses of body systems to high altitude

Initial responses of body to high altitude

The body's initial responses to being at high altitude are:

- An increase in respiratory rate (hyperventilation).
- An increase in heart rate (tachycardia).
- Hypoxia which is where the body has lower levels of oxygen than required.

When a person arrives at high altitude, their respiratory rate and depth increase. The increased breathing rate has the effect of causing more carbon dioxide to be expired and more oxygen to be delivered to the alveoli. The respiratory rate peaks after about one week of living at high altitude, and then slowly decreases over the next few months, although it tends to remain higher than its normal rate at sea level.

Heart rate also increases because the body's cells require a constant supply of oxygen. As there is less oxygen available in the blood, the heart beats more quickly to meet the cells' demands. However, heart rate will also start to decrease as more time is spent at high altitude.

Reduced VO$_2$ max

Due to the fact there is a lower partial pressure of oxygen in the air, a person's VO$_2$ max will be reduced when they arrive at altitude. VO$_2$ max is a measure of the body's ability to uptake and use oxygen. However, if there is less oxygen available in the air then the ability to uptake oxygen is reduced which results in a reduced VO$_2$ max.

Altitude sickness

A person may suffer from altitude sickness initially, but a person's fitness levels do not appear to have any effect on whether they will suffer from this condition or not.

Altitude sickness includes the following symptoms:

- Headache
- Nausea
- Dizziness
- Exhaustion.

D3 Adaptations of the body systems to high altitude

After a person has spent a number of weeks at high altitude, their body undergoes a number of changes in order to increase oxygen delivery to cells and improve efficiency of oxygen use. This response usually begins immediately and continues for several weeks.

The adaptations of the body systems to high altitude include an increase in:

- red blood cell production
- haemoglobin concentration
- capillarisation
- mitochondria
- oxidative enzymes.

Red blood cell production and haemoglobin concentration

The bone marrow contributes to acclimatisation by increasing red blood cell production and, therefore, the blood's haemoglobin concentration. This increase is triggered by the kidneys' increased production of erythropoietin (EPO). New red blood cells become available in the blood within four to five days, and have the effect of increasing the blood's oxygen-carrying capacity. An acclimatised person may have 30%–50% more red blood cells than a counterpart at sea level.

Capillarisation

The cardiovascular system also develops more capillaries in response to altitude. This has the effect of improving the rate of diffusion of oxygen from the blood into the muscles by shortening the distance between the cells and the capillary.

All these adaptations in the weeks following exposure are aimed at increasing oxygen transport to the body cells. This results in a reduction in the cardiac output required for oxygen delivery during rest and exercise compared with pre-acclimatisation.

Increase in the number of mitochondria and oxidative enzymes

The increased number of mitochondria and oxidative enzymes appears to be due to the switch in the body's preferred fuel for energy production. At low altitude, carbohydrate is the usual energy source; however, at altitude fat is the preferred fuel. This change is not well understood, but may be due to the fact that a reduced oxygen supply causes a higher lactate level in the muscles and blood stream. Carbohydrate metabolism also leads to increased production of lactate, but fat metabolism does not produce lactate as a by-product. Therefore, the change of the main metabolic fuel from carbohydrate to fat results in a reduced level of lactate production.

Impact of adaptations on sport and exercise performance

Aerobic performance

The body's adaptation to high altitude helps significantly, but does not fully compensate for the lack of oxygen in the air. There is a drop in VO_2 max by 2 % for every 300 m elevation above 1500 m, even after full acclimatisation

Anaerobic performance

As the impact of high altitude is mainly due to the reduced amount of oxygen available, and anaerobic performance does not require oxygen, there is limited effect on anaerobic performance at altitude. In fact, due to the reduced partial pressure of air, there is less resistance to movement. This means that some anaerobic performances may be increased if performed at altitude, such as throwing or jumping events. This was seen in the 1968 Mexico City Olympic Games where the world record for the long jump was set at 8.9 m and remained in place for 23 years.

Promoting equivalent adaptations to high altitude to enhance sport and exercise performance at sea level

The effects of altitude training will all contribute to higher levels of performance in aerobic endurance events which take place at sea level due to the increased oxygen carrying capacity of the blood and increased ability to deliver the oxygen to the working muscles. This has resulted in types of altitude training being included in elite athletes' training programmes before significant competitions.

However, as living at altitude prevents an athlete from being able to train to such a high intensity as when they are at sea level, because of the reduction in oxygen molecules in the air which results in a reduced VO_2 max, altitude training can take different forms.

Figure 1.19 A high altitude chamber

Some athletes acclimatise by training at a low altitude and then sleeping in simulated high altitude in a high altitude chamber. A high altitude chamber replicates the same conditions as being at high altitude with lower partial pressures of gases.

This allows the athlete to train at maximal levels when they are at low altitude, and then be exposed to hypoxic stress while sleeping, thus increasing the production of red blood cells and other physiological adaptations.

Key term

Hypoxic stress means lower than normal oxygen levels.

If the person is competing at high altitude, then they may live at high altitude for a number of weeks before the competition, in order for their body to adapt appropriately prior to competition. They may also sleep and train in a hypoxic chamber before they go to live at high altitude to speed up the process of adaption.

D1, D2 and D3 Check your understanding

1 Describe what happens to the air at high altitude.
2 Identify two ways the body initially responds to being at high altitude.
3 Describe why a person's VO_2 max is reduced at altitude.
4 Identify three symptoms of altitude sickness.
5 Describe how the release of EPO helps a person to acclimatise to high altitude.
6 Explain why a javelin thrower's performance could be improved at high altitude.
7 Describe how a high altitude chamber could help to improve a 5000 m runner's performance.

D4 Thermoregulation

> ### Key term
>
> **Thermoregulation** is the process of maintaining a constant body core temperature. In humans this temperature is 37°C.

The core of the body consists of the head, chest and abdomen.

Figure 1.20 The body core

Activity: Core temperature and skin temperature

Aim
The aim this activity is to determine what the core temperature and the skin temperature of a person are.

Equipment
Oral thermometer

Sterilising fluid

Skin thermometer

Pen and paper

Method
1 Place a sterile thermometer under your tongue and leave it there for a few minutes.
2 Take the thermometer out of your mouth and record the temperature reading.
3 Place a skin thermometer on your hand and record the temperature reading.
4 Place the skin thermometer on your neck and record the temperature reading.
5 If you have time, take external readings from other parts of your body.
6 Disinfect/sterilise all thermometers before allowing another person to use them.

Results
Record your results in the table below.

Core temperature (°C)	
Hand temperature (°C)	
Neck temperature (°C)	

Conclusion
Try to answer these questions in your conclusion:

1 Is your core temperature the same as that of the person sitting next to you? If not, why do you think this is?
2 Why is your skin a different temperature to your core temperature?
3 Is there a difference between skin temperature readings taken from different sites of your body? Try to explain why this is.

The skin temperature of the body can vary a great deal; however, if the core temperature is increased or decreased by 1 °C or more, this will effect a person's physical and mental performance. Larger changes in core temperature will lead to hypothermia or hyperthermia, both of which can be fatal.

> **Key terms**
>
> **Hypothermia** means lower than normal core temperature.
>
> **Hyperthermia** means higher than normal core temperature.

In order to assess the core temperature of a person, there are a number of places a specialised thermometer can be placed: the mouth, the ear, the rectum or under the arm. For sports scientists, the ear is the most common site for measuring core temperature, or, if the exercise allows, the rectal thermometer is used as this gives the most accurate readings of the true body core temperature.

Heat transfer

There are four different methods of heat transfer, some of which can be used to rid the body of excess heat and others which can be used to gain heat.

1 **Conduction** – Place your hand on the desk in front of you. How does it feel? If it feels cold then you are losing heat to it via conduction; if it feels hot then you are gaining heat by conduction. Conduction involves the direct transfer of heat from one object to another. Normally this method of heat loss is not significant unless a person is exercising in cold water. This is because water conducts heat away from the body approximately 25 times more quickly than air. At the same temperature, a person in water will lose heat from the body two to four times faster than in air.

2 **Convection** – Blow air over your hand. How does your hand feel? Your hand probably will have felt cooler after having air blown over it. This blowing of air molecules across your hand is the basis of convection. As air molecules are moved across the body, heat will be lost because convective air currents carry the heat away. Wind will increase the flow of air over the skin, thus increasing the

amount of heat lost through convection. This is why a breeze feels good on a hot day and why we use fans to help keep us cool.

Figure 1.21 We use fans to keep us cool

3 **Radiation** – At rest, radiation is the main method of heat loss. It is the process by which heat is lost (via electromagnetic waves) to cooler objects in the environment, such as the floor, walls, trees, and so on. How much heat a person loses through radiation is determined by their size, mass and body composition.

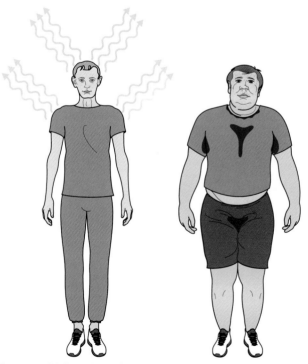

Figure 1.22 People with a high body fat percentage will lose less heat through radiation than a person with a low body fat percentage

People with a high body fat percentage will lose less heat through radiation than a person with a low body fat percentage, because body fat acts as an insulator to radiative heat loss. In contrast, a tall slim person will lose more heat through radiation than a short stocky person. In warm climates, the sun radiates heat to the body, which will increase its temperature. This makes getting rid of excess heat during exercise more difficult, because the sun's heat must also be dissipated.

4 **Evaporation of sweat** – In humans, evaporation of sweat from the body is the major method of heat dissipation, particularly during exercise. Heat is transferred continually to the environment as sweat evaporates from the skin's surface and produces a cooling effect. However, if the environment is humid, evaporative heat loss is reduced. Heat is only lost when sweat evaporates, which it will not do in humid conditions. Therefore, on a hot, humid day, an athlete can be dripping with sweat, but because the sweat is not evaporating, it does not cool them down.

Figure 1.23 Evaporation of sweat from the body is the major method of heat dissipation

Activity: The effect of blood vessel dilation and constriction on the skin

Aim

The aim of this activity is to see how blood vessel dilatation and constriction affect the colour of the skin.

Equipment

Large beakers	Thermometer
Hot water	Paper towels
Ice cubes	Skin thermometers (if available)

Method

1 Working in small groups, fill a large beaker with warm/hot water. Ensure the water is not too hot for you to place your hand in! Take the temperature of the water and write it down.

2 Look at your hand and make a note of its colour.

3 Place your hand in the water for about 3 minutes.

4 Remove your hand from the water, towel it dry, and then record the skin temperature. Note down the colour of your hand.

5 Fill a large beaker with cold water and add a few ice cubes. After 2 minutes, take the temperature of the water and note it down. Ensure the water is not too cold for you to bear.

6 Place your hand in the water for about 3 minutes.

7 Remove your hand from the water, towel it dry, and then record the skin temperature. Note down the colour of your hand.

Results

Record your results in the table below.

Temperature of water (°C)	Colour of hand
Hot	
Cold	

Conclusion

Try to answer the following questions:

1 Why did your hand turn the colour it did after having been placed in hot water?

2 Why did your hand turn the colour it did after having been placed in cold water?

3 By what process was your hand trying to lose heat when it was placed in the hot water?

D5 Excessive heat

Exercise increases metabolic rate by 20–25 times, and could increase core temperature by 1 °C every six minutes if heat loss did not take place. This would result in death from hyperthermia if exercise continued. Therefore, with the added stress of a hot environment, an exercising athlete has to maximise heat loss in order to perform optimally and to avoid hyperthermia.

The hypothalamus acts as a thermostat and initiates the responses that protect the body from overheating. It receives information about the temperature of the body via two sources:

- indirectly from the thermoreceptors in the skin
- directly by changes in blood temperature detected by thermoreceptors in the blood vessels.

Methods of heat loss in a hot environment

Heat loss through radiation is not possible if the environment is hotter than the person exercising. Therefore, there are only three forms of heat loss available to a person exercising in a hot environment.

Conductive heat loss occurs by the peripheral blood vessels dilating and bringing blood close to the skin's surface.

This results in the rosy-coloured skin associated with hot athletes. The heat from the blood warms the air molecules around the person and any cooler surfaces that come into contact with the skin. Conductive heat loss works in conjunction with convective heat loss.

Figure 1.24 Conductive heat loss results in the rosy-coloured skin associated with hot athletes

Convective heat loss occurs much more rapidly if there is increased air flow around the body, e.g. if it is windy or a fan is being used. If there is little air movement, the air next to the skin is warmed and acts as a layer of insulation that minimises further convective heat loss. However, if the warmed air surrounding the body is frequently changed due to increased air currents, heat loss through convection will continue to remove excess body heat.

Evaporative heat loss provides the main source of heat dissipation. As the sweat evaporates, it cools down the skin surface. This has the effect of cooling the blood as it travels through the blood vessels that are close to the skin surface. In order for evaporative heat loss to occur maximally, the person must be hydrated and have normal levels of salt and electrolytes in their body.

Children are much more prone to overheating than adults. This is partly because they do not have a fully developed sweating mechanism and also because they have a much higher surface area to volume ratio. This fact means that they will gain (or lose) heat much more quickly than adults. Therefore, when children are taking part in sports or exercise on a hot day, they should be given lots of rest periods and drinks and where possible kept out of direct sunlight.

Women usually have lower sweat rates than men, therefore, on average, males are able to lose more heat through evaporative heat loss than females. However, as females have a higher body surface area to volume ratio than males, they are able to lose more heat through radiation. Research has shown that these variations in heat loss between the sexes evens out, so that there is no real difference in the ability to dissipate heat between males and females.

Activity: Heat loss

Name the main method(s) of heat loss in the following conditions and try to explain your answers:

1 Swimming in cold water
2 Running on a cloudy, windy day
3 Cycling on a hot, sunny day.

The circulatory system is vitally important in ensuring that these three methods of heat loss can occur. Not only does the blood have to supply the muscles with oxygen and nutrients, it also plays a major part in thermoregulation. The blood is redirected to the periphery by dilatation of peripheral blood vessels. In extreme conditions, 15%–25% of the cardiac output is directed to the skin. As a result of these two cardiovascular demands, the heart rate is higher when exercising in the heat than in normal conditions.

Responses of the body to excessive heat during sport and exercise performance

Hyperthermia
If the body is unable to lose the excess heat generated from exercising and/or from the environment, the person will suffer from hyperthermia.

There are three major forms of hyperthermia:

- heat cramps
- heat exhaustion
- heat stroke.

Heat cramps are muscle spasms caused by heavy sweating. Although heat cramps can be quite painful, they usually do not result in permanent damage.

Heat exhaustion is more serious than heat cramps. It occurs primarily because of dehydration and loss of important minerals. In order to lose body heat, the surface blood vessels and capillaries dilate to cool the blood. However, when the body is dehydrated during heat exhaustion, the blood volume is reduced so there is not enough blood to supply both the muscles and the skin with their required blood supply. This results in the peripheral dilated blood vessels constricting which significantly reduces heat loss. This can be observed by looking at the face of an athlete suffering from heat exhaustion – it will suddenly change from a red, rosy appearance to a much paler colour or white.

If a person ignores the symptoms of heat exhaustion and continues to exercise, they will suffer from heat stroke, which is a life-threatening condition and has a high death rate. It occurs because the body has depleted its supply of water and salt, and results in the person's body temperature rising to deadly levels. If the core temperature of the body reaches 43 °C or more, the proteins start to break down and change their structure permanently. Imagine cooking an egg: the egg white is mainly made up of protein; when the egg white reaches a certain temperature (around 43 °C), its structure changes from a runny viscous medium to a solid. The same principle applies to the body's proteins, such as the enzymes and hormones. Once heated to a certain temperature, the structure of the body's proteins will permanently change and will no longer be able to function. Therefore, it is vitally important that the core temperature is not elevated to this degree.

Dehydration
Heart rate is also elevated because of the slight to severe dehydration that often occurs while exercising in the heat. If the person is dehydrated, then plasma volume is decreased. A decreased plasma volume will lead to a decreased stroke volume. Therefore, as we know:

Cardiac output = heart rate x stroke volume

Q (l per min) = HR (bpm) x SV (ml)

In order for cardiac output to remain the same, heart rate has to increase to make up for the decreased stroke volume.

Q = HR x SV

Activity: Exercising in hot conditions

Aim

The aim of this activity is to see how the effect of exercising in hot conditions affects the cardiovascular system. You should ensure this activity is supervised by a qualified tutor and that a risk assessment has been carried out prior to participation.

Equipment

Bleep test

Tape recorder

Heart rate monitors

Results table

Sports kit – shorts and T-shirt for test 1; tracksuit bottoms, sweatshirt, woolly hat, gloves for test 2

Weighing scales

Sports hall

Method

Test 1 – normal conditions

1   Each person is weighed wearing shorts and T-shirt.

2   Working in pairs, place a heart rate monitor on the first person taking the test.

3   The first person takes part in the bleep test. At the end of each stage, the exercising person calls out their heart rate while their partner records this number and the appearance of the exercising person.

4   Once the exercising person has exercised to voluntary exhaustion, they towel down, put on a clean T-shirt and record their body weight.

5   The process is repeated for the second person.

Test 2 – hot conditions

This test should be carried out at least 72 hours after test 1. Ensure that each person taking part is fully hydrated before taking part in this test.

1   Each person is weighed wearing shorts and T-shirt.

2   Working in pairs, place a heart rate monitor on the first person taking the test.

3   This person then puts on tracksuit bottoms, a sweatshirt, woolly hat and gloves.

4   This person then takes part in the bleep test. At the end of each stage, the exercising person calls out their heart rate while their partner records this number and the appearance of the exercising person.

5   Once the exercising person has exercised to voluntary exhaustion, they remove their tracksuit bottoms, sweatshirt, hat and gloves, towel down and put on a fresh T-shirt and shorts. The person is then weighed.

Results

Copy the table below to record your results.

Stage	Heart rate	Appearance	Test 1	Test 2
1				
2				
3				
4				
5				
6				
7				
8				
9				
10				

Now plot the heart rates for the normal and hot conditions on a line graph.

You should also record your weight results, as shown below.

Test 1

Weight before: _____

Weight after: _____

Weight difference: _____

Test 2

Weight before: _____

Weight after: _____

Weight difference: _____

Conclusion

Try to answer the following questions:

1   Was there a difference in the heart rates at each stage in the two tests?

2   Was there a difference in the person's appearance in the two tests at each stage of the bleep test? Was there any difference between the weight loss in test 1 and test 2?

3   Did the person manage to reach the same stage in the bleep test in both tests? Try to explain your results.

Adaption to excessive heat on the body during sport and exercise performance

Adaptation to excessive heat takes around 14 days for full acclimatisation; however, in the first 1–5 days the body will start to adapt in the following ways:

- **Increased sweat production**

  The body is able to produce at a faster rate, so more sweat is produced to have a greater cooling effect on the body through the evaporation of the sweat.

- **Reduced electrolyte concentration in sweat**

  The body starts to conserve the electrolytes sodium and chloride so not as much is lost in sweat, which helps with water retention.

- **Increased blood plasma volume**

  Plasma volume expands, which means there is more water in the blood that can be used to produce sweat to cool the person down.

- **Earlier onset of sweating**

  The body is able to produce sweat at a lower core temperature, which helps the body to start cooling down sooner.

Impact of adaptations on sport and exercise performance

Aerobic performance

Aerobic performance is the main type of performance negatively affected by excessive heat because of dehydration. Dehydration causes a significant loss of performance. This is because dehydration will cause a loss of blood plasma affecting blood flow and the ability to sweat. When we sweat it is predominantly blood plasma that is lost and thus cardiac output (the amount of the blood leaving the heart per minute) is reduced. Therefore, rehydration is important to improve the circulation of the blood and the body's ability to control temperature. The effects of adaption to heat help a person to produce more sweat to help to cool them down through evaporation. Any athlete competing in a hot environment will need to go through a full acclimations process to ensure their body is able to cope with the demands of exercising in the heat.

Anaerobic performance

Anaerobic performance will only last for short periods of time and not rely to the same extent on the volume of blood in the body as aerobic exercise. Therefore, athletes competing in anaerobic sporting events are not affected to the same degree as those competing in aerobic events.

D4 and D5 Check your understanding

1 Define what is meant by thermoregulation.
2 Identify what is meant by hyperthermia.
3 Describe four methods of heat transfer.
4 Identify what happens to a person's metabolic rate during exercise.
5 Describe how the body signals an excess of heat.
6 Explain how conductive heat loss can occur in a hot environment.
7 Describe how dehydration increases a person's heart rate.

D6 Extreme cold

When humans are exposed to a cold environment at rest, the body attempts to prevent heat loss, as well as to increase heat production.

Methods of reducing heat loss during sport and exercise performance

The three main methods a person uses to reduce their heat loss are:

- Vasoconstriction
- Shivering thermogenesis
- Non-shivering thermogenesis.

Vasoconstriction

First of all, the body will decrease the blood supply to the peripheral circulation by vasoconstriction of the peripheral blood vessels. The purpose of this is to keep the blood close to the body core and redirect the blood away from the body's extremities and skin surface, where it would be cooled down by the environment. In humans, vasoconstriction can reduce heat loss by up to a third. The presence of subcutaneous fat also aids in maintaining the heat of the blood as fat is a very good insulator.

Shivering thermogenesis

A person will experience a rapid involuntary cycle of contraction and relaxation of skeletal muscles, which is called shivering. The process of shivering can actually increase metabolic rate to four to five times above resting levels.

Non-shivering thermogenesis

Secondly, a person will experience an increase in their metabolic rate, which is brought about by an increased release of the hormones thyroxin and adrenaline. An increased metabolic rate will generate body heat. This process is called non-shivering thermogenesis.

A person can also conserve heat by adding clothing, which is a behavioural mechanism for minimising heat loss.

Effects of cold on the body during sport and exercise performance

The effect of a cold environment on exercise performance depends largely on the severity of the cold and the type of exercise performed. Exposure to a moderately cold environment may actually have a positive effect on performance, as the cardiovascular system no longer has to divert blood to the periphery for heat loss in addition to supplying the exercising muscles with blood. This results in less stress being placed on the heart than when exercising in the heat. Therefore, it is not surprising that record performances during long-distance running and cycling are usually achieved in cool climatic conditions.

Exposure to a very cold environment may cause frost bite or hypothermia

Hypothermia is defined as a drop in the body's normal core temperature to 35 °C or below. The condition usually comes on gradually and its severity varies in relation to how low the body core temperature drops – if it drops to 30 °C or below, this can lead to cardiac and respiratory failure that is soon followed by death.

Frostbite usually occurs in a person's fingers or toes. It happens when a part of the body becomes extremely cold, significantly reducing blood supply to the area, which results in the body tissue freezing. The ice crystals that form will rupture and destroy the body's cells. The involved region turns a deep purple or red colour and has blisters, which are usually filled with blood. This tissue will then have to be amputated to prevent infection spreading to other parts of the body.

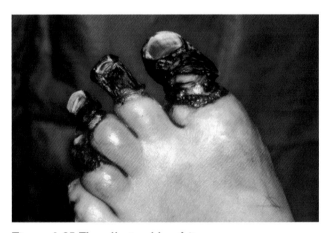

Figure 1.25 The effects of frostbite

D6 Check your understanding

1 Identify three ways a person can reduce their heat loss.
2 Explain why a person who is going to swim the English Channel puts on body fat as part of their preparation.
3 Explain the difference between shivering and non-shivering thermogenesis.
4 Describe why a cold climate can increase marathon running sporting performance.

Exam Practice

The Check your understanding questions will provide revision for each topic in each learning aim. However, in the external assessment you will be asked questions on the interrelationship of the body systems in line with AO4 Make connections between how the body systems work together in response to the demands of sport and exercise and to enhance performance.

To help you to prepare for this, some revision questions on this AO are included below.

1   A basketball player takes part in a fitness training programme and their VO_2 max increases over the 8-week training period.

The training programme includes the following:

Monday: 30 minutes Fartlek running

Tuesday: 30 minutes swimming

Wednesday: resistance training

Thursday: 30 minutes Fartlek running

Friday: resistance training

Saturday: 30 minutes continuous running.

Evaluate how the training programme would improve the cardiovascular and respiratory system to lead to the increase in VO_2 max. (10 marks)

2   A marathon runner takes part in a race in a hot climate and gets a slower time compared to previous race in a cooler climate.

Analyse why her performance could be slower due to the change in climate. (10 marks)

3   A 400 m runner trains every day for 5 weeks and has noticed that they are getting slower times to complete the 400 m run.

Evaluate how the muscular and endocrine system could have an effect on the other body systems to produce this decline in performance. (10 marks)

4   A Tour De France cyclist takes part in high altitude training in order to help improve their cycling performance in a race that is due to take place at sea level.

Evaluate how adaptations to high altitude training of the cardiovascular and respiratory system could improve cycling performance at sea level. (10 marks)

Further reading

Howley, E.T. and Franks, B.D. (2003). *Health Fitness Instructor's Handbook (Fourth Edition),* Human Kinetics.

Palastanga, N., Field, D. and Soames, R. (2006). *Anatomy and Human Movement: Structure and Function (Fifth Edition),* Butterworth-Heinemann.

Sharkey, B.J. and Gaskill, S.E. (2006). *Fitness and Health (Sixth Edition),* Human Kinetics.

Tortora, G.J. and Derrickson, B.H. (2008). *Principles of Anatomy and Physiology (12th Edition),* John Wiley & Sons.

American College of Sports Medicine's Health and Fitness Journal

British Journal of Sports Medicine Exercise and Sport Sciences

Reviews International Journal of Sports Science & Coaching Medicine

Science in Sports and Exercise Research Quarterly for Exercise and Sport

References

Howley, E.T. and Franks, B.D. (2003). *Health Fitness Instructor's Handbook (Fourth Edition),* Human Kinetics.

Palastanga, N., Field, D. and Soames, R. (2006). *Anatomy and Human Movement: Structure and Function (Fifth Edition),* Butterworth-Heinemann, 2006.

Sharkey, B.J. and Gaskill, S.E. (2006). *Fitness and Health (Sixth Edition),* Human Kinetics.

Stafford-Brown, J. and Rea, S. (2010). *BTEC National for Sport and Exercise Sciences (Third Edition),* Hodder Education.

Tortora, G.J. and Derrickson, B.H. (2008). *Principles of Anatomy and Physiology (12th Edition),* John Wiley & Sons.

Useful websites

1st4Sport
www.1st4sport.com

American College of Sports Medicine
www.acsm.org.uk

The British Association of Sport and Exercise Sciences (BASES)
www.bases.org.uk

The Human Kinetics website
www.humankinetics.com

Sport Science journal
www.sportsci.org.uk

Sports Coach UK
www.sportscoachuk.org.uk

Topend Sports
www.topendsports.com

2 Functional anatomy

About this unit

Functional anatomy is the study of the body systems and how they produce movement. Therefore, the focus of this unit is mainly on the skeletal and muscular systems. However, the cardiovascular system, respiratory and energy systems will also be considered, as they clearly play a key role in providing the muscular system with the nutrients and oxygen that it needs, as well as removing waste products so that muscles can contract to produce movement. In order to understand the function of the cardiovascular, respiratory, skeletal and muscular systems, this unit will examine the anatomical structure of each. The physiology of each system (including the energy systems) will also be introduced, however, the physiology of each of these systems is covered in much more detail in Unit 1 Sport and exercise physiology.

How will I be assessed?

External assessment

This unit will be assessed externally, meaning that at the end of the unit you will complete a written examination that has been set by Pearson and will be marked by Pearson examiners.

The paper contains short- and long-answer questions and covers the anatomy of the cardiovascular, respiratory, skeletal, and muscular systems. The questions will require you to use your knowledge and understanding of each of these systems to analyse how they produce movements in sport and exercise-related contexts. You will also need to demonstrate your understanding as to how each system works together to carry out sport and exercise-related movements.

You will be given 1 hour and 30 minutes to sit the exam and the number of marks available is 80.

The exam will be available twice a year from May/June 2017.

Key term

Functional anatomy is the study of the structures of the different body systems and how they contribute to producing movement.

How will I be graded?

The assessment outcomes show you the knowledge and skills that you are expected to be able to demonstrate in the exam. It is important when you are covering the unit content that you keep these objectives in mind, as they show what you need to be able to do with the information you are learning about. In this case, the words demonstrate, apply and analyse are particularly important, as they tell you the skills that you will need to show in the external assessment.

Assessment outcomes

The exam is split into four different assessment outcomes (AOs) and each will be covered in varying amounts within the paper. The command words that will be used for each assessment outcome are also provided, to help you to gain an understanding of the depth and breadth that you will need to include in your responses for each AO.

→

How will I be graded?

AO1 Demonstrate knowledge and understanding of the language, structure, characteristics and function of each anatomical system.

Command words: describe, give, identify, name, state

Marks: range from 1 to 5 marks

AO2 Apply knowledge and understanding of the structure, characteristics and function of the anatomical systems in context.

Command words: describe, explain

Marks: range from 2 to 5 marks

AO3 Analyse the anatomical systems' effectiveness in producing sport and exercise movements and evaluate their impact on performing movements successfully.

Command words: analyse, assess, evaluate, discuss, to what extent

Marks: range from 8 to 20 marks

AO4 Make connections between anatomical systems and how they interrelate in order to carry out different exercise and sporting movements in context.

Command words: analyse, assess, evaluate, discuss, to what extent

Grade descriptors

Grade descriptors are provided by Pearson to give an idea of what sorts of skills and knowledge need to be shown to achieve a pass or a distinction grade. However, further grades are available including:

U – Unclassified

Level 3 Pass

Learners demonstrate knowledge of functional anatomy and apply it to exercise and sports performance. They have a sound understanding of the structures, functions and characteristics of the anatomical systems and are able to apply this to a range of familiar and unfamiliar contexts. Learners can interpret information related to exercise and sports performance and make judgements on how the anatomical systems allow for movements to be carried out.

Level 3 Distinction

Learners demonstrate thorough knowledge and understanding of the anatomical systems in exercise and sports performance and can apply this to a range of familiar and unfamiliar contexts. Learners are able to analyse how the body carries out exercise and sporting movements.

Learners will be able to interpret information on exercise and sports performance and be able to make reasoned judgements on how anatomical systems carry out exercise and sporting movements in a range of different contexts, demonstrating understanding of the interrelationships between those systems.

Command words meanings

In your external assessment, each question will start with one of the possible command words or terms, so it is important that you know what each means so that you know how to answer each question. Look at page 8 for a table of these.

A Anatomical positions, terms and references

A1 Anatomical language

The terminology used in anatomy stems from Greek and Latin origins. It is therefore important for you to have an understanding of what some of these key terms mean so that you are able to locate and describe different parts of the body in reference to their correct location.

Anatomical standing position

This is the point of reference in relation to anatomical terms and all other locations of different parts of the body, and movements are related this position.

In the anatomical standing position, the body stands up straight with the feet parallel and the arms hanging at the sides with the palms facing forward.

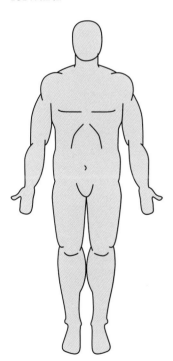

Figure 2.1 Anatomical standing position

Anterior – Towards the front of the body, e.g. the nose is on the anterior side of the head.

Posterior – Towards the back of the body, e.g. the heel of the foot is located on the posterior of the body.

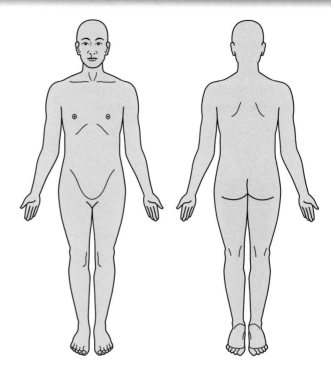

Figure 2.2 Anterior and posterior views of the body

Lateral – Away from the midline of the body, e.g. the shoulders are lateral to the chest.

Medial – Close to the midline of the body, e.g. the neck is medial to the shoulders.

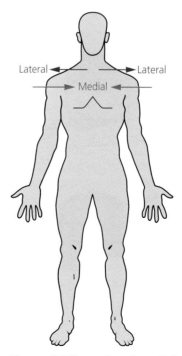

Lateral · Lateral
Medial

Figure 2.3 Lateral and medial

Proximal – Closest to the main part of the body (main part of body includes the shoulders or the hip), e.g. the knee is proximal to the ankle.

Distal – Further away from the main part of the body, e.g. the wrist is distal to the elbow.

Superior – Higher or closer to the head, e.g. the eyes are superior to the nose.

Inferior – Lower or closer to the feet, e.g. the ankle is inferior to the knee.

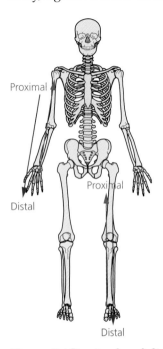

Figure 2.4 Proximal and distal

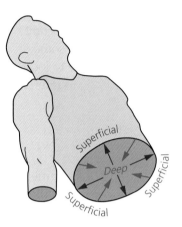

Figure 2.5 Superficial and deep

Peripheral and superficial – Both of these terms mean close to the surface of the body, e.g. the finger nails are peripheral to the phalanges.

Deep – Further away from the surface of the body, e.g. the stomach is deep in relation to the abdominal muscles.

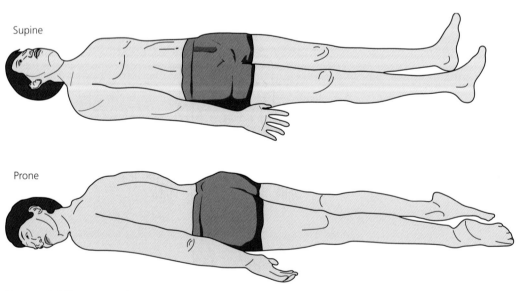

Figure 2.6 Supine and prone

Supine – Lying down on your back with your face pointing upwards. This term can also be applied to the hand, with the palm facing upwards.

Prone – Lying down on your stomach with your face pointing downwards. This term can also be applied to the hand, with the palm facing downwards.

A1 Check your understanding

Answer the following questions using your knowledge of anatomical terminology:

1 Which of the following statements describes the 'anatomical position'?

   a) Standing erect, facing forwards, arms at side, palms facing the person's side

   b) Standing erect, facing forwards, arms at side, palms facing forward

   c) Standing erect, facing forwards, arms at side, palms facing backward

   d) Standing erect, facing forwards, arms at side, palms facing outward.

2 Which of the following are correct statements?

   a) The neck is superior to the pelvis.

   b) The chest is inferior to the stomach.

   c) The hip is superior to the shoulder.

   d) The ribs are superior to the chin.

3 When a person is walking towards you, what view are you seeing of them?

4 Complete the missing words with either **lateral** or **medial** in the following sentences:

   a) The inside of the thigh is _____ to the outside of the thigh.

   b) The shoulder is _____ to the neck.

   c) The knee is _____ to the hip.

5 Complete the missing words with either **distal** or **proximal** in the following sentences:

   a) The hip is _____ to the knee.

   b) The shoulder is _____ to the elbow.

   c) The knee is _____ to the ankle.

6 Complete the missing words with either **superior** or **inferior** in the following sentences:

   a) The elbow is _____ to the knee.

   b) The ankle is _____ to the knee.

   c) The mouth is _____ to the chin.

7 Identify if a person is supine or prone in the following sports activities:

   a) swimming breast stroke

   b) swimming back crawl

   c) performing press-ups.

B Anatomy of the cardiovascular system

B1 Location, anatomy and function of cardiovascular components

Close your hand into a fist and look at it. Your fist is approximately the same size as your heart, around 12 cm long, 9 cm wide and 6 cm thick. It is located behind the sternum and tilted to the left. The heart is made up mainly of cardiac muscle, which is also known as myocardium.

Function and anatomy of the heart

The heart is divided into right- and left-hand sides by the septum. The two sides are separate and have no communication with each other. Each side is further divided into two chambers. The upper chambers are called the atria (atria pleural, atrium singular) the lower chambers are called the ventricles.

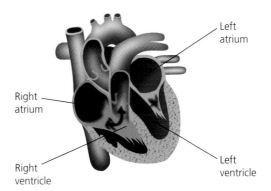

Figure 2.7 The anatomy of the heart

Blood flow through the heart

- **Right atrium (RA)** – This receives deoxygenated blood from the organs of the body.

- **Right ventricle (RV)** – This pumps deoxygenated blood to the lungs.

- **Left atrium (LA)** – This receives oxygenated blood from the lungs.

- **Left ventricle (LV)** – This pumps oxygenated blood to all organs of the body; it is larger and therefore stronger than the right ventricle as it has to pump the blood through the body.

The heart is made of cardiac muscle called the myocardium. Blood circulation is dependent upon the action of the myocardium, which varies in thickness: it is thickest in the left ventricle to produce power to pump oxygenated blood around the body, and is thinner in the right ventricle and thinnest in the atria.

Coronary arteries

These are the blood vessels that supply the blood with oxygen and nutrients and remove the waste products. Remember, the blood that is pumped by the heart does not provide any oxygen or nutrients to the heart itself as the blood just flows through it and then, as the heart contracts, blood is pumped from the heart and around the body and to the lungs.

Valves of the heart

The heart uses valves to ensure the blood flows in the right direction. The valves consist of cusps made of muscle and fibrous tissues that are attached to several fine, tendinous cords called chordae tendinous, which keep the valves in place and prevent the cusps from being forced back into the atrium.

There are four main valves:

- The **tricuspid valve** is located on the right side of the heart. It opens up to allow blood to flow in one direction from the right atrium to the right ventricle.
- The **bicuspid valve** opens up to allow blood to flow in one direction from the left atrium to the left ventricle.

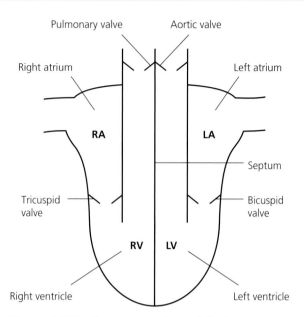

Figure 2.8 The four main valves of the heart

- The **semilunar valves** are located between the ventricles and the blood vessels that take blood away from the heart and prevent blood flowing back into the heart after the ventricles have contracted.

Location and anatomy of blood vessels

There are four main blood vessels that take blood into and out of the heart. These are the:

- aorta
- superior vena cava
- pulmonary artery
- pulmonary vein.

The **aorta** carries oxygenated blood out of the left ventricle to the body.

The **superior vena cava** returns deoxygenated blood to the right atrium from the head and upper body; the inferior vena cava returns deoxygenated blood to the right atrium from the lower body.

The **pulmonary vein** carries freshly oxygenated blood from the lungs to the left atrium.

The **pulmonary artery** carries deoxygenated blood from the body to the lungs.

In order to make its journey around the body, blood is carried through five different types of blood vessel:

- arteries
- arterioles
- capillaries
- venuoles
- veins.

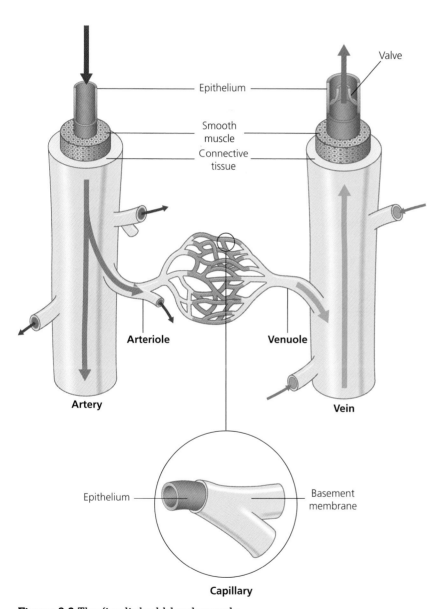

Figure 2.9 The five linked blood vessels

Activity: Heart dissection

Aim

The aim of this practical is to examine the structure of a mammalian heart.

Equipment

Sheep or pig heart	Scissors	Disposal bag/bin for hearts and used gloves
Dissection boards	Lab coats	Worksheets
Tweezers	Latex gloves	Goggles
Scalpels	Disinfectant	

Method

Working in groups of three or four put on lab coats, goggles and latex gloves, then complete the following activities.

1   Examine the outside of the heart and make a note of its texture and appearance.
2   Try to determine the orientation of the heart in the body.
3   The valves inside the heart should still be intact and can be shown to still work. Go to a sink and pass running water into the left and right atria; it should be possible to see the valves close.
4   Place the heart back onto the dissection board, dome-side up, and make an incision with the scalpel or with the scissors from the right atrium right down to the right ventricle. This should expose the whole of the inside of the right-hand side of the heart. Make a note of the appearance and texture of the inside of the heart.
5   The tendons that hold the valves in place can be seen clearly. Use the tweezers to pull on these, and make a note of their strength.
6   Dissect the left-hand side of the heart, from the left atrium down towards the left ventricle. Compare the thickness of the right- and left-hand side ventricle walls.
7   Try to ascertain which blood vessel is which by pushing your finger down the blood vessels into the heart. Where your finger appears should give you enough of a clue to work out which blood vessel is which.

Results and conclusion

In your conclusion, look back at the comments you have made throughout the dissection, then write down what you have found out about the heart's anatomy and try to explain why it has these anatomical features.

Activity: The heart

Fill in the blanks below.

1   The heart is split into _____ sides and has _____ chambers. The top two chambers are called _____ and the bottom two chambers are called _____. The heart is split into two separate sides by the _____.
2   There are _____ valves that allow the blood to pass through the heart in one direction.
3   The valve between the atrium and ventricle on the right side of the heart is called the _____ valve. The valve on the left side of the heart between the atrium and the ventricle is called the _____ valve. The valve between the pulmonary artery and right ventricle is called the _____ valve. The valve between the left ventricle and the aorta is called the _____ valve.

Arteries and arterioles

Arteries are the large blood vessels that leave the heart. They have thick, muscular walls which contract and relax to send blood to all parts of the body. The main artery leaving the heart is the aorta and it quickly splits up into smaller vessels, which are called the arterioles. Arterioles mean 'little arteries'. Artery walls contain elastic cartilage and smooth muscle. This flexible wall allows the vessels to expand and contract, which helps to push the blood along the length of the arteries. This action is called peristalsis and is how smooth muscle contracts.

Arteries do not contain any valves as they are not required and they predominantly carry oxygenated blood. The exception to this is the pulmonary artery, which carries deoxygenated blood away from the heart.

- Arteries carry blood away from the heart.
- Arteries have thick, muscular walls.
- Arteries carry predominantly oxygenated blood.
- Arterioles are the small branches of arteries.

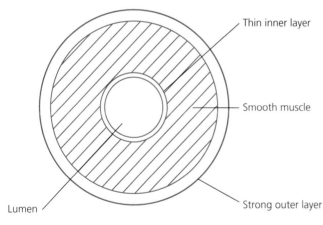

Figure 2.10 The structure of arteries and arterioles

The aorta and pulmonary artery are examples of the main arteries in the body.

Capillaries

Once the arteries and arterioles have divided, they will eventually feed blood into the smallest blood vessels, called capillaries. These are found in all parts of the body, especially the muscles, and are so tiny that their walls are only one cell thick. These walls are semi-permeable, which means there are tiny spaces within these thin cell walls, which allow oxygen and carbon dioxide to pass into and out of the blood stream by a process called diffusion (when gases move from a high concentration to a low concentration). Their walls also allow nutrients and waste products of metabolism such as lactate to flow into and out of the blood stream. The blood flows very slowly through the capillaries to allow for this process. There are more capillaries than any other type of blood vessel in the body.

- Capillaries are tiny blood vessels, one cell thick.
- Small spaces in the thin walls of capillaries allow for diffusion.
- Oxygen and nutrients will diffuse into the cells.
- Carbon dioxide and lactic acid will flow from the cells into the capillaries.

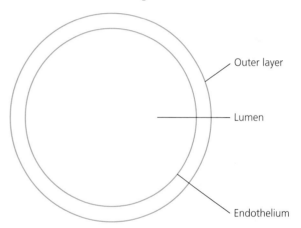

Figure 2.11 The structure of a capillary

Veins and venuoles

The capillaries will eventually feed back into larger blood vessels called venuoles, which are the smallest veins, and these eventually become veins. These veins are thinner and less muscular than arteries, and they carry blood back to the heart. They also contain smooth muscle and contract to send the blood back to the heart. The veins are generally acting against gravity, so they contain non-return valves to prevent the blood flowing back once the smooth muscle has relaxed. These valves prevent the pooling of blood in the lower limbs. Veins predominantly carry deoxygenated blood, with the exception of the pulmonary vein, which carries oxygenated blood to the heart from the lungs.

- Veins always take blood towards the heart.
- Veins have thin, muscular walls.
- Veins have non-return valves to prevent backflow.
- Veins predominantly carry deoxygenated blood.
- Venuoles are smaller branches, which feed into veins.

The vena cava and pulmonary vein are examples of main veins in the body.

Composition of blood

Blood is the medium in which all the cells are carried, to transport nutrients and oxygen to the cells of the body. Among other things, blood will transport the following: oxygen, glucose, proteins, fats, vitamins, hormones, enzymes, platelets, carbon dioxide and electrolytes.

Blood is made up of four components:

- red blood cells – erythrocytes
- white blood cells – leucocytes
- platelets – thrombocytes
- plasma.

Blood can be described as a thick, gloopy substance due to the high concentration of solids it carries. Blood is made up of 55% plasma and 45% solids, which is why it is quite a thick liquid substance.

Red blood cells – erythrocytes

Of the blood cells in the body, around 99% of them are red blood cells or erythrocytes. They are red in colour due to the presence of a red-coloured protein called haemoglobin. Haemoglobin has a massive attraction for oxygen, and thus the main role of the red blood cells is to take on and transport oxygen to the cells. There are many millions of red blood cells in the body; for example, there are 5 million red blood cells for 1 mm^3 volume of blood.

White blood cells

White blood cells are colourless or transparent and are far fewer in number (1:700 ratio of white to red blood cells). The role of white blood cells, or leucocytes, is to fight infection; they are part of the body's immune system. They destroy bacteria and other dangerous organisms and remove disease from the body.

Platelets

Platelets are not full cells but rather parts of cells; they act by stopping blood loss through clotting. They become sticky when in contact with the air to form the initial stage of repair to damaged tissue. Platelets also need a substance called factor 8 to enable them to clot. A haemophiliac is a person whose blood does not clot; this is not because they are short of platelets but rather factor 8, which enables the platelets to become active.

Plasma

Plasma is the liquid part of the blood, which is straw-coloured in appearance. It is the solution in which all the solids are carried.

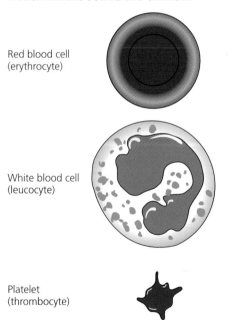

Red blood cell (erythrocyte)

White blood cell (leucocyte)

Platelet (thrombocyte)

Figure 2.12 Three different types of blood cell

Lymphatic system

This system is part of the cardiovascular system and consists of lymphatic vessels and lymph nodes. This system collects fluids from the body's tissues that are not reabsorbed back into the blood stream and its main function is to fight infection. The fluid circulating through the lymphatic system is called lymph and is a pale yellow fluid, and contains lymphocytes. The lymphatic vessels have one-way valves to ensure the lymph flows in one direction around the body. The lymph nodes are located in various places around the body including the jaw, neck, elbow, knee, armpit and groin, and their function is to deal with any infection arriving via the lymphatics.

B1 Check your understanding

1 Describe the process of blood flow through the heart and around the body and lungs.
2 Explain how blood can only flow in one direction around the heart.
3 Describe how oxygen is carried in the blood.
4 Describe the function of white blood cells.
5 Explain why it is essential for capillaries to have semi-permeable membranes.

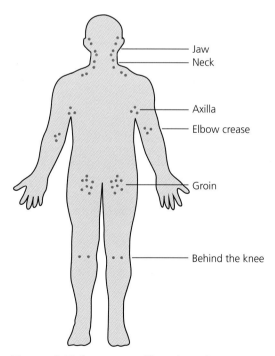

Figure 2.13 Locations of lymph nodes in the body

B2 Function of the cardiovascular system

The cells of the body need a steady and constant supply of oxygen. Blood is responsible for carrying and delivering oxygen to all the body's cells, and this blood is pumped around the body and to the lungs by the heart. The left-hand side of your heart pumps the oxygenated blood to the cells of the muscles, brain, kidneys, liver and all the other organs. The cells then take the oxygen out of the blood and use it to produce energy. This is called metabolism and it produces waste products, such as carbon dioxide. The deoxygenated blood then continues its journey back to the heart, enters the right-hand side and is pumped out of the right ventricle to the lungs. At the lungs, the blood becomes oxygenated and the waste product carbon dioxide is 'unloaded' and breathed out.

Cardiac cycle

Pulmonary circulation

The right ventricle pumps blood through the pulmonary artery to the lungs. Here, the blood picks up oxygen and carbon dioxide is released into the lungs. From the lungs, the oxygenated blood is carried to the left atrium. This short loop is called the pulmonary circulation.

Systemic circulation

From the left atrium the blood flows down to the left ventricle. The left ventricle pumps oxygenated blood through the aorta to all tissues of the body. Oxygen and nutrients are released from the blood to nourish cells, and carbon dioxide and other waste products are carried back to the heart via the two venae cavae. The blood enters the right atrium. Carbon dioxide is carried to the lungs and removed from the body.

Control of blood flow

Blood flows through the body through arteries, arterioles, capillaries, veins and venuoles. However, not every one of these blood vessels are in use at the same time. Blood is directed to where it is needed, so for example, after we have eaten some food, more blood is directed to the stomach to help us to digest it. When a person is exercising or taking part in a sport, blood is directed to the muscles that are working – if a person is running, more blood will be directed to flow around the leg muscles so that oxygen and nutrients can be delivered to these muscles so that they can function.

During exercise or sports participation, blood is also directed to flow through blood vessels that are close to the skin surface to help to cool the body down. You will have no doubt experienced the colour change in your face when you are taking part in an energetic sport – it will turn from a paler colour to a pink or red colour.

The process of redirecting blood occurs through the ability of blood vessels to narrow (constrict) or get larger (dilate). Where blood vessels increase in size, this is called vasodilation and this allows more blood to flow through them; where blood vessels decrease in size this is called vasoconstriction and this reduces or stops blood flow through them.

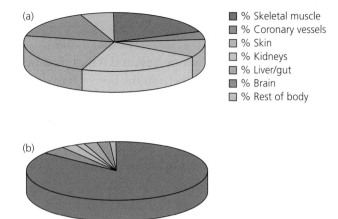

Figure 2.15 Distribution of cardiac output at rest and during exercise

Fight infection

The cardiovascular system fights infection by two methods: using the blood stream and the lymphatic system. The white blood cells destroy bacterial

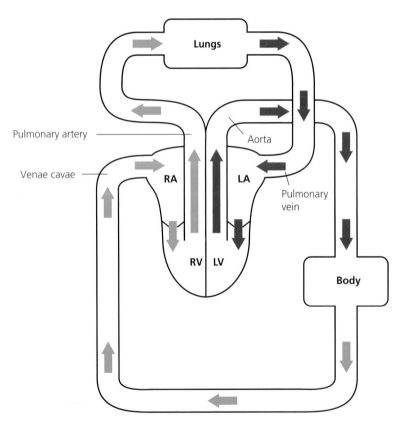

Figure 2.14 Blood flow through the heart

infections and the lymphatic system also helps to fight infections. If a person become unwell, these systems work together to help the person to recover from the disease or infection.

Clot blood

If you get injured, such as grazing your knee, the injury site will bleed for a short period of time and then, usually, the blood will clot which stops any further bleeding. Blood clots by changing from a liquid to a gel which then forms a scab. The platelets in the blood stream release chemicals which act on proteins called fibrinogens that are already circulating in the blood. These chemicals cause fibrinogen proteins to join together to form fibrin fibres which start to form a mesh across the injury site. As more and more fibrin fibres form they stick together and act as a plaster to seal the wound.

B2 Check your understanding

1   Describe how the cardiovascular system delivers oxygen and nutrients to the body.
2   Describe how carbon dioxide is removed from the body.
3   Explain how blood flow to parts of the body can be increased.
4   Identify why it is important for blood to be able to clot.

B3 Cardiac cycle

Blood flow through the heart

The cardiac cycle is the process that the heart follows in terms of it contracting and relaxing in order to pump blood around the body and lungs.

When the heart contracts this is called systole and when the heart relaxes this is called diastole.

Neural control of the cardiac cycle

The heart muscle has its own independent nerve supply via a specialised tissue called the sinoatrial node (the pacemaker of the heart), which is situated close to the point where the vena cava enters the right atrium. When a nervous impulse is produced it will pass through both atria to the atrioventricular node positioned in the septum where the atria and ventricles meet. The nervous impulse pauses slightly and then enters the ventricles through the atrioventricular bundles (Bundle of His), one into each ventricle. The Bundle of His leads to the purkinje fibres, which carry nervous impulses to all parts of the ventricles.

The heart is controlled by the autonomic nervous system. First, the vagus nerve slows down the heart rate and decreases the power of ventricular contraction by delivering impulses through the sinoatrial node. Second, the sympathetic nerves increase the heart rate and the force of contraction of the ventricles. This innervation of the heart is controlled through the cardiac centre of the brain, which is positioned within the medulla oblongata.

B3 Check your understanding

1   Describe the process of the cardiac cycle.
2   Identify the name of the process of the heart contracting.
3   Identify the name of the process of the heart relaxing.
4   Describe how the heart rate is increased.

C Anatomy of the respiratory system

The respiratory system is responsible for transporting the oxygen from the air we breathe into our body. Our body then uses this oxygen in combination with the food we have eaten to produce energy. This energy is then used to keep us alive by supplying our heart with energy to keep beating and pumping blood around the body; it allows us to move and take part in sports and many more different types of activities.

C1 Location, anatomy and function of respiratory system components

The aim of the respiratory system is to provide contact between the outside and internal environments so that oxygen can be absorbed by the blood and carbon dioxide can be removed. It is made up of a system of tubes and muscles delivering the air into the lungs. The average person takes around 26,000 breaths a day to deliver the required amount of oxygen to the cells of the body.

The passage of air through the respiratory system

1   Air enters the body through the mouth and nose. The nose acts to warm and filter the air.

2   It passes through the pharynx which is the back of the throat area.

3   It then passes through the larynx which is responsible for voice production.

4   Air passes over the epiglottis. The epiglottis closes over the trachea when we swallow food to stop the food going down 'the wrong way' into our trachea and lungs.

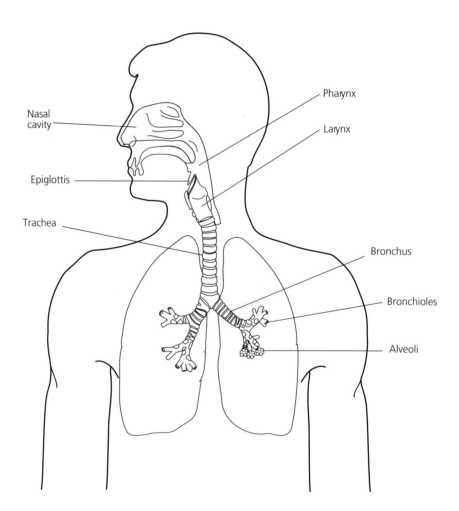

Nasal cavity

Epiglottis

Trachea

Pharynx

Larynx

Bronchus

Bronchioles

Alveoli

Figure 2.16 Location of the respiratory system components

5   The air enters the trachea which is a cartilaginous tube that delivers air to the lungs. The trachea contains a number of horseshoe-shaped rings of cartilage to keep the tube from collapsing and to ensure the airway remains open.

6   The trachea then divides into two bronchi, one into each lung.

7   The two main bronchi further divide into bronchioles which will further subdivide 23 times and result in 8 million terminal bronchioles in each lung.

8   Around the bronchioles you will find the groups of air sacs called alveoli. There are around 600 million alveoli in each lung and it is here that the exchange of gases (oxygen and carbon dioxide) occurs. Each alveolus is in contact with a capillary where the blood is present.

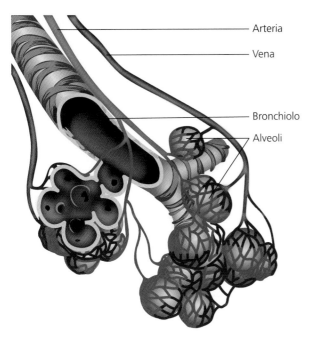

— Arteria

— Vena

— Bronchiolo

— Alveoli

Figure 2.17 The capillary network surrounding alveoli in the lungs

The lungs are covered in a membrane called visceral pleura. The thoracic cavity is lined by parietal pleura. Between both of these membranes there is as fluid-filled space called the pleural cavity. These membranes and the fluid-filled pleural cavity all help to provide lubrication to allow the lungs to glide easily over the surface of the thoracic cavity as they expand during inspiration.

The respiratory system also includes two types of muscles which work to move air into and out of the lungs: the diaphragm and the intercostal muscles.

Diaphragm

The diaphragm is a large dome-shaped muscle which covers the bottom of the ribcage.

Intercostal muscles

There are internal and external intercostal muscles. These muscles attach between the ribs and assist in the process of breathing. If you like to eat spare ribs, these are actually bones and intercostal muscles!

The function of the diaphragm and intercostal muscles will be described in more detail in the next section on the mechanisms of breathing.

C1 Check your understanding

1   Identify the function of the nasal cavity.
2   Identify the function of the epiglottis.
3   Explain why the trachea contains cartilage.
4   Describe the function of the visceral and parietal pleura.
5   Identify the three main muscles involved in breathing.

C2 Function of the respiratory system

Mechanisms of breathing (inspiration and expiration)

Breathing is the term given to inhaling air into the lungs and then exhaling air out. The process basically works on the principle of making the thoracic cavity (chest) larger which decreases the pressure of air within the lungs. The surrounding air is then at a higher pressure which means that air is forced into the lungs. Then the thoracic cavity is returned to its original size which forces air out of the lungs.

Breathing In (inhalation)

At rest

The diaphragm is dome-shaped but when contracted, it flattens and pushes the two sides of the ribcage away from each other. This results in an increase in the size of the thoracic cavity and air is forced into the lungs.

Exercise

During exercise, the diaphragm contracts and also the intercostal muscles contract to push the ribs upwards and outwards to increase the size of the chest cavity. This draws more air in than just the diaphragm contracting alone.

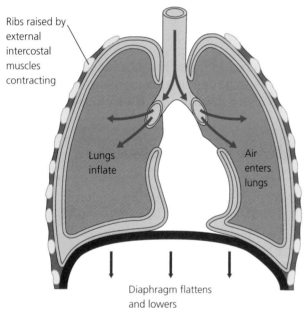

Ribs raised by external intercostal muscles contracting

Lungs inflate

Air enters lungs

Diaphragm flattens and lowers

Figure 2.18 Inhalation - diaphragm and intercostal muscles

Breathing out (exhalation)

At rest

The diaphragm relaxes and returns upwards to a domed position. The thoracic cavity gets smaller, which results in an increase in air pressure within the lungs, so air is breathed out of the lungs.

Exercise

During sport and exercise, additional skeletal muscles aid with the process of breathing. During inspiration, the sternocleidomastoid muscles aid by contracting to raise the upper half of the chest.

During expiration the internal intercostal muscles, rectus abdominis, transverse abdominis and the oblique muscles all contract to force air more quickly and more forcibly out of the lungs ready for the next inspiration of air.

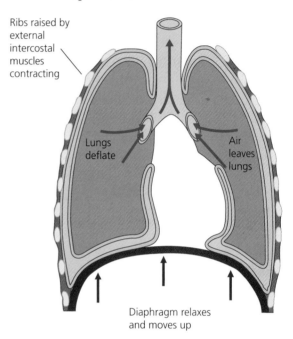

Ribs raised by external intercostal muscles contracting

Lungs deflate

Air leaves lungs

Diaphragm relaxes and moves up

Figure 2.19 Exhalation – diaphragm and intercostal muscles

Gaseous exchange

The aim of gaseous exchange is to get oxygen into the blood stream where it can be delivered to the cells of the body and for carbon dioxide to be removed from the body.

The body uses oxygen to produce energy and then carbon dioxide and water are produced as waste products.

Food + oxygen ⟶ energy + carbon dioxide and water

Composition of air

The air that is inspired is made up of a mixture of gases, and the air exhaled is different in its composition of gases.

Gas	Inhaled air	Exhaled air
Nitrogen	79.04%	79%
Oxygen	20.93%	17%
Carbon dioxide	0.03%	4%

Table 2.1 The composition of inhaled and exhaled air

We can see that oxygen is extracted from the air that is breathed in and replaced by carbon dioxide which is produced by the body in order to produce energy.

Diffusion is how gases move from one area to another – by moving from a high concentration to a low concentration – and it is because of this that the process of gaseous exchange takes place.

Key Term

Diffusion is the movement of a gas from an area of high concentration to an area of low concentration.

Gaseous exchange in the lungs

In the lungs there is a high concentration of oxygen from the air that has been breathed in. In the blood stream there is a high concentration of carbon dioxide as it is bringing blood from the muscles that have been producing carbon dioxide, so oxygen diffuses into the blood stream and carbon dioxide diffuses out of the blood and into the lungs. Oxygen then attaches to the haemoglobin in the red blood cells and is carried to back to the body and carbon dioxide is breathed out.

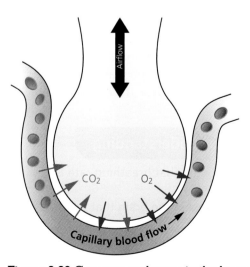

Figure 2.20 Gaseous exchange in the lungs

Gaseous exchange in the muscles

In the muscles there is a high concentration of carbon dioxide and a low concentration of oxygen due to the process of energy production. As a result, the oxygen diffuses into the muscles and the carbon dioxide diffuses into the blood stream. It is then taken to the lungs to be breathed out.

Lung volumes

In order to assess an individual's lung function we can use a spirometer to find the size of a variety of lung volumes.

An individual will have a lung capacity of around 5 litres which is similar to the amount of air in a basketball. It will be slightly lower for a female and slightly higher for a male, due to the differing sizes of the male and female ribcage.

Tidal volume

This is the amount of air breathed in with each breath. This volume will increase during exercise as more air is breathed in and out when a person exercises.

Vital capacity

This is the maximum amount of air that can be breathed in and out during one breath which includes the maximal inhalation of air before blowing out as much air as possible.

Residual volume

This is the amount of air left in the lungs after a full exhalation. Around 1 litre will always remain otherwise the lungs will deflate and breathing will stop.

Total lung volume

This is the vital capacity plus the residual volume and measures the maximum amount of air that could be present in the lungs at any moment.

C2 Check your understanding

1. Explain why air enters the lungs when the diaphragm contracts.
2. Explain how oxygen enters the blood stream from the lungs.
3. Describe what happens to the tidal volume during exercise.

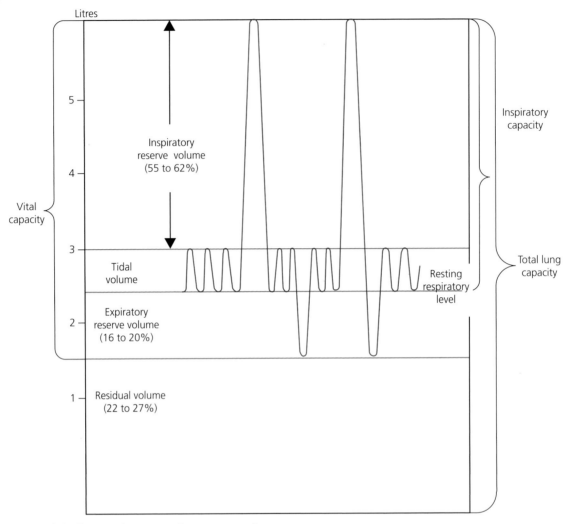

Figure 2.21 Lung volumes as shown on a spirometer trace

C3 Control of breathing

Breathing rate is controlled by both neural and chemical mechanisms.

The neural control is from the respiratory centre in the brain which is located in the medulla oblongata. During exercise, when the body needs to produce more energy, the amount of carbon dioxide increases and dissolves in the blood stream to produce a weak acid. As levels of carbon dioxide in the blood rise, this in turn increases the acidity of the blood. This increase in acidity of the blood is sensed by chemoreceptors which are specialised cells within the arteries that detect chemical changes in the blood. As the body does not like the acidity of the blood to increase, the chemoreceptors

signal the medulla oblongata. This area of the brain then sends signals to the diaphragm and intercostal muscles, by the phrenic nerves, to increase the breathing rate in order to get rid of the excess carbon dioxide. Therefore, during exercise, breathing rate increases because carbon dioxide levels rise rather than because the cells demand more oxygen.

C3 Check your understanding

1. Identify two ways that breathing rate is controlled.
2. Identify the area in the brain that controls breathing.
3. Describe how breathing rate is increased during exercise.

D Anatomy of the skeletal system

The skeletal system is the central structure of the body and provides the framework for all the soft tissue to attach to, in order to give the body its defined shape. The skeleton is made up of bones, joints and cartilage and enables us to perform simple and complex movements such as walking and running.

D1 Anatomy of the bone

Structure of a long bone

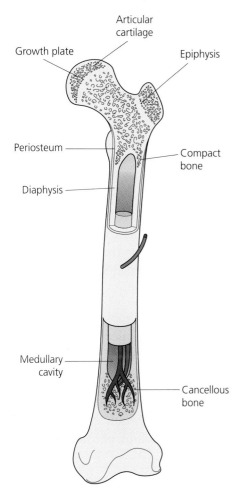

Figure 2.22 The structure of a long bone

Epiphysis – These are the ends of the bone.

Diaphysis – This is the long shaft of the bone.

Articular cartilage – This is the thin layer of bluish cartilage covering each end of the bone.

Periosteum – This is the thin outer layer of the bone. It contains nerves and blood vessels that feed the bone.

Compact bone – Compact bone is hard and is resistant to bending.

Cancellous bone – Cancellous (spongy) bone lies in layers within the compact bone. It has a honeycomb appearance and gives the bones their elastic strength.

Medullary cavity – This is the hollow space down the middle of the compact bone and contains bone marrow. There are two types of bone marrow: red marrow, which produces blood cells, and yellow marrow, which stores fat.

Growth plate – This is the area where bones grow in length until a person reaches maturity and they then stop growing.

Bone minerals – Bones take up minerals from the diet to make them strong and hard so that they are able to withstand impacts. Both calcium and phosphorous are important minerals to ensure the strength of bones.

Bony landmarks

The skeletal bones contain grooves and notches which help a person to identify various areas of the bones of the skeletal system. Each of these features are given names to identify the shape and size of the feature. The bony landmark terms that you will need to know include:

Notch – This is an indentation of the bone.

Fossa – This is a shallow dip in the bone.

Condyle – This is a round prominence at the end of a bone.

Border – This is the edge of the bone.

Process – This is a part of the bone that projects out from the main body of the bone.

Tuberosity – This is a projection of bone that is used for muscle or tendon attachment.

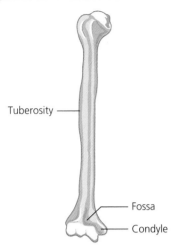

Tuberosity

Fossa

Condyle

Figure 2.23 The structure of the humerus

D2 Process of bone growth and remodelling

As a foetus, most of the skeleton consists of cartilage which is a tough flexible tissue; as the foetus develops minerals are laid down in the cartilage and the bones become harder and less flexible. This process is called ossification and it continues until we are adults. Bones keep growing until between the ages of 18–30, depending on the bone and the body part. When a bone grows it occurs at the epiphyseal plate which is an area just behind the head of the bone at each epiphysis; as a bone grows the two ends of the bone are slowly pushed away from each other.

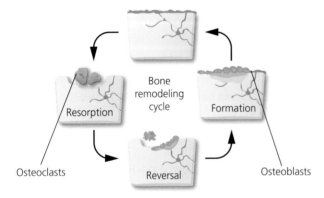

Bone remodeling cycle

Resorption

Formation

Reversal

Osteoclasts

Osteoblasts

Figure 2.24 Ossification: the process of cartilage turning into bone

Key term

Ossification is the process of cartilage turning into bone.

Bones are very much alive and full of activity. We know bones are living material because they can repair if they are damaged, grow when we are young and they produce blood cells. Bone is continually being broken down and replaced, which is a process called bone remodelling, and this process is done by different cells: osteoblasts and osteoclasts.

- **Osteoblasts** – are cells that will build bone.
- **Osteoclasts** – are cells that destroy or clean away old bone.

The process of remodelling starts by osteoclasts destroying areas of older bone and the tissue is then reabsorbed by the body. This process by the osteoclasts activates the osteoblasts to start to lay down collagen and minerals in the area that was destroyed to start the process of remodelling. The osteoblasts turn into osteocytes which are bone cells and form the new bone.

Osteoclasts and osteoblasts will replace around 10% of bone every year and this means that no matter how old we are, our skeleton is no older than 10 years of age.

In order to ensure our bones remain strong and able to withstand impacts, it is important that a person has an adequate intake of calcium, phosphorus and vitamin D.

Calcium is found in a variety of foods including dairy products; phosphorous is found in meat, chicken and dairy products; and vitamin D is found in oily fish, liver and eggs. Vitamin D can also be made naturally by the body if it is exposed to sunlight.

D3 Location of skeletal bones

The skeleton consists of 206 bones, over half of which are in the upper and lower limbs. Babies are born with around 300 bones and over time they fuse together, so reducing the number.

Cranium

The cranium consists of eight bones fused together which act to protect your brain. There are 14 other facial bones which form the face and jaw.

Sternum

This is the flat bone in the middle of the chest which is shaped like a dagger. It protects the heart and gives an attachment point for the ribs and the clavicles.

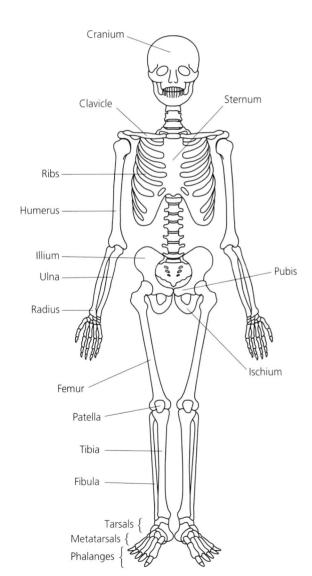

Figure 2.25 Anterior view of a skeleton

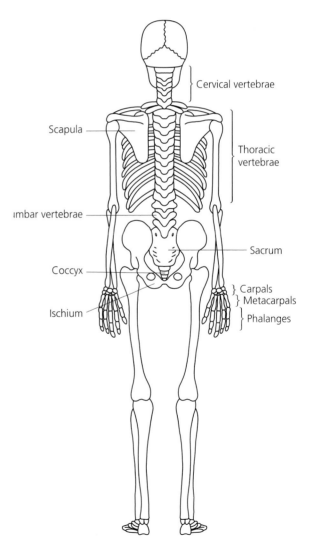

Figure 2.26 Posterior view of skeleton

Ribs

Adults have 12 pairs of ribs which run between the sternum and the thoracic vertebrae. The ribs are flat bones that form a protective cage around the heart and lungs. An individual will have seven pairs of ribs that attach to both the sternum and vertebrae (true ribs), three which attach from the vertebrae to a cartilage attachment on the sternum and two which attach on the vertebrae but are free as they have no second attachment (floating ribs).

Clavicle

This bone connects the upper arm to the trunk of the body. One end is connected to the sternum and the other is connected to the scapula. The role of the clavicle is to keep the scapula at the correct distance from the sternum.

Scapula

This bone is situated on the back of the body. The scapula provides points of attachment for many muscles of the upper back and arms.

Arm

This consists of three bones: the humerus (upper arm), the radius and the ulna (lower arm). The ulna forms the elbow joint with the humerus and runs to the little finger. The radius is positioned beside the ulna and runs to the thumb side. When the hand moves, the radius moves across the ulna.

Hand

The hand has three areas made up of different types of bones. Firstly, the wrist is made up of eight carpals which are small bones arranged in two rows of four; the five long bones between the wrist and fingers are the metacarpals and the bones of the fingers are called phalanges. There are 14 phalanges all together with three in each finger and two in the thumb. There are a total of 30 bones in the upper limb.

Pelvis

The pelvis protects and supports the lower internal organs, including the bladder, the reproductive organs and also (in pregnant women) the developing foetus. The pelvis consists of three bones: the ilium at the head of this (the iliac crest),

as well as the pubis and ischium, which have become fused together to form one area.

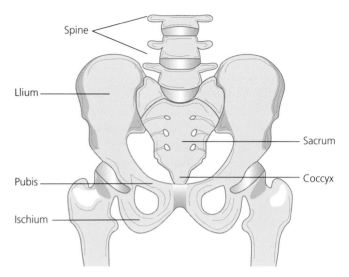

Figure 2.27 The pelvic bones

The leg

The leg consists of four bones. The femur is the longest bone in the body and forms the knee joint with the tibia which is the weight bearing bone of the lower leg. The fibula is the non-weight bearing bone of the lower leg and helps form the ankle. The patella is the bone which floats over the knee; it lies within the patella tendon and smooths the movement of the tendons over the knee joint.

Foot

Like the hand, the foot has three areas: the seven tarsals which form the ankle, the five metatarsals which travel from the ankle to the toes and the 14 phalanges which make up the toes. There are three phalanges in each toe with only two in the big toe. Again the lower limb has 30 bones; it has one less tarsal but makes up for it with the patella. The heel bone of the foot is called the calcaneus bone.

Vertebrae

The spine is made up of five areas:

- cervical – 7
- thoracic – 12
- lumbar – 5
- sacrum – 5
- coccyx – 4.

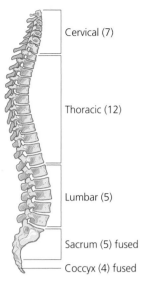

Figure 2.28 Structure of the vertebral column

The **cervical vertebrae** make up the neck and run to the shoulders. The top two vertebra are the atlas and axis which allow the head to move up and down and from side to side.

The **thoracic vertebrae** make up the chest area and protect the heart and lungs.

The **lumbar vertebrae** are the largest vertebrae in the spinal column and make up the lower back. The sacrum consists of five vertebrae which are fused together and form joints with the pelvis and form the sacroiliac joint.

Lastly, the **coccyx** are four fused bones joined together, which are the remnants of when we had a tail.

The vertebrae all have a hollow ring in the middle which is where the spinal cord passes through. The vertebrae act to protect the spinal cord, as damage to this can result in paralysis.

Between each vertebra there are discs of fibro cartilage which act as shock absorbers. The vertebrae form two curves in the spine which helps to increase its strength.

Axial and appendicular skeleton

The axial skeleton is the central core of the body or its axis. It consists of the skull, the vertebrae, the sternum and the ribs. It provides the core the limbs hang from.

The appendicular skeleton is the parts hanging off the axial skeleton. It consists of the shoulder girdle (scapula and clavicle), the pelvic girdle, upper and lower limbs.

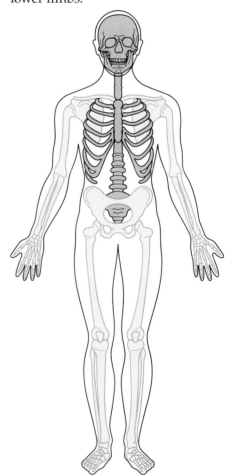

Figure 2.30 Bones that form the axial skeleton

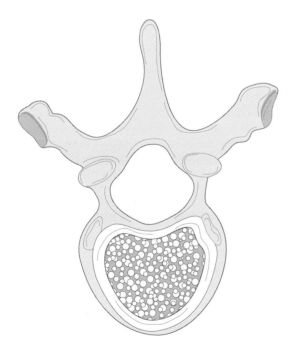

Figure 2.29 The thoracic vertebra

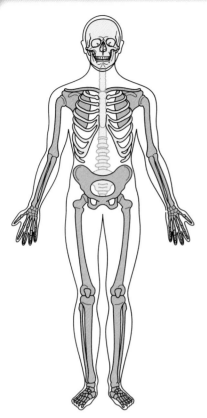

Figure 2.31 Bones that form the appendicular skeleton

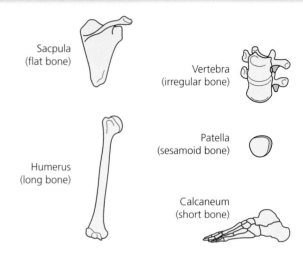

Figure 2.32 Five types of bone

Types of bone

The bones of the body fall into five general categories based on their shape (see Figure 2.32 and Table 2.2).

D4 Ligaments

Function of ligaments

Ligaments are a form of connective tissue and their function is to:

- attach bone to bone
- give stability to joints.

They are made of tough white fibres which are inelastic. They have a very poor blood supply which is why they are a whitish colour. This limited blood supply also means that they will take a long time to repair if they become damaged.

Location of ligaments in stabilising and restricting joint movements

Some of the joints in our body have a number of ligaments holding the joints in place in order to increase the stability of the joint.

The hip joint is a ball and socket joint which has a large range of movement. However, the placement of the ligaments around this joint ensure that it is stable and does reduce the movement permitted at this joint. The shoulder joint is also a ball and socket joint but there are less ligaments holding it in place in comparison to the hip joint. If you compare the amount of movement permitted at the hip and the

Type of bone	Example in body	Description
Long	Femur, tibia, humerus	Cylindrical in shape and found in the limbs. Main function is to act as a lever
Short	Carpals, calcaneum	Small and compact, often equal in length and width. Designed for strength and weight bearing
Flat	Sternum, cranium, pelvis	Protection for the internal organs of the body
Irregular bones	Vertebrae, face	Complex individual shapes. Variety of functions, including protection and muscle attachment
Sesamoid	Patella	Found in a tendon. Eases joint movement and resists friction and compression

Table 2.2 Different types of joint

shoulder joints you can see this difference in amount of movement permitted. This does also mean that the shoulder joint is less stable than the hip joint, so is more prone to dislocation compared to the hip joint.

Some ligaments only allow joints to move in certain directions, such as at the knee joint. The collateral ligaments of the knee prevent side-to-side movements and only allow flexion and extension.

Ligaments can also prevent hyperextension at joints.

D3 and D4 Check your understanding

1   Labels the bones in the diagram of a skeleton.

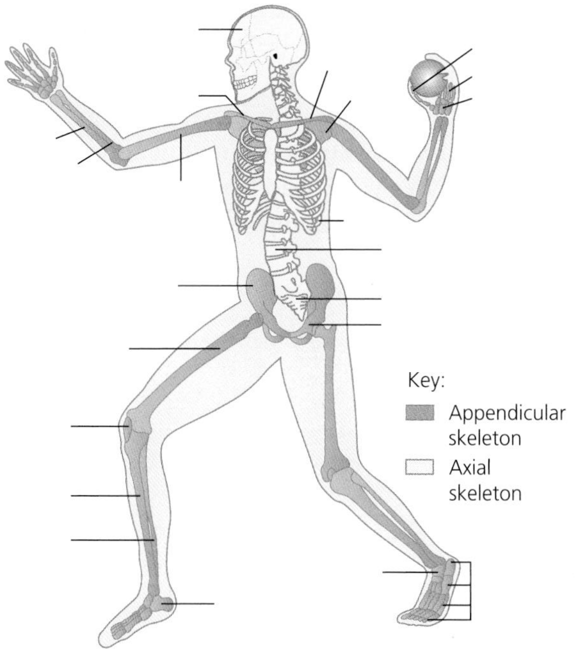

Key:
- ■ Appendicular skeleton
- □ Axial skeleton

Figure 2.33 A skeleton

2   Identify the type of bone found at the patella.
3   Identify a long bone.
4   Identify the function of ligaments.

D5 Joints

The place where two or more bones meet is called a joint or an articulation. A joint is held together by ligaments which give the joints their stability.

Key term

A **joint** is a place where two or more bones meet.

Classification of joints

Joints are put into one of three classifications depending upon the amount of movement available:

1   Fibrous, also known as fixed or immovable.
2   Cartilaginous, which are also known as slightly moveable.
3   Synovial, which are also known as moveable.

1. Fibrous joints

These joints allow no movement. These types of joints can be found between the plates in the skull.

2. Cartilaginous joints

These allow a small amount of movement and are held in place by ligaments and cushioned by cartilage. This kind of joint can be found between the vertebrae in the spine.

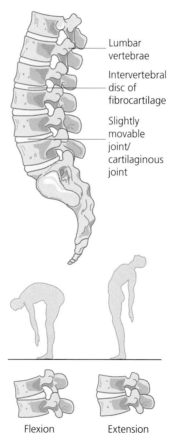

- Lumbar vertebrae
- Intervertebral disc of fibrocartilage
- Slightly movable joint/ cartilaginous joint

Flexion   Extension

Figure 2.34 A cartilaginous joint

3. Synovial joints

There are six types of these joints and all allow varying degrees of movement. These are hinge, ball and socket, pivot, condyloid, sliding and saddle.

Types of synovial joint and range of movement permitted at each

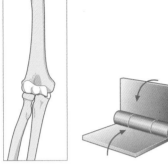

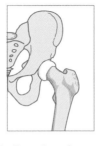

Figure 2.35 The hinge joint, e.g. elbow joint

Figure 2.36 The ball and socket joint, e.g. hip joint

Figure 2.37 The pivot joint, e.g. spine (between atlas and axis)

Hinge joint

These can be found in the elbow (ulna and humerus) and knee (femur and tibia). They allow flexion and extension of a joint. Hinge joints are like the hinges on a door, and allow you to only move the elbow and knee in one direction.

Ball and socket joint

These types of joint can be found at the shoulder (scapula and humerus) and hip (pelvis and femur) and allow movement in almost every direction. A ball and socket joint is made up of a round end of one bone that fits into a small cup-like area of another bone.

Pivot joint

This joint can be found in the neck between the top two vertebrae (atlas and axis). It only allows rotational movement; for example, it allows you to move your head from side to side as if you were saying 'no'.

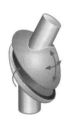

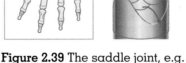

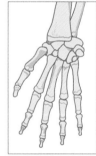

Figure 2.38 The condyloid joint, e.g. radio-carpal joint

Figure 2.39 The saddle joint, e.g. carpo-meta carpal joint of thumb

Figure 2.40 The gliding joint, e.g. carpals

Condyloid joint

This type of joint is found at the wrist. It allows movement in two planes, this is called biaxial. It allows you to bend and straighten the joint, and move it from side to side. The joints between the metacarpals and phalanges are also condyloid.

Saddle joint

This type of joint is only be found in the thumbs. It allows the joint to move in three planes, backwards and forwards, and from side to side and across. This is a joint specific to humans and gives us 'manual dexterity', enabling us to hold a cup and to write, among other skills.

Gliding joint

This type of joint can be found in the carpal bones of the hand. These types of joints occur between the surfaces of two flat bones. They allow very limited movement in a range of directions.

Structure of a synovial joint

Joint capsule – Keeps the contents of the synovial joint in place.

Synovial membrane – Releases synovial fluid onto the joint.

Synovial fluid – A thick 'oil like' solution which lubricates the joint and allows free movement.

Articular cartilage – A bluish-white covering of cartilage which prevents wear and tear on the bones.

Ligaments – These hold the two or more bones making up the joint in place.

Bursa – This is a fluid-filled sac that helps to reduce friction in the joint.

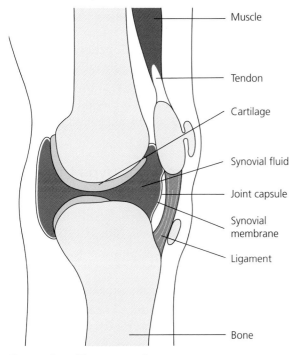

— Muscle

— Tendon

— Cartilage

— Synovial fluid

— Joint capsule

— Synovial membrane

— Ligament

— Bone

Figure 2.41 The synovial joint

D6 Function of skeletal system

The different functions that the skeletal bones perform are as follows:

1   Supporting framework
2   Protection
3   Attachment for skeletal muscle
4   Source of blood cell production
5   Store of minerals
6   Movement.

1. They provide a supporting framework for the body

The bones give the body a distinctive shape and a framework to attach muscles and other soft tissue to. Without bones, we would just be a big sac of fluids!

2. They offer protection to the organs found within the skeleton

The bones will support and protect the vital organs they contain. For example, the skull will protect the brain, the ribs offer protection to the heart and lungs, the vertebrae protect the spinal cord and the pelvis offers protection to the sensitive reproductive organs.

3. Attachment for skeletal muscle

Bones provide surfaces for the attachment of muscles and also tendons and ligaments. This is why they are often irregular shapes and have bony points and grooves to provide attachment points.

4. Source of blood cell production

Certain bones in the skeletal system contain red bone marrow. Bone marrow produces red blood cells, white blood cells and platelets. The bones that contain marrow are the pelvis, sternum, vertebrae, costals, cranial bones and clavicle.

5. Storage of minerals

The bones themselves are made of minerals stored within cartilage; therefore, they act as a mineral store for calcium, magnesium and phosphorous which can be given up if the body requires the minerals for other functions.

6. Movement

The skeletal system allows movement of the body as a whole and in its individual parts.

The bones will act as levers and by forming joints, they will allow muscles to pull on them and produce joint movements. This will enable us to move in all directions and perform the functions we need on a daily basis.

E Anatomy of the muscular system

E1 Muscle types

The muscular system will work in conjunction with the skeleton to produce movement of the limbs and body. The muscular system always has to work with the nervous system because it will produce a nervous impulse to initiate movement. There are three types of muscle tissue: cardiac, skeletal and smooth.

Cardiac muscle

The heart has its own specialist muscle tissue which is called cardiac muscle; it makes up the heart muscle or myocardium and is an involuntary muscle. The heart has its own nerve supply via the sinoatrial node and it works by sending the nervous impulse through consecutive cells. The heart will always contract fully; that is, all the fibres contract. The cardiac muscle contracts around 60–80 times a minute. The function of the cardiac muscle is to pump blood around the body.

Skeletal muscle

Skeletal muscle is the muscle that is attached to the skeleton across joints. It is under voluntary control as we decide when to contract muscles and produce movement. Skeletal muscle is arranged in rows of fibres and is also called striated or stripy due to its appearance. The coordinated contractions of skeletal muscle allow us to move smoothly and produce sports skills. There are over 700 skeletal muscles in the human body and they make up around 40% of our body weight (slightly less for a female).

Skeletal muscle is responsible for the following functions:

- producing movement
- maintaining body posture
- generating heat to keep us warm
- storing of glycogen for energy.

Smooth muscles

Smooth muscles are called involuntary muscles because they are out of our conscious control. They can be found in the digestive system (large and small intestine), the circulatory system (artery and vein walls) and the urinary system. Smooth muscles contract with a peristaltic action in that the muscle fibres contract consecutively rather than at the same time and this produces a wave-like effect. For example, when food is passed through the digestive system, it is slowly squeezed through the intestines.

Skeletal muscle fibre types (type I, type II, type IIa, type IIx)

Within our skeletal muscles we have different types of muscle fibre including type I, type II, type IIa and type IIx.

Type I

Type I fibres are also called slow twitch fibres as they contract slowly and produce low levels of force. They are red in colour as they have a good blood supply. They have a dense network of blood vessels, making them suited to endurance work, and they are slow to fatigue. They also contain many mitochondria to make them more efficient at producing energy using oxygen.

> **Key term**
>
> Mitochondria is the energy-producing organelles within cells.

Type II

These types of muscle fibres are also called fast twitch fibres. They contract twice as quickly as type I fibres and are thicker in size. They have a poor blood supply, are whiter in appearance and due to the lack of oxygen they will fatigue fairly quickly. Their faster, harder contractions make them suitable for producing fast, powerful actions such as sprinting and lifting heavy weights.

Type II fibres are split into two different types, type IIa and type IIx as they have slightly different properties.

Type IIa

These types of fibres contract with a slightly lower intensities and produce slightly less force than the type IIx fibres. A 400 m runner would use type IIa fibres for the majority of their race.

Type IIx

These types of fibres contract when a person is working very close to their maximum intensity. A 100 m runner would use type IIx fibres for the majority of their race.

Every muscle in the body will contain a mixture of type I and type IIa and IIx muscle fibres depending on its role in the body. Postural muscles, which keep us standing upright, such as the muscles in the legs, back and abdominal areas will be predominantly type I. For example, 90% of the muscles in the back are type I. Postural muscles need to produce low forces over a long period of time. The arms tend to have more type IIa and type IIx as they will need to move quickly but over much shorter periods of time. The types of muscle found in the legs will determine whether we are more suited to sprinting or endurance running; you will know which you have most of based on your own athletic performances. According to Bursztyn (1997), well trained middle runners will have around 80% type I fibres while well trained sprinters may have up to 75% type II a and IIx muscle fibres.

Anatomy of the skeletal muscle

Each muscle is covered by a layer of epimysium. This epimysium then continues on to form the tendons for that muscle which attach the muscle to the skeleton.

Within the muscle there are bundles of muscle fibres called fascicles. Perimysium surrounds each bundle of fascicles. Within each fascicle are singe muscle fibres, and each of these single muscle fibres are covered by endomysium.

Characteristic	Type I	Type IIa	Type IIx
Speed of contraction (ms)	Slow (110)	Fast (50)	Fast (50)
Force of contraction	Low	High	High
Size	Smaller	Large	Large
Mitochondrial density	High	Lower	Low
Myoglobin content	High	Lower	Low
Fatiguability	Fatigue resistant	Less resistant	Easily fatigued
Aerobic capacity	High	Medium	Low
Capillary density	High	High	Low
Anaerobic capacity	Low	Medium	High
Motor neuron size	Small	Large	Large
Fibres/motor neuron	10–180	300–800	300–800
Sarcoplasmic reticulum development	Low	High	High

Table 2.3 Skeletal muscle fibre types (Source: Adapted from Sharkey 'Physiology of Fitness', Human Kinetics 1990)

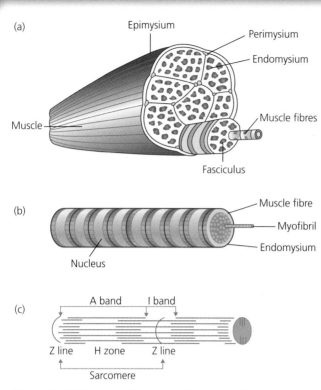

Figure 2.42 The structure of skeletal muscle

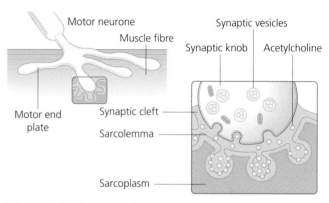

Key term

A **synapse** is the connection between two neurones.

Figure 2.43 The neural transmission process

E1 Check your understanding

1 Identify the three types of muscle.
2 Describe the different muscle fibre types.
3 Explain which muscle fibre types a sprinter would use in a 100 m run.
4 Explain which muscle fibre types a long distance runner would use in a 5 km race.

E2 Neuromuscular process of muscle contraction

Muscle contracts in response to stimulation from the nervous system. The central nervous system includes the brain and spinal cord and is responsible for stimulating the nervous system to carry messages called nervous impulses to the required muscle in order to produce movement. The nervous impulse is carried through neurones. Some neurones stretch all the way from the central nervous system to the muscle, whereas others are shorter and connect to other neurones in order to transmit the stimulation to the correct muscle group. The connection between two neurones is called a synapse.

The nervous impulse travels down the axon of a nerve, which is covered in a myelin sheath –

the thicker the myelin sheath, the faster the nerve impulse will travel. When the impulse reaches the end of the axon the electrical signal is converted into a chemical signal as a chemical neurotransmitter called acetylcholine is released at the neuromuscular junction.

The neuromuscular junction is the place at which the nerve and muscle meet. The nerve transmits its signal to make the muscle contract in the following manner:

1 The pre-synaptic membrane reacts to the signal by its vesicles releasing acetylcholine.
2 Acetylcholine diffuses across the gap between the nerve and the muscle (the synaptic cleft) which allows calcium ions to enter the muscle fibres and produces an electrical signal called the excitatory post-synaptic action potential.
3 If the excitatory post-synaptic potential is big enough it will make the muscle tissue contract.
4 Once the muscle has carried out its desired movement the enzyme cholinesterase breaks down the acetylcholine to leave the muscle ready to receive its next signal.

Acetylcholine is released into the muscle fibre and calcium ions also enter the muscle fibres. If there is enough acetylcholine released then this has the effect of allowing sodium and potassium ions into the muscle tissue; the presence of these ions allows the muscle to contract. When there is sufficient acetylcholine released this is called the action potential, and means enough acetylcholine has been produced for a nerve impulse to make the muscle contract.

The nerve that connects with the muscle fibre is called a motor neurone.

Sliding filament theory

Muscle contraction requires energy but how does this energy enable our muscles to contract? The contraction process occurs in four steps and is known as the sliding filament theory.

A myofibril is made up of two main components, actin and myosin. Actin is also referred to as the thin filaments and myosin is referred to as the thick filaments. The smallest part of a muscle is called a sarcomere.

1   At rest, troponin and tropomyosin cover the actin and myosin filaments and prevent myosin from binding to actin. When we give the signal for our muscles to contract, calcium is released into the sarcoplasm. Calcium binds to troponin and takes it away from the myosin binding site. As it moves away, it moves the tropomyosin molecule with it. Therefore, as the troponin and tropomyosin bind to calcium, the myosin binding site is exposed.

2   The myosin heads bind to the actin filament to form cross bridges and slide it across the myosin filament, which results in the sarcomere getting shorter.

3   ATP is used to break the attachment of the actin and myosin filaments. The myosin heads then re-attach at a site further up the actin filament which results in further shortening of the sarcomere.

4   When the stimulus to the muscle ends, calcium ions are released from the troponin and are pumped out of the sarcoplasm. This causes the troponin and tropomyosin to bind to the myosin heads once again, which means they cannot bind to the actin molecule and contraction cannot occur.

The entire process is extremely fast and only takes a fraction of a second. The cycle then repeats itself until the muscle relaxes.

During a muscle contraction, different parts of the sarcomere can be shown to change length.

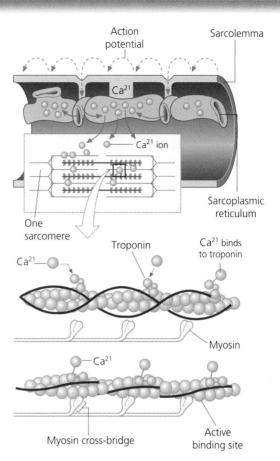

Figure 2.44 The structure of actin and myosin

Each part of a sarcomere is identified by letters which are:

● **H zone** – this only includes the myosin filaments.

● **Z line** – this is at the edge of each sarcomere.

● **A band** – this is a zone that contains the length of the sarcomere with the myosin filaments and does not change size during contraction. It can contain just the myosin filaments or can contain both actin and myosin filaments.

● **I band** – this is a zone around the Z lines and includes part of two separate sarcomeres. It only contains actin filaments and gets smaller when the muscle contracts.

During contraction the H zone gets smaller, the I band gets bigger and the sarcomere gets shorter.

Types of muscle contraction

Muscles can contract or develop tension in three different ways:

1   Concentric contraction

2   Eccentric contraction

3   Isometric contraction.

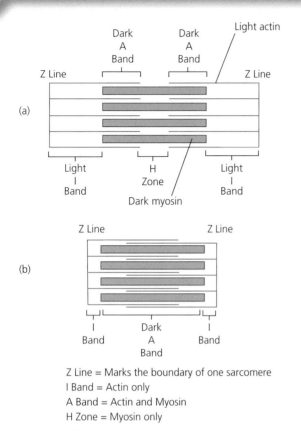

(a)

(b)

Z Line = Marks the boundary of one sarcomere
I Band = Actin only
A Band = Actin and Myosin
H Zone = Myosin only

Figure 2.45 A sarcomere from resting (a) to muscle contraction (b)

Concentric contraction

A concentric contraction involves the muscle shortening and developing tension. The origin and insertion of the muscle move closer together and muscle becomes fatter. To produce a concentric contraction a movement must occur against gravity.

Eccentric contraction

An eccentric contraction involves the muscle lengthening to develop tension. The origin and the insertion move further away from each other. An eccentric contraction provides the control of a movement on the downward phase and it works to resist the force of gravity.

If a person is performing a bench press they will produce a concentric contraction to push the weight away from their body. However, on the downward phase they will produce an eccentric contraction to control the weight on the way down. If they did not gravity would return the weight to the ground and hurt them in the process. The agonist muscle will produce concentric and eccentric contractions while the antagonist muscle will always stay relaxed to allow the movement to occur.

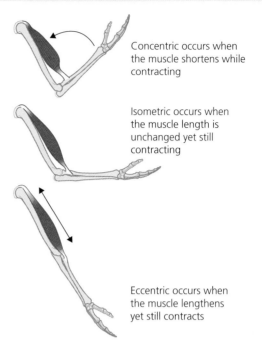

Concentric occurs when the muscle shortens while contracting

Isometric occurs when the muscle length is unchanged yet still contracting

Eccentric occurs when the muscle lengthens yet still contracts

Figure 2.46 Types of muscle contraction at the biceps brachii

Isometric contraction

If a muscle produces tension but stays the same length then it will be an isometric contraction. This occurs when the body is being fixed in one position. For example, a gymnast on the rings in the crucifix position. When we are standing up our postural muscles will produce isometric contractions.

Figure 2.47 A gymnast holding the crucifix position

Muscle fibre type recruitment

The nerve that connects with a muscle fibre, the motor neurone, only stimulates a part of that muscle – this part is called the motor unit.

Key term

The motor unit is the part of a muscle stimulated by a motor neurone.

The number of muscle fibres that a motor neurone stimulates varies between different muscles; for example, muscles that produce large movements, such as the quadriceps, will have more muscle fibres per motor unit whereas muscles that need to produce fine movements, such as moving the eye, will have less muscle fibres per motor unit. Each motor unit will consist of the same muscle fibre type.

Different muscle fibres will be stimulated at different intensities; this process is called muscle fibre recruitment. When the muscles need to produce a large force such as lifting a very heavy weight, the type IIx muscle fibres will be recruited in order to produce these large amounts of force. However, when a person is walking, slow contractions and low forces are required so type I muscle fibres will be recruited. See Figure 1.1 on page 11 of Unit 1.

E2 Check your understanding

1   Describe the process of muscle contraction.
2   Explain the three different types of muscle contraction.
3   Asses what type of muscle contractions occur in the quadriceps during:
    a) the downwards phase of a squat
    b) the upwards phase of a squat.

E3 Location of skeletal muscles

You will need to know the location of each of the following major muscles in the muscular system:

- deltoids (posterior, anterior, medial)
- medial and lateral shoulder rotators
- biceps brachii
- triceps brachii
- wrist flexors
- wrist extensors
- forearm supinators
- forearm pronators
- sternocleidomastoid

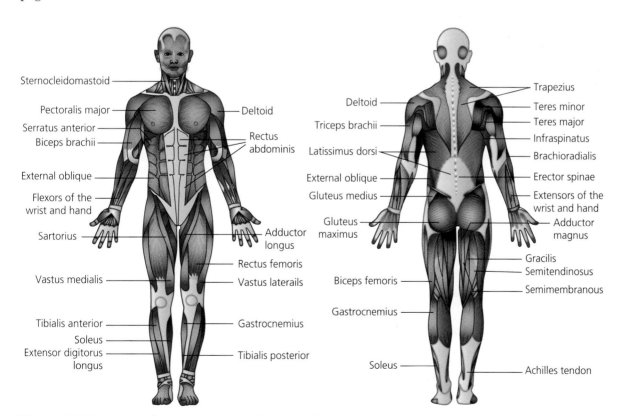

Figure 2.48 Anterior and posterior view of the muscular system

- pectoralis major
- rectus abdominis
- obliques
- transverse abdominis (TVA)
- quadriceps (rectus femoris, vastus medialis, vastus lateralis, vastus intermedius)
- iliopsoas
- tibialis anterior
- erector spinae
- trapezius
- rhomboids

- latissimus dorsi
- gluteals (gluteus maximus, gluteus medius, gluteus minimus)
- hamstrings (biceps femoris, semitendinosus, semimembranosus)
- gastrocnemius
- soleus.

Some of these muscles are shown on Figure 2.50.

The transverse abdominis and iliopsoas are deeper muscles and are shown in the Figures 2.51 and 2.52.

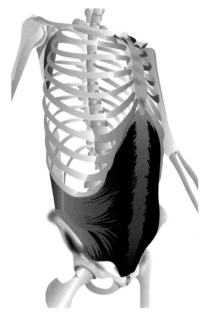

Figure 2.49 Traverse abdominis (TVA)

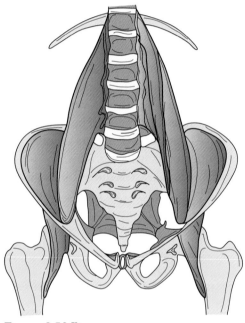

Figure 2.50 Iliopsoas

Muscle	Position	Action	Exercise
Trapezius	Upper back	Elevation, retraction and depression of shoulder girdle	Bent over rows
Rhomboids	Upper back	Retraction of the shoulder	Bent over rows
Sternocleidomastoid	Neck	Flexes the neck	Neck retraction and side neck rotations
Latissimus dorsi	Lower back	Adduction and extension of shoulder	Lateral pulldown
Pectoralis major	Chest	Horizontal flexion and adduction of shoulder	Bench press
Deltoid	Shoulder	Abduction, flexion and extension of shoulder	Lateral raises
Medial shoulder rotator	shoulder	Moving the arm inwards towards the body	Arm rotations with a dumbbell
Lateral shoulder rotator	shoulder	Moving the arm outwards away from the body	Arm rotations with a dumbbell

Muscle	Position	Action	Exercise
Biceps brachii	Front of upper arm	Flexion of elbow and shoulder, supination of forearm	Bicep curls
Triceps brachii	Back of upper arm	Extension of elbow and shoulder	Tricep extension
Wrist flexors	Back of the lower arm	Flex the wrist	Wrist curls
Wrist extensors	Front of lower arm	Extend the wrist	Wrist curls
Forearm supinators	At the top on the back of the lower arm	Supinates the lower arm and hand	Using a dumbbell to supinate and pronate the hand
Forearm pronators	One at the top and one at the bottom of the lower arm	Pronates the lower arm and hand	Using a dumbbell to supinate and pronate the hand
Rectus abdominis	Front of abdomen	Flexion of vertebrae	Swiss ball sit-ups
Obliques	Sides of the abdomen	Rotation of vertebrae	Side bends
Transverse abdominis (TVA)	Deep layers of muscle at the front and to the side of the rectus abdominis	Pelvic stability	The plank
Erector spinae	Up and down the spine	Extension of vertebrae	Dorsal raises
Iliopsoas	Vertebral column, T12, L1- L3 to front of the femur	Hip flexion	Walking and running
Gluteus maximus	Bottom	Extension of hip	Squats
Rectus femoris	Front of upper leg	Extension of knee	Leg extension
Vastus lateralis	Front of upper leg	Extension of knee	Leg extension
Vastus medialis	Front of upper leg	Extension of knee	Leg extension
Vastus intermedius	Front of upper leg	Extension of knee	Leg extension
Semimembranosus	Back of upper leg	Flexion of knee	Leg flexion
Semitendinosus	Back of upper leg	Flexion of knee	Leg flexion
Biceps femoris	Back of upper leg	Flexion of knee	Leg flexion
Gastrocnemius	Back of lower leg	Plantarflexion of ankle, knee flexion	Calf raises
Soleus	Back of lower leg	Plantarflexion of ankle	Calf raises
Tibialis anterior	Front of lower leg	Dorsiflexion of ankle	Walking
Iliopsoas	Vertebral column, T12, L1–L3 to front of the femur	Hip flexion	Walking and running

Table 2.4 Muscles and their position and actions, and how to exercise these

E3 Check your understanding

Label each of the following muscles on the diagram:

- sternocleidomastoid
- pectoralis major
- rectus abdominis
- obliques
- quadriceps
- tibialis anterior
- trapezius
- latissimus dorsi
- gluteus maximus
- biceps femoris, semitendinosus, semimembranosus
- gastrocnemius
- soleus.

Figure 2.51 The muscular system in action

E4 Antagonistic muscle pairs

A muscle can only contract and pull on a bone. Therefore, in order for a body part to return to its previous position, another muscle needs to be in place to pull the body part back to its original position. This is called an antagonistic muscle pair. One muscle in the pair contracts to produce movement and the other muscle does not contract to allow the movement to occur. For example, the biceps brachii and triceps brachii are an antagonistic muscle pair. When you perform a bicep curl the biceps brachii will contract to produce the movement, while the triceps brachii does not contract to allow the movement to occur.

Hamstrings	Quadriceps
Pectorals major	Trapezius
Deltoids	Latissimus Dorsi
Biceps brachii	Triceps brachii
Wrist flexors	Wrist extensors
Forearm pronators	Forearm supinators
Erector Spinae	Rectus abdominis
Gluteals	Iliopsoas
Tibialis anterior	Gastrocnemius

Table 2.5 Antagonistic muscle pairs

When muscles contract they work as a group in that the muscle contracting is dependent on other muscles to enable it to do its job. A muscle can play one of four roles:

1 **Agonist (or prime mover)**

This muscle contracts to produce the desired movement.

2 **Antagonist**

This muscle does not contract to allow the agonist to contract.

3 **Synergist**

This muscle assists the agonist in producing the desired movement.

4 **Fixator**

These muscles will fix joints and the body in position to enable the desired movement to occur.

For example, in the upwards phase of a bicep curl, the following muscles play the following rules:

1 **Agonist** – the biceps brachii are producing the movement at the elbow

2 **Antagonist** – the triceps brachii are relaxing to allow the agonist to contract

3 **Synergist** – a muscle called the brachioradialis assists the biceps during the lifting phase of the movement

4 **Fixator** – trapezius fixes the shoulder in place to keep the arm in place.

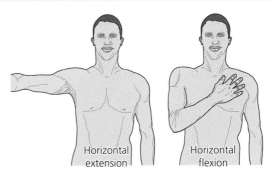

Figure 2.52 Horizontal extension and flexion

E5 Types of movement

Learners must understand the different types of movement with application of anatomical terminology:

- flexion (horizontal flexion, hip flexion, shoulder flexion, plantarflexion, dorsiflexion, lateral flexion)
- extension (hyper-extension, horizontal extension, hip extension, shoulder extension)
- abduction
- adduction
- rotation (medial and lateral)
- circumduction
- pronation
- supination
- elevation
- depression
- protraction
- retraction.

Types of joint movement

To enable us to understand sporting movements, we need to able to describe or label joint movements. Joint movements are given specific terms.

Flexion

This occurs when the angle of a joint decreases. For example, when you bend the elbow it decreases from 180 degrees to around 30 degrees.

There are other types of flexion and these are:

- **Horizontal flexion** – this occurs at the shoulder and hip. The shoulder is abducted and the arm moves across the body. At the hip the hip is abducted and the leg moves across the body.

- **Shoulder flexion** – this occurs with the arm moving upwards in front of the body.

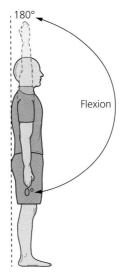

Figure 2.53 Shoulder flexion

- **Hip flexion** – this occurs with the thigh moving upwards in front of the body towards the body.

Plantarflexion

This means that the foot moves away from the shin bone and you will be pointing your toes or raising onto your tiptoes. It is specific to your ankle joint and occurs when you walk.

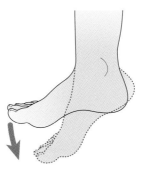

Figure 2.54 Plantarflexion

Dorsiflexion

This means that the foot moves towards the shin as if you are pulling your toes up. It is specific to the ankle joint and occurs when you walk.

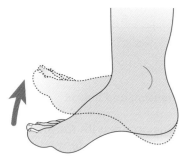

Figure 2.55 Dorsiflexion

Lateral flexion

This is movement of the spine to the left or to the right while standing upright.

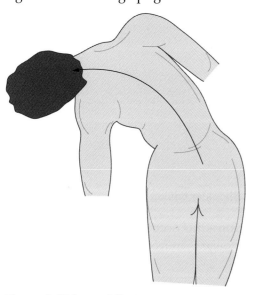

Figure 2.56 Lateral flexion

Extension

This occurs when the angle of a joint increases. For example, when you straighten the elbow it increases from 30 degrees to 180 degrees.

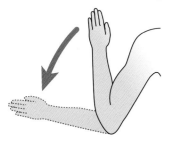

Figure 2.57 Extension

Hyperextension

This is the term given to an extreme or abnormal range of motion found within a joint; for example, at the knee or elbow.

- **Horizontal extension** – this occurs at the shoulder and the hip. The shoulder is abducted and the arm moves away to the side of the body. At the hip, the hip is abducted and the leg moves away to the side of the body.
- **Hip extension** – this occurs with the leg moving backwards behind the body.
- **Shoulder extension** – this occurs with the arm moving backwards behind the body.

Adduction

This means movement towards the midline of the body.

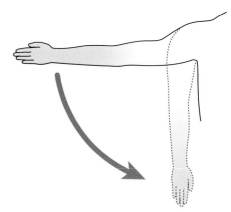

Figure 2.58 Adduction

Abduction

This means movement away from the midline of the body. This occurs at the hip during a star jump.

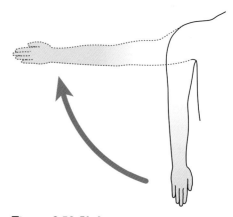

Figure 2.59 Abduction

Circumduction

This means that the limb moves in a circle; this occurs at the shoulder joint during an overarm bowl in cricket.

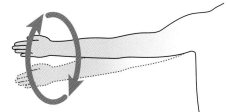

Figure 2.60 Circumduction

Rotation

This means that the limb moves in a circular movement.

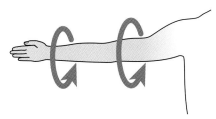

Figure 2.61 Rotation

There are two types of rotation:

- **Medial rotation** is where the limb moves towards the middle of the body. This occurs in the hip in golf while performing a drive shot.
- **Lateral rotation** is where the limb moves away from the body.

Pronation

This means when the hand is facing down while the elbow is flexed. Pronation occurs as the hand moves from facing up to facing down and is the result of the movement of the pivot joint between the ulna and radius. This would happen when a spin bowler delivers the ball in cricket.

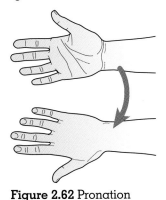

Figure 2.62 Pronation

Supination

This means when the palm of the hand is facing up. Supination occurs as the hand moves from facing down to facing up and is the result of the movement of the pivot joint between the ulna and radius.

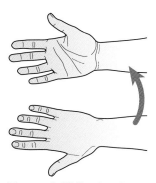

Figure 2.63 Supination

Inversion

This means that the soles of the feet are facing each other. It occurs at the gliding joints between the tarsals rather than at the ankle joint.

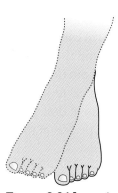

Figure 2.64 Inversion

Eversion

This means that the soles of the feet are facing away from each other. It occurs at the gliding joints between the tarsals rather than at the ankle joint.

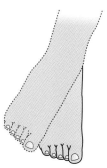

Figure 2.65 Eversion

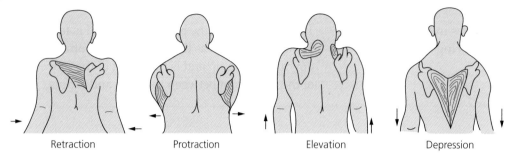

Retraction   Protraction   Elevation   Depression

Figure 2.66 Four movements at the shoulder

The next four movements all occur at the shoulder:

- **Elevation** – this is where the shoulders are lifted towards the head.

- **Depression** – this is where the shoulders are brought downwards towards the body.

- **Protraction** – this is where the shoulders are moved towards the front of the body.

- **Retraction** – this is where the shoulders are moved towards the back of the body.

It is important to remember that it is the joint that moves, not the body part. For example, if a person said that their arm was flexed, the arm contains three joints, the shoulder, the elbow and the wrist. Therefore, which of these joints are flexed, all or some? To be accurate, in anatomical terms you should always refer to the movement that is taking place at the joint, for example, flexion at the shoulder and elbow.

E6 Planes of movement

The body is divided into three anatomical planes:

- sagittal plane

- frontal plane

- transverse plane.

The **sagittal plane** divides the body into the right- and left-hand side. Flexion and extension movements such as bicep curls, knee extension and sit-ups occur in this plane.

Frontal plane divides the body into the front and back or anterior and posterior in anatomical terms. Abduction and adduction movements such as star jumps, and lateral flexion such as side bends occur in this plane.

Transverse plane divides the body into an upper and lower half. Rotational movements such as pronation, supination and rotation occur in this plane.

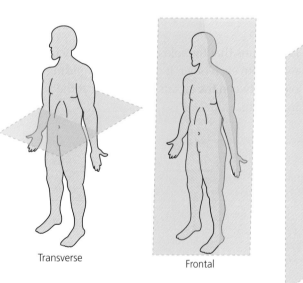
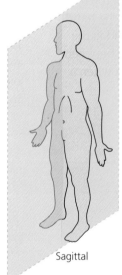

Transverse   Frontal   Sagittal

Figure 2.67 Three planes of motion

1 Give examples of sporting movements in which you would see the sports person perform each of the types of movement listed below.
   a) horizontal flexion of the shoulder
   b) shoulder flexion
   c) plantarflexion at the ankle
   d) lateral flexion at the spine
   e) hyper-extension at the spine
   f) hip extension
   g) shoulder abduction
   h) hip adduction
   i) hip medial rotation
   j) shoulder circumduction
   k) hand pronation
   l) shoulder retraction.
2 Identify:
   a) the types of movement permitted at the knee joint
   b) the types of movement permitted at the shoulder joint
   c) the types of movement permitted at the ankle joint
   d) the types of movement permitted at the spine
   e) which plane of motion supination takes place in
   f) which plane of motion the knee can only move in
   g) the planes of motion and the type of movement performed the hip can move in
   h) the plane a somersault takes place in
   i) the plane a cartwheel takes place in
   j) the plane a tennis backhand takes place in.

F Analysis of the skeletal and muscular systems and how they produce movements in sport and exercise

F1 Phases of sport and exercise movement

When analysing a sport or exercise-related movement, it is important that you know about the different phases of the movement so that you are able to analyse each appropriately.

There are three phases of movement that you will need to be aware of.

Learners must understand the application of the muscular and skeletal systems to each of the following:

1 preparation
2 execution
3 follow through.

For example:

1 In the preparation phase, the body has moved into a position in order to be prepared to execute the movement.
2 Execution is the part of the movement when the performer carries out the desired movement, such as making contact with a ball.
3 Follow through is the part of the movement where the performer completes the movement, which in some cases can help to put the object that they have made contact with go in the right direction.

Figure 2.70 shows an example of three phases of movement.

F1 Check your understanding

1 Describe the three phases of movement in a netball pass.
2 Draw a stick man to represent the three phases of movement in a netball pass.

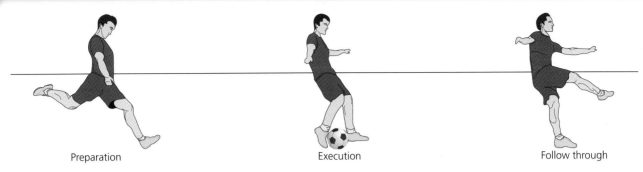

Preparation   Execution   Follow through

Figure 2.68 Three phases of movement

F2 Interrelationship of the muscular and skeletal systems in movement analysis

When analysing the movements that take place at the muscular and skeletal systems, the body will be divided into three sections:

1 upper body

2 trunk

3 lower body.

The **upper body** consists of the head, neck, arms, wrists, hands, and chest area.

The **trunk** consists of the abdomen and lower back.

The **lower body** consists of the hips, legs, ankles and feet.

You will also need to know about the movement efficiency during each phase of different sporting movements and exercises. Movement efficiency includes the following:

● dynamic (balanced) stability at joints and mobility at other joints

● kinetic chain

● transfer of movement across body segments

● transfer of loads and maintain force

● muscle balance

● mechanical efficiency.

Stability and mobility at joints

During a sport or exercise movement, some joints will need to be kept stable in order for others to be able to move fully through the range of motion required for optimal performance. For example, when bowling a cricket ball, the shoulder needs to be able to move through its full range of movement in order to gain the maximum power behind the bowling action. The spine remains stable to keep the body in the best position to perform the shot.

Kinetic chain

The kinetic chain is used to describe the sequence of events in a movement and how the movement transfers powers to different parts of the body. For example, when bowling a cricket ball, the kinetic chain includes the following parts:

1 The bowler runs up to the bowling area.

2 As they get closer to the bowling area they extend and circumduct their shoulder.

3 They plant their foot on the ground and release the ball.

Transfer of energy across body segments

The processes involved in sport and exercise movements require a preparatory phase in order to transfer energy across the body segments in order to help the person to perform such actions as throwing an object or jumping as far as possible. Many sports will require a run up, as in a javelin throw. When the thrower plants their foot ready to throw, the energy that they have gained from their run up is transferred to the rest of the body. The hip of the planted foot rotates medially which then transfers the energy to the upper body and to the throwing limb to help the person to throw the javelin as far as possible.

Muscle balance

It is important for sports and exercise performers to have balanced antagonistic muscle pairs, otherwise it can lead to injury. For example, a number of football players suffer from hamstring injuries. This can be due to the quadriceps muscle being stronger than the hamstring muscle. When the footballer strikes the ball, the quadriceps contract with too much force which results in the hamstrings over stretching and tearing.

Carrying out a movement analysis

When carrying out a movement analysis you will need to include the following areas:

1 Bones involved in movement including the type of bone.
2 The muscles involved in movement including the:
   ● role and/or function of antagonistic pairs
   ● role and/or function of synergist muscles
   ● role and/or function of fixator muscles
   ● types of contraction of the muscles.

3 The joints involved in movement including the:
   ● type of joint
   ● bones forming each joint
   ● range of movement permitted at each joint.
4 The type of movements including the planes of movement.
5 Movement efficiency which includes:
   ● dynamic (balanced) stability at joints and mobility at other joints
   ● kinetic chain
   ● transfer of movement across body segments
   ● transfer of loads and maintain force
   ● muscle balance
   ● mechanical efficiency.

When carrying out an analysis such as this, you may find it useful to present your work in a table to start with. This will help to ensure you have included all the main points to start your analysis.

For example, if you were analysing a football player kicking a ball, your analysis table could be shown in the following way:

Lower body

Joint	Bones at the joint	Types of bone	Type of movement	Agonist	Antagonist	Type of contraction	Plane of movement
Preparation: Knee	Femur Fibula Tibia patella	Long Long Long sesamoid	Flexion	Hamstrings	Quadriceps	Concentric	Sagittal
Preparation: Hip	Femur Pelvis	Long Flat	Extension	Gluteus maximus	Iliopsoas	Concentric	Sagittal
Preparation: Ankle	Fibula Tibia tarsals	Long Long Irregular	Plantar flexion	Gastroc-nemius	Tibialis anterior	Concentric	Sagittal
Execution: Knee	Femur Fibula Tibia patella	Long Long Long sesamoid	Extension	Quadriceps	Hamstrings	Concentric	Sagittal
Execution: Hip	Femur Pelvis	Long Flat	Flexion	Gluteus maximus	Iliopsoas	Concentric	Sagittal
Execution: Ankle	Fibula Tibia Tarsals	Long Long Irregular	Dorsiflexion	Tibialis anterior	Gastroc-nemius	Concentric	Sagittal

→

Joint	Bones at the joint	Types of bone	Type of movement	Agonist	Antagonist	Type of contraction	Plane of movement
Follow through: Knee	Femur Fibula Tibia patella	Long Long Long sesamoid	Extension	Quadriceps	Hamstrings	Concentric	Sagittal
Follow through: Hip	Femur Pelvis	Long Flat	Flexion	Gluteus maximus	Iliopsoas	Concentric	Sagittal
Follow through: Ankle	Fibula Tibia Tarsals	Long Long Irregular	Dorsiflexion	Tibialis anterior	Gastroc-nemius	Concentric	Sagittal

Table 2.6 Analysis of movement: a football player kicking a ball

You will then need to write a response around this table to show your understanding of what is happening in the body during each phase of the movement. You should add into this part of your response any contractions from relevant synergist and fixator muscles as well as the information in the table. This section should also include the movement efficiency section of the unit content.

For example:

Additional factors responsible for movement
All three joints are synovial joints, allowing a specific range of movement.

The muscles that work across each joint are connected to the bone via tendons.

The bones of each joint are held together securely by ligaments, to provide stability at the joint.

Hip: ball and socket joint
- The joint is formed by the articulation of the femur and pelvis.
- A great range of movement is possible at the hip, due to the shape made by the articulating bones.

Knee: hinge joint
- The joint is formed by the articulation of the femur, fibula and tibia.
- As the knee is a hinge joint, movement is only possible in one plane, the sagittal plane.

Ankle: hinge joint
- The joint is formed by the articulation of the tibia, fibula and tarsals.
- As the ankle is a hinge joint, movement is only possible in one plane, the sagittal plane.

Preparation phase
During the preparation phase, the person is preparing to kick the ball. They need to flex their knee to do this. During this movement, the agonist is the hamstrings which are made up of the biceps femoris, semimembranosus, and semitendinosus. These muscle shorten as they produce a concentric contraction to flex the knee and bring the foot upwards behind the body. The quadriceps are the antagonist muscle. The quadriceps consist of the rectus femoris, vastus lateralis, vastus medialis and vastus intermedius. During this flexion of the knee, the synergist muscles is the gastrocnemius to help produce the knee flexion. The fixator muscle is the abdominals.

The hip is extended by concentric contraction of the gluteus maximus muscle which moves the thigh backwards behind the body. The antagonist muscle is the iliopsoas. The synergist muscles are the hamstrings and the fixator are the abdominals.

The ankle is plantar flexed by contraction of the gastrocnemius acting as the agonist muscle and the tibialis anterior acting as the antagonist. The soleus acts as the synergist muscle in this movement.

These concentric contractions allow the football player to correctly align their foot with the ball so that they can produce an accurate shot.

Execution phase

During this phase the foot makes contact with the football. The knee is extended by concentric contraction of the quadriceps muscle which act as the agonist, and the hamstrings now do not contract and are the antagonist. The fixator muscles are the gluteus maximus muscle, to help to stabilise the area. The hip is flexed with the iliopsoas acting as the agonist muscle which contracts concentrically. The gluteal muscle group are the antagonistic muscles and the hamstrings acting as synergists. The abdominals acts as the fixator muscles.

Lastly, at the ankle joint there is dorsiflexion for the foot to move up towards the ball and make contact with it in order to strike it. The tibialis anterior is the agonist muscle; the gastrocnemius is the antagonist.

These concentric contractions allow the football player to complete the kicking of the ball, ensuring the ball follows the correct line to either a team mate or to try to score a goal.

Follow through

After the person has kicked the ball, they will continue to produce movement to complete the activity. The knee continues to extend further by concentric contraction of the quadriceps muscle which act as the agonist, and the hamstrings now do not contract and are the antagonist. The fixator muscles are the gluteus maximus muscle to help to stabilise the area. The hip is further flexed with the iliopsoas acting as the agonist muscle which contracts concentrically. The gluteal muscle group are the antagonistic muscles and the hamstrings acting as synergists. The abdominals acts as the fixator muscles.

Lastly, at the ankle joint there is further dorsiflexion for the foot to move up after it has struck the ball. The tibialis anterior is the agonist muscle, the gastrocnemius is the antagonist.

It is important that the footballer has muscle balance between the antagonistic muscle pairs, the hamstrings and quadriceps, so that the hamstrings muscles do not get injured if the quadriceps are stronger and the footballer strikes the ball with a lot of power.

The kinetic chain of this process is from the footballer running to the ball, planting their foot and flexing their knee to bring the other foot backwards to allow it to follow through at speed as the knee extends to then make contact with the ball and kick the ball with force.

Other muscles will act as synergists and fixators to stabilise the hip joint throughout the movement, increasing functionality of the movement and maximising the force generated.

F2 Check your understanding

Look at the images below of a person performing a tennis serve.

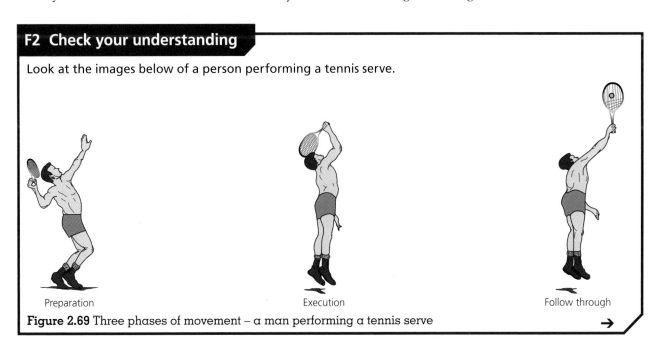

Preparation   Execution   Follow through

Figure 2.69 Three phases of movement – a man performing a tennis serve →

F2 Check your understanding

Copy and complete the table below and then write an analysis of the movement.

Movement phase	Joint	Bones at the joint	Types of bone	Type of movement	Agonist	Antagonist	Type of contraction	Plane of movement
Preparation	**Shoulder**	Scapula Clavicle Humerus		Extension				
	Elbow	Radius Ulna Humerus		Flexion				
	Wrist	Radius Ulna Carpals		Flexion				
Execution	**Shoulder**							
	Elbow							
	Wrist							
Follow through	**Shoulder**							
	Elbow							
	Wrist							

Table 2.7 Analysis of movement – performing a tennis serve

Further reading

Howley, E.T. and Franks, B.D. (2003). *Health Fitness Instructor's Handbook (Fourth Edition)*. Human Kinetics.

Marieb, E. and Hoehn, K. (2015). *Human Anatomy & Physiology (10th Edition)*. Pearson Education.

Milner, C. (2008). *Functional Anatomy for Sport and Exercise*. Routledge.

Sharkey, B.J. and Gaskill, S.E. (2013). *Fitness and Health (Seventh Edition)*. Human Kinetics.

Tortora, G.J. and Derrickson, B.H. (2014). *Principles of Anatomy and Physiology (14th Edition)*. John Wiley & Sons.

American College of Sports Medicine's Health and Fitness Journal

British Journal of Sports Medicine Exercise and Sport Sciences

Reviews International Journal of Sports Science & Coaching Medicine

Journal of Anatomy

Useful websites

1st4Sport

www.1st4sport.com

American College of Sports Medicine

www.acsm.org.uk

Sport Science journal

www.sportsci.org.uk

Sports Coach UK

www.sportscoachuk.org.uk

Topend Sports

www.topendsports.com

References

Marieb, E. and Hoehn, K. (2015). *Human Anatomy & Physiology (10th Edition)*. Pearson Education.

Milner, C. (2008). *Functional Anatomy for Sport and Exercise*. Routledge.

Palastanga, N. (2006) *Anatomy and Human Movement (Fifth Edition)*, ButterworthHeinemann.

Stafford-Brown, J. and Rea, S. (2010). *BTEC Level 3 National Sport and Exercise Sciences (Third Edition)*, Hodder Education.

Tortora, G.J. and Derrickson, B.H. (2014). *Principles of Anatomy and Physiology (14th Edition)*, John Wiley & Sons.

3 Applied sport and exercise psychology

About this unit

Sport and exercise psychology is the study of how people behave in sport and exercise environments. Sport environments are quite unique, as they place people in competitive situations and put them under pressure to succeed. As a result, they will experience changes in the way that they think and the feelings they are experiencing, which impact on behaviour. When placed in stressful situations, people can react in ways that you wouldn't normally. For example, the mildest natured people can become very competitive and even show signs of aggression; very confident people can start to have self-doubts and make uncharacteristic mistakes. Sport psychology has a wide scope and looks at the behaviour of human beings, the characteristics of the environments they are playing in and the effects of playing in different types of groups.

Sport psychologists work with athletes to offer them skills or interventions that they can use to manage their thoughts and feelings and the impact that these have on their behaviour. They also work with athletes to help them understand their sporting experiences and interpret why they achieved the results that they did. Sport psychologists are now a common feature of most high-performing sports teams.

According to British Association of Sports Sciences (BASES), sport psychology is one of the three core disciplines within the study of sports science. Physiology and biomechanics are identified by BASES as the other two core disciplines, and the study of these three subjects are key to understanding performance in sport and exercise activities. The study of sport psychology can be highly rewarding, as it can help you to understand your own experiences in sport and the results you achieved, or didn't achieve. It can help you to prepare mentally for sport and exercise and ensure that you approach sporting competition with an appropriate mindset. The more time you spend understanding theories and their application then the greater understanding you will gain about the behaviour of sports people, their coaches and managers, and the effectiveness of the teams that they are playing in.

How will I be assessed?

External assessment

This unit will be assessed externally, meaning that at the end of the module you will complete a task that has been set by Pearson and will be marked by Pearson examiners. The task will ask you to respond to a scenario that describes the experience of individual sports people or a team, and you will have to use your knowledge of psychological theories and psychological interventions to address the scenario. The scenario will cover large amounts of the unit content, so you will have to understand as much of the unit as you possibly can.

The task will be partly seen. This means that you will be given some pre-release material to read and then, based on the content of this material, you will be able to complete some preparation work. You are able to make research notes that you will be able to bring into the assessment session with you. This will be the only assessment you complete for this unit – you are not required to complete assignment work as you would for internally assessed units.

Key term

Sport and exercise psychology is the study of how people behave in sport and exercise environments.

How will I be graded?

The assessment outcomes show you the knowledge and the skills that you are expected to be able to demonstrate in the external assessment. It is important when you are covering the unit content that you keep these objectives in mind, as they show what you need to be able to do with the information you are learning about. In this case, the words demonstrate, apply and analyse are particularly important, as they tell you the skills that you will need to show in the external assessment.

Assessment objectives

The exam is split into four different assessment outcomes (AOs) and each will be covered in varying amounts within the paper. The command words that will be used for each assessment outcome are also provided, to help you to gain an understanding of the depth and breadth that you will need to include in your responses for each AO.

AO1 Demonstrate knowledge and understanding of psychological factors, concepts, interventions and theories in sport and exercise activities.

AO2 Apply knowledge and understanding of psychological factors, concepts, interventions and theories, and their influence in sport and exercise activities on real-life sporting contexts.

AO3 Analyse and evaluate information related to individuals or teams to determine appropriate psychological interventions.

AO4 Be able to recommend psychological interventions underpinned by theory and in context with appropriate justification.

Grade descriptors

Grade descriptors are provided by Pearson to give an idea of what sorts of skills and knowledge need to be shown to achieve a pass or a distinction grade. However, further grades are available including:

U – Unclassified

Level 3 Pass

Learners are able to demonstrate knowledge and understanding of psychological factors and concepts, and can apply these in context. They can identify factors and interpret the impact and influence that these have on the performance of an individual or team in context. They will be able to rationalise the approach required in different sport and exercise situations. Learners will be able to apply psychological theories to propose and rationalise psychological interventions that are relevant to the scenario, demonstrating an understanding of the principles behind those interventions.

Level 3 Distinction

Learners are able to critically evaluate information in context, relating to improving the performance of a team or individual. They can identify psychological factors and provide a detailed interpretation of the impact and influence that these have on the performance of an individual or team in context. Learners can prioritise the psychological factors based on their significance in relation to the effect on individual and/or team performance. They show a thorough understanding of psychological theories and can apply these to propose, prioritise and justify psychological interventions that are relevant to the scenario, demonstrating a detailed understanding of the principles behind those interventions.

Command words meanings

In your external assessment, each question will start with one of the possible command words or terms, so it is important that you know what each means so that you know how to answer each question. Look at page 8 for a table of these.

A Motivation for sports and exercise

A1 Types of motivation

While many factors are important for success at sport, the factor that influences athletic success the most is probably motivation. Motivation is the force that underlies our behaviour and influences the choices and decisions we make. Motivation is what causes an athlete to train harder than other athletes, to train in all weathers and make sacrifices (such as nights out and holidays) to train and work towards achieving their goals. Despite being such an important factor in success, it is difficult for some sports people to accurately explain why they are motivated for one thing but not for another.

What is it that makes one athlete show more desire and hunger for success than another?

Motivation is not a consistent commodity in that it fluctuates from day from day. You have probably noticed that some days you jump out of bed and are fully motivated for what you need to do that day, and other days you want to stay in bed and find it very difficult to force yourself into action. Even the most highly motivated athletes must wake up some days full of aches and pains and think that it might not hurt them if they just had one day off.

There are many definitions of motivation, most of which describe how we move from inaction to action. In a classic definition, Sage (1977) describes motivation as the direction and intensity of one's effort. This is a simple definition but it shows two facets of motivation:

- The direction of motivation, which refers to the activities and situations that an individual seeks out (or avoids);
- The intensity of effort, which refers to how much effort and attention they give to the activity and by extension how much persistence they show the activity.

These two factors are different and just because an individual chooses an activity, it does not mean they will put much effort into it. For example, two athletes may train five times a week but one of the athletes may put a lot more effort into each session. Likewise, your classmates and you have all chosen to study sport and exercise science, but some may work a lot harder than others. It is likely accounted for by the motivating factors you have for studying this subject.

> **Key term**
>
> Motivation is the direction and intensity of effort.

Amotivation

Amotivation is the complete absence of any motivation. It would be characterised by a lack of attraction to an activity or a complete lack of effort expended on an activity. The person would see no value in the activity and have no reason to participate in it. Amotivation is only a temporary state, as an individual's motivation may change if they can see value in participating in an activity. For example, an individual may have no motivation to take part in exercise until they are advised by a doctor that unless they become more active they are at risk of having a heart attack. Almost immediately amotivation could change into very high levels of motivation.

Intrinsic and extrinsic motivation

Motivation can come from sources internal to the body or sources external to the body. Internal factors create intrinsic motivation where rewards come from the activity itself. These include motives such as fun, pleasure, enjoyment, feelings of self-worth, excitement and self-mastery. They are often the reasons why we play sport and keep playing it. Those who are intrinsically motivated will engage in an activity for the pleasure and satisfaction they experience while learning, exploring or trying to understand something new (Weinberg and Gould, 2007).

Motivation can also come from sources outside the activity and these are called extrinsic rewards or sources of extrinsic motivation. This would include the recognition and praise we get from other people, such as our coach, friends and family. It could also be the approval we get from the crowd who support us. Extrinsic motivating factors would also include trophies, medals, prizes, records and any money derived from success. Those who are extrinsically motivated engage in the activity because of the valued outcome rather than the interest in the activity solely for itself (Weinberg and Gould, 2007).

> ## Activity: Types of motivation
>
> 1 Think of examples of activities for which you have the following types of motivation:
>   - Amotivation
>   - Intrinsic motivation
>   - Extrinsic motivation.
> 2 Then think of examples of activities where your motivation has changed from:
>   a) Amotivation to intrinsic motivation
>   b) Intrinsic motivation to extrinsic motivation.

Relationship between different types of motivation

Your motivation for different activities can change from day to day. You may not have even of heard of a sport until you heard that one of your friends was doing it, or they told you how much fun it was. In this case, you have gone from amotivation to motivation for the sport. It is likely that you started playing the sport because you found it to be fun and that you enjoyed playing – you played it because you were intrinsically motivated. However, as you got better you heard about competitions for the sport and you joined a club so you could improve and play in these competitions. The more you played these competitions the more you wanted to win and gain medals and trophies. Now you have become more extrinsically motivated.

A similar thing happens with professional sports people who probably start playing the sport because they enjoy it. A footballer may notice that professional footballers seem to get paid very large amounts of money and spend it on houses, cars and holidays. Slowly they realise that they would like these things as well, so it increases the intensity of their effort. Their motivation

has changed from being intrinsic to extrinsic as they feel these external factors are driving them onwards. If a professional footballer was told that they were no longer to be paid or would have to take a pay cut, they may get very angry and refuse to play. This may seem strange as they initially started playing football for the love of it and now they are refusing to play it.

Sports coaches and anyone involved in sport with young people need to be aware that providing extrinsic rewards can have a negative effect on intrinsic motivation. If a coach gave an individual a reward for playing an activity, they may find that in the future the individual becomes motivated only to gain another external reward.

> ## Key terms
>
> **Amotivation** refers to the complete absence of any motivation to participate in an activity.
>
> **Intrinsic motivation** refers to motivation arising from sources inside the body.
>
> **Extrinsic motivation** refers to motivation arising from sources outside the body.

> ## A1 Check your understanding
>
> 1 Identify why motivation is such an important subject in sport psychology.
> 2 Describe the two main facets of motivation.
> 3 Describe how a person showing amotivation to an activity would behave.
> 4 Explain, using examples, what is meant by intrinsic motivation.
> 5 Explain, using examples, what is meant by extrinsic motivation.
> 6 Explain why it may be dangerous to offer extrinsic rewards to an intrinsically motivated person.

A2 Theories of motivation

Theories of motivation have been researched and developed to help us to understand motivation and why people are motivated to be involved in sport and exercise and be successful at these activities. All motivation theories view motivation in different ways and thus will increase our understanding of this complex subject.

Need achievement theory

Need achievement theory is a theory of achievement motivation which describes whether we are motivated primarily to succeed or to avoid failure. To illustrate this, answer the following questions:

1   Would you rather compete in a race where you are better than your competitors, worse than your competitors, or one where you are all evenly matched?

2   Would you rather take an exam that was very hard, very easy or in the middle?

The choices you make tell us something about your personality as well as your motivation. The choice you made would tell us whether you are motivated to be successful or avoid failure, or whether you like the competition.

Need achievement theory (Atkinson, 1974; McClelland, 1961) was an early theory of motivation and it considers that both our personality traits and the situation we find ourselves in are important to motivation. It also considers three other factors that will predict achievement behaviour – resultant tendencies, emotional reactions and achievement behaviour.

Personality factors

Consider the previous questions about the type of opponent you would like to compete against or the difficulty of the exam you would like to take. Your choice would tell us something about your personality and whether you would be described as a high or low achiever. High achievers have high motivation to achieve success and low motivation to achieve failure while low achievers have high motivation to avoid failure and low motivation to achieve success. This is due to the emotions associated with success and failure. Success is likely to bring pride and satisfaction while failure will be accompanied by feelings of shame and low self-worth.

Situational factors

Situational factors describe how likely we are to be successful in a specific situation and this is based on two factors: the probability of success and the incentive value of success.

Probability of success is influenced by the skill level of the opposition and environmental factors such as whether the competition is at home or away or the weather on the day.

Incentive for success is the value of success in that situation. A good example of this is in open competitions, such as the FA Cup, where teams from lower leagues are drawn to play against Premiership teams. The probability for success for the lower ranked team is low but the incentive for success is incredibly high and as a result their motivation levels should be very high. Conversely, the probability for success for the Premiership team is very high but the incentive for success is quite low as it something that is expected of them. As a result their motivation levels may be relatively low and we end up with a team with high skill level but low motivation playing against a team with low skill level but high motivation. Often these matches are much closer than they should be and occasionally result in shock results or giant killings.

Resultant tendencies

This describes the tendencies of high and low achievers to favour different types of opponents. High achievers will seek out opponents who are close to their skill level where they have roughly a 50:50 chance of winning. They like challenges against others of equal ability rather than playing against competitors who have much higher or much lower skill levels. In contrast to this, low achievers will favour opponents who are ranked much higher or much lower as in these situations they have a much greater certainty of success or failure. This is called an ego-protective strategy as they are unlikely to experience the shame and embarrassment of losing and there is no shame in losing to an opponent you are expected to lose to. A situation where there is a 50:50 chance of success is the worst situation for a low achiever as it offers maximum uncertainty and the greatest possibility of demonstrating their lack of competence.

Emotional reactions

An individual's emotional reactions consist of the amount of pride and shame they feel at their success or failure. Both high and low achievers want to feel pride and minimise shame but the focus is different for each group. High achievers focus on maximising pride while low achievers focus on minimising shame.

Achievement behaviour

This relates to how an individual behaves in competitive situations and summarises the factors that we have explored.

The high achiever prefers challenging tasks that are not too hard or too easy and like situations where their performance is being evaluated.

The low achiever prefers difficult or easy tasks where success or failure is more certain and they dislike situations where their performance is being evaluated.

Need achievement theory is useful to us as it explains the behaviour of two different personality types in selecting tasks and opponents but it doesn't look specifically at the factors, apart from pride and shame, which may motivate us.

Achievement goal theory

Achievement goal theory looks at two different types of orientation. They are task orientation and outcome (or ego) orientation. An individual who is task-oriented has the goal to master a particular skill. They will consider that their ability has improved if they are able to perform a skill better now than they did a week ago. A task-oriented person will continue to be motivated to improve their mastery of the skill and will show improvements in self-confidence as their skill level improves.

An outcome- or ego-oriented individual will measure their ability in comparison to the ability of another individual. An ego-oriented individual will continue to be motivated to keep their ability higher than other people's and will gain self-confidence for as long as they achieve this.

These two types of motivation are also referred to as self-referenced and externally-referenced. A self-referenced person measures their achievements against their previous achievements while an externally-referenced person measures their achievements against those of other people.

This theory has implications for athletes and their coaches. For coaches it is important to develop environments where athletes will improve their own skills in relation to their own ability, as they have little control over the amount of effort their opponents or teammates expend on improving their skills. Nicholls (1989) identified that athletes with an ego-orientation showed higher levels of anxiety before practice and competition as they felt they were being evaluated by other people.

Self-determination theory

Self-determination theory (Deci and Ryan, 1985) relates to different types of motivation, intrinsic and extrinsic, but specifically to whether an activity is freely chosen by an individual or has been enforced on them.

An activity that is self-determined is one chosen by the participant and they will have control over their experience. This is in opposition to activities that are enforced on an individual where they have little choice in how they are conducted. There is a relationship between intrinsic and extrinsic forms of motivation and the level of self-determination present in an activity.

It is likely that an individual who shows amotivation towards an activity would only engage in it if they are forced to and thus their participation can never be self-determined. A person's participation in an activity is only fully self-determined if they are doing it for the pure enjoyment of participating rather than for any form of external reward. These activities are engaged in freely with the individual having full control over how the activity is conducted. Intrinsically motivated individuals participate in activities to gain new skills and knowledge, to gain the pleasure of achieving a goal and to experience interest and excitement from an activity (Cox, 2012).

Extrinsic motivation

Deci and Ryan (1991) classified extrinsic motivation into four types, rather than just regarding it as a single concept. They said that it is rare for an individual to be fully extrinsically or intrinsically motivated, but they will be motivated by varying amounts of each type of motivation. They identified the following four different types of extrinsic motivation:

1 **External regulation** – where an individual participates to gain an external reward, such as a trophy or prize, rather than for a personal desire to participate.

2 **Introjected regulation** – where an individual participates to please other people, such as their coach or parent, or to avoid feeling guilty or anxious.

3 **Identified regulation** – where an individual freely chooses to participate in an activity that they don't view as pleasant or interesting but realise it may be important for them to help them achieve another goal. For example, a runner completes weight training exercises because they know they will help them prevent injury.

4 **Integrated regulation** – where an individual freely chooses an activity despite it being suggested or controlled by their coach. It is still an example of extrinsic motivation, but only just, because it is hasn't been fully chosen by the individual.

Self-determination theory is a useful theory in sport because self-determined behaviour has been shown to lead to greater persistence in a sport, an increased ability to cope with stress and an increased likelihood that peak performance will be achieved (Vallerand, 2001). In simple terms you are more likely to be motivated to participate in activities that you have chosen (or think you have chosen) yourself, rather than those that have been enforced on you. Often children are involved in sports activities because their parents want them to be successful at them rather than because they enjoy the activity. Children are often afraid to say that they don't want to play a certain sport anymore because they know it will make their parents angry or disappointed.

> **Key term**
>
> **Self-determination theory** reflects the extent to which participation in an activity is freely chosen.

Weiner's attribution theory

Attribution theory focuses on the explanations or reasons that people give for their successes and failures and attempts to categorise them. Look at the following reasons given for success or failure in sport and exercise activities:

- I played well today – the hard training is paying off.
- We worked much harder than the opposition today.
- The referee made a series of bad decisions in favour of the opposition.
- I can't play backhand shots – they are too difficult.
- My instructor really wasn't able to motivate me.
- My back was painful so I had to stop early.

These reasons/excuses may be familiar to you, but why do athletes/coaches attribute their successes or failures to specific reasons? Firstly, they are important because they affect our motivation levels and secondly, they will affect our future expectations of success (self-confidence). Thirdly, they fulfil the need to interpret our performance and learn from our experiences. Some of the attributions made relate to ability ('I played well today'), some refer to effort ('We worked much harder than the opposition'), some to task difficulty ('I can't play backhand shots') and others to luck ('The referee made a series of bad decisions').

Attributions can be placed into two categories:

1 **Stable or unstable** – a fairly permanent trait (skill or ability) or one subject to change (luck).

2 **Internal or external** – one which is under your control (effort) or out of your control (difficulty of opposition).

Generally speaking, attributions can be organised into four types, dependent on their level of stability and locus of control, as shown in Table 3.1.

	Internal	External
Stable	Skill, ability	Task difficulty
Unstable	Effort	Luck

Table 3.1 Four types of attribution

Application of Weiner's attribution to sport

Research shows that successful athletes usually attribute their success to internal, stable factors (skill, ability) and failure to external or unstable causes (luck). It makes sense that we want to take responsibility for our victories and distance ourselves from our failures. It also explains why so many sports managers are keen to blame the referee for the failure of their team. It has the effect of protecting their ego and also steering the blame away from the lack of ability or effort of their players.

Attributions of success to ability or effort are described as being ego-enhancing, as they make the athlete feel even better about their victory, while attributions to task difficulty or luck are ego-protective, making the athlete feel not so bad about themselves. Stable attributions for success will also help maintain the athlete's expectations of future success. If they attributed their success to luck or the lack of ability of their opponents, then success would have no impact on their self-performance. Conversely, an athlete attributing their failure to luck would protect their future chances of success and not reduce their self-confidence.

Key term

Attributions are the reasons that athletes and coaches give for their success or failure.

A2 Check your understanding

1 Explain how need achievement theory can account for our choice of opponents.
2 Identify the difference between an individual who is self-referenced and one who is externally-referenced.
3 Explain what is meant by self-determination and why it is important in sport.
4 Explain the four types of attribution an individual can make to account for their success or failure.

A3 Motivational environment and its influence on sports performers

A motivational environment is about creating conditions where athletes will feel motivated.

Rather than referring to just the physical conditions of an environment it mainly concerns the actions of people involved with athletes and the impact that they have on them. In this respect the coach or instructor has a vital role in ensuring that their behaviour has a motivational effect on their athletes.

The influence of the coach, teacher or instructor on motivation

Coaches, teachers and instructors find themselves in leadership positions and as a result in a position where their behaviour can have a significant impact on the motivation of others. Leaders need to lead by example, meaning that if they don't care about their performance then it is unlikely that they will be able to motivate the people they coach, teach or instruct. Firstly, leaders need to pay attention to their own behaviour and be aware that as a role model their behaviour can impact on the motivation of others.

The aim of a leader is to develop a 'mastery climate' where participants are encouraged to master skills. To create a mastery climate, a framework has been developed that is best known by the acronym **TARGET** (Treasure, 2001). TARGET stands for task, authority, recognition, grouping, evaluation and timing (Duda and Balauger, 2007), and Table 3.2 summarises these six areas and the strategies that can be used by leaders in each area.

Influence of family and peers

As well as the influence of their own behaviour on people they coach, teach or instruct, a leader needs to be aware of the influence of other people on the motivation of the people they are leading. This includes the family and their peers or friendship groups. The family and peers are described as social influences as they can impact of an individual's attitudes, opinions and behaviours with either beneficial or detrimental effects. In exercise environments it has been shown that people who receive the support and encouragement of their family are more confident about their ability and likely to be more successful in maintaining their exercise programme (Howley and Franks, 2003).

TARGET	Structure	Strategy
Task	What tasks athletes are given to help them learn	Provide athletes with a variety of tasks that are moderately demanding and emphasise individual challenges
Authority	Athletes should have some authority in the decision-making process (regarding training sessions and setting rules and boundaries)	Encourage participation by athletes in the decision-making process
Recognition	Practices used to motivate athletes and recognise them for their progress and achievements	Recognise individual progress, effort and improvements through praise and external rewards (if appropriate)
Grouping	How athletes are brought together or kept separate during training sessions and competitions	Use flexible arrangements and groups of mixed abilities
Evaluation	Procedures for monitoring athletes' performances and progress	Develop criteria based on effort, improvement, persistence and progress towards goals
Timing	Appropriateness of time demands placed on learning and development	Training programmes need to recognise that athletes do not all develop at the same rate

Table 3.2 Adapted from Duda and Treasure (2006), p.73

Parents will influence their children's participation in sport through role modelling, social influence and social support. It may come down to basic arrangements such as travel and providing equipment, up to offering support when the young athlete is struggling or unsuccessful. These things are vital to the success of young athletes, but they may be influenced by their friends as well, including pressure to conform to their behaviour. This can be problematic if the athlete's peer group are not athletes themselves, and the individual athlete may find it difficult to conform to the expectations of both their coach and their peer group.

The influence of personality on motivation

There are different views of personality referred to as trait theory and social learning theory. Trait theory suggests that an individual's personality is made up of a series of traits, or relatively consistent ways of behaving. If you know an individual's traits then you know their personality. A trait view of motivation would say that an individual is either motivated or not, and a motivated individual may be described as 'driven' or 'a winner'. It is assumed that these types of individuals will thrive in all

environments as their behaviour is internally driven rather than the result of external influences.

The social learning approach says that personality is learnt through modelling behaviour on other people, particularly role models like parents, and through reinforcement. Reinforcement occurs when a behaviour is positively or negatively rewarded or feedback is provided. In this case, the individual's behaviour is dictated by the environment that they are in and thus their motivation will be affected by what they observe and copy (modelling) and the feedback or reinforcement they are given. This theory suggests that motivation can be moulded by the behaviour of the leader and the feedback they provide.

The influence of the physical environment on motivation

It is likely that you would prefer to find yourself in modern, well-designed facilities that have up-to-date equipment and comfortable changing rooms rather than old, run down, cold facilities. It is no surprise that gyms are designed to be aesthetically attractive as well as functional, so that people enjoy training in them and look forward to visiting them. The more attractive gyms are made, then the increased likelihood that people will keep visiting them.

Football stadiums often have pictures of previously successful teams on the walls to inspire the team and intimidate the opposition. Liverpool F.C. have a large plaque stating 'Welcome to Anfield' in the tunnel that the players pass through to get to the pitch, to intimidate the opposition. Often coaches will place posters and inspiring quotes in the gym or changing rooms to generate motivation within athletes and players.

In summary, the leader plays an exceptionally important role in influencing the motivation levels of the people they are coaching, teaching and instructing. Everything that a coach does will have an impact and this offers the leader the opportunity to be able to positively influence other people.

Activity: Motivational environment

Think of two sports and exercises that you have experienced and answer the following questions to consider the effect that the environment had on your motivation and success.

1 Give examples of how the behaviour of the coach affected your behaviour.
2 Which parts of the TARGET framework did the coach use and how?
3 How did the actions of your family and friends impact on your motivation level in the environment?
4 Explain whether you think that your motivation levels were the result of your personality traits or affected by modelling and feedback.
5 Give examples of how the coach modified the physical environment to enhance motivation.

A3 Check your understanding

1 Describe why the behaviour of the leader affects the motivation of individuals they lead.
2 Identify the six areas covered by the acronym TARGET.
3 Explain how friends and family could have positive and negative effects on motivation.
4 Briefly outline two theories of personality and their differing impact on motivation.

A4 Signs and effects of over-motivation

Over-motivation

Over-motivation occurs when an individual has unrealistically high goals or their behaviour changes because they want to achieve something so much that they work towards it in an obsessive way.

Signs of over-motivation

Over-motivation can show itself in over-training, meaning that the individual is working harder than the body can cope with and is not allowing time for rest and recovery. It is closely linked to exercise addiction, which is defined as a psychological and physical dependence on exercise where withdrawal symptoms occur 24–36 hours after exercise (Weinberg and Gould, 2015). Withdrawal symptoms would include anxiety, irritability, guilt and muscle twitching. While a certain level of addiction may be beneficial for people who have to train six days a week, it can have serious negative implications as well. These would be the result of an individual organising their life around exercise and allowing their work and home life to be less important, causing their relationships to deteriorate as a result. The addiction would result in social withdrawal, where an individual would not spend as much time with friends and family and make excuses not to attend family events or to meet up with their friends.

Effects of over-motivation

An athlete who is over-motivated may experience over-confidence where they feel that due to the amount of work and effort they are expending on their sport then they are sure that it will result in increased success and improved performances. Of course, this is not always the case as their over-training may result in a decrement in performance as they are not giving their body time to rest and recover. Rest and recovery gives the structures of the body the opportunity to adapt to the training they are undertaking, and the brain will need a rest from training as well.

Over-training can lead to a syndrome called 'burnout' which is a condition due to prolonged exposure to physical and psychological stress. The characteristics of burnout are physical and emotional exhaustion, low self-esteem, increased injuries, anxiety and even depression. Burnout often results in social withdrawal as well as the individual finding that they don't have the energy to cope with social situations and the response of their friends to this can make it even harder for the individual to recover.

Key term

Over-motivation occurs when an individual has unrealistically high goals and works towards them in a way that could cause them damage.

A4 Check your understanding

1 Explain what is meant by 'over-motivation'.
2 Identify two signs over over-motivation.
3 Explain the relationship between over-motivation and burnout.
4 Describe why an over-motivation person may have high levels of self-confidence.

B Competitive pressure in sport

B1 Theories of arousal-performance relationship

Arousal describes how excited or motivated we become by something. Arousal level can be seen on a scale where the lowest level of arousal would be asleep up to the highest level which would be in a very excited, frenzied state. You may have played in competitions where you were not interested or motivated at all and in other competitions where you were intensely focused and excited.

Weinberg and Gould (2015) identify that arousal is both physiological and psychological and relates to the intensity of feelings of motivation towards an activity. As arousal levels increase, we feel more energised and ready to take on a challenge. We can see how some athletes, such as weightlifters, get themselves into a state of high arousal before attempting a lift so that they produce the energy they need to perform a heavy lift.

Arousal levels are closely linked to performance, as we shall see in the following theories examining the relationship between arousal and performance.

Key term

Arousal describes how excited and motivated we are about a specific task. It has physiological and psychological dimensions and provides us with energy needed to complete a task.

Theories of the arousal-performance relationship

Drive theory

Drive theory is the work of Hull (1943), who showed that there is a linear (straight line) relationship between arousal level and performance. As arousal levels increase then so will performance level, as can be seen in Figure 3.1. A key feature of this theory is that increased arousal levels will result in an increase in performance if the skill is well learnt.

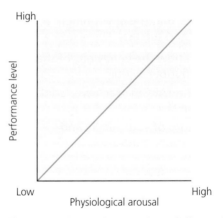

Figure 3.1 Drive theory when skill is well learnt (*Source*: Stafford-Brown and Rea, 2010, p. 63)

Key term

Drive theory says that increases in arousal will result in improvements in performance.

But drive theory is a little simplistic, particularly if we consider the effect of arousal level increases on a novice or someone with a low skill level.

Increases in arousal for a novice are unlikely to have any effect on their performance as the skill is poorly learnt and they will not be able to perform beyond their current skill level. If arousal level becomes even higher it is likely to make their performance worse (McMorris, 2004). This relationship is shown in Figure 3.2.

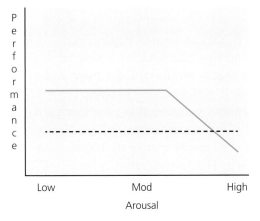

Figure 3.2 Drive theory when skill is poorly learnt (*Source*: McMorris, 2004, p. 247)

Drive theory is able to explain the effect of increased arousal levels on well-learnt tasks. It works well when applied to simple or strength-based tasks, such as pushing hard or lifting weights, but what about when more complex tasks are performed?

Inverted U hypothesis

The inverted U hypothesis is based on the classic work of Yerkes and Dodson (1908). They showed that the relationship between arousal level and performance was curvilinear, as shown in Figure 3.3, rather than the linear relationship shown by drive theory. This theory states that as arousal increases so will performance level up to a point where the arousal state is optimal for the task being performed. Once this point, called the optimal point of arousal or ideal performance state (IPS), has been reached, any further increases in arousal state will result in a decrease in performance level. If you are at the IPS it is often said that you are experiencing a 'flow state' where everything seems to be easy and you perform without feeling there is any effort or feelings of fatigue.

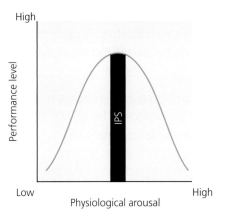

Figure 3.3 The inverted U hypothesis (*Source*: Stafford-Brown and Rea, 2010, p. 63)

This makes sense, as you may well have experienced situations where you were under-aroused and not really interested in an activity and this lead to a poor performance; alternatively, you may have found that there were occasions when you were too motivated and excited and this led you to make mistakes and perform poorly. Hopefully, you may have experienced the optimal point of arousal where your arousal level matched the demands of the task; at this point you experience an optimal performance and everything seems to flow easily.

Key term

Inverted U hypothesis says that increases in arousal will lead to an improvement in performance but only up to a certain point, called the optimal point of arousal. Once the optimal point of arousal has been reached, any further increases in arousal will result in a performance decrement.

Catastrophe theory

Catastrophe theory (Fazey and Hardy, 1988) presents an adaptation to the inverted U hypothesis. This theory says that the curve will not be regular in shape. Figure 3.4 shows that once arousal levels have gone just past their optimal point, any further increase in arousal level can lead to a sudden drop in performance level. This is in contrast to the steady fall-off of performance shown by the inverted U hypothesis. It may be due to an athlete becoming worried about their performance. The point where performance levels drop is described as 'the point of catastrophe' and is indicated with an arrow in Figure 3.4.

This theory helps to explain the phenomenon of 'choking'. Choking is characterised by an athlete suddenly starting to make large errors and being unable to control their performance. It can be seen when tennis players start missing the back line by metres, golfers start hitting wild shots and missing easy putts or cricketers are unable to make contact with the ball. Usually, the athlete has too much muscle tension, so they have lost their coordination. Also, their attentional focus may have narrowed excessively. From being in a position where they were performing well they are now playing like a novice.

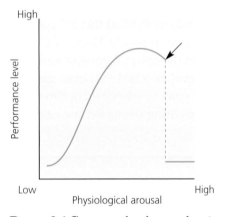

Figure 3.4 Catastrophe theory showing the point of catastrophe (*Source*: Stafford-Brown and Rea, 2010, p. 63)

> ### Key term
>
> **Catastrophe theory** states that once the optimal point of arousal has been reached then any further increases in arousal may lead to a serious decrement in performance.

Individual zones of optimal functioning (IZOF)
Hanin developed individual zones of optimal functioning (IZOF), as seen in Figure 3.5, when he found that athletes have a zone of state anxiety that is comfortable for them and where their best performances happen. Once an athlete is above or below this zone there is a detrimental effect on performance. This theory was presented as an alternative to the inverted U hypothesis as Hanin states that optimal performance does not always happen at the midpoint of the curve for all athletes but it varies from athlete to athlete.

Effects of changes in arousal on sports performance

Improvements or decrements in performance

Changes in arousal level can provide improvements or decrements in performance and it depends on three things:

1 the performer's original arousal level
2 the location of their optimal point of arousal
3 the task they are performing.

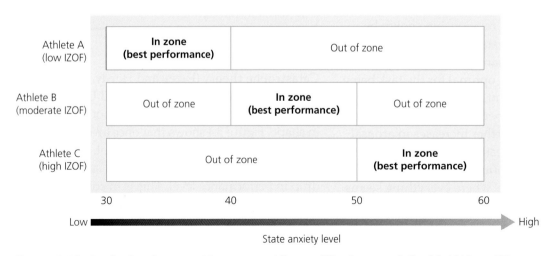

Figure 3.5 Individualised zones of functioning (*Source*: Weinberg and Gould, 2015, p. 87)

In summary, it depends on the characteristics of the performer and the task. The different theories show how changes in arousal level can have differing impacts on performance.

Increased arousal levels impact on performance for several reasons. Firstly, increased arousal levels can produce increases in muscle tension, fatigue and coordination (Weinberg and Gould, 2015). Muscle tension makes it more difficult to produce coordinated movement as a muscle that is already tense cannot contract anymore and it interferes with the contraction of other muscle groups. This is why the best sports people are able to remain relaxed under pressure and only contract the muscle groups that they need to contract for movement. When an individual has high arousal levels and is tense and anxious, it can make them feel fatigued. Fatigue can detract from producing skilled performances and it can interrupt concentration.

Changes in attentional focus

As arousal levels change, they can affect a performer's attention span. If a performer has a broad attention span they are able to pick up information from a wide field of vision. The narrower the attention span becomes, the less information the performer will pick up and the more they will miss. The attention span can be too broad as the performer may try to pick up too much information.

Increased arousal levels cause the attentional span to narrow. This can have a beneficial impact on performance because it means the performer will focus only on relevant cues in the environment and filter out any irrelevant cues. However, it can happen that the attention span becomes too narrow and then important cues may be missed. There is an optimum attention span where it is broad enough to pay attention to all relevant cues and narrow enough to filter out the irrelevant material. This is closely related to concentration levels as well and the relationship is shown in Figure 3.6.

You may well have experienced these different attention spans. If you consider a sports match or a film that you have become totally engrossed in, you find that you stop noticing background noise and other distractions. You may even have such a narrow attention span that you don't notice

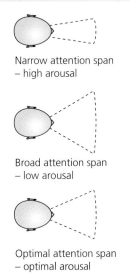

Narrow attention span – high arousal

Broad attention span – low arousal

Optimal attention span – optimal arousal

Figure 3.6 Three attention spans

someone talking to you. Alternately, you may be watching a film or game that you find very boring and you become distracted by things happening around you as your attention span is very wide.

Flow states and choking

Attention span is also closely related to two psychological phenomena – flow states and choking. Flow states were mentioned in the section about the inverted U hypothesis as they are experienced when you are performing in your ideal performing state (IPS). At this point your arousal level has produced an optimum attention span and you feel absorbed in the activity and then everything is flowing easily. Alternately, choking occurs once your arousal level has increased and you have moved beyond your IPS. It is when you start to make large errors and find that your performance has seriously deteriorated. Choking is associated with high arousal levels which cause the attention span to become too narrow, meaning that you start to miss crucial information you need to perform. For example, you might start to miss the ball completely when you try to kick it or hit it, and if you do contact the ball it misses the intended target by large margins.

Increased stress and anxiety levels

Stress and anxiety are generally unpleasant emotions that are experienced at high levels of arousal. They both will have an effect on performance as will be examined in the next section.

B1 Check your understanding

1 Define the term 'arousal'.
2 Explain what drive theory says about the relationship between arousal level and performance. What are the theory's weaknesses?
3 Explain what inverted U hypothesis says about the relationship between arousal level and performance. What are the theory's weaknesses?
4 Identify how an athlete experiencing 'choking' would perform.
5 Describe three reasons why increased arousal levels are associated with improvements in performance.
6 Describe what an athlete in a flow state would be experiencing.

B2 Stress and anxiety on sports performance

Stress is a concept closely associated with arousal, but it differs slightly. When your arousal levels increase, your body experiences increased stress. For example, an individual's arousal levels will rise in response to being asked to complete an activity, such as demonstrating a skill to the rest of the class or doing a presentation. When the individual has been asked to complete a task they will make a judgement whether they feel they have enough energy and skill to meet the challenge. Stress occurs when the individual perceives that they don't have the physical and psychological resources needed to meet the challenge and that there will be important consequences for their success or failure. As stress levels increase, anxiety may also be experienced.

Stress is often best explained by the stress process that shows the stages an individual goes through when they are placed in a situation that causes stress. The stress process is shown in Figure 3.7.

Stage 1: Environmental demand

The first stage of the process is when a demand is placed on the individual, such as being chosen for a team or to demonstrate a skill.

Stage 2: Individual perception of demand

The individual makes a perception about whether they have the resources (skill and ability) to be successful at this task. They either view the task as challenging or threatening.

Stage 3: Stress response

Depending on how they have viewed the task they will produce a stress response. If they

Stage 1
Cause of stress
An emotional demand places physical or psychological pressure

Stage 2
Individual perception of demand
The person produces an individual view of the situation and whether it is threatening to them

Stage 3
Stress response
Production of physical and psychological changes in the individual

Stage 4
Behaviour consequences
Any positive or negative changes in performance resulting from the perceived threat

Figure 3.7 The stress process

think that they will be able to complete the task successfully the stress response will be low; if they think that they are in danger or feel threatened by the task as they don't have the resources to be successful, they will have an increased stress response. This will make them feel scared and anxious.

Stage 4: Behavioural consequences

The stress response that they produce will have an impact on their success or failure of the task in hand.

This process shows that stress is the result of how an individual perceives a task. Two people may be set the same task, for example completing a parachute jump, and one will find it exciting and enjoyable while the other will find it threatening and stressful.

Eustress and distress

The terms eustress and distress are used to show that stress may have positive and negative aspects. Selye (1983) labelled positive stress as 'eustress' and negative stress as 'distress'. He claimed that eustress brings excitement and stimulation and gives you the energy and focus you need to move into action and get things done. For example, sporting situations can be exciting and offer you a pleasurable form of stress as your skills and abilities are put under pressure. Some sports people, such as rock climbers or skiers, actually seek out stressful situations as they enjoy these stressful experiences. Eustress can be seen as being positive because without any stress in our lives most of us would become psychologically stale or bored.

This leads us on to look at sources of stress and remembering that sources of stress and the stress response are different for every individual.

Sources of stress

Sources of stress can be divided into those that are internal or personal sources of stress and those that are external or situational. It must be remembered that while stress can come from these two sources they only become stressful if we perceive them to be, or react with a stress response.

Internal sources of stress

Internal sources of stress come from our thoughts, feelings and beliefs about ourselves. Scanlan (1986) identified that individuals with high trait anxiety and low self-esteem will experience more stress. Trait anxiety is a personality disposition where an individual views many situations as stressful and experiences anxiety in a lot of situations.

For example, they would find all competitions to be stressful and have doubts as to whether they have the resources to be successful in those situations. Self-esteem is a description about how we feel about ourselves and those with low self-esteem will have less confidence in a range of situations and increased doubts about whether they will be successful. These doubts lead to increased stress and feelings of anxiety in a range of situations.

External sources of stress

In sport there are two main external factors that cause an increased stress response. Firstly, the more important the event then the more stress it is likely to produce. It makes sense that cup finals and matches to decide who wins the championship and who gets relegated are more important than regular games. These matches will increase arousal levels in players and that may result in them playing at their optimum point of arousal or their arousal may have gone beyond this point and resulted in stress and a decrement in performance.

Secondly, the uncertainty of the outcome can increase the stress response. If an athlete is fairly certain that they will win or lose they can adopt a more relaxed attitude but if they are closely matched to the skill level of their opponent they are likely to experience more anxiety about the outcome. If this is coupled with high event importance then there will be an increased stress response.

It is worth saying that these sources of stress have been applied to sport here but they apply equally to life situations as well. Some people find taking exams to be stressful, particularly if they view the exam as being a high-stakes assessment, where the outcome has an impact on their life. In the workplace, people are put under stress by being given tasks that they cannot be sure they have the skills to achieve, or they have so many tasks that they are unsure they will be able to complete them all on time. Of course, different people will react in different ways. For some people the stress gives them energy and motivation to succeed and for others it causes so much anxiety that they react by avoiding the situation.

Anxiety

Anxiety is defined as a negative emotional state where an individual experiences feelings of nervousness, worry and apprehension (Weinberg and Gould, 2015). Anxiety is an uncomfortable state to experience and is viewed as a negative emotion but this does not mean that it always has a negative impact on sports performance, as this depends on how it is interpreted.

Anxiety is associated with high levels of arousal and with high levels of stress, or more specifically, distress. The relationship between arousal, stress and anxiety are shown in Figure 3.8. As arousal levels increase, so do stress levels. Eustress would be experienced on the left-hand side of the graph up to the point of ideal performing state (IPS), but when arousal levels increase beyond the point of IPS an individual will start to experience distress and feelings of anxiety. However, the point where distress and anxiety start to be experienced will be individual to each person and this figure only provides a generalised example.

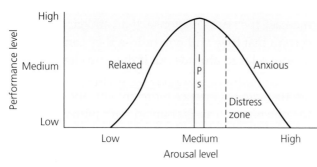

Figure 3.8 The relationship between arousal level, stress and anxiety

State and trait anxiety

Trait and state anxiety are different types of anxiety. A person with high trait anxiety would find that many situations made them anxious. They tend to worry a lot and view many situations as being threatening. They would worry about taking part in sports competitions and think that they were going to fail. They would also find things such as taking an exam, speaking in public and doing their driving test cause them anxiety. We would say that this person has high trait anxiety meaning that they have anxiety as a personality trait. A trait is a relatively stable way of thinking and behaving. A person who does not usually worry about things would have low trait anxiety. They would be described as laid-back or generally relaxed and would not find many situations that made them anxious.

However, there are situations that will cause an anxiety response in almost everyone. For example, being faced by a snake, tiger or large spider will create feelings of anxiety in most people and rightly so as our survival is at risk. This is called state anxiety and describes our anxiety response in a certain situation. For example, if we were to progress from playing sport at school level to county level and then on to national and international level, we may find each level makes us more anxious than the previous one. We have experienced an increased state anxiety response.

State anxiety is influenced by trait anxiety as an individual who has higher levels of trait anxiety is likely to experience an increased state anxiety response in all situations. A person with low trait anxiety will experience lower levels of state anxiety. For example, double Olympic Champion, Usain Bolt, probably has low levels of trait anxiety as he seems very relaxed when competing. He is often seen joking with officials and other competitors in contrast to other athletes who seem tense and anxious in the high-pressure situation.

Key terms

Trait anxiety describes anxiety when it is an aspect of an individual's personality.

State anxiety describes the anxiety response of an individual to a specific situation.

Symptoms of stress and anxiety

When we come under stress we activate our 'fight or flight response', which means that our body is preparing either to fight against a threat or to run away from it. It is an inbuilt human response that is designed to protect us from danger and our response is based on how seriously we take the threat. If we take the threat seriously our sympathetic nervous system is activated causing stress hormones (adrenaline and cortisol) to be

Cognitive effects	Somatic effects	Behavioural effects
Reduced concentration	Racing heart rate	Talking, eating and walking quickly
Unable to make decisions	Faster breathing	Fidgeting
Sleep disturbance	Butterflies in the stomach	Moodiness and grumpiness
Unable to relax	Chest tightness	Interrupting conversations
Quick losses of temper	Dry mouth	Accidents and clumsiness

Table 3.3 Cognitive, somatic and behavioural effects of anxiety

released into the blood stream. These hormones will cause physical and mental changes to occur to prepare to fight back against the threat. We will experience increases in anxiety and symptoms of cognitive, somatic and behavioural anxiety.

Cognitive, somatic and behavioural anxiety

Anxiety has many effects on the body and it will impact on an individual's thoughts (which is called cognitive anxiety) as well as their feelings (which is called somatic anxiety) and their behaviour. Due to these three aspects of anxiety, it is described as being multidimensional. Some of the cognitive, somatic and behavioural aspects of anxiety are shown in Table 3.3. This view that anxiety has cognitive, somatic and behavioural components is the basis of multidimensional anxiety theory (Martens *et al.*, 1990).

Competitive anxiety

Competitive anxiety describes the anxiety of an individual in competitive situations, such as sports events. How anxious a person becomes in sports events depends upon several factors, such as their level of trait anxiety and the importance of the event. It is interesting to watch sports performers before a match or race and to see how they look and behave as some look very tense and focused and others look quite relaxed and playful.

Multidimensional anxiety theory

Martens *et al.* (1990) Multidimensional Anxiety Theory (MAT) presented the relationship between competitive state anxiety and performance. They proposed that cognitive state anxiety, somatic state anxiety and self-confidence will all have a different relationship with performance.

Cognitive state anxiety describes the mental component of anxiety (Cox, 2012) and somatic state anxiety describes the physical response to anxiety. These two components, along with self-confidence make up the dimensions of anxiety. If an athlete is experiencing high fear of failure and insecurity, it is likely that their self-confidence (expectations of success) will be eroded. However, if they feel they are likely to be successful and are positive about their performance their self-confidence should be high.

MAT shows that increases in cognitive state anxiety will result in decrements in performance and that increases in somatic anxiety will be beneficial up to a certain point where any further increases cause a decline performance. Increases in self-confidence will produce improvements in performance. As cognitive anxiety increases self-confidence will decrease but as cognitive anxiety decreases self-confidence will increase.

Reversal theory

Reversal theory is an arousal-performance theory but it increases our understanding of anxiety and its influence on performance. Reversal theory says that that the effect arousal has on performance is dependent on how high arousal levels are interpreted by an individual. If you consider an athlete in the moments before an important race or match they may be experiencing high levels of arousal and they could interpret these feelings as pleasurable excitement or unpleasant anxiety. This is influenced by the athlete's personality and the level of arousal they are comfortable with.

Reversal theory predicts that if athletes interpret their high arousal levels as pleasurable excitement rather than unpleasant anxiety it can improve their performance. In practice, the athlete may say that 'my feelings of anxiety are telling me that this race is important and I am physically and psychologically ready for it'. This is in contrast to them saying 'my anxiety levels are high because I am terrified of failing'. If interpreted positively high anxiety levels can benefit performance rather than be detrimental to it.

B2 Check your understanding

1 Define the term 'stress'.
2 Identify the relationship between arousal and stress.
3 Describe the four stages of the stress process.
4 Explain the difference between eustress and distress.
5 Identify two internal sources of stress and two external sources of stress.
6 Define the term 'anxiety'.
7 Explain the multidimensional anxiety theory.
8 Describe how reversal theory would help an athlete interpret anxiety.

B3 Consequences of stress and anxiety

As we can see, the relationships between stress and anxiety and sports performance are complex. Whether increases in stress and anxiety are beneficial is dependent on an individual's personality, how they respond to stress, the skill or task they are doing and how they interpret stress and anxiety. In general, there are consequences of stress that are positive to sports performance and there are consequences that are negative.

Positive consequences of stress

As arousal levels increase so will stress levels, and at a point anxiety levels will increase as well, causing an increase in energy, focus and motivation for an activity. These increases can produce a positive mental state and increased self-confidence resulting in improvements in performance.

Negative consequences of stress

If arousal levels increase too much for an individual, they will experience increased stress and anxiety levels that may rise to a point where they become debilitating. In this situation, performance will be negatively affected as self-confidence is reduced and the individual enters a negative mental state

characterised by worry and even fear. These high levels of arousal, or over-arousal in relation to the activity at hand, can put the individual at risk of injury as they may be playing in an over-excited and frenzied way. They are also more likely to commit acts of aggression, risking injury to other players as well as to themselves.

B3 Check your understanding

1 Identify four factors that influence how stress and anxiety affect behaviour.
2 Describe how stress and anxiety can have beneficial consequences for performance.
3 Describe how stress and anxiety can have negative consequences for performance
4 Explain why an individual with high arousal levels may be at increased risk of injury.

B4 Aggression as a response to competitive pressure

Aggressive acts can be the result of high levels of arousal and stress in an athlete brought about by the competitive environment that they are operating in. However, aggression is a complex area and aggressive acts can be caused by a range of factors and for a range of intended outcomes. In this section we will explore the different types of aggression and a range of theories that try to account for aggressive behaviour in sporting environments.

In general, we refer to behaviour where a person is being over-physical as being aggressive, but often these actions are mislabelled. Baron and Richardson (1994) defined aggression as 'any form of behaviour directed towards the goal of harming or injuring another living being who is motivated to avoid such treatment'.

In sport psychology, aggression has a specific meaning in that it is behaviour where an individual is aiming to harm or injure an opponent to gain an advantage, rather than just playing in a hard, upbeat manner. Gill (2000) gives us four criteria which must all be met to allow us to label an action as aggressive:

1 There must be a physical or verbal behaviour.
2 It must involve causing harm or injury, whether it is physical or psychological.
3 It must be directed towards another living thing.
4 There must be the intention to cause harm or injury.

To expand on these statements, to be categorised as 'aggression', the act must actually involve a behaviour that is either physical or verbal in nature. Rather than just thinking or feeling that you want to do something, there must be an action to follow on from these thoughts. The result of the aggressive action can be experienced either physically or psychologically (emotionally) and it must result in harm or damage to another person. While an act of physical aggression, such as throwing a punch, has a clear outcome of harm, so can saying something hurtful or offensive to another person. It is important that the actions are carried out on another living thing because only they have feelings. So to throw your bat down when you are out is not an aggressive act, although it might be seen as unacceptable behaviour. Finally, the most difficult aspect is that the act to cause harm must be intentional. If harm is caused by accident then it is not aggressive, but if there is intent to cause harm it clearly is aggressive. The reason this is difficult is because only the individual knows what their intentions are and the officials have to make a judgement on their intention.

You should be starting to realise that when examining aggression there are some grey areas. We cannot tell whether an act is aggressive unless we know the motives of the person who produces the act. Plenty of sports people are injured, but not necessarily through acts of aggression. In order to be more specific about this area we need to split aggressive acts into four distinct categories.

Types of aggression

Assertive behaviour
Assertive behaviour is when a person plays with high energy and emotion but within the rules of the game. For example, a footballer puts in hard,

uncompromising tackles, or a tennis player is playing in a very tough and upbeat manner but always within the rules. This is assertive play because it is not intended to do any harm or cause any injury to their opponent, and uses force that is legitimate and within the rules. It is often mislabelled as 'aggression'.

Key term

Assertive behaviour is playing in an upbeat and energetic manner but within the rules of a sport.

Instrumental aggression
Instrumental aggression is when acts of aggression are used to achieve a non-aggressive goal, such as improving a team's chances of victory. They are not usually accompanied by feelings of anger. For example, if you target the opposition's star player for rough treatment by one of your team, but you are willing to accept the punishment, then you are committing instrumental aggression. This also explains the sport of boxing, where the aim is to hurt your opponent to win the fight, rather than because you do not like your opponent. Also, in a rugby scrum, ruck or maul, players use a legitimate amount of force, but this may actually harm or injure an opponent.

Hostile aggression
Hostile aggression is when acts of aggression are conducted where the primary goal is to inflict harm or injury on an opponent purely for the sake of it. Hostile aggressive acts are usually accompanied by feelings of anger. It often occurs when an individual is continually blocked from achieving a goal and their frustration and anger build up. For example, if a player is continually fouled or verbally abused they may eventually respond aggressively as a result.

Relational aggression
Relational aggression involves the use of spreading negative rumours or ostracising someone socially. This can cause harm as it can lead to the rejection of an individual by their peer group. The use of social media has increased the prevalence of relational aggression as rumours and malicious gossip are now easier to spread and there are many platforms that can be used to spread them.

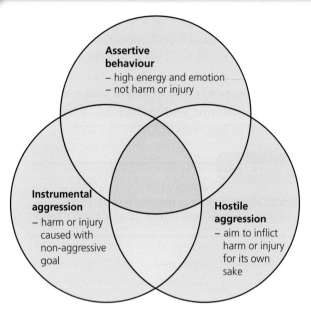

Figure 3.9 Three of the categories of aggression

Aggression can be instrumental when aggressive acts are performed for a non-aggressive goal, hostile where aggression is purely aimed at the outcome of harming an opponent, or relational where malicious rumours are spread with the aim of psychologically hurting an individual.

Theories of aggression

Instinct theory

Instinct theory says that all people have an instinctive, inborn need or tendency to be aggressive that will build up until it needs to be expressed (Gill, 2000). However, aggressive behaviour is not always inevitable – it can be directed towards another person or it can be displaced. This release of aggression is called catharsis. People will say they play rugby or football at the weekend to get rid of the tension and aggression that builds up during the week. Other people will go swimming or running to achieve the same release of aggressive tendencies in a socially acceptable manner. This theory has also been used to explain why people fight at football matches as an outlet for their aggression, albeit in a less socially acceptable manner.

There is little research to support this theory, and it cannot explain why some people are more aggressive than others. Indeed, you may know some people who never show aggressive behaviour. It also differs across cultures and this suggests there must be external influences which make the chances of aggression more likely.

Social learning theory

This theory offers an opposing view to the instinct theory and says that aggression is learnt through modelling and imitative behaviour, rather than being an inborn instinct. Albert Bandura (1973) conducted research involving groups of children watching groups of adults playing with a doll. The children who watched the adults punching and beating up the doll produced this reaction more than the group who watched the adults playing passively with the doll. Incidents of aggressive behaviour were increased when the children were positively rewarded for their actions. Research has shown that aggressive acts are more likely to be imitated if produced by a person of the same sex and if they are witnessed live rather than on television or in cartoon form.

It is easy to see how a young footballer may learn to be aggressive. At a football match he sees a player making hard tackles, some of which are illegal and dangerous, and being cheered on by the crowd and his coach. The harder the player tackles, the more praise he gets and he develops a following among fans who like this type of player. The young footballer learns that this is a positive way to behave and mimics the play in his own matches. Ice hockey has attracted a lot of research due to the regularity of fighting and fouling in the sport. Smith (1988) found that the violence in the game is the result of young amateur players modelling the professionals' behaviour.

Social learning theory is a very convincing theory, and we can see how the levels of aggression in sport are accompanied by rises in the level of violence in society, particularly on television and in films. However, it fails to explain how different people can witness the same events and yet the majority of them will not produce an aggressive response, while a minority will mimic the behaviour. For example, a boxing match will have a cathartic effect on some supporters and will cause an aggressive response in others.

Frustration–aggression theory

This theory states that aggression is the direct result of frustration that has built up due to goal blockage or failure. This theory was first proposed by Dollard *et al*. (1939), who claimed frustration would always produce aggression. However, in 1989, Berkowitz revised this theory by saying that frustration will lead to anger rather than aggression, particularly if we feel we have been unfairly treated, but we will not always produce an aggressive action. He went on to say that an aggressive action is more likely if aggressive cues are present (things related to aggression), but a person may be able to control their anger.

Adapted frustration–aggression theory

The frustration–aggression theory was adapted to include aspects of social learning theory. It acknowledges the role of socially learned cues on aggression. These cues may be the presence of particular opponents or particular behaviour by opponents. Aggressive behaviour can be modified though its negative reinforcement. For example, a player who lashes out at an opponent and discovers that this behaviour results in a three-match ban or being dropped for the next match, becomes much less likely to repeat the aggressive behaviour.

B4 Check your understanding

1 Define the term 'aggression'.
2 Identify four characteristics that an action must have to be labelled as aggression.
3 Describe how assertive behaviour differs from aggressive behaviour.
4 Explain the difference between instrumental and hostile aggression.
5 Discuss how the instinct and social learning theories of aggression differ.
6 Explain the weaknesses in frustration–aggression theory.

Exam Practice

This activity will cover aspects of learning aims A and B, and its purpose is to provide preparation for the external assessment.

Read the following case study and then answer the questions that follow:

Oliver is a 16-year-old tennis player whose play is characterised by moments of brilliance mixed with temper tantrums. When Oliver trains in the gym he enjoys lifting weights to increase his strength and he finds that the more up for it he is then the heavier weights he can lift, so he spends time psyching himself up before lifting weights. Oliver loves the excitement of playing a match and he feels that it gives him energy and helps to focus his attention. Oliver particularly likes playing in tournaments where he feels he has a good chance of winning the event. If he can win the trophy he thinks that it shows his friends and parent what a good player he is and he enjoys the praise and adulation that it brings him.

When Oliver plays tennis he usually starts off quite relaxed but sometimes he is too relaxed to play well and will start to lose points. However, when he is in a losing situation he starts to become worried and he gets butterflies in his stomach and this spurs him on to play better and get back into the match. Sometimes, he wants to win so much that he starts to miss the service box or the base line and often by quite large margins. This can make him really angry and when he loses his temper he shouts at himself, his opponent and the umpire. He also tends to throw his racket to the ground and has broken several racket heads on the court.

1 Explain, using theories of motivation, what factors may be motivating Oliver.
2 Describe how need achievement theory can account for Oliver's choice of opponents.
3 Identify any symptoms of stress and anxiety that Oliver is showing.
4 Explain how theories of arousal-performance relationship account for Oliver's performance.
5 Describe how changes in arousal level affect Oliver's performance.
6 Categorise any possible examples of Oliver's aggressive behaviour and analyse whether these types of behaviour are beneficial to his performance.

C Effects of self-confidence, self-efficacy and self-esteem on sport and exercise performance

C1 Self-confidence and sport and exercise performance

Self-confidence is the belief that you can perform a desired behaviour (Weinberg and Gould, 2015). Self-confidence has trait and state forms. A person with high trait self-confidence would be said to be confident over a range of situations and generally expect to be successful at whatever they were doing. State self-confidence would be confidence that varies from task to task and would be affected by how the individual perceives their ability at that task. Self-confidence is said to be a self-fulfilling prophecy in that if you think that you are unlikely to achieve something and then don't achieve it you have proved yourself right. Alternately, if you expect to achieve something and then do, once again you have proved yourself right.

Self-confidence is seen as a beneficial trait to possess because how you think will affect your emotions (how you feel) which will in turn impact on behaviour. Positive emotions are associated with staying calm under pressure, improving concentration, increasing effort and setting challenging but realistic goals.

> **Key term**
>
> **Self-confidence** is the belief that you can perform a desired behaviour.

Impact of different levels of self-confidence on sport and exercise performance

The belief that you will be successful is critical to performance, but self-confidence will not make you perform higher than your skill and ability levels allow. High levels of self-confidence will only allow an athlete to succeed up to a certain point. The relationship between self-confidence and performance is represented by an inverted U shaped graph that is skewed to the right (Weinberg and Gould, 2015), as can be seen in Figure 3.10.

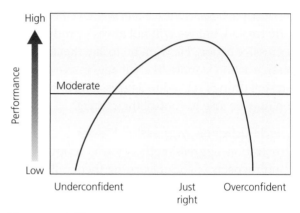

Figure 3.10 The relationship between self-confidence and performance (*Source:* Weinberg and Gould, 2015, p. 327)

The graph shows that as confidence levels rise so will performance, up to the point where the self-confidence level matches the demands of the task. Any further increases in self-confidence will start to cause decrements in performance.

Optimal self-confidence

When you reach the optimal point of self-confidence you will feel sure that you can achieve your goals and will work hard to give yourself the best chance of doing so. However, it does not necessarily mean you will be successful, but that you are giving yourself the best chance to be so. The performance of an athlete will always be limited by their current skill level; however, a person with strong self-belief will be able to deal with errors and overcome obstacles put in front of them. Athletes such as Serena Williams and Rory McIlroy have kept showing confidence in their abilities when they have been struggling in a competition and it can help to turn momentum in their favour.

Lack of confidence

It is not uncommon to see athletes who have the physical skills needed to be successful at their sport fail because they lack the self-confidence to perform their skills in pressurised environments. You may have seen athletes who look great in practice and during practice matches but when it comes to the match situation they start to make mistakes and become full of doubts when their play fails to have the desired effect.

Self-doubts will quickly undermine an athlete's performance as they create anxiety, affect concentration, and interfere with decision making. Athletes with low self-confidence will start to focus on their weaknesses rather than their strengths and they take this negative mindset into their performances, expecting their weaknesses to be found out rather than their strengths. That said, a few self-doubts can be beneficial to an individual as they can provide motivation and energy to work on any weaknesses and ensure they don't affect performance.

Over-confidence

Over-confident people are people who exude false confidence or confidence that is not backed up by their skills or knowledge. Often over-confidence leads to complacency, where an individual or team feel that their ability is so great that they don't need to put in any effort to succeed. This mindset can cause them not to prepare properly and quickly leads to a decline in performance level.

For example, when a top-rated team are playing a lower-level team in a cup competition they may take it for granted that their superior skill level will be enough to ensure success; however, it doesn't always come out that way as the lower-level team can be highly motivated and expend extra effort to give themselves a chance of success.

Vealey's self-confidence model

Vealey *et al.*'s (2002) multidimensional self-confidence model that developed Vealey's original model (1986, 1988) showed that the relationship between self-confidence and performance was complex. There are four layers to the model, as seen in Figure 3.11.

Layer 1 – Factors influencing sport confidence

Demographic factors such as age, gender, socio-economic status and ethnic background, and personality factors such as traits, attitudes and beliefs, will affect self-confidence, as will the organisational culture an individual is operating within. This refers to expectations of coaches and leaders, the motivational climate and level of competition.

Layer 2 – Sources of sport confidence

There are three sources of sport confidence: mastery (current level of skill and ability; self-regulation (physical and mental preparation) and social climate (support from coaches and other significant others).

These two layers impact on the three constructs of sport confidence which are the three types of sport confidence.

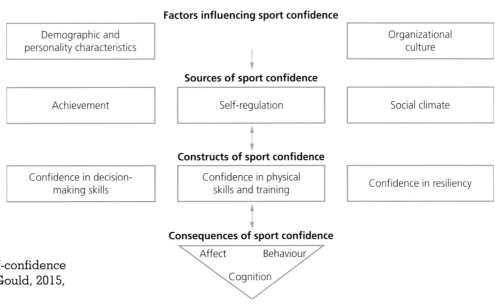

Figure 3.11 Model of self-confidence (*Source:* Weinberg and Gould, 2015, pp. 330)

Layer 3 – Constructs of sport confidence

Cognitive efficiency describes confidence in making decisions and maintaining focus, physical skills and training describes how well an athlete can execute their skills, and resilience describes an athlete's persistence in overcoming setbacks and working against adversity.

Layer 4 – Consequences of sport confidence

These three layers will influence how an athlete feels (affect), how they think (cognition) and how they behave (behaviour). These three aspects of self-confidence have been affected by the three upper layers and will impact on performance and the outcomes of an athlete.

The model shows that self-confidence is influenced from a variety of sources rather than just from the internal thoughts of an individual. Self-confidence is derived from the attitudes and behaviour of an athlete's coach, their friends and family, the environment they find themselves in and their own perception of their skill level.

Influence of expectations on sport and exercise performance

Self-confidence is a belief in yourself and your ability to be successful rather than a concrete fact and it produces expectations of success. If you think that something is likely to happen it increases the chances that it actually will. It is like taking a medicine that we have been told will cure our illness, and because we believe it will cure us it often does.

Expectations of self

Research into the relationship between expectations of self and performance have shown high expectations can give an individual the energy and direction that they need to be successful. In a classic study by Nelson and Furst (1972), they paired 12 sets of subjects who were instructed to arm wrestle but they told the weaker member of the pair that they had superior strength compared to their opponent. They found that in 10 of the 12 cases the weaker partner won the arm wrestle bout because they believed they were stronger than their opponent. In summary, expecting to beat a stronger opponent can lead to psychological barriers being overcome and extraordinary achievements being accomplished.

Expectations of coach

The expectations of a coach have an impact on the self-confidence of an athlete as they will affect the way the coach behaves towards the athlete and how they speak to them. A coach who has high expectations of an athlete will give them more coaching time, higher quality instruction and more positive feedback. Because the coach expects them to be successful it provides psychological support for the support and develops their self-confidence.

C1 Check your understanding

1. Describe how a person with high self-confidence would behave.
2. Explain, using a graph, the relationship between levels of self-confidence and performance.
3. Explain the four layers of Vealey's self-confidence model.
4. Describe the relationship between expectations of success and performance.
5. Identify how a coach with high expectations of their athlete would behave.

C2 Self-efficacy in sport and exercise performance

Self-efficacy is an individual's expectations of success specific to a certain situation rather than self-confidence which relates to expectation of success across a range of situations. An individual who expects to be successful at a task will show greater levels of willingness to be involved in that task and they will respond by persisting for longer to achieve it. A person with low self-efficacy will be less motivated as they do not think they will be successful and are less likely to persist if their participation results in failure.

Key term

Self-efficacy is an individual's expectations of success in a specific situation.

Bandura (1977, 1986, 1997) identified six sources of information that would affect an individual's self-efficacy. The six sources are shown in Figure 3.12.

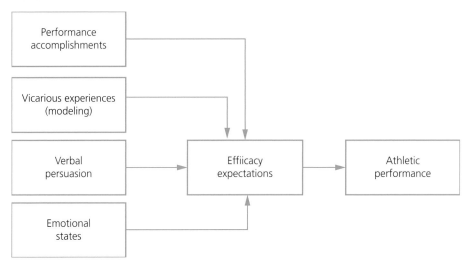

Figure 3.12 Six sources of self-efficacy and how they relate to efficacy expectations and athletic performance (*Source:* Adapted from Feltz, 1984, p. 192)

Performance accomplishments

Previous success at an activity is the strongest factor in influencing efficacy expectations (Bandura, 1997) because any self-doubts that you can be successful will have been removed. On the other hand, failures, or repeated failures, at a task will reduce efficacy expectations. For example, consider a footballer who has recently missed a penalty kick; as they prepare for another penalty kick their mindset will be affected by their previous failure.

The effect of success on self-confidence has implications for teachers and coaches as well as performers. It is important for teachers/coaches to ensure that when they introduce a new skill, the participants have a high chance of success early in their initial practices. Otherwise repeated failures may lead them to concluding that they will 'never be able to do this' and quickly withdraw.

Vicarious experiences

Vicarious experiences are second-hand experiences or watching someone else being successful at a task. Vicarious experiences have most impact if the person you are watching is someone of similar skill and experience level. For example, if you were to watch a friend of yours abseiling down a steep cliff it may give you the view that 'if they can do it so can I'. However, if you were to watch the instructor

completing the abseil you may reason that 'just because they can do it doesn't mean that I can'.

Demonstrations are vicarious experiences that can used by teachers and coaches to increase participants' self-efficacy to help them learn new skills.

Verbal persuasion

Coaches and teachers will regularly use persuasive techniques to influence the behaviour of participants. Pep talks where a coach may say 'I know you can do this as I've seen you do it hundreds of times in practice' may increase efficacy expectations in competition. Verbal persuasion in sport is particularly effective if it comes from someone that the athlete views as credible and knowledgeable.

Emotional states

Your thoughts and feelings at a particular time and particularly in relation to a task will have an influence on your self-efficacy. An athlete who is feeling energetic and positive is likely to experience high self-efficacy in comparison to one who is anxious or depressed (Weinberg and Gould, 2015).

These six factors work together to influence efficacy expectations, which are expectations of success and these impact on athletic performance.

Application of the model and its impact on sport and exercise performance

Research has consistently shown that higher levels of self-efficacy are associated with higher performance levels (Morris and Keohn, 2004); therefore, we can say that our perception of our ability to perform a task successfully has a real impact on performance. Performance accomplishments are the strongest factor and a reciprocal relationship exists between performance accomplishments and self-efficacy. A successful performance increases self-efficacy which in turn increases the further likelihood of a successful performance.

C2 Check your understanding

1 Explain how self-efficacy differs from self-confidence.
2 Explain how self-efficacy will impact on athletic performance.
3 Describe why performance accomplishments have the most impact on efficacy expectations.
4 Describe what is meant by vicarious experiences and why they can affect efficacy expectations.

C3 Self-esteem and its impact on sport and exercise performance

Definition

Self-esteem is a description of what we think of ourselves, our overall sense of self-worth or personal value. It would include the emotions we experience and our beliefs which are the things we believe to be true about ourselves, for example, 'I believe I am good student' or 'I believe I am a talented athlete'. When assessing yourself and your self-esteem you can look at your self-concept which is a description of yourself across the different roles that you have in life. There is your physical self which includes your skills and abilities at sport, as well as how you assess your own physical appearance; your social self which covers your relationships with family and friends, and your academic self which would cover how good you think you are at a range of subjects (English, maths, science).

Key term

Self-esteem is a description of what we think of ourselves or our self-worth.

Impact of self-esteem

Athletes with low self-esteem have less self-confidence and experience more state anxiety than those athletes with high self-esteem. Low self-confidence and increased state anxiety are both problematic for successful athletes and are likely to impact on their chances of success. Low self-esteem is also an indication of emotional stability, which describes how easily affected you are by feelings, and it impacts on life satisfaction, how you deal with stress and achievement levels. Once again, having emotional stability is important in sports performance as is being resilient to stress in pressurised environments.

C3 Check your understanding

1 Identify what is meant by self-esteem.
2 Describe, using an example, what beliefs are.
3 Explain how athletes with low self-esteem differ from those with high self-esteem.

D Mindset in sport and exercise performance

D1 Fixed versus growth mindset

Fixed and growth mindset

Mindset is a term used to describe how you think and feel about something. For example, a person with a 'positive mindset' is generally having positive thoughts and feelings and expects to be successful. In this case we will look at mindset as being what you think about the extent to which a person can improve their sports performance.

Firstly, answer the following questions with a simple yes or no:

1 'I believe that those with more natural talent will always be better than me.'
2 'It is better to have natural intelligence than to work hard.'

3 'I believe there are some things that I will never be any good at.'

4 'My success in sport will always be limited by my ability.'

If you answered 'yes' to all or most of the question we say you have a 'fixed' mindset and if you answered 'no' to all or most of them then you have a 'growth' mindset. If you answered 'yes' we might also say that you believe in the 'talent myth', or the belief that ability rather than practice is what influences whether you achieve excellence. Why would you spend time and effort working hard to improve if success has already been determined by how much talent a person possesses?

Key terms

The **fixed mindset** encompasses the belief that performance is due to the amount of talent or ability that an individual possesses.

The **growth mindset** encompasses the belief that performance is the result of practice and hard work rather than talent.

A growth mindset encompasses the belief that skill level and performance are not fixed but are the result of the amount of effort and practice an individual devotes to a task.

Dweck's theory

One of the major researchers into the influence of mindset is American Psychologist Carol Dweck. She led a team of researchers who investigated intelligence and development in primary school children. She chose a sample of 330 students aged 11 to 12 and used a questionnaire about ability and talent to split them into two groups – one group who believed that intelligence was most important for success in school (fixed mindset) and one group that believed that intelligence can be developed through effort (growth mindset). She then gave each group a set of twelve tasks, eight of which were easy and four of which were very difficult.

Dweck (2006) discovered large differences between the behaviour of the two groups.

Students in both groups completed the first eight tasks fairly easily but the students in the fixed mindset group gave up quickly when faced with the four difficult tasks. When questioned they blamed their intelligence for their failure – 'I guess I am not very smart' or 'I'm not good at things like this'. However, the growth mindset group carried on with the difficult tasks for much longer and kept trying different strategies to solve the tasks. Their success rate was much higher than the fixed mindset group and when asked about why they thought they had failed they replied by saying that they hadn't failed but had just not found the correct solution yet.

This experiment shows that performance is not solely due to intelligence or motivation but down to mindset as well. The fixed mindset group believed that because the intelligence they are born with is the most important factor in success then their performance level will reach a point they can't go beyond. This relates very clearly to ability beliefs in sport, as the fixed mindset view would be that to be successful at sport you need to be naturally gifted or have talent. The growth mindset would suggest that you can always improve at sport if you put enough effort in to learn skills and practise them regularly.

Talent versus effort

This is an important lesson to take for sport and education: that if you are willing to put in the effort you will improve at whatever you are doing. Initial differences in talent cannot predict where you might get to and what you can achieve they just show where you are at the moment. The brain is like a muscle that develops with hard work and it will change as more time is spent on a task.

Application and its impact on sport and exercise skill development

Mindset will influence how a person approaches learning new tasks or skills. Table 3.4 summarises the influence that Dweck found mindset has on different aspects of learning a new task or skill.

Fixed mindset – intelligence remains stable	Factors	Growth mindset – intelligence can be developed
Avoid challenges	**Challenges**	Embrace challenges
Give up easily	**Obstacles**	Persist despite any setbacks
See effort as pointless	**Effort**	See effort as the key to success
Ignore any feedback they see as negative	**Criticism**	Encourage and learn from criticism
Feel threatened by others' success	**Success of other**	Learn from the success of other people

Table 3.4 The influence of a fixed or growth mindset on learning new skills

Having learnt about fixed and growth mindset you will start to see these attitudes in people around you and understand the damaging effect a fixed mindset can produce. If a person has been taught that their talent is fixed it can take away their motivation to push beyond their current level. Also, if a person thinks they are talented then why would they bother putting in any effort?

Mindset attitudes can be seen in teams as well, for good and for bad. For example, throughout a long period of success Barcelona Football Club was built around smaller players, such as Lionel Messi, Andres Iniesta and Xavi. These were players who may have been deemed 'too small' by other clubs yet Barcelona developed a style to incorporate the specific skills of these players, as did the very successful Spanish national team.

10,000 hours practice

A view that has become popular in recent years is the 10,000 hours rule. This states that if you want to achieve excellence in any field then you to accumulate 10,000 hours of practice. It is based on a study of a violin student who began playing at the age of 5 and by the age of 20 had reached elite level having practised for around 10,000 hours. This view was adopted by Malcolm Gladwell who wrote a book called 'Outliers' that had a chapter titled '10,000-hour rule', and also by some coaching organisations who hold it up as a standard for young players to achieve.

This view has been heavily criticised recently with contrary views pointing out that this is just an average number and some skills will take a much shorter time to master. Also, the type of practice is very important as well. While the rule has been discredited slightly it does make the important point that effort and practice are more important in success than relying on natural talent. Talent will get you so far but it won't be long until the talented people get overtaken by those willing to put the effort in practice.

Learned helplessness

Learned helplessness is an attitude that is characterised by an individual saying 'I am no good at this activity and never will be'. It is caused by a fixed mindset and the individual attributing their failure to a lack of talent. If they were to think differently about the activity they are not mastering they may say 'this is a very difficult but if I work hard enough then I will be successful'. It is another example of the limiting effect of having a fixed mindset.

D1 Check your understanding

1   Explain the difference between a fixed and growth mindset.
2   Describe how an individual with a growth mindset would approach learning a new skill.
3   Explain how a coach could use the principles of Dweck's theory during coaching sessions.
4   Explain the 10,000-hour rule and why it may be flawed.
5   Explain how you would deal with an athlete showing learned helplessness.

D2 Resilience in sport

Resilience is described as a personality trait that is a force within an individual that drives them to overcome adversity (Richardson, 2002). Adversity would include situations such as injury, slumps in form, illness, burnout and transitions between teams and standards of play.

Key term

Resilience is an internal force that helps an individual overcome adversity.

Overcoming adversity

Adversity is something that every athlete is going to have to face, and how they deal with it will influence their career in the present and the future. Adversity can produce stress and anxiety and the development of a negative mindset. Research into how athletes dealt with adversity and developed resilience showed four main themes:

- Coping strategies
- Focus on positive outcomes
- Identification of personal coping resources
- Social influences to support coping strategies.

Richardson (2002) stresses the importance of the individual identifying their own coping resources and those around them at times of adversity. The use of psychological interventions, such as self-talk and goal setting can help to build resilience in athletes.

D2 Check your understanding

1 Identify what is meant by the term 'resilience'.
2 Identify four situations where resilience is required from athletes.
3 Explain how athletes can build their resilience.
4 Identify two ways a sport psychologist could support athletes in times of adversity.

D3 Perfectionism

Traits of a perfectionist

Perfectionism in sport is exhibited by performers who are searching for the perfect performance rather than just success or excellence. Perfectionists will tend to set very high standards in their work and expect other people to live up to those standards. They often have high trait anxiety as they worry about the standards of their work and they often set themselves unrealistic targets.

Key term

Perfectionism is shown when an individual seeks for a perfect performance rather than just winning.

Functional and dysfunctional perfectionism

There are different types of perfectionism but it can be reduced into two types: functional and dysfunctional perfectionism (Sager and Stoeber, 2009).

Functional perfectionism is positive in nature and a functional perfectionist will set high personal standards, desire organisation in their life, be persistent in working towards their goals and strive for the perfect performance.

Dysfunctional perfectionism is negative in nature and a dysfunctional perfectionist will be concerned about the mistakes they make, parental expectations and parental criticism. They will also have self-doubts about their actions and feel other people have high expectations of them (Anshel and Sutarso, 2010).

Perfectionism is linked to anxiety because dysfunctional pessimists will show higher levels of cognitive state and somatic state anxiety (Stoeber *et al.*, 2007). A dysfunctional perfectionist will experience and be motivated by a fear of failure and the fear of experiencing shame and embarrassment. They will also show increased anger and react angrily to their own and other people's mistakes (Vallance, Dunn and Dunn, 2006). In contrast, a functional perfectionist will show lower levels of state anxiety and higher levels of self-confidence (Stoeber *et al.*, 2007).

Impact of perfectionism on performance

While functional perfectionism can contribute to a commitment to high performance standards, dysfunctional perfectionism needs to be addressed by the coach and the athlete. This can be done if the athlete breaks the link between their performance and their self-worth and reduces the irrational sense of importance that they place on being successful (Hill, Hall and Appleton, 2010).

D3 Check your understanding

1 Identify what is meant by the term 'perfectionism'.
2 Identify how a functional perfectionist would behave.
3 Explain the difference between a functional and a dysfunctional perfectionist.
4 Describe how dysfunctional perfectionism can be managed.

E Group dynamics in sport

E1 Group processes

Many activities in sport and exercise take place as part of a team or a group. For example, hockey, rugby, netball and cricket all involve playing as a team. Some sports such as gymnastics and golf can still involve being part of a team (or group) but are somehow different as they are not so reliant on all the members of the team working together all the time. It might make you ask the question:

What is it that makes a team?

Let's compare three teams – a netball team, a rowing four and a golf team, and see what the differences are. The members of a netball team will all have to work together by passing the ball and then moving when attacking and coming back and blocking when defending their goal. Team members will each have their own responsibilities and are expected to perform these during different phases of play. The success of the team is dependent on them working effectively together. The rowing four will also have to work together to be an effective team. They actually have to do the same thing at the same time to move the boat as quickly as they can. If they lose synchronicity, then it will act to decelerate the boat with negative effects. The golf team will, at times, be playing together and, at times, playing individually. They won't have to be coordinated in their play as they will be playing different shots at different times; however, the success of the team is the sum of all the efforts of the individual members so there is still a team output.

Interactive and coactive groups and teams

Interactive teams and groups are where the outcome of their performance is dependent on the team members working together so the members of netball, rowing and golf teams are all interactive. Coactive teams are where the team members are all doing the same thing at the same time and the rowing team are the only truly coactive team of the three. Not all coactive teams or groups are interactive. For example, if you consider an exercise group where the members are doing an aerobics session, the members of the group are all doing the same thing at the same time so it is coactive but they are not dependent on each other for success so it is not interactive.

> **Key terms**
>
> **Interactive teams** are those whose success is dependent on the members working closely together.
>
> **Coactive teams** are those where the members are performing the same skills at the same together.

Tuckman's stages of group development

A group of people coming together does not necessarily form a team. Becoming a team demands a process of development. Tuckman and Jensen (1977) proposed a five-stage model of group development:

1 **Stage 1** – forming
2 **Stage 2** – storming
3 **Stage 3** – norming
4 **Stage 4** – performing
5 **Stage 5** – adjourning.

Every group will go through the five stages but the length of time they spend in each stage is variable. Each stage involves the group going through different processes:

Forming: the group comes together, with individuals meeting and familiarising themselves with the other members of the group. The structure and relationships within the group are formed and tested. If it is a team, the coach may develop strategies or games to 'break the ice' between the group members. At this point the individuals are seeing whether they fit in with this group.

Storming: a period of conflict will follow the forming stage as individuals seek their roles and status within the group. This may involve conflict between individual members, rebellion against the leader or resistance to the way the team is being developed or managed, or the tactics it is adopting. This is also a period of intense inter-group competition, as group members compete for their positions within the team.

Norming: once the hostility and fighting has been overcome, either by athletes leaving the group or accepting the common goals and values of the group, a period of norming occurs. Here, the group starts to cooperate and work together to reach common goals. The group pulls together and the roles are established and become stable.

Performing: in the final stage, the group members work together to achieve their mutual goals. The relationships within the group have become well established, as have issues of leadership and strategies for play. It is unrealistic to see the group as being stable and performing in a steady way. The relationships within the group will change and develop with time, sometimes for the good of the group and sometimes to its detriment. As new members join the group there will be a new period of storming and norming, as this person is either accepted or rejected. This re-evaluation of the group is often beneficial and stops the group becoming stale. Successful teams seem to be settled and assimilate two or three new players a year to keep them fresh. Bringing in too many new players can disrupt the group and change the nature of the group completely.

Adjourning: once the group has achieved its goals or come to the end of its useful purpose the team may break up. This may also be caused by a considerable change in the personnel involved or the management and leadership of the group.

Ringelmann effect and social loafing

The aim of a group is to be effective by using the strengths of each person to better the effectiveness of the group. However, the outcome is often not equal to the sum of its parts. Steiner (1972) proposed the following model of group effectiveness:

Actual productivity = Potential productivity – Process losses

In this model actual productivity is the actual performance achieved, whereas potential productivity is the best possible performance that could be achieved by that group based on its resources (ability, knowledge, skills). Process losses are then the losses due to working as part of a group, these can include losses due to coordination, communication problems and losses in motivation. For example, in a tug-of-war team each member can pull 100 kg individually and as a team of four they pull 360 kg in total.

Why do you think this would happen?

The lower productivity of a group or team is often to do with a concept called 'social loafing' whereby individuals working as part of a team tend not to give as much effort as they would do individually because working in groups tends to affect individual motivation. Research shows that rowers in larger teams give less effort than those in smaller teams:

- 1 person gives 100% effort
- 2 people give 90% effort each
- 4 people give 80% effort each
- 8 people give 65% effort each.

This phenomenon is also referred to as the Ringelmann effect.

> **Key term**
>
> **Ringelmann effect** describes the tendency of individuals to expend less effort when working as part of a team that when they work individually.

> **E1 Check your understanding**
>
> 1 Describe the difference between interactive and coactive teams.
> 2 Identify two interactive and two coactive teams.
> 3 Explain briefly Tuckman's stages of group development.
> 4 Explain how Steiner's model of group development accounts for teams that underperform.
> 5 Describe the Ringelmann effect.

E2 Cohesion

Cohesion is concerned with the extent to which a team is willing to stick together and work together. The forces causing people to stick together tend to cover two areas:

- the attractiveness of the group to individual members
- the extent to which members are willing to work together to achieve group goals.

To be successful in its goals, a group has to be cohesive. The extent to which cohesion is important depends on the sport and the level of interaction needed.

Key term

Cohesion describes the willingness of team members to work together and stick together.

Carron's conceptual model of cohesion

Albert Carron is a key author in the study of sports groups and teams and their cohesive qualities. He presented a conceptual model of cohesion that provided a framework for examining cohesion in sports teams. The framework is shown in Figure 3.13.

Figure 3.13 Carron's (1982) framework for examining cohesion in sports teams

1 **Environmental factors** would include the level of competition the team are playing at, how close together they live and their closeness to each other when they do meet up.

2 **Leadership factors** would include the behaviour of the leader, how secure their leadership position is and how well respected they are. In particular, the decision-making style of the leader is important, as teams where decisions are taken by the team members themselves rather than having decisions imposed on them by the leader, tend to be more cohesive, and members have a stronger sense of being important.

3 **Team factors** will include the extent to which team members have to interact or coact with each other. Also teams where the members have clear understanding of their role within the team and accept this role will have higher levels of cohesion, as they will all be working towards the same objective.

4 **Personal factors** include the age, gender and social background of the team members. Teams who have greater similarity in these factors tend to have higher levels of cohesion and avoid the development of smaller friendship groups called cliques.

Task and social cohesion

There are two types of cohesion within a group – task cohesion and social cohesion. Task cohesion, or group integration, is the willingness of a team to work together to achieve its goals. Social cohesion, or individual attraction, refers to the extent that the members of the team like each other and want to socialise together.

Relationship between cohesion and sports performance

Research says that cohesion is important in successful teams, but that task cohesion is more important than social cohesion. It does depend on the sport being played, as groups that need high levels of interaction need higher levels of cohesion. Research also suggests that success will produce increased cohesion rather than cohesion coming before performance. Being successful helps to develop feelings of group attraction, and this will help to develop more success, and so on. This can be seen by the cycle of success, in that once a team has been successful it tends to continue being successful – success breeds success.

E2 Check your understanding

1 Explain what is meant by the term 'cohesion'.
2 Identify a cohesive team that you were part of and what factors made it cohesive.
3 Identify the difference between task and social cohesion.
4 Explain whether task or social cohesion are most important in successful sports teams.

E3 Leadership in sport

The choice of a manager, coach or captain is often the most important decision a club's members have to make. They see it as crucial in influencing the club's chances of success. Leadership has been defined as the 'behavioural process of influencing individuals and groups towards goals' (Barrow, 1977). Leadership behaviour covers a variety of activities, which is why it is called 'multidimensional' in nature. Some of the different activities include:

● decision-making processes
● motivational techniques
● giving feedback
● establishing interpersonal relationships
● confidently directing the group.

Key term

Leadership is the process of influencing teams and individuals towards achieving their goals.

Types of leaders

Emergent versus prescribed

People become leaders in different ways as not all are appointed. Prescribed leaders are appointed by a person in authority – a chairperson appoints a manager, a manager appoints a coach, a principal appoints a teacher. Emergent leaders emerge from a group and take over responsibility. For example, Wayne Rooney emerged to become the leader of the England football team, just as Alistair Cook emerged to become the England cricket captain. Emergent leaders can be more effective as they have the respect of their group members.

Autocratic versus democratic

The term '-cratic' at the ends of the two words refers to power, so an autocratic leader is one who retains the power to make all the decisions while a democratic leader will allow the members of the group to make the decisions or have a say in the decision-making process. These two represent the opposite ends of a scale and often leaders will show aspects of each style. The style of leadership is based on many things such as the personality of the leader but also the situation that the leader finds themselves in. For example, if your team is losing with just a couple of minutes to go in an important game it can be difficult to consult all the members of a team before deciding what to do. In this situation it is best for the leader to trust their ability to make a decision. The multidimensional model explores many of the factors that influence whether a leader of a specific group will be successful or not.

Chelladurai's multidimensional model of sport leadership

Chelladurai's (1990) multidimensional model of leadership has been developed specifically to help us understand leadership and give guidance on how to be an effective leader. There are seven stages to the model, as can be seen in Figure 3.14.

Antecedents, leader behaviour and consequences

The model is split into three parts. Antecedents are the factors that the leader needs to consider before they make a decision; leader behaviour looks at the leadership behaviour they adopt and consequences shows the outcomes for the group.

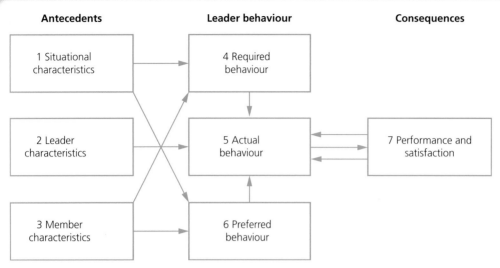

Figure 3.14 The multidimensional model of leadership (Chelladurai, 1990)

The seven stages are summarised in Table 3.5 below.

Stage number	Stage title	Summary of each stage
1	Situational characteristics	The characteristics of the situation the group is in, such as size, type of sport, winning or losing.
2	Leader characteristics	The personal qualities of the leader. Some of the qualities needed are confidence, intelligence, assertiveness and self-motivation.
3	Member characteristics	The different personality types of different groups of athletes, including age, gender, ability level and experience.
4	Required behaviour	The type of behaviour required of a leader in a particular situation. For example, if a team is losing with five minutes to go, it is best for the leader to make a decision themselves rather than discuss it with their teammates.
5	Actual behaviour	The behaviour the leader actually displays.
6	Preferred behaviour	The preferred leadership of the group, depending on their characteristics.
7	Performance satisfaction	The extent to which the group members are satisfied with the leader's behaviour and with the outcome of the competition.

Table 3.5 Stages of the multidimensional model

Application to the performance of sports groups and teams

This model shows that for a coach in sport or an exercise instructor to be successful they need to be very flexible in their leadership approach. They will need to adapt their behaviour to meet the needs of the different groups they are coaching or instructing. For example, the style a coach uses would be different when they were coaching a group of children who were beginners compared to a group of adults who were elite athletes. Likewise, an exercise instructor would need to be adaptable and would instruct a circuits class of beginners with low fitness levels differently to a military style circuits session. Often the coach will have a style that they are happiest with but, rather than forcing this style on the group, they must be aware of the preferred leadership style of the group members and lead them that way.

1 Explain what is meant by 'leadership'.
2 Identify three activities a leader would need to cover.
3 Describe, using an example, the difference between autocratic and democratic leaders.
4 Explain Chelladurai's multidimensional model of leadership.
5 Describe what implications the multidimensional model of leadership would have for an exercise instructor with different client groups.

Exam Practice

This activity will cover aspects of learning aim E, and its purpose is to provide preparation for the external assessment.

Read the following case study where George, a former professional football player, talks about two teams he played for in his career and then answer the questions that follow.

'I played for several teams in my career, but when I was a young player I was lucky to have a brilliant manager who had recently been appointed to this job after managing a different club. At the beginning of the season he told each player what their role was in the team and then he would bring the team together and told us how he wanted us to play together. We each knew our individual role and as long as we performed it, we were kept in the team. The team was never friendly outside of training and playing as the personalities were so different, but we all worked well together on the pitch.

My second team was managed by an ex-player that I knew from the first club and he put together a team of

players that he had played with and trusted. He had played for this team and everyone wanted him to be manager after the previous manager was sacked. We were never the most talented group of individuals, but once we were on the pitch, we all worked for each other and achieved more than the individual sum of our talents should have achieved. The manager always took us out on Monday nights and we would go for a meal, go bowling or play darts – this helped to build a solid bond between us and we cared for each other on and off the pitch. This manager would always discuss tactics with the team members and listen to our suggestions about how we should play against each opponent.'

1 Identify whether managers are emergent or prescribed.
2 Describe whether each manager is an autocratic or democratic leader.
3 Explain the types of cohesion that are present in each group and how they impact on team performance.

F Psychological interventions for sport and exercise

Psychological interventions are skills and techniques that athletes can learn to enhance their performance, increase their enjoyment and provide support. The learning and practise of psychological interventions are often referred to as psychological skills training (PST) and these techniques are generally taken from mainstream psychology and then applied in sporting environments.

F1 Aims of psychological interventions

Athletes are often told by coaches that they need to stay relaxed or keep concentrating which may be sound advice but if they don't have these skills then they are not going to be able to take the advice. Psychological interventions aim to provide athletes with a set of skills that they can use when they need them. They will be taught and practised alongside physical skills and then implemented in the sport or exercise environment.

The aim of psychological interventions is to develop characteristics of high-performing athletes by modelling the skills that have made them successful. In particular, successful sports performers will have the following psychological skills:

- high levels of motivation
- self-regulation of arousal levels
- positive thoughts
- high levels of self-confidence.

Coaches and instructors often refer to the value of mental toughness in athletes. Mental toughness covers all mental processes but in particular an athlete's ability to keep focus, bounce back after failure, cope with pressure and show persistence at a task (Bull *et al.*, 2005).

F1 Check your understanding

1 Explain why athletes may benefit from psychological interventions.
2 Identify what the aim is of psychological interventions.
3 Identify four psychological traits of successful sports performers.
4 Explain what is meant by 'mental toughness'.

F2 Performance profiling

Performance profiling is a technique that can be used in different ways. The aim of performance profiling is for athletes and their coaches to identify the psychological characteristics needed to be successful in their chosen sport. Once these characteristics have been identified the athlete can assess how closely they match the profile and thus identify their psychological strengths and weaknesses. As a technique it allows a certain amount of self-determination because the athlete is in control when deciding the characteristics and then assessing their own skills; however, the same process could be done by their coach and then they could match up their profiles and discuss any differences in assessment. Performance profiling can be used to assess strengths and weaknesses in other factors influencing performance, such as physical, biomechanical or technical characteristics.

Applications of performance profiling

While performance profiling can give an overall picture of an athlete's mental skills it can be used in other ways as well. The information generated can be used as a basis for the motivation of the athlete to improve their skills and their profile can be reviewed regularly. It can be used in conjunction with other techniques, such as goal setting, so that specific weaknesses can be worked on and then progress can be monitored. In summary, the following are some of the applications of performance profiling:

- provides motivation to improve
- providing a basis for goal setting
- identifying strengths and weaknesses
- develops athlete's self-awareness
- can be used to monitor and evaluate progress.

The visual nature of performance profiling often appeals to athletes and their coaches, and it can give them a clear picture of their position at any point in time.

Process of performance profiling

Introducing performance profiling

Performance profiling may represent a new concept for an athlete and explaining the process and value of the technique would be useful. The technique could be introduced by covering the following information:

- the aim of performance profiling
- the steps that are taken in completing the performance profile
- the benefits of performance profiling to athlete and coach
- how the results can be applied
- show examples of completed performance profiles (anonymous).

Eliciting constructs

The athlete will come up with ten psychological factors which are central to their success by answering a question such as 'What psychological factors do you consider to be most important in helping you to achieve your best performance?'

The ten factors they come up with are called the 'constructs' and these will be plotted on the performance profile.

Assessment of constructs

The athlete is asked to rate themselves on a scale of 1 to 10 to show their current level on each construct where a rating of 10 would represent their idea of perfection.

Then they would rate how far they would like to progress towards their idea of perfection. They may feel that a score of 10 is not necessary and they would be happy to get to 7. The information can be presented on a grid such as the one shown in Figure 3.15.

In this performance profile the dark bars show the athlete's current levels on each construct and the lighter bars show their desired levels.

Utilising results from assessment

The information in the performance profile can be used in the following ways:

- to assess the athlete's strengths and weaknesses
- to assess the athlete's view of what is important in their sport
- to assess what the athlete needs to work on.

The coach may have different ideas from the athlete about what is important for success in their sport and their current level of skill. This exercise will highlight any differences in points of view.

This information can be gained from the performance profile:

- **Any areas of perceived strength** – any construct where they score 5 or more (aggression control).
- **Any areas of perceived weakness** – any construct where they score less than 5 (arousal control).
- **Any areas that are resistant to change** – where there is little difference between their current rating and the rating they would like to achieve (attitude).

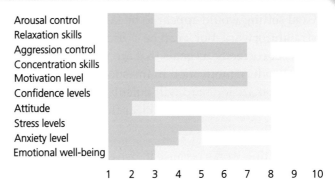

Figure 3.15 Example of a performance profile

Performance profiling is a useful intervention because it can be used to consider a range of aspects of performance. A technique such as goal setting tends to focus on one or two aspects of performance. Most importantly, it considers what the individual considers to be important and focuses the process on their responses.

F2 Check your understanding

1 Explain how performance profiling can be used with athletes.
2 Identify five psychological constructs that could be assessed during the process of performance profiling.
3 Explain three ways the results from performance profiling could be used.
4 Identify any benefits that performance profiling may have over goal setting.

F3 Goal setting

Goal setting is a common technique that is used to develop motivation in an individual or team. Goals are what an individual is aiming to achieve. It is the outcome they want their actions to produce, for example:

- Our goal is to finish in the top three of the league.
- My goal is to score 20 goals this season.
- I want to lose 5 kg in weight.
- I want to make 20 appearances this season.
- I want to run 100 m in 11.0 seconds.
- I want to bench press 90 kg.

Goal setting would appear to be fairly straightforward, but it can be difficult to get a goal set correctly, as goals that are too easy will only produce motivation in the short term and goals that are too hard will quickly produce demotivation as it becomes clear they won't be achieved.

Goal setting works because it gives our wants and desires a specific outcome and can provide us with steps we need to take towards this outcome. It gives our daily actions a meaning or framework to work within and gives us clear direction. Goals will work to direct our energy and efforts.

Timescale for goals

Goals can be set over different time periods. You usually have a long-term goal that is something you may want to achieve over a season or a year. However, these are often broken down into short- and medium-term goals.

Short-term goals are set over a brief period of time, usually from between one day to three months. A short-term goal may relate to what you want to achieve in one training session or where you want to be by the end of the month.

Medium-term goals will bridge the gap between short- and long-term goals and are set from three to six months.

Long-term goals will run from six months to over several years. You may even set some lifetime goals which run until you retire from your sport. In sport you may set long-term goals to cover a season or a sporting year.

Usually short-term goals are set to help achieve the long-term goals. It is important to set both short-term and long-term goals because short-term goals will give you more motivation to act now. For example, if you have to give in a piece of coursework tomorrow it will make you work hard tonight but if you have to submit it in one month then you are unlikely to stay in tonight and complete the work. Short-term goals will have the most powerful effect because they influence what you are doing now, at this moment.

Key terms

Short-term goals are set with a timescale of between one day to three months.

Medium-term goals are set between three to six months.

Long-term goals are set between six months to over several years.

Types of goal

Performance, outcome and process goals
Outcome goals focus on the outcome of a competition or event, such as winning a race or beating an opponent. Achieving an outcome goal is not solely dependent on your own actions as they are also dependent on the performance and effort of your opponent. It is possible to play the best you have ever played and still not achieve your goal as it is not totally self-determined.

Performance goals focus on achieving a certain standard of performance. They are usually based on a comparison with your own previous performance rather than the actions of your opponents. As a result, performance goals are less dependent on the actions of your opponent and are more under your own control. For example, aiming to increase your bench press from 80 kg to 90 kg is a performance goal.

Process goals focus on the processes or actions that an individual must produce to perform well. For example, a runner may set process goals to train five times a week, eat correctly every day, gain eight hours sleep a night and have a weekly sports massage. The process goals will be the small steps we take towards the larger outcome goal.

All three types of goal are important and we find that short-term goals are normally process goals while long-term goals are outcome goals.

Key terms

Outcome goals focus on the outcome of a competition or event, performance goals focus on achieving a specific standard and process goals focus on the actions that are needed to perform well.

Mastery and competitive goals

Mastery goals are set with the aim of mastering specific skills or techniques. For example, a footballer may break down their performance into a set of techniques that they need to master to improve their performance, such as goals set for short passing, long passing, clearing, shooting, attacking heading, defensive heading and tackling. Competitive goals are set for achieving specific things in competition. These may relate to the outcome of the competition but they could also relate to the individual skills that underpin the overall performance. For example, the footballer may aim to be successful with 85% of their passes and be on target with 75% of their shots inside the box.

Principles of goal setting

When setting goals you need to use the **SMART** principle to ensure that they are as effective as they can be and that they actually work to achieve the outcomes that you want. SMART stands for:

- **S**pecific
- **M**easurable
- **A**ction-oriented
- **R**ealistic
- **T**ime-constrained
- **S**elf-determined

Specific: the goal must be specific to what you want to achieve. This may be an aspect of performance or fitness. It is not enough to say 'I want to get fitter.' You need to say 'I want to improve strength, speed or stamina'. This describes the difference between subjective goals, such as 'I want to have fun' that are not easily measured, whereas a specific goal to improve strength is objective as its success or failure can be assessed.

Measurable: goals must be stated in a way that is measurable, so they need to state figures. For example, 'I want to improve my first serve percentage' is not measurable. However, if you say 'I want to improve my first serve success by 20%' it has become measurable.

Action-oriented: goals must be related to the actions that you have to take during performance (performance goals) or to improve performance (process goals).

Realistic: we need to be realistic in our goal setting by setting goals that are moderately difficult to achieve and are challenging but which are still

possible to achieve. When setting goals you also need to look at factors that may prevent you from achieving the goal. For example, time, energy and resources may be three factors to consider.

Time-constrained: there must be a timescale or deadline on the goal. This gives you a specific point at which you can assess whether you have been successful or not. This can be done by stating a date by which you wish to achieve the goal.

Self-determined: the goals need to be decided by the individual who is going to work towards the goal. This means that they will feel that they have ownership over the goals rather than working towards something that has been imposed on them.

How to set goals

The best way to do this is to answer three questions:

1 What do I want to achieve? (desired state)
2 Where am I now? (present state)
3 What do I need to do to move from my present state to my desired state? (actions)

Then present this on a scale:

Figure 3.16

1 Write in your outcome goal at point 5 and your present position at point 1.
2 Decide what outcome would be achieved at halfway between points 1 and 5. This is your goal for point 3.
3 Then decide what outcomes would be achieved halfway between your present state and point 3. This is your short-term goal for point 2.
4 Then decide what outcome would be halfway between point 3 and the desired state; this is the goal for point 4.

All these goals are outcome goals and must be set using the SMART principle.

5 Work out what actions need to be taken to move from your present state at point 1

to point 2. These are your process goals and must again use the SMART principle.

Once the outcome that you wanted to achieve at point 2 has been achieved you can then set more process goals to enable you to move from point 2 to point 3. The same would happen as you achieve the outcome at points 3 and 4 as you would set new outcome goals to enable you to move to the next point.

It is also good practice to use a goal-setting diary to keep all goal-setting information in the same place, and to review your goals on a weekly basis.

F3 Check your understanding

1 Explain what is meant by a 'goal'.
2 Describe the difference between short-term and long-term goals.
3 Describe the difference between process and outcome goals.
4 Identify what is meant by the acronym 'SMART'.
5 Explain why goal setting can be an effective method of influencing motivation.

F4 Imagery in sport

Imagery is a skill that involves creating or recreating experiences in your mind (Weinberg and Gould, 2015). It is referred to by different terms, including visualisation and mental rehearsal, but all refer to a form of mental preparation where you recall information from memories and previous experiences and use them to influence your performance in the future.

Imagery would seem to refer to developing images or pictures in your head but it includes other senses as well.

Types of imagery

Visual
Visual imagery involves seeing yourself performing skills or behaving in certain ways, such as confidently or when dealing with problems. Many athletes use visual imagery to mentally rehearse the skill they are about to perform. You can see this when rugby kickers are preparing for a penalty, a high jumper is preparing for their jump or a golfer is mentally practising their shot.

When using the visual sense you can either have an internal perspective where you are seeing with a perspective from your own eyes or an external perspective when you are outside your own body looking at yourself performing a skill. If you were playing a golf shot you would see the ball in front of you and then you would see the club coming down and hitting the ball. You would then see the ball fly towards the hole and land. From an external perspective you would see yourself as if in a film performing the golf shot and then follow the flight of the ball. Generally speaking the internal perspective will have more effect but the external perspective can be useful if you want to observe your body language or behaviour.

Auditory
Imagery has most effect if you can include more than one sense into the experience so hearing the sounds that you heard when you were performing well are useful too. You might hear the clean noise when a golf ball or cricket ball is well struck or it might be the sounds of the crowd as you are running down the home straight to victory.

Kinaesthetic sense
Kinaesthetic sense describes the feelings that you have when you are performing a skill. It involves the feelings of holding a piece of equipment and then the feelings in your body as you move around and get into different positions. It also relates to the feelings or emotions that you experience, such as energy and joy as you perform well.

Imagery works because when you imagine yourself performing a skill the brain is unable to differentiate between a real experience and an imagined experience. As a result, the brain sends impulses to the muscles via the nervous system. These impulses are not strong enough to produce a muscular contraction, although you may see twitches. As the impulses are passed down the nervous system so the pattern becomes imprinted on the nervous system and is there for whenever you physically perform the skill.

Uses of imagery

Imagery can be used in several different ways.

Reducing anxiety and stress

Imagery is an effective means for reducing stress and anxiety as you can imagine yourself in an environment that is very relaxing, such as somewhere that you have been to on holiday. You can recreate the relaxing environment in your mind and then when you need to relax you can take yourself there.

Influencing self-confidence

Imagining yourself successfully performing skills and performing well can help to build your feelings that you will actually be successful. Also, you can imagine yourself behaving in a self-confident way with positive body language.

Imagining goals

As part of the process of goal setting, you can imagine yourself achieving your goal. You might see yourself crossing the finish line of a half marathon and draw up images of the feelings associated with the success. When imagining success it is important that the images you create are big, bold and colourful as the more vivid the images are then the greater the impact they will have on you.

Mental rehearsal

Mental rehearsal, where you imagine yourself performing skills, or recreating a performance, is one of the key uses of imagery as it embeds your positive feelings. A popular technique is recalling past experiences when you played particularly well or performed skills and then applying these images and the associated feelings into the performance you are about to produce. Many athletes will spend some time each day using imagery to mentally rehearse the skills they will perform. For example, a gymnast may mentally rehearse the floor routine that they will complete or a 100 m runner rehearses the stages of their upcoming race.

Pre-performance routines

Pre-performance routines are the steps that a sports person goes through before they perform a specific skill. You may notice that tennis players or golfers do exactly the same things before they execute a skill. Some of the routine may be physical but it will also involve imagery as they rehearse their skill. This helps sports people to concentrate and ensure that their focus is on the task in hand.

Imagery is a skill that different people will find hard or easy. Some people will find it difficult to draw up visual images in their head but that they can recreate the feelings associated with sport quite easily. It is a skill and it can be improved significantly with practice.

F4 Check your understanding

1 Explain what is meant by 'imagery'.
2 Explain three different types of imagery.
3 Explain how imagery can be used to reduce stress and anxiety.
4 Explain how imagery can be used as mental rehearsal.

F5 Self-talk in sport and exercise

Self-talk relates to the conversations that we have with ourselves. They are mostly internal conversations, but sometimes we do talk to ourselves out loud. Everyone talks to themselves in different ways, but examples of self-talk in sport would include:

- 'Come on, you can do this.'
- 'Keep going, there's just one more mile to go.'
- 'Don't let them know you are hurt and get on with it.'
- 'You have done this before and you can do it again.'
- 'I am going to do this successfully.'

Types of self-talk

Self-talk can be positive and negative and will both have different effects on you. If you are feeling anxious and tired, your self-talk can often become negative as you start to doubt your ability to achieve your aim. This can be very damaging to you as it starts to diminish your motivation or affect your self-confidence.

Positive self-talk includes affirmations which are phrases we use to reassure ourselves that have the skills and abilities needed in a specific situation.

Also we use command words to help with the timing of skills, such as 'turn now' or 'swing slowly' and mood words that help to create feelings, such as 'play hard' or 'burn bright' to increase arousal levels.

Generally speaking, people use twice as much negative self-talk as positive self-talk so you need to be aware when you are talking to yourself in a negative way and either stop the talk or change it to positive talk.

Uses of self-talk

Self-talk has many uses and here are three of them:

Building self-confidence

Self-talk can help to create feelings and thoughts that help you to believe that you can be successful and have the competency to achieve the task in hand.

Arousal control

Self-talk can help you to calm down when arousal levels become too high and might lead to you being aggressive or experiencing a decline in performance. Alternatively, self-talk can provide a pep talk to yourself to increase your energy levels and encourage yourself to work harder.

Pre-performance routines

As part of a pre-performance routine you may use self-talk to encourage yourself to do certain things during performance and concentrate on certain aspects of the performance. For example, telling yourself to keep relaxed and move smoothly.

F5 Check your understanding

1 Explain what self-talk involves.
2 Describe why negative self-talk can be damaging to performance.
3 Explain how self-talk can be used to increase self-confidence.
4 Explain how self-talk can be used as part of a pre-performance routine.

F6 Arousal control techniques in sport and exercise

The arousal-performance theories show that your performance is related to your arousal level. For example, the inverted U hypothesis showed that as arousal levels increase so does performance level, up to an optimal point of arousal (ideal performing state). Once the optimal point of arousal has been reached, any further increases in arousal will cause decrements in performance. Therefore, it is essential that you control your arousal level to ensure that it matches the demands of the situation that you are in.

There are two types of arousal techniques: those that will lower your arousal level, and consequently also reduce your stress and anxiety levels, and those that increase your arousal levels if you are too relaxed and lacking focus.

These techniques are only useful if you are aware of your optimal point of arousal and how it differs depending on the situation you find yourself in.

Relaxation techniques

Relaxation skills are useful to sports performers who have high levels of arousal and anxiety that are having a negative effect on their performance. Or they may be playing a sport, such as golf or shooting, where lower levels of arousal are needed.

Progressive muscular relaxation

Progressive muscular relaxation (PMR) was initially developed by Jacobsen (1938) and is an important relaxation technique. PMR involves the tensing and relaxing of muscles. It is done using a recorded script that takes you through the muscles of the body, usually starting at the hands and moving up to the arms and shoulders, into the face and neck, down the back and buttocks and finally to the legs and feet.

You will learn the difference between tensed and relaxed muscles and experience an increased relaxation effect each time you practise the programme. The aim is that you understand what tension and relaxation feel like so that when you become tense during sporting competition you can quickly relax your muscles.

PMR is particularly effective for sports performances with high somatic anxiety (racing heart rate, butterflies in the stomach) and negative stress (distress). As the body becomes relaxed the mind will become more relaxed as well. However, for individuals with high cognitive anxiety, imagery or mental relaxation techniques may be more effective.

Mind-to-muscle techniques (imagery)

Mind-to-muscle techniques involve the development of images in your mind and can be used for relaxation. Mind-to-muscle techniques are particularly good for individuals who experience high levels of cognitive anxiety (mental worry and poor concentration). To use imagery for relaxation you need to think of a specific time or situation when you felt really relaxed and recreate this situation in your mind. It is often related to a place or activity; for example, somewhere you went to on holiday or a special place that you go to so you can get away from everything. When you recreate the situation you need to engage all your senses so it is about seeing the place where you are, hearing any sounds specific to the place (sound of the sea or a river) and feeling any related feelings, such as the heat of the sun.

The aim is that as your mind becomes more and more relaxed these feelings of relaxation spread to your body and your whole body becomes relaxed. Then when anxiety or arousal levels become too high you can quickly recreate these feelings of relaxation by visualising your relaxing place. The feelings of relaxation will replace the tension in the mind and the body and lower arousal levels to the optimum point of arousal.

Breathing control

Breathing control is a method used to reduce muscle tension and to lower anxiety levels. When you become stressed and anxious you experience short, shallow breathing, and when you are relaxed your breathing deepens.

To become relaxed you can breathe deeply and slowly to produce mental and physical relaxation. If you are focusing on your breathing it will shift your attention from the cause of stress and anxiety. Breathing control can then be used at the appropriate time during a competition to control arousal levels.

> **Key term**
>
> **Relaxation skills** are used to lower levels of arousal and anxiety and include PMR, imagery and breathing control.

Energising techniques

Energising techniques are the opposite of relaxation techniques and are used when a sports person's arousal levels are too low or below the optimal point of arousal. If you are experiencing low arousal levels it may be that you are feeling tired and lethargic and can't concentrate on what you are meant to be concentrating on. These feelings can happen before or during a performance and will result in a relatively poor performance. If this is the case then techniques are needed to raise arousal levels but care must be taken that they do not increase too much and result in over-arousal.

> **Key term**
>
> **Energising techniques** are used to increase arousal levels and feelings of energy. They include increasing breathing rate, pep talks and using energising music.

Increasing breathing rate

Slowing your breathing rate resulted in reductions in arousal and anxiety so the opposite will result in an increased arousal level. Short deep breaths will produce energy and help to raise arousal levels.

Pep talks

Pep talks take different forms and can involve your coach talking in a very animated and upbeat way about how you should feel and act on the sports field. They may even shout and create positive, upbeat emotions. You can use self-talk as a pep talk by using emotive or confirmatory phrases, such as 'you can do this', 'be confident' or 'show them what you can do'.

Listening to music

Listening to upbeat, energetic music can produce energy before training or a competition. This is why we often see athletes with headphones who are listening to music to either energise or relax themselves. Some athletes will listen to music during training to keep them energised and working hard.

Use of energising imagery

Positive feelings and energy can be created by creating certain images in your mind. Often athletes will think about animals that have attributes that relate to their sport. For example, a sprinter may visualise a cheetah running swiftly and effortlessly and a rugby player may visualise a lion who is strong and fearless.

Positive statements

These are a form of self-talk as they will be phrases that you use to energise yourself. They may be written down or repeated using self-talk. For example, you might use words such as tough, strong, invincible or statements such as 'burn hot' or 'tackle hard'.

F6 Check your understanding

1 Explain why an athlete may need to use arousal control techniques.
2 Explain how an athlete would use PMR as a relaxation technique.
3 Explain how an athlete would use imagery as a relation technique.
4 Identify the different types of anxiety that PMR and imagery can help control.
5 Describe when an athlete would use energising techniques.
6 Explain one type of energising technique.

Exam Practice

Addressing a case study – applying psychological interventions in practice

Psychological interventions can be used in a variety of ways. When you complete your external assessment you will have to select appropriate psychological interventions to meet the needs of an athlete.

Table 3.6 below summarises the use of psychological techniques by matching them to potential issues that athletes may face.

When you select a psychological intervention you will need to justify why you have selected that

one and how it would be used with an athlete. It is also worth considering what you are aiming to achieve with an intervention – what will be the expected outcome of the psychological intervention?

Addressing a case study question to achieve a distinction grade

The external assessment will take the form of a case study question so you will need to be prepared for this type of answer.

	Performance profiling	Goal setting	Imagery	Self-talk	Relaxation techniques	Energising techniques
Controlling arousal			✔	✔	✔	✔
Managing stress		✔	✔	✔	✔	
Reducing anxiety		✔	✔	✔	✔	
Motivation	✔	✔	✔			
Controlling aggression		✔	✔	✔	✔	
Developing self-confidence		✔	✔	✔		

Table 3.6 Psychological interventions athletes use

→

There are three stages to dealing with a case study type question:

Stage 1 – Define the problems/issues the athlete is facing

Stage 2 – Applying theory to understand the case study

Stage 3 – Generating a solution.

When addressing the case study it is beneficial to do it in a logical and organised way. The following steps expand on the three stages and take you through working on a case study in a series of logical steps. This will ensure that you address the case study in the best possible way.

1   Read the case study through at least twice.

2   Underline what you think are the key parts.

3   Put yourself in the shoes of the athlete in the case study and experience what they are experiencing.

4   Decide on the key problems/issues that the athlete is facing.

5   Identify how these issues are affecting their performance.

6   Identify which theories may explain their experiences.

7   Explain how these theories help to make sense of the athlete's experiences.

8   Identify which psychological interventions would help the athlete.

9   Explain how the selected interventions would help the athlete and how you would use the intervention.

Case studies involve putting theory into practice which is an important academic skill. It is also a skill that improves with practice. You can practice by looking at other case studies but also by examining your own experiences and athletes that you watch and read about. Sport psychology can be applied in every competition you play in or watch.

Here is a case study for you to use as practice.

Motivation case study

Laura is an 18-year-old field hockey player who plays at left wing. Laura is a very fast, skilful player who loves to beat her opponent and play the ball into the shooting circle. She loves to dribble with the ball and make shooting opportunities for herself.

She is the star player of her school team and she also plays for a local, senior team where she is youngest player.

Laura plays hockey for the sheer enjoyment of the sport and she loves the feeling of being good at a sport and the success it brings. At school she is known by the other students because she is such a good sports person. Laura enjoys playing against tough opponents that she knows will provide a hard challenge for her. When she plays for the school team she finds that her opponents are often much weaker than her and that victory comes too easily. This is the reason that she joined a senior team.

The senior team are totally focused on trying to win the league and they welcomed Laura as they needed a player who could cover the left wing position. Laura is told exactly how to play so that the team have the best opportunity to win. In particular, she is given specific defensive responsibilities and is encouraged to do as much tackling as possible.

While Laura is progressing well with the senior team she has started to find that she can't sleep well before a match as she is constantly thinking about the match and the strong opponents she will be facing. Her heart is often racing and her chest feels tight. Her parents are concerned that she seems distracted, does not get involved in conversation and is often moody. Her coach reassures her that feeling nervous is totally normal and that she should use it as proof that she is motivated and ready to play.

However, during one match against one of the best teams in the senior league Laura keeps making mistakes and losing the ball. She starts to doubt her ability to play for the senior team. Unfortunately in this match she is constantly being fouled by

→

her opponent and she thinks the umpires are not noticing this. After being hit by her opponent's stick she retaliates by whacking her opponent across her legs with her hockey stick. The umpire gives her a red card for serious foul play.

Laura is distraught at this turn of events and she tells the team captain that she wants to leave the team. The club captain calms her down and recommends that she consults a sport psychologist as she had been helped by one in the past.

1   Identify how Laura is motivated and how this may change between her school and senior teams.

2   Identify the main psychological issues that Laura is experiencing and the impact they are having on her performance.

3   Using three theories from sport psychology to explain Laura's experiences as presented in the case study.

4   Identify three psychological interventions that the sport psychologist could use to help Laura with her issues and explain how these interventions could be used.

Further reading

Cox, R. (2011). *Sports Psychology: Concepts and Applications*. Wm C. Brown Communications.

Perry, J. (2016). *Sport Psychology: A complete introduction.* London, John Murray Learning.

Rea, S. (2015). *Sports Science: A complete introduction.* London, John Murray Learning.

Tod, D., Thatcher, J, and Rahman, R. (2010). *Sport Psychology.* Basingstoke, Palgrave MacMillan

Weinberg, R.S., and Gould, D. (2007). *Foundations of Sport and Exercise Psychology (Fourth edition)*, Champaign, Human Kinetics.

Weinberg, R.S., and Gould, D. (2015). *Foundations of Sport and Exercise Psychology (Sixth edition)*, Champaign, Human Kinetics.

Useful websites

Mind Tools

http://www.mindtools.com/page11.html

The Sport in Mind

http://www.thesportinmind.com/

Association for Applied Sport Psychology

http://www.appliedsportpsych.org/

Exercise and Sport Psychology

http://www.vanguard.edu/psychology/amoebaweb/exercise-psychology/

Sport Psychology Portal (University of Essex)

http://orb.essex.ac.uk/bs/sportpsy/

References

Anshel, M.H., and Sutarso, T. (2010). Conceptualising maladaptive sport perfectionism as a function of gender. *Journal of Clinical Sport Psychology, vol.4*, pp.263–281.

Atkinson, J.W. (1974). 'The mainstream of achievement oriented activity' in Atkinson, J.W. and Raynor, J.O. (eds.). *Motivation and Achievement.* New York, Halstead.

Bandura, A. (1973). *Aggression: A Social Learning Analysis*. Prentice Hall.

Bandura, A. (1977). Self-efficacy: Toward a unifying theory of behavioural change. *Psychological Review, vol. 84*, pp.191–215.

Bandura, A. (1986). *Social foundations of thoughts and actions: A social cognitive theory.* Eaglewood Cliffs, NJ. Prentice Hall.

Bandura, A. (1997). *Self-efficacy: The exercise of control.* New York. Freeman.

Baron, R. and Richardson, D. (1994) *Human Aggression*, New York, Plenum.

Barrow, J. (1977) The variables of leadership: a review and conceptual framework. *Academy of Management Review*, 2, pp.231–251.

Bull, S., Shambrook, C., James, W., and Brooks, J. (2005) Toward an understanding of mental toughness in elite English cricketers. *Journal of Applied Sport Psychology*, 17, pp.209–227.

Carron, A. (1982) Cohesiveness in sports groups: Interpretations and considerations. *Journal of Sport Psychology*, 4, pp.123–138.

Chelladurai, P. (1990) Leadership in sports: A review. *International Journal of Sport Psychology*, 21, pp.328–354.

Deci, E.L., and Ryan, R.M. (1985). *Intrinsic motivation and self-determination in human behaviour.* New York. Plenum.

Deci, E.L., and Ryan, R.M. (1991). A motivational approach to self: Integration in personality. In R. Dienstbier (ed.) *Nebraska symposium on motivation:* vol.38, *Perspectives on motivation* (pp.237–288). Lincoln, NE: University of Nebraska Press.

Duda, J.L. and Balauger, I. (2007) Coach-created motivational climate. In Jowett, S. and Lavallee, D. (eds.), *Social Psychology in Sport* (pp.117–130). Leeds: Human Kinetics.

Duda, J.L. and Treasure, D.C. (2006) Motivational processes and the facilitation of performance, persistence and well-being in sport. In Williams, J.M. (ed.), *Applied Sport Psychology* (pp.57–81). London, McGraw-Hill.

Dweck, C.S. (2006) *Mindset*, New York, Random House.

Fazey, J., and Hardy, L. (1988). *The inverted U hypothesis: A catastrophe for Sport Psychology?* British Association of Sports Sciences Monograph, no.1. NCF, Leeds.

Gill, D. (2000) *Psychological Dynamics of Sport and Exercise,* Champaign, Human Kinetics.

Hill, A.P., Hall, H.K., and Appleton, P.R. (2010). A comparative examination of the correlates of self-oriented perfectionism and conscientious achievement striving in male cricket academy players. *Psychology of Sport and Exercise, vol. 4*, pp.162-168.

Howley, E.T. and Franks, B.D. (2003) *Health Fitness Instructor's Handbook.* 4th edition. Leeds, Human Kinetics.

Hull, C.L. (1943). *Principles of Behaviour.* New York, Appleton-Century-Crofts.

Jacobsen, E. (1938). *Progressive relaxation.* Chicago, University of Chicago Press.

Martens, R., Vealey, R.S. and Burton, D. (Eds.) (1990). *Competitive anxiety in sport.* Champaign, IL, Human Kinetics.

McClelland, D. (1961). *The Achieving Society.* New York, Free Press.

McMorris, T. (2004). *Acquisition and Performance of Sports Skills.* Chichester, John Wiley and Sons.

Morris, T., and Keohn, S. (2004). Self-confidence in sport and exercise. In T. Morris and J. Summers (Eds.), *Sport Psychology: theory, applications and issues* (Second edition, pp.175–209. Queensland, Australia, Wiley.

Nelson, L.R. and Furst, M.L. (1972) An objective study of the effects of expectation on competitive performance. *Journal of Psychology*, 81, pp.69–72.

Nicholls, J.G. (1989). *The competitive ethos and democratic education.* Cambridge, Harvard University Press.

Richardson, G.E. (2002) The meta theory of resilience and resiliency. *Journal of Clinical Psychology*, 58, pp.307–321.

→

Sage, G. (1977). *Introduction to motor behaviour: A neurophysiological approach (Second edition).* Reading, MA, Addison-Wesley.

Sager, S.S., and Stoeber J. (2009). Perfectionism, fear of failure and affective responses to success and failure: The central role of fear and experiencing fear and embarrassment. *Journal of Sport and Exercise Psychology, vol. 11,* pp.177–187.

Scanlan, T.K. (1986) Competitive stress in children. In Weiss, M.R. and Gould, D. (eds.), *Sport for children and youths* (pp.113–118). Champaign, Human Kinetics.

Selye, H. (1983) The stress concept: Past, present and future. In Cooper, C.L. (ed.), *Stress research* (pp.1–20). New York, John Wiley and Sons.

Steiner, I. D. (1972) *Group Processes and Productivity*, Cambridge, Massachusetts, Academic Press.

Stoeber, J., Otto, K., Pescheck, E., Becker, C., and Stoll, O. (2007). Perfectionism and competitive anxiety in athletes: Differentiating striving for perfection and negative reactions to imperfection. *Personality and Individual Differences, vol. 42,* pp.959–969.

Tuckman, L. and Jensen, M. (1977) *Stages of Small Group Development Revisited*, Group and Organisational Studies.

Vallance, J.K.H., Dunn, J.G.H., and Dunn, J.L.C. (2006). Perfectionism, anger and situation criticality in competitive youth ice hockey. *Journal of Sport and Exercise Psychology, vol. 28,* pp.383–406.

Vallerand, R.J. (2001). 'A hierarchical model of intrinsic and extrinsic motivation in sport and exercise' in Roberts, G.C. (ed.) *Advances in Motivation in Sport and Exercise,* Champaign, Human Kinetics.

Weinberg, R.S., and Gould, D. (2007). *Foundations of Sport and Exercise Psychology,* Fourth Edition. Champaign, Human Kinetics.

Weinberg, R.S., and Gould, D. (2015). *Foundations of Sport and Exercise Psychology,* Sixth Edition. Champaign, Human Kinetics.

Treasure, D.C. (2001) Enhancing young people's motivation in youth sport: An achievement goal perspective. In Roberts, G.C. (ed.), *Advances in Motivation in Sport and Exercise,* Champaign, Human Kinetics.

Vealey, R.S., Knight, B.J and Pappas, G. (2002) *Self-confidence in sport: Conceptual and psychological advancement.* Paper presented at the annual convention for Advancement of Applied Sport Psychology, Tucson, AZ.

Vealey, R.S. (1986) Conceptualisation of sport-confidence and competitive orientation: Preliminary investigation and instrument development. *Journal of Sport Psychology,* 8. pp.221–46.

Vealey, R.S. (1988) Sport-confidence and competitive orientation: An addendum on scoring procedures and gender differences. *Journal of Sport and Exercise Psychology,* 20, pp.54–80.

Yerkes, R.M., and Dodson, J.D. (1908).The relation of strength of stimulus to rapidity of habit formation. *Journal of Comparative Neurology of Psychology, vol. 18,* pp.459–482.

4 Field- and laboratory-based fitness testing

About this unit

This unit will enable you to explore the applications of sports science within the context of a field and laboratory testing environment. It will allow you to appreciate the stages a sports scientist will follow in order to prepare, test and evaluate a performer's physiological profile. From the evaluation, judgements can be made to identify strengths and weaknesses, along with enabling the sports scientist to make recommendations on how a training programme may be developed to enhance performance. It is essential that the sports scientist ensures their testing individual, more formally known as a subject or participant, remains safe throughout the testing process. Furthermore the sports scientist should understand the testing procedures used and be able to provide constructive feedback from the results gathered. Data collection may be statistically analysed to help draw conclusions from the testing conducted and this unit aims to introduce you to how this may be applied. The function of the sports scientist is diverse and wide-ranging. This unit will introduce you to their applied role, enabling you to appreciate their importance when supporting an aspiring performer.

Learning aims

This unit is split into four learning aims, each addressing the applications of a sports scientist. The learning aims include:

A Examine the preparation required prior to sport and exercise field- and laboratory-based testing

B Undertake anthropometry and somatotype testing procedures in sport

C Explore the use of field- and laboratory-based protocols in sport and exercise science

D Explore profiling of a sports performer following practical research design using field- and laboratory-based testing.

Within each learning aim there includes an assessment outcome that divides the content into key areas, sub-dividing the learning aim and allowing you to appreciate each of its components.

How will I be assessed?

The unit of field and laboratory fitness testing will be assessed by assignments that have been designed internally by your tutors. It is likely that there will be three assignments for you to complete. Each assignment will enable you to apply the knowledge you have learnt to a range of activities.

Learning aim A achievement

For distinction standard, learners will evaluate the stages necessary for the safe preparation and application of testing, and justify its importance. They will demonstrate an excellent understanding of the procedures and policies that should be in place prior to laboratory testing – for example, clear evidence of health screening with appropriate data recorded, PAR-Q, evidence of a comprehensive ethics form, participant consent information and a thorough risk assessment. Learners will clearly explain the procedures in detail and then justify their importance by making links to a code of practice and appropriate legislation, such as safeguarding and child protection policies. Learners will demonstrate a thorough understanding of validity and reliability, and will clearly define the terms as well as apply them in a practical context.

Learning aim B achievement

For distinction standard, learners will consider the use of anthropometric assessment and somatotype testing protocols, making judgements and drawing conclusions about the advantages and significance of these forms of measurement. They will give reasons to support how their results can be used to predict sporting performance. Learners will demonstrate a sound understanding of somatotyping and its use in sport and exercise. They will independently perform the appropriate assessment techniques with accuracy and correctly map the body for skinfold testing sites to gain reliable repeated measures during the data-gathering stage. Learners may provide appropriate diagrams to illustrate their knowledge of the sites. They will apply appropriate testing protocols with accuracy to produce reliable data that will be used to calculate an individual's somatotype. Evidence of an accurate Heath-Carter assessment record will be shown along with their calculations and resulting somatochart.

Learning aims C and D achievement

For distinction standard, learners will make judgements about the strengths, weaknesses and significance of the outcomes, in relation to the prediction of sport performance and the relevance of field- and laboratory-based testing protocols.

Learners will provide clear evidence of accurate preparation and planning of a mini case study that includes the presentation of six individual testing methods, two of which could be aerobic. Learners will implement testing procedures independently using the correct protocol and equipment, while ensuring the data collected is both valid and reliable. Data will be recorded using formal a spreadsheet, and statistical calculations will be completed using either Microsoft Excel or SPSS. Such calculations could include standard deviation, Pearson's product moment correlation coefficient (r), and t-tests and also use a range of graphical display methods such as correlation charts, graphs and tables.

Learners will use appropriate units of measurement when recording data, including the correct labelling of axis on graphs/charts and correct presentation of tables. All data and graphs/charts must be clear for interpretation, e.g. professionally displayed and of an appropriate size, correctly labelled and annotated.

Learners will carefully consider how effective the creation and use of client profiles from field- and laboratory-based testing is in predicting sport performance. Learners will make judgement on the key strengths of the types of data collected from testing and draw conclusions on the value of creating profiles for the subjects from this, supported by well-considered examples.

How will I be graded?

The table below shows the grading criteria for this unit. To achieve a pass grade you must meet all the P criteria; to achieve a merit grade you must achieve all the P and all the M criteria; to achieve a distinction grade you must achieve all the P, M and D criteria.   →

How will I be graded?

Pass	Merit	Distinction
Learning aim A: Examine the preparation required prior to sport and exercise field- and laboratory-based testing		
A P1 Explain the procedures that should be completed prior to laboratory testing. **A P2** Explain how validity, reliability and ethical considerations impact on field and laboratory testing.	**A M1** Recommend pre-test procedures that can be used to ensure testing is conducted in a safe, valid, reliable and ethical way.	**A D1** Evaluate pre-test procedures that can be used to ensure testing is conducted in a safe, valid, reliable and ethical way, justifying their choices.
Learning aim B: Undertake anthropometry and somatotype testing procedures in sport		
B P3 Explain how anthropometric assessment and somatotype testing protocols are used in laboratory-based testing.	**B M2** Assess the suitability of anthropometric assessment and somatotype testing protocols that are used in laboratory-based testing.	**B D2** Evaluate the use of anthropometric assessment and somatotype testing protocols, justifying how their own results could predict sport and exercise performance.
B P4 Perform three contrasting anthropometric assessment protocols and a somatotype assessment protocol following the correct procedures, recording the results in an appropriate format.	**B M3** Perform three contrasting anthropometric assessment protocols and a somatotype assessment protocol, calculating the test results with accuracy.	
Learning aim C: Explore the use of field- and laboratory-based protocols in sport and exercise sciences		
C P5 Conduct six field- and laboratory-based testing protocols following the correct procedures and record the results in an appropriate format.	**C M4** Conduct six field- and laboratory-based testing protocols, ensuring the test results are calculated with accuracy.	**C D3** Evaluate the data produced from six field- and laboratory-based testing protocols using statistical calculations, justifying the protocols used with reference to the prediction of sport and exercise performance.
Learning aim D: Explore profiling of a sports performer following practical research design using field- and laboratory-based testing		
D P6 Create a profile for a selected sports performer following the implementation of a practical research design using appropriate laboratory- and field-based protocols.	**D M5** Analyse the practical research design followed when creating the profile, making recommendations for future testing.	**D D4** Evaluate the effectiveness of creating performer profiles from anthropometric assessment, somatotype testing and field- and laboratory-based testing protocols in the prediction of sport and exercise performance.

Table 4.1 Assessment criteria

A Examine the preparation required prior to sport and exercise field- and laboratory-based testing (A P1, A P2, A M1, A D1)

A1 Health and safety in a sport and exercise laboratory

Ensuring that all individuals are safe during any practical testing is very important. It is essential that any risks are minimised to both the participant and the administrator. To avoid danger you should complete a number of checks to ensure your testing remains safe and successful.

Health and safety

To ensure that those taking part in field- and laboratory-based testing remain free from harm, it is important that every precaution is taken to avoid any potential dangers. These dangers could create an injury to both the participant, also referred to as the subject, and you as the administering sports scientist. It is important that you take time to carefully plan and prepare your testing to avoid potential hazards, ensuring that no harm comes to all.

Prior to testing you should take the opportunity to reflect on potential dangers that could cause your participant harm. It is important that all those involved with carrying out the testing have clearly defined roles and responsibilities, as they may be required to oversee part of the testing or more often, the complete testing process. These roles and responsibilities may cover:

- **Participant safety** – Ensuring they are happy to continue and identify any signs or reasons as to why the test should stop, e.g. feeling faint or unable to cope with the demands of the activity.
- **Safe administration of method** – Ensuring that the activity is completed for the duration that is set out and agreed upon with the participant.
- **Equipment safety** – Ensuring that equipment is used appropriately to avoid damage or injury.

- **Recording data** – Ensuring data is safely recorded using appropriate measuring techniques.
- **Safe equipment handling** – Ensuring equipment is safely used during the testing and packed away after the testing procedures.

Each role will have a specific responsibility that will allow a sports scientist to safely apply and manage the testing both during and after, enabling them to restrict the potential dangers.

A dedicated sports technician may perform a number of these duties. They may provide a supporting role to a sports scientist, ensuring that precautions are taken to manage any potential dangers. They may manage the field or laboratory testing environment, checking for safety and that the equipment is used appropriately. It is essential that all equipment is maintained to the highest standard in order to avoid causing potential injury to both the sports scientist or testing subject.

Risk management

A risk may be referred to as any situation whereby there is a potential danger that could create harm or injury. For example, if a test requires you to run on an uneven surface, there could be a potential 'risk' of suffering an ankle injury due to the additional stress that may be placed on the joint, or even falling over during the activity.

When preparing for testing it is important we take sufficient steps to avoid these dangers. Avoidance strategies may include carrying out a risk assessment that can identify any concerns which may be of a potential danger during testing. It is important to note that not all risks can be eliminated; however, attempts need to be made to minimise them to an acceptable level.

Using a risk assessment will enable you to list potential hazards. The assessment allows you to identify:

- who is at risk during the testing
- the action that needs to be taken to avoid the potential danger

Risk Assessment					
Potential hazard	**Who is at risk?**	**Existing control measures**	**Risk rating**	**Preventative measures**	**Responsibilities**

Table 4.2 Risk assessment template

Risk Assessment Matrix

Matrix below provides leaders a process to assess risk based on severity and probability of each hazard. The point where the severity row and probability column intersect defines the level of risk of a hazard. Taking unnecessary risk is unacceptable.

Severity \ Probability		Frequent	Likely	Occasional	Seldom	Unlikely
		A	B	C	D	E
Catastrophic	I	E	E	H	H	M
Critical	II	E	H	H	M	L
Moderate	IV	H	M	M	L	L
Negligible	V	M	L	L	L	L

Definitions of Severity
- **Catastrophic**: Death or permanent total disability, system loss, major property damage
- **Critical**: Permanent partial disability, temporary total disability in excess of 3 months, major system damage, significant property damage
- **Moderate**: Minor injury lost workday accident, compensable injury or illness, minor system damage, minor property damage
- **Negligible**: First Aid or minor supportive medical treatment, minor system impairment

Definitions of Probability
- **Frequent**: Occurs often, continuously experienced
- **Likely**: Occurs several times
- **Occasional**: Occurs sporadically
- **Seldom**: Unlikely, but could occur at some time
- **Unlikely**: Can assume it will not occur

Definition of Risk Levels (combining severity and probability)
- **E = Extremely High**: Loss of ability to accomplish mission if hazards occur during mission
- **H = High**: Significant degradation of mission capabilities if hazards occur during mission
- **M = Moderate**: Minor injury, lost workday accident, compensable injury or illness, minor system damage, minor property damage
- **L = Low**: Little or no impact on mission accomplishment

Figure 4.1 Traffic light risk assessment

- a scale to rate the risk and determine how much of a threat it is to the testing process
- steps that can be taken to try and minimise the effects of the identified risk
- the individual who has the responsibility for dealing with the action taken.

There are a range of risk assessment templates that can be used. One way to assess risk is demonstrated in Table 4.2, by considering all potential hazards, who is at risk, the 'risk rating', and the measures that are or could be put in place to reduce risk. The traffic light assessment (Figure 4.1) uses green, amber and red to identify potential areas of risk, with red representing high levels of risk and green low levels. As already mentioned, not all risks may be overcome; however, like the risk rating system, the traffic light colours can identify the dangers involved, and help you to decide upon a level of acceptability when testing.

If an unforeseen risk has caused harm or danger during a testing activity, it is important that it is reported and recorded using an accident report form – see Figure 4.2. By recording the accident, it can help you avoid any future reoccurrences. To reduce the potential for another repeated accident, you can:

- reflect on the testing protocol used
- identify changes in future safety
- make the appropriate adjustments to safety procedures, and
- minimise potential harm in the future.

If the accident is serious then the Reporting of Injuries, Diseases and Dangerous Occurrences Regulations (RIDDOR, 2013) state that by law the Health and Safety Executive must be informed.

Activity: Risk assessment

Carry out your risk assessment in a testing environment. Ensure that all the risks are identified and note of how each of them may be overcome.

Accident report form

These details should also be recorded in the Accident Book, where one exists.

About the person who had the accident			
Full Name			
Address			
Postcode		Age if under 16	
Occupation			
Activity being undertaken at time of the accident			

About the person reporting the accident (if not the same as above)			
Full Name			
Address			
Postcode		Age if under 16	
Occupation			
Role being undertaken at time of the accident			
Signature		Date	

About the accident – when and where			
Date it took place		Time	
Where it took place; room or location			

Activity: Risk assessment

About the accident – what happened	
How did the accident happen? What was the cause?	
If there were any injuries – what were they?	
Signature of employer or person in charge	

Figure 4.2 Accident report form template

If there is a potential for harm, it is important that you are aware of first aid procedures and where they are available at the testing centre. A qualified first aider or a facility to contact emergency services must be accessible in case an incident requires immediate medical attention. Should there be an accident, it is important to raise the alarm before any attempt is made to support the participant. Once you have raised the alarm you should consider **D**anger, **R**esponse, **A**irway, **B**reathing and **C**irculation. Rolling the patient into the recovery position may be required until emergency help arrives. CPR could be carried out if you have been trained to do so. Further information may be found online at the St. Johns Ambulance website. However, reading about first aid and emergency responses is no substitute for attending a first aid course.

www.sja.org.uk

It is important that all those taking part in the testing procedure, including both you as the sports scientist and the participating subject, remain safe throughout the activities. If there has been harm or there is a potential for danger to anyone involved within the testing, it is important that the test is terminated. It is the responsibility of the sports scientist to ensure no harm comes to those participating within the testing. For example, if a test requires a subject to run on a treadmill and they are at risk of collapse, it is important that the test is stopped in order to avoid them falling and being propelled off the machine.

Testing environment

During any testing, the environmental conditions can have a significant influence on the results.

It is important that we use every opportunity to ensure the environment remains sterile and stable for testing. Hygiene is extremely important as not only does it prevent unwanted germs and potential diseases, it can also affect the outcomes of the recorded results. By sterilising all equipment we are able to reduce the risk of cross-contamination which could affect another participant's results during the testing process. For example, when conducting a test for Peak Flow, it is important we sterilise the mouthpiece thoroughly following each test or use a disposable mouthpiece. By blowing through the measuring equipment, the mouthpiece can transfer many germs that can cause unwanted sickness, colds, and in extreme cases, hepatitis B.

Conducting your testing in a stable environment will allow you to gather results which have the greatest potential to be more accurate and/or reliable. These are of greater importance to us when conducting a study, as they can allow you to make more accurate conclusions and determine the testing outcomes more clearly. For example, exercising in changeable surface conditions can have a considerable effect on the outcome of results. Sprinting on a wet running track can cause the foot to slip during each running stride leading to a loss in power. Inevitably this will affect speed and sprint time therefore it would not be suitable to compare these results against a time set in dry track conditions. Another example can be seen when there are changes in temperature and humidity. If you were to participate in testing during high temperatures, your body's sweat rate, muscle performance and even your motivational desire to succeed, can all change which could influence the outcome of your results. It is important that every effort is made to ensure the environment remains stable in order to gather results that are more accurate and reliable.

Equipment preparation

Prior to testing it is important to check the condition of all the equipment. Basic checks may include checking for batteries, stock-check of items that are regularly used (e.g. stopwatches), checking that equipment is correctly fixed into position, and ensuring that data capture devices are communicating correctly with computers, e.g. chest belt and watches are in contact with heart rate monitors. In this way you will ensure that all of the equipment is fit for purpose and ready for the session you intend to run. These kind of checks are vital to ensure that a session doesn't become interrupted and its outcome is accurate.

It is also important that safety checks are carried out frequently both prior to and following testing activities. Some safety checks will be specific to the piece of equipment, so you should ensure you are familiar with its safe operation. As the sports scientist, you and a sports technician should ensure that all equipment is returned, it is checked and packed away following each of the testing activities. If any equipment is faulty, it should be reported and returned to full working order immediately.

So that testing remains accurate, it is important that the equipment is checked regularly and calibrated. The calibration resets the accuracy of the measure, ensuring consistency and reliability for future testing. Inaccurate measurements can affect the outcome of the study which can lead to a misleading conclusion. Therefore it is essential that the equipment is well maintained, checked and calibrated regularly.

Testing questionnaires

Once a subject has agreed to take part in a study, it is important that you carry out a number of pre-test checks to assess whether they are fit enough to take part. This process is more commonly referred to as health screening, whereby a subject is provided with a questionnaire and asked a number of relevant questions about their health to check their suitability for participation. The information gathered regularly is qualitative, meaning that the responses are more descriptive in response than numerical (quantitative).

Assessments that are more frequently used include a Physical Activity Readiness Questionnaire (PAR-Q), and health and lifestyle questionnaires.

Typical questions in a PAR-Q form are:

1 Has your doctor ever said that you have a heart condition and that you should only do physical activity recommended by a doctor?

2 Do you feel pain in your chest when you do physical activity?

3 In the past month, have you had chest pain when you were not doing physical activity?

4 Do you lose your balance because of dizziness or do you ever lose consciousness?

5 Do you have a bone or joint problem (for example, back, knee or hip) that could be made worse by a change in your physical activity?

6 Is your doctor currently prescribing drugs (for example, water pills) for your blood pressure or heart condition?

7 Do you know of any other reason why you should not do physical activity?

If your subject has answered yes to any of these questions, then it is essential they seek medical advice from their GP before taking any further part. You will always have the overall responsibility for the health and safety of your participant, and may be liable for any harm or injury caused as a result of neglect prior to, during, or after the testing process. Questionnaires on health and lifestyle may assess a participant's background to activity, their exercise habits, and diet. They may also take basic health measures such as heart rate, blood pressure, height, weight, and estimate BMI. Medical questionnaires may focus more on identifying conditions such as diabetes, epilepsy, cardiovascular related conditions, and medical family history.

These questionnaires may focus upon a specific capability, e.g. injury or medical history. While they are more specific, they do not provide a general overview of the participant's health, therefore they should only supplement the pre-test screening questionnaires. The information gathered helps to keep both the subject and you safe, while enabling the risk assessment to be updated to identify any further considerations when administering the testing procedure.

Assessments can identify health issues, such as heart related problems or lung conditions such as asthma, or long-term injuries. All of these may affect the testing outcomes. When providing a subject with a questionnaire, you should encourage them to answer it truthfully and be as accurate as possible. By gaining accurate information, it will allow you to be prepared for most eventualities.

HEALTH QUESTIONNAIRE

Have you, or do you suffer from any of the following?

Asthma ☐	Constipation ☐	Rheumatic fever ☐
Angina ☐	Diabetes ☐	High cholesterol ☐
High blood pressure ☐	Frequent colds ☐	Palpitations ☐
Low blood pressure ☐	Dizziness/fainting ☐	Headaches ☐
Epilepsy ☐	Heart disease ☐	Migraines ☐
Arthritis ☐	Shortness of breath ☐	Joint pains ☐

Please provide details where applicable. _____

Have any of your first-degree relatives experienced the following conditions?

Heart attack ☐   Heart operation ☐   Congenital heart ☐   High cholesterol ☐
disease

Have you ever had surgery?   Yes ☐   No ☐
If yes, give details.

Please list any injuries you've had in the past, e.g., broken bones, sprains, etc.

Figure 4.3 Example of a medical questionnaire that may be used prior to testing

Subject preparation

Once you have chosen your subject, they have agreed to participate and they have been screened, it is important that they receive a medical health check. While this health check may be dependent on the fitness testing being carried out, the measures will help you determine whether the subject is fit to participate.

Pre-test health check measures are more frequently quantitative measures that are numerically recorded. The data aims to identify the suitability of the participant based on physical health measures. For example, if a test requires maximal strength heavy lifting, a subject who has high blood pressure problems would not be suitable due to health concerns. High blood pressure and heavy lifting should be avoided due to a number of life-threatening health conditions such as a stroke and heart attack.

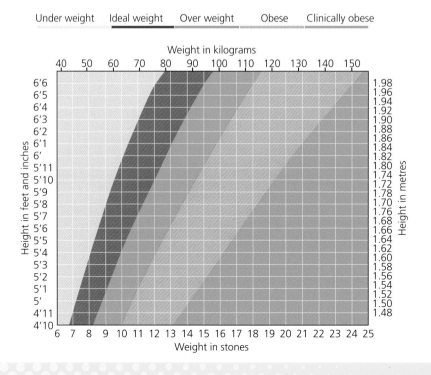

Figure 4.4 BMI body composition estimate table

Examples of health check measurements may include height, weight, blood pressure, heart rate, Body Mass Index (BMI), and forced lung expiration. The equipment that may be used includes a stadiometer (height), body weighing scales (weight), a sphygmomanometer (blood pressure), a heart rate monitor (heart rate), weight and height calculations (BMI) and a Peak Flow meter (forced expiration). The BMI calculation formula is:

$$BMI (\%) = Weight (kg) / Height^2 (m)$$

Along with the pre-test health check measures, it is important that you inform the participant subject of all the procedures that are to be performed. For some tests it may not be suitable as it could interfere with, or cause the subject to change their behaviour. For example, if your psychological belief in your own ability does not reflect your physiological ability, it could affect your motivation which cause you to underperform.

When your subject has been informed of the testing protocol, an informed consent and subject disclaimer will need to be completed. Informed consent is a procedure whereby a subject provides a signed agreement to participate in the testing activities, that will be administered by you as the sports scientist. This may also be referred to as a subject disclaimer and can be considered as a legally-binding document. It is important to remember that the subject only agrees to perform the tests that you have planned for, it will not cover any other additional unplanned activities. If your study requires a change to the protocol, a new agreement is usually required to avoid any potential safety concerns.

Once the initial preparations have been completed, you can prepare your subject for test participation. It is important that your subject dresses appropriately for testing. The wearing of unsuitable clothing may influence the outcome of your results. For example, if a subject was to wear jeans when

Informed Consent		
(Title of the project)		
Participant's name		
We intive you to take part in_____ which seeks to _____on the _____ /20_____ . Participating in this project is totally voluntary.		
The purposes of this project are		
You are being offered this opportunity because		
An estimated_____ number of people will participate in this _____. The duration of this project will be_____ . If you agree to participate in this project, your involvement will last for_____ and you may also be required to_____ By signing below, you agree to take in the project.		

Name	Signature	Date

Figure 4.5 Example of an Informed Consent form that may be used prior to testing

completing a sit and reach test to assess their hip flexibility, this would not be suitable as they can restrict the movement needed to complete the test. If the subject was to wear appropriate loose fitting clothing, this would give them the freedom of movement needed to accurately perform the test.

A2 Ethical considerations when conducting sport and exercise testing

As we know, the safety of both the participating subject and you as the sports scientist, is very important during any testing activities. To ensure you all remain protected throughout, it is important you follow appropriate standards and legislations. The following of standards and legislations is often referred to as the planning and use of ethical testing.

Ethical testing is a moral code of guidelines that ensure the sports scientist conducts their tests professionally during any practical assessments. The guidelines may govern the application of a testing protocol, age of the subjects used, types of test to be performed, the sports scientist behaviour and relationship with the subjects, medical practices to be used, the sharing of sensitive information and confidentiality. The list in non-exhaustive as there are many considerations that must be examined and agreed upon prior to commencing the testing.

Security

The recording of sensitive information may be required in many field and laboratory tests and it is very important that it is safely stored to protect confidentiality. All data should be recorded a anonymously, with each individual being referred to as a 'subject' or 'participant'. By using these terms, the participant subject cannot be identified by any other individual involved except for the managing sports

scientist. While there are legislations regarding the sharing of sensitive information, without the use of anonymity some subjects may be reluctant to provide sensitive information.

For example, subjects may feel reluctant to provide information on their bodyweight, body fat, heart rate and blood pressure, in fear of being ridiculed by their peers. By keeping all information anonymously, we are able to maintain subject confidentiality which is essential for many testing procedures.

When data is collected it is important that it is stored in a secure environment. The security facility may vary from a lockable cupboard or cabinet, to a password protected electronic document. Any facility that is used should only be accessed by the managing sports scientist and not be shared, for example with friends or unrelated organisations.

The Data Protection Act (1998) controls the use of personal information across organisations and businesses. The Act prevents the unlawful sharing of people's personal information and outlines the expectations for its secure storage. It is the responsibility of the sports scientist to follow these regulations and securely store all information in a protective facility. Should any information be shared unlawfully, the sports scientist may be at risk of prosecution.

Protocol familiarisation and ethics forms

Before testing it is important that you become familiar with the protocol being used. This may involve a rehearsal or a practice with specific equipment. By practising with the equipment it may also allow you to:

- make additional safety checks
- identify any additional risks for their assessment
- ensure all equipment is working correctly
- identify areas that may require a specific skills-set.

Subject	Resting Pulse (bpm)	Blood Pressure (mmHg)	Height (cm)	Weight (kg)	BMI (%)	Waist/Hip Ratio	Peak Flow (L.min⁻¹)	Age (Yrs)
1	68	131/89	187	94	27	0.83	590	18
2	66	129/79	172	56	19	0.67	450	17
3	61	141/71	170	61	21	0.82	450	17
4	65	127/67	177	76	24	0.82	500	18

Figure 4.6 Example of data collection with 'subject anonymity'

All testing within sports science should be rigorously checked before you begin testing. To achieve this, you would be expected to complete a detailed ethics form. It is a complex process that provides an in-depth justification of the testing to be carried out and requires a presentation to a panel of experts who will decide upon its suitability. This panel may consist of selected research specialists, professors and doctors. The panel may consider a number of options including:

- the type of subject participants to be tested (age, gender, disability)
- the protocol to be used
- the study aims and outcomes
- the facility required.

The ethics panel may provide further guidance on the testing procedures, identifying where changes could be made, or even feel that the study is not appropriate for testing. The panel aims to ensure that the testing is functional, appropriate, and safe for all those taking part.

Subject welfare

Subject welfare should remain paramount during any testing. It is the responsibility of the sports scientist to ensure the safety of the subject is maintained throughout the testing. Any neglect or failure to maintain appropriate care could lead to prosecution. Prior to testing the sports scientist should assess whether the participant is fit enough to take part. During the testing it is essential that they continue to monitor their progress and make regular checks on their progress. When testing children or vulnerable groups, it is essential that you complete and pass a DBS (Disclosure and Barring Service) application, previously known as a CRB (Criminal Records Bureau) check. By completing this application it will enable you to work with children or vulnerable groups which may be essential to complete your testing. The DBS assesses an individual's previous criminal history and can identify a risk that may be caused to others.

It is important that rigorous child protection policies are in place prior to any testing. The lead sports scientist should always be familiar with child protection and safeguarding policies, as they will protect the safety of children and vulnerable groups at all times.

Any testing should take into consideration the needs of an individual or a group. These might be related to age, disability or injuries. For example, tests that rely on heavy weightlifting or regular impact jumping would not be suitable for a child who is still growing due to the damage it may cause. Therefore, special consideration should be made and alternatives selected.

A3 Validity and reliability of testing protocols when conducting sport and exercise assessments

When conducting field and laboratory testing, it is important that you collect accurate results for analysis. The accuracy is dependent on a variety of factors, however, and the use of an appropriate protocol and collection technique can have a significant effect on the testing outcome. To ensure you gather accurate data, it is important that the testing protocol is valid and reliable.

Validity

Validity may be defined as the extent to which a test measures what it has been designed to measure. When applied to field and laboratory testing, it refers to the sports scientist selecting the most suitable test to identify a component they wish to investigate.

For example, if your aim is to test a subject's maximum oxygen uptake (VO_2 max), the test you could choose is a multi-stage fitness test rather than a vertical jump test. The multi-stage fitness test requires the subject to make repeated shuttle runs without stopping over 20 metres, keeping in time with a recorded bleep which increases in frequency throughout the duration of the test. This test requires the subject to run at a sub-maximal pace, challenging their aerobic capabilities and providing an estimate of their maximum oxygen uptake.

Unlike the multi-stage fitness test, the vertical jump test does not require an aerobic component to complete the test. As a consequence this would not be suitable in providing an accurate measure of maximum oxygen uptake. If you were to try and use a vertical jump test, it would not be a valid measure as it does not test what it aims to test.

Being familiar with a test can help you identify and apply the most valid testing procedure. By using the most appropriate testing procedure, correctly carrying out pre-test preparations and calibrating all equipment, you can improve the likelihood that your testing is valid during data collection. Validity may be statistically analysed to check for acceptable data differences in results. The differences may be used to check the accuracy of a testing protocol. The calculations we produce can help us examine the significance of a testing protocol and help us to accept or reject the results produced.

Reliability

Reliability may be defined as a characteristic of a measurement that produces consistent results. The reproduction of results implies that when your testing is repeated, you will be able to reproduce similar results within an acceptable range. Like validity, the selection of suitable equipment is important in order to produce reliable results. The test must be able to reproduce results consistently and not arrive at results with luck, i.e. a one-off result. This feature is very important to a sports scientist as it allows them to collect results with accuracy and draw conclusions with greater certainty.

Reliability and validity are often confused and misunderstood. While they are closely related, both have different applications when preparing a test. It is important to remember that validity focuses on the appropriateness of a testing protocol, whereas the reliability focuses on the consistency of a protocol to deliver similar results. Understanding this, it is important that a sports scientist chooses a reliable test in order to make it valid. However, it is possible to select a test that is not valid, though can still be reliable.

To ensure testing protocols are reliable, it is important you take repeated measures. For example, the reliability of measuring body fat skinfold data is mainly down to the skill and consistency of the measurer. If a subject has their measurements taken by an inexperienced sports scientist, they are less likely to record consistent readings due to the specialist skill needed to be accurate. This would not reflect the true values of the subject. If the same person tried to measure the same person again the next day they would get different results. In this way the data they have collected is unreliable, and the test has become invalid.

While skinfold measures require a high level of skill, even the most experienced sports scientist will take slightly different measurements each time. Taking repetitive measures can help to minimise this problem, as taking the mean of a number of measurements reduces the risk that one of the measurements is unreliable.

Like validity, reliability can also be statistically analysed in order to determine its accuracy. Calculations on the similarity of results can be made to identify correlations. These can recognise potential trends and show links between data. As with validity, all consistencies are subject to acceptable data differences when analysing its outcome.

Testing variables

All protocols used within field and laboratory testing are influenced by a range of testing variables. A testing variable is a changeable component that may influence an experimental protocol to influence the final results.

Environmental conditions can be one variable that may be difficult to control when conducting field-based testing. As temperature and weather conditions cannot be controlled during field testing, it is something that needs to be considered when planning a study. In order to overcome these conditions, it is important to make attempts to use situations where environmental conditions may remain relatively consistent, e.g. similar weather conditions. Environmental changes can influence a range of physiological and psychological responses that can impact on the results collected.

Performer motivation can prove difficult with subject participation. If a subject is poorly motivated, this may influence the experimental outcomes. It is important that you try to keep all subjects positive and engaged in testing throughout a study.

Another variable in a test is the **pre-test physical condition** of the performer. Your test may of course be investigating the effect this variable has on a performance, however, if your test is assuming that all performers are at the same level of skill or physical fitness, then you need to be aware that this is not the case.

In order for a protocol to be used, it should be robust and reliable. It is important that clear boundaries are set with clear instructions provided. The protocol should be **suitable** to the level of participant subjects. For example, a group of subjects may respond more positively if the protocol explanation is direct with few instructions; however, others may require more of a detailed explanation to understand the testing expectations. The protocol suitability should consider the subject's capabilities. If the protocol is perceived as too complex, too difficult or unattainable, this could affect motivation and the success of the study.

When testing subjects who are still undergoing **growth and maturation**, it is important to consider the protocol to be used. Firstly, the testing needs to be carefully planned to avoid any potential harm coming to the participants. This harm may affect both physical and psychological attributes. As their body has not fully matured, tests need to be carefully considered to avoid any potential injury. High intensity strength-based tests should be avoided as this can impact upon skeletal development. Furthermore, the use of repetitive weight bearing activities should also be restricted as this can have a similar effect on musculoskeletal development. All testing should be appropriate as the outcome can have a significant influence on the validity and reliability of the study results.

A Check your understanding

1. Define the term 'validity' and explain how it relates to a testing method.
2. Define the term 'reliability' and explain how it relates to a testing method.
3. A tester begins to use a piece of equipment, however, on three separate occasions they gather very different results. What could be the problem and how may it be overcome?
4. Why is ethical testing crucial to the safety of those being tested?
5. What is the function of a PAR-Q and why is it important?
6. Why is it important that we don't share testing data that's been collected from our subject participants?

Distinction activity: Preparation for fitness testing (A D1)

You are planning to conduct a series of physical fitness tests within a field- and laboratory-based environment. You must ensure that all health and safety procedures are followed and that your testing is both valid and reliable.

1. Prepare and conduct a detailed risk assessment of your testing environment. Identify any concerns you feel could cause harm to your participants and how they may be overcome.
2. Prepare and carry out a health and lifestyle questionnaire on your subject to check they are fit to participate. Evaluate the results to check their suitability and record all observations.
3. Complete an ethics form that details your research proposal, how you will conduct it and the stages involved. Within the report explain why the reasons will be both valid and reliable.

B Undertake anthropometry and somatotype testing procedures in sport (B P3 , B P4 , B M2 , B M3 , B D2)

B1 Anthropometric assessment methods applied within the sport and exercise laboratory

The analysis of the human body has long been associated with both health identification and sporting success. Within sports science, body shape can be assessed using a range of methods which can help profile an individual's sporting success. The methods need to provide accuracy so that the sports scientist can draw reliable conclusions from the information provided.

Anthropometry

The term anthropometry may be defined as the measurement and study of the body's dimensions and proportions. It is a long established science and not something which is limited to sports science as it has many health and industry applications. Anthropometry is used within a number of sectors including health assessments, e.g. medical assessments; safety wear, e.g. fitting of safety equipment such as a helmet; and product design, e.g. seating.

Health applications can enable medical professionals to identify future health risks based on their body size and measurements. For example, it has long been established that individuals who carry too much fat around their waist, have a greater increased risk of suffering heart disease, type 2 diabetes and cancer. Understanding this, many health professionals are able to use a range of anthropometric techniques to help identify people who may potentially develop future health conditions.

Sports performers are often able to be categorised into a size and proportion. Their body composition has a significant role in determining their success alongside their fitness, skills and psychological traits. For example, in a game of rugby the heavier and larger players predominantly engage within the scrum whereas the faster and lighter players stand at the back, waiting to run onto a pass. The scrum can be used to drive an opponent's team backwards using the larger and heavier players, as both their weight and strength can help to generate the momentum needed for movement. When passing the ball from the scrum, the faster and lighter players make fast breaks and attack the opposing team using their speed and agility. Due to their body composition, both groups of players have different responsibilities on the pitch though must work together as a team to score a try.

In sports science we are able to categorise performers based on their composition and in some cases, identify future international and Olympic-winning performers. Many physical characteristics can determine success therefore sports scientists are able to profile individuals in order to help them with their competitive career goals.

Testing guidelines

As we know, you as the sports scientist are responsible for the care and safety of your subject participant throughout any testing procedure. It is important that you pay attention to their needs and responses throughout the testing in order to avoid any harm. All participants will have different support needs as understandably, everyone is different. As the sports scientist you should try to take reasonable steps to accommodate these needs. For example, some participants may need extensive instructions to complete a testing protocol whereas others may require a simple demonstration.

However, it is important that we stick closely to the protocol planned in order to avoid any misunderstanding during the testing process. As we know, it is important we inform the subject of the testing procedures and follow the guidelines of the testing process. The guidelines will be approved by the subject participant when they sign their subject disclaimer, which provides an agreement to take part in the activity set out. It is important we do not deviate from this protocol or change the testing midway, as this could cause conflict and the subject then has the right to withdraw from the testing process.

Skinfold analysis and methods of measurement

In field- and laboratory-based testing there are a range of assessment methods we can use to determine the body composition of an individual. One such method includes the measurement of the skinfold thickness from various sites around the body. By measuring the subcutaneous fat, we are able to calculate body density and body fat percentage.

> ### Key term
>
> Subcutaneous fat is the fatty deposit known as adipose tissue, which is found directly under the skin's surface. It is more visual and often associated with the only source of fat within the human body. However, additional fat may also be found deep within the body around the organs. This is known as visceral fat and is another source that can cause an individual to be overweight.

The guidelines for collecting this anthropometric skinfold measurement requires the use of a skinfold calliper which takes a skin pinch of the top layer of skin, which is pulled away from the muscle underneath. It is important that the layers are separated as grabbing muscle will give an inaccurate measure for their skinfold assessment.

Skinfold measurement technique

All measurements should be taken on the right side of the body, with the subject standing.

1 From a predetermined marked location on the body, gently pick up skin between your thumb and forefinger and ease it away from the main body. The sample you have is now the subcutaneous fat and not the muscle which lays beneath.

2 Using the skinfold calliper, gently clamp the jaws around the skin sample, ensuring that the jaws are of equal depth around the sample in order to take a reliable measure. While the measure is being taken you should maintain the grip of the skin with your thumb and forefinger.

3 Once attached, relax the grip and allow the calliper to apply its full closing force to take the sample.

4 After two seconds, record the measure to the nearest millimetre and remove the callipers gently, and release the skin with your thumb and forefinger.

5 Repeat steps 1 to 4 an additional two times and take an additional measure if the results show significant variation.

There are a number of methods that may be used to estimate body fat percentage, each of which varies depending on the number of measures and locations taken. Ultimately, each of the methods should be both valid and reliable, therefore we should always ensure we follow the protocol test guidelines in order for the results to remain consistent.

Activity: Assessing the skinfold measures

1 Using the skinfold measurement technique, take measures from your partner around the body to examine their total measures.
2 Use all the sites in Figure 4.8.
3 Record all of your data into a clear table for interpretation.
4 Compare your results against that of your partner and comment on the differences.

Methods of measurement

Durnin and Womersley assessment measure method

The Durnin and Womersley assessment method uses four sites of measurement. Collecting skinfold measures from the biceps, triceps, subscapular and suprailiac, you can calculate body density and body fat percentage. Having followed the protocol and

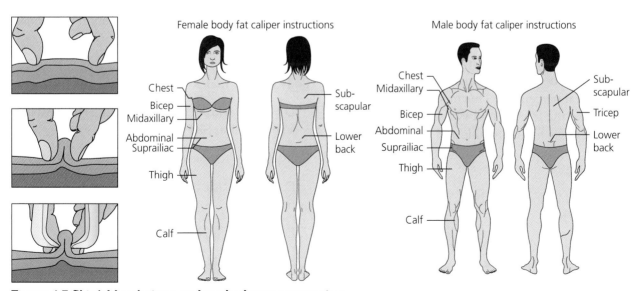

Figure 4.7 Skinfold technique and method assessment sites

Age (years)	Equations for males	Equations for females
< 17	D = 1.1533 – (0.0643 X L)	D = 1.1369 – (0.0598 X L)
17–19	D = 1.1620 – (0.0630 X L)	D = 1.1549 – (0.0678 X L)
20–29	D = 1.1631 – (0.0632 X L)	D = 1.1599 – (0.0717 X L)
30–39	D = 1.1422 – (0.0544 X L)	D = 1.1423 – (0.0632 X L)
40–49	D = 1.1620 – (0.0700 X L)	D = 1.1333 – (0.0612 X L)
>50	D = 1.1715 – (0.0779 X L)	D = 1.1339 – (0.0645 X L)

Table 4.3 The Durnin and Womersley assessment method, **D** = Predicted density (g/ml), **L** = log of the total of the 4 skinfold measurements (mm) (*Source:* Topend Sports)

taken the data recordings you need to firstly calculate the body density. To do this you must follow a set equation which is shown in Table 4.3.

Having calculated body density we then need to use this data to calculate the body fat percentage. To do this we use a separate equation, known as the Siri Equation, which enables you to divide the body density into fat mass and fat-free mass, e.g. bones.

Siri Equation

% Body Fat = [(4.95 / Body Density) – 4.5] x 100

Having followed both formulas, we now have an estimated body fat percentage which enables us to assess our body composition.

Jackson and Pollock assessment measure method

A second method you can use is the Jackson and Pollock assessment method which requires you to use seven measurement sites. The areas to be measured are the triceps, chest, midaxillary, subscapular, suprailiac, abdominal, and mid-thigh. When we have collected this data we are able to calculate the body density, and then calculate the body fat percentage. This method is slightly different to the Durnin and Womersley as it is able to differentiate between male and female subjects by using different calculations to estimate their body density.

Jackson and Pollock 7-site body density equation for male subjects:

D = 1.112 – (0.00043499 x ΣSKF) + (0.00000055 x ΣSKF2) – (0.00028826 x age)

Jackson and Pollock 7-site body density equation for female subjects:

D = 1.097 – (0.00046971 x ΣSKF) + (0.00000056 x ΣSKF2) – (0.00012828 x age)

D = Density (g/ml)

SKF = Skinfold measurements (mm)

Σ = sum

Having calculated the body density using this 7-site method, we are able to then calculate the body fat percentage using the Siri Equation which again separates the body fat from the fat-free mass.

Using an alternative method, you are able to differentiate between male and female subjects by using the Sloan Equation. Using this calculation you can gain additional body density results that may also be used to assess the body fat percentage. Again, you would use the Siri Equation to calculate the body fat percentage.

Sloan Equation

Body density males:

D = 1.1043 – (0.001327 x mid-thigh SKF) – (0.00131 x subscapular SKF)

Body density females:

D = 1.0764 – (0.0008 x iliac crest SKF) – (0.00088 x tricep SKF)

D = Density (g/ml)

SKF = Skinfold measurements (mm)

With different calculations we are able to make a comparison against norms data, that enables us to identify acceptable differences within a given population or against a group of sports performers. If there are significant unacceptable differences, it can allow you to develop strategies to ensure that the body composition is returned to its ideal standard.

Key term

Norms data is the ideal standard which is estimated for a given population. The norms data is an average value which is set to acceptable standards. Health applications may include obesity where a population is recommended to maintain body fat levels in order to avoid premature death or related illnesses.

Body fat chart for men (%)

Age																	
18–20	2.0	3.9	6.2	8.5	10.5	12.5	14.3	16.0	17.5	18.9	20.2	21.3	22.3	23.1	23.8	24.3	24.9
21–25	2.5	4.9	7.3	9.5	11.6	13.6	15.4	17.0	18.6	20.0	21.2	22.3	23.3	24.2	24.9	25.4	25.8
26–30	3.5	6.0	8.4	10.6	12.7	14.6	16.4	18.1	19.6	21.0	22.3	23.4	24.4	25.2	25.9	26.5	26.9
31–35	4.5	7.1	9.4	11.7	13.7	15.7	17.5	19.2	20.7	22.1	23.4	24.5	25.5	26.3	27.0	27.5	28.0
36–40	5.6	8.1	10.5	12.7	14.8	16.8	18.6	20.2	21.8	23.2	24.4	25.6	26.5	27.4	28.1	28.6	29.0
41–45	6.7	9.2	11.5	13.8	15.9	17.8	19.6	21.3	22.8	24.7	25.5	26.6	27.6	28.4	29.1	29.7	30.1
46–50	7.7	10.2	12.6	14.8	16.9	18.9	20.7	22.4	23.9	25.3	26.6	27.7	28.7	29.5	30.2	30.7	31.2
51–55	8.8	11.3	13.7	15.9	18.0	20.0	21.8	23.4	25.0	26.4	27.6	28.7	29.7	30.6	31.2	31.8	32.2
56 & UP	9.9	12.4	14.7	17.0	19.1	21.0	22.8	24.5	26.0	27.4	28.7	29.8	30.8	31.6	32.3	32.9	33.3
	Lean				Ideal				Average					Above average			

Body fat chart for women (%)

Age																	
18–20	11.3	13.5	15.7	17.7	19.7	21.5	23.2	24.8	26.3	27.7	29.0	30.2	31.3	32.3	33.1	33.9	34.6
21–25	11.9	14.2	16.3	18.4	20.3	22.1	23.8	25.5	27.0	28.4	29.6	30.8	31.9	32.9	33.8	34.5	35.2
26–30	12.5	14.8	16.9	19.0	20.9	22.7	24.5	26.1	27.6	29.0	30.3	31.5	32.5	33.5	34.4	35.2	35.8
31–35	13.2	15.4	17.6	19.6	21.5	23.4	25.1	26.7	28.2	28.6	30.9	32.1	33.2	34.1	35.0	35.8	36.4
36–40	13.8	16.0	18.2	20.2	22.2	24.0	25.7	27.3	28.8	30.2	31.5	32.7	33.8	34.8	35.6	36.4	37.0
41–45	14.4	16.7	18.8	20.8	22.8	24.6	26.3	27.9	29.4	30.8	32.1	33.3	34.4	35.4	36.3	37.0	37.7
46–50	15.0	17.3	19.4	21.5	23.4	25.2	26.9	28.6	30.1	31.5	32.8	34.0	35.0	36.0	36.9	37.6	38.3
51–55	15.6	17.9	20.0	22.1	24.0	25.9	27.6	29.2	30.7	32.1	33.4	34.6	35.6	36.6	37.5	38.3	38.9
56 & UP	16.3	18.5	20.7	22.7	24.6	26.5	28.2	29.8	31.3	32.7	34.0	35.2	36.3	37.2	38.1	38.9	39.5
	Lean					Ideal			Average						Above average		

Figure 4.8 Body fat charts for men and women (*Source:* **www.bodyfatcharts.com**)

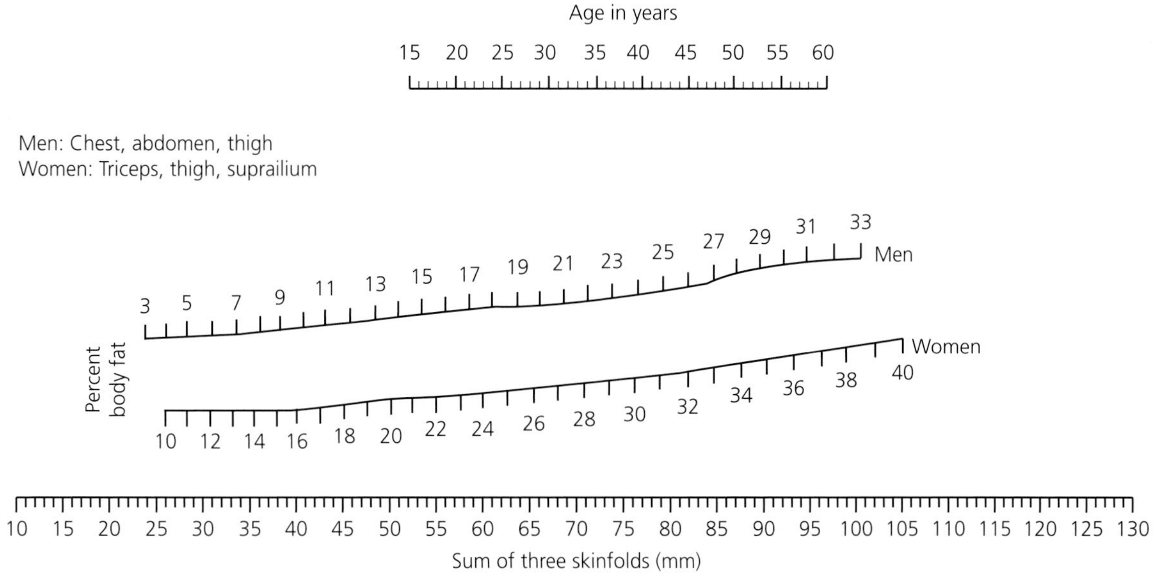

Figure 4.9a a and b Nomogram examples for body fat percentage prediction

Alongside the calculations we are also able to use predictive tables that can be used to estimate body fat percentage by collecting measures and avoiding complex calculations. They can be useful when assessments are completed quickly, however can be less accurate than the calculation methods.

Activity: Comparison of testing methods

1 Measure the body skinfold sites for both the Durnin and Womersley assessment measure method and the Jackson and Pollock assessment measure method.
2 Compare the results. Are there any differences?
3 Explain the outcome of the testing.

Body mass measures

Additional body mass measurements may also be used to estimate body composition. The **Ponderal Index** is a measure of leanness of an individual, making a calculation based on their height and weight. While it can be less accurate than the skinfold measures, it is a simple calculation which like the **Body Mass Index**, can quickly be performed to gain an understanding of body leanness.

To calculate the Ponderal Index we should follow the formula:

$$PI = \text{Weight (kg)} / \text{Height}^3 \text{ (m)}$$

Like the Ponderal Index, **Body Mass Index (BMI)** requires the use of a calculation to provide an estimation of mass. BMI quantifies tissue mass (bones, muscle and fat), and then makes an estimation against agreed normative data. The calculation estimates whether a subject is underweight, normal weight, overweight or obese. It should be emphasised that BMI focuses on mass and not body fat percentage. Many athletes have a high BMI, however have little body fat, therefore, like Ponderal Index, it should not be relied on as a sole estimate of performer body composition. The BMI measures mass and not just fat.

To calculate BMI:

$$BMI (\%) = \text{Weight (kg)} / \text{Height}^2 \text{ (m)}$$

(You can also look at the BMI body composition estimate table on page 158, Figure 4.4.)

Tissue calculations can also identify the body's **Lean Body Mass** alone. By calculating muscle mass you can estimate the total muscle composition in the body and if necessary alter a performer's training plan to improve their performance. Muscle mass is important as it allows us to disregard fat within the calculation and focus primarily on the muscle. Muscle and fat tissue do not weigh the same so the calculations may be more accurate than BMI.

To calculate lean body mass we follow the formula:

Male calculation:

$$LBM \% = (0.32810 \times W) + (0.33929 \times H) - 29.5336$$

Female calculation:

$$LBM \% = (0.29569 \times W) + (0.41813 \times H) - 43.2933$$

W = Weight (kg)

H = Height (cm)

Another assessment on body composition is **Bioelectrical Impedance (BIA)**, which uses a mild electrical current to flow through the body to estimate body fat tissue. The process measures the intensity and speed of the current as muscle, blood and fluid transfer a signal faster than when travelling through bone and fat. To carry out the test, two electrical charge plates must be in contact with the skin and a signal is passed between them. While its accuracy is limited, you are able to use it to predict body fat percentage.

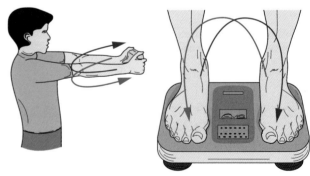

Figure 4.10a and b Bioelectrical impedance measure examples

Hydrostatic weighing is another method which we can use to estimate an individual's fat mass. The procedure requires the use of a dunk tank, allowing you to submerse your subject underwater to make an assessment of fat percentage.

The procedure is based upon Archimedes' principle which states that the buoyant force of a submerged object is equal to the weight of the fluid it displaces. The difference between the scale and underwater weight can be used to calculate body volume. As lean tissue, e.g. bones and muscle, have greater density than water, when they are submerged they will try to sink, creating a weight. However, fat mass is less dense than water and therefore floats. The measurement works by weighing the individual, and if they are significantly lighter underwater than they are on land, this could indicate that there is little muscle mass contained within the body. In essence, muscle sinks and fat floats in water.

Calculating the **Waist to Hip** ratio is also another method that may be used to estimate body composition or more importantly fat distribution. By taking a measurement around the hips and the waist, we can locate where the body mass is mostly located.

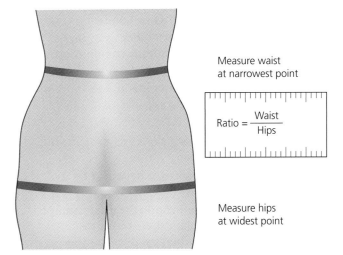

Measure waist at narrowest point

$$Ratio = \frac{Waist}{Hips}$$

Measure hips at widest point

Figure 4.12 Measurement sites and calculation for waist to hip ratio

The test is useful as it can help identify potential health conditions that may be associated with the specific body shape. It is able to identify the 'apple' and 'pear' shaped body which are prone to specific illnesses or conditions. For example, individuals with more of a rounded body shape are more likely to suffer from obesity, type 2 diabetes and heart related problems. By making the calculation we are able to make a comparison against norms data.

Figure 4.11 Example of hydrostatic weighing

Waist to hip circumference ratio standards for men and women

	Age (years)	Disease risk related to obesity			
		Low	Moderate	High	Very high
Men	20–29	<0.83	0.83–0.88	0.89–0.94	>0.94
	30–39	<0.84	0.84–0.91	0.92–0.96	>0.96
	40–49	<0.88	0.88–0.95	0.96–1.00	>1.00
	50–59	<0.90	0.90–0.96	0.97–1.02	>1.02
	60–69	<0.91	0.91–0.98	0.99–1.03	>1.03
Women	20–29	<0.71	0.71–0.77	0.78–0.82	>0.82
	30–39	<0.72	0.72–0.78	0.79–0.84	>0.84
	40–49	<0.73	0.73–0.79	0.80–0.87	>0.87
	50–59	<0.74	0.74–0.81	0.82–0.88	>0.88
	60–69	<0.76	0.76–0.83	0.84–0.90	>0.90

Figure 4.13 Health norms data for waist to hip ratio

B2 Somatotype profiling applied within the sport and exercise laboratory

Somatotype characteristics and appearance

A performer's characteristic shape and physical appearance may be described as their somatotype. There are three categories of somatotype, each of which have their own characteristics of appearance.

1   Endomorphy

2   Ectomorphy

3   Mesomorphy.

Endomorphs are characteristically shorter and rounder in body shape with fat located around the body, upper arms and thighs. They are frequently overweight due to the excessive fat, have wider hips and shoulders. Sports where power-based activity is required, such as powerlifting, benefit from this body size as their endurance can be limited.

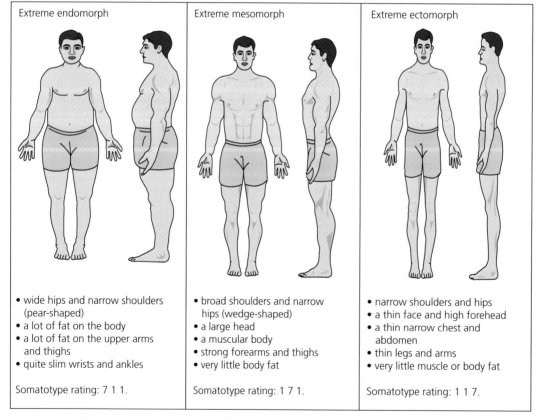

Extreme endomorph

• wide hips and narrow shoulders (pear-shaped)
• a lot of fat on the body
• a lot of fat on the upper arms and thighs
• quite slim wrists and ankles

Somatotype rating: 7 1 1.

Extreme mesomorph

• broad shoulders and narrow hips (wedge-shaped)
• a large head
• a muscular body
• strong forearms and thighs
• very little body fat

Somatotype rating: 1 7 1.

Extreme ectomorph

• narrow shoulders and hips
• a thin face and high forehead
• a thin narrow chest and abdomen
• thin legs and arms
• very little muscle or body fat

Somatotype rating: 1 1 7.

Figure 4.14 Example of somatotype body characteristics (*Source:* www.precisionnutrition.com)

Ectomorphs are slimmer and taller in stature, have limited fat stores and muscle mass. Characteristically they have narrow shoulders and chest, along with a slim waist. These individuals are best suited to distance running and endurance events as fat and muscle requirements are limited.

Mesomorphs appear more muscular and defined in stature. They have limited fat stores and have a larger frame. Similar to ectomorphs, the mesomorph has limited fat body fat though differ in that they have much more muscle mass. They usually have broader shoulders, narrow hips and a larger chest size. These individuals tend to excel in sports that require speed and strength as their muscles and low fat mass enable them to be more dynamic.

Somatotype assessment

Your somatotype can be assessed using the Heath-Carter method which uses the collection of data to calculate your bodies shape and size. The method requires you to measure specific areas of the body and record them onto a Heath-Carter Rating Form. From the data collected you can then perform a series of calculations to establish your body size. The measures you need include:

- Weight
- Height
- Skinfold measures (triceps, subscapular, supraspinale, calf)

HEATH-CARTER SOMATOTYPE RATING FORM

NAME .... AGE .... SEX: M F NO: ....

OCCUPATION .... ETHNIC GROUP .... DATE ....

PROJECT : .... MEASURED BY: ....

SUM 3 SKINFOLDS (mm)

Skinfolds nwn			
Triceps	=	Upper Limit	10.9 14.9 18.9 22.9 26.9 31.2 35.8 40.7 46.2 52.2 58.7 65.7 73.2 81.2 89.7 98.9 108.9 119.7 131.2 143.7 157.2 171.9 187.9 204.0
Subscapular	=	Mid-point	9.0 13.0 17.0 21.0 25.0 29.0 33.5 38.0 43.5 49.0 55.5 62.0 69.5 77.0 85.5 94.0 104.0 114.0 125.5 137.0 150.5 164.0 180.0 196.0
Supraspinale	=	Lower Limit	7.0 11.0 15.0 19.0 23.0 27.0 31.3 35.9 40.8 46.3 52.3 58.8 65.8 73.3 81.3 89.8 99.0 109.0 119.8 131.3 143.8 157.3 172.0 188.0

SUM 3 SKINFOLDS = [ ] x ($\frac{170.18}{ht-}$)   (height corrected skinfolds)

Calf =

| Endomorphy | 1 | 1½ | 2 | 2½ | 3 | 3½ | 4 | 4½ | 5 | 5½ | 6 | 6½ | 7 | 7½ | 8 | 8½ | 9 | 9½ | 10 | 10½ | 11 | 11½ | 12 |

Height cm	[ ]	139.2 143.5 147.3 151.1 154.8 158.8 162.6 166.4 170.2 174.0 177.0 181.6 185.4 189.2 193.0 195.9 200.7 204.5 208.3 212.1 215.9 219.7 223.5 227.3
Humerus width cm	[ ]	5.19 5.34 5.49 5.64 5.78 5.93 6.07 6.22 6.37 6.51 6.65 6.80 6.95 7.09 7.24 7.38 7.53 7.67 7.82 7.97 8.11 8.25 8.40 8.55
Femur width cm	[ ]	7.41 7.62 7.83 8.04 8.24 8.45 8.66 8.87 9.08 9.28 9.49 9.70 9.91 10.12 10.33 10.53 10.74 10.95 11.16 11.36 11.57 11.78 11.99 12.21
Biceps girth [ ] – T*		23.7 24.4 25.0 25.7 26.3 27.0 27.7 28.3 29.0 29.7 30.3 31.0 31.6 32.2 33.0 33.6 34.3 35.0 35.6 36.3 37.0 37.6 38.3 39.0
Call girth [ ] – C^A		27.7 28.5 29.3 30.1 30.8 31.6 32.4 33.2 33.9 34.7 35.5 36.3 37.1 37.8 38.6 39.4 40.2 41.0 41.7 42.5 43.3 44.1 44.9 45.6

| Mesomorphy | ½ | 1 | 1½ | 2 | 2½ | 3 | 3½ | 4 | 4½ | 5 | 5½ | 6 | 6½ | 7 | 7½ | 8 | 8½ | 9 |

Weight Kg	=	Upper limit	39.65 40.74 41.43 42.13 42.82 43.48 44.18 44.14 45.53 46.23 46.92 47.58 48.25 48.94 49.63 50.33 50.99 51.68
Ht. / ∛wt.	= [ ]	Mid-point	and 40.20 41.09 41.79 42.48 43.14 43.84 44.50 45.19 45.89 46.32 47.24 47.94 48.60 49.29 49.99 50.68 51.34
		Lower limit	below 39.66 40.75 41.44 42.14 42.83 43.49 44.19 44.85 45.54 46.24 46.93 47.59 48.26 48.95 49.64 50.34 51.00

| Ectomorphy | ½ | 1 | 1½ | 2 | 2½ | 3 | 3½ | 4 | 4½ | 5 | 5½ | 6 | 6½ | 7 | 7½ | 8 | 8½ | 9 |

	ENDOMORPHY	MESOMORPHY	ECTOMORPHY	
Anthropometric Somatotype				BY : ....
Anthropometric plus Photoscopic Somatotype				RATER : ....

* Biceps birth in cm corrected for fat by subtracting triceps skinfold value expressed in cm.
^A Calf birth in cm corrected for fat by subtracting medial calf skinfold value expressed in cm.

Figure 4.15 Heath-Carter Somatotype Rating Form

- Bone breadth (humerus, femur)
- Limb girths (bicep tensed, calf in standing position).

Having collected the data and completed a series of calculations we are able to plot the resulting anthropometric somatotype onto a **somatochart**.

A somatochart is a multi-axis graph which enables your somatotype rating to be plotted in order to determine your body size and structure. To accurately plot your somatotype you need to complete the following calculations.

To plot your data along the *x*-axis you should follow the formula:

X = ectomorphy – endomorphy

X = _____

To plot your data along the *y*-axis you should follow the following formula:

Y = 2 x mesomorphy – (endomorphy + ectomorphy)

Y = _____

Somatotype profiling

As many athletes share similar characteristics in terms of their build and structure, you will be able to identify many using the somatochart. Due to many performances requiring the same muscles, the body becomes trained in the same area as other performers, leading to many being of a similar build. For example, many dynamic agile performers such as a gymnast, will be a

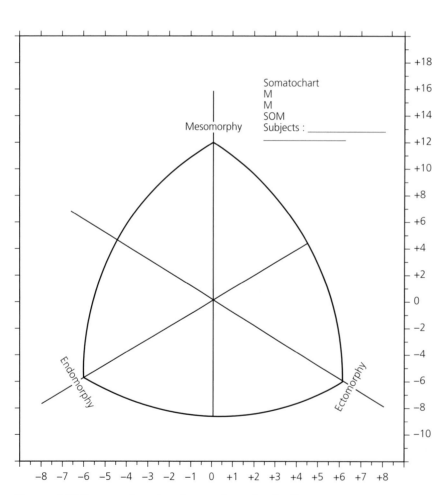

Figure 4.16 Somatochart for plotting the individual's somatotype

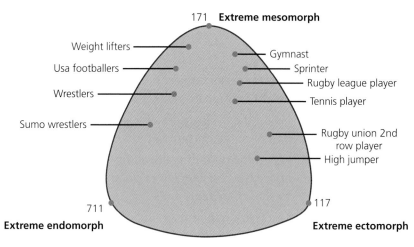

Figure 4.17 Somatotype chart – average athletes

combination of mesomorph and ectomorph in order to allow them to achieve rapid coordinated movements. In power-based activities such as a power-lifter, you will remember that the endomorph body shape is important to its success. As a result, many power-lifters will be more endomorph and mesomorphy in body shape as this allows them to move the heavy weight with their large muscles and continue with the momentum using their personal body size.

Somatotype can help to identify potential health issues and even potential life threatening illnesses. For example, many people who are close to the endomorph category have a greater chance of suffering from type 2 diabetes, heart related illnesses and blood pressure problems. For this reason you will be able to use the somatotype assessment method to identify people who may be at risk of death or future health problems.

B Check your understanding

1 Define the term 'somatotype' and how it may be assessed.
2 Define the term 'anthropometry' and how its meaning is different to 'somatotype'.
3 Explain why body shape and size is crucial to human sports performance.
4 Why is BMI not suitable when testing sports performers?

Distinction activity: Preparation for fitness testing (B D2)

A group of college students have approached you to try to work out their anthropometric and somatotype body shapes. They would also like you to advise them on the best sports you think they should play based on their somatotype. You therefore decide to measure them and should complete the necessary calculations.

Part 1

1 Conduct both the Durnin and Womersley and Jackson and Pollock skinfold assessment measure methods on a testing individual.
2 Present all your data in a clear table to make it easy to interpret.
3 Analyse the results for similarity and explain any differences you may find.

Part 2

1 Conduct the Heath-Carter somatotype assessment procedure on your partner.
2 Present your data using the appropriate form for analysis.
3 Produce a somatotype chart that represents your partner.

Part 3

Using the results you gained in Part 1 and Part 2, identify the types of sport and exercise that would be suitable for your partner and justify your reasons why.

C Explore the use of field- and laboratory-based protocols in sport and exercise sciences

()

C1 Applied laboratory and experimental testing

As you now know, when conducting research it is important you take time to complete a full assessment of your participant and ensure they remain safe at all times. You will be aware that the use of a pre-planned protocol will enable you to be fully prepared when conducting your research. There are a range of testing protocols that we can use to assess fitness components, therefore it is important we are familiar with them prior to testing.

Laboratory-based testing protocols

Prior to conducting any testing protocols it is essential that health screening, informed consent and ethical procedures are completed in order to safely conduct the activities. It is also important that you familiarise yourself with the equipment and check it is in good working order to ensure the results will be as accurate as possible.

Astrand-Ryhming cycle ergometer test

This test aims to predict the oxygen uptake of a subject participant using an aerobic test. It is a sub-maximal test, requiring the subject to participate at a low intensity, though enabling you to predict the maximal capacity outcome.

> **Key term**
>
> **Aerobic** is when exercise occurs in the presence of and requires oxygen. For example, when jogging we require lots of oxygen to keep our muscles working efficiently. To do this we must exercise aerobically, requiring us to run slower than a sprint to allow us to breathe more deeply.

For this test you will require a heart rate monitor, cycle ergometer, stopwatch, and calculator.

Method

1. Measure your subject participant's body weight, height and record their resting heart rate.

2. Using the cycle ergometer, start your subject pedalling at 50 rpm.

3. When the pedalling speed has been reached, apply the resistance workload to the ergometer as shown in Table 4.4.

4. The workload aims to increase the heart rate between 130 and 160 beats.min⁻¹ (bpm) depending on their age.

5. Start the clock and your subject will then pedal for six minutes at the steady pace of 50 rpm.

6. Using Table 4.5, make adjustments to the resistance setting if the heart rate after the initial 3 minutes is above or below the target heart rate of 130–160 bpm.

7. In the last 15 seconds of each minute, record the heart rate of your subject. For minutes 5 and 6, average these heart rates and if there is a greater difference of 5 bpm continue for further minutes until it stabilizes.

The results and oxygen uptake calculations

To predict the oxygen uptake we now need to use a series of calculations which will enable us to understand the outcomes.

1. Work intensity after 3 min of exercise: _____ kg _____ W

2. Average Heart Rate from 5th + 6th minute:_____ beats.min⁻¹

3. Calculate your sub-maximal VO_2 (L.min⁻¹) based on your current test performed:

   VO_2 (L.min⁻¹) = [Power (in W) x 0.012] + 0.3

   VO_2 (L.min⁻¹) = _____

4. Now calculate your VO_2 max (L.min⁻¹)

   Male:

   VO_2 max (L.min⁻¹) = [VO_2 x ((220 – age) – 61) / (HRss – 61)]

   VO_2 max (L.min⁻¹) = _____

Age (years)	Male Mass (kg)	Power (W)	Female Mass (kg)	Power (W)	Target HR beats.min⁻¹
<30	3	150	2	100	150–160
30–39	2	100	1.5	75	145–155
40–49	2	100	1.5	75	140–150
50–59	2	100	1	50	135–145
60–69	2	100	1	50	130–140

Table 4.4 Starting resistance workload table

Female:

$$VO_2 \text{ max (L.min}^{-1}) = [VO_2 \times ((220 - \text{age}) - 72) / (\text{HRss} - 72)]$$

VO_2 max (L.min⁻¹) = _____

HRss = average heart rate from the 5th and 6th minute of the Astrand-Rhyming Test

5 VO_2 max (L.min⁻¹)_____ L.min⁻¹

6 Body mass: _____ kg

7 VO_2 max (relative to body mass) = VO_2 max (L.min⁻¹)

   Weight (kg)

   VO_2 max _____ ml kg⁻¹min⁻¹

The results will show your subject's aerobic fitness with the highest value indicating a higher level of aerobic fitness. The test indicates your subject's maximal oxygen uptake per minute during the exercise test. If they are able to breathe in and consume lots of oxygen during exercise, it could indicate that they are able to work harder for longer as all muscles require oxygen to perform.

A. Raise Power level by:		
Power (W)	**Mass (kg)**	**Heart rate (beats.min⁻¹)**
75	1.5	If HR is < 110
50	1.0	If HR is 110–130
25	0.5	If HR is 130–139
B. Lower Power level by:		
Power (W)	**Mass (kg)**	**Heart rate (beats.min⁻¹)**
50	1.0	If HR is >160
25	0.5	If HR is 150–159

Table 4.5 Power adjustments after the third minute of the Astrand-Rhyming test, (if required)

Activity: Calculating aerobic capacity using the Astrand-Rhyming cycle test

1 Using the Astrand-Rhyming cycle test, conduct the method on a partner and collect the testing data in the form of a table.

2 Perform calculations to establish the results of their aerobic capacity.

3 Repeat the test on another individual and compare the results.

4 What were the outcomes of the test? Explain the results.

30-second Wingate cycle test

The Wingate cycle test is a maximal anaerobic test that measures power from the legs. Like the Astrand-Ryhming test, it requires the use of a cycle ergometer; however its difference is that it's a short sprint on the bike over a 30 second period.

Key terms

Anaerobic is an activity which takes part without the presence of oxygen. For example, when sprinting at high intensity, we are unable to breathe in enough oxygen to keep us working for a long period of time before we become fatigued. To gain more oxygen we need to slow down and work aerobically. Working at such a high intensity means that the muscles must rely on oxygen already stored in the body until it runs out. When this occurs you become fatigued and have to stop.

Power is the rate that energy is generated per unit of time. It is a key component within many sporting events and extremely important in events that require an explosive performance such as throwing the javelin, performing a tennis serve, or performing a volleyball smash shot.

Age (Yrs)	Very high (VH)	High (H)	Good (G)	Average (Ave)	Fair (F)	Low (L)
Men						
20–29	>61	53–61	43–52	34–42	25–33	<25
30–39	>57	49–57	39–48	31–38	23–30	<23
40–49	>53	45–53	36–44	37–35	20–26	<20
50–59	>49	43–49	34–42	25–33	18–24	<18
60–69	>45	41–45	31–40	23–30	16–22	<16
Women						
20–29	>57	49–57	38–48	31–37	24–30	<24
30–39	>53	45–53	34–44	28–33	20–27	<20
40–49	>50	42–50	31–41	24–30	17–23	<17
50–59	>42	38–42	28–37	21–27	15–20	<15
60–69	>39	35–39	24–34	18–23	13–17	<13

Table 4.6 Norms data for evaluation of the Astrand-Rhyming cycle test
Aerobic fitness (maximal fitness categories – ml kg^{-1} min^{-1})

The equipment you require for this test includes a Monark resistance adjustable cycle ergometer, Wingate assessment computer and software, weighing scales and height measurement.

Method

1   Weigh (kg) and measure the height (cm) of your subject and input them into your recording software.

2   Adjust the height of the saddle on the ergometer so that their leg is extended and ankle is at right angles to the pedal. This will allow for a full leg strike during the pedalling phase.

3   Adjust the cycle resistance required for testing. The resistance is based on the subject's bodyweight. You should calculate 7.5% of their bodyweight in kilograms, and add this value as a resistance to the flywheel for when the test begins. For example, a 100 kg subject will require a resistance weight of 7.5 kg.

4   When the test is to begin, the subject should cycle at maximum speed and then the weight is applied to the flywheel, at which point the Wingate software should automatically begin.

5   The subject will cycle at maximum intensity for 30 seconds.

6   When 30 seconds has passed the weight should be removed and the subject should slow down but continue to cycle at a gentle pace in order to cool down.

Figure 4.18 The Wingate test

The results and power performance

In your results you should be able to identify:

1   Peak power (PP)

2   Relative peak power (RPP)

3   Anaerobic fatigue (AF).

1. Peak power (PP)

Peak power is the maximal power output performed by the muscles in the opening seconds of the Wingate test. It is usually at its greatest

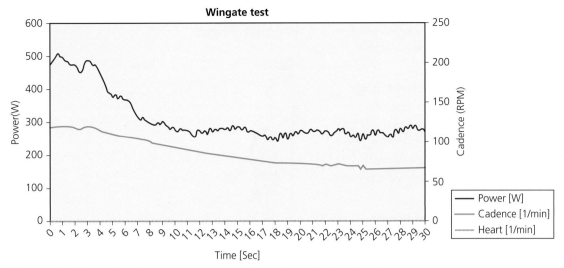

Figure 4.19 Example of test data that may be collected using the Wingate test

within the initial 5 seconds. It is the explosive element of the test where muscles are at their most powerful of the performance. For example, when a performer throws a javelin it requires an explosive power performance from the arm and body to propel the implement over a great distance.

2. Relative peak power (RPP)

The relative peak power is determined by the bodyweight of the subject. The value of peak power is divided by the bodyweight of the subject which indicates the power to weight ratio. It is possible not to have the greatest power output from the test, though be the most powerful for body size. For example, gymnasts are typically light in bodyweight though their power performance is exceptionally high in order to perform jumps and somersaults during their routines.

3. Anaerobic fatigue (AF) or fatigue index

Anaerobic fatigue is an indication of the rate at which a subject's power performance declines or drops. The slower the decline, the greater ability the subject has at maintaining their anaerobic performance. This may be particularly important in events such as the 400 m, as a high intensity of activity is needed over a long period of time. The slower they fatigue, the longer they can run at a high intensity.

Anaerobic fatigue may be calculated:

AF = [(Peak Power Output – Min Power Output) / Peak Power Output] × 100

The final result indicates the amount the performance declined throughout the duration of the test. The greater the decline, the quicker the performer becomes fatigued.

Percentile norms for relative peak power for active young adults (Maud and Shultz, 1998) is:

	Male	Female
%Rank	**Watts. kg**	**Watts. kg**
90	10.89	9.02
80	10.39	8.83
70	10.20	8.53
60	9.80	8.14
50	9.22	7.65
40	8.92	6.96
30	8.53	6.86
20	8.24	6.57
10	7.06	5.98

Table 4.7 Peak power per kg (*Source:* www.brianmac. co.uk)

The Vertec jump or Sargent jump test

This test aims to examine the explosive power of the legs, requiring your subject to leap vertically into the air from a standing position using both legs to take off.

The equipment used for this test is a Vertec jump measuring stand.

Method

1 When the athlete is ready to start, they should stand with both hands on their hips directly under the Vertec measuring stand.

2 When ready to jump, the subject should jump with both feet in a stationary position and hands remaining on their hips. The fixed hands position will reduce the contribution of the upper body, isolating the leg action and reducing the momentum of the arms which can generate increased height.

3 When taking off, the subject should release their hand from their hip and reach up as high as possible to try and swipe the highest measurement vane. The jump height is taken from the difference between standing height and jump height.

Figure 4.20 Vertical jump using the Vertec

Calculating Power from the vertical jump test

Power = **2.21 × Weight** in kgs × **Height jumped** in cms
(2.21 = a constant based on the weight of falling bodies)
eg. A 67 kg person who jumped 50.8 cm =
Power = 2.21 × 67 kg × ' /0.508 m
   = 148 × 0.713
   = 105 kgm.s^{-1}

Vertical jump scores of college men and women				
	Height Difference			
Percentile	Men		Women	
	In.	Cm	In.	Cm
90	25	64	14	36
80	24	61	13	33
70	23	58	12	30
60	19	48	10	25
50	16	41	8	20
40	13	33	6	15
30	9	23	4	10
20	8	20	2	5
10	2	5	1	2.5

D (cm)	P (kgm·s^{-1})	Wt (kg)
80	200	
70	180	100
		90
60	150	
	140	
	130	
50	120	80
40	100	
		70
	90	
30	80	
	70	
		60
	60	
20	50	50
	40	45
15		
	30	40
10	25	36

Figure 4.21 Power results that may be gained from the test

Rating	Males (cm)	Females (cm)
excellent	>70	>60
very good	61–70	51–60
above average	51–60	41–50
average	41–50	31–40
below average	31–40	21–30
poor	21–30	11–20
very poor	<21	<11

Table 4.8 Example of vertical jump norms data

The measurement aims to determine the peak power generated from the legs in order to propel the body as high as possible. This is particularly important in sports such as basketball and high jump, where the legs are required to generate the power needed to drive the body high into the air.

Activity: Comparison of tests – Wingate test and the Vertec jump

1 Conduct the Vertec jump test three times, collect the results and rest for 10 minutes.
2 Using the Lewis Nomogram calculate the results of the peak power and record into a table.
3 Conduct the Wingate cycle test, collect the results and rest.
4 Using the readout record all results into a table.
5 Analyse the results. Explain any differences you can see and justify the reasons as to why this may have occurred.

1 Repetition Max (1-RM) test

The 1-RM is a strength test that aims to measure the maximal weight an individual can lift. The test is frequently used in weight training programmes to measure training progression. Within a laboratory environment we can use it in a similar way or as a one-off test measure.

Method

1 Having selected the 1-RM exercise, the subject participant should warm up thoroughly as this is a maximal activity. Due to the intensity, the individual is at greater risk of becoming injured without appropriate stretching and warm-up activities.

2 Following the stretching, your subject should perform between five and ten warm-up lifts with a weight you consider is 40–60% of their estimated 1-RM.

3 Following the initial warm-up lifts, the weight should be increased to approximately 60–80% of their estimated 1-RM, and three to five repetitions should be performed, after which the subject should rest for 3–5 minutes.

4 Increase the weight, lifting just once until the maximum is reached. If one lift is successful the subject should rest for 5 minutes before commencing their next increased lift.

Repetitions	% 1 RM
1	100
2	95
3	93
4	90
5	87
6	85
7	83
8	80
9	77
10	75
11	70
12	67
15	65

Table 4.9 1-RM repetitions prediction table
(*Source:* Baechle & Earle, 2008)

The results gathered are subject specific, however the percentage change whether they improved or not, can be shown against other performers. Norms data differences are therefore difficult to compare against one another, however you should maintain accurate record keeping in order to monitor the progress of a subject participant. Strength is particularly important in weightlifting events and also many events which require a high level of power such as the shot putt.

Isometric leg strength test (back dynamometer)

This test aims to assess the static isometric strength of a muscle group. While the 1-RM test also assesses strength, this test requires no significant movement other than the pressure being applied to the equipment.

For this test, the equipment required is a back dynamometer.

Method

1   Place the back dynamometer on a stable, solid floor.
2   Stand on the dynamometer directly over the measuring equipment, back straight, head up, legs slightly bent and hands firmly gripping the pulling bar. Ensure that the height of the bar has been adjusted to approximately mid-thigh height.
3   Without leaning back, the subject must straighten their legs and pull the bar upwards in one smooth motion, avoiding any jerky movements. It is very important that during this phase the head is kept up and the back remains straight at all times in order to avoid injury.
4   Having completed the movement, the subject should relax and the result recorded.

The test will show the maximal force that can be applied using the legs and back with the highest measurement being the greatest force. Like the 1-RM, this test may be suitable for measuring the strength and force of performers that require these components such as in rugby. This is particularly important when contesting the scrum, as force must be applied to drive back the opponents and win the ball.

Isometric grip strength test (grip dynamometer)

Like the isometric leg strength test, the grip strength test aims to measure the force that can be generated by the hand during one single contraction. The movement should be constant and not be jerky in motion.

The equipment needed for this test is a grip dynamometer.

Method

1   Adjust the handle so that it is comfortable for your subject to grip the dynamometer tightly.
2   With their arm held by their side, the subject should squeeze their hand as tight as possible without any jerky movements.
3   Record the result and repeat the procedure using the other hand.
4   Rest for 2 minutes and take a second attempt.

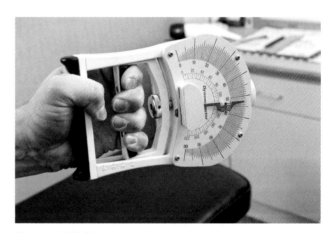

Figure 4.22 Grip strength activity

Gender	Excellent	Good	Average	Fair	Poor
Male	>56	51–56	45–50	39–44	<39
Female	>36	31–36	25–30	19–24	<19

Table 4.10 Normative data for the isometric grip strength test (*Source:* www.brianmac.co.uk)

Like the isometric leg strength test, the grip strength test avoids the use of momentum by remaining static throughout the test. A firm grip that is able to generate much force may be important in a number of sports such as weightlifting and gymnastics. As both activities require the performer to grip tightly onto a bar, their strength can prevent them from dropping a weight or falling off the apparatus.

One-minute press-up test

The press-up test is a strength endurance test that requires the muscles to work at a high intensity over a long period of time. The test requires the subject to lift the body from just above floor height which demands strength. When the movement is repeated frequently over one minute, this becomes endurance.

Key term

Strength endurance is the ability of the muscle to contract repeatedly at a high intensity over a long duration of time. Individuals who have good strength endurance are able to resist becoming fatigued, therefore able to work harder for longer.

To perform the test the equipment you will need is a stopwatch.

Method
1 Your subject will lay face down with hands placed at shoulder height and width apart.
2 With their legs and body straight, your subject must push their body off the floor so that they fully extend their arms.

Press-up test (men)

Age	17–19	20–29	30–39	40–49	50–59	60–69
Excellent	>56	>47	>41	>34	>31	>30
Good	47–56	39–47	34–41	28–34	25–31	24–30
Above average	35–46	30–39	25–33	21–28	18–24	17–23
Average	19–34	17–29	13–24	11–20	9–17	6–16
Below average	11–18	10–16	8–12	6–10	5–8	3–5
Poor	4–10	4–9	2–7	1–5	1–4	1–2
Very poor	<4	<4	<2	0	0	0

Press-up test (women)

Age	17–19	20–29	30–39	40–49	50–59	60–69
Excellent	>35	>36	>37	>31	>25	>23
Good	27–35	30–36	30–37	25–31	21–25	19–23
Above average	21–27	23–29	23–30	18–24	15–20	13–18
Average	11–20	12–22	10–21	8–17	7–14	5–12
Below average	6–10	7–11	5–9	4–7	3–6	2–4
Poor	2–5	2–6	1–4	1–3	1–2	1
Very poor	0–1	0–1	0	0	0	0

Figure 4.23 Example of norms data for the press-up test

3 Keeping their back and legs straight, your subject will flex their arms to lower their chest to approx. 3–4 inches (a fist width) from the floor, and then extend their arms to return back to the original starting position. This completes one single press-up.

4 The subject has 1 minute to complete as many press-ups as possible.

The press-up test is specific to the upper body and cannot be used as an appropriate test for all over strength endurance. However, as a general measure, it can be of use in assessing performers who rely on this area for their performance. These performers may include a kayaker who will use their upper body strength to drive their body through the water when moving along a river or rapids.

One-minute sit-up test

Like the one minute press-up test, the sit-ups require your subject to perform as many as they can within one minute. Therefore, this test also measures strength endurance of this region. The exercise tests the abdominal muscles, requiring them to contract repetitively over a duration of time.

The equipment you will need for this test is a stopwatch.

Method

1 Your subject should start by laying on their back with their knees bent at 90° and feet flat on the floor. Your subject's hands should be touching just behind the ears and not gripping the back of the head as this may cause injury during the sit-up activity.

2 When starting, the subject should squeeze their abdominal muscles so that their shoulders leave the ground and move towards their knees.

3 On reaching the knees, the subject should touch them with their elbows and lower themselves to the ground. This completes one sit-up.

4 The subject should repeat the sit-ups and complete as many as possible in one minute.

Figure 4.24 A sit-up test activity

As we know, the sit-up test is specific to the central region of the body, therefore it is best used to assess any activities that rely on this area for their performance. An example of a sports performer where the core abdominal strength is important is a gymnast. A gymnast must have strong abdominal

Female (Age)	Very Poor	Poor	Fair	Good	Excellent	Superior
Under 20	> 28	28–31	32–35	36–45	46–54	< 54
20–29	> 24	24–31	32–37	38–43	44–50	< 50
30–39	> 20	20–24	25–28	29–34	35–41	< 41
40–49	> 14	14–19	20–23	24–28	29–37	< 37
50–59	> 10	10–13	14–19	20–23	24–29	< 29
60 and over	> 03	03–05	06–10	11–16	17–27	< 27

Female (Age)	Very Poor	Poor	Fair	Good	Excellent	Superior
Under 20	> 36	36–40	41–46	47–50	51–61	< 61
20–29	> 33	33–37	38–41	42–46	47–54	< 54
30–39	> 30	30–34	35–38	39–42	43–50	< 50
40–49	> 24	24–28	29–33	34–38	39–46	< 46
50–59	> 19	19–23	24–27	28–34	35–42	< 42
60 and over	> 15	15–18	19–21	22–29	30–28	< 38

Figure 4.25 Sit-up test norms data

muscles that can contract regularly without fatigue. If the gymnast was to complete a floor routine and tire too quickly, this could affect the success of their performance. By tiring and not having the strength to complete the necessary movements, it could cause them to achieve a low performance score and therefore be less successful.

The sit and reach test

The aim of this test is to assess the range of movement or flexibility around the lower back and hip regions. It is a simple test which is easy to perform and requires limited equipment. Your subject is assessed by them being seated and leaning forward for a measure to be taken.

The equipment you will require for this test is a sit and reach box.

Method

1 The sit and reach box should be placed against a firm surface or wall.
2 The ankles of your subject should be placed against the edge of the box and side-by-side. All footwear should be removed as this can affect the final result.
3 Your subject is required to lean as far forward as possible, keeping both their hands parallel to one another. The movement should be slow and smooth with no jerk action. The legs must be kept straight throughout the test.
4 As soon as they can reach no further they should hold the position momentarily and the measurement be taken, then relax.

Figure 4.26 A sit and reach test

Hip flexibility test with goniometer

The aim of this test is to assess the range of movement or flexibility around the hip region. Like the sit and reach test it requires minimal equipment. From a laying position your subject will be assessed as to how far they can raise their leg above the floor and as it is held back towards their head.

The equipment needed is a goniometer and recording sheet.

Method

1 Warm up thoroughly prior to testing.
2 Subject lays down flat on their back with both legs together and straight.
3 With the assistance of a partner one leg is raise while the other is kept flat on the floor. It is important that the partner assists the lift and does not pull the leg further, to make it a fair test. Also the subject must remain flat and not try to twist their body during the movement.
4 When the leg is unable to be moved anymore, an angle measurement of the hip is recorded.
5 Repeat the test three times on each leg and record the results.

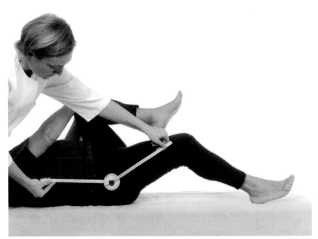

Figure 4.27 A goniometer test

Gender	Excellent	Above average	Average	Below average	Poor
Male	>16	11–16	7–10	4–6	<4
Female	>17	12–17	7–11	4–6	<4

Table 4.11 Example of normative data for sit and reach

Field-based testing protocols

Multistage fitness test

The multistage fitness test is an **aerobic** test which requires your subject to run continuously in time with a bleep. It is regularly used as it is simple to perform and requires a limited area of 20 metres to shuttle run. As the test begins your subject will be expected to keep in time with the bleep which starts at 8.0 km/hr and increases by 0.5 km/hr every 60 seconds.

To perform this test you will need cones, a sound system with a copy of the test to play, and a measuring tape.

Method

Your subject should warm up thoroughly before the test, ensuring they have fully stretched and performed a light jog.

1 Place two cones 20 metres apart on a flat running surface.
2 Line your subject up at the start line and await the first starting bleep.
3 On hearing the starting tone, your subject should jog to the next cone which will be 20 metres apart from the start. The subject should arrive at the cone at approximately the same time as the bleep so that they jog continuously.
4 Subject will turn and run in the opposite direction, continuing to run to the bleep which will gradually increase in speed. Subject will be expected to keep in time, if they fall behind on three occasions they will be withdrawn from the test and their last achieved score will be recorded.
5 Once the subject drops out, their level can be compared against normative data and VO_2 max predicted.

As the test is continuous, it is aerobically-based and relies heavily on your subject's endurance ability. Those individuals that have good endurance fitness will perform well in this test, achieving a high level score and running the furthest distance.

The Cooper 12-minute run fitness test

The Cooper run is an aerobic test that requires a subject to run continuously over a duration of 12 minutes. The aim of the test is to cover as much distance as possible. Like the multistage fitness test, the Cooper run relies heavily on your subject's endurance ability, therefore those who excel in this fitness component should perform well in this test.

To conduct this test you will require cones, a measuring tape/wheel, stopwatch, and whistle. If a running track is available then this would also be suitable.

Method

1 Mark out a 400 metre square on a flat running field, placing cones at 50 metre intervals. If you have access to a running track then place cones at similar intervals.
2 Warm up your subject, ensuring they are well stretched and ready to run the test.
3 Prepare your subject at the start line ready to run the 12-minute test.
4 Blow the whistle and start the stopwatch at the start of the test and monitor your subject as they run for 12 minutes around your running track. Count how many laps they complete and record on your data sheets.
5 When 12 minutes has finished, blow your whistle a second time and ask your subject to stand still.
6 Add up the laps and any additional distance they may have completed.

For example, if a 400 m track was used:

6 laps completed = 6 × 400 m

300 m achieved in final lap = + 300

Total distance covered = 2700 m

Age	Gender	Very good	Good	Average	Below average	Poor
13–14	M	2700+ m	2400–2700 m	2200–2399 m	2100–2199 m	>2100 m
	F	2000+ m	1900–2000 m	1600–1899 m	1500–1599 m	>1500 m
15–16	M	2800+ m	2500–2800 m	2300–2499 m	2000–2299 m	>2200 m
	F	2100+ m	2000–2100 m	1700–1999 m	1600–1699 m	>1600 m
17–20	M	3000+ m	2700–3000 m	2500–2699 m	2300–2499 m	>2300 m
	F	2300+ m	2100–2300 m	1800–2099 m	1700–1799 m	>1700 m
20–29	M	2800+ m	2400–2800 m	2200–2399 m	1600–2199 m	>1600 m
	F	2700+ m	2200–2700 m	1800–2199 m	1500–1799 m	>1500 m
30–39	M	2700+ m	2300–2700 m	1900–2999 m	1500–1899 m	>1500 m
	F	2500+ m	2000–2500 m	1700–1999 m	1400–1699 m	>1400 m
40–49	M	2500+ m	2100–2500 m	1700–2099 m	1400–1699 m	>1400 m
	F	2300+ m	1900–2300 m	1500–1899 m	1200–1499 m	>1200 m
50+	M	2400+ m	2000–2400 m	1600–1999 m	1300–1599 m	>1300 m
	F	2200+ m	1700–2200 m	1400–1699 m	1100–1399 m	>1100 m

Figure 4.28 Example of Cooper run norms data

Using the distance covered, we can now calculate your subjects VO_2 max using the following formula:

$$VO_2 \text{ max} = \text{(Distance covered in metres} - 504.9) / 44.73$$

$$VO_2 \text{ max} = (2700 - 504.9) / 44.73$$

$$VO_2 \text{ max} = 49.07 \text{ mls/kg/min}^{-1}$$

While both the multistage fitness test and Cooper 12-minute run fitness test assess aerobic fitness, the methods used may be more suitable for different types of performers. For example, as the Cooper run requires a limited change in direction, it may be more of a suitable for athletes who perform in a similar single direction such as a marathon runner. Alternatively, a performer such as a football player may be best tested using the multistage fitness test to assess aerobic endurance, as the frequent change in direction may resemble a game situation.

Running-based anaerobic sprint test

The aim of this test is to measure a subject's **power** and anaerobic fatigue, otherwise known as the Fatigue Index. The test requires your subject to run repeatedly over a distance of 35 metres with a 10-second recovery period in between each sprint. The test assesses the similarity of running times as this can indicate that very little fatigue has occurred. For the test to be accurate, it is important that you encourage your subject to work as hard as they can throughout the test.

To perform this test you will require cones, three stopwatches, a 35-metre tape measure and an assistant.

Method

1 Measure a distance of 35 metres on a flat running surface, ensuring you have sufficient additional run off space at either end. Place cones at each end of the 35 metres.

2 Warm up your subject using appropriate stretching and exercises.

3 Have your subject stand at one end of the 35 metres, ready to start the test. When they are ready, countdown and begin the first sprint test.

4 Start the stopwatch when your subject's first foot touches the floor and press stop as soon as they have sprinted through the finish line, covering the 35 metre distance. The stopwatch should only be started when the first foot touches the ground as this will avoid reaction time influencing the result. The sprint time should be recorded following each sprint.

5 Having completed the run, the subject should then return to the finish line within 10 seconds and stand waiting to start the next sprint. The subject will now sprint back to the start line following the 10 second rest interval. This will now be their second sprint and the time should be recorded.

6 Again within a 10 second rest, the subject must return to the start line and await the command to start the third sprint.

7 Repeat stages 4–6 until they have completed a total of six sprints, and record all the sprint times throughout.

Using the data collected we are now able to perform a series of calculations to find your subject's Velocity, Acceleration, Force, and Power.

$$\text{Velocity} = \text{Distance} \div \text{Time}$$

$$\text{Acceleration} = \text{Velocity} \div \text{Time}$$

$$\text{Force} = \text{Weight} \times \text{Acceleration}$$

$$\text{Power} = \text{Force} \times \text{Velocity}$$

Using the calculations for Power we can now identify your subject's maximum, minimum and average power, and then calculate your subject's anaerobic fatigue or fatigue index.

Maximum power = The highest value

Minimum power = The lowest value

Average power = Total of all six values / 6

Fatigue Index = (Maximum power – Minimum power) / Total time for the 6 sprints

The flying 30 m sprint test

The 30 m sprint test is an assessment of maximum speed over the set distance. Unlike a standing 30 m sprint, this test measures speed rather than acceleration as your subject will be running at full speed when they pass through the start line. Acceleration can be assessed using an alternative method.

To perform this test you will require a 60 m measuring tape, cones and a stopwatch.

Method

1 Measure a distance of 60 metres, placing a cone at the start, another at the 30 metre mark and a final cone at the 60 metre distance.

2 Warm up your subject using appropriate stretching and exercises.

3 Have your subject stand at one end of the 60 metres, ready to start the test. When they are ready, countdown and begin the first sprint.

4 To complete the sprint test, your subject must gradually increase their speed and pass through the 30 metre cone at their maximum. At this point the stopwatch should start and timing begin.

5 From the 30 metre mark your subject should keep sprinting at maximum speed through the 60 metre mark at which point the clock is stopped.

6 The time taken from the 30 metre to the 60 metre point is to be recorded as this will be their maximum speed during the sprint activity.

7 Rest for 3–5 minutes and repeat the test two more times.

Activity: Calculated example of the running-based anaerobic sprint test (RAST)

Below are the sprint times gathered from a RAST test:

Sprint	Time (secs)	Power (watts)
1	4.52	1008
2	4.75	869
3	4.92	782
4	5.21	658
5	5.46	572
6	5.62	525

Table 4.12 Sprint times gathered from a RAST test

Athlete weight = 76 kilograms

Using the calculations for each test, calculate the following:

Maximum power = watts

Minimum power = watts

Average power = watts

Fatigue index = watts/sec^{-1}

Now perform the test yourself and compare your results. Who has the greatest fatigue index and why?

With the subject having completed the series of sprints, you will see that the results drop considerably. This will also be shown in the fatigue index which shows the rate of decline in power during the test. For example, in this test the subject fatigued by 15.8 watts every second of the activity. This may be important in athletic events such as the 400 m as the athlete would want to resist tiring throughout the race. Therefore the sprinter would train hard to lower the rate at which they fatigue as this could make them faster over the whole race.

Gender	Excellent	Above average	Average	Below average	Poor
Male	<4	4.0–4.2	4.3–4.4	4.5–4.6	>4.6
Female	<4.5	4.5–4.6	4.7–4.8	4.9–5.0	>5.0

Table 4.13 Example of normative data for the flying 30 m sprint test (*Source*: www.brianmac.co.uk)

Using similar calculations as shown in the RAST test, you will be able to calculate your subject's sprint Velocity, Force, and Power throughout the test. You will also be able to compare sprint times against norms data.

This test is very useful for sports performers who need to maintain their speed over a long period of time. For example, a 100 m sprinter needs to be able to accelerate out of the blocks; however, they must also be able to maintain their speed once they reach their maximum. Therefore, sprinters must train hard to ensure their speed does not drop as they race towards the finish line.

Illinois agility test

This test assesses your ability to change direction while travelling at speed. It measures your **agility** which is particularly important in a number of sporting events. Your subject is timed and required to run around a series of cones, using their legs to power their body in different directions while running as fast as they can.

Key term

Agility is the body's ability to rapidly change direction while at speed, avoiding any loss of coordination or balance. The speed at which the body can change direction is related to power as the movement of the limb in an opposite direction requires a strong force in another direction.

To perform this test you will require cones, a stopwatch and a level running surface with sufficient grip.

Method

1 Set out a grid, 5 metres in width, 10 metres in length with four cones equally spaced along the centre (see Figure 4.29).

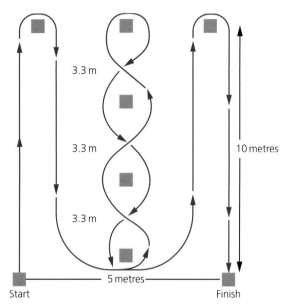

Figure 4.29 The Illinois agility test grid

2 Warm up your subject using appropriate stretching and exercises.

3 Assemble your subject at the start line and prepare them to begin.

4 On 'go', the sprinter is to sprint around the cones as fast as possible. The stopwatch should only be started when their first foot touches the floor as this avoids reaction time influencing the result.

5 When their torso has passed the finish line you stop the clock. If your subject fails to sprint around any of the cones the result must be disallowed.

Gender	Excellent	Above average	Average	Below average	Poor
Male	<15.2 secs	15.2–16.1 secs	16.2–18.1 secs	18.2–18.3 secs	>18.3 secs
Female	<17.0 secs	17.0–17.9 secs	18.0–21.7 secs	21.8–23.0 secs	>23.0 secs

Table 4.14 Example of norms data for the Illinois agility test (*Source*: www.brianmac.co.uk)

The agility test is useful when assessing individuals whose sport requires them to frequently change direction. Sporting performers that may benefit from using this test may include football players, racket sport players and gymnasts. These activities require a frequent change in direction and they would be expected to perform this test very quickly. The quicker the time the greater the agility of the performer.

The T-Drill test

Like the Illinois agility test, the T-Drill test measures your subject's ability to change direction while travelling at speed. Cones are marked into the shape of a 'T' and require the subject to sprint and shuffle in different directions as quickly as possible.

For this test you will require a stopwatch, cones, a tape measure and a flat non-slip surface.

Method

1   Cones should be placed into a 'T' shape. It should measure 10 metres in length and 5 metres each side at right angles at one end (see Figure 4.30).

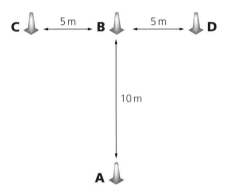

Figure 4.30 Cone layout diagram of the T-Drill test

2   Instruct your subject to sprint as fast as they can to cone B, then shuffle left to cone C, then shuffle right to cone D, shuffle back to cone B and finally run backwards to cone A.

3   Start the watch when your subject's first foot touches the floor. This will avoid reaction time influencing the final result.

4   Record the result and repeat a further two times.

Similar to the Illinois test, the T-Drill test is useful when assessing performers who need to change direction during their sporting activities. The use of power and speed will enable a sports performer to be successful and this test is a useful field measure of these fitness characteristics.

Advanced field- and laboratory-based testing protocols

There are a range of testing protocols that we can use to assess the body. Some require more specialised equipment that is frequently found within universities or specialist testing facilities.

While the use of an Astrand-Ryhming cycle ergometer test, the multistage fitness test and Cooper run test are able to assess your subject's VO_2 aerobic capacity, we can use an alternative that takes a direct sample of air from your subject's lungs. Using a mouthpiece, your subject is able to breathe directly into a collection device known as a Douglas bag, allowing for air to be breathed in but not allowed to escape through the use of controlled valves. This method allows you to measure the carbon dioxide and oxygen that is leaving the body and from which we are able to determine how hard your subject is working. If they are working very hard, the Douglas bag will contain a high concentration of carbon dioxide as this is a waste product. A high carbon dioxide level will indicate that they are using more energy to exercise at that intensity. If they are working at a low intensity, their breath will contain little carbon dioxide and a high concentration of oxygen as this has not had to be used when exercising. This will indicate that the subject is working at a low intensity. If we do not need to use much oxygen for exercise, we can then simply remove it by breathing it back out again. Therefore as a measure, we can not only use the Douglas bag method to assess oxygen consumption, but also measure the amount of energy used during the exercise. This helps us to measure metabolic rate which is a key determinant of how quickly a subject breaks down their dietary intake and uses it for energy. The Douglas bag technique is more accurate than the alternative methods, therefore most sports scientists prefer to use this if the facilities are available.

Sports performance results from this testing will be dependent on a range of factors including children and team positions. It is important to remember that children's aerobic capacity has not yet fully developed. A sports scientist should consider this when planning any physical activity for a young performer. Typically, children will have a significantly lower aerobic capacity when being assessed using the Douglas bag method.

The type of sports performer will also have a significant impact upon their aerobic capacity. It should be remembered that team performers have different roles and responsibilities, therefore it will be expected that there will be some variation in their aerobic performance. For example, football players are divided into four key areas: the goalkeeper, defenders, midfielders and attackers. Each of these performers will have their own physical fitness demands. Midfielders are responsible for travelling the furthest around the pitch. In contrast, goalkeepers will travel the least, though are required to have the shot stopping strength and power along with the ability to dive and change direction. As a result, it would be expected that the midfield position would have the greatest aerobic capacity due to their positional needs.

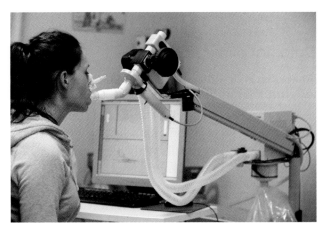

Figure 4.31 Douglas bag testing

As carbon dioxide is a waste product, if it is allowed to stay within the body it can gradually increase the concentration of lactic acid within your muscles. We are able to measure lactic acid by tacking a small sample of blood from a pin-prick. Using a specialist device we can gain a measure of the lactic acid in your subject's body, which can indicate how hard your subject is working. If your subject is working very hard they will have a very

high concentration of lactic acid in their blood. If they are working at a low intensity, the sample would indicate a very low concentration.

As we are aware, strength can be assessed using isometric methods and 1-RM, however another method you can use is protocol known as isokinetic testing. One of the most common uses of this method is when assessing leg strength of a performer. To conduct this test you will strap your subject tightly to a chair and their leg will be strapped to a knee bar. Your subject will then start to flex and extend their knee several times which is monitored by a computer. The equipment measures the force generated by the knee with the reading calculated directly by a computer. This method is helpful for assessing your subject's leg strength and is frequently used by physiotherapists to monitor stages of recovery.

Figure 4.32 An isokinetic knee strength assessment

C2 Experimental data collection methods used within the sport and exercise laboratory

Units of measurement

When conducting research it is important you use units when presenting your data. Without units a measurement has no meaning. For example, if you have measured your subject performing the vertical jump and they achieve 30, you must indicate the units used as this could mean 30 cm or 30 inches. Another example can include the throwing of an implement. If we threw the implement 30 (?), would you mean 30 cm, 30 inches, 30 feet, 30 yards or 30 metres? Without the use of units the data may be misinterpreted, therefore it is very important you include them.

The SI units are the most widely used system of measurement.

- Mass – measured in kilograms, kg.
- Weight and force measured in newtons, N.
- Length and distance measured in metres, m.
- Work and energy are measured in joules, J.
- Power is measured in watts, W.
- Speed and velocity are measured in metres per second, m/s or m s^{-1}.
- Angular velocity is measured in radians per second, rad/s or rad s^{-1}.
- Torque is measured in newton-metres, N m.
- Volume is measured in cubic metres, m^3.
- Pressure is measured in newtons per square metre, N/m^2 or N m^{-2} – this unit of measurement is known as a pascan, Pa. (Remember, 1 N/m^2 = 1 Pa).

Data-recording techniques

As a sports scientist, it is very important you keep clear records of all data that's recorded. This means that prior to testing you should always be prepared with appropriate tables what may be completed during the test. Using make-shift scraps of paper is not suitable as you can easily confuse data or find it hard to read your writing having rushed with the recordings. Always try to design an appropriate data recording sheet that can be easily completed as the test progresses.

When preparing tables, ensure that the data is correctly presented within a table. Correctly grid the tables boxes, avoid floating data as this can be difficult to read. Consider how many rows and columns you will need and add them neatly. Always take pride in your data presentation as it can be key to the outcome of field and laboratory testing. The use of ICT can provide clarity and be more efficient when recording data so always try to take the opportunity to use this technique where possible. Data analysis often uses ICT too, so collecting data in a digital format can speed up the analysis.

When collecting data it is important we take it carefully and with accuracy to avoid any potential risks or incorrect reporting. Identifying experimental errors may be achieved using both a review of the testing process, but also an analysis of the date collected. The review may identify protocol variations that could affect the outcome of the results, and the statistics could analyse any significant difference in the results. It is the identification of these errors and variations that can affect our overall testing validity and reliability, therefore it is important they are corrected throughout any research testing.

Data handling

As we have already covered, data handling remains an important process throughout the testing process. An appropriate testing design is needed that is both valid and reliable, which will enable us to collect results with greater accuracy and precision. It is evident that normative data is able to help us with our evaluations along with the use of nomograms. Using a variety of manual calculations we can analyse our data, as shown within the unit.

Subject	Age	Height (cm)	Weight (kg)	Brake weight (kg)	Peak power (W)	Peak power per kg (W/kg)	Average power (W)

Figure 4.33 Example of a student prepared data recording sheet

Ethical guidelines

Individuals should be referred to as 'subjects' or 'participants' as information disclosure can make some individuals reluctant to participate. You must seek the consent of your subject participant if you want to share the information with additional people and organisations beyond the agreed testing. Keeping records of information will enable you to prepare appropriately for any physical testing. Many methods are tried and tested therefore are ethically sound when it comes to their use. As with all human testing, ethical guidelines still need to be followed. However, having clear records of previous testing can help speed up the considerations needed for ethical testing. Furthermore, if using the same subject for multiple tests then this can avoid recording the same information several times over. As you will recall, when we collect data it is important we keep it safe and secure to prevent any information being shown to others without consent. It is important that the collection is safely stored in a location that is either password protected or in a lockable storage area.

C3 Data handling and evaluation of outcomes when conducting laboratory experimentation

Quantitative data is the most frequent set of information a field and laboratory sports scientist will analyse. From the range of tests you will use, your data will be more often numerical. Quantitative data can be assessed using a range of statistical tests that will allow us explore the outcomes and how we can respond. For example, if a subject performer has poor aerobic fitness, you as the sports scientist can explain that to a coach who can then adjust their training. Similarly, you could test individuals for their BMI and identify those who may be at risk of health problems.

Statistical interpretation of results

For information on data calculations for interpretation, mode, mean, median, range, relationships and differences, standard deviation, t-tests, critical values, Pearson product-moment correlation coefficient (Pearson's r) and comparative norms testing, please see Unit 5 Section D3.

Data evaluations

When analysing the data calculations, it is important you draw conclusions which are accurate and meaningful. Statistical analysis can be a valuable tool in exploring unknown scientific developments, helping you explain the study outcomes. Each calculation can aid you in identifying the success or failure of the study or whether the study aims and objectives have been reached. The evidence and findings of your study can aid you in explaining whether validity and reliability requirements are adequate within the testing.

As we now know, correlations help us analyse the consistency of data which can be particularly important when we are examining reliability issues. If the data is more consistent then it is reasonable to surmise that it shows greater reliability. The validity can be examined using a t-test (see page 214) as it explores the potential difference in data. If there is a significant difference this could be linked to the application and validity of the study methods used.

Therefore, if we summarise the key points we look for when evaluating our data, we should include:

- What are the outcomes of the testing?
- Was the test a success or failure?
- Did you achieve your aims and objectives?
- Is there sufficient evidence on your findings?
- Is your data valid and reliable?
- Were there any difficulties with the testing?
- What conclusions can you make from the testing?

Significance of findings

Following the evaluation you should always explore the meaning of the outcomes. It is important that time is taken to reflect on the results and potentially identify any areas of development. For example, if your study question analysed the responses to heart rate following training, you could begin to explore which type of training is more beneficial. A good evaluation can not only produce results, but it can help explain the limitation of a study and identify areas for development when planning future investigations.

Results are understandably important for coaches and health practitioners as they allow them to interact with the outcomes. For example, a coach could reflect upon varying fitness characteristics and make adjustments to training programmes. Health practitioners could analyse data to support their research and development in creating healthy living lifestyles, reducing the risk of life threatening illnesses such as diabetes or heart conditions.

Therefore, if we summarise the key points we look for when evaluating the significance of our findings, we should:

- Review our study aims
- Apply our research results to future work
- Identify the health implications of a study
- Identify the limitations of our investigation
- Suggest changes and improvements we could make to our testing.

C Check your understanding

1. Which test would we commonly use to assess similarities in data?
2. Which test would we commonly use to assess differences in data?
3. Explain how understanding a data correlation can enable us to make future sporting predictions.
4. Explain why you think statistics are key to sports science.

Distinction activity: assessing aerobic performance C D3

You have been asked by a group of athletes to assess their aerobic performance using two fitness tests. The results you gather are:

Subject	Cooper run	Multistage Fitness test
Reg	44	52
Jackie	40	40
Chris	57	56
Dave	39	43
Joanne	43	45
Suzie	59	62
Simon	63	61
Jenny	54	50

Table 4.15 Results of fitness tests

Using the data taken from two different tests, evaluate the results and explain your findings.

Task 1

1. Reproduce the table and make it presentable using the appropriate units.
2. Produce a correlation chart to evaluate the outcomes of your data.
3. What could be the reasons for these outcomes?

Task 2

1. Perform a t-test (see page 214) to analyse whether there is any significant difference between the sets of data you have collected.
2. Evaluate the data you've collected and justify the answers gained.

D Explore profiling of a sports performer following practical research design using field- and laboratory-based testing (D P6, D M5, D D4)

D1 Scientific application of experimental protocols in sport and exercise science

As a sports scientist you are aware of the importance of looking after your subject participant. With the initial stages requiring the completion of questionnaires, health assessments, a risk assessment and an ethics form, you will also take the opportunity to brief your subject on the testing protocol to be used.

With an understanding of the protocol and its practical application you will be confident enough to start testing with your subject participant. However, before you start, it is important you have a purpose for your testing otherwise all activity becomes meaningless. To do this you must identify what you are aiming to study, how you will apply the testing, and be able to conduct an analysis of the results. By completing these tasks your case study will have a purpose and will observe any changes in a performance throughout your testing.

Practical research design

A case study does not necessarily have to be a large research project as it can focus on a small subject area. However, case studies can be built on and many can be explored further in order to analyse a study area in greater detail. For example, you may choose to study the power performance from a particular group of individuals. To develop this further you may wish to expand your study and increase study numbers, use a greater variety of equipment or focus towards a specific group of sports performers.

Regardless of the size of the case study, it is important we report your work in a basic format for a reader to appreciate.

1   **Title**: This is always the difficult stage, what it is you propose to study. Always keep the title explanatory but clear and concise. There is no need for a long drawn out title, however you should provide sufficient information to provide immediate guidance as to what the study will examine. For example, instead of 'A study on fitness', we could say 'The effects of BMI on aerobic performance'. By providing a little extra detail, you have made it more specific and informative to the reader.

2   **Aims**: You should always try to consider what you are trying to find out. Identify something you want to know, otherwise the study can become meaningless. A hypothesis can be used which states the objective of the study. You should be clear about what you're trying to find out.

3   **Introduction**: Prior to conducting any testing you should always try to provide a background on the study area. For example, using our original title, we could begin to explain the importance of BMI and aerobic performance. As a sports scientist, you could explain the health risks and why it is important we remain fit and healthy. Within this section you are beginning to tell the story, setting the scene for the case study you're about to perform. Within the introduction you should try to reference any information you have used whether that be text, diagrams, tables, charts or pictures. While a formal research project would be in greater depth, you should always try to provide background knowledge to inform and create interest for the reader of your study.

4   **Method**: The method should be clear and concise throughout. It simply explains what you did but not what you are going to do. It is very important you record the method in the past tense, it's what happened and not what you are going to do. It can be divided into subsections. In the first section you can explain details about your subjects, how many were used, what groups were there, provide details on their average age, on what sports they play or their current fitness level. This will give a good indication of the subjects that you are using in your project. Next, include your research design, how you collected your information. After the research design give a list of the equipment you needed to use. The final section of the method is to report the procedures you undertook. Provide

enough information so that anybody reading it could reproduce exactly what you did with little difficulty.

5   **Results and analysis**: The results should contain the data of what you collected during and after the testing process. It should be word processed, clear and concise with the correct use of units throughout. All tables and charts should be correctly titled so that a reader can clearly see what they are showing. Ensure titles are descriptive as it will allow the reader to understand what is being shown.

Using Excel and SPSS, the results should be analysed using statistics in order to establish patterns of change or areas which are not at first obvious from an initial analogy. Patterns in the data could be observed such as the greater the BMI, the lower the aerobic fitness. With the use of appropriate analysis techniques such as correlations and t-tests (if applicable), you can start to build up a picture of what's been shown from the data. Remember at this stage the analysis is only commenting, building up evidence and demonstrating observations. It is within your discussion where you critically evaluate your findings. From the results you can describe what they show.

6   **Discussion**: This is the in-depth analogy of your results, therefore it crucial to your case study. You should reflect on your results and identify what you think has happened. Within the results you should simply report observations; however, within the discussion you should then start to examine why they could have occurred. For example, if BMI is linked to aerobic performance, is there any reason why this may have occurred? Provide details and explore using research references. This will help to build a critical analysis of your results which is excellent practice for a sports scientist.

Always refer back to the aim of your case study and to what you stated in the introduction. Did your idea of what was going to happen come true, if not why not? Also explain what went wrong and why. What could you have done better or were there things beyond your control? Explain how your study could be improved, perhaps additional tests or different types of tests. Finally, give some ideas for future research – as sports science evolves so new suggestions can help to develop a wider understanding.

7   **Conclusion**: This is a round-up of what your case study demonstrated. Summarise the main findings of the study, referring back to the aims and title. The conclusion does not need to be too long or detailed. Simply outline the findings and summarise what has been discovered.

8   **References/bibliography**: Here you will list the references you have used within your report. In the text of your introduction and discussion you should have quotes or citations referring to other people's work which should be recorded in a list at the end of your work. The Harvard system of referencing is commonly used in sport and exercise science academic work. A sports scientist will be expected to demonstrate this throughout their work therefore it is good practice to ensure this skill is developed.

9   **Appendix**: In this section you should include any information that does not readily fit into the rest of your report. Details such as the original raw data sheets, questionnaires, and additional supplementary information can be included. You can refer to any of the details in the appendix in the main body of the report. The appendix should be labelled (example: Appendix A). If you do refer to the appendix in your report, you could do it like this: 'Appendix A shows that … (See Appendix A)'.

Testing protocol

As we have already covered within our testing protocols, it is important we implement clear research designs. The application of appropriate methods will enable us to maintain safe working practices when testing. See page 152 for details.

Data collection

When collecting our data, we should ensure that we use appropriate methods of collection. It will be remembered that using ICT can help us prepare and record our data in an appropriate format. The use of clearly labelled tables, ensuring that we maintain anonymity throughout the recording process, will ensure that the data remains confidential and is not in breach of the Data Protection Act. See page 160 for details.

Data presentation

With the collection of data it is important you present it in a format which makes it easy for interpretation. If data is difficult to understand due to problems with its presentation, it can be misleading which could ultimately lead to inaccurate conclusions being drawn. Always look for the most appropriate method and ensure it is correctly presented.

- **Tables**: Ensure all tables are clear and concise. They should be titled, labelled and numbered above the table throughout. A title should appear above the table, but a figure number can either appear above or below. You should ensure that each box of data is surrounded by a boarder to avoid any free-floating data which can make it difficult to read clearly. The use of appropriate units for data is extremely important, otherwise it can become meaningless. Try to avoid excess information within a table, keeping it focused on the experimental data needed for your study.

- **Graphs**: Ensure all graphs are clear and can be interpreted easily. They should have a title and a figure should be provided below the display. It is extremely important that appropriate units and a scale or label is provided for all the axes. Graphs do not necessarily need to take up the whole page; however, they should be large enough for them to be easily read. The scale does not necessarily need to start at zero, however this should be clearly indicated on the graph. If a legend is required then ensure one is provided and if in colour, ensure that a colour printer is used. Remember, a black and white printer will only print colour

in grey scale which means that all colours will be similar and difficult to interpret the differences.

- **Bar charts**: Like graphs and tables, all bar charts should be clear and concise. Data should not be excessive as this makes them difficult to interpret. All axes should be correctly labelled with appropriate units applied. If they are completed in colour, a colour printer should be used to present them. If numerous bars are being provided, avoid grey scale as this can make them difficult to compare. Ensure they are correctly titled and an appropriate figure is used so that are easy to follow.

- **Histograms**: Like the graphs, histograms should be presented with appropriate use of axis labels, units and colours (if applicable). The histogram focuses on the frequency of the data presented. The data can be recorded into a scatter plot, allowing for a chart to be gained from the recordings. For example, Table 4.16 and Figure 4.36 could show the amount of people who enjoyed running at school.

Age	Frequency
5–10	6
11–15	14
16–17	4
>17	0

Table 4.16 Example of histogram table

- **Cumulative frequency**: Similar to histograms, cumulative frequency relies on the amount of times a value is present, i.e. frequency. It is obtained by continually adding up the

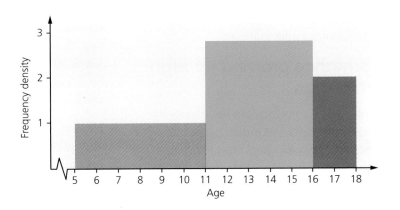

Figure 4.34 Example of histogram chart

frequency at set points, gradually providing a running total until all data has been accounted for. For example, if conducting a sit and reach test we can use the frequency table to see how many participants are able to perform a test over set distances.

Length	Frequency	Cumulative frequency
21–24	3	3
25–28	7	10 (= 3 + 7)
29–32	14	24 (= 3 + 7 + 14)
33–36	6	30 (= 3 + 7 + 14 + 6)
37–40	2	32 (= 3 + 7 + 14 + 6 + 2)

Table 4.17 Example of cumulative frequency

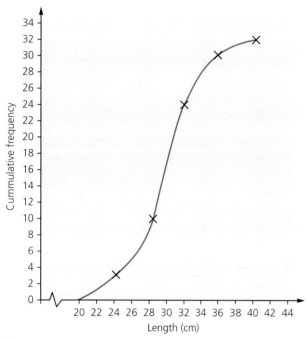

Figure 4.35 Example of cumulative frequency graph

Normal distribution and skewness

See page 213 for more information.

D2 Performance profiling through research design

Athletes and exercise performers have long been profiled with different anthropometric somatotypes and physiological characteristics significantly contributing towards their success. As a sports scientist, your research can help to support a coach improving their athlete's performance. The use of field and laboratory testing methods can enable you to identify performer strengths and weaknesses, which can allow a coach to agree targets for development during their training activities.

Stages of profiling can vary, however the principle remains the same:

- Selection of key performance characteristics
- Testing data analysis
- Identification of strengths and weaknesses.

Development strategies

When considering the characteristics, it is important that you discuss them with both the athlete and the coach, as together you can begin to devise a strategy for development. Also, by identifying the characteristics of success, you can focus your training and development needs and plan accordingly. For example, a 200 m sprinter may concentrate too heavily on their upper body strength rather than their leg power. Through discussion, you may consider that their training programmes could be adjusted to focus more on leg power rather than create bulk in the upper body.

The next phase using testing can help the athlete and coach reflect upon the changes needed. Having conducted the testing, the results can be analysed to identify the strengths and weaknesses of the performance. As the sports scientist, you can use the data to make comparisons to norms data, which may help identify any development needs. For example, against comparative data, you may identify appropriate fitness components such as their peak power being poor, however, their strength endurance is good. As a result, you will identify that your 200 m sprinter clearly has the strength endurance to carry them through to the line, but their initial power drive from the blocks needs to be improved upon. This initial phase could be a crucial characteristic to the race therefore this weakness would need to be addressed.

Having analysed the data and identified performer strengths and weaknesses, you will be in the best position to advise the coach and athlete of their development needs. As a group you will be able to identify performance priorities and agreed goals to work towards. Future planning may require ongoing testing to monitor progress which can motivate the performer, should positive performances develop. If there are changes required, then the testing procedures will enable you to make alterations to the training which can help to develop new training strategies. This process is very important for international performers. For example, many athletes refer to the Olympic Games as a four-year plan. This process begins with early development goals, establishing training priorities, identifying their strengths and weaknesses, and then adapting their training for future successful performances. All this takes time, which is why many athletes plan over a long period to reach success.

Activity: Examining a research design

1 Using the internet, search for a research article on a sports science subject area of your choice.
2 Summarise the research design and its outcomes, referring to the study title, its aims, method, results, and summary of findings.
3 Examine the design and provide a number of improvements you could make to develop it further if you were to repeat it in the future. For example, greater number of participants, varying ages, different tests, etc.
4 Complete the summary and your recommendations on a PowerPoint presentation and present your findings to the class.

D Check your understanding

1 How can the use of field and laboratory fitness testing help us to profile potential athletes of the future?
2 How can profiling help a coach to develop the performances of their athlete?
3 Explain how physiological characteristics can help determine performance success.
4 When presenting tables and graphs, name five important inclusions in presentation and recording that we must always follow in order to enable our data to be fully understood.

Distinction activity: Preparing for case-study (C D3 , D D4)

A research scientist has approached you to provide them with ideas and a plan for their up and coming research project. They need help on how to prepare the study, what should be included within each section and how it should be analysed.

Task 1

Follow the study template and include within each section what you believe should be included. Propose a research problem that links to sporting performance and the prediction of performance outcome. You should provide an overview of the relevant statistics that could be used and analyse what they would show.

Remember you should include:

1 Title
2 Aims
3 Introduction
4 Protocol
5 Results
6 Discussion
7 Conclusion
8 References
9 Appendix.

Task 2

Your scientist is studying anthropometry and somatotype, so provide an outline of how to perform these methods, evaluating their effectiveness.

Task 3

In your plan evaluate the use of somatotype and anthropometry as methods of performance prediction.

Further reading

American College of Sports Medicine (ACSM), (2013), *ACSM's Guidelines for Exercise Testing and Prescription (Ninth Edition)*, Lippincott Williams and Wilkins.

Beam, W.C. and Adams, G.M. (2013). *Exercise Physiology Laboratory Manual (Seventh edition)*, London, McGraw Hill Higher Education.

Baechle, T., Earle, R. (2008). *Essentials of Strength Training and Conditioning (Third Edition)*, Human Kinetics.

Coolican, H. (2014), *Research Methods and Statistics in Psychology (Sixth edition)*, London, Routledge.

Eston, E. and Reilly T. (2008). *Kinanthropometry and Exercise Physiology Laboratory Manual: Tests, Procedures and Data*, London, Routledge.

George, D. and Mallery P. (2013). *IBM SPSS Statistics 21 Step by Step: A Simple Guide and Reference (13th edition)*, London, Pearson.

Useful websites

American College of Sports Medicine

www.acsm.org

Brianmac

www.brianmac.com

BBC Bitesize

www.bbc.co.uk/education

British Association of Sport and Exercise Sciences

www.bases.org.uk

Human Kinetics

www.humankinetics.com

Sport Science

www.sportsci.org

Sports Coach UK

www.sportscoachuk.org

References

American College of Sports Medicine (ACSM), (2013). *ACSM's Guidelines for Exercise Testing and Prescription (Ninth Edition)*, Lippincott Williams and Wilkins.

Beam, W.C. and Adams, G.M. (2013). *Exercise Physiology Laboratory Manual (Seventh edition)*, London, McGraw Hill Higher Education.

Baechle, T., Earle, R. (2008). *Essentials of Strength Training and Conditioning (Third Edition)*, Human Kinetics.

Coolican, H. (2014). *Research Methods and Statistics in Psychology (Sixth edition)*, London, Routledge.

Eston, E. and Reilly, T. (2008). *Kinanthropometry and Exercise Physiology Laboratory Manual: Tests, Procedures and Data,* London, Routledge.

Foss, M.L. (2000). *Fox's Physiological Basis for Exercise and Sport*, London, McGraw-Hill.

George, D. and Mallery, P. (2013). *IBM SPSS Statistics 21 Step by Step: A Simple Guide and Reference (13th edition)*, London, Pearson.

Heyward, V.H. and Gibson, A.L. (2014). *Advanced Fitness Assessment and Exercise Prescription (Seventh revised edition)*, Human Kinetics.

Heyward, V.H. and Stolarczyk, L.M. (1996). *Applied Body Composition Assessment*, Human Kinetics.

Kent, M. (2007). *Oxford Dictionary of Sports Science and Medicine (Third edition)*, Oxford, Oxford University Press.

Maud, P.J. and Foster, C. (2005), *Physiological Assessment of Human Fitness*, Human Kinetics.

Reiman, M.P. and Manske, R.C. (2009). *Functional Testing in Human Performance: 139 Tests for Sport, Fitness, Occupational Settings*, Human Kinetics.

Thomas, J.R. Silverman, S. and Nelson, J. (2015). *Research Methods in Physical Activity (Seventh edition)*, Human Kinetics.

Walker, I. (2010). *Research Methods and Statistics, London*, Palgrave MacMillan.

5 Applied research methods in sport and exercise science

About this unit

This unit will enable you to explore the importance of research when analysing performance. It will enable you to appreciate how we examine sports science and make sense of the results it can produce through testing. Sports science is just that, a science. This is often forgotten and confused, with it often being thought of as simply participation rather than its examination. Understanding the science requires us to reflect on performances and make a scientific judgement on what has happened, how and why. This unit will help to develop your research skills and enable you to appreciate the true outcomes of sport and exercise performance.

It is essential that we are able to use a range of assessment methods and this unit will introduce you to the investigative techniques we can use to help us make sense of what's going to or has happened. Understanding the difference between quantitative and qualitative methods is essential for us to appreciate how to effectively use our research methods. This unit will help you to understand these terms and enable you to confidently apply them to research projects and testing activities.

Learning aims

This unit is split into four learning aims, each addressing the applications of a sports scientist. The learning aims include:

A Understand the importance of research in sporting environments

B Examine key issues that impact on the effectiveness and quality of research

C Examine the three main approaches to research in the sport and exercise sciences

D Apply appropriate research methods to a selected sport or exercise sciences-based research problem.

Each learning aim includes an assessment outcome that divides the content into key areas, sub-dividing the learning aim and allowing you to appreciate each of its components.

How will I be assessed?

The unit of research methods will be assessed by assignments that have been designed internally by your tutors. It is likely that there will be three assignments for you to complete. Each assignment will enable you to apply the knowledge you have learnt to a range of activities.

For Learning Aims A and B, the awarding body recommend learners write a report that examines the importance of research when working with clients in sport-based settings and the key issues that affect the effectiveness of research. For Learning Aims C and D, the awarding body recommend learners prepare a presentation that introduces the three main approaches to research in sport and exercise sciences and then presents the methods and results from an in-class mini-investigation.

Learning aims A and B achievement

For distinction standard, learners will show the importance of the relationship between the different types of research, the factors affecting the quality of research, ethics, and how these affect a sport and exercise scientist's ability to adopt evidence-based practice with clients. Evidence – such as relevant textbooks, websites or appropriate level peer-reviewed journals – to support learners' suggestions is required for the award of this criterion. There will be a clear conclusion to the learner's work. For example, only working in their own area of competence is important for the welfare and safety of the research participant, as well as for ensuring that collected data is valid, reliable, accurate and precise, which will then affect the conclusions and interpretations possible from the research.

Learning aims C and D achievement

For distinction standard, learners will evaluate why they chose the overall approach to research (quantitative, qualitative or mixed), research design, data collection method(s) and data analysis method(s). This reasoning must be supported with evidence from an appropriate resource (for example, sport and exercise science-based research methods textbook unit or appropriate-level journal) and should be clearly linked to the advantages and/or disadvantages of the overall approaches, design and methods. Learners will also demonstrate proficient use of skills in complex or advanced situations – for example, showing that they are able to collect data in a laboratory-based setting, then analyse the data integrating appropriate descriptive, inferential and practical meaningfulness statistics.

How will I be graded?

The table below shows the grading criteria for this unit. To achieve a pass grade you must meet all the P criteria; to achieve a merit grade you must achieve all the P and all the M criteria; to achieve a distinction grade you must achieve all the P, M and D criteria.

Pass	Merit	Distinction
Learning aim A: Understand the importance of research in sporting environments		
A P1 Explain the importance of research in sporting environments. **A P2** Explain the importance of using research to inform your own work with clients in a sport or exercise science context.	**A M1** Analyse the importance of different types of research to inform your own work with clients in a sport or exercise science context.	**A D1** Evaluate the importance of research in sport or exercise science contexts, making justified conclusions.
Learning aim B: Examine key issues that affect the effectiveness and quality of research		
B P3 Explain validity, reliability, accuracy and precision and their importance in sport and exercise sciences-based research. **B P4** Explain research ethics and their importance in sport and exercise sciences-based research.	**B M2** Analyse the relationship between validity, reliability, accuracy, precision, and the ability to conduct ethical research in sport and exercise sciences.	**B D2** Evaluate the importance of key issues that impact on the effectiveness and quality of research.
Learning aim C: Examine the three main approaches to research in sport and exercise sciences		
C P5 Explain the three main approaches to research in the context of sport and exercise sciences. **C P6** Explain the advantages and disadvantages of the three main approaches to research in the context of sport and exercise science.	**C M3** Compare quantitative, qualitative and mixed-methods research in the context of the sport and exercise sciences.	**C D3** Evaluate the choice of research approach, design and methods for a selected sport or exercise sciences-based research problem, justifying the research skills used.
Learning aim D: Apply appropriate research methods to a selected sport or exercise science-based research problem		
D P7 Explain the appropriate research methods for a sport or exercise science-based research problem. **D P8** Explain the research skills used to address a selected sport or exercise science-based research problem.	**D M4** Analyse the research methods for a sport or exercise science-based research problem and the research skills used to address a selected research problem.	

Table 5.1 Assessment criteria

A Understand the importance of research in sporting environments
(A P1 , A P2 , A M1 , A D1)

A1 Introduction to research and the different types of research

Definitions of research

A research method may be considered as a technique we use to investigate a study area. There are a range of methods that can be used, each of which aim to solve problems or discover new skills so that we can make continued advances in our knowledge of sports science. The type of method we use will always be dependent on the research topic. There is never one method that is suitable for every research question. Each study has its own research question. Each question has its own hypothesis which we aim to examine and answer. The hypothesis identifies and challenges relationships between variables, providing a focus point for a study investigation.

Types of research

As a researcher, we have two summary forms of data that we can use to base a study on:

- Primary data
- Secondary data.

Primary data is that which has been collected directly by the researcher and is therefore original data. The researcher has been the individual who has developed and collected the data for the specified study. Secondary data differs in that it uses data that has been collected from already established information from existing sources. For example, if a study examined the responses of heart rate to a fitness test, the researcher can easily conduct the test and collect the data. This would therefore be primary data. However, if the researcher wants to compare their data to that of another similar study by a different researcher, they will have to rely on the other researcher's data. This data from the separate researcher would be known as the secondary data.

A2 The importance of research for individuals involved in sport and exercise science

Literature searching and reading appropriate sources of information

Understanding secondary data can be very helpful when deciding on developing a research question. While it is not always necessary to include secondary data, background reading of previous research can help to decide on a topic to explore in greater detail. It is therefore important that we search relevant literature from appropriate sources which can help to develop our sport or exercise science-based projects. This stage of research may involve quick basic searches using internet search engines; to the use of more advanced techniques including the internet, published journal and textbook sources. Journal articles are particularly important as they contain ever evolving up-to-date research, published from the most recent studies so are at the cutting edge of sports science. They can be found either within your local library or online journal databases. Discuss with your library as to whether they are able to provide access to these resources using an online journal database. The use of key words to filter through all the different subjects and topics when searching is essential as it will help to find exactly what you're looking for. Remember not all information will be listed exactly as your work is titled therefore it's important to look for key words that can be used to search and use within your work.

Examples of how research has been used to develop knowledge and understanding

Research reviews are often key to the development of new studies and theories. Many sports scientists conduct research reviews to understand the latest theories and concepts. Training practices and research into environmental responses are ever changing within exercise performance. Many coaches use research opportunities to keep themselves up to speed with the latest developments in order to keep ahead of their competitors. As sports science evolves, it is important we are up-to-date with our knowledge and understanding.

A3 The importance of using research to inform work with clients

How research has been used to benefit clients

Study research continues to allow us to reflect on our understanding of sports science and help us develop strategies to improve our knowledge further. It has continued to benefit clients by offering them the latest technology, the most up-to-date training developments and enhanced competitive performances throughout the years. For example, the combination of new training techniques and our understanding of nutritional supplements, has continued to enable us to train harder and recover faster. Psychological studies have helped us appreciate the influence of stress, and understand why some athletes become more aggressive than others. Research has enabled us to identify the causes of aggression and develop strategies that may be used to overcome it during competitive situations.

By using the latest research, we are able to apply the latest technology, training techniques and supplementary support to enhance sports performance. This application is often referred to as evidence-based practice (EBP) where studies can demonstrate responses from research (evidence), and these are developed and applied within a sports performance setting (practice). It is the use of these evidence-based practices which continue to improve sport and exercise performance. Careful research will provide evidence of success on a small scale, however when applied within a competitive situation, we begin to put the theory into practice.

B Examine key issues that affect the effectiveness and quality of research (B P3 , B P4 , B M2 , B D2)

B1 Validity, reliability, accuracy and precision in research

Validity may be defined as the extent to which a test, measurement, or investigation achieves what it has been designed to do (Kent, 2007). Choosing a valid test can be a problem in sport and exercise science research. Frequently people measure and try to make general statements and interpretations about what they have found. For example, the sit and reach fitness test is often used as a measure of flexibility. It requires the participant to reach as far forward as they can, stretching their legs and lower back, as they move their hands towards their feet. Keeping their legs straight, the test can measure the flexibility of the joints and muscles in this region. However, while the test can measure the legs and lower back, it is does not measure flexibility across the whole body. Therefore, when we consider whether the test is a valid measure of total body flexibility, the obvious answer is no! If an individual has very good flexibility in their lower legs, we should never assume that this is the case across the whole body.

It can be difficult to find any test that is totally valid due to the number of variables that can affect the outcome. So for us to accurately interpret results and draw meaningful conclusions, our test must be specific and relevant to the component which it is testing. Valid tests are very important to sports science, as they can enable us to draw good, accurate conclusions from what we have measured. By trying to make our research as valid as possible, we will be able to have greater certainty in making our study more successful.

Impact of accuracy and precision on validity

Validity may be statistically analysed, which will allow you to check the accuracy and precision of the testing protocol. If any testing has been carried out using an inaccurate procedure, or there has been a failure to follow precise methods, then this will be reflected within the result. This can in turn provide a false outlook of the study conducted, causing a sports scientist to draw conclusions that do not reflect the true outcomes.

The calculations used to examine validity can focus upon the significance of a test and help us to accept or reject the results produced. Poorly prepared methods and data can cause a sports scientist to draw wrong conclusion. Therefore, the impact of both the accuracy and precision can be considerably damaging if not carefully considered throughout a research study.

Types of validity

1 **Internal validity** – where we consider whether the effects of the study have manipulated a variable. For example, the research has created something to change.

2 **External validity** – the extent whereby we consider whether the outcomes of a study reflect that of a generalised population. For example, does the outcome of a study into sugar intake and the development of diabetes, reflect that of a generalised population?

3 **Face validity** – the most traditional understanding of validity. We simply consider on face value, whether the test appears to measure what it claims to.

4 **Ecological validity** – the extent to which the research study reflects that of the real world. For example, if a study examines an athlete exercising in an environmental condition, then this condition should be constructed to replicate the same situation. Ecological should not be confused with external validity as this is a generalised representation of results.

Reliability may be defined as a characteristic of a measurement which produces consistent results. In other words, if we were to repeat a test, we can be certain that the next set of results will be similar to those from the previous test. We can say that the results gained show greater consistency and that their repeatability will provide more accurate results in future testing. This feature is very important to a sports scientist as it allows them to collect results with accuracy and draw conclusions with greater certainty.

Reliability and validity are often confused and misunderstood. While they are closely related, both have different applications when preparing a testing protocol. It is important to remember that validity focuses on the appropriateness of a testing protocol, whereas the reliability focuses on the consistency of a protocol to deliver similar results. Understanding this, it is important that a sports scientist chooses a reliable test in order to make it valid. However, it is possible to select a test that is not valid, though can still be reliable.

Types of reliability

To ensure testing protocols are reliable, it is important you take repeated measures which are referred to as test re-test reliability. For example, when collecting body fat or skinfold data for analysis, its reliability comes from the consistency of the measurer. If a subject has their measurements taken by an inexperienced sports scientist, their results could be inconsistent and not reflect the true values of the subject. With the data being unreliable, the test becomes invalid as a different protocol has been applied on each occasion, i.e. the measures are inconsistent. To accurately record skinfold measures, the sports scientist must be highly skilled therefore the results are only as accurate as the skill of the sports scientist taking them. Repetitive measures can help to minimise this problem as the sports scientist can become more skilled and reliable when performing this testing procedure.

Other forms of reliability include inter-observer reliability which measures the consistency of measure between humans, such as the scoring by judges in a boxing match or gymnastics performance. Another example is known as internal consistency reliability, which measures the same component using a different test to gather a similar result. In reality this reliability looks for a correlation, checking whether one test is just as accurate at determining a variable as another. For example, both the 12-minute Cooper run and multistage fitness test are used to try and determine aerobic endurance. These tests use different methods, however we would need to check whether they are able to determine a similar result. Therefore, if the results are similar, there is a good indication of a correlation which could help us decide whether the results have internal consistency reliability.

Impact of accuracy and precision on reliability

Like validity, reliability can also be statistically analysed in order to determine its accuracy. Calculations on the similarity of results can be made to identify correlations. These can recognise potential trends and show links between data.

As with validity, all consistencies are subject to acceptable data differences when analysing its outcomes.

It is important to remember that it is very difficult to be totally certain that the results we gather are completely accurate. We are only able to measure variables to a certain degree of precision and accuracy.

Differences between reliability and validity

Accuracy may be defined as how close something is to its actual value whereas precision may be defined as the degree of agreement of a measure. They can be affected by a range of factors including both the equipment and/or the sports scientist using it. For example, if you weighed somebody using a set of bathroom weighing scales, they may provide a slightly different result to that taken from a set of clinical laboratory scales which are finely calibrated. Understanding this, both the accuracy and precision of a test are very important when we consider the concepts of validity and reliability. If we are trying to establish the bodyweight using clinical laboratory scales that have been regularly calibrated, the method we use could be considered as valid. By being precise we can repeat collect similar measurements in agreement therefore can consider the results as being reliable.

When testing it is important to be aware that if testing is conducted with a lack of accuracy and precision, then this can have a significant effect on the validity and reliability of the research study.

B2 Ethical issues

Research ethics and ethical issues as outlined by the BASES Code of Conduct

Research ethics may be defined as a process whereby there is an application of ethical practices to protect all participants. To ensure it is carried out to respectable standards, studies are frequently required to follow the British Association of Sport and Exercise Sciences (BASES) code of conduct which ensures the safety and acceptability of participation. Following such standards can enable a study to gain ethical clearance which deems the research to be acceptable, safe, confidentially appropriate and suitable.

As noted in Unit 4, it is important to respect the rights of others and ensure that they are not negatively affected by the tests or research that you plan to perform. The participant's safety and well-being is paramount during the study, which is especially enforced when working with children or vulnerable adults.

Ethical testing should always ensure that any participant provides informed consent to participate in the testing activities. The consent provides an agreement of willingness to take part in the testing activities, while allowing them to ask any questions about the testing process. All participants should have the right to confidentiality and full privacy during testing activities, meaning that no unauthorised viewing of their personal details is allowed. Any data collection should be stored securely in line with the Data Protection Act (1998), otherwise this may lead to legal prosecution. Further prosecution may be enforced should unskilled assessments take place, putting the participant in danger. All sports scientists should be competent in their role and act appropriately to avoid any personal discomfort for the participant.

Ethical issues as outlined by other professional sporting bodies and organisations

Many organisations such as Sport England, the Football Association, the Rugby Football Union, the Amateur Swimming Association, and many other sporting bodies will have extensive ethical practices and policies in place in order to allow for the safe participation of their athletes. These procedures may include the conduct of coaching staff and athletes, the application of training practices, or the application of child protection policies.

The impact of ethical issues in research settings

During any research testing, a participant has their own rights and responsibilities and their safety and well-being should be of utmost importance throughout the study. A participant should be aware of their right to withdraw from testing at any time. They must give informed consent whereby the testing process has been clearly explained to them (informed) and they

Subject	Resting Pulse (bpm)	Blood Pressure (mmHg)	Height (cm)	Weight (kg)	BMI (%)	Waist/Hip Ratio	Peak Flow (L/min)	Age (Yrs)
1	68	131/89	187	94	27	0.83	590	18
2	66	129/79	172	56	19	0.67	450	17
3	61	141/71	170	61	21	0.82	450	17
4	65	127/67	177	76	24	0.82	500	18

Figure 5.1 Example of data collection with 'subject anonymity'

agree to take part (consent). They must be willing to continue to take part and not be under any duress or pressure to continue. Research often requires the recording of sensitive information and it's very important that it is safely stored to protect confidentiality. Any information should be anonymously recorded with each individual being referred to as a 'subject' or 'participant'. By using these terms, the participant subject cannot be identified by any other individual involved within the testing except for the managing sports scientist. While there is the Data Protection Act (1998) that restricts the sharing of sensitive information, the use of anonymity can enhance a study's credibility as it can avoid any bias reflection throughout the analysis procedures.

The preparation of clear data tables and use of subject or participant labels can enable data to be recorded with great accuracy throughout. While carrying out any testing is important, the quality of the data collection can enable a study to have the maximum potential to draw effective conclusions and interpretations.

Distinction activity (A D1 , B D2)

1   Research a journal article that analyses the effect something has upon an exercise performance. Your article must show a physical test and a collection of data using an appropriate method.

2   Read the article and make a summary of the aims, objectives, methods, results, and conclusive findings.

3   Analyse the article.
    a) Explain whether you would consider the research to be valid.
    b) Explain whether you would consider the research to be reliable.
    c) Explain how you would consider the research to have been collected with accuracy.
    d) Explain how you would consider the research to have been collected with precision.
    e) Identify how the research has been conducted ethically.

4   Evaluate the importance of these terms in determining the quality of the research.

A and B Check your understanding

1   Explain the term 'validity'.
2   Explain the term 'reliability'.
3   Define research ethics and explain why it is important to research testing.
4   Explain why it is important to maintain confidentiality when conducting physical testing.
5   Explain the advantages and disadvantages of primary and secondary research.
6   Provide an example of evidence-based practice and explain how it can help make advances in sports science.

C Examine the three approaches to research in sport and exercise science (C P5 , C P6 , C M3 , C D3)

While understanding the different research approaches is key, it is important that we try to use them within a practical setting. Research methods when applied can help us to appreciate the true outcomes of a sports science research study. Throughout this learning aim, we should always consider how to apply rather than just to understand. Application is key within any study in order for us to fully investigate its outcomes.

C1 Quantitative research

Quantitative research refers to the collection of numerical data through measurement and statistical analysis. For example, if we were to collect data on the heart rate responses experienced by a group of individuals and find out their average, the data would be the beats per minute and we could calculate the average from the total gathered. Testing accuracy and precision are extremely important with quantitative research as it relies solely on the data to make an interpretation. If the data is incorrect then this will lead to inaccurate calculations and conclusions being drawn, also referred to as deductive research.

We can use a range of methods to collect this data including questionnaires, for example 'how many hours a week do you exercise?', observations such as how many shots on goal during a game of football, and taking physical data measures such as heart rate or body weight. As quantitative is numerically-based, we can perform calculations on larger sample sizes as the data is easy to manage if we use appropriate recording techniques.

Advantages of using quantitative research

Quantitative research allows the research scientist to measure the cause and effect of a testing procedure. For example, if we are analysing the heart rate response to exercise, the change in response would be caused by the exercise and the effect would be for it to either increase or decrease. As quantitative research enables us to test large numerical sample sizes (i.e. large groups), we can be more objective with our conclusions. By being more objective we can test our test hypothesis and theories (i.e. what we think will happen), as well as our null hypothesis (i.e. the opposite of the hypothesis) with greater accuracy.

Quantitative research allows us to measure potential performance influences or causes, and measure strategies as to how we can change or affect them. As a result it is often viewed as being more credible research and seen as a more accurate method to determine a research answer.

Disadvantages of using quantitative research

A disadvantage of quantitative research can be that the knowledge we gain can be too general and not enable us to probe for further responses in various scenarios. For example, some studies may have influencing factors that are unable to be assessed using quantitative measures. If the researcher requires information on beliefs and attitudes to exercise, it may be difficult to reflect this within a numerical quantitative assessment.

C2 Qualitative research

Qualitative research differs to quantitative research in that it is more question-based and uses non-numeric data such as words, images or behaviours. The use of interviews and discussion-based questionnaires are good examples of this method where words and images are particularly important to its outcome. It is often a technique we use to gain information on emotions, opinions and beliefs. As a result it may be referred to as indicative research as it measures the mood or psychological feelings that may be expressed throughout the research. As this research requires the assessment emotional opinions, it is more suitable for smaller sample sizes. Along with this, its success is highly dependent on the trust and rapport that is built up between the researcher and participant, as this can be an important component in helping them to open up and be more responsive to questions.

Advantages of using qualitative research

The advantages of the qualitative technique is that it can provide a deeper understanding of a subject topic. Unlike quantitative research, qualitative research allows us to be more flexible and dynamic in response to the needs of participants, and our researchers' findings (or interim findings), enabling us to follow up with further questions should there be a need for additional information. Furthermore, we can also use this research alongside quantitative research to understand why a phenomenon occurs, such as identifying the psychological behaviours based on quantitative responses. For example, we could ask:

How many hours do you exercise in the gym per week? (*Quantitative research*)

1–2   2–3   3–4   4–5   5–6   6+

What motivates you to go to the gym? (*Qualitative research*)

Disadvantages of using qualitative research

The disadvantage of using qualitative method is that the collection and analysis of data can be very time-consuming. If 20 participants require an interview, this can take much more time than if they were each to complete a quantitative questionnaire and return individually. Along with this, the research can be very subjective as it is open for interpretation and relies heavily on the interaction of the researcher and participant. As already noted, the rapport and trust can have a significant effect on the overall outcome of the results that are gathered. With the responses relying heavily on personal experiences, the research gathered may not be generalised to other settings as it is built on emotion, opinion and beliefs. Responses could be determined on personal experience rather than simply a reflection of a questionnaire. As a result, qualitative research can provide a subjective analysis rather than objective outcome.

C3 Mixed-methods research

The mixed-methods research is very common within many studies as it combines both quantitative and quantitative techniques (within the same study). These studies allow the researcher to gain quantitative data which can be explored further in a discussion-based context or through more descriptive responses, e.g. descriptive questioning on a questionnaire. Using our previous example, we can use quantitative research techniques to identify how many hours an individual attends the gym per week, and then use qualitative research techniques by asking the participant about their motivation to go to the gym.

Advantages of mixed-methods research

An advantage of this method is that it uses both quantitative and qualitative research techniques. The use of mixed-methods of research can strengthen a study, as it enables us to overcome potential problems of missing key information that may be essential to understanding the outcomes. For example, if a researcher was to use a qualitative research method, they could ask a participant questions about their overall health and blood pressure. From the research gathered, the results may show that the respondent believes that they're fit and healthy with no immediate health problems. However, if we were to combine this research with a quantitative method, the results may indicate that their blood pressure is very high and therefore their health is at risk. This is in direct contrast to the qualitative results, therefore the combined use of these methods has helped to uncover information that one method, the qualitative, may have missed without the use of a quantitative measure. The outcome could be that, despite the participant feeling healthy, the reality is that the measures provide a different outlook. The use of both tests strengthens the project's findings and overcomes the weaknesses of the other. In this example, the qualitative research has identified that despite the participant feeling healthy (the study's weakness), the blood pressure is evidently very high which strengthens the accuracy of our research.

Disadvantages of mixed-methods research

While the use of both techniques can improve the study accuracy, a disadvantage of the mixed-methods research is that it can be time-consuming as it uses multiple tests. Furthermore, the additional tests may be expensive which can be a significant drawback where studies are run on tight budgets, as is frequently the case. Additional problems may be that due to the varied range of methods that may be used within the testing, some research sports scientists may not have the necessary skills to accurately conduct and conclude the study outcomes. As a result this could lead to problems with the validity and reliability of the study procedures. To overcome this, a research team could be employed. However, the study success may be governed by the skills of the additional researchers and the financial demand it may cost the overall project.

D Apply appropriate research methods to a selected sport or exercise science-based research problem (D P7 , D P8 , D M4 , C D D3)

D1 Quantitative research designs

Experimental research design

Quantitative research is a study technique whereby we collect experimental data for analysis. The research design uses random participants and examines their responses to a variable. This variable could be an object, stimulus, environment and many other examples. The main focus is to control all the variables that could create a response and manipulate one which could affect the person's response. For example, a group of athletes are provided with two pairs of running spikes and timed over a set distance. One set would be their normal training pair and the other would be a brand new lightweight shoe with exceptional grip for sprinting. The test would aim to compare the training pair against the lightweight high grip shoe to see if they made a difference. The training pair would be known as the control as these will be the results that the new shoes will be compared against. Control groups are essential as they can enable the sports scientist to make a comparison of the before and after effect, which can help us to understand what has happened and why. The changed pair would be known as a variable which has been changed to conduct the test. All other variables during the test should be controlled to avoid any other additional influences. For example, the sprints could be conducted indoors wearing the same clothing and soon after one another. The changed variable would isolate the use of different running spikes which avoids other influences on the results. The use of a control now becomes very important as the variable of the new spikes would be compared and results analysed to assess for any potential differences. The outcome of the results may show the change in sprint spikes caused the athlete to improve their sprint time therefore indicating that they could be the best shoe to wear for competitions. This research design can be developed further by using what is known as a cross-sectional/survey design.

Cross-sectional/survey design

This design examines the trends of a population and analyses their characteristics. For example, a study may analyse the trends in human diet and the development of diabetes. Research has shown that women who eat too many complex carbohydrates during pregnancy have a higher risk of developing diabetes prior to giving birth. As this is a study, it is unable to examine the whole population to establish the true results. To overcome this medical practitioners conduct tests on small populations to identify trends in a sample of pregnant women. While it does not necessarily mean that every person will develop the same condition, evidence suggests that from a cross-section sample of the population, there is a trend and relationship with poor diet and diabetes. The results for this research were gathered using questionnaires and surveys that analysed the individual's lifestyle and diet. This research technique often uses questionnaires and surveys as they allow for large quantities of data to be analysed and the outcomes can easily be reviewed.

Longitudinal design

A longitudinal research design involves the measuring of a component or experimental variable over a long period of time to see how they change. This could include measurements that last over a number of weeks, months or years depending on the project. For example, it is possible for studies to measure the body's response to nutritional supplements or changes in training methods using this technique. As the design involves an analysis of data over a long period of time, it can be more helpful when we are trying to draw conclusions over long-term performance. As a result we use this method to measure gradual change rather than a one-off performance, as you would expect with an experimental research design.

D2 Quantitative data collection methods

Common quantitative data collection methods

As we are aware, quantitative measures involve the collection of a data component which can be used in a statistical analysis. Common tests that are used include laboratory and field testing methods and surveys. For example, using tests such as the 12-minute Cooper run can enable us to calculate the distance run, performer average running speed, and more importantly their aerobic capacity (VO_2 max). If a group was to be tested then the quantitative data collected could enable us to examine group performances across the class. It is important that any research uses appropriate data recording methods. These may include initial paper-based copies that may be used on the field and copied up when in a laboratory facility, or online password protected spreadsheets that aim to keep all the data private and confidential.

Whichever method is chosen, it is very important that the recording of data is both clear and concise to avoid any misinterpretation of the data at a later stage.

Uses, benefits and limitations

There are many uses, benefits and limitations when choosing a data recording method, each of which should be considered when preparing the testing methods. For example, while the benefits and use of paper-based data recording sheets can be convenient, their limitation is that they have the potential to being easily damaged, lost or poorly interpreted when returned back for online data transfer. A benefit is that they can easily be adapted and require no specialist equipment other than a pen to record the data information. However, it is not acceptable for any data recording to be collected on a 'scrap' of paper which is often the case during testing at school or college environments. Paper copies should be clear, easy to use and easy to read to ensure the results remain accurate. Due to their ease of use, transportation and adaptability, paper-based collection methods are often used during field-based testing and transferred when back within a laboratory setting.

The use of online password-protected spreadsheets can also be useful when collecting data for analysis. Their benefits include providing clarity of presentation, ease for further data analysis, and ease of safe storage online. However, their limitations can include failure of computer software, forgetting passwords to access work, failing to save the work correctly, or preparing confusing spreadsheets that make interpretation difficult. Password-protected spreadsheets understandably require specialist equipment to record information, therefore are often limited to a laboratory setting.

Surveys: While surveys are an excellent method of collecting large quantities of data, their limitation is that they can take much time to prepare and interpret their final outcome. Furthermore, it is not uncommon for some surveys to produce a low return rate. By returning such low levels of data, this can lead to inaccurate conclusions being drawn based on the limited returns. To overcome this problem, researchers can use 1:1 surveys whereby they individually ask a participant questions face to face. However, this technique also has additional limitations in that the researcher has the potential to influence an individual's response, e.g. make them feel guilty about their unhealthy lifestyle.

D3 Quantitative data analysis methods

When you have completed your testing, it is now important to interpret what it means. We can use a number of methods, from making comparisons to norms data, to performing various appropriate statistical calculations. The analysis of the data can enable us to:

- compare to normative data
- make comparisons to different populations (e.g. gender, age)
- make predictions on sports performance
- compare different kinds of sports performers and athletes
- identify trends in health.

In doing this we can also:

- consider the accuracy of the data
- examine the reliability of data
- assess the similarity of data.

It is essential you collect your data as accurately as possible and take time to ensure it can be understood, so that you can interpret its findings.

Descriptive analysis and organising data

As we know, when collecting the data it is important you place it all clearly into tables, ready for interpretation. During the initial analysis you can reflect on what it shows using the basic tests of mode, mean, median, and range.

Mode

The number that represents the mode, is that which appears the most within a group of data. For example, when collecting skinfold measures from nine subjects, the following data has been collected:

Subject	Skinfold (mm)
1	6
2	3
3	9
4	6
5	6
6	5
7	9
8	6
9	3
Mode	6

Table 5.2 Subject measurement of skinfold with mode value

From looking at this data it is possible for us to see that the most frequent measurement number is 6 mm, therefore you will be able to identify that 6 mm is the mode value.

Mean

The mean value of data is more commonly referred to as the average. This is the central value of all the data, the number that falls between the highest and lowest values. To calculate the average we simply add up all the data and then divide by the number of results.

Subject	Skinfold (mm)
1	6
2	3
3	9
4	6
5	6
6	5
7	9
8	6
9	3
Mean	5.89

Table 5.3 Subject measurement of skinfold with mean value

Total = 53 mm

Mean = 53 mm/9

= 5.88 mm

Median

The median value is the middle number taken from the sample. This is less commonly used for data analysis, however it can allow you to sort the numbers in order should this be required.

Subject	Skinfold (mm)	Subject	Skinfold (mm)
1	6	2	3
2	3	9	3
3	9	6	5
4	6	1	6
5	6	4	6
6	5	5	6
7	9	8	6
8	6	3	9
9	3	7	9
		Median	6

Table 5.4 Subject measurement of skinfold with median value

As can be seen, using our original data we can rearrange it into numerical order, and then find the entry that is midway between the first and last entry. In this case there are nine results so we need to find the fifth result. The midway result belongs to subject number 4 and its value is 6 mm.

Analysing the range

When analysing the range of data we are identifying the difference between the highest and lowest values. Using the original data, you can see that the lowest measurement was 3 mm and the highest was 9 mm. We can calculate the range from taking the highest recorded value and subtracting the lowest value. In this case, the data shows that this highest is 9 mm and the lowest is 3 mm. As a result the range will be 6 mm.

Standard deviation

The standard deviation measures the variation of data from the mean value. Using this method you are attempting to identify how much data is dispersed each side of the mean. It can be calculated by the square root of the mean of the square of all the deviations away from the mean. We would record this calculation as a value plus or minus around the mean $\pm$ SD. For example, if we had a small group and we weighed each individual, we may find that the average weight is 70 kg. By carrying out our standard deviation calculations, we may identify that the variation of data is 2.5 kg each side of the mean. To record this we would show our data as 70 ± 2.5 kg, which represents the mean value and the data spread around it.

Whereas range considers all of the data and provides us with the lowest to the highest value, standard deviation focuses primarily on the majority of the data which is located around the average. The benefit of this is that you are able to concentrate on the main bulk of the data, two-thirds, which allows you to draw more accurate conclusions on the data trend. The outliers, which are the unusual data falling outside the two-thirds (65%), can distort your study results and not necessarily provide a true reflection of the testing. Situations where this may occur could include inaccurate data entry, faulty equipment, and poor data collection technique.

Rank order distribution

Rank order distribution is where data is ranked from the lowest value through to the highest. For instance if you have measured VO_2 max across ten subjects, you can rank the person with the lowest VO_2 max measurement as '1', the second lowest '2', right through to the person with the highest VO_2 max who is ranked '10'.

Simple frequency distribution

Simple frequency distribution is where data is arranged in order based on its frequency of measure. For example, if a football team scores a number of goals per game we can measure how often they scored 1, 2, 3, 4, 5 goals. Using this method we may find the following results:

Scores:
1, 1, 2, 2, 2, 2, 3, 3, 3, 3, 4, 4, 5

Score	Frequency
1	2
2	5
3	4
4	2
5	1

Table 5.5 Frequency of goals scored per game

From this data we can produce a graph or chart to help illustrate the results outcome.

Grouped frequency distribution

Grouped frequency distribution is a very similar to that of simple distribution, however it uses a range of frequencies that are arranged into number order. Whereas simple frequency focuses on the distribution of the values attained, grouped frequency aligns the data into order across a range. This enables you to identify the peak point of the data as it can show a spike in data if a trend was to be shown.

In Table 5.5 above the grouped frequency would be:

Score	Frequency
1–2	7
3–4	6
5–6	1

Table 5.6 Grouped frequency

Grouped frequency distribution is useful when you have a lot of data.

You can display this kind of data by using a frequency distribution scatter plot. This format allows you to plot data by frequency instead of using individual bars per data, as would be the case on a conventional bar chart. The frequency scatter plot uses a series of plots which can then be summarised using a histogram (see Figure 5.2, which has been created using Statistical Package for Social Scientists (SPSS)). SPSS is similar to EXCEL in that it allows you to record and display data. It is often used due to its versatility when using statistics and can perform a range of complex statistical tests through data entry.

The presentation of data is very important. It should displayed in the most effective format – for instance, there is rarely any need to include raw data. Tables of data should contain units and must have a suitable title. Graphs should also incorporate units and labels and contain a title. Any picture, photograph or diagram, including graphs and histograms but not tables, is referred to as a figure.

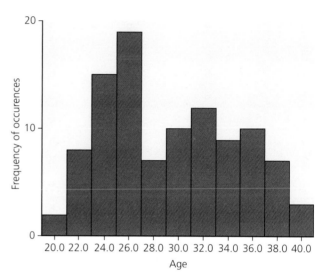

Figure 5.2 A frequency of occurrence bar chart

Activity: Calculating data

Using the following data from a Vertec jump, calculate the following from the group's results:

- Mode
- Mean
- Range
- Frequency distribution.

Subject	Height jumped (cm)
1	62
2	50
3	50
4	43
5	39
6	56
7	39
8	53

Table 5.7 Results from a Vertec jump test

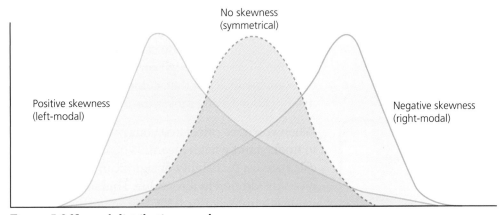

Figure 5.3 Normal distribution graph

Distribution curves

Normal distribution

While standard deviation focuses on the bulk distribution of data around the mean, normal distribution analyses the location of the majority of the data. The location can indicate whether there is an equal grouping around the mean or whether there is an unequal alignment either side. If the majority of the data is located to the right of the mean, this indicates that there is a negative skew, whereas if bunched to the left this is known as a positive skew.

Normally distributed data is described as bell-shaped when plotted on a graph. In an exact true normal distribution, the mean, median and mode are all the same. If the distribution is asymmetrical the data is not normally distributed.

In a normal distribution 68% of the data should fall within one standard deviation from the mean, referred to plus or minus 1 standard deviation (+1 SD or –1 SD). 95% of the data will fall within plus or minus 2 standard deviations from the mean (+2 SD or –2 SD) and 99% will fall within plus or minus three standard deviations (+3 SD or –3 SD). Most data that we collect we would expect to be normally distributed. Therefore, we would always want 68% of our data to fall within 1 SD of the central mean to show true normal distribution.

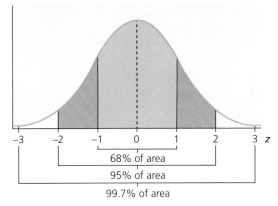

Figure 5.4 Normal distribution showing standard deviation

Selecting appropriate inferential statistics

Data correlations

When analysing statistical data we can use what are known as parametric and non-parametric tests. Parametric statistics make assumptions that your data collected is normally distributed and is interval or ratio data. This is the most common analysis method and is used when we can confidently assume that a normal distribution is shown within your data.

Our second analysis tests are non-parametric which are used when we examine data that is not normally distributed. An indicator is that your results could be noticeably skewed or not showing the consistent bell shape around the mean. This form is less common as in sports science we can often see data patterns in existence. To perform these tests we use ordinal or nominal data.

By understanding the type of data, we can begin to perform an appropriate statistical test. It is important that we take time to consider which test should be used, as it can determine the whole outcome of the research study.

Key terms (forms of data)

Interval is a group of data that is measured in equal units, e.g. temperature.

Ratio is a form of interval data, however there is a natural zero point, e.g. measuring your height from the ground.

Ordinal is a ranking or positioning of data, e.g. result across the finishing line.

Nominal is a basic category which could be numerical or descriptive data.

How to conduct appropriate inferential statistical tests

Parametric tests

A correlation may be defined as a measure of similarity between at least two sets of data. Relationships look at how one thing affects another and can be analysed using correlations. Differences decide if one group is different from another. Using scatter diagrams we are able to identify trends also known as linearity. The linearity can show whether there is an ongoing pattern whereby one set of data shows a similar pattern to that of another.

For example, in a study we could measure the effects of jogging on heart rate. If you created a study question, 'Is heart rate affected by jogging?' you can investigate whether the speed of a treadmill is proportional to the speed of the heart rate, i.e. the faster the treadmill the faster the heart rate.

If there is a link identified, you can calculate how much of a relationship there is, known as the correlation coefficient (r). If you identify that the heart rate beat per minute correlates to the treadmill speed, you can conclude that there is a positive correlation. Using a statistical calculation, the correlation coefficient (r) for a positive relationship would be represented as +1. If there is no relationship, r would be calculated as 0. However,

if the relationship is the other way around, one goes up as the other goes down, this is a negative correlation. Therefore, you can see that r can be between +1 and –1. A high correlation, association or relationship is just that; it does not necessarily mean that one thing causes the other.

When you have calculated your r value, you need to understand what it means. When a correlation is calculated, a probability or significance value is also given in addition to the r value. This significance value is a number (e.g. 0.10). The value gives the likelihood of what you are testing being true. For example, if you were testing a relationship and you had a significance value of 0.10, this would indicate that 10 times in 100, you would be wrong if you said there was a relationship. However, the flip side is that 90 times in 100, you would be correct. In social science (e.g. sports science or psychology) the largest allowed significance value is normally 0.05 (being wrong 5 times in 100). If the significance value is higher than 0.05, then it is considered that any relationship between the values is not statistically significant. Mathematically, the specific significance value of 0.05 is written as $p < .05$.

The use of data correlations are valuable to sports science as they enable us to make predictions on potential responses. We are able to track progress and identify links between components that may otherwise have been missed. The process of assessing samples and making chance predictions based on relationship probability is known as inferential statistics and is frequently used by sports scientists when analysing data.

Dependent and independent t-test

With parametric statistics, the most frequent difference test we can use is the t-test. An independent t-test is used when we are investigating differences within a group, e.g. a performance from the same person. A dependent t-test is used when we are investigating a difference inside the group, e.g. comparing a person against others.

Difference tests are used for studying the effect of something on a group of individuals, for example, how training affects fitness levels. The outcome of difference tests is reported the same as a correlation, but rather than a relationship we aim to identify a significant difference. For example, if you were investigating whether there is a significant difference between the heart rate of a group of individuals that exercise and those who do not, we can use a t-test which calculates the difference by providing us with a T value which can be analysed with certainty. The T value uses tables of significance, enabling you to conclude whether there is a reasonable certainty that the results are different.

Pearson product-moment correlation

A Pearson product-moment correlation is one type of test that can be performed to analyse association or relationship. In order to perform this test a number of criteria must be met.

Firstly, the data used must be taken from related pairs, meaning that it should be collected from the same individual. For example, if using data for height and weight, all the data must come from the same individual, we are unable to pick and choose individual values from other subjects.

Secondly, the data should be either interval or ratio level data. Interval data is that where the difference between two data has some meaning. For example, a 10 degrees celsius difference between two measurements of temperature actually means something. Note that temperature in degrees celsius does not have a defined 'zero point' where the measurement has to stop, i.e. temperature can get extremely hot or cold forever. Ratio data is similar to interval data except there is a clearly defined 'zero point'. For example, when measuring your height, your start point will be zero on the floor and your end point will be the top of your head. This is a start and end measurement point which is unlike the interval data.

Finally, the data used should be normally distributed, and we discussed these characteristics earlier in the unit.

The significance of the results gathered using this correlation calculation are dependent on the closer the value is to +1. For a strong significance to occur, your results would be expected to show a value of +0.874, indicating a 'high positive correlation'. The strength of the relationship is dependent on group size therefore this should always be considered when you are calculating this result.

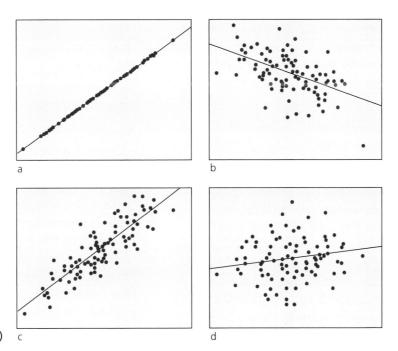

Figure 5.5 Scatter diagrams indicating typical correlation meanings (*Source:* interpret a correlation, **www.dummies.com**)

Activity: Creating a correlation chart

Using the data below, taken from two different tests for aerobic performance, compare the results and explain their findings, using the most appropriate method. Consider what you are trying to do and which statistical analysis technique would be most suitable.

Subject	Cooper run (mls/kg/min⁻¹)	Multistage fitness test (mls/kg/min⁻¹)
1	44	52
2	40	60
3	57	53
4	39	49
5	43	45
6	59	42

Table 5.8 Calculation of aerobic capacity using aerobic-based fitness tests

1. Does the correlation show any similarities between the data you have collected?
2. What could be the reasons for this?
3. Explain the outcomes of the testing procedure.

Non-parametric tests

As we are aware, non-parametric tests examine statistical data where there is no assumption that the data is normally distributed. We can analyse such data using alternative statistical tests. These tests include:

- Wilcoxon matched pairs signed rank test
- Mann-Whitney U test
- Spearman's rank order correlation.

The **Wilcoxon matched pairs** signed rank test measures data at an ordinal level, i.e. in a numerical order. It is used when we need to examine paired data from within a testing group. For example, if we were to examine performance data based on the results gathered from using 'coaching programme A', against the results of using 'coaching programme B', we would be assessing whether one programme was more successful than the other. The Wilcoxon can help us identify whether there was a difference in the outcomes of the programme, or that they both simply produced similar performances. As is shown from a t-test, we are attempting to establish whether a difference in programme used by the same person has been shown between the two programmes. However, unlike the t-test, the Wilcoxon makes no assumption that any change has taken place therefore may be used instead. The Wilcoxon uses a T value which can be calculated using Excel or SPSS. For there to be evidence of a significant difference between the programmes, we would require this calculation value to be as high as possible when plotted on a critical value table. It is the critical value which measures the level of significance and the overall certainty of a result.

Like Wilcoxon match pairs test, the **Mann-Whitney U test** uses ordinal data, is non-parametric and examines samples of data for differences. However, the two methods differ as they are reliant on the design of the experiment from which the data is produced. For a Mann-Whitney U test to be used, the data should come from unrelated samples whereas the Wilcoxon will use related samples. For example, when we examined the differences in performance caused by our changes in a coaching programme, we used the Wilcoxon test. The reasoning for this was because we took repeated measures from the same group to calculate the difference or change. If we now aim to compare differences between different groups of individuals, referred to as an unrelated design with independent measures, we then use the Mann-Whitney U test to examine our differences. In essence the Mann-Whitney compares groups whereas Wilcoxon compares internal performance.

Non-parametric data can also be used to analyse its strength of association with another variable, or more commonly referred to as its correlation. While we discussed the use of a Pearson's correlation earlier in the unit, a **Spearman's rank correlation** aims to assess a similar concept but using non-parametric ordinal data. The important component becomes the use of ordinal data which is the ranked order of data rather than interval/ratio data which as we know is based on equal scale. Whereas a Pearson's correlation uses data dispersed across a chart based on its measured values, a Spearman's rank uses the results order for plotting. For example, if we were to analyse the performance of athletes' javelin throw and shot put results, we could plot their personal best positions on a graph to provide us with our correlation.

Athlete	Javelin throw (m)	Javelin ranking	Shot put throw (m)	Shot put ranking
1	38.10	6	12.50	6
2	39.56	5	15.56	3
3	58.01	2	14.10	5
4	42.50	4	16.01	1
5	51.48	3	15.92	2
6	65.68	1	15.13	4

Table 5.9 Athlete performances within the javelin and shot put events

Therefore, using the ranking order of performance, we can plot our correlation based on performance. While we can consider that the individual results were good, this procedure ignores this component. The main focus here is the ordinal rank and not the actual performance.

As can be seen, it is very important that we select the most appropriate method to analyse our data and statistics. When conducting inferential calculations, it is important to familiarise yourself with statistical software such as SPSS and Microsoft Excel for support. These are very supportive in aiding the calculations as well as accurately developing appropriate tables, charts and graphs. It is important that any statistical calculation be considered in terms of its relationship and differences. When analysing the data calculations, it is important you draw conclusions which are accurate and meaningful. The statistical outcomes and their meaningfulness may be dependent on the recorded change and the effect size it has had. Drawing a result from a larger sample can have greater meaning should there be an indication of change. Understanding this, statistical analysis should always try to use an appropriate sample size to accurately measure the impact of percentage change, and the magnitude the effect may have had. Statistical analysis can be a valuable tool in exploring unknown scientific developments, helping you explain the study outcomes.

D4 Qualitative research designs

Common qualitative research designs used within sports science include:

- Case studies
- Historical/Retrospective studies
- Grounded theory
- Ethnographic design.

Case studies involve an investigation of a single case. They aim to analyse a specific situation or case and explore it in greater detail. Case studies may involve the analysis of individuals, or groups (such as a single team, or class within a school); or multiple cases (involving two or more cases) but all stemming from the same fundamental phenomenon. For example, if a study was to examine people's attitudes to watching sport before and after the Olympic Games, the single focus of the case study would be to examine how our interest changes due to support participation. The case study may identify how the Olympic Games inspires people to take part in sport which is the overall aim of the investment legacy.

Historical or retrospective research studies aim to collect and analyse data relating to past events to try and identify why they happened. These studies are often used when we are aiming to make sense or comparisons of historical events against that of current day outcomes. For example, historical research studies may examine knee arthritis problems in competitive football players in comparison to non-players. The outcomes of the study would assess the relative risk of over-use injury through performing repetitive historical activities.

The use of **grounded theory** research involves the gathering and analysis of qualitative research in order to generate new theories. This research may be in the form of interviews and observations which are analysed for their importance. As a research method, it is supportive in understanding social studies as it can help to investigate how an individual responds during different environmental circumstances. Grounded theory often develops through reflection rather than identifying instantaneous results such as in a qualitative study. The theory involves stitching together other research to enable us to develop new or simply extend existing theories.

An **ethnographic design** is a method we can use to study a group or culture without the need to become immersed within the group. This research often focuses on an in-depth study of members of a culture, in an attempt to understand the wider picture. It is often used to reflect on everyday life and practice in order to reflect on the overall culture. For example, a study could examine sports culture in different countries and how participation and health are viewed as important components of living.

D5 Qualitative data collection methods

Interviews

This is where the researcher will ask a series of questions to a person. Interviews tend to be used mainly with qualitative research. A good individual interview will rely on trust and rapport to obtain information. Interviews are good at assessing somebody's attitude towards something. They can allow for probing or follow-up questions (e.g. 'What do you mean by …?'). This can lead to a deeper level of understanding which may not come across on a quantitative study. On the negative side interviews are time-consuming, they can be open to biases on the part of the interviewer and can result in the interviewee giving answers that are socially acceptable.

An interview may be structured, unstructured or semi-structured. A **structured interview** involves the use of a set of standardised questions that are all the same in each interview and used in the same order. An interviewer would simply ask all the questions, using the exact same questions in the exact same order. This is a very common technique in qualitative analysis as it can limit bias that could be gained by asking any additional, more probing questions, beyond that of the original planned by the interviewer.

An **unstructured interview** involves the use of questions that are not prearranged prior to collecting the research. On many occasions the unstructured interview can appear to be more discussional rather than a formal interview due to its unplanned approach. It is very reliant on the interaction and rapport between the researcher and interviewee. With poor communication it can affect the outcome of the interview with the results and feedback from the questioning. Good interpersonal skills such as being able to relate to the interviewee can help to draw more in-depth answers during the interview. As a result, the unstructured interview can be less consistent when focusing on a topic due to its lack of structured content.

A **semi-structured** interview is a very good middle ground between the use of structured and unstructured. It benefits from the use of standardised questions which then allow the researcher to explore the responses provided by the interviewee. For example, a researcher may be investigating the health and fitness of a sample population. They may ask the structured question 'What would you consider to be a healthy diet?' Following the response, the researcher could ask an unstructured question linked to their response such as, 'Would you consider yourself as having healthy diet? And why?' The response enables the researcher to explore the topic in detail, allowing a greater amount of information to be collected which can then be analysed following the questioning.

During interviews information is usually recorded via a voice recorder or filmed footage. A voice recorder is less obtrusive (some people feel nervous faced with a camera); however, the use of camera recordings can give some non-verbal information that may prove beneficial. If a voice recorder or camera is not available, the interviewer will have to record responses by hand. To become a good interviewer requires both ability and practice. If the answers obtained are to be valid, it is essential that the respondent is relaxed and at ease. It is vital that the answers given are genuine and, for this reason, it is important that the interviewer does not influence the response by the nature of their questioning or even by their presence. As with face to face surveys, the researcher is relying on what the subject says, which may or may not be the truth. Techniques can be used to test the validity of a person's answer (i.e. repeated or similar questions can be asked to see if the answers are the same).

Focus groups

Interviews are more frequently based on a 1:1 encounter involving the researcher and interviewee. These differ from a focus group which involves the use of a group of people (5–10 people) who focus on a specific topic. The researcher will guide the session so that issues discussed are relevant to the research. Focus groups are very good for exploring people's ideas, beliefs and values. Again, as with interviews, issues can be probed in more detail and a debate can be formed. Due to the group situation people may feel less self-conscious than when being interviewed one to one, therefore they may be more open and honest with their feedback. You could consider this as safety in numbers. Similar to the interview information can be recorded and analysed after the event.

Advantages and disadvantages of interviews

Interviews and focus groups do have their advantages and disadvantages which should be considered prior to any research event. The **advantage** of an interview is that it can research specific topics that can be guided by the researcher. Depending on the type of interview used, the feedback provided can be supportive in investigating thoughts and responses in a qualitative format. A comprehensive interview with a good technique can draw much information out of the interviewee which can be assessed during an analysis of the feedback. Information can easily

be recorded and reviewed whether that be voice or camera footage recording depending on what is felt comfortable. Focus groups also have their advantages in that they can promote debate and discussion. They can encourage interviewees to bounce ideas, thoughts and feelings from one another to come to an agreeable group response.

The **disadvantages** of interviews are that they can be influenced by the researcher or additional external factors such as the environment or influencing audiences, e.g. friends. For example, the interviews may provide the researcher with inaccurate or dishonest information. If an individual is asked questions about their lifestyle, such as drinking and smoking habits, they may feel ashamed about their unhealthy living therefore provide less accurate information. This is a common outcome, with many individuals only reflecting on their lifestyle when asked to directly reflect on it through questioning. Despite interviews having the advantage of gaining much more information through probing questions, they can be time-consuming and therefore can take many days, weeks or months to gain sufficient information. Additionally, they can be very reliant on the ability of the researcher. The interview technique, body language and their personality can all influence the responses given by an interviewee. The rapport is key between the researcher and interviewee so a level of trust must be built between the two in order to successfully gain accurate results.

Focus groups also have their disadvantages. Leading the group and facilitating discussion is a difficult skill. Often, one or two people have a tendency to dominate the group and others are happy to watch. As there are larger numbers, the group has the potential to discuss unnecessary information. It is important that a focus group is carefully monitored to encourage all contributions and that the subject matter remains the key focus of discussion.

Conducting effective interviews

The use of an effective interview can have a considerable influence on a qualitative study outcome. It is important that the key theme and topic of the interview is clear and concise in order for the interviewee to understand its purpose. The interviewer should try to avoid leading questions, that is, ones that are leading the response to an answer. 'Do you think football players receive too much money?' could be considered a leading question, as it almost implies that footballers are paid too much money. Also avoid unclear terms throughout the interview in order to avoid any potential misunderstandings. If a question begins with 'usually' or 'mostly', you may get a vague and unhelpful response. It is important to be specific. Once a day, once a week, or maybe something different? Also good interviews try not to use technical terms to again avoid confusion or as much interaction by the researcher during the questioning. If you ask a member of the public, 'How many times per week do you take part in aerobic exercise?' they may not understand the term aerobic. They may not answer the question or may answer it incorrectly. You could instead ask them about how often they run, cycle or swim in the gym. This could be followed up with 'How long do you perform this activity?' to gain a response to a similar question. Remember, it is important to allow the interviewee to respond to the questions and not lead them to a response.

When conducting the interview it is always important to consider who will complete it, your target interviewees (e.g. is the interview age-specific?), where you will conduct the interview and how it will be completed. Conducting interviews in busy areas may lead to information being withheld due to other people being able to hear responses. If held in front of peers it could encourage their unnecessary interaction which should be avoided. The body language of the researcher could determine the openness of the interviewee. Threatening or dominating body language could influence the interviewee's responses so it is important to remain patient, encouraging and appreciative of their time at the end of the interview.

Observations

A further means of gaining information or data for research is to observe the subject in a given situation. Observations are common in psychology-based research – seeing what a person will do in different situations. This method is used because it

is less obtrusive than conducting a questionnaire or asking questions in an interview. Also, people do not always do what they say they will do! Coaching is another area that relies on observations for obtaining information. Many sport and leisure qualifications require the use of extensive observations in order to judge competence at performing the chosen activity. When assessing performance, observations can be used by researchers to analyse coach or player behaviour, which can be reflected upon to help players improve future performance.

A good example of this is in football, where notational analysis systems can be designed to examine the amount of physical activity (walking, running, jumping, etc.) performed during a match. Using this technique we can analyse players of different positions and identify player work-rates and physical performance levels. The observation analysis can help us to examine performance needs and make changes to training or positional play.

Non-participant observation

There are many methods of observation. For example, when an observer remains external from the group, they observe participants without engaging with them or the activity, they are known as a **non-participant observer.** An example of this is a coach who observes their own player performances. This observation technique requires the observer to be totally remote from the participants, while reflecting on their performance throughout. The **advantages** of this technique are that it enables the observer to analyse the performance of a large group of individuals or players and make an overall analysis. Furthermore, the observer is able to gain a wider picture of observation, being able to view all and individual participant performances. By not being part of the performance the observer is also able to avoid any bias from their involvement which could influence the final outcome of a result. While there are advantages, the **disadvantages** can include the observation technique causing performers to behave differently, leading to an unnatural performance. This experience is known as the Hawthorne Effect whereby individuals behave differently in the presence of influencing factors.

Along with this, the observation outcome can be heavily influenced by the understanding of the person performing the observation. For example, the success may come from the observer's ability to identify key parts of a performance. The most experienced researchers may have the most accomplished understanding of the key points to look for during this qualitative observation. Having a sound understanding of a qualitative measure can enable a researcher to provide the most accurate results during a long-term study.

The second type of observer may be part of the activity or performance group. This technique is known as a **participant observer**. The **advantages** of this method are that it enables the observer to be part of the action. As a player-manager, a performer is able to reflect on both the performances and game dynamics from first-hand experience. Commonly referred to as observing 'from the inside', in sport it is more commonly practised at amateur level allowing for a coach or manager to observe the game while continuing to participate. As a technique it is a very effective as it allows the observer to experience the action of the performance and gain an understanding 'from the inside'. It enables the observer to gauge the performance experience and the stresses that may be involved. This can allow for judgements and conclusions being drawn with greater accuracy that can be based upon real-time performances. However, while being part of the activity has its benefits, the **disadvantages** are that it requires the observer to be attentive to their own performance along with that of those around them. For a participant observer to be effective, they must be able to concentrate on their own performance and accurately observe. If they are unable to perform and observe together this could lead to their performance being detrimental others, or missing key parts of a performance. Furthermore, this technique is very difficult for the observer to focus on the non-action zones in a game of play. For example, while the ball positioning in netball may be located in one area of the court, the observer would need to be able to make an observation on the remaining players in order to make judgements or an effective analysis. Also, it is very difficult to use this method to assess individual performances such as those mentioned above for notational analysis.

D6 Qualitative data analysis methods

Appropriate methods of data analysis

When examining data there are a number of methods that can help us gain the maximal feedback from the feedback presented. The methods include:

- **Content analysis** – A method whereby we take qualitative information and analyse it using a quantitative measure. It is a useful technique when we are trying to analyse and understand a large collection of text. For example, if we are analysing a coaches response during a game, we may describe a similar action throughout the game, e.g. feedback on positioning or defending during a match. From the content of the feedback given, we can identify how often the same or similar phrases were used. From analysing the frequency of feedback, the coach can examine how often they communicated the same comments throughout a match, enabling them to evaluate the overall team performance.

- **Coding** – A method that identifies a key term or phrase and categorises it for analysis. For example, if asking a participant to explain about why they feel it important to attend the gym, the phrases they use can be highlighted as a key word response. This phrase or description will be qualitative, however may be given a data value that can be analysed using quantitative measures, e.g. statistics.

- **Thematic analysis** – This is the most common and simplistic methods of analysing qualitative information. Very similar to content analysis, thematic analysis involves the researcher reviewing their information and sorting it into relevant categories based on its findings. For example, when a participant has explained the reasons why they think it is important to attend a gym, the codes they produce may have key themes. The themes that are produced may be categorised. For example, many of the participants' responses may be about health and medical benefits. Whereas another participant may identify the health and body image benefits of participation. Another may report the psychological benefits, and so on. From the single subject of attending the gym, we have been able to categorise the general themes as to why people may be attending the gym.

Stages of qualitative analysis

Having generated much data, it is important that it is handled correctly to avoid us from analysing it incorrectly. Sometimes we can have too much data therefore may need to use data reduction techniques to make sense of the experimental outcomes.

Data reduction is not a procedure of throwing information into the bin! It is a process whereby we can compress the data into meaningful parts. For example, if we have interviewed 100 people about healthy living, we would have key parts of the research that may be more influential than others. We can summarise key sections to reduce and compress the initial study findings. Using our qualitative data analysis techniques, we can reduce the quantity of data into a smaller report. The full set of data testing data, known as the raw data, should always be kept as a full record of the study results.

It is important that qualitative data is accurately stored for analysis. The use of tables are essential when displaying or presenting data. They should be clear and concise, allowing for an easy interpretation of a study outcome. When presenting statistics it is important to label units correctly in order to avoid lack of clarity. It is possible to provide example statement responses should an interview technique be used; however, the information should be summarised using the most appropriate data analysis technique, reducing the overall data content. Presenting data accurately can enable us to draw on conclusions with greater accuracy. The use of an appropriate accurate coding and thematic analysis techniques can enable a researcher to provide conclusions with greater certainty. Being able to identify the key elements that are important to a study is extremely important, therefore time should be taken when evaluating qualitative research. This

can allow for future studies to verify its outcomes, check its accuracy and assess its authenticity. The validity and reliability of a study is always paramount within any testing, therefore it is essential that any conclusions can be verified to assess the overall success of the study.

D7 Mixed-research designs

Sequential research design

While we are able to produce research using qualitative and quantitative research methods alone, in some circumstances we can use them together in what's known as a sequential research design. This design involves the use of a qualitative data collection and analysis technique, followed by a quantitative data collection and analysis technique, or vice versa.

This type of study is a very thorough design, as it reflects on both the quantitative numerical and qualitative discussional feedback from the performer. For example, when examining the benefits of health supplements, many studies base their research on how they make the individual feel while taking a dietary addition. Claims of improved endurance performance or recovery rates are often assessed with qualitative questionnaires and interviews. The researcher may ask an athlete to report on how they feel, have they felt any physical benefit from consuming the supplement, and do they feel that they are performing better while taking the product, etc. The consumption phase of a dietary supplement may be researched over a period of weeks, during which time the researcher will be able to analyse how the performer responds to the dietary addition. After a specified period of time, physical tests may be used to gain the quantitative research data, and the results would then be analysed. In this example the application of the sequential design has led to the initial research being collected using qualitative measures, and the following physical measures being gathered using a quantitative assessment. In this instance, the experimental study could help us to analyse whether there has been any physical benefit from the supplement (quantitative measures), or whether the change is a result of psychological perception (qualitative measures).

Parallel research design

Like the sequential research design, the procedure involves using qualitative and quantitative data collection and analysis techniques but running alongside each other at the same time.

An example of this could be shown with the use of lifestyle assessment procedures that are often used by dieticians and nutritional experts. These research studies can consist of a series of **qualitative** interviews and questionnaires, coupled with **quantitative** medical health assessments. These research designs are valuable when examining people's perception of their eating habits. They enable us to monitor dietary progress, as often we underestimate the content and quantity of the food consumed within our daily diet. The qualitative measure may measure a daily response to questionnaires that may require information on what an individual has eaten and when. Should they over- or under-eat, then this would be shown within a quantitative measure, which would be running parallel during this research study. By using this design, we can analyse an individual's diet while gathering measures on blood sugar or blood pressure.

D8 Mixed-research data collection

Using appropriate data collection methods

The methods of data collection during mixed research design should be appropriate to the study outcomes. For example, if conducting a study into **concussion** in sport, it would not be suitable for the researcher to ask participants to become concussed during an activity. This would be ethically wrong, therefore alternative measures would be needed.

Research studies both parallel and sequential could use an analysis of interviews, questionnaires or surveys on the rating of concussion, how it occurred, and the movement pattern that caused the concussion. Qualitative questions and interviews could examine whether there were behavioural changes as a result of the concussion including memory loss, confusion or emotional changes. Using quantitative data analysis measures, a study could examine the frequency of concussion in sport, identify sports that have

a higher incidence of concussion or even death. Quantitative data may also enable a researcher to analyse the current statistics of concussion in sport and making a comparison between that of previous research data in previous years. As we have already identified, using appropriate display methods can help us draw conclusions with accuracy and enable us to understand the full extent of this condition in sport.

D9 Mixed-research data analysis

Using appropriate data analysis methods

As we already know, when collecting our qualitative and quantitative measures it is important we select the correct method of data analysis. For qualitative assessments we can analyse the results using content analysis, coding, and thematic analysis techniques to examine our questionnaires, interviews and surveys. For quantitative measures we can use a range of inferential statistics to analyse the accuracy of our results including their significance and correlation of frequency. Using our sequential and parallel study methods we can analyse our data to draw our conclusions. A study analysis could identify the frequency of a type of concussion injury along with its severity. A parallel study could examine this incidence throughout a competitive season whereas a sequential study could analyse retrospective incidences such as previous season injuries to make comparisons against today's performances. Regardless of the analysis method, it is important to examine people's attitudes to concussion in sport and it is the use of these techniques that aim to achieve this. It will be remembered that one method of study may not reflect the true outcomes of people's understanding and belief of this injury. The use of mixed methods can help us appreciate the dangers associated.

In summary, concussion in sport is a very frequent and dangerous injury. Much research using sequential and parallel studies has gone into reducing its frequency. Injuries such as severe brain injury and even death continue to be a part of some sporting activities, however ongoing research studies have continued to develop safer playing practices.

C and D Check your understanding

1   Using a sporting example of your choice, identify how observations may be used to analyse a performance.
2   Explain how interviews can be an advantage and a disadvantage when conducting qualitative research.
3   Prepare a research plan and analyse the research methods you would use to achieve it.
4   Explain the advantages and disadvantages of mixed-methods research.
5   With the following data conduct a Mann-Whitney U test and explain the outcomes.

Athlete	Javelin throw (m)	Javelin ranking	Shot put throw (m)	Shot put ranking
1	38.10	6	12.50	6
2	39.56	5	15.56	3
3	58.01	2	14.10	5
4	42.50	4	16.01	1
5	51.48	3	15.92	2
6	65.68	1	15.13	4

Table 5.10 Competitive performances within the javelin and shot put events

6   Conduct two experimental tests and examine the data using a Pearson's correlation test and t-test. Explain the outcome of your results.

Case study

Applying mixed research methods to evaluate gym membership (D D3)

Fitness gyms are often busy in January and frequently numbers begin to drop in the following months. There may be many reasons as to why this could happen, and as a researcher, it is your job to try to find out. The gym has provided you with its attendance figures and needs to understand the data to make potential changes in their marketing campaign.

The monthly attendance data is shown below.

Month	Total members	Attendance
Jan	4152	3520
Feb	4100	3621
Mar	3998	3454
Apr	3704	3102
May	3704	3054
June	3339	2909
July	3008	2305
Aug	3000	2102
Sept	3145	2352
Oct	3100	2600
Nov	3012	2408
Dec	2989	2207

Table 5.11 A gym's attendance data

Case study (continued)

Using the data, you have been asked to construct a survey and questionnaire to help you to analyse the reasons why people attend.

Task 1

Using a variety of statistical tests, identify the mode, median, mean, range, standard deviation, produce a Pearson's correlation chart, and any other data analysis techniques you feel are appropriate.

Task 2

Having understood the data for those attended, construct a mixed-research design questionnaire for your peers to answer so that you can understand the reasons why people attend and how often. Remember your questionnaire should be both qualitative and quantitative. Your questionnaire should focus on gym use and exercise participation.

Task 3

With the data you have collected, evaluate the research you have gathered.

Task 4

Compare the quantitative and qualitative measures you have used and evaluate which one you feel has provided you with the most suitable information. Justify your reasons why.

Distinction activity (D D3)

You have been asked to work alongside a researcher to develop a study that investigates a group of javelin throwers' performances throughout their competitive season. The researcher has noted that their performances have been inconsistent and changes may be needed to their training programme. While the training programme is not your concern, the research and recommendations you make are. Throughout the season, you need to examine as many variables as possible to ensure that you avoid missing key information that may cause you to draw inaccurate conclusions. That way you won't need to start the project all over again next year!

Your first problem is that you need to decide upon the research design you will follow, along with the information you wish to gather. You are aware that the throwing problems may not just be because of the distance achieved – there may be additional technique problems such as the run-up speed, delivery angle of the javelin, and speed of release. Additionally, problems could include how the athlete feels each day, the weather or environmental changes, and how the athlete has prepared for the competition.

Task

1 Understanding your research problem, decide upon a potential research design that you may wish to use to examine your study.
2 Using a word-processed research proposal, evaluate the choice of research approach, design and methods, justifying the research skills.
3 You should consider how you will research the problem, along with how you could evaluate the outcomes from your research.

Further reading

Coolican H., (2014), *Research Methods and Statistics in Psychology* (*6th edition*), Routledge.

George D. and Mallery P,. (2013) *IBM SPSS Statistics 21 Step by Step: A Simple Guide and Reference* (*13th edition*), Pearson.

Kent M., (2007), *Oxford Dictionary of Sports Science and Medicine* (*3rd edition*), OUP Oxford.

Thomas J R., Silverman S., Nelson J., (2015), *Research Methods in Physical Activity* (*7th edition*), Human Kinetics.

Walker I., (2010), *Research Methods and Statistics*, Palgrave MacMillan.

References

Clegg F., (1983), *Simple Statistics*, Cambridge University Press.

Coolican H., (2014), *Research Methods and Statistics in Psychology* (*6th edition*), Routledge.

George D. and Mallery P., (2013) *IBM SPSS Statistics 21 Step by Step: A Simple Guide and Reference* (*13th edition*), Pearson.

Kent M., (2007), *Oxford Dictionary of Sports Science and Medicine* (*3rd edition*), OUP.

Thomas J R., Silverman S., Nelson J., (2015) *Research Methods in Physical Activity* (*7th edition*), Human Kinetics.

Walker I., (2010) *Research Methods and Statistics*, Palgrave MacMillan.

Useful websites

BBC Bitesize

www.bbc.co.uk/education

Explorable – Think outside the box

explorable.com

Maths is Fun

www.mathsisfun.com

Sports Science

sportsci.org.uk

6 Coaching for performance and fitness

About this unit

Sports coaches are vital to the success of the modern athlete with many hours dedicated to support their journey to success. Coaches exist in all sporting activities and their role can vary from supporting the elite to developing new talent at grass roots level. While their contributions are often overlooked, they are instrumental in supporting and motivating the athlete as they strive to improve their performance. Their contributions can help with making tactical decisions, understanding the rules of the game along with developing progressive training programmes to enhance physical performance. Whether the coach of an after school club or a top international performer with support staff, it will be the coach who is at the very centre of developing the modern athlete.

This unit will assist those starting on the coaching ladder, learning how to develop coaching sessions to improve an athlete's fitness and technical understanding of performance. It will help to recognise the key characteristics that are essential for effective coaching and enable you to reflect on your own coaching performance.

With a combination of theoretical and practical application, it will help you prepare for a future successful career in coaching.

Learning aims

This unit is split into four learning aims, each addressing the applications of a sports coach in fitness and performance. The learning aims include:

A Investigate coaching for performance and fitness

B Explore practices, adaptations and measures used to develop performance and fitness

C Demonstrate effective planning of coaching to develop performance and fitness

D Explore the impact of coaching for performance and fitness.

Within each learning aim are assessment outcomes that divide the content into key areas, sub-dividing the learning aim and allowing you to appreciate each of its components.

How will I be assessed?

The unit of coaching will be assessed by assignments that have been designed internally by your tutors. It is likely that there will be three assignments for you to complete. Each assignment will enable you to apply the knowledge you have learnt to a range of activities.

Learning aim A achievement

For distinction standard, learners can complete an analysis of the skills, knowledge, qualities and best practice required to deliver coaching for performance and fitness. They will also analyse the use of technology and supporting professionals to support athlete development. Learners will include practical examples to support the analysis, and these can be drawn from coaching activities or relevant life experiences. Within their analysis, learners will identify clear reasons for the inclusion of each element and how they sit within coaching for performance and fitness sessions.

Learning aim B achievement

For distinction standard, learners can evaluate the practicality, suitability, effectiveness and relevance of the practices and measures, making judgements on advantages and disadvantages of each. They will then make recommendations, derived from the advantages and disadvantages, for adaptations to meet the differing performance and fitness needs of individual athletes or teams. Learners will justify the relevance or significance of each adaption in relation to coaching for performance and fitness.

Learning aims C and D achievement

For distinction standard, learners can evaluate the impact of their planning and coaching for performance and fitness on the athlete and/or team. The evaluation will detail strengths and weaknesses, and how each one has contributed towards athlete and/or team performance and fitness during and after the session. During the evaluation, it is essential that learners reflect on the session delivered and their own coaching performance, as well as the impact of their own performance. They will also draw on valid information from the planning and delivery to support their conclusions. In addition to this, learners will evaluate how they could develop their planning and personal coaching abilities for future coaching, suggesting actions to achieve this goal (for example, coaching courses). Learners can also justify the relevance or significance of each action to their personal development as a performance coach.

How will I be graded?

The table below shows the grading criteria for this unit. To achieve a pass grade you must meet all the P criteria; to achieve a merit grade you must achieve all the P and all the M criteria; to achieve a distinction grade you must achieve all the P, M and D criteria.

Pass	Merit	Distinction
Learning aim A: Investigate coaching for performance and fitness		
A P1 Describe coaching for performance and fitness and the methods used to support athlete development. **A P2** Describe the role technology and professionals may have to support athlete development when coaching for performance and fitness.	**A M1** Explain coaching for performance and fitness, the methods used to support athletes and the role technology may play in athlete development.	**A D1** Analyse coaching for performance and fitness, and the use of technology and supporting professionals to support athlete development.
Learning aim B: Explore practices, adaptations and measures used to develop performance and fitness		
B P3 Explain practices and adaptations used to develop athletes when coaching for performance and fitness. **B P4** Explain measures used to develop athletes when coaching for performance and fitness.	**B M2** Analyse practices and adaptations used to develop athletes when coaching for performance and fitness. **B M3** Analyse measures used to develop athletes when coaching for performance and fitness.	**B D2** Evaluate the practicality, suitability and effectiveness of practices and measures used to develop athletes when coaching for performance and fitness.
Learning aim C: Demonstrate effective planning of coaching to develop performance and fitness		
C P5 Produce a detailed plan for an individual performance and fitness coaching session that reflects planning considerations and measures, and fits within an overall series plan.	**C M4** Discuss the interrelationship between own individual plan, planning considerations, measures and the overall series plan.	**C D D3** Evaluate the impact of the planning and delivery of the performance and fitness session, justifying adaptions to future sessions and personal coaching developments.
Learning aim D: Explore the impact of coaching for fitness and performance		
D P6 Deliver the individual performance and fitness session, showing consideration of health and safety factors. **D P7** Review the delivered performance and fitness session, reflecting on own planning and coaching performance.	**D M5** Analyse the impact of the planning and delivery of the performance and fitness coaching session, suggesting adaptions to future session and personal coaching developments.	

Table 6.1 Assessment criteria

A Investigate coaching for performance and fitness (A P1 , A P2 , A M1 , A D1)

A1 Skills and knowledge for coaching for performance and fitness

General skills for coaching

The role of a coach is ever-changing, with many demands placed upon their skill, expertise and supportive capabilities. For a coach to be successful, they must have an abundance of qualities that can be drawn on to cope with a range of scenarios. The key components of a good coach will include:

- being well-organised
- having good rapport with their athletes
- possessing excellent communication skills
- being an excellent motivator
- having good diplomacy
- having a good understanding of the athlete
- having good knowledge of event.

Organisation

Effective organisation skills are crucial to the success of a coach, as each session should be progressive and able to build upon the last. Few coaches have the privilege of just turning up, coaching and going home. Any coach who does not take the time to organise their coaching sessions may risk their success, to paraphrase, 'fail to prepare; prepare to fail'. Organisation serves a number of purposes, including:

- identifying the aim and objective of the coaching session
- planning to meet the participant's needs
- planning for equipment and facilities that may be needed
- identifying outcome achievements.

During the session good organisation enables the coach to be adaptable, reflective and responsive to needs which allows the session to flow smoothly and continues to keep it enjoyable. Remember, it is important that the athlete wants to be coached rather than told they must be coached.

A good means of keeping organised is to write it down. Many coaches keep coaching records, usually in the form of a diary and separate training logbook. Many coaching qualifications require prospective coaches to complete logbooks and maintain a full record of their coaching group for formal assessments. The records can help you track progression, identify strengths and weaknesses, and consider future athlete developments.

Often coaches are also involved in booking facilities, arranging equipment or contacting participants, which involves a great deal of organisation. Some coaches may delegate these responsibilities to team members, such as in the following example.

Senior Women's Volleyball Team

Role	Responsibility
Coach	Team-specific coaching and team selection
Assistant Coach	Warm-up/cool-down/general preparation
Player 1 (Capt.)	Contact players to arrange meeting times and place
Player 2	Washing and looking after kit
Player 3	Contacting officials prior to games
Player 4	Maintain website/travel arrangements
Player 5	All communication with league
Player 6	Introducing new players/school liaison
Player 5	General equipment preparation

Table 6.2 The responsibilities of individual team members

Rapport

For the session to be enjoyable, it is important that the coach and athlete have a good rapport with one another. Many coaches spend much time with their athletes, therefore it is essential there is a good working relationship which can be built through effective communication. The coach is instrumental in motivating the athlete to build on previous achievements for future success.

The most important aspect of the coach and athlete's relationship is wanting to achieve. Achievement does not necessarily mean to win a competition or be the world's best performer; it could be a personal battle from improving a skill to regaining full fitness.

Communication and diplomacy

Communication is perhaps the single most valuable skill we have. The ability to convey your thoughts and ideas to an athlete or group can provide the essential instruction, motivation and encouragement to succeed. It must always be easily understood rather than just opinions. Remember, the coach's opinion is not always right; they must guide the athlete and reflect upon the feedback they are presented with.

The coach must:

1   **Be able to provide clear messages.**

    These are mostly **non-verbal** signals. For example, consider the body language of a coach, is it positive and confident or negative and inappropriate? Does the body language inspire progress or show limited motivation to achieve? Standing at the side with their hands in their pockets and focus elsewhere does not provide much encouragement to the athlete. The main feedback a performer receives in almost every sport is the non-verbal therefore presentation is very important when coaching.

    Avoid overusing **verbal** communication as this can lead to confusion. If the coach provides too much information, it can become forgotten so it is important to keep it specific. The pace, tone and volume of the spoken word will all have a significant effect on participants' engagement. If the coach sounds bored and uninterested, this could lead to the athlete feeling this way. The coach who spends most of their time shouting abuse will quickly lose the respect of their participants and will be less likely to be successful. It is important to remember that the participants want to be coached rather than have to be there so be **diplomatic** and supportive as it will help to motivate them.

2   **Be able to receive incoming messages.**

    This particular skill is concerned with understanding and interpreting the signs and signals of others, player, officials, etc. Listening to valued opinions such as from players regarding tactical decisions, drills in practice or perhaps even concerning opponents. There are many different coaching styles, however reflecting on the information from others can help develop fresh ideas and coaching strategies.

3   **Be able to check message reception.**

    If coaching a particular skill or component, it is important to check the participant's understanding. This is often referred to as a 'learning check'. It is important to avoid treating athletes or participants like robots. Being able to think for themselves and make independent decisions can make for a good performer. Good coaches will question their players regularly to check for their understanding. If something is misunderstood, it must be reinforced as it could be a crucial part of the overall performance. One way of ensuring understanding is to ask players to explain concepts in their own words.

Motivation

Motivation is key for learning and coaching. An athlete needs to have the desire to learn or develop their performance in order to get the most out of a coaching session. A positive coaching environment with stable consistent conditions can help keep the athletes focused. Negativity can have an opposite effect in that it can cause the athlete to become disinterested in developing skills or create performances that are below their best. In the long term this can potentially cause the athlete to become despondent and suffer a reduction in self-confidence and improvement.

Knowledge of sport's technical, tactical and fitness characteristics and demands

Confidence can be greatly increased in a performer by being coached by someone who has good knowledge about the sport's characteristics, technical and tactical demands. Athletes are mentored by their coach, have belief in their decision making and trust their skills to achieve. A good coach must be able to understand the sport, including both the physical and technical demands of the activity. Much experience may come from participation, not necessarily at a high level, however sufficient enough to understand the performance characteristics.

a

b

Figure 6.1a and b Boris Becker as a player (1985) and as a coach of Novak Djokovic (2016)

By having such specialist knowledge, coaches who have experienced the performance are able to identify tactics that may influence play, skills needed to achieve them along with the fitness demands placed upon them.

With each sport having its own physical fitness demands, the fitness component they rely on for success will vary.

We can divide fitness into two areas, each of which has their own individual components:

- physical fitness
- skill-related fitness.

Physical fitness is the ability to work efficiently and be able to cope with the varied demands of activity without becoming excessively fatigued. In a sporting context, this may apply to a 400 m runner who is able to sprint at a fast pace to win in a quick time. They have been able to achieve their time as their fitness capacity has enabled them to continue to run at a quick pace, avoiding them having to slow down because of premature fatigue.

While physical fitness focuses on the ability to work efficiently and cope with the demands of an activity, skill-related fitness differs as it is more activity specific. Skill-related fitness may be defined as the abilities of the functional underlying skills when participating in sport. While they are not focused on one particular sport, they are the fundamental abilities needed to be successful.

Details of the component of physical fitness is given in Unit 8 Section A2. These components will apply in different ways to different sports, as illustrated in Table 6.3 below.

Sport	Key components of fitness
Tennis	• Strength • Muscular endurance
Rugby	• Strength • Muscular endurance
Athletics – 100 m sprint	• Strength • Muscular endurance
Athletics – 5000 m	• Cardiovascular endurance • Muscular endurance
Football	• Strength • Muscular endurance

Table 6.3 The key components of fitness in various sports

Challenge and develop performance and fitness with a range of activities and sports adaptations

For sports performance, it is important that coaching sessions reflect that of the activity. A coach should have a thorough understanding of the rules and techniques needed to deliver stimulating practice sessions. These sessions should aim to replicate game or event situations, adapting the skills needed for a competitive performance. For example, when coaching a badminton serve, a beginner could practise both a short or long serve. The coach would need to understand the rules and techniques needed to place the shot. A points scoring system could be used as a target, adapting the skills necessary for effective accuracy. The ability to be flexible with training practices is an important component of a coach. Effective use of space can challenge and develop a performance. It can be achieved with the adaptation of training activities, training or coaching time, pace and speed of an activity, the people used including the quantity, along with the exercise intensity and duration. Fundamentally the changes aim to develop skills with greater difficulty that may be suitable for a range of activities. The adaptation of games can help to coach basic skills which can then be developed in greater difficulty. For young children the key component is to develop enjoyment of the sport, such as tag rugby rather than full contact tackles. By providing adapted games it can stimulate the love of the sport, inspiring future participation and progress in the sport over a longer period of time.

Planning for changing conditions

An important skill of a coach is to be adaptable as not everything goes completely to plan. For this reason it is useful to plan for the unexpected, therefore contingency plans are always a valuable asset. While it is not possible to prepare for all unexpected situations, efforts should be made to try and prepare a coaching session that could cover many of these issues. For example, participant numbers could be very high and equipment and resources may be inadequate due to a lack of facilities. As an alternative, larger groups and adapted games could be prepared to use the space and equipment available which may require some last minute decision making.

A planned session could be influence by a number of factors, including:

- the weather conditions
- the participant numbers (team games)
- the facility availability
- the equipment availability

- the rate of progress (whether skills are found to be easy or difficult)
- whether the coaching session is too tedious and not varied enough
- the location – whether practice conditions are safe.

Planning for progression

Coaching an athlete or participant to make any progress to improve within their chosen sport takes time. Progression does not happen overnight. Coaching and training takes patience and in most cases it can take many years. Whatever the standard the performer aspires to be, it is always important to start any activity with the basics. For example, badminton is a very mobile and active sport. Many people think they can hit a shuttlecock if they swing wildly at it for a smash and then look surprised when they miss it. To achieve success it is important that we take time to break the skill into its technical components and perform it in a controlled manner. With careful control we can improve the smash action which can lead to us becoming more successful.

The tactical demands can come from when it is appropriate to use the smash. It is not always a suitable shot, therefore as we progress we begin to understand the tactical elements of shot choice and placement.

Progression in fitness is one element that is more commonly referred to as making progress. While it is an important component it is not the only one. Fitness progression can come from the development of training programmes that become progressively difficult over the weeks and months of training. While it is event specific, the basic principle is to progressively overload the body with an intensity of exercise to make it fitter and stronger.

Maintaining safety in changing conditions

The safety of both the athlete and coach is the coach's responsibility throughout a session. The coach should consider the safety of:

- **The athlete** – Is the performer correctly dressed to take part? The coach should ensure that there is no jewellery which could cause harm or damage to the equipment. Is there any medical health history that the coach should be aware of prior to the athlete taking part in the session, such as epilepsy when taking part in swimming?

- **The equipment** and resources – Has the equipment been correctly serviced and is it in an appropriate condition for use? Are there any sharp points that could cause injury, e.g. a javelin?

- **The location** – Is the coaching facility suitable for use? It is important to check for hazards such as an uneven surface, rubbish, obstructions from other equipment, poor lighting.

- **The weather conditions** – Are the weather conditions a danger to participation? Golfers should avoid playing in storm conditions as they could be struck by lightning.

A2 Qualities for coaching for performance and fitness

A good coach should have range of qualities that are not just limited to their coaching specialist knowledge. Many coaches need to possess the same qualities as parenting, whereby they need to show the understanding and empathy to support their athlete's needs. It is often found that some participants are more willing to discuss personal issues with their coach rather than their parents, therefore it is important coaches are able to show a positive attitude and be approachable in such situations.

> **Key term**
>
> Empathy means to understand someone's feelings and to offer support.

Coaches are a role model, someone who is respected and listened to. A coach should build the trust needed for the participant to believe in their performance as well as the confidence to succeed. Sports participation is a character building process. It teaches discipline, team building and communication skills, which are essential for everyday living as well as within competitive sport.

Children are the most impressionable individuals through coaching. They often imitate the behaviour, language and manner of their coach. For this reason, it is vital that coaching is safe, responsible and that the coach's behaviour is considered good practice.

The coach can influence player development in a number of ways:

1 **Social** – Sport offers a code of acceptable social behaviour, teamwork, citizenship, cooperation and fair play.

2 **Personal** – Players can be encouraged to learn life skills, promote their own self-esteem, manage personal matters like careers or socialising and develop a value system including good manners, politeness and self-discipline.

3 **Psychological** – Coaches can create environments that help performers control emotions and develop their own identities, confidence, mental toughness, visualisation and a positive outlook on life that can be developed or improved.

4 **Health** – In taking care to design coaching or training sessions to include sufficient physical exercise, good health and healthy habits can be established and maintained.

Typical qualities that a coach must have include:

- **Personal prep/appearance** – Your coach should demonstrate a level of professionalism within their coaching activities. They should be appropriately prepared for activity, wearing appropriate clothing and footwear to interact within the session, e.g. provide demonstrations, etc.

- **Timekeeping** – Your coach should be punctual, setting the standard of expectations for the performers. They should start coaching sessions on time and finish on time, along with preparing their performers in a timely fashion, before competitions and activities.

- **Positive attitude** – Your coach should show a positive attitude that inspires all of those he/she are working with. Positivity can help bring motivation with the enthusiasm to succeed and help to develop a positive role model in front of the coaching group.

- **Knowledgeable** – Your coach should have a good understanding of the activity which they are coaching. They should be able to be analytical and observe a performance, reflect on how successful it was, and provide clear and accurate feedback.

- **Proactive** – Your coach should be a self-starter in that they have a level of confidence to independently lead and take control of activity sessions. They should be able to problem-solve and be adaptable in order to draw the best out of their performers. Having a good awareness of their individual athlete's ability can help to develop coaching practices that are tailored to individual needs. This is also referred to as differentiation.

- **Approachable** – Your coach should be easy to communicate with, and someone who is trusted and able to share ideas, thoughts and knowledge. They should be able to be listen and show empathy for your feelings, reacting and responding with positivity to inspire you for further achievements.

- **Fitness** – Your coach should demonstrate a level of fitness that is required to coach. This is relative, and does not mean they have to be elite performers themselves. On the contrary, not all coaches are necessarily extremely fit, however they are able to communicate, demonstrate and interact with their performers to provide an enjoyable, motivating and enthusiastic activity session.

A3 Best practice for a coach for performance and fitness

Safeguarding, DBS and equal opportunities

When working with young children or vulnerable groups, it is essential that you complete and pass a **DBS (Disclosure and Barring Service)** application, formally known as a **CRB (Criminal Records Bureau)** check. The DBS assesses an individual's previous criminal history and can identify a risk that may be caused to others. By completing this application it will enable you to work with children or a vulnerable group which is now standard procedure across many sports and coaching awards. It is important that rigorous child protection policies are in place to not only protect the participants, but also yourself as the coach. All coaches have a safeguarding responsibility which they must adhere to. Safeguarding is the protection of children from maltreatment which is the responsibility of any adult who supervises children. All coaches should act in the best interests of a child to ensure they have the best outcomes during their sporting participation. There are many laws and regulations that protect children and these must be followed at all times to avoid prosecution.

The safety of the group participants is very important, as is providing **equal opportunities** for participation. All coaches must respect and champion the right of every individual to participate in sport. Coaches should ensure that everyone has equal opportunity to participate regardless of age, gender, race, ability, faith or sexual orientation. Coaches have a responsibility, both legal and moral, to ensure that no discriminating behaviour occurs during their coaching sessions. It is very important that every member of the coaching group should have the right to feel part of the group and free from prejudice.

Qualifications and CPD

As we know, coaching qualifications are essential to updating our understanding of equal opportunity and how it may be incorporated into a coaching session. As sports and training practices continue to evolve, it is important that the coach builds on their already established knowledge. Coaches should have the commitment for continual learning or **continuing professional development (CPD)**. This may include:

- attaining higher grade academic qualifications
- attending workshops/seminars
- update coaching knowledge through social media, readings and journals
- gaining additional supporting qualifications such as BASES accreditation, UKSCA or YMCA Fitness awards.

The skills and knowledge gained from CPD enable the coach to develop new coaching strategies and include them within their activity plans. Any new coaching techniques will enable the coach to understand new methods that can enhance an athlete's performance along with reducing the risk of injury or harm.

Risk assessment and emergency procedures

A risk may be referred to as any situation where there is a potential for danger which could create harm or injury to an individual. For example, if you're coaching gymnastics it is important to have sufficient matting to protect the performer on landing. Without such equipment the risk could include minor injuries such as a bruise or cut, to severe including a broken neck and death.

To avoid risk, you must carry out a **risk assessment** to identify any concerns that may be of a potential danger to your athlete. It is important to remember that not all risks can be prevented, however attempts need to be made to minimise them.

If there is potential for harm or injury, it is important that you are aware of first aid **emergency procedures** and where they are available. A nominated qualified first aider should be available in case of an accident and access to contacting the emergency services should they be required. If available, an Automated External Defibrillator (AED) should also be within easy access in case of a cardiac arrest. If an accident was to occur on a playing field, be familiar with the road access in case an ambulance needs to drive directly to the patient. As a coach it is important you have the confidence to assist with their land and evacuation procedures.

More information on Risk Assessment and Emergency Procedures is given in Unit 4 Section A1.

Administration for coaching

Effective administration is essential for an aspiring coach. It is important for all coaches to develop, keep and maintain a full record of the coaching plans and other such related material. This information is essential as it can help the coach reflect on previous training sessions as well as prepare for those in the future. Alongside this, a coach should try to keep a full record of preparation materials which may include technical information and examples of drills and activities. This information will continue to enhance the training experience and will also help to develop coaching practice. For legal cover, it is expected that all coaches have sufficient insurance to coach their sport. Some organisations will provide this when you qualify as a coach, however this would need to be checked with the individual organisation body. As a precaution, some coaches take out an additional policy to ensure they are fully covered for any potential accidents or difficulties.

Further information that may be recorded and stored by a coach include health related history, e.g. a PAR-Q form, or coaching consent forms so that the coach is fully informed of their athlete's desire for participation. Alongside this the coach should keep a **register** of participants as this can help to prepare and plan for future training sessions.

A4 Methods of supporting the development and performance

Feedback

Performance may be developed using a number of methods, however it is important that a coach provides adequate feedback to the performer. A coach should always aim to keep the performer informed of progress, such as any technical or tactical adjustments.

When providing feedback it is important we identify positive information and carefully identify the athlete's weaknesses. Evidence suggests that performers who receive praise and positive feedback are likely to remain motivated to perform. There are many different types of feedback we can use in coaching:

- **Sandwich feedback** – A style where positive feedback is provided in a sequence of positive–constructive–positive. We can use football as an example:
  - **Positive** – 'Well done, your movement and support around the pitch was superb. You made some positive contributions to the attacking play and accurate passes.'

o **Constructive** – 'When defending, try to mark your player tight to restrict their possession and ability to shoot.'

o **Positive** – 'Work on these development points and I'm sure your performance will continue to improve.'

Figure 6.2 Sandwich feedback
(*Source:* www.athleteassessments .com)

- **'Two stars and a wish'** – An effective method of one-to-one feedback to motivate younger athletes. This technique highlights two initial positive points about the performance (two stars), and then identifies the point to develop (the wish).

Understanding this, it can be seen that the main purpose of feedback is to reinforce positive performance and help correct negative errors. It should be generous, clear and concise. Feedback needs to develop technical and tactical decisions while being able to reflect on weakness or defeat. Feedback should be able to provide constructive criticism or praise, and evaluate success. It is important that feedback can reflect on fitness, identify the components needed to perform and can focus on how they may be improved in relation to its intensity and effort needed to successfully complete the event. The key elements to consider when we provide feedback are when to give it (as timing can be vital), what to give, how much to give, and how to give it. Groups of athletes may need to be dictated to, as it is hard to have a discussion when numbers are large but individuals may response better to a conversation along with the feedback. Much is dependent on the rapport with the group, and their interaction with the coach; however, whatever the choice it should always have a purpose.

Hot and cold feedback

The timing of the feedback can be crucial to its success. Feedback during the event can be of short notice and provides limited time to create a new response. Therefore, if a coach provides feedback immediately post-event, it can be more supportive in order to gain greater performance change in the future. It is important that the coach limits the time delay following the session or event in order to fully reflect on the feedback provided.

Goal setting

When developing a coaching session or a coaching programme, it is important we understand the personal goals of the performer. When goal setting we need to consider both the primary and secondary goals:

- **Primary goal** – Usually the first stage of goal setting. It is the ultimate aim of achievement and will be composed of a number of secondary goal components.

- **Secondary goals** – Usually the second stage of goal setting. These are component-based goals in that they will help you to work towards your primary goal. They are mini-targets and the foundations of the primary goal. While individually they may not have much value, collectively they can enable you to achieve the ultimate primary goal. Secondary goals are particularly useful as they can help encourage the performer to reach their primary goal. The goal setting process helps the coach to:

  o focus the attention of the athlete participant

  o encourage determination to achieve

  o motivate learning

  o increase the effort needed throughout participation.

The type of goal will vary depending on the achievement desired. Process goals are those that take an already established skill and try to refine its performance. While they may also be competitive, they are frequently used within a coaching programme to create a potential outcome of the session. For example, a football player may work on keeping their head positioned over the ball when shooting at the goal to avoid hitting the ball over the bar. It is simply taking a skill or task and refining it during the coaching process.

Performance-based goals differ from process goals in that they can be more competitive based. Also referred to as outcome or competitive goals, they use the progress of process goals to aid the individual to achieve the final competitive outcome. They may be more manageable as they can be adjusted throughout a competitive season based on the progress made. Session and training goals are inevitably based around each training session. A performer may have personal goals to complete a training activity that may be technical or physically-based. For example, a hockey player may aim to hit a certain amount of penalty shots into the back of the goal by the end of the session, or a basketball player may aim to shoot successfully a planned number of 3-pointer shots during a practice session. Regardless of the activity, it is important that each participant has something to aim for as it will give them a constant aim for each individual session.

While session or training goals deal with the immediate training activity, long-term and short-term goals for the season can help to continue an athlete's future development. Long-term goals can be season-focused, they may be the achievements that the performer aspires to by the end of the year. They will always follow the process of SMART targets as it is essential they are something which the athlete/performer has the ability to reach and achieve. Short-term goals are often the mini-components of a long-term goal. Many short-term goals may make up a long-term goal. Short-term goals could consist of what the performer aims to achieve in a number of weeks' time. While they are longer than session goals, they are still relatively short but of sufficient length to make progress for achievement. The goal setting process will always aim to work towards future developments of the performer. These developments will enable the performer to continue to develop their individual skills and understanding of their sport with the ultimate aim of progressing their performance to higher levels.

As with all targets, they should be progressive in order to build upon towards the long-term primary goal. All targets should be **SMART**:

- **Specific** – All targets should be as specific as possible. They should be clear and focused as to what is being achieved and how. For example, the target could focus on a key goal of what needs to be achieved.

- **Measureable** – Any activity or performance needs to be measured. A coaching session should measure a baseline performance or success to help reflect on progress. For example, a tennis player could count their serving success rate and reassess themselves after a period of coaching activities.

- **Achievable** – Any target set should always be achievable. Having targets becomes meaningless as if they can't be achieved, there becomes little point in taking part. The target should be something that an individual can aim for and ultimately reach.

- **Realistic** – When setting training exercises it is important to consider whether it is realistic for the athlete to achieve it. For example, if coaching a novice freestyle swimmer, how realistic would it be for them to reach the finals of the county swimming championships? If it is unrealistic it could cause a negative outcome, potentially de-motivating the athlete as they may not reach the standard required.

- **Timely** – All targets should be time bound in that there should be a deadline for them to be achieved. Having a focal point as to when they need to be completed can help us plan for a long-term primary goal.

By setting SMART targets and breaking them down, we can identify secondary short- and medium-term goals, and long-term primary goals. By measuring the athlete's progress over time, checking whether the targets are specific enough to be realistically achievable, we can identify whether the time available is sufficient to complete the primary goal. If there is a fault with this process, new SMART targets should be considered and set for future success.

A5 Technology and sports professionals

Technology has continued to enhance sports performance throughout the decades. These advances have made significant improvements in skill and achievements which has embraced the Olympic motto of 'Faster, Higher, Stronger'.

Supporting technologies

Global Positioning Satellite (GPS) technology has made a significant impact on sport with performers and coaches being able to track their athletes' movements during both training and competition situations. While its use in cycling is commonplace, sports such as rugby and football are also using this technology with increasing popularity. In rugby the tracking device consists of a small GPS unit that is worn in the boot or jersey so as to not interfere with the player's performance. For example, many rugby teams sew a small device into the shirt between the shoulder blades where contact or tackle activity is limited. While they can be expensive, the benefits of these units are that they can provide the coaching staff with a range of data and statistics such as:

- performer speed
- distance run
- player acceleration
- location on a pitch
- player activity.

From the pitch side, coaches can analyse the physiological responses of the players, including their work rate and rate of fatigue. This information can be invaluable to the coach as it can help them pick the most fresh and optimal performing team.

Figure 6.3 A player wearing a GPS tracker (under their shirt at the top of the shoulder blades)

Video technology has been widely used for many years as it allows a coach to analyse team and individual sports performances. Unlike **GPS**, the players do not need to have additional equipment attached to their person as all videoing takes place away from the performance area. Its most obvious application can be to identify performance highlights such as goals, engagement, errors and success. The analysis can help with coaching and evaluating team performances as it provides real-time feedback that can be judged for future tactical decisions. However, without the use of a statistical analogy, the feedback is based on verbal opinion and is less scientific. As a result, this technology is only as good as the coach.

With the use of additional software, we can use video footage to create data feedback for biomechanical analysis. This process is able to quantify a performance, meaning we are able to gain various measures. Its use is that we are able to:

- identify performance strengths and weaknesses
- observe technique and movement efficiency
- measure acceleration and deceleration
- measure movement velocity
- measure power
- support injury management.

For example, video footage can help us assess the take-off velocity and technique of a long jumper. The footage can be used to make changes to technique or adapt training practices that will enable us to jump further.

There are a range of software applications which can analyse a video performance. Examples include:

- Quintic
- Dartfish
- Kinovea
- Sports Coach
- Kandle.

Advances in software technology have enabled coaches to analyse a range of information during both training and competitive performances. With modern technology, much is now available to download on mobile phones and tablet devices. Examples of these applications include:

- Mapmyrun – GPS tracking system for running and walking
- Strava – GPS tracking system used for runs and cycle rides
- MyFitnessPal – A calorie counter and diet tracker
- Fitbit – Monitoring app that tracks all day activity, workouts and health
- Instant Heart Rate – Heart rate monitoring app

Figure 6.4 Video analysis of a long jumper using Dartfish technology

- Ski Tracks – GPS tracker for mountain skiing
- Hudl Technique – Slow motion video analysis software.

With many applications being available as free downloads or at a minor cost, a modern day coach has access to data which would have previously been limited to specialist exercise professionals. While these applications examine individual performances, complex team performances can also be analysed. Using advanced techniques, we can examine games with technology such as Prozone and EyeVision. Before their development, performance was analysed using video footage alone and as we know, this is only as good as the feedback given. The use of this technology enables a coach to be more scientific, creating statistics on individual and team contributions. Understanding this information the coach is able to rethink coaching strategies and perhaps additional fitness needs of the team.

With the widespread development of specialist online resources, there are many websites that continue to offer ideas, chat forums and support for coaches. With the use of social media and online video streaming such as YouTube, many coaches are able to pick up fresh ideas and keep abreast of the latest development techniques. Sport and activity continues to evolve, therefore the online up-to-date resources share the ideas and information at a faster rate than traditional textbook resources.

Power meters are popular devices in cycling training, and measure the energy output per second of a rider. It is another measure that can be useful, alongside heart rate monitors and so on, to understand how a cyclist is performing. Working alongside a sports scientist a coach may have access to more specialist Laboratory-based testing technology, that can enable them to perform VO_2 max assessments and lactate threshold testing. VO_2 max is the maximum oxygen uptake of the body and it can be assessed using a procedure of gas analysis that can measure how hard we are working during exercise. The harder we work the greater the demand for oxygen which can be measured using a gas analyser. If we work very hard we then begin to form lactic acid which can then cause us to fatigue and slow down. Due to its specialist nature and cost, it's more frequently found within a laboratory-based environment with the feedback given to the sports coach. Athletes with high levels of fitness will produce less lactic acid at high intensities whereas the unfit will fatigue faster. If the athlete continues to fatigue quickly a coach is able to reflect on the outcomes and make adjustments to a potential training programme.

Supporting professionals

The types of technology discussed here are more likely to be available to elite performers and coaches, who will be able to use a sports scientist specialist to help with their training and preparation for an event. It is not unusual for the elite athletes to be surrounded by a team of supporting individuals that can be used to help enhance their performance. These specialists may include:

- Sports scientist
- Sports nutritionist
- Sports therapist (specialist in massage / osteopath / chiropractor)

- Personal physiotherapist
- Sports psychologist
- Strength and conditioning coach.

While these specialists are very supportive and effective in supporting the performer, they can be costly. A coach would often need sufficient funding to be able to justify their use and travel to competitions which may not always be possible. Therefore, while these individual practitioners are relevant to the sports performer, the practicality of their use can be difficult. All will have a valuable place in preparing and monitoring a performer's season. Both a coach and athlete will value the support they are able to provide, however this is not always possible due to the logistics and cost of their time and availability.

A Check your understanding

1 Explain how technology has had an influence on coaching in recent years.
2 Using a sports coach of your choice, identify the technology that may be available to them and how they may use it to enhance their athletes.
3 Explain why SMART targets are essential to a coach and their athletes.
4 Explain feedback and the methods in which it is provided.

Distinction activity (A D1)

You are a coach who has been approached to support an athlete with their sports performance. You have been asked to film their performance and help them evaluate it against a technical model.

Task 1
Using a visual recording device, film a partner performing an activity or skill of your choice, e.g. a lay-up free kick, shooting a ball, throwing an implement, etc.

Task 2
Use the technology to analyse the performance when coaching, making comparisons to the technical model.

Provide four bullet points that evaluate the performance strengths and weaknesses of the performance you have observed.

Provide four coaching drills that you could use for each of the weaknesses, to try and increase your performer's success.

B Explore practices, adaptations and measures used to develop performance and fitness (B P3 , B P4 , B M2 , B M3 , B D2)

B1 and B2 Practices to develop skills and techniques and tactics for performance

Skill may be defined as 'the learned ability to bring out the pre-determined results with maximum certainty, often with the minimum outlay of time, energy or both' (Knapp, 1963). For a coach to develop an athlete's skill and performance, it is essential that sufficient practice is available to make the improvements needed for success. Practice may take place in a number of situations.

Isolated practices enable the athlete to perform parts of a skill repeatedly in separation. An example could be a tennis coach who uses a machine to feed a ball to their player's forehand who then returns it with an accurate shot. The isolated practice enables the performer to focus on one technical skill at a time, to practise in a non-competitive environment at a controlled tempo. It is particularly useful with novice performers as it helps them break down an activity into component parts, making it easier to manage and develop for the future.

To place greater emphasis on competitive performance, we can use **conditioned situations** which can develop **skills and tactics** using smaller versions of a full game. For example, we could use 5-a-side football or mini tennis to develop the skills necessary to play in a full size game. While the game size is greatly reduced, it allows the performer to work on the basic control needed to be successful in a full game. A 5-a-side game would develop passing and ball control, and mini tennis could develop body positioning and racket control. Similarly these games can help to develop tactical decisions. For example, in 5-a-side game the players may develop an understanding of positioning on the pitch, attacking and defending play, and counterattacking. Mini tennis can help the player decide on shot selection, shot placement, and attacking net play. As these games are on a smaller scale, they can help the coach monitor the performer closely and offer feedback as the competitive game progresses.

Conditioned games are used when a coach wants to create **competitive situations** which are likely to happen within a game, e.g. practising ball control in football, or simply adding a condition that emphasises a teaching point, such as choosing a target area on a tennis court. Competitive situations should artificially create a particular condition that may be likely to happen in a competitive situation.

A basketball coach might consider the merits of initially removing defenders, or perhaps outnumbering them in a practice situation that is aimed at improving a particular attacking focus. Defenders can be added when the technique is well practised, conversely, extra defenders could be added so that the attacking technique could be practised under greater pressure. Similarly, defenders in these practices could be asked to take one of three roles according to the conditions required by the coach:

1 passive, offering little resistance other than presence
2 active, playing under normal conditions, tempo, intensity, etc.
3 pressure, playing with extra intensity.

This allows the coach to focus on particular aspects of the team or individual, such as offence or defence.

Success should regularly be evaluated, focusing on the progression and achievement of the coaching activity. It is important to remember that conditioned games are not full size competitive situations, so they should be built on to develop the final performance. Practice is just that, practice. For it to be effective it must successfully develop the performance in order for you to progress. It is important to consider that any adapted game needs to be practical, suitable, effective and relevant. The practical activity should be suitable to meet the needs of the performance activity which we are being coached for. Any activity should therefore be effective in helping us to perform at a higher level or progress. Therefore, if the practical activity is effective and suitable, then it should be relevant to meet the needs of the performance.

B3 Adaptation of practices to promote development of performances and fitness

Using isolated and conditioned sports practices, the adaptation of games and activities is essential to replicating sport and competition fitness. The changes could involve modifying a range of areas such as:

- **The use of the participants**

  This could involve the restriction of group size such as the number of players or technique of play. Games such as 5-a-side football are a good example where the full size team numbers are reduced and the ball must be played below shoulder height. The restriction in technique encourages the performer to control the ball, develop close play strategies, improve communication skills, along with controlling passing and possession. Therefore, as a result the role of the individuals during the practice changes as different skills need to be applied in order to be successful. The process of technique restriction causes performers to play in a modified environment which makes it more difficult to perform. As is shown in the football example, the technique restriction encourages individual performance progressions due to the additional thinking and communication skills need to effectively perform. The benefit of this development may be used when applied within a non-restrictive activity such as a full size match where these skills can become supportive to a successful performance.

  Game modifications to basketball may also be used such as half-court 3-on-3 players to develop the skills of marking, movement, attacking and defending strategies.

- **The coaching environment**

  This could involve the modification of a game into a smaller space. For example, mini tennis promotes the skills needed for the full size game. Tactical play, coordination of footwork and racket control may all be developed by restricting the playing environment. This restriction also reinforces the competitive element so allows the game to be played using a normal tennis point scoring system.

- **The equipment used**

  Equipment modifications may be used to help develop games and activities. For example, seated volleyball could use a badminton court for small number groups, e.g. pairs. The restriction of space and reduced height of the net encourages the player to control their hitting along with its placement around the court. This skill of control and placement may be transferred into the full size game, potentially leading to an improved future performance.

- **The physical fitness demands of the session**

  The intensity could be modified by having unbalanced team players. For example, instead of playing 3-on-3 in basketball, the game could consist of three attackers and two defenders. Due to the additional attacking player, the defenders would be expected to work intensely to perform their role. This may replicate a game based situation as it could imitate a fast-break scenario whereby only two players are able to defend the quick attacking team. This drill may also be modified further to greatly increase the distance and duration of the fast break. As with any fast break situation, they regularly start from underneath the opposing team's basket. To replicate a game-based scenario, defending players can begin the defensive play from the opposing end to increase both the duration and distance they must travel in order to successfully defend the basket.

- **The psychological demands of the session**

  As with the basketball adaptation, disadvantaging teams can promote tactical awareness and encourage a positive response to a stressful defensive situation. The introduction of a competitive element to coaching is crucial to mental rehearsal. This process can help to develop a competitive mental rehearsal to practice for the stresses of competitions. Activities such as the use of pressured games and races can help to increase mental pressure. These games could include basket shooting in a set period of time. Further additional pressures could be added with changes in distance, e.g. from the free-throw line to the 3-point line, to increase both the accuracy and distance for a successful shot to be completed. Modifying games and enforcing changes, such as giving an opposing player/team a head start, can provide both advantages when rehearsing performance stress. Through the use of applying pressure on their performance, a coach can help the performers rehearse scenarios where points are needed to level a game score.

Alternatively, they could encourage players to think quickly, make appropriate decisions to respond to the surrounding players which could benefit their performance during a game. However, the disadvantages of this head start could be that it may have a negative effect on performance, causing players to give up, panic or become demotivated due to inaccuracies. This would understandably have a negative effect on a game/performance, therefore a coach needs to consider any modifications carefully before applying them within a coaching session.

You always need to evaluate the adaptations you devise, thinking about how practical they are to run, how suitable they are for the purpose in question, how effective they were, and how relevant they are.

B4 Measures of performance and fitness

From adapting performance and fitness practices, it is important that we are able to measure the progress made. Known as a benchmark, it enables you to make a comparison between the current performance and that of others. The comparison may be against another performer such as a competitor or someone who competes at national, regional, school, or club level. The main aim is to try and identify any performance differences which could be seen as a potential advantage to performance. However, whatever the comparison, the process aims to observe the differences between higher levels of performance, compare against previous records on all levels, and class or group performances.

Measures can be gained using a range of field tests, such as:

- **Technical** – e.g. measurements of accuracy and distance.
- **Tactical** – e.g. notational analysis using written notes on patterns of performance.
- **Fitness** – e.g. measurements of speed; running distance; aerobic capacity; agility; strength; power.
- **Coach-devised** – e.g. measurements of shot tally; conduct an observation analysis and give feedback on the performance.

Each of these field tests are activity-specific so there is no one template fits all. The coach should decide on the relevance when measuring performance and fitness. The tests are a valuable process in understanding an athlete's progress. Remember, 'progression' is a key term that needs to be applied within all coaching sessions. It is important these tests are evaluated to identify whether any activities have been successful and effective. On reflection we can discover whether the coaching practices are suitable and relevant rather than non-functional or practical. For example, were the adapted and conditioned games suitable to the performance? Using the benchmark and fitness measures, has there been any gain or improvement in the athlete's performance? If not, why not? Asking questions will help you to find answers which will potentially lead to progression.

B Check your understanding

1 Explain the differences between isolated and conditioned practices.
2 Select a sporting activity of your choice and analyse how the training practices may be adapted to develop a skill within the activity.
3 Suggest and explain two skill-based measures that may be used to assess the progress of your sports performer.
4 Using your skill-based measures, select a drill that could improve the success of this skill achievement.

Distinction activity (B D2)

A newly qualified coach has approached you and is after some coaching tips. They know you're very experienced so will explain the points clearly and in great detail. They'd like to know which coaching techniques are best to use in different coaching situations. They would like to know about practices and how we can develop skills and tactics, as well as how you would measure and develop performances.

Task

Evaluate the practicality, suitability and effectiveness of practices and measures used to develop athletes when coaching for performance and fitness.

Feedback your response using a small PowerPoint presentation.

C Demonstrate effective planning of coaching to develop performance and fitness (C P5 , C M4 , C D D3)

C1 Planning considerations

When preparing the coaching plan it is important we consider a number of points in order to allow our session to run smoothly. Prior to planning sessions and a series of coaching sessions, we need to:

- **Understand the group**

  Consider the number of the group that will be in the coaching session, how will you need to plan the session based on the numbers? Would there need to be group or team work? If so, decide how this could be divided up within the group.

  Consider the standard and performance ability, and fitness level, of your performers. At what level do they compete at, e.g. school, county, national or international level? How could this affect their personal goals, their aim and objectives, or their needs?

  Consider the age of the group. If the group is young, what physical training needs should we consider? Will they be able to cope with the physical training demands as an adult performer? Think about how we could change the intensity to differentiate across the age range, however still enable them to take part in similar activity.

- **Be familiar with the coaching environment**

  Be aware of your coaching surroundings. It is rare that you will always have a coaching venue to yourself as many facilities are used by other groups. Consider the size and type of the space. How could you plan to maximise this space to enable to you deliver an effective coaching session? For example, if coaching rugby you may be limited to half a pitch with over a full squad. How could you coach a session that involves all team players but in a restricted area? Similarly, you should consider whether the playing surface is suitable to the activity. Rugby would need to be adapted to tag-rugby if only a tarmac surface was available.

- **Have a good understanding of the equipment used**

  Consider the equipment that's to be used when planning a coaching session. How may it be adapted to suit the needs of your activity? You should plan to ensure you have some spare in case something does not go to plan or there are some last minute changes to the session. For example, if using team bibs, include some extra in case you want to divide the teams into greater numbers. Think about the colours of the bibs and equipment as this could help your participants understand the coaching task.

- **Be able to select a range of skills and techniques, and differentiate to encourage progress**

  Consider the skills and techniques that are needed to successfully complete the coaching activity. Are they relevant to the sport or fitness programme aims and objectives? You should try to think about the technique involved and be able to recognise the technical model for performance. For example, if coaching the clean and jerk lift in power lifting, it is essential that the coach is familiar with the correct technique and movement of the bar to avoid injury. An inexperienced coach who has little knowledge of the activity could be a danger to both the athlete and those surrounding them.

- **Be aware of the suitable exercise intensities and field tests**

  A coaching plan should try to replicate the duration and intensities of the sport. Suitable adjustments should be made to ensure they are relevant to the activity. For example, consider how long the event lasts for. What are the physical fitness demands? What are the skill-based fitness demands? How long do they last for? As the coach you should try to break the sport or fitness activity into key components to help structure the plan. Set clear learning aims and outcomes to develop performance.

  A coach should have a clear understanding of what needs to be achieved both during a coaching session and throughout the year. Each session should have an aim for achievement, something that both the coach and athlete wish

to gain from its completion. The long-term aims will reflect those which the athlete will aspire too and may also be referred to as long-term targets. A coach should have clear knowledge of their future goals in order to improve the performance of their performers and show progression throughout the sessions.

- **Consider a selection of practices to develop performance and fitness and relevant adaptations to challenge/develop individuals**

  When developing a coaching session it is essential that the learning practices are relevant to the performer. Activities that may be too easy may cause demotivation. A successful coach should take the time to develop activities which are both challenging and stimulating for the participants. Tasks that are of a low level may restrict the speed of progression as the performer may be learning very little. Practices should continue to stretch and challenge their performance to make them improve their abilities.

- **Differentiate through adaptation of activities**

  Understanding the need for challenging activities, it is important that they can be adapted should they need to be. It should be remembered that we all progress at different speeds and are not all as gifted as each other. Therefore it is important that any coaching session may be modified to support or differentiate between each individual performer.

- **Consideration of benchmarks and field testing**

  As we know, benchmarks are a level at which we can make comparisons against. During field testing we can use those of normative data for performances or make comparisons to other performers. The use of benchmarks during testing and a coaching activity can be beneficial as they can motivate performers to try and beat pre-existing performance levels. This is important. Benchmarks can also be used by the coach to try and identify gifted and talented individuals as these may excel in their performances which may be compared against the established standards.

When coaching, it is important to remember that nothing ever goes completely to plan. We should always think of a 'worst case scenario' where the unexpected may happen. It is good practice to have a contingency back-up plan to avoid any potential issues which could affect the coaching session. Consider the following as examples of what can happen and what you could plan for:

1 weather threatens your outside session
2 you fall ill and are no longer able to continue as coach
3 there are not enough participants for the session
4 the facility is double-booked when you arrive for the session
5 the group are not responding to your style of coaching or the practices that you have chosen.

By preparing or being aware of additional ideas, we can ensure that the coaching session runs smoothly and is challenging. Being disorganised can have a negative effect on the athlete participants so it is important to keep them interested and motivated. Alongside this, it is also important we keep our participants safe and a back-up plan can help to avoid any potential accidents.

Health and safety

The health and safety of all involved in sport should be the most important of considerations of the coach. In most cases it is necessary to ensure that the facilities and equipment are safe. Checks may need to be made on the maintenance service history such as with gym equipment. Remember it is the responsibility of the coach to ensure that the athlete performers remain safe during their coaching sessions so they all need to be aware of key health and safety issues that could affect them taking part.

Coaches should consider the following as a checklist for health and safety, although by no means is it an exhaustive list:

1 **The facilities and equipment**
   - Does the provider have a Normal Operating Procedure and an Emergency Action Plan? This should cover; number of players allowed, coach:learner ratio, conduct and supervision, hazardous behaviours, fire and evacuation procedures.

2 **The nature of the sport, for playing and training**
   - What to do when rules are not observed, what to do with injured players.
   - Not teaching activities beyond the capabilities of the performers.
   - In competitive situations, matching performers where appropriate by size, maturity or age.

3 **The athlete/performers**
   - Are you aware of any special individual medical needs, and the types of injuries common to the sport?
   - Safety education – informing players of the participation risks and establishing a code of behaviour.
   - Teammates and opponents to be aware of their responsibilities to each other.
   - Players should be discouraged from participating with an existing injury.

4 **The coach**
   - Safe coaching practices.
   - Safe numbers for the area.
   - Arranging appropriate insurance.
   - Dealing and reporting accidents.
   - Being aware of emergency procedures.

C2 Planning for an individual session for performance and fitness

As we are aware, target and goal setting is a key component to coaching success. Our targets should be SMART, whether that is for a single or multiple series of coaching sessions. Regardless of the number, the main focus is to achieve something from each session and use it to progress to the next.

Session planning should therefore always have an aim. We need to consider exactly what we want to achieve from the session. Using cricket as an example, young children may aim to achieve a basic skill such as catching a ball. For the more elite, their skill may involve hitting the middle stump during a fast bowl delivery. Therefore, each aim and target will be specific to the performer and we should adjust them to meet the skill level. It is good practice to list the initial targets at the beginning of a coaching plan, keeping them clear and concise. Depending on the length of the session and target, typically we should aim for three to five targets to be achieved by the end.

The planning phase should take into consideration both the **equipment** needs and availability. The equipment can help to determine the targets as these should be specific to its availability. Therefore it is important we check the equipment prior to planning and starting a coaching session. Equipment failure can lead to a disorganised session so it is always worthwhile preparing for all eventualities.

When preparing a plan the equipment should be clearly shown so that there is clarity as to what is needed. Try to remember, if you were absent and someone else was to use your coaching plan, would they know exactly what's needed? A clear list of equipment will help the replacement coach understand your plan and continue with the planned session you've prepared.

There are many different types of **warm-up** we can use depending on the sport. A 'warm-up' should not be considered as simply stretching. It is important that the muscles become warm before any stretching takes place as it will make them more pliable. The use of a light jog or other similar aerobic activity can help increase your muscle temperature as it causes the warm blood to circulate around your body faster. It is this warm blood that causes the muscle temperature to increase, preparing them for the stretching phase.

Once the aerobic phase has been completed, **static stretching** should be used to initially warm-up and lengthen the muscle fibres. It is important that stretches are held for between 5–10 seconds, repeating the same stretch on the same muscle at least twice depending on the sport activity being participated in. When selecting the stretch it is important that the intensity, duration and technique of the event are considered. As some areas of the body may be more in demand that others, it is important that they are stretched thoroughly to avoid the stress that may be placed on the muscles.

Following static stretching, **dynamic stretching** can be used to loosen the muscle further. The movement continues to increase the blood flow throughout the muscle tissue, helping it move and stay warm. It is important that the muscle is not overworked at this stage as it can cause fatigue which defeats the purpose of the warm-up.

Once your athlete(s) are warm and ready to take part in the coaching session they will need a technical or tactical introduction. For example, if coaching the javelin throw to a group of novices, the coach should go through the basic technique. Within the introduction they should explain:

1 safety procedures

2 the grip

3 the stance

4 the foot placement

5 the throwing action

6 the recovery.

Following the introduction, the athlete should go through the performance phase whereby they try to apply their understanding to a practical performance. It is helpful for the coach to monitor progress and provide initial 1:1 feedback on early performances where necessary. Interaction is key as it both supports and motivates the performers to improve on their next attempt of the activity.

Using **performance analysis,** a coach can provide feedback on not only the actual performance, but also plan for future **strategies, techniques or tactical** changes depending on the sport. By using **conditioned games** and **competitive scenarios**, it is possible for the coach to identify a performer's strengths and weaknesses and make any **adaptations** to their performance. For example, if a football coach were to analyse their team play, it may be found that they are weak on the counterattack. Having identified this as a weakness they will then need to plan and prepare coaching sessions to overcome this performance problem. Using a performance analysis, competitive games and drills on the training pitch, a defensive strategy could be formed. The identification and adaptation will then go to help the team during their next game.

A **cool-down** should perform the reverse of a warm-up. It is important that we start to cool down approximately 10–20 minutes following the sporting activity. From the activity there should be a period of a light continuous exercise followed by a period of dynamic and static exercises. The aim of the light continuous exercise is to gradually reduce the heart rate and keep the blood circulating around the body. As the blood continues to circulate, waste products such as lactic acid are able to be removed which speeds up the recovery process.

Both dynamic and static stretches are important to the recovery process. The stretches reduce the tightening of the muscle fibres which could limit the movement and potentially cause future injuries. It is important that we do not simply collapse and lay on the floor following the exercise as this will not help with the recovery. Light continuous movement such as a slow jog or cycle, followed by controlled stretching is a sufficient cool-down after activity.

During the cool-down there is an ideal opportunity to gain some **feedback** on the coaching session. Listening to ideas and reflecting on the activities can help make future adjustments and keep the sessions progressive. It is good practice to identify what went right and what could be improved on. Making a written log of session outcomes can be a good method of remembering and adapting changes where and when necessary.

The **training intensity** is dependent on the training frequency, type and method being used. It is important that an athlete is not overloaded beyond their capacity as this could cause them to become injured or de-motivated. As explained within the SMART targets, all coaching sessions should be achievable. Any session that is beyond the athlete's capabilities could lead to them becoming potentially injured so it is important that a balance is found. The progress of the intensity can be monitored through the use of field testing. These may be fitness or skill focused and dependent on the type of activity your athlete is performing. Fitness tests could include the multistage fitness test for events that have a considerable aerobic requirement, or the Illinois agility test for performers who require rapid speed and the ability to change direction. All tests are event and activity specific so one test will not suit all coaching events.

C3 Planning for an overall series of sessions for performance and fitness

When planning coaching sessions it is important to identify the aims and objectives of the training. There should always be an aim, otherwise the coaching activity may become repetitive and non-functional. Therefore, as we know from this unit, goals, aims and objectives are key to coaching performer success.

For the coaching sessions to make a significant impact on performance, i.e. show progression, we should try to plan for a minimum of four sessions. This period enables sufficient development to take place and develops our coaching sessions further. It is important that performers are given time to adjust to the coaching sessions and allow for sufficient learning in the process. To monitor its progress it is important to provide a comparison of baseline measure. This can be achieved through field fitness and skill-based test or through the use of event specific measures. By testing, coaching over a series of sessions and then retesting, we can make a comparison of progress.

For example, a discus throwing coach could measure the maximum distance their athlete throws during the first coaching session. With an established measure, the following sessions could then contain a range of drills and activities that could develop the skills and fitness of the technical components. The sessions could coach the skills needed for body positioning, or coach the turn around the circle for added power of delivery. The fitness component of power may be developed by power-based training such as plyometric training and weight ball throwing. Each of the sessions should be progressive and focus on an end-product, e.g. the event/activity performance.

Following a series of coaching sessions the athlete performer may then be retested to assess their performance following the coaching sessions. This may be weeks after the original test, however these should be sufficient time for the adaptations to occur. Having trained extensively it would be envisaged that the performance would have progressed significantly, improving the athlete's performance. If there has been limited or no progression, the coaching plan should be analysed for changes should it be felt necessary.

C Check your understanding

1 Explain six planning considerations needed when preparing a coaching session.
2 Explain why a contingency plan is important when preparing coaching sessions.
3 Explain the term 'benchmark' and analyse its strengths and the weaknesses of its use.
4 Explain what is meant by a 'conditioned situation'.

D Explore the impact of coaching for performance and fitness
(D P6 , D P7 , D M5 , C D D3)

D1 Delivering coaching for performance and fitness

Preparing a fantastic coaching plan is one thing; delivering it successfully is quite another. Some coaches can produce a great plan but have difficulty implementing it. Similarly, some coaches are very good at delivering a session but have poor planning skills. A good coach is someone who can do both: effectively plan their session(s) and deliver to the performer(s) confidently.

Some general coaching dos and don'ts:

- **DO – Lead by example**. You are a role model for many therefore you should act accordingly. A coach has a significant influence over their performers so should encourage good morals and characteristics.

- **DO – Be knowledgeable about your subject area**. If this is not a sport or activity you've significant experience in, read up on it and be confident for when you coach the session. Always ensure you are fully planned and prepared before the coaching session. Keep records of your coaching plans and outcomes.

- **DO – Be positive throughout the session including both your voice tone and body language**. There is nothing worse than having a coach that portrays a negative attitude, such as poor motivation, monotone voice or boredom. If the coach feels that way then so will the performers. Being positive can make you more approachable and help to make the session more enjoyable.

- **DO – Ensure you provide clear communication to the athletes/participants**. This will make you easier to understand and enable you to get your points across.

- **DO – Engage within the activities**. Be prepared to take part in the activity to demonstrate how to perform a skill.

- **DO – Performance analyse throughout the session**. Be prepared to simplify skills for those who struggle and stretch and challenge those

more able for the same activity, i.e. backup activities. Regular analysis can help to progress the session, for example the athlete participants may find the plan too easy which could lead to tedium. Be prepared to make some advanced additions should it be skill-based.

- **DO – Dress appropriately for the activity you are taking part in**. If you are a coach or are educating a group of performers and there is a kit to wear, embrace it to reinforce your unity with the team. Wearing alternative clothing can cause a break down in team unity and leadership.

- **DON'T – Ignore your athlete participants**. Listen to their feedback as to how they are progressing. This can help you prepare for both current and future coaching sessions.

- **DON'T – Talk to just your friends or those you get on best with**. Some individuals may feel isolated and more likely to drop out if they feel neglected or lack worth.

- **DON'T – Use inappropriate language as this shows a lack of respect and professionalism**. Keep your focus task-based because if you show the appropriate language, your performers will repeat your good practice.

- **DON'T – Keep your hands in your pockets**, as this provides very poor body language of non-engagement. Keep your hands and arms working throughout the session whether demonstrating or engaging with the activity.

- **DON'T – Be impatient**. We all progress at different speeds therefore be prepared to support the needs of all. Young children can take longer to master complex coaching activities, therefore be patient and motivated throughout.

- **DON'T – Forget to pack equipment away**. As a coach it is your responsibility that all equipment is accounted for and correctly stored for the next coaching activity. If there are any faults they should be reported immediately to the maintenance representative.

D2 Reflection on session and planned series

Once completed it is important to reflect on the success of the coaching session. It is important to identify a number of key points including:

1 **Impact of planning** on the session – Here we can review whether the planning of the session was sufficient to make it successful. We should focus on the plan.

   a) Was it sufficient to meet the session aims and objectives?

   b) Was it clear as to what you had to do and when you were meant to do it?

   c) Are there any adjustments needed?

   d) Could it be replicated with ease should it be necessary in the future?

2 **Impact of practices and measures** of development – Having reviewed the planning preparation, we should now review the success of the practice activities.

   a) Were the activities appropriate?

   b) Were there a sufficient number of activities?

   c) Did the activities enable the athlete performer to progress?

   d) Was there a measured performance change, e.g. success rate?

3 **Coaching delivery on athletes** – Here as the coach, we can review our own performance.

   a) What went well?

   b) What could be improved upon?

   c) How did the performers respond?

   d) Were the performers positively engaged throughout or appear bored or restless?

   e) Did the coach behave acceptably?

4 **Progress towards aims and targets** – Having reviewed our performance, we should review the athletes' performance to help us plan for future sessions.

   a) How well did the performers learn the skills or techniques introduced to them?

   b) What performance developments were evident for each participant?

   c) Are the performers ready to progress to the next session?

   d) Are there additional needs that should be included to reach the aims?

With a sound overview of the session outcomes we can make adaptations to the planned future series of sessions. From the answers we can gather from both the questions and the feedback of the athlete participants, we can prepare effective long-term coaching activities. Any potential adaptations could help to develop their understanding and ensure faster progression in performing the activity.

Finally, the review can reflect on health and safety. We should try to focus on all areas and not just the participants. For example, were the facilities up to standard? Was it a safe exercise environment? Was a risk assessment carried out prior to the coaching session? Were there sufficient precautions in place in order to avoid potential dangers?

By reviewing your own and the athletes' progression it can be helpful for us to prepare the long-term series of training activities. We can reflect on our session, adjust potential coaching aims and continue to make the session enjoyable throughout.

D3 Coaching development based on reflection

As a coach we can reflect upon our personal skills and knowledge of the activity. What could be learnt or developed to aid your long-term coaching abilities? Coaching continues to evolve therefore there are always new techniques and skills to be learnt. The techniques of today are very different to those of 20 years ago. It is important that as a coach, you recognise the areas for development and base any future needs around them. Continuous professional development is a must in order to stay on top of the latest practices that are being coached nationwide.

Consider whether you feel you had the correct qualities needed to coach, were you patient and communicated the tasks clearly to the participant? If this could be improved on you should try to self-assess the reasons why and consider how they could be developed. For example, if you stood on the side-line shouting at the performers, it may have been more supportive to gather them into a small group and explain the expectations. If explaining a task it could be over complicated and communication too complex. It may be more suitable to break the skills into small practices and then piece the activities together.

Reflect on whether you performed in line with best practice guidelines for a coach, e.g. did you follow appropriate standards such as safeguarding, offer support and guidance equally to all of your performers, did you offer equal opportunities throughout your session? From reflection we can focus on the session development for future planning. From all the feedback we gather, we should consider measures of progress and how effective the practices were. For example, were they appropriate to meet the session aims and targets? Were they manageable and could they be easily repeated? Would they need any further adaptation?

By completing a comprehensive review we can evaluate the session and future sessions' strengths and weaknesses. We can make adaptations to help the coaching activities be more successful and improve participation.

D Check your understanding

1 Create a coaching plan and coach it to your peers.
2 Evaluate how your session went, identifying its strengths and the areas for improvement.
3 Identify the adaptions you would make and justify your reasons why.
4 Reflect on your own personal coaching skills – what do you see as your areas for development?

Distinction activity (C D3 , D D3)

All successful coaches continue to develop their strategies, to improve their athlete/participant's performance. Like all top level coaches, they are happy to reflect on their performance and make changes should they feel it necessary. Any coach that thinks they know all there is to know about coaching, clearly doesn't. To explore the impact of planning and coaching on fitness, you decide to produce and use a session plan.

Task 1

Prepare a coaching session plan that lasts for approximately 30 minutes.

Your plan should include all the activities that you may use and how they can be applied.

Task 2

Evaluate the outcomes of your session plan.

Focus on the delivery of the plan and justify any adaptations you would make in order to improve it next time around.

Further reading

Jones, R.L., Kingston, K., (2013), *An introduction to Sports Coaching: Connecting Theory to Practice*, Routledge.

Kent, M., (2006), *Oxford Dictionary of Sports Science & Medicine*, Oxford University Press.

Nash, C., (2014), *Practical Sports Coaching*, Routledge.

Stafford-Brown, J., Rea, S., (2010), *BTEC National Sport: Development, Coaching and Fitness (Second edition)*, Hodder Education.

Useful websites

1st4Sport

www.1st4sport.com

BBC Bitesize

www.bbc.co.uk/education

BrianMac – Sports Coach

www.brianmac.co.uk

Sports Coach UK

sportscoachuk.org.uk

Teach PE

www.teachpe.com

References

Jones, R.L., (2006), *The Sports Coach as Educator: Re-conceptualising Sports Coaching*, Routledge.

Jones, R.L., Kingston, K., (2013), *An introduction to Sports Coaching: Connecting Theory to Practice*, Routledge.

Kent, M., (2006), *Oxford Dictionary of Sports Science & Medicine*, Oxford University Press.

Lyle, J., Cushion, C., (2010), *Sports Coaching: Professionalism and Practice*, Churchill Livingstone.

Matens, R., (2012), *Successful Coaching*, Human Kinetics.

Nash, C., (2014), *Practical Sports Coaching*, Routledge.

Stafford-Brown, J., Rea, S., (2010), *BTEC National Sport: Development, Coaching and Fitness (Second edition)*, Hodder Education.

7 Biomechanics in sport and exercise science

About this unit

Biomechanics studies human movement and the movement of objects that humans propel when they play sport. The term biomechanics means 'the mechanics of living beings' and biomechanists apply scientific principles to achieve optimal sports performance. For example, they can analyse how humans move when they are running, swimming or cycling and improve the efficiency and effectiveness of an athlete's movement. They can analyse specific sports techniques such as throwing, kicking, tackling, bowling or weight training techniques and make recommendations about how they could be done more efficiently and to prevent possible injuries. Biomechanists can also apply scientific principles to the design of sports equipment, clothing and footwear.

According to The British Association of Sport and Exercise Sciences (BASES), biomechanics is one of the three core disciplines within the study of sports science. Physiology and psychology are identified by BASES as the other two core disciplines and the study of these three subjects is key to understanding performance in sport and exercise activities. Due to its scientific nature and use of mathematical formulae biomechanics can be a subject that takes more effort and commitment to understand; however, time spent on biomechanics will reward you with an increased understanding of sport and how to improve sports performance.

Learning aims

The aims of this unit are to:

A Investigate linear motion in sport and exercise activities

B Examine forces acting on sports performers and their equipment

C Investigate angular motion in sport and exercise activities.

How will I be assessed?

The biomechanics unit will be assessed by assignments that have been designed internally by your tutors. It is likely that there will be three assignments for you to complete where you will be able to apply the knowledge you have learnt to a range of sport and exercise activities.

Learning aim A achievement

For distinction standard, learners will analyse speed, velocity, acceleration and deceleration in detail. They will break down motion in sport and exercise activities into their component parts, showing changes in each type of linear motion. Learners should be able to calculate each type of linear motion and show the relationships between the different types. Both activities will be analysed in detail, demonstrating a clear understanding of the principles of linear motion as applied to sport and fitness activities.

Learning aim B achievement

For distinction standard, learners will analyse in detail how reaction forces, friction forces, air resistance and aerodynamics impact on sports performers and sports equipment by breaking down sport and exercise activities to show exactly how the forces are acting. They will examine how the negative and positive impact of forces can be manipulated to promote optimal sports performance and make connections between the impact of forces and the design of sports clothing and equipment. Both activities will be analysed in detail, demonstrating a clear understanding of the action and impact of forces as applied to sport and fitness activities, and the interrelationships between the different forces.

Learning aim C achievement

For distinction standard, learners will analyse in detail the impact of changes in the centre of mass and break down sport and exercise activities into their component parts, showing how the centre of mass of a body is affected by changes in its shape and position. They will analyse the relationship between the position and movement of different types of levers on the location of the centre of mass and the stability of the body. They will analyse the selected activity in detail, demonstrating a clear understanding of the principles of centre of mass and different types of levers as applied to sport and fitness activities.

How will I be graded?

The table below shows the assessment criteria for this unit. To achieve a pass grade you must meet all the P criteria; to achieve a merit grade you must achieve all the P and all the M criteria; to achieve a distinction grade you must achieve all the P, M and D criteria.

Pass	Merit	Distinction
Learning aim A: Investigate linear motion in sport and exercise activities		
A P1 Describe speed, velocity, acceleration, deceleration and momentum in sport and exercise contexts.	**A M1** Explain speed, velocity, acceleration, deceleration and momentum in sport and exercise contexts.	**A D1** Analyse speed, velocity, acceleration, deceleration and momentum using relevant calculations from sport and fitness contexts.
Learning aim B: Examine forces acting on sports performers and their equipment		
B P2 Describe how forces impact on sport and exercise performance referencing Newton's three laws of motion.	**B M2** Explain how forces impact on sport and exercise performance referencing Newton's three laws of motion.	**B D2** Analyse, using examples, how forces impact on sport and exercise performance.
Learning aim C: Investigate angular motion in sport and exercise activities		
C P3 Describe how different types of levers and axes of rotation are used in sport and exercise activities.	**C M3** Explain how different types of levers and axes of rotation are used to complete different movements.	**C D3** Analyse how levers and changes in the centre of mass combine to affect performance in sport and exercise activities.
C P4 Describe how changes in the centre of mass affect performance in sport and exercise activities.	**C M4** Explain how changes in the centre of mass affect performance in sport and exercise activities.	

Table 7.1 Assessment criteria

A Investigate linear motion in sport and exercise activities (**A P1**, **A M1**, **A D1**)

A1 Linear motion

Linear motion refers to the movement of the body along a line that may be straight or curved. Linear motion occurs when all the parts of the body are moving in the same direction and at the same speed. Motion of the body can either be rectilinear, which means along a straight line, or curvilinear, which means along a curved line. A 100 m runner would have rectilinear motion but if they ran 200m the first part of the race where they run around a bend would be curvilinear. Movement in most sports involves both rectilinear and curvilinear motion.

When studying linear motion, we will be exploring the qualities of moving bodies in terms of their speed or velocity, whether they are accelerating or decelerating and their inertia and momentum. Before we look at these qualities of linear motion, we need to understand what is meant by scalar and vector quantities.

Key terms

Linear motion refers to the movement along a straight or curved line.

Rectilinear motion refers to movement along a straight line.

Curvilinear motion refers to movement along a curved line.

Vector and scalar qualities

A scalar quantity is one described purely by its size (or magnitude) while a vector is a quantity that is described by its size and its direction. Mass is a scalar quantity because it is a figure that describes the amount of matter a body possesses. Mass is measured in kilograms (kg). Weight is a vector quality because it is a measure of the effect that gravity has on the mass of the body, and that effect has a particular direction. Mass is a representation of size and the force of gravity is a representation of the direction of the force. Under normal circumstances gravity is downwards into the Earth and thus weight is a downwards force. Weight is measured in newtons (N) and is calculated by multiplying mass by acceleration due to gravity (9.81 m/s^2).

In everyday language when people talk about weight they are usually discussing mass and referring to it incorrectly. For instance, a person who is defined as 'overweight' is actually being told that their body contains too much matter and they would benefit from having a lower body mass.

Weight will change depending on an individual's location as you will become lighter the higher up you are or the further away from Earth. For example, if you were to find yourself on the Moon your mass would be unchanged but your weight would be reduced because the force of gravity acting on you would be much lower. If anyone ever asks you how to lose weight tell them to go on the live on the Moon; however, they will be disappointed as their mass will be unchanged and that is what they really want to reduce.

> ### Key terms
>
> **Scalar quantities** are ones described by their size or magnitude.
>
> **Vector quantities** are described by their size and direction.
>
> **Mass** is a scalar quantity and measured in kilogrammes, kg.
>
> **Weight** is a vector quantity and is measured in newtons (N), downwards.

A2 Speed and velocity

Distance and displacement

Before examining speed and velocity we need understand the difference between distance and displacement. Distance describes how far a body or object has moved from its starting position. For example, a 400 m runner will cover 400 m during their race around one lap of the athletics track. Displacement describes how far a body has moved away from its starting position. The 400 m runner who ran one lap has started and finished at roughly the same place and although they have covered a distance of 400 m they will have a displacement of 0.

The difference between distance and displacement can be seen in all sports where sports people change position. For example, a footballer or hockey player may dribble the ball over a long distance but it may be that their actual displacement may be much lower.

Distance is a scalar quality because it only considers the size of the quantity of ground covered while displacement is a vector quality because it considers size but also direction in which the displacement has occurred.

> ### Key terms
>
> **Distance** describes how far a body has moved.
>
> **Displacement** describes how far a body has moved in relation to its starting position.

Speed

Distance and displacement are important when examining the difference between speed and velocity. Speed measures how quickly a body or object has moved from their start to finish position. It can be calculated by dividing the distance covered by time taken in seconds:

$$Speed = \frac{\text{distance covered in metres (m)}}{\text{time taken in seconds (s)}}$$

Speed will be measured in metres per second (m/s). If a 400 m runner completed the race in 55 seconds, then their speed would be calculated in the following way:

$400 \div 55 = 7.27 \text{ m/s}$

Because speed only considers distance covered and not the direction of displacement or change in position it is a scalar quantity. However, velocity is a vector quantity because it considers both distance covered and changes in displacement.

Velocity

Velocity is different from speed as it focuses on the change in position, or displacement, that a body or object has undergone. It is calculated by dividing displacement by the time taken in seconds:

$$\text{Velocity} = \frac{\text{displacement in metres (m)}}{\text{time taken in seconds (s)}}$$

If a 400 m runner runs around one lap of the athletics track then they would have a displacement of 0 m and their velocity would be calculated in the following way:

$$0 \div 55 = 0 \text{ m/s}$$

That might look odd, but remember it is an average velocity over the entire lap. And if a runner, after one lap, comes back to exactly where they started then they have the same displacement as if they had just stood still instead! Hence the average velocity is zero. Note, however, that a runner's instantaneous velocity at some point in the lap would not equal zero.

Activity: Calculating speed and velocity

Part 1

Table 7.2 shows real data from Usain Bolt's world record breaking 100 m run at the World Championships in 2009.

1   Calculate Usain Bolt's speed over the sections that are missing in Table 7.2:

Section	Split time	Speed
0–10 m	1.89 s	5.29 m/s
11–20 m	0.99 s	
21–30 m	0.90 s	11.1 m/s
31–40 m	0.86 s	
41–50 m	0.83 s	12.0 m/s
51–60 m	0.82 s	
61–70 m	0.81 s	
71–80 m	0.82 s	
81–90 m	0.83 s	12.0 m/s
91–100 m	0.83 s	12.0 m/s

Table 7.2 Split times for Usain Bolt's 100 m run at 2009 World Championships

2   Calculate Usain Bolt's speed over the first 50 m and the second 50 m of the 100 m race.

Part 2

1   Table 7.3 shows data from a 400 m runner who completes the one lap race in 51 seconds.

Calculate the runner's speed and velocity at each 100 m segment of the race. The first row is completed for you as an example.

Distance covered	Displacement	Time to point	Speed	Velocity
100 m	85 m	13.5 s	7.41 m/s	6.3 m/s
200 m	170 m	25.5 s		
300 m	85 m	38.0 s		
400 m	0 m	51.0 s		

Table 7.3 Data from a 400 m run

Velocity can be positive or negative as it is possible to end up in a position behind where you started from. For example, a rugby player may run with the ball but then be driven backwards by the opposition to a position behind where they started from and record a negative value for velocity.

A3 Acceleration and deceleration

Acceleration describes the change in velocity of a body or object over a specific period of time. When acceleration has a negative value it is described as deceleration.

Calculating acceleration and deceleration

To be able to calculate acceleration you need to know the velocity of the body or object at the start of the period of time (v1) and the velocity at the end of the period of time (v2). The difference between the two velocities (v2–v1) is divided by the length of the period of time:

$$\text{Acceleration} = \frac{\text{change in velocity (v2} - \text{v1)}}{\text{change in time}}$$

Acceleration is measured with the units m/s^2 (metres per second squared). For example, a 100 m runner who ran their race in 12 seconds would have a starting velocity of 0 and a final velocity of 8.3 m/s (100÷12) and the change in time would be 12 seconds (12–0). The equation would look like this:

$$\text{Acceleration} = 8.3 \div 12 = 0.69 \ m/s^2$$

However, while this figure is an average across the whole race, acceleration will not be uniform across a 100 m race. In reality, the sprinter will accelerate in the early stages of the race and reach peak speed around 50–60 metres into the race; after this point they will start to decelerate and their aim is to minimise the amount of deceleration they are experiencing. Often in a 100 m race it looks like one athlete is accelerating away from the pack

---

Distinction activity: Calculating acceleration and deceleration (A D1)

Table 7.4 shows real data from the women's 100 m final in 2009 which was one of the fastest women's 100 m races ever run.

Shelly-Ann Fraser-Pryce (won in 10.73 s):

Section of race	Time to end of section (s)	Time to complete section (s)	Velocity (m/s)	Acceleration (m/s²)
0–20 m	3.03	3.03		
20–40 m	4.98	1.95		
40–60 m	6.88	1.90		
60–80 m	8.77	1.89		
80–100 m	10.73	1.96		

Table 7.4 Split times for Shelly-Ann Fraser-Pryce

→

Distinction activity: Calculating acceleration and deceleration (A D1)

Kerren Stewart (second place in 10.75):

Section of race	Time to end of section (s)	Time to complete section (s)	Velocity (m/s)	Acceleration (m/s²)
0–20 m	3.11	3.11		
20–40 m	5.07	1.96		
40–60 m	6.96	1.89		
60–80 m	8.82	1.86		
80–100 m	10.75	1.93		

Table 7.5 Split times for Kerren Stewart

Answer the following questions:

1   Which sprinter has the highest peak velocity and highest peak acceleration?
2   What is the difference between the acceleration of the two sprinters in the first 20 m section of the race?
3   Does Shelly-Ann Fraser-Pryce show acceleration or deceleration over the last 20 m of the race?
4   Using figures for acceleration, what would you see at the start of the race and the finish of the race in terms of the gap between the two runners?
5   Using the statistics available, which sprinter do you think would win if the race carried on for another 20 m? Explain why you think this.

when in actual fact they are the athlete who is showing the least deceleration as the other athletes are decelerating faster. Most sporting objects, such as a tennis ball, cricket ball, discuss or javelin, will reach peak velocity at the point they leave contact with a racket, bat or hand and then start to decelerate.

Deceleration is expressed as negative acceleration.

A4 Inertia and momentum

Inertia is a description of the resistance to change in the position of a body or object or the resistance of a body to change its current state of motion. If you consider a weight of 2 kg lying on the gym floor it will have less inertia than a weight of 70 kg. The 70 kg weight is going to need a much greater force to cause it to change its position than the 2 kg weight. The amount of inertia a body has is directly proportional to its mass and the more matter it contains then the more difficult it becomes to change its position. Inertia does depend on the surface that a body or object is resting on as a body resting on ice is easier to move than one resting on a rubber surface.

> **Key terms**
>
> **Inertia** describes the resistance of a body or object to change to its position. Bodies of a higher mass will show greater inertia.
>
> **Momentum** is described as the quantity of motion a body or object possesses and depends on its mass and velocity.

Momentum is described as the quantity of motion a body or object possesses and is dependent on the mass of a body or object and its velocity at any point.

Calculating momentum

Momentum is a vector quantity calculated by multiplying mass by velocity:

Momentum in kg·m/s = mass (kg) x velocity (m/s)

An object that is resting on the ground, such as a golf ball, has momentum of 0 kg·m/s as its velocity is 0 m/s. It is in a state of inertia until it is struck by a club that will produce a change in velocity and give the ball the quality of momentum. Momentum is important in sports where there are head on collisions between two bodies. For example, in wrestling one wrestler will move towards their opponent with a momentum based on their mass and velocity and they aim to knock their opponent over. This will happen if their momentum is greater than their opponent and is more likely if they can move at a velocity as close to their maximum as possible. Momentum is also an important quality in sports where tackling is a key feature as the person entering the tackle with the greatest momentum has the higher possibility of winning the tackle.

Distinction activity: Calculating momentum (A D1)

Table 7.6 shows the mass and peak velocity for three rugby players. Calculate the peak momentum of each player and then answer the questions that follow.

Player name	Mass (kg)	Peak velocity (m/s)	Peak momentum (kg·m/s)
Eddie	90	8	
Harry	85	9	
William	80	10	

Table 7.6 Mass and peak velocities for three rugby players

1 Which player will have the greatest inertia?
2 Which player would you least like to tackle and why?
3 Which player would you be least likely to pass the ball to if all three played for your team?
4 How much mass would William have to gain to have a higher peak momentum than Eddie?

Meeting distinction criteria

To achieve a distinction for learning aim A, you will need to be able to analyse how qualities of speed, velocity, acceleration and momentum apply to a range of sport and fitness activities. You will also have to show that you can calculate these qualities using data from sport and fitness activities. For example, you may look at rugby and show that speed is an important quality for a rugby player because you need speed to be able to run past and away from players when you are in possession of the ball. However, velocity is much more important because the quality of your running is dependent on the displacement that it produces rather than just relying on the speed at which it happens. Momentum is a very important quality because, while you may be able to produce high peak velocity, it is possible that unless you have a high mass to accompany the velocity it is likely that the momentum you produce will not be high enough to break through the tackles of the opposition. Acceleration is also an important quality, particularly acceleration from the point that you take possession of the ball, as the higher your acceleration then the increased chance you will have of running around your opponent who is accelerating towards you with the intent of tackling you.

Distinction activity: Linear motion in sport and exercise (A P1 , A M1 , A D1)

Choose two activities, one which is a sport and one which is a fitness/exercise activity. Using these two activities summarise each of the qualities of linear motion – speed, velocity, acceleration, deceleration, inertia and momentum, and provide examples of each quality from the two activities of your choice. To achieve a distinction grade, you will need to include examples of how you have calculated speed, velocity, acceleration and momentum in these activities.

A Check your understanding

1   Explain the difference between a scalar and a vector quantity.
2   Identify two scalar quantities and two vector quantities.
3   Explain the difference between speed and velocity.
4   If a sprinter covered 60 m in 7 seconds, what would be their acceleration over the duration of the race?
5   Describe why momentum is often more important in sport than acceleration or velocity.
6   Explain, using an example, the quality of inertia of a body or object.

B Examine forces acting on sports performers and the equipment they use
(B P2 , B M2 , B D2)

The study of forces that act on the human body and the effects of these forces is one of the central focuses of biomechanics in sport (Hay, 1993). There are two distinct types of forces acting on the human body. Firstly, there are forces that are produced inside the body, such as muscle contractions, which either produce movement to run and swim or they produce forces that are passed onto sporting objects, such as balls, rackets or weights. Secondly, there are forces that act on the body as it moves or attempts to stay in position. These forces would include air resistance, gravity and friction and they will be the main focus of Section B.

B1 Newton's three laws of motion

Before you can start to have full understanding of forces you need to have knowledge of Newton's three laws of motion. Sir Isaac Newton (1642–1727) was an English physicist and mathematician who went on to introduce the theory of gravity. His laws underpin our knowledge of mechanics and as a result biomechanics as well.

Newton's first law – the law of inertia

Newton's first law, the law of inertia, states that:

A body will maintain a state of rest or constant velocity unless acted on by an external force that changes its state.

Inertia was described as the resistance of a body or object to change to its position and it will stay in a state of rest until a force is applied to attempt to move it. The size of the force needed to move it is dependent on the mass of the body or object. However, once a body or object is in motion it is resistant to change its direction and velocity. It will only do so if it comes into contact with a force and it will then be accelerated, decelerated or diverted. Think about how when you hit a hockey ball it will continue in a straight line until it comes into contact with another hockey stick that either stops it, deflects it or increases its velocity in the direction that you hit it. Hopefully, its motion will only be overcome when it hits the back of the hockey goal.

Note that if you roll a hockey ball on a pitch eventually it will come to a stop. This is because air resistance and friction forces from contact with the grass act on it to decelerate it. If there were no air resistance and the pitch was completely frictionless then the ball would not slow down!

Newton's second law – the law of acceleration

Newton's second law examines the relationships between force, mass and acceleration. The size of a force is measured in Newtons (N), while the mass of an object is a measure of how much matter it contains in kg. The law of reaction states:

A force applied to a body causes an acceleration of that body of a magnitude:

Proportional to the force, in the direction of the force, and inversely;

Proportional to the body's mass.

This means that if a ball is struck it will travel in the direction that the force has been applied in. If you serve in tennis then the ball will travel towards your opponent in the direction that you hit it at a velocity dependent on how much force you applied to the ball. If you applied twice as much force to the ball it would accelerate twice as quickly as the slower ball and have twice as much velocity. This is because its acceleration is proportional to the size of the force applied on the ball.

However, if the ball was twice as heavy and an equal force was applied to the ball during the serve it would only accelerate at half the velocity of the lighter ball. This is an example of an inverse relationship. The relationship between force, mass and acceleration can be expressed as:

Force = mass x acceleration

So if a ball of with a mass of 3 kg was hit with a force of 30 N it would accelerate at 10 m/s^2 but if the ball had a mass of 6 kg and was hit with a force of 30 N it would only accelerate at 5 m/s^2.

Newton's third law – the law of reaction

Newton's third law of motion states that for every action there will be an equal and opposite reaction. When this is used in the context of forces it states that:

When one body exerts a force on a second body, the second body exerts a reaction force that is equal in magnitude and opposite in direction on the first body.

This means that if a force is applied by the body on another object or surface then that object or surface will apply an equal force that pushes back on the athlete. If you think about when you are running, every time your foot your strikes the ground a force of equal size is sent back up your leg – the force is equal and opposite to the force created by your body weight landing on the ground through your foot. This force is called a ground reaction force and can cause damage if you are wearing inappropriate footwear or have poor running technique.

This law also applies to when you strike a sporting object; for example, if you take a shot in snooker you are sending a force down the cue to the ball but when the cue strikes the ball, the ball will also send a force back up the cue into your arm. If you hit the ball hard you can often feel this equal and opposite force in your arm so the cue has to be held securely.

Key point

Newton's three laws of motion

1 A body at rest or moving with a consistent velocity will remain in that state unless an external force is applied to it.
2 The acceleration of a body is proportional to the force that caused it and will take place in the direction that the force is applied. It is inversely proportional to the mass of the body or object to which it has been applied.
3 For every force that is applied there will be an equal and opposite reaction force.

Activity: Newton's three laws of motion

1 Briefly describe Newton's laws of motion.
2 Using examples, illustrate how Newton's three laws can be used to explain how forces impact on sport and fitness activities.

B2 Reaction forces

Forces

Forces act on a body or object by exerting a push or pull effect on them. All forces are trying to overcome the inertia of a body or object and change its state of movement. Forces can produce motion in a stationary body or object, and if it is already moving they can cause the body or object to speed up, slow down or change its direction. Forces will either be generated internally in the body through muscle contractions or applied externally through the application of gravity, air resistance or friction to a body or object. Forces make movement possible but they can also resist movement and cause problems for athletes to overcome.

Activity: Forces

Figure 7.1 Rowers in action

Look at the picture of the rowers in action and write down four forces that are either being produced by the rowers or that the rowers have to work against. Divide the forces up into internally and externally produced forces.

Forces are central to all sport and exercise activities. Forces will be specific to the activity and the environment where it is done. If you think about rowing indoors on a rowing machine the forces will be very different as the rower is rowing against resistance from the fly wheel rather than from moving water. They also don't have to stabilise the boat on the water or work against wind that may be pushing against them.

Forces are vector quantities as they are described by their direction and their size. For example, air resistance will be in a certain direction depending on the direction of motion of the body or object and the direction of movement of the air/wind; the size of the air resistance force is dependent on how quickly the body or object is moving and how quickly the air is moving.

All forces will be measured in Newtons (N). One newton represents the force required to accelerate a mass of 1 kg by $1 m/s^2$. This section will go on to look at the different types of forces acting on a body or object during sport and exercise performance.

Key term

A **force** is a push or a pull that is exerted on a body or object. Forces can act to move a body, accelerating and decelerating it, or changing its direction.

Ground reaction forces

When we are standing still we will be applying a force on the ground or surface underneath our feet. The force is due to gravity acting on our mass. A person with a larger mass will feel a larger gravitational force and hence apply a greater force on the ground. The forces exerted on the ground by an athlete are shown in Figure 7.2.

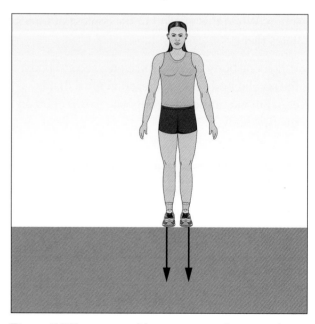

Figure 7.2 Forces an athlete exerts on the ground

The forces produced by the athlete on the ground will, according to Newton's third law, produce forces that are equal and opposite. This force will be upwards into the athlete's body and is described as a reaction force, or in this case a ground reaction force, as it is produced by the surface the athlete is standing on. The direction of the reaction forces can be seen in Figure 7.3.

Figure 7.3 Forces the ground exerts on an athlete

When the athlete starts to move two things will happen. Firstly, the direction of the force will change as the athlete's foot will push downwards at a different angle. Secondly, the size of the force will increase as the foot is being accelerated towards the ground by muscular contractions and the effect of

gravity. This will mean that the size of the reaction forces will increase as well. The human body is designed to deal with reaction forces as our bones can bend slightly and our joints are cushioned by cartilage; however, if the reaction forces do become too great then damage can be done to the structures of our body.

Action and reaction forces

Ground reaction forces are just one example of reaction forces and they are present in every contact that is made in sport and exercise activities. Action and reaction forces will occur in all sports and examples of these forces can be seen in Figure 7.4. In this figure the forces are labelled 'A' for the action force and 'R' for the reaction force produced as a result of the action force.

In the example of the footballer in Figure 7.4 we can see him imparting an action force on the football to set it in motion. This action force will produce an equal and opposite reaction force that is felt in the foot and leg. The greater the action force imparted on the ball then the further the ball will travel and the greater the reaction force produced then the greater the force that has to be withstood by the footballer's leg.

Key terms

Reaction forces are the equal and opposite forces that are exerted on the object or body in response to an action force.

Action forces are forces that are imparted on an object or a body by another object or body.

Figure 7.4 Three examples of forces and reaction forces

Impact on sport and exercise activities (Distinction content)

Action forces are important for producing movement of the body and for propelling sporting objects. For example, in the second picture of Figure 7.4 we see a shot putter who is producing forces internally to then apply these forces on the shot put that will propel it forwards. The greater the forces that the athlete's muscles can produce will directly impact on the size of the action force and how far it will travel away from the athlete. However, the shot put will come under other forces once it has been released as it has to travel through the air and it will be subject to the force of gravity that will attract it towards the ground. The distance the shot put travels will also depend on the angle that it is released at.

Performance in the high jump is dependent on reaction forces. When a high jumper runs up towards the bar they will increase their velocity as they get closer to the bar and the forces they are producing increase with velocity. However, the direction of these forces is horizontal but when they produce their jump the direction of these forces becomes vertical. When they take their last stride they exert a large force into the ground with the aim of producing a ground reaction force that will produce an upward force to enable them to gain height. For the high jumper to accelerate upwards the reaction force must be greater than the weight of the athlete and the difference in the size of the force and the mass of the jumper will directly influence how high they can jump.

Distinction activity: Action and reaction forces (B D2)

Using a sports skill of your choice, analyse the skill by assessing how action and reaction forces are acting during the movement. Answer the following question about the sports skill:

1 What is the direction of the action forces?
2 How are the action forces being produced?
3 What is the direction of the action and reaction forces?
4 Are the forces being produced horizontal or vertical?
5 What impact are reaction forces having on the performer's body?
6 What would happen to performance if the size of the action forces was increased?

B3 Friction

Friction is described as a force that will oppose the efforts to slide or roll one body over another (Hamilton, Weimar and Luttgens, 2008). We are able to walk due to the friction created between our shoes and the ground. If in sport we need to create more friction then we change our footwear as a lack of friction can be hazardous, such as when we walk on a wet or icy surface.

Most sports rely on friction or friction being created between two surfaces; for example, when a gymnast puts chalk on their hands to increase their chances of staying on a piece of apparatus or a hockey player chooses footwear appropriate to a surface. Sliding sports, such as snowboarding and skeleton bobsleigh are concerned with minimising friction so that velocity can be maximised.

Friction occurs when two surfaces come into contact and each exert a force on the other. If you were to rub the palms of your hands together you would feel some resistance to the movement. Friction is the resistance force that opposes the movement of the hands. If your hands were wet there would be less friction and if they covered in chalk there would be more friction.

Key term

Friction is a force that acts when two surfaces come into contact with each other.

Types of friction

There are different types of friction that are produced, depending on the situation. The three main types are:

- **Static friction** is produced when two objects push against each other but neither one moves, e.g. a runner's foot as it pushes into the track surface.
- **Rolling friction** is produced when a curved object, such as ball or a wheel, moves across a flat surface, e.g. when a hockey player passes a hockey ball to a team mate.
- **Sliding friction** is produced when a body moves across a surface, e.g. a skier moving down a slope.

Each of these involves a difference in the movement between two surfaces. Static friction may become sliding or rolling friction if the size of the force exerted increases. The change from static to sliding friction depends on the size of the force applied. A runner's foot will not slide backwards as long as the force they exert does not overcome the friction forces. If they exert too much force in relation to the friction between the two surfaces their foot will move backwards. Running shoes and particularly spiked shoes are designed to maximise friction relevant to specific surfaces. The amount of friction created between two surfaces is represented by the coefficient of friction.

Coefficient of friction

The coefficient of friction is a measure of the amount of friction between two bodies or objects. It represents the relative ease of sliding between two surfaces in contact with each other (Hall, 2007). It is a dimensionless number (i.e. has no units) that is affected by a number of factors:

- the mass of the object in contact with a surface
- the type of surface (its roughness or hardness)
- size of the contact area between two surfaces
- dryness or wetness of surfaces in contact
- presence of oils or lubricants.

Table 7.7 shows the coefficient of friction for a variety of surfaces:

Types of surfaces	Coefficient of friction
Rubber on concrete	1.0
Ice on ice	0.1
Waxed wood on snow	0.14
Copper on steel	0.53

Table 7.7 (*Source:* Serway and Jewett, 2014)

Implications of frictional forces for sports performance (Distinction content)

Frictional forces have implications for every sport. Runners will use frictional forces to decide on their choice of footwear as spiked running shoes will create more friction than normal training shoes. Spikes are worn on tartan athletics tracks to maximise friction and ensure that no energy will be lost due to slipping backwards. Runners will also tend to choose tight clothing so there are fewer loose areas of clothing that could cause friction between the material and the skin and create chafing that is very uncomfortable. Marathon runners use lubricants to ensure that the skin on their limbs does not rub as they move backwards and forwards.

Tennis courts have different surfaces that produce different amounts of friction to suit different players. Grass and hard courts produce low amounts of friction when the ball strikes the surface and as a result these surfaces are fast. This means that players with fast serves who hit the ball hard will find that these surfaces suit their game as the ball will lose little speed when it is in contact with the surface. For example, Novak Djokovic has a fast serve and powerful game and he has been successful at Wimbledon which uses grass courts and the US Open which uses hard courts. On the other hand, clay courts produce a lot more friction between the tennis ball and the surface and they favour players who spin the ball as they negate the speed that a ball is hit with. Rafael Nadal is a player who benefits from clay courts as his game in based on staying in long rallies and moving his opponent around the court until he can play passing shots. He won the French Open nine times between 2005 and 2014.

In motor racing the contact between a racing car's tyres and the track surface is key. Even the best car in Formula One cannot go quickly if there is not enough friction between the tyres and surface. Consequently, sophisticated engineering technology is required to develop high performance tyres that can produce enough friction for the high cornering speeds of racing cars.

Distinction activity : Frictional forces

Select a sport and exercise activity of your choice and analyse the activity by answering the following questions:

1 How do frictional forces impact on this activity?
2 Which frictional forces are beneficial to performance and which are detrimental?
3 What attempts are made to maximise and minimise friction?

B4 Air resistance

Air resistance is a force that affects the movement of any object as it moves through the atmosphere. Although we can't see them air is made up of atoms and molecules that strike an object as it passes through them. The object has to move the atoms and molecules aside to enable it to move forwards. Thus, air provides a force acting in the opposite direction to an object's direction of travel.

If a ball was moving through a vacuum there would be no air resistance and its velocity would remain the same; however, in real life situations air resistance will affect how far a ball, or other sporting body, travels. If there is a tailwind then air resistance will push the body further than if there is a head wind that decelerates the body more quickly. You are probably aware of this and if you have either run or cycled into a head wind you will know how much more energy you expend to keep moving forwards.

> **Key term**
>
> **Air resistance** is the resistance that a body or object will come under when it moves through air.

Effect of air resistance on projectiles

When running, cycling or rowing air resistance will act on the body but it acts on sporting objects, particularly projectiles, as well. Air resistance will impact on projectiles in different ways depending on the mass, size, shape and design of the projectile. Figure 7.5 shows the expected trajectories of a range of projectiles.

If you compare the shot and the discus, the shot has a much steeper curve in its trajectory. This is due to its higher mass meaning that the effect of acceleration downwards due to gravity is greater than the effect on the discus. The shape of the shot also means that there is smaller surface area than a discus for air particles to strike and so keep it in flight.

The flight of the shuttlecock in badminton is very different from that of a tennis ball. Due to its lightness the shuttlecock will be accelerated very quickly off a badminton racket and can leave the racket at speeds over 200 mph; however, by the time

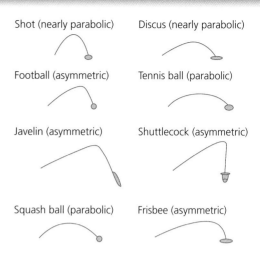

Figure 7.5 Expected trajectories of a selection of projectiles.

it has reached its opponent it will have decelerated considerably due to its shape and design. This deceleration is due to the feathers of the shuttlecock that provide a high level of air resistance and quickly decelerate the shuttlecock and eventually cause it drop quickly from the air.

Implications and effect of air resistance for design of sports equipment and clothing (Distinction content)

Air resistance is also referred to as drag and is of particular interest to designers of sportswear and sports equipment. The equipment and clothing of cyclists and runners have undergone huge changes over the last 20 years as the effects of air resistance have become more appreciated. As can be seen from Figure 7.6, the helmet and clothing of the cyclist have been specially designed to reduce the force produced by air and the cyclist's position on the bike is also recommended to reduce the contact area between the cyclist and air.

The cyclist will adopt a crouched position and keep their elbows close to their body so that there is less surface area travelling forwards to make contact with the air. The outcome of this technique, called streamlining, is that the cyclist is able to travel through air more quickly and do so with reduced energy expenditure.

Cyclists and swimmers will also shave body hair from their arms and legs and apply oil to reduce any friction between air and their skin and this

Factors affecting speed of flow around an object

Flow around an object depends on three main factors:

1 the shape of the object
2 the speed of the object
3 the nature of the object's surface.

The greater the surface area that is travelling towards the flow, the air will find it more difficult to flow around it. A shot put will have poorer aerodynamics than a discus as it has a greater surface area travelling into the path of the air and a javelin will have even better aerodynamics as it has a pointed end providing even less air resistance. Objects travelling at fast speeds or those with rough, textured surfaces will have poorer aerodynamics because they produce turbulence or turbulent flow which is examined in the next section.

Types of flow

Air can flow around an object in two different ways. These are called laminar flow and turbulent flow. When an object, such as a ball, is travelling through air it will carry with it a layer of air molecules on its surface and they will make contact with the molecules in the air it is moving through and disrupt their flow. Figure 7.7 shows a ball travelling through layers of air. When a ball is moving slowly the layer of air in contact with the ball, called the boundary layer, is slowed down as the ball is exerting a force on it. This layer of air will slow down the layer next to it and so on. As the ball is moving forwards slowly air will flow past the ball in a smooth symmetrical fashion which is known as laminar flow. The flow of air will quickly return to the way it was flowing before it made contact with the ball.

However, flow does not always happen this way, particularly if the ball is travelling at a fast speed or the surface of the ball is rough or dimpled. As the fast moving object passes through air the layers of air further down the boundary layer become thicker and this causes the air on the boundary layer to become unstable and it starts to get mixed up. This can be seen in Figure 7.8 where the air goes from flowing in parallel lines (laminar flow) to flowing in a violent, mixed up way (turbulent flow).

Figure 7.6 A cyclist showing specially designed equipment and a crouched position to minimise air resistance.

will also reduce air resistance. Streamlining has played a huge part in the design of clothing for swimming, running and rowing as any seam or loose area of clothing will increase the effect of air resistance. The result of reducing air resistance is that energy can be preserved and over the course of a 2–3 hour run or cycle it will have an impact on the time achieved by the athlete. It may be a small gain but success in sport is often the result of a series of marginal gains.

B5 Aerodynamics

Although it is related to air resistance, aerodynamics specifically studies how air flows around an object. The shape of an object will influence how air flows around it and this has an impact on sports performance. For example, aerodynamics has major implications for sports such as motor racing and cycling. In motor racing a car's fuel consumption is affected by air flow around it and a more aerodynamic car will have greater fuel efficiency. It is similar in cycling where increased air resistance will cause the cyclist to use their fuel stores more quickly. Aerodynamics will work in favour of the cyclists behind the first rider as the first rider will experience high levels of air resistance but air will flow over the riders behind the front rider and mean they can expend less energy when riding in second or third place in the peloton.

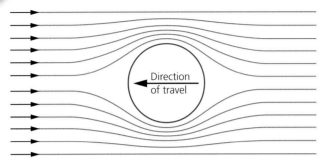

Figure 7.7 Laminar flow of air around a slow moving ball

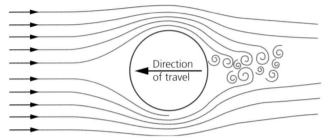

Figure 7.8 Turbulent flow of air around a fast moving ball resulting in a drag force

This turbulent flow creates drag, or more specifically, surface drag. Drag is a resistant force and will act to slow the object down as it moves around and behind an object. This is because the air at the back of the ball has a relatively lower pressure in comparison to air at the front of the ball and will produce a force that pulls the ball backwards.

Key terms

Aerodynamics is the study of how air flows around a body or object and the disruption it can cause.

Laminar flow occurs when air flows around a body in a smooth, symmetrical fashion.

Turbulent flow occurs when air flows around a body in a disrupted and mixed up way.

Implications of turbulence for sports performance

Turbulence is an unavoidable hindrance to performance in sports involving objects moving at fast speeds but there are ways of minimising drag or turbulent flow. Take the example of cyclists who are travelling in a peloton, as seen in Figure 7.9. The proximity of cyclists to each other ensures that air will flow around them as if they were a single object rather than three separate objects.

The cyclists must be positioned close together because the leading cyclist will disrupt the flow of air molecules at the boundary layer and create turbulence behind them. The second cyclist has to be really close to the first cyclist so that the turbulent air flows directly over them and not behind the first cyclist. This effect will occur down the length of the chain of cyclists, or the peloton, as long as they each ride with their front wheel as close as possible to the rider in front's back wheel.

If the cyclists left large gaps between them they would find that they were affected by turbulence, as can be seen in the third figure in Figure 7.10.

Similar principles apply in running – for middle and longer distance races, running in a pack will reduce some of the air resistance for those in the middle of the pack. While the effect is nowhere near as important as in cycling, it still has a small effect which could be crucial in elite competitions.

In motor racing the effect is very pronounced because of the high speeds. If a car can get close enough to the car in front then the air resistance can be reduced enough to allow the car behind to gain speed and overtake.

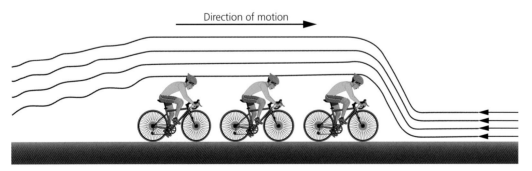

Figure 7.9 Air flow around three cyclists in close proximity to each other

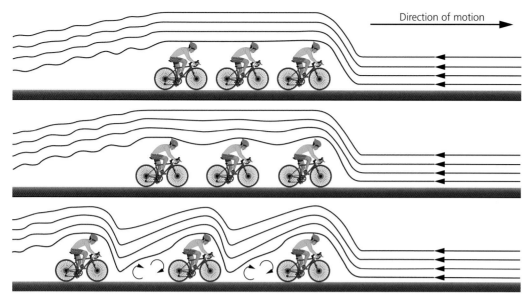

Direction of motion

Figure 7.10 Air flow over three cyclists at different distances apart from each other

Cricket balls are designed with a raised seam down the middle of the ball and this means that the surface is not totally smooth. A smooth cricket ball would flow through the air with predominantly laminar flow but the seam disrupts the flow of air at the boundary layer and causes turbulent flow. This turbulent flow will cause the ball to move around in the air. Also, as the ball gets older the shiny surface will become rougher and more worn and this causes more turbulence and the movement of the ball will become even more unpredictable, giving bowlers an advantage over the batters.

Golf balls also benefit from turbulent flow. In the 19th century it was discovered that golfers could hit balls that had a scuffed surface further than if the surface was smooth. A totally smooth golf ball will cause turbulent flow behind it if it is hit hard but if the golf ball has small dimples on its surface the separation of air flow that causes turbulent air flow is reduced. The small dimples actually create some turbulence on the boundary layer but reduce the amount of turbulence behind the ball that sucks it back. However, if the dimples are too deep it will actually increase the amount of turbulence produced. Thus it is very important that the dimples on a golf ball are very shallow.

Distinction activity: Air resistance and aerodynamics (B D2)

Research an activity of your choice and analyse how air resistance and aerodynamics impact positively and negatively on performance by answering the following questions:

1 How does air resistance affect performers in this sport?

2 What attempts are taken to minimise air resistance?

3 Will laminar or turbulent flow be created when bodies or objects are moving?

4 How could the effects of turbulent flow be minimised?

B6 Lift and Bernoulli's principle

Lift is a force created by a difference in pressure below and above a body that causes it to be pushed upwards. Lift can be seen in Figure 7.11 where a body, in this case an aerofoil, is moving forwards into air flow. The shape of the aerofoil means that the air flow around the foil is disrupted. The air above the foil has further to travel to reach the back of the foil than the air below. As a result the air flow above the foil is quicker than that below. The increased velocity of air flow causes pressure to drop above the foil, so that there is a pressure difference between the air below and above the foil. Because the air pressure is greater below the foil there will be a lift force acting which will cause the foil to move upwards.

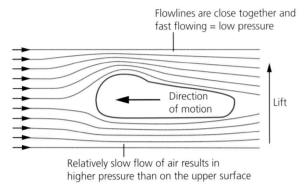

Figure 7.11 The different velocities of air flow above and below a foil will cause a pressure differential between its lower and upper surfaces resulting in lift

This is referred to as Bernoulli's principle and has application and implications for many sports activities.

> **Key term**
>
> **Lift** is a force that is caused by a pressure differential in the air flow above and below a body with the result of pushing a body upwards.

Factors affecting lift

Lift is affected by two main factors: the shape of the body or object and its position relative to the air flow. A good example of the principle of lift in action is flying. Aeroplane wings are designed to be similar to the shape of the foil so that the air flows with greater velocity above the wings than below and creating an upward force for take-off. When the aeroplane has gained enough height the angle of the wings is changed so that the pressure above the below the wings is equal and the aeroplane neither loses nor gains height.

Bernoulli's principle and its impact on sports performance – Lift (Distinction content)

There are many applications of this effect in sport. Firstly, discus throwers will release the discus at a specific angle with the bottom to maximise the force of lift. The discus should be tilted to an angle of 30–40° so that the bottom of the discus is the first part to make contact with air flow. The tilt of the discus ensures that a pressure differential is created and that the flight of the discus will be maximised. However, the discus has a large mass and as a result its lift is quickly negated by the force of gravity which returns it to the ground. The shape of a shot put means that a pressure differential cannot be created and thus it will not experience lift; however, the angle of release of a javelin is important in creating lift forces.

Figure 7.12a and b Ski jumpers and long jumpers assume shapes to create lift

The aim of ski jumping and long jumping is to remain in the air at speed for as long as possible as the length of the jump is the result of the length of hang time. Figure 7.12 shows that ski jumpers hold their skis at a slight tilt to create a pressure differential above and below the skis and thus create lift. Likewise, the long jumper aims to get their body at an angle where the air pressure below their body is higher than the air pressure above the body so that lift is created. While speed of take-off is the main factor for their performance, angle of take-off and the angle their body moves through the air at will also impact on the length of the jump.

Formula 1 cars have an aerofoil, or spoiler, on the back which is angled in the opposite direction to the discus or ski jumper's skis because its aim is to produce a downwards force to improve road holding as the car goes around corners.

Figure 7.13 The aerofoil on the back on an F1 car produces downwards forces

In this case the position of the aerofoil means that the air flows with greater velocity above the foil than below and the pressure is lower below the aerofoil causing downward pressure.

Magnus effect

The Magnus effect applies the principles of the Bernoulli effect of pressure differentials to spinning objects. When an object spins the air molecules forming the boundary edge spin with it. The air molecules at the boundary edge will come under resistance from the air flow that it is travelling into. This is shown in Figure 7.14 where a ball is moving forwards into an air flow but is also spinning in a clockwise direction. The collision between these two sets of moving air molecules causes changes in pressure. As the ball is spinning clockwise the air molecules on the left-hand side of

the ball are colliding head on with the air flow and creating high pressure and a lower velocity. The air molecules on the right-hand side are flowing in the same direction as the air flowing over them so the collision between the two is minimal, creating a higher velocity and lower pressure than on the left side. As a result the ball will move, or spin, to the right. This movement has been caused by the creation of a Magnus force.

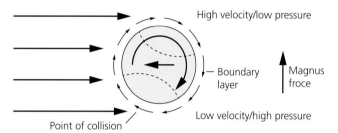

Figure 7.14 The collision between air molecules at the boundary layer and in the air flow creates a Magnus force

Bernoulli's principle and its impact on sports performance – Magnus effect (Distinction content)

This Magnus effect has application to all sports involving a ball. Some balls are more susceptible to spin than others. For example, tennis balls are covered in felt which acts to trap a large area of boundary air to collide with the air flow and thus creates a heightened Magnus effect. This explains why new tennis balls spin more than older balls where the felt has become damaged or flattened.

It will also explain how free kicks in soccer can be made to swerve. The 'banana shot' involves the footballer hitting the ball off-centre so that it starts to rotate as well as travel forwards and this sideways spin can make it curve around the wall of players and into the net.

> ### Key term
>
> The Magnus effect explains why balls deviate from a straight path when they are rotating, or spin. Spin is caused because the air molecules at the boundary layer are moving in different directions in relation to the air flow.

B Check your understanding

1 Describe what is meant by a force.
2 Explain Newton's three laws of motion.
3 Explain, using a sporting example, what is meant by reaction forces.
4 Identify three types of friction.
5 Describe why different projectiles have different trajectories.
6 Explain why moving objects can produce turbulence.
7 Describe three ways a cyclist can improve their aerodynamics.
8 Explain, using a sporting example, the concept of lift.

Case study

Meet Paul Brice

Paul is a biomechanist working at the English Institute of Sport. This is what he said about his work:

Biomechanics is primarily concerned with enhancing and optimising the way we move. Sports biomechanics therefore uses the scientific principles of mechanics to study the effects of various forces on sporting performance. It is directly concerned with the forces that act on the performer during all sports, in particular velocities, time, accelerations, torque, momentum, displacements and inertia.

Biomechanical techniques can be used within any sport to define the characteristics of skills, to gain an understanding of the mechanical effectiveness of their execution and to identify the factors underlying their successful performance. This knowledge and understanding can then assist the coach and athlete to enhance the learning and performance of sport specific skills.

Work may involve a diverse range of duties ranging from performance analysis through to in-depth 3D video kinematic analysis.

(*Source:* BASES Career Guide, available online at: www.bases.org.uk/write/documents/BASES%20 Career%20Guide%20revised%20edition%20 Jan%202010.pdf)

1 How do you think you could use principles of biomechanics to improve other people's performances in your own sport?
2 What skills would you need to work as a sport biomechanist?

C Investigate angular motion in sport and exercise activities

C1 Centre of mass

The centre of mass is the point through which gravity acts. It is the point in a body or object where there are equal amounts of mass on both sides. If you try to balance a ruler on your finger you will find its centre of mass at the exact point where it becomes balanced. The centre of mass is also referred to as the centre of gravity.

Key term

The **centre of mass** is the point where its mass is equally balanced and is the point that gravity acts through.

Location of centre of mass

The centre of mass of round or other regular shaped objects is fairly easy to find but not all objects are regularly shaped.

Activity: Centre of mass

Look at the different types of racket and place a mark with a pencil where you think the centre of mass of each racket would be positioned.

Figure 7.15 Different types of racket – where is the centre of mass?

Then place a mark on the human body where you think the centre of mass is located.

→

Activity: Centre of mass

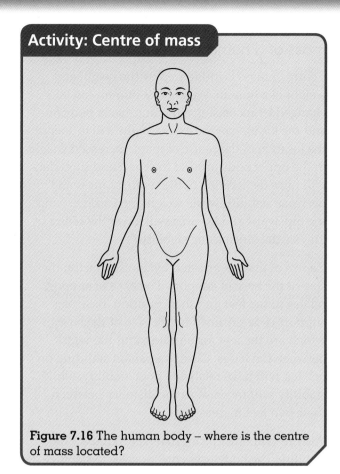

Figure 7.16 The human body – where is the centre of mass located?

The centre of mass for a human body is usually around the navel but it would be halfway between the front and back of the body. However, the location of the centre of mass is dependent on the height and mass of the individual and the position that they are in. If you were to raise your arms the location of the centre of mass would rise and if you were kneeling on all fours the centre of mass would be just in front of the body.

It is important to note that the centre of mass can be outside an object or body and it can move around if the shape of a body changes.

Impact of changes in centre of mass on performance

The centre of mass is important when considering the balance of the body. If it travels too far forwards, backwards or to one side of the body then balance will be lost. Rugby players and footballers are often praised if they have a low centre of gravity because it means that they don't fall over so easily and can assume greater ranges of motion without losing their balance.

In sports, such as gymnastics, where maintaining balance is central to performance, we tend to find athletes who are short of stature, with centres of mass relatively close to the ground. A gymnast on a beam needs to keep their centre of mass over the beam because if it moves outside the beam they become unstable and are likely to fall off, unless they can move it back above the beam very quickly.

Activity: Impact of changes in centre of mass on performance

Choose two out of the three sports below and explain how changes in the position of the athlete's centre of mass will affect their performance:

1   A striker playing football.
2   A trampolinist completing a routine.
3   A judoka during a judo match.

Centre of mass and the high jump

While gymnasts tend to be of short stature so that their centre of mass stays relatively close to their body, the opposite is true for high jumpers. High jumpers are usually relatively tall with long limbs and this means that their centre of mass will be relatively higher in their body. Figure 7.17 shows the technique that is currently most popular amongst high jumpers. It is known as the Fosbury flop, after Dick Fosbury who developed the technique and used it to win the gold medal at the 1968 Olympic Games.

Figure 7.17 A high jumper using the Fosbury flop technique

The major factor for success in the high jump is velocity at take off as this influences the height the athlete will gain. However, once the athlete is in the air they can manipulate the location of their centre of mass so that while the body goes over the bar the centre of mass will pass below it. The technique involves bending the back as much as possible and keeping the legs hanging until the point where the hips could dislodge the bar and then rapidly raising the hips and pulling the legs over the bar. Because the top athletes have long bodies and limbs it enables them to move their centre of gravity further away from their body than a shorter person.

C2 Centre of mass and stability

Stability is a term that is closely related to the concept of balance and is described as resistance to the disruption the body's balance (Hall, 2007). Stability is vital to a rugby player trying to resist a tackle or a wrestler trying to remain on their feet. Sprinters will be at the last point before unbalance when they are in the start position on the blocks and the tiniest of movements forwards will cause them to lose their balance and fall forwards.

Key term

Stability is described as a body's resistance to the disruption of its balance.

Relationship of the centre of mass and stability

Stability is dependent on the location of the centre of mass with a lower centre of mass increasing stability and a higher centre of mass decreasing stability. This can be seen in two sports used as examples in this section. Gymnasts need stability and benefit from a centre of mass close to the ground, while high jumpers need to become unstable to move their centre of mass outside their bodies and they benefit from being tall.

Factors affecting the centre of mass of a human

Centre of mass is influenced by the height and weight of a human. Weight of a human can be changed by increasing either muscle or body fat and the location of the extra weight will influence the location of the centre of mass. Increased weight in the upper body around the chest and shoulders will raise the location of the centre of mass and decrease stability, while weight increased around the hip, waist and leg area will lower the centre of gravity thus increasing stability.

Centre of mass is affected by another factor, the size of the base of support. The base of support relates to the feet and their position. Base of support is determined by the size of the bases, which are the feet for humans, and the width between the bases. Clearly a person standing on one leg will have relatively poor stability, while stability will increase as the distance between their two feet increases.

Posture is another factor that has an impact on stability. The body uses core muscles to stabilize the spine and give the body central strength. If these muscles are well conditioned and activated then the body will be more resistant to changes in the centre of mass and be more balanced.

Manipulation of centre of mass to improve sports performance (Distinction content)

Martial artists and boxers are aware that the location of their centre of mass will affect their stability and ensure a wide stable base, as seen in Figure 7.18, is adopted as a means of providing stability for their defence and a stable base from which to attack their opponent. A split position where one foot is in front of the other while maintaining a wide base is also relatively stable. This stance is often used by weightlifters to improve their stability and the amount of weight they can lift.

Figure 7.18 Position of a judoka is important to keep the centre of mass low and a wide base of support to support stability

Sprinting provides a good example of different foot positions for different periods of the race. When a sprinter leaves the blocks their feet will be positioned relatively widely because the aim is to produce as much power as possible and this can cause the body to be less stable so it requires a wider, more stable base. However, once the power has been generated the feet become closer together to try and maintain speed for as long as possible.

C3 Levers

When muscles develop tension they pull on bones to overcome resistance that is created by the weight of a body part and the weight of any added load. The bones, muscles and a joint are acting as a lever system. A lever is a rigid bar (in this case, the bone) that moves about an axis (the joint), also called a fulcrum. The muscles provide a force that moves a weight or resistance.

A basic understanding of the different types of lever system can help us to understand human movement more deeply and explore ways that technique can be modified.

Functions of levers

The arms and legs of the human body act as levers and they have three main functions:

1 to increase the amount of resistance that can be moved

2 to increase speed of movement

3 to increase mechanical advantage.

An example of the effect of levers is changing the speed of movement. If you have two people, one with shorter legs and one with longer legs, you will find that the person with shorter legs has to move their legs (levers) more quickly than the one with longer legs. Also, if the person with longer legs moved their legs at the same speed as the person with shorter legs, their feet would be moving with greater velocity as the increased lever length multiplies the velocity that the foot moves at. This also explains why, if you want to hit a golf ball a long distance then you choose a longer golf club as the velocity of the club head will be increased due to the length of the club (lever). Swimming is another sport where participants benefit from having long levers as they can create more force with each stroke giving them a mechanical advantage over shorter rivals. Generally speaking, longer strokes at a lesser speed will beat shorter, faster strokes.

Types of lever

There are three classes of lever depending on the relative positions of the lever, fulcrum and resistance. The three classes of lever are shown in Figure 7.19.

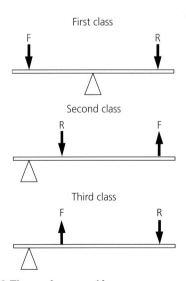

Figure 7.19 Three classes of lever

A **first class lever** is when the force and resistance are found on opposite sides of the fulcrum; for example, like a seesaw which has a seat on each end and a moving joint in the middle. First class levers are rare in the human body but the skull sitting on top of the cervical vertebrae enabling you to nod your head forwards and backwards, is an example of a first class lever.

Second class levers are found when the force and resistance are both on the same side of the fulcrum with the resistance closer to the fulcrum. For example, when you use a wheelbarrow the wheel is the fulcrum and the weight of the wheelbarrow is the resistance with you applying the force on the handles at the end. There are no complete second class levers in the body and the closest example is provided when you do a calf raise exercise. The fulcrum is the balls of your feet, the resistance is the weight of the body and the force is provided by your calf muscles to raise the body upwards.

Third class levers are very common in the body and account for nearly all weight training techniques. They occur when the resistance and force are on the same side of the fulcrum but the force applied is closer to the fulcrum. If you think about a bicep curl the elbow is the fulcrum, the bicep that attaches below the elbow (on the radius) is the muscle providing the force and the resistance is a weight held in the hand. As the force is applied on the radius the elbow flexes and the weight moves upwards. In this case, and many others, the biceps muscle is above the elbow but its attachment is below the elbow causing the force and the resistance to be on the side of the lever.

Meeting distinction criteria

Third class levers also apply to all racket and bat type sports. If you think about playing tennis with a racket – the shoulder will act as the fulcrum, the force will be applied to the handle of the racket and the resistance will be applied by the ball on the strings of the racket. If you want to hit the ball harder you can either extend the length of the lever by having a longer racket or holding the racket further up the handle. Alternately, you can swing the racket with increased velocity thus increasing the velocity of the lever. Lever length accounts for the reason why taller tennis players are able to apply higher velocities to the tennis ball as the increased lever length can create increased speed of movement.

It does not equate that all people with longer levers will be better sports people. For example, most weightlifters are fairly short in stature and have shorter levers. This is because in order to lift a weight above the head, the weight will have to travel a distance according the length of a lever. A weightlifter with shorter levers will not need to produce as much muscular force to move the weight a shorter distance than a person with longer levers. This also applies to kicking a football as a taller player will create more speed on the ball but it will take longer for their leg to complete the movement and this gives their opponent more time to block the shot or get a tackle in.

Turning effects

Levers in the human body are only able to produce rotational movement so the majority of sporting movements involve angular motion around a joint. The twisting or turning effect of a force is known as the moment of force, or torque. Moment of force is directly related to the distance between the point where the force is applied (the muscle insertion point) and the fulcrum (joint). The largest turning effect will occur when the distance between the point where force is applied and the fulcrum is at its longest or the applied force is at its greatest.

The moment of force is calculated by multiplying the size of the force by the distance between the point where force is applied and the fulcrum.

C4 Axes of rotation

Movement in each axis of rotation

There are three axes of rotation: they are the transverse (mediolateral), frontal (anteroposterior) and the longitudinal axes. They can be seen in Figure 7.20 and they represent the three ways that the body rotates in space.

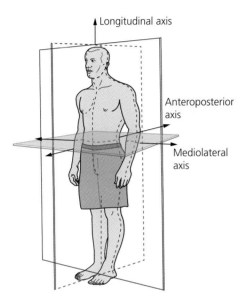

Figure 7.20 The three axes of rotation

The **mediolateral axis** goes through the middle of the body and bending forwards would use this axis. A diver performing a front somersault rotates around this axis.

The **anteroposterior axis** goes from the front of the body to the rear and it passes through the body between the hips and the shoulders. A gymnast rotates around this axis when performing a cartwheel. Jumping jacks involve the hips and shoulders moving in the anteroposterior axis.

The **longitudinal axis** runs from the top of the body to the bottom of the body and movements involving rotation of the body occur through this plane. An ice skater rotates around this axis when spinning.

Distinction activity: Levers and axes of rotation (C P3 , C M3 , C D3)

Task 1

1 Select an example of how each of the three types of lever are used in sport/exercise activities and explain the function that each example performs in relation to performance in sport and fitness activities.

2 Select a sport and give examples of movement through each of the axes of rotation from that sport. Explain what movement in each of the axes of rotation enables the performer to do in that selected activity.

Task 2

3 Select a sport and analyse the effects of changes in centre of mass and the roles of different types of lever on sports performance. You will need to analyse the sport by breaking it down into smaller parts and looking at how changes in the centre of mass and different types of lever affect performance in the different skills involved in the sport.

C Check your understanding

1 Define the term 'centre of mass'.

2 Explain where the centre of mass of the human body is located and what causes it to move.

3 Explain why it may be beneficial for a rugby player to have a low centre of mass.

4 Describe three factors that will affect the body's stability.

5 Describe the three classes of lever.

6 Explain how the length of a lever can impact on performance in a sport of your choice.

Further reading

Bartlett, R. (2007). *Introduction to Sports Biomechanics* (*Second edition*). Abingdon, Routledge.

Blazevich, A. (2007). *Sports Biomechanics – The Basics: Optimising Human Performance.* London, A&C Black.

Burkett, B. (2010). *Sports Mechanics for Coaches* (*Third edition*). Champaign, IL, Human Kinetics.

Hall, S.J. (2007). *Basic Biomechanics* (*Fifth edition*). New York, McGraw-Hill.

Hamilton, N., Weimar, W., and Luttgens, K. (2008). *Kinesiology: Scientific Basis of Human Motion.* Boston, McGraw-Hill.

Payton, C.J., and Bartlett, R.M. (eds.) (2008). *Biomechanical Evaluation and Movement in Sport and Exercise.* Abingdon, Routledge.

Sewell, D., Watkins, P., and Griffin, M. (2005). *Sport and Exercise Science.* Abingdon, Hodder Arnold.

Wirhed, R. (2006). *Athletic Ability and the Anatomy of Motion,* (*Third edition*). London, Elsevier.

References

BASES Guide to careers (2015), Career Profiles: Biomechanist [online]. Available at: www.bases.org.uk/write/documents/BASES%20Career%20Guide%20revised%20edition%20Jan%202010.pdf (accessed 26th October, 2015).

Hall, S.J. (2007). *Basic Biomechanics* (*Fifth edition*). New York, McGraw-Hill.

Hay, J.G. (1993). *The Biomechanics of Sports Techniques* (*Fourth edition*). New Jersey, Prentice-Hall.

Hamilton, N., Weimar, W., and Luttgens, K. (2008). *Kinesiology: Scientific Basis of Human Motion.* Boston, McGraw-Hill.

Serway, R.A., and Jewett, J.W. (2014). *Physics for Scientists and Teachers,* (*Ninth edition*). Boston, Brooks/Cole.

Useful websites

British Association of Sport and Exercise Science
www.bases.org.uk/Biomechanics
International Society of Biomechanists
http://isbweb.org/
Australian Institute of Sport
www.ausport.gov.au/participating/coaches/videos/intermediate/basic_biomechanics
Gait and Clinical Movement Analysis Society
www.gcmas.org/about
Sports Training Advisor
www.sports-training-adviser.com/sportbiomechanics.html
Quintic software for analysis of sports
www.quintic.com/

8 Specialised fitness training

About this unit

Fitness training has a very diverse meaning, with many people applying it to their individual, particular needs. As a result, every person has their own specialist needs based on what they aim to achieve. For example, what may be considered as high intensity by one individual may be considered as low intensity by another. Each training programme should always be carefully planned with individual needs taken into consideration. This unit will aim to explore the fitness requirements and components that can be trained within a sporting context. Every sport will have its own specific need, therefore a thorough understanding of its development can be the difference between success and failure. The unit will explore the methods we can use to train skill-related components whereby combined fitness characteristics can define a functional performance. Finally, the unit will help you to apply the characteristics, enabling you to develop training programmes which may be suitable for individual specialist needs.

Learning aims

This unit is split into three learning aims, each addressing the applications of a sports scientist. The learning aims include:

A Examine the fitness requirements, physical characteristics and demands of sport that contribute to effective training and performance
B Investigate methods of training for physical and skill-related fitness
C Explore the planning of fitness programming.

Each learning aim includes an assessment outcome that divides the content into key areas, sub-dividing the learning aim and allowing you to appreciate each of its components.

How will I be assessed?

The unit of fitness training will be assessed by assignments that have been designed internally by your tutors. It is likely that there will be two assignments for you to complete. Each assignment will enable you to apply the knowledge you have learnt to a range of activities.

Learning aim A achievement

For distinction standard, learners will consider the fitness demands, characteristics and movement patterns of a specific sport, exploring the relevance and significance of each. They will draw conclusions about the influence that each aspect has on the planning of training for an athlete performing that sport. Learners will include specific examples in their work, to support their conclusions. They will use appropriate terminology and provide examples to illustrate their points.

Learning aim B achievement

For distinction standard, learners will consider the advantages, disadvantages and relevance of methods of training for physical and skill-related fitness components in order to make judgements on their effectiveness. They will draw conclusions that are supported by examples, justifying how the methods contribute to the enhanced performance in a chosen sport. Learners suggest ways in which training methods may be adapted to maximise effectiveness of training for their specific chosen sport. They will articulate their arguments coherently throughout.

Learning aim C achievement

For distinction standard, learners will consider the effectiveness of the periodised training programme in improving sports performance. They will make judgements about the advantages, disadvantages and relevance of the programme in relation to the whole performance cycle, and the training plan in relation to the specific phase. Learners will draw conclusions about the programme's effectiveness supported by well-considered examples. They will also make justified recommendations for adaptation or alternatives to the programme, training methods and plan. Learners will use appropriate terminology and provide examples to illustrate their points.

How will I be graded?

The table below shows the grading criteria for this unit. To achieve a pass grade you must meet all the P criteria; to achieve a merit grade you must achieve all the P and all the M criteria; to achieve a distinction grade you must achieve all the P, M and D criteria.

Pass	Merit	Distinction
Learning aim A: Examine the fitness requirements, physical characteristics and demands of sport that contribute to effective training and performance		
A P1 Explain how the fitness demands, characteristics and movement patterns of the sport influence the planning of an athlete's training.	**A M1** Analyse how the fitness demands, characteristics and movement patterns of the sport influence the planning of an athlete's training.	**A D1** Evaluate how the fitness demands, characteristics and movement patterns of the sport influence the planning of an athlete's training.
Learning aim B: Investigate methods of training for physical and skill-related fitness		
B P2 Explain methods of training and their effectiveness in improving physical fitness for a chosen sport.	**B M2** Analyse methods of training and their effectiveness in improving physical fitness for a chosen sport.	**B D2** B.D2 Evaluate the effectiveness of methods of training used to improve physical and skill-related fitness, justifying how they contribute to enhance performance in a chosen sport.
B P3 Explain methods of training and their effectiveness in improving skill-related fitness for a chosen sport.	**B M3** Analyse methods of training and their effectiveness in improving skill-related fitness for a chosen sport.	
Learning aim C: Explore the planning of fitness programming		
C P4 Explain the principles of training to be considered when planning for periodised training and fitness programming.	**C M4** Analyse the design of the training session plan as part of the periodised programme.	**C D3** Evaluate the effectiveness of the training programme towards enhancing sports performance, making justified suggestions for adaptations or alternative methods of training.
C P5 Produce a detailed periodised training programme to improve performance for a chosen sport.		
C P6 Produce a detailed training session plan for a selected aspect of the periodised training programme.		

Table 8.1 Assessment criteria

A Examine the fitness requirements, physical characteristics and demands of sport that contribute to effective training and performance

(**A P1** , **A M1** , **A D1**)

A1 Characteristics of sport

As sports vary in terms of their physical and mental demands, it is important that a performer is able to train in a way that allows them to achieve success.

The **duration** of the event will always have an impact upon the training needs of your performer. With events lasting seconds, minutes, hours or days, it is important that any training is able to enhance the performance **characteristics**. For example, in athletics an elite male 200 m sprinter will be expected to exercise for between 19–20 seconds in order to win their event. A male 400 m sprinter will be expected to exercise for between 44–46 seconds to win their event. While both are sprinting events, the duration characteristic will have a significant impact on the type of training they complete. Similarly, athletes in impact sports such as rugby, judo and boxing require repetitive short bursts of explosive power to be successful at their event. In contrast, throwers require an individual explosive power performance to complete their event. Again, while both require power, the duration and characteristic of the activity will be a major determinant of the training programme to be followed.

As many athletic events require heats, finals or rounds, the rate of recovery will also be as important to the final performance. As recovery is crucial both within and after a competition, any training programme should try to increase the recovery rate in order to bring home gold winning success. The main focus of many repetitive sports is recovery. Without quick recovery, you may perform your next exercise bout already fatigued, which could lead to a substandard performance.

Similar principles apply to an athlete's **performance cycle**. Many athletes perform in leagues or tournaments that will require adequate recovery in between each performance. The performance cycle refers to the demands of the competition year. Is it a one-off performance or a tournament? For example, it is essential that tennis players are able to recover quickly in between matches during the Wimbledon tennis championships. The recovery enables the player to be fully prepared for their next match and avoid excess fatigue. Any fitness training programme should focus on the performance demands and its key physical characteristics.

Types of activity

Games such as football, rugby, netball and hockey are referred to as **multi-sprint activities**. These games require the player to perform varying activity bursts from walking, jogging, sprinting and jumping. As the event is inconsistent, the athlete must use multiple changes in speed and direction in order for them to be successful. The ability to coordinate these changes, combining several together to develop a movement makes them **skill-based activities.** A practical example may be seen within gymnastics, whereby a series of coordinated skills help to provide an accomplished performance. Gymnasts are required to make movements that are direct, controlled and precise in order to demonstrate a high level of skill. Floor routines require periods of powerful leaps and bounds to power the gymnast into controlled somersaults or cartwheels, and variations of gentle floor movements that demonstrate grace and poise. Each of these skills requires the combination of a range of skills from agility, power, and body awareness.

As these performers need to be agile, have great speed and power, they need to coordinate many fitness components into a skill. The greater the ability to control and coordinate these components, the greater the potential the performer has for success.

Similar skill-based activities that require multi-discipline performances include events such as the decathlon, modern pentathlon and triathlon. These events require an athlete to master a number of different activities, however each require their own individual fitness and skill component. For example, the triathlon requires the athlete to swim, cycle and run. For a triathlete to be successful they must be able to master the fitness and skill components to a high standard in order to complete a fast time. As each of the race components are very different, each will require an ability to coordinate them together to perform to a high standard.

The trained combination of fitness-based components such as muscular endurance, strength and power, can enable an athlete to complete the multi-discipline activity with the skill-based activities they require. For example, when a weightlifter performs the clean and jerk exercise, they must combine a number of skill movements that enable them to raise the bar off the floor. Having the ability to coordinate these movements, which include the application of power, balance and strength, will enable them to successfully complete the lift. During a training programme where a series of lifts may be required, the ability to recover is just as important, therefore muscular endurance also becomes an important factor. By training these components, identifying the skills' basic fitness elements, we can significantly increase our ability to continue to perform at a high standard in future lifts to come. It is important to remember, fitness is the fundamental component of any physical-based activity.

A2 Fitness demands of sports

With each sport having its own physical demands, the fitness component they rely on for success will vary. We can divide the fitness into two parts, each of which have their own individual components:

- physical fitness
- skill-related fitness.

Physical fitness is the ability to work efficiently and be able to cope with the varied demands of activity, without becoming excessively fatigued.

Physical fitness

Physical fitness is composed of five components:

1 cardiovascular endurance
2 strength
3 muscular endurance
4 flexibility
5 body composition.

Cardiovascular endurance is your ability to exercise over a long period of time. Good endurance comes from the heart, vessels and lungs working together efficiently, being able to deliver large quantities of

oxygen which in turn makes energy. The oxygen is key as it is an important ingredient for creating new energy, known as adenosine triphosphate (ATP).

> **Key term**
>
> ATP is known as adenosine triphosphate. It is pure energy and is used within the cells to produce a reaction such as a muscle contraction.

If there is a lack of oxygen being delivered to the working tissues, it can cause the concentration of carbon dioxide in your blood to increase, which in turn causes an increase in lactic acid production. This can be harmful to the cell and it causes fatigue which will eventually lead to the athlete needing to stop exercising. A good supply of oxygen can slow the rate of fatigue which can be an indicator of good aerobic endurance.

Strength may be defined as the maximal force generated by a single muscle contraction. In muscle fibres, the intensity of a contraction comes from the number of muscle fibres recruited to shorten the muscle length.

There are three main types of strength:

1 dynamic
2 static
3 explosive.

Dynamic strength is ability of the muscle to make repetitive movements over a long period of time. It is also referred to as strength endurance as it requires the muscle to make a series of intense muscle contractions throughout the duration of an activity. For example, a gym user may perform an exercise that requires the completion of a high repetition exercise. The strength applied would be dynamic in movement and as many repetitions are being performed, it makes the exercise endurance-based.

Often referred to as isometric strength, **static strength** is the maximal force exerted from a muscle for between 2–6 seconds. Unlike dynamic strength, static strength is shorter in duration with a gradual force applied to its maximum. An example can be seen when performing the rugby scrum. As the scrum is engaged, both opposing teams apply a gradual force to drive the opposing team backwards. The scrum lasts for a short duration of time and does not involve the players making any fast explosive movement as would be expected in explosive strength.

Explosive strength differs from both static and dynamic strength as it is the maximal force applied in a single contraction in a very short duration of time. The contraction is regularly referred to as explosive power. Examples of these movements include the javelin event where a competitor is required to throw the implement as far as possible. The event is one of the most demanding on the body requiring the thrower to deliver the javelin off a fast run-up. Explosive strength enables the competitor to not only use their arm, but also drive their legs, hips and shoulders through the throwing action to accelerate the implement to speeds of 60–70 mph.

Muscular endurance is very similar to that of aerobic endurance, however it is more localised to the muscle being used. Muscle endurance focuses on the performance of the individual muscle to contract repetitively over a long period of time. As it is endurance-based, the exercise needs to be sub-maximal, however of a sufficient intensity to make the muscle work above and beyond its resting state. Similar to cardiovascular endurance, a good supply of oxygen can prevent fatigue. A steady flow of oxygen to meet the demands of the exercise will enable your athlete to work harder for longer. Understanding this, the ability to deliver oxygen is a major determinant of endurance fitness.

Flexibility may be defined as the range of movement around a joint. The movement can be determined by a number of factors including joint, muscle elasticity and bone structure. At a young age, muscle and ligament tissue will be more elastic, therefore we have greater flexibility during these early years. As we age we begin to lose our flexibility as the joints and surrounding tissues can tighten to enable us to remain stable and control our movements. Good flexibility can help reduce the occurrence of injury if maintained during sporting activities. Examples of athletes who require good flexibility include high divers and gymnasts. With good flexibility these performers are able to tightly tuck their body position, enabling them to rotate faster through the air during somersaults.

Figure 8.1 Divers with good flexibility in the tuck position

Body composition is particularly important to both an athlete and the health and well-being of the general population. Body size and structure is often linked to the success of a performer. For example, gymnasts are generally light, stocky and powerful performers. Due to the nature of their event, they need to be agile which is helped by their significant muscle mass to body size. Having a high muscle mass for the lightness of frame provides the gymnast with a very high power-to-weight ratio. It is the power that enables the gymnast to leap or tumble across the floor, driving their legs downwards to propel the body and rotate in the air.

Skill-related fitness

While physical fitness focuses on the ability to work efficiently and cope with the demands of an activity, **skill-related fitness** may be defined as the underlying skills used when participating in sport. While they are not focused on one particular sport, they are the fundamentals that need to be mastered to be successful.

Skill-related fitness is composed of six key components:

- speed
- power
- agility
- balance and proprioception
- coordination
- reaction time.

Speed may be defined as the body's ability to move quickly over a measured distance. While it is often measured as a sprint, it can also be measured as body movements, e.g. the measurement used in biomechanics. Speed is often confused with acceleration which would be the ongoing increase in speed. An example of this would be when an athlete sets off from the starting blocks. Speed is a constant measurement of movement, measuring the performers travel over a unit of time. In sport it could be the measurement of a sprinter as they travel over the final 50 m of a 100 m race. At this point the speed can be measured as the acceleration phase would have ceased with the athlete now travelling at their maximal pace. Events such as sprinting use this component with the elite having been recorded at speeds of 20–25 mph.

Power is closely linked to strength and speed. As mentioned above, one of the components of strength is explosive strength which requires a performer to apply a maximal muscle contraction in a very short period of time. Using the javelin as an example, the performer is able to quickly contract their arm and body in the final delivery of the throw to propel the implement over the greatest distance. While technique is an important factor, it is the generation of power to accelerate the javelin that creates much of the distance thrown.

Like power, **agility** is related to speed and explosive strength. It may be defined as the ability to change direction at speed, quickly and efficiently. A sporting example where this is important is within tennis where the player must change direction to strike the ball over the net. If the player arrives at the shot too late, this could cause them to miss-hit or poorly direct the ball out of court. For this reason it is important the player is able to quickly power their legs towards the ball early and position themselves ready for the shot.

Balance may be defined as the ability to maintain a controlled stable position in relation to the surrounding environment. Balance may be stable when stationary or when performing a dynamic movement, however it should be controlled throughout. Balance is very closely linked with agility and power as for them to be applied the performer must be in a controlled balance posture. For example, when a gymnast needs to perform a flip on a beam, it is important they apply both power and agility in a controlled direction. This will allow them to direct their body along the beam, maintaining their balance and prevent them from falling off.

For an individual to be defined as having good **coordination**, they should be able to perform smooth controlled movements using a number of body parts. Coordination is very event specific, however similar skills may be applied to other sports. Many sports rely on good coordination such as hand–eye coordination in cricket or racket sports. Being able to control the body and hands when striking the ball requires great skill that is learnt through practice. Strongly linked to co-ordination, **proprioception** is one's sense of the position of different parts of the body relative to each other.

Finally, **reaction time** can be defined as the interval taken to respond to a stimulus. It is particularly important in sports such as badminton where a response to strike the shuttle with good hand–eye coordination can determine the outcome of a point. With some players being able to strike a shuttlecock at speeds of over 150 mph, it is vital that a player has quick reactions in order to return the shot.

A3 Movement patterns

Human movement patterns are key to the success of a sporting performer. It is important that an athlete coordinates their limbs in a pattern to perform an exercise. It is the joints that enable the body to move using the muscle contractions to provide control.

The body is divided up into two anatomical sections:

- the core
- the periphery.

The core is the central region of the body which is where the major organs can be found. It is the centre of all movement as it creates and controls all of the limbs attached. Using the many muscle attachments it has, the core is able to balance your posture and its positioning during static or dynamic movements. This is achieved by using the spine and surrounding muscles which enable the core to stand upright but also bend and twist when performing an activity. Static movements are typically movements where the posture or core is held in a fixed position. A good example of this is the plank exercise where the body is held in a static position and not able to collapse. Dynamic movements are, as described, dynamic and able to move. An example of this type of movement could be a tennis serve where the player arches their back and then flexes forward to create power when striking the ball toss. The rapid flexion and extension is achieved due to a dynamic movement pattern of the core.

The periphery, or the peripheral region, is composed of the leg and arm attachments to the central core. It is the peripheral region that provides much of the movements in sport. The periphery enables us to reach beyond the core and use the joints to perform a movement. The type of movement and its direction is limited by the force of the muscle contraction and structure of the joint that is being used.

The movement of both the core and peripheral regions can be individual or combined depending on their complexity. During an exercise, the core provides the fixed point for movement. The centre of balance is frequently based within the core. The use of the limbs and an external mass often counter balances a movement. With changes in posture, the core is able to provide a fixed point such as in the spine and hips during a golf swing, or be a dynamic component such as in the tennis serve. The movement pattern is exercise specific and a training programme should reflect this when designed for fitness training.

As the core remains a central component, it is the control region of movement. Peripheral movements can be unilateral or bilateral depending on the performer needs.

Both unilateral and bilateral movements are specific to the exercise being performed and can be limited by the range of movement provided at the joint. For true unilateral and bilateral movements to occur, there must be a clear single or both sided exercise activity being performed. For example, a chest press exercise using both arms to press individual dumbbells rather than a barbell does not make the exercise unilateral. While one arm is pressing one dumbbell and the other is pressing the second, it is important to remember that both arms are being used in the one movement. For true unilateral movement to be performed, the one sided region should be isolated within a single movement.

As many sports perform unilaterally, training programmes should always include single isolated components. For example, when a runner performs their running stride, the individual leg powers them onto the next to create momentum. Each leg is working unilaterally as they perform the power phase on their own.

The movement patterns associated with an activity will vary depending upon its demands. Many sports may contain:

- **Repetitive movements** – such as walking and jogging.
- **Changes in direction** – such as netball and basketball where we need to receive or intercept the ball.

Figure 8.2 Unilateral running

- **Pre-programmed movements** – such as familiar, instinctive movements that are learnt through performer experience, e.g. technique changes on different surfaces.
- **Reactive movements** – where there is an immediate response to a stimulus, such as ducking from an object.

A4 Energy systems and expenditure

Details of aerobic and anaerobic energy production, and energy expenditure are given in Unit 1: A7 Energy systems.

A5 Importance and influence on training programme design

There are many details that should be considered when preparing a training programme. Some may be referred to as barriers to fitness whereby adherence to a programme may be affected due to a range of factors. Further considerations could be the demands of the performer. What do they want to achieve? What are their needs? And some may have more specific considerations that may be specific to a sport.

Any programme should take into consideration the **time** it takes to complete training, and the frequency of which it will be followed. The programme should be realistic and lifestyle factors need to be considered. Without careful thought an excellent programme could be designed, however not be achievable due to the time pressures on the athlete. It is also important that sufficient rest be given in between each training session. Without adequate rest, the programme could potentially cause overuse injuries, therefore making it counterproductive.

A successful training programme may be used for **injury prevention.** Fitness training is able to support the healing of injuries by strengthening the muscles and joints that are involved in movements. While it should be very light, training can help speed up recovery time as it increases the blood flow around an injury site so helping it to repair. Furthermore, an effective training programme can help avoid joint related problems such as arthritis and increase bone density, avoiding the condition of osteoporosis.

At the planning and preparation phase it is essential that a training programme takes into account the **performance outcomes** that need to be achieved. If a performer aims to increase their strength, endurance or flexibility, this should be reflected within the programme. This may be shown within the type of exercises selected, the intensity and the rest periods provided. Whatever the programme, it is important that the outcomes are understood before it is constructed.

There are many influences that could affect the training programme of a competitive athlete. These may include:

- Is the programme for **pre- or post-season** training?
- What are the **coach and manager demands** of the performer?
- Are there any **personal team or positional needs** for the performer?

Training cycles for pre- and post-season training can determine the type of activity that's completed. For example, while the javelin throw event is predominantly anaerobic power-based, in the early stages of their pre-season training, much of the preparation phase will include a significant level of aerobic endurance. The aim is to prepare the athlete for further training demands and help them recover faster between training sessions.

A Check your understanding

1 Explain the differences between physical fitness and skill-based fitness.
2 Evaluate how the movement of an athlete can influence the type of physical fitness characteristics.
3 Select four sporting events and explain the physical demands of their performance.
4 Select four sporting events and explain the movement patterns that can influence the planning of training for each performer.
5 Explain the terms 'bilateral' and 'unilateral', providing at least two examples per term as examples of your answer.

Meeting distinction criteria A D1

You are just starting your coaching career and have been given a small group of potential volleyball players to train. Before you start the training, you need to consider the players' training demands and when they have their first competition.

Evaluate the fitness training demands required for your players' event. **Hint** – Consider the movement patterns that are regularly performed within their particular event and the demands of these.

B Investigate methods of training for physical and skill-related fitness (B P2 , B P3 , B M2 , B M3 , B D2)

B1 Training for physical fitness

Flexibility training

Flexibility may be defined as the range of movement around a joint. It is sub-divided into two parts, **static** and **dynamic flexibility**. The term we usually associate with flexibility is static flexibility. This is the passive movement of a joint to determine the range of motion and its flexibility, e.g. reach and hold. Dynamic flexibility differs from static as it is the range of movement during an active movement, such as during a sports performance. While both are a form of flexibility, dynamic flexibility can provide the greatest measure of flexibility as it is the stretch caused when the body is opposing an external force such as gravity or implement.

The extent as to how much movement is achieved at the joint is dependent on a number of factors, including:

- the joint structure, e.g. bone structure
- muscle and tendon elasticity
- temperature of the tissue
- the age of the joint
- the gender of the performer.

Flexibility is extremely important within all sporting activities. It is able to assist with a number of roles such as reducing injury occurrence, maintain body figure and form along with enhancing muscle force and the production of power. The length of muscle and tissues surrounding a joint is important for injury prevention. If a muscle is more pliable and supple, as it would be with a warm-up, it is able to avoid over-stretching which could lead to injury. The muscle fibre length can also assist with postural balance such as helping the spine stand in a neutral position. Poor postural flexibility is often shown within inadequate weight training programmes whereby an individual may over-exercise the chest region of the body. This lack of training balance causes the chest muscles to tighten and shorten, pulling the chest forward and spine to stoop which leads to poor posture. Therefore it is important that muscles remain balanced and flexible in order to maintain good postural form.

There are three main methods that can be used to develop flexibility:

- Static flexibility stretching (active and passive)
- Dynamic and ballistic stretching
- Proprioceptive neuromuscular facilitation (PNF) stretching.

Static flexibility training involves the controlled lengthening of the muscle tissue which is held for approximately 30 seconds. An example can be shown using the toe touch hamstring stretch. During this stretch an individual would sit on the ground and gradually reach forward towards their toes until they feel significant discomfort. At this point the performer should hold this position for 30 seconds and then return back to their resting position.

Static stretching may be sub-divided into two types of stretching which are **active and passive stretching**. An **active stretch** occurs when the individual who is performing the stretch creates the force needed to increase the length of the tissue fibres. For example, without any help the athlete reaches forward to touch their toes and hold the position themselves. This is different to a **passive stretch** as this occurs when a force is applied to hold the stretch or enhance it further. For example, a partner could gently push the shoulders of the individual further forward and help hold the position for 30 seconds. The advantage of this method is that it allows the individual to increase the range of the stretch, making it more beneficial for flexibility training.

Dynamic stretching involves the controlled movement of the body to carefully stretch it to the limits of its range. It should not be confused with ballistic training as this is a bouncing movement whereas dynamic is controlled. The movement should be repetitive and slow at the end of each movement so as to avoid a bouncing motion. An example of this type of activity can be seen when completing a leg swinging action. As the leg moves side to side it is able to swing to the maximum range and then return back in the opposite direction. As soon as the leg reaches the maximum range it is slowed as to avoid any bouncing action. This form of stretching is more often used as part of a warm-up or cool-down rather than as a specific form of flexibility training.

Ballistic flexibility training involves the use actively bouncing during the stretch. During the stretch the muscle is not held and therefore it has limited benefit to flexibility training. While not suitable for training the range of movement around a joint, it is often used as a part of warm-up activities. However, this dynamic stretching motion can be counterproductive as it mainly stretches tendons and ligaments rather than muscle tissue. This can lead to joint instability and therefore defeats the purpose of stretching. Care should always be taken with this stretch

as it can cause over-stretching leading to joint damage. Due to the problems associated with this stretch, it is not suitable for flexibility-based training.

Proprioceptive neuromuscular facilitation (PNF) training differs from both static and ballistic training as it involves a passive holding of a stretch, applying a period of resistance from the stretching individual, and then extending the passive stretch further. For example, if performing a hip extension stretch from a laying position, the athlete will raise their leg and maintain a passive stretch with the aid of a partner. The passive stretch will be held for 10 seconds after which a resistance will be applied by the athlete to lower the leg. The contraction of pushing the leg back to the ground is an isometric contraction as the partner resists any effort made to move the leg in the opposite direction. Following 6 seconds of resistance, the athlete should relax the contraction and allow the partner to extend the leg further. At the point of significant discomfort, the stretch should be passively held by the partner for 30 seconds, after which the leg should be gently lowered to the ground.

Figure 8.3 The hip stretch

When using this training technique it is important that only one exercise is used on one muscle group. The exercise should be repeated approximately three times over 2–5 sets, allowing for sufficient rest periods in between. Due to the additional over-stretch placed on the joint, this should be used when training rather than as a warm-up.

Strength training

Strength may be defined as the maximal force generated by a single muscle contraction. There are three main types of strength, which are dynamic, static, and explosive. See section A3 in this unit for more details.

The term strength is more often associated with **maximum strength** which refers to the force that can be generated in one single muscle contraction. When we focus on an individual's strength we often believe that their maximal strength is their true ability. However, strength may also come from **strength endurance** or muscular endurance which is the repetitive contraction of a muscle over a period of time. This may involve a high intensity exercise which takes place over a long period of time, e.g. 400 m. Finally, strength may also be applied to **core stability** where force is applied to maintain posture and positioning. Muscles around the trunk are particularly important as they are able to maintain the body posture during dynamic movements or help us maintain static positional holds. Poor core stability can lead to lack of stability at the spine, poor posture and back injuries, a decrease in joint integrity, and a decrease in force production. It is important that any training exercises include a range of core activities to avoid these problems.

There are many different methods we can use to train muscle strength. Each method is specific to the muscles used, however the basic principle is to overload a muscle and allow it sufficient time for recovery. This repeated process of exercise and recovery follows the more common **traditional** route of training that has been tried and tested over many years. For example, a bench press exercise will develop the chest and the athlete may choose to complete 8 repetitions over 3 sets (3 sets of 8 repetitions). The rest period between the set would be determined by the type of training. For example, strength endurance programmes may have more repetitions with shorter recover periods in between each set. Programmes that aim to build on maximal strength may have lower repetitions and longer recovery periods. However, in comparison, maximal strength programmes will have a higher intensity to the strength endurance programme. The recovery period will always be dependent on the exercise intensity.

Like traditional strength training programmes, **core training** follows a similar method whereby the exercise plan should follow an exercise and rest period. While maximal activities may train a range of areas across the body, core training focuses on the muscles that surround the main body structure. This may include muscles that support the spine and pelvis which stabilise the body during activity. Traditional exercises on the abdominals, obliques, and lumbar extensors which surround the spinal column are very supportive in the development of the core, however the use of unstable surfaces where constant adjustment of the core is needed to maintain stability is also a useful method. The varying surface causes ongoing contractions, which aim to maintain balance and posture, therefore placing greater demand on the core muscles.

Another method that can be used to develop strength and strength endurance is **circuit training**. An exercise circuit can consist of up to 12 individual exercises which are dependent on what the athlete aims to achieve. Typical general bodyweight circuits could consist of a number of exercises including:

- press-ups
- sit-ups
- burpees
- squats
- shuttle runs
- dips
- shoulder press
- hyperextensions.

The exercise difficulty can be adapted depending on the fitness of the individuals taking part. For example, press-ups could be performed incline with the feet raised to shoulder height; the shoulder press weight could be increased; and hyperextensions can be performed off a Swiss exercise gym ball instead of from the floor. Any exercise adaptations can increase the intensity of the exercise which will inevitably lead to an improved strength endurance performance.

A circuit will consist of a work and rest period. For example, an athlete may complete an exercise within the circuit for the duration of 30 seconds, followed by 45 seconds of rest. The aim is to perform as many repetitions within the exercise rather than complete a set number and stop. During the 45 second rest, the athlete should move to the next exercise station in preparation to start again. The full circuit of exercises should be completed and the athlete would have a 5 minute rest in between repeating the circuit again. To increase the difficulty, the exercise time may be increased and rest period reduced, both between the sets and each exercise within the circuit.

Finally, **complex training** is another method that may be used to develop strength. It involves the completion of a combination of strength and plyometric power-based exercises. The strength exercises are performed prior to the power-based exercises and should involve the use of a similar muscle group. For example, an athlete may complete 3 sets of 10 squats (3 x 10) which will be followed by 3 sets of 10 drop down squat jumps. Each set will have a 60 second rest period in between, and there will be a 90 second rest period in between the start of the strength activity and plyometric activity.

This type of training is particularly useful with strength and power-based athletes such as sprinters and throwers. A range of exercises can be used all over the body, however it is essential that the same exercise group is worked on during both the strength and plyometric phase.

> ### Key term
>
> Plyometric training is a form of training that consists of the lengthening of a muscle fibre followed by an immediate shortening to create power. The movement is dynamic and should involve minimal contact time with the object or surface. For example, a plyometric application can be shown using a double-footed hurdle bound. As the athlete jumps the hurdle, they will land with both feet and immediately jump to clear the second hurdle. The contact time of the feet on the floor should be minimal and there should be no pause following the first jump.

Cardiovascular training

Cardiovascular endurance is the body's ability to exercise over a long period of time. Commonly referred to as **aerobic endurance**, cardiovascular endurance is important to an athlete as it can enable them to work harder for longer and recover faster. As the body can deliver more O_2 and fuels to the working tissues, it is able to make more ATP energy and remove more CO_2, which helps us to resist fatigue. **Anaerobic endurance** differs from aerobic endurance in that it is the repeated performance at a high intensity. For example, this may include repeated training sprints over 60 m whereby the speed is a full pace sprint and the recovery time is restricted. This is a form of interval training which will be discussed further in this unit.

Cardiovascular endurance serves many purposes within the body. Firstly, it is important in allowing us to maintain a sustained performance over a prolonged period of time. For example, elite marathon runners are able to sustain a running pace of approximately 5-minute miles throughout the duration of over 26 miles. To achieve this they must have significant cardiovascular endurance to sustain such a fast pace.

Following the race it is important that the athlete is able to quickly recover in order to avoid any exercise related stress. Furthermore the recovery will enable the performer to prepare for their next training bout following the race. While many fun runners and charity runners continue to ache for many days after the race, elite runners recover much quicker and are soon back training after the race. It is their superior cardiovascular endurance that enables the elite performers to recover faster and cope with the intensity of the training following the race they have only just competed in.

There are many methods that can be used to train cardiovascular endurance. These include:

- continuous training
- interval training
- Fartlek training.

Continuous training is the most traditional method used by many leisure and exercise performers. The method involves the completion of a 'continuous' activity over a long period of time with no rest interval. For example, this exercise could compose of a 45 minute jog, whereby the athlete will exercise at a sub-maximal level throughout the duration of the activity.

The benefits of this exercise is that it requires little preparation and is simple to follow. The adaptations to fitness can be improved by simply increasing the exercise time or the speed at which the athlete completes the distance.

Interval training differs from continuous training in that it requires the athlete to exercise at a moderate to high intensity, followed by a relatively short rest period in between. For example, a sprinter may complete 6 repetitions of a 50 m sprint with a 30 second rest interval in between each run. The exercise period would be a high intensity exercise whereas the recovery period would be low intensity. By varying the intensity, it causes the workout to exercise both the aerobic and anaerobic endurance components of the body. By spacing the rest periods throughout the exercise period, the training enables the athlete to complete more work than would have been possible at the same intensity during continuous training.

Fartlek training follows a similar principle to continuous whereby an athlete completes an activity over a continuous period of time. Its difference is that it follows an unstructured period of fast and slow bursts of activity throughout the training session. For example, a runner may complete a 45-minute session within which there will continuous activity. The session may consist of jogging, fast bursts of running and even slower periods such as walking. The focus is for the movement to be continuous but varied in intensity. The session should not stop and be consistent as this will then become an interval training session. Fartlek training is often used by cross country and orienteering competitors due to is varied approach in speed and intensity.

B2 Training for skill-related fitness

Agility training

Agility can be defined as the ability to change direction at speed, quickly and efficiently while maintaining balance and control. Many sports contain an agility component therefore it is important we train it thoroughly prior to competition. Agility can perform a number of functions from allowing us to quickly change direction, complete a tackle, complete a shot, make a save, lose an opponent or create space on the field of play. The ability to quickly change direction at speed is an important component and can make the difference between success and failure, e.g. run past an opposing player and score a goal.

There are a range of methods that can be used to train agility. Examples include:

- zig-zag drill
- agility ladders
- four cone drill
- Speed Agility and Quickness (SAQ®) training
- agility shuttle runs.

The **zig-zag drill** requires the use of a series of cones that are placed into a diagonal zig-zag formation. From a standing start position the athlete will move diagonally forwarded around the first cone and then diagonally sideways to the next cone. This will continue until all cones have been passed and be completed as fast as possible. The speed and change in direction will help to develop the agility of the athlete using this exercise.

Agility ladders are able to develop the movement of quick feet. Using the ladders an athlete is able to travel across them, placing their feet inside each rung as they move. The foot placement should be fast and precise so that their movement is quick and controlled. Athletes can run forwards over the ladders or sideways depending on the needs of the sporting activity.

Figure 8.4 Agility ladders

The **four cone drill** uses a large square that requires the athlete to run facing in different directions. As the athlete moves to each cone, they should change direction from initially running backwards, side shuffles (both sides), alternate carioca leg shuffle and then finally a sprint to the end. The quick movements and directional changes help to develop the movement and positioning of the body needed for good agility skills.

Speed Agility and Quickness (SAQ) training may consist of the use of low level hurdles, barriers, speed and conditioning drills. The training requires the athlete to complete a series of movement patterns that are specific to their sporting performance. These patterns could consist of rotation drills, fast feet, acceleration and deceleration movements that develop reactivity, balance and movement which is directly linked to their sporting activity.

Finally, **agility shuttle runs** consist of a procedure which requires an athlete to sprint at full speed over a distance of 10 metres while collecting and placing wooden blocks at each end of the marked parallel lines. Each block must be placed on the line and not thrown, therefore the performer travels at speed and then changes direction in a controlled manner.

Speed training

Speed may be defined as the body's ability to move itself, or its limbs, quickly over a measured distance. The speed or cadence, is often applied to the leg action as it is the movement of these limbs that determine how fast the body can travel. Understandably the faster you travel then the faster your leg cadence will be.

Speed is often confused with acceleration which is the ongoing increase in speed, e.g. as an athlete sets off from the starting blocks. Acceleration is also important and it can be included within speed training. Like agility, speed has a number of applications in sport. Not only is speed crucial for a measured event like the 100 m, but it can also be useful to help overtake players when chasing the ball, help score a goal or defend from an opposing team's attacking play. While an individual may have great speed, it does not mean they will be

agile. Both speed and agility are two separate fitness components and any training would need to consider this.

There are a range of training methods that can be used to develop speed. Examples include:

- acceleration sprints
- hill sprints
- overspeed training.

Acceleration sprints use a gradual increase in speed from initial jogging, to striding and then up to top speed for approximately 50 m. It is a rolling start for the athlete to build up to their maximum speed. Due to its progressive increase, it can help to reduce muscle injury. Sudden maximal muscle contraction can make you more susceptible to injury, therefore this type of training would avoid this problem.

Hill sprints are exactly as titled, sprinting up a hill. The training principle is similar to interval training whereby you complete a series of sprints but up a hill which increases the intensity. The hill should be between 50–100 m in length, depending on the experience of the athlete. Ideally you should aim to complete 6–8 sprints with a minute rest in between each run. As the sprint requires the athlete to drive their legs harder to move their body quickly up the hill, it promotes the training adaptation of power. With the development of greater power it can be used by the athlete to increase their sprint speed.

Overspeed training uses a method of accelerating the muscle action which makes it work faster than it would have previously been capable of. Techniques such as down-hill running or accelerated towing with bungee cords can assist with this training. These training methods accelerate the natural speed of muscle contraction and help it become more forceful. Overspeed training also has the ability of educating the muscles to work faster, helping them increase their contraction speed.

Balance training

Balance may be defined as the ability to maintain a controlled stable position. When stable and balanced in relation to the surrounding environment, this may be referred to as proprioception, as you are in control of your own body's sense of orientation. It is a key component of agility where speed and power must be combined to enable the athlete to change direction. Balance is important for coordination too as it helps to control the movement of the body. For example, when a sprinter powers out of the blocks, it is important they keep their body balanced low and forward. The posture enables the full power from the leg action to be transferred through the body to coordinate the accelerated start. If the athlete was poorly balanced, e.g. leaning back as they powered out of the blocks, this could lead to a poor transfer of energy which may lose valuable time in the race.

There are a range of training methods that can be used to develop balance. These include:

- wobble balance board exercises
- heel–toe walking exercises.

There are many different types of **wobble balance boards** available, each of which train the body's coordination and core strength. The basic shape consists of a flat board that has a central pivot point. There are many variations of exercises that can be used to develop specific skills. If stood on, the board requires the performer to apply equal pressure from both feet to maintain balanced stability. The athlete needs to not only control the board movement side-to-side, but also forward and back as it can travel in all directions. The board may be used with both feet together or with just **one foot** placed centrally at the pivot point for greater difficulty.

Due to the ease of use, the wobble board can also be used for **press-ups**, and **side plank exercises**. Both require careful balance and tightening of the core muscles to maintain the strength needed for the position. The wobble board is often used for athlete rehabilitation as it educates the muscles for control which may have been lost through injury. For example, the stress that the wobble board places upon the ankle joint, can help to support walking gait as the repetitive correcting action strengthens the supportive muscles. Similarly, for additional difficulty and corrective rehabilitation, lunges may be used to place the leading leg onto the unstable pivoting platform. This action again encourages the leg to make adjusted movements, placing greater stress on the core and lower limbs for balance.

Heel–toe walking exercises are also useful when developing the skill of balance. It is a very simple method whereby the athlete walks in a straight line placing each walking step with the heel in close contact with the previous toe. As the steps are short and narrow, the body must remain balanced in order to avoid it toppling from side-to-side. The skill success would be developed from the athlete's ability to maintain balance throughout the exercise. For additional difficulty, the athlete could perform the exercise with their eyes shut as it can disorientate the less able.

Figure 8.5 Using a wobble board

Figure 8.6 A heel-toe walking balance exercise

Power training

Power is closely linked to strength and speed. As mentioned above, one of the components of strength is explosive strength which requires a performer to apply a maximal muscle contraction in a very short period of time. Many sports require the use of power as a part of their success. For example, a field hockey player requires a high level of power when striking the ball during a penalty corner to avoid the goalkeeper from saving it. The power comes from the generation of momentum from the stick that strikes the ball with great force.

There are a range of training methods that can be used to develop power. These include:

- power-based weightlifting exercises
- plyometrics.

Prior to any power-based training, it is important to have built up the basic component of strength. Typical strength exercises may include:

- squats
- lunges
- calf raises
- bicep curls.

It is important that base strength is well conditioned prior to explosive power work. The base strength provides you with the ability to perform the lift or move your body in a controlled forceful movement. These movements will then enable you to generate explosive movements and subsequent power.

There are many different types of **power-based weightlifting exercises** that can be used. Ultimately, their aim is to move the weight quickly by contracting the muscle as fast as possible. Examples of power-based exercises include:

- the clean
- the snatch
- squat jumps.

These exercises require the quick movement of the weighted bar in order to successfully perform the exercise. To perform the clean and snatch exercises, the athlete must accelerate the weighted barbell from the floor to shoulder height (clean), or above (snatch). When performing the squat jump, the athlete must power both the body and the weighted barbell upwards to leave the floor for the jump. As the exercises require the weight to be accelerated quickly, they train the muscles to generate a greater force than they would have otherwise gained using just strength-based exercises.

Plyometric training consists of a stretch and contract muscle action. There are a range of exercises that may be used all over the body. The basic principle is that a movement is dynamic and involves a quick muscle contraction as soon as it becomes stretched. For example, when performing a double booted hurdle bound the athlete lands bending their legs causing the quadricep muscles to be stretched or lengthened. To counteract this the athlete should immediately contract the quadricep muscles to propel themselves back into the air and clear the next hurdle. The contact time of the feet on the floor should be minimal, and there should be no pause following each jump. The stretch and contract action causes the muscle to develop power by counteracting against the muscle stretching process.

Figure 8.7 An athlete performing a plyometric hurdle exercise

Further plyometric-based training exercises may include:

- power lunges
- bounding
- incline explosive press-ups
- hopping
- jumping.

Reaction time training

Reaction time can be defined as the interval taken to respond to a stimulus. While it can be instinctive, it can be improved through practice. Training can involve a repetitive process of reacting to a starter's gun, clap board, practice event-based object, or a coach's signal. A performer's reaction time is extremely important within a variety of events including team games, athletics, and racket sports.

B3 Effectiveness and suitability of training methods to athlete's goals

In order for a training programme to be effective it is important that it be made specific to the desired goals. A coach or athlete should consider a needs analysis which identifies the key components of the sporting performance to help to develop future training goals. For example, if an athlete requires power and strength-based fitness improvements, the programme should include exercises to develop these components.

Having identified the training component, it is important that the training method reflects the sporting performance. The training should aim to be specific which enable the fitness training adaptations to be successfully transferred into the performance. Any training should take into account both the recovery and performance needs as this can determine its overall success.

For a training programme to be suitable it is essential that the athlete is given an appropriate amount of time to recover. Athletes who exercise without adequate recovery are at risk of injury or a sub-standard performance. Any training should consider its intensity in order for the athlete to progress from the previous training activity. Along with recovery, the training method should consider the performance demands. The competitive needs should be identified to fully prepare an athlete for their sporting event. For example, is the sport individual or team-based? Are their tactical considerations, attack and defend? How long is the event?

B Check your understanding

1   Discuss the differences in flexibility training methods and how they are used.

2   Power training is particularly useful for sprint-based events. Explain at what point in a race that power is crucial to the performance and speed.

3   Endurance training techniques such as continuous and Fartlek training are useful in developing aerobic capacity. Using sporting examples other than track and cross country running, explain how this training can contribute to the success of your examples.

4   Explain an example of plyometric training and how it may be performed.

5   Explain the different types of agility training we can use to develop our performance. Analyse each one, making reference to the sport it is most applicable to.

Meeting distinction criteria B D2

A basketball player has approached you for some support with their training. Select five different fitness components (physical and skill-related), and evaluate how effective these will be to the basketball player's performance.

Justify why you have chosen these activities and how you think they will contribute to the overall performance.

C Explore the planning of fitness programming (C P4 , C P5 , C P6 , C M4 , C D3)

C1 Collecting personal information to aid programme design

When developing a training programme it is important we understand the personal goals of the performer along with their aims and objectives. The suitability of the training programme should also be based on their medical health, attitudes to exercise, and motivation towards training as this could influence the safety and participation.

When preparing **personal goals**, we need to consider the short-, medium- and long-term outlook.

- **Short-term goal** – Immediate goals that are set over a period of between one day and one month. For example, a weightlifter commences a training programme and aims to complete a specific training session(s) by the end of the month.

- **Medium-term goal** – Usually the second part of goal setting, it is the development of progressive goals that extend beyond the short-term goal. They build on the existing short term and provide the foundations of the long-term goal. For example, a weightlifter will plan to make progressive improvements over a number of months to reach their personal best.

- **Long-term goal** – Usually the first stage of goal setting as it is the complete focus of achievement. It should total all of the short- and medium-term goals for what you are working towards. For example, the deadline a weightlifter wants to lift their personal best, e.g. at the Olympic Games.

By setting the goals, the athlete has determined their performance **aims** which include the basic details of what they would like to achieve, e.g. long-term goal. The **objective** has been identified within the medium-term goal as it focuses on the key stages that will be followed to achieve the aim. With the weightlifter identifying the progress they need to make to be successful in the long term, they have provided evidence of how they will achieve their aim.

Prior to an individual taking part in any activity, it is important that they are assessed. Firstly we should assess their **medical and lifestyle history**. The aim is to check whether specific training methods are suitable for their needs. For example, it would not be suitable for a weight training programme to be completed by an athlete who has high blood pressure as this could cause a stroke or heart attack. An initial assessment may include a Physical Activity Readiness Questionnaire (PAR-Q), and health and lifestyle questionnaire. More specific questionnaires can also be used that focus upon a specific capability, e.g. injury or medical history. See Unit 4 Section A1 for more on questionnaires.

Assessments can identify issues such as heart related problems, lung conditions such as asthma or long-term injuries which may affect the individual's participation in different types of training. When providing them with a questionnaires, it's important they are encouraged to answer them truthfully and be as accurate as possible. The accuracy will not only help to keep the individual safe, but also allow you as a coach, to make realistic long-term goals.

Further information that could also be gathered during the planning phase is the athlete's attitude and motivation to physical activity. When deciding on a training programme, it is important that the attitudes and motivation are carefully considered as they can affect the participation outcome. For example, an athlete may be more responsive and inclined to continue with a fitness training programme if they enjoy it and feel comfortable with exercises it contains. If an athlete has a negative attitude to activity due to poor experiences, it could cause them to become quickly de-motivated and more likely to stop taking part.

Any information or data collected should be analysed and interpreted prior to setting out a training plan. It is important that the personal goals are based on the baseline measures which are the initial starting point. By understanding and interpreting the individual's base measures, it can enable them to look at what they need to achieve and how they will achieve it. It is important that before any training commences, baseline measures are taken in order to review any performance gains as a result of training adaptation.

C2 Principles of training and their application to training programming

Training is the key to the development of any performer. While sporting events are varied, the training principles remain the same. The fundamental aim is to select an appropriate physical fitness, skill or psychological component and develop it further. This includes:

- specificity
- adaptation
- progression
- overload
- reversibility.

The concept of **specificity** concerns the training of a specific fitness component in order to enhance its performance. For example, aerobic-based training such as running or cycling, has the potential to develop the aerobic fitness. In practice the aerobic system is required to work harder than its usual resting state. The regular changes in exercise cause the body to **adapt** in the long term, to cope with the extra demands.

Progression is a key component to any training as it is the ultimate aim of training. As with any exercise programme, we try to develop our body to cause it to adapt to training. To enable the body to make steady increases in performance, we must gradually increase the intensity it works at. Progression is therefore the gradual increase in the exercise intensity that causes the body to adapt over a period of time. As a programme increases in intensity, the greater the progressive adaptations will occur.

The training principle of **overload** concerns the intensity at which a training programme is set. In many circumstances, an increase in overload can make the exercise activity more difficult to complete. For example, if an individual has never taken part in any significant physical activity in the past, any light jogging or fast walking would be an increase in exercise intensity. The overload level is achieved by a combination of the **FITT principle**:

Frequency – The number of overload sessions completed in a given time period.

Intensity – The difficulty there was in completing them (how hard were they?).

Time – The duration of the overload activity session.

Type – The type of activity chosen to complete the session (e.g. weights, running).

Reversibility is a key problem for many individuals who are unable to keep up their exercise programme. The expression 'if you don't use it then you'll lose it' is often paraphrased. If training was to abruptly stop after a number of weeks/months of training, this can often lead to many of the adaptations being reduced. For example, if a weightlifter was to leave the gym and give up training, the adaptations they gained throughout their programme would slowly decrease, which will inevitably lead to them losing their trained physical strength.

In addition to these principles are the essentials of training **variation** and **recovery**. Whenever training, it is important that sufficient **rest** and **recovery** is provided between each activity session. The length of recovery will be determined by the activity. For there to be sufficient adaptation and to avoid injury occurrence, it is important that the rest be suitable to the training demands. For example, recovery rest periods during a training activity could vary from minutes to seconds based on fitness levels and activities. Using circuit training as an example, a performer may use 8 exercise stations for 30 seconds and then rest for 45 seconds. Once completed, the performer may rest for 3 minutes before repeating the same circuit a further 2 times. The training allows for sufficient rest in between exercise bouts, however short enough to prevent full recovery. For full recovery, the circuit could be repeated days later to allow the muscles to fully rest before the next overload, reducing the risk of injury.

Training **variation** is particularly important as it can help stimulate both physiological and psychological performance. With a lack of exercise variation it can promote boredom or tedium which can reduce an athlete's motivation to train. Many people use a variation of an exercise to help train a specific fitness component. For example, the dumbbell flies exercise may be used as an alternative to the cable cross-over exercise. Both exercises place a significant overload on the chest, however there is a variation in the exercise used.

Following continued training the body will begin to change and develop which is known as **adaptation**. This is a process whereby the body begins to significantly change, however it will be reliant on the intensity, frequency, duration and type of exercise performed. The body adapts as it is trying to cope with the stress of the exercise each time you train. If you over-train then you can become injured. If you under-train then you will experience very little adaptation, therefore there is a fine balance needed when planning a training programme. Typical adaptation examples may include an increase in muscle size and strength due to free weight training, or an increase in aerobic endurance as a result of regular jogging.

C3 Designing periodised training programmes

With the use of baseline measures and **personal information** it is important that we are able to design a training programme that suits the needs of the individual. If sporting-based, it is important that the training relates to the performance activity, i.e. specific. The training should match the event needs and aim to make an improvement in their performance.

It is important that a training programme uses a needs analysis that identifies the **performance priorities** in order to set future targets. The targets should be progressive in order to build upon towards the long-term goal. All targets should be **SMART**:

- **S**pecific – All targets should be as specific as possible. They should be clear and focused as to what is being achieved and how. For example, the target could focus on a key goal of what needs to be achieved.
- **Me**asureable – Any activity or performance needs to be measured. A training programme would use baseline measures to help check progress. For example, an athlete could measure their aerobic fitness prior to starting a training programme and then retest a number of weeks later. The difference in performance is measured and it can help establish the progress gained by the training programme used.
- **A**chievable – Any target set should always be achievable. Having unachievable targets become meaningless as if they can't be achieved, there becomes little point in taking part. The target should be something that an individual can aim for and ultimately reach during the training process.

- **R**ealistic – When setting training exercises it is important to consider whether it is realistic for the athlete to achieve it. For example, if a training programme sets a very heavy workload, it is important to consider whether it will be completed. If it is unrealistic it could cause the athlete to potentially become de-motivate or cause future injury as a result of over exertion.
- **T**imely – All targets should be time-bound in that there should be a deadline for them to be achieved. Having a focal point as to when they need to be completed can help us plan for a long-term goal.

By setting SMART targets and breaking them down into short-, medium- and long-term goals, we can use them to review progress over time. If we review the athlete's progress regularly, we can check that the programme is working effectively.

When designing a training programme for a sports performer, it is important we break down the year into phases. Within the year we can identify key stages as to where training, competitions and recovery or transition phases take place. By doing this we can prepare the athlete to achieve the previous targets and goals which were set at the beginning of the year. For many sports performers, a training year does not necessarily begin in January. Any **training calendar** is worked back from the competitive phase in order to prepare the athlete adequately for competition.

If we identify athletics as an example, we can see how we can develop a training plan to prioritise key components throughout the year. Athletes will typically begin to start their preparation for the following outdoor season in early autumn of the previous year. This allows them to train throughout the winter in readiness for the start of the competitive season in April the following year. The type of training and competition calendar will be dependent on their season's goals for the year. The competition phase will typically last throughout the summer months until late August, completing the competitive year. This would differ from other activities such as rugby whereby the competitive season is during the winter months therefore requiring much of the training to be complete in the summer months.

Using the athletic example, we can see that the season is divided up into distinct phases:

- **Preparation phase** – Winter Training.
- **Pre-competition phase** – Weeks leading up to competition season.
- **Competition-tapering phase** – Competitions until August.
- **Recovery phase** – End of season rest.

The breakdown of a training year is referred to as **periodisation**, where key stages are broken up into small sub-sections. The basic principle is to vary the intensity, duration and frequency of a training programme.

The periodised phases are known as:

- the macrocycle
- the mesocycle
- the microcycle.

The **macrocycle** lasts for a few months, or more often the full competitive year. It is the training template within which other key phases are included. The **mesocycle** is a smaller phase that can last from several weeks to several months. A training programme may include a number of mesocycles within the complete macrocycle plan. Finally, the **microcycle** divides the mesocycle into even smaller components. They can last for 1 to 4 weeks, which is dependent on the type of programme being followed.

In summary, the macrocycle is the complete training programme with both the mesocycle and microcycle sub-diving it into smaller pieces. Simplified, it could be considered as a pie. The complete macrocycle (the pie), is divided in to mesocycle pieces (quarter slices), which in turn are sliced into smaller microcycle pieces (eighth slices).

When deciding on the training content, it is important to select the appropriate method that will complete each cycle. The method will be based on the personal fitness testing data and needs of the sport. For example, if the athlete's requirement is to develop maximal strength and power, they would need to choose the appropriate exercises to support these needs. The athlete may wish to choose exercises such as:

- the clean
- the snatch
- front squat
- bench press
- pullovers
- military press.

All exercises would be dependent on the region of the body that is in need of development as well as the intensity required. Whatever exercises are chosen, it is important that the **FITT principle** is considered as this can help the athlete make steady progress throughout their training (see page 295).

Once the programme has been designed and cycles agreed on, it is important to keep reassessing the athlete to **monitor progress** through fitness testing. If it is found that there is insufficient change or that the programme is having a negative effect on their performance, it is the reassessment process that will identify this. Therefore, it is very important that training programmes are regularly reassessed throughout their use which can be achieved by regular testing of your athlete.

Macrocycle (entire season)					
Meso 1	Meso 2	Meso 3	Meso 4	Meso 5	

Microcycle 1	Microcycle 2	Microcycle 3	Microcycle 4	Microcycle 1	Microcycle 2	Microcycle 3	Microcycle 4	Microcycle 1	Microcycle 2	Microcycle 3	Microcycle 4	Microcycle 1	Microcycle 2	Microcycle 3	Microcycle 4	Microcycle 1	Microcycle 2	Microcycle 3	Microcycle 4

Preseason ⟶ Race season ⟶ Offseason

Figure 8.8 A training template

C4 Planning training sessions

Every training session should ensure that the athlete participant is safe throughout. It is important that any training programme reflects safety within the type of training activities chosen. In order to avoid injury during participation it is important that a full and comprehensive warm-up is used to prepare the athlete for exercise.

There are many different types of **warm-up** we can use depending on the sport. A 'warm-up' should not be considered as simply stretching. It is important that the muscles become warm before any stretching takes place as it will make them more pliable. The use of a light jog or other similar aerobic activity, can help increase your muscle temperature as it causes the warm blood to circulate around your body faster. It is this warm blood that causes the muscle temperature to increase, preparing them for the stretching phase.

As we have previously mentioned, there are three main categories of stretching which include:

- Static stretch
- Dynamic and ballistic stretching
- Proprioceptive neuromuscular facilitation (PNF) stretching.

Once the aerobic phase has been completed, **static stretching** should be used to initially warm-up and lengthen the muscle fibres. It is important that stretches are held for between 5–10 seconds, repeating the same stretch on the same muscle at least twice depending on the sport activity being participated in. When selecting the stretch it is important that the intensity, duration and technique of the event are considered. As some areas of the body may be more in demand that others, it is important that they are stretched thoroughly to avoid the stress that may be placed on the muscles.

Following static stretching, **dynamic stretching** can be used to loosen the muscle further. The movement continues to increase the blood flow throughout the muscle tissue, helping it move and stay warm. It is important that the muscle is not overworked at this stage as it can cause fatigue which defeats the purpose of the warm-up.

As a warm-up, **PNF stretching** may not be considered as a suitable method. As PNF requires a significant overstretch of the muscle, it can lead to the muscle tension being lost prior to the competition. For this reason static and dynamic stretches are more suitable on top of the initial light continuous aerobic activity. PNF stretching is more suitable for a standalone training method rather than as a warm-up.

In contrast, a **cool-down** should perform the reverse on a warm-up. It is important that we start to cool down approximately 10–20 minutes following the sporting activity. From the activity there should be a period of a light continuous exercise followed by a period of dynamic and static exercises. The aim of the light continuous exercise is to gradually reduce the heart rate and prevent blood pooling. As the blood continues to circulate around the body, waste products such as lactic acid are able to be removed which speeds up the recovery process.

> **Key term**
>
> Blood pooling is when a large volume of blood is held within the muscles and its flow around the body is limited.

Both dynamic and static stretching are important for recovery as they help to maintain the range of movement in the joints. The stretches reduce the tightening of the muscle fibres which could limit the movement and potentially cause future injuries. While they both have their benefits, research has shown that dynamic stretching is of more benefit when improving flexibility after exercise in comparison to static stretches. However, whatever the stretches used, we should always use a full cool-down following exercise. It is important that we do not simply collapse and lay on the floor following the exercise as this will not help with the recovery. Light continuous movement and controlled stretching has been shown to improve long-term flexibility, decrease recovery time and enable you to be in peak fitness for the next training session.

Figure 8.9a, b and c Various warm-up stretching exercises

The **training intensity** and **duration** are dependent on the training type and method being used. It is important that an athlete is not overloaded beyond their capacity. All repetitions and sets should be realistic. As explained within the SMART targets, all training sessions should be achievable. Any session that is beyond the athlete's capabilities could lead to them becoming potentially injured so it is important that a balance is found.

Strength-based training is typically based from an athlete's 1 rep max (1RM). The training intensity uses a percentage of their maximum lift with anything from 90% and above being high. Training is completed using repetitions and sets. The repetitions are the number of times an exercise is completed during one sitting. For example, the bench press exercise will be repeated 10 times. The sets account for the number of times the group of repetitions will be performed. The bench press exercise will be performed three times (sets) using ten repetitions. Therefore the bench press would be completed '3x10'. Pure strength-based training may consist of high intensity low repetition exercises. Strength endurance training would consist of a medium intensity exercise but use high repetitions. Endurance-based athletes may perform distance running at a medium intensity over a long duration. For speed endurance the athlete may choose to complete medium-high intensity activity over a short-medium duration. Whatever the choice of exercise, the intensity and duration is athlete specific and performance needs should be considered when selecting an appropriate level.

The **selection of any training equipment** should be appropriate and meet the needs of the session. At no point should the athlete be in danger of harm or injury as a result of training therefore it is important that any exercises are appropriate and safe. The progress of the performer cannot only be by observation but also by the use of **heart rate monitors** and **RPE scales**.

An RPE scale is more formally known as a **Rating of Perceived Exertion**. It is a scale that an athlete can use to determine how hard they are working in relation to the exercise intensity. From a scale of 1 to 10 the athlete can provide ongoing feedback as to how difficult they are finding the training workload which can then be used to make adjustments to a programme. While they can be helpful for progress assessments, they are very subjective and require the athlete to be honest and in touch with their physical abilities throughout the training.

Monitoring feedback is extremely important as it allows us to make adjustments where and when necessary. We need to listen and monitor progress as this will help you gain the most out of a training session.

RPE scale	Rate of perceived exertion
10	**Max effort activity** Feels almost impossible to keep going. Completely out of breath, unable to talk. Cannot maintain for more than a very short time.
9	**Very hard activity** Very difficult to maintain exercise intensity. Can barely breathe and speaks only a few words.
7–8	**Vigorous activity** Borderline uncomfortable. Short of breath, can speak a sentence.
4–6	**Moderate activity** Breathing heavily, can hold short conversation. Still somewhat comfortable, but becoming noticeably more challenging.
2–3	**Light activity** Feels like you can maintain for hours. Easy to breathe and carry a conversation.
1	**Very light activity** Hardly any exertion, but more than sleeping, watching TV, etc.

Figure 8.10 An RPE scale

C5 Evaluating the effectiveness of programming and training plan design

The analysis of a training plan helps us review its progress and effectiveness. This is important as we need to check the success of the training activities in relation to the sporting performance. When we review we must reflect on:

- the methods of training
- the specific exercises used in relation to the sport
- the intensities and duration of the training activities performed
- the scheduling of the session and periodised year.

For training to be successful it is important that the methods are considered as appropriate. We need to understand whether they were specific enough to make the body adapt and sufficient enough to alter its performance. For example, if an athlete is trying to develop the power component of their performance, we should consider whether they have completed both the appropriate power-based exercises as well as gained sufficient base-strength. We should consider whether the intensity and duration are too

demanding as this could cause ongoing fatigue, or is it too easy therefore causing the body to under-perform. If an athlete is over-worked and unable to recover they will not perform at their best during each training session. This could potentially lead to them underachieving or sustaining an injury.

Evaluating the **periodised programme** can allow you to identify the success of its components. You can consider whether the training activities were appropriate. Were the various mesocycles of sufficient length, too long or short? Were the macrocycles sufficient? What could be done to adjust it? Are there any additional exercises that could be included within the programme? Throughout the evaluation phase we should consider each of these questions and adjust the future programme where and when necessary.

The evaluation may **suggest adaptations to the plan** that could include the choice of alternative training activities. For example, you may decide to change a **training method** from Fartlek to Interval training. While both methods require changes to a variable pace, it will be remembered that they have different programme structures and therefore different adaptations to performance. In your evaluation of your programme you may identify **alternative exercises** that may be more suitable to the performance you're trying to achieve. For example, kettlebell training could be used as an alternative to circuit training activities; or changes to free weight training as opposed to resistance machine; or speed endurance interval training as opposed to long duration continuous running. These variations may affect the **intensity and/or the duration** of the training, however they should be important enough to consider for future changes. While these changes may be subtle, they may be able to help us make a significant or fractional change which could determine success or failure.

Our final evaluation component should consider the success of the season's outcome. Did we achieve what we set out to achieve? Were our targets met? If not, why not? We should consider the training plan and identify its strengths and weaknesses. Evaluate whether its periodised components reflect the season's aims and objectives. You should break down each element of the season phases and reflect on their function. If they're not suitable then they should be removed or potentially replaced. However, regardless of the evaluation, we should always take time to review and evaluate our training. The body will continue to adapt as long as it's trained. Making changes to our training programme can only continue to develop it further for future competitions.

C Check your understanding

1 Design a periodised training programme for an athlete of your choice. You must consider the macrocycle, mesocycle and microcycles over a competitive season.

2 Evaluate your programme and justify the selection of training exercises you have included.

3 Produce a training session plan and complete it as a part of your training regime.

4 Evaluate your training session, focusing on its strengths and areas for improvement.

Case study C D3

You have been approached by an international athlete who has asked you to prepare a training programme for them to qualify and take part in the Olympic Games. They have important qualifying championships in early June and the Olympics are in mid-August. For this reason, they must be performing at a high standard in June to qualify, but be even better come the Olympics.

As a coach, you need to consider how you can prepare a programme for them to be in top shape leading up to these key dates. It is important to remember that they will need four competitions prior to competing in June to get them into competition mode and two more before the Olympic Games. They have left these for you to decide, but have given you strict instructions that they get enough rest between each competition. The competition season will start early April, so you need to plan from this time onwards.

Task

You need to plan and prepare a full training plan for your athlete from September through to completion of the Olympic Games. You need to consider:

- the periodised plan (macro/meso/microcycles)
- types of training
- competitive season
- the event.

Justify your training programme and make suggestions for alternative training methods that may be used.

Further reading

Baechle T., Earle R., (2008), *Essentials of Strength Training and Conditioning (Third Edition)*, Human Kinetics.

Bompa T., Buzzichelli C., (2015), *Periodization Training for Sports (Third edition)*, Human Kinetics.

Kent M., (2007), *Oxford Dictionary of Sports Science and Medicine (Third edition)*, Oxford University Press.

National Strength & Conditioning Association, (2011). *Developing Agility and Quickness (Sport & Performance)*, Human Kinetics.

Useful websites

Brianmac

www.brianmac.co.uk

Livestrong

http://www.livestrong.com

Men's Fitness

http://www.mensfitness.com/training/workout-routines

Netfit

www.netfit.co.uk

NHS Health and Fitness

http://www.nhs.uk/LiveWell/Fitness/Pages/Fitnesshome

Peak Performance Online

www.pponline.co.uk

Sportsci

www.sportsci.org

Women's Fitness

http://www.womensfitness.co.uk/workout-routines

References

Baechle, T., Earle, R., (2008). *Essentials of Strength Training and Conditioning* (*Third edition*), Human Kinetics.

Bompa, T., Buzzichelli, C., (2015), *Periodization Training for Sports* (*Third edition*), Human Kinetics.

Cardinale, M., Newton, R., Noska, K., (2010), *Strength and Conditioning: Biological Principles and Practical applications*, Wiley-Blackwell.

Hoffman, J., (2014), *Physiological Aspects of Sport Training and Performance* (*Second edition*), Human Kinetics.

Joyce, D., Lewindon, D., (2014), *High Performance Training for Sports*, Human Kinetics.

Kent, M., (2007), *Oxford Dictionary of Sports Science and Medicine* (*Third edition*), Oxford, Oxford University Press.

National Strength & Conditioning Association, (2011). *Developing Agility and Quickness (Sport & Performance)*, Human Kinetics.

9 Research project in sport and exercise science

About this unit

Research is about finding solutions to problems, obtaining facts, and determining what is the truth. A research project allows you to bring different areas of study together. You can use your knowledge of sport and exercise science to investigate a particular topic or question you have an interest in. It could be related to a certain sport (e.g. fitness in football referees), general issues in sport and exercise (e.g. the amount of physical activity undertaken by school children), or it may arise from one of the disciplines within sport and exercise (e.g. sports injuries). Whatever topic you choose, you will have to spend a large amount of time working independently. This will include reading literature, collecting and analysing data and writing up the whole project. The aim of this unit is to help you achieve such a project.

Learning aims

This unit is split into three learning aims, each addressing the applications of a sports scientist. The learning aims include:

A Plan a sport or exercise science-based research project

B Carry out a sport or exercise science-based research project

C Produce a sport or exercise science-based research report.

Each learning aim includes an assessment outcome that divides the content into key areas, sub-dividing the learning aim and allowing you to appreciate each of its components.

How will I be assessed?

The unit of research project will be assessed by assignments that have been designed internally by your tutors. It is likely that there will be two assignments for you to complete. Each assignment will enable you to apply the knowledge you have learnt to a range of activities.

Learning aim A achievement

For distinction standard, learners will provide reasons and evidence to support the appropriateness of their selected research methodology. As part of this, learners will consider the quality of their research, for example specific types of validity and reliability, accuracy, precision and trustworthiness, appropriate for the research methodology. Justifications should be supported with evidence such as research methods texts. Additionally, this evidence may come in the form of published precedents where previous studies have adopted a particular methodological approach.

Learning aims B and C achievement

For distinction standard, learners will draw on varied sources of information, for example different journal articles, appropriate textbooks, and government agency documents, theories or concepts to examine the relevance of their research findings. This relevance can be expressed through practical implications, research considerations or a combination of both. Learners should clearly demonstrate how the interpretations of research findings are linked with the strengths and limitations of the research project, which must, in turn, form the foundation of future research directions. Strengths, limitations and future research directions must be supported by appropriate evidence, for example research methods texts or journals that will support learners' arguments about how the future research directions will increase the overall quality of future research.

How will I be graded?

The table below shows the grading criteria for this unit. To achieve a pass grade you must meet all the P criteria; to achieve a merit grade you must achieve all the P and all the M criteria; to achieve a distinction grade you must achieve all the P, M and D criteria.

Pass	Merit	Distinction
Learning aim A: Plan a sport or exercise science-based research project		
A P1 Produce an appropriate rationale, research aims and research questions for a self-selected sport or exercise science-based research project.	**A M1** Interpret literature in order to support and develop the rationale for a self-selected sport or exercise science-based project.	**A D1** Justify the research methodology for a self-selected sport or exercise science-based research project.
A P2 Explain an appropriate research methodology for a self-selected sport or exercise science-based research project.	**A M2** Analyse an appropriate research methodology for a self-selected sport or exercise science-based research project.	
Learning aim B: Carry out a sport or exercise science-based research project		
B P3 Complete appropriate data collection and analysis for a self-selected sport or exercise science-based research project.	**B M3** Analyse the process of data collection and data analysis for a self-selected sport or exercise science-based research project.	**B D2** Evaluate the data collection and data analysis for a self-selected sport or exercise science-based research project.
B P4 Complete a research diary that documents the data collection, data analysis, and reflects on the research process using an established model of reflection.		
Learning aim C: Produce a sport or exercise science-based research report		
C P5 Explain the research, from a sport or exercise science-based project, using an appropriate writing style.	**C M4** Analyse the research findings, quality of research, and future directions arising from the sport or exercise science-based research project.	**C D3** Evaluate the research findings and the quality of the sport or exercise science-based research project using an appropriate evidence-base.
C P6 Produce a sport or exercise-based research report that uses a standard structure.		

Table 9.1 Assessment criteria

A Plan a sport or exercise science-based research project
(A P1 , A P2 , A M1 , A M2 , A D1)

A1 Selecting a research topic and creating a rationale

Thinking of a good idea takes time, so getting a project started can be difficult. It is useful to have a number of ideas that you're interested in just in case one proves impractical. A good research question is something that you can answer, e.g. are netball players fitter than basketball players or is body weight related to aerobic fitness?

It's important to remember that your project needs to be practical and viable so that you can actually test it. Many project ideas look wonderful on paper, however, without the appropriate facility, participants or equipment, it will never develop any further. When thinking of ideas you should always consider:

- the timeframe available
- the resources you need
- the equipment you have
- the subjects you can use.

The selection of your subjects is very important, as they should have a relationship to the final conclusion. In other words, they should be part of what you are aiming to find out. For example, when considering the netball players' fitness against that of basketball players, the relationship here is the athletes being used. The fitness is being tested with the comparisons being made between the two groups, the netball and basketball players. Within the study you're identifying them as the important component of the test.

To develop a project idea, it's important to consider what your interests are, as it will be you who will be studying it further. Creating a title and the direction you want to take it in can be difficult, so consider all of the options available. Using literature and discussing your ideas with your peers and tutors can help to create an interesting project for both yourself and a reader.

A good start can be to use a **mind map** that can help you to think about sport or a type of exercise.

A mind map is a useful technique in creatively jotting your ideas onto paper. From the map, you can start with a central topic and then identify its major components. With each strand from your centre point you can draw further ideas. Eventually, your map will begin to resemble the roots of a tree, from which you can begin to establish what you already know or have an existing interest in. For example, if you're a keen cyclist, you may wish to create a project on an aspect of cycling. Another way to narrow this topic further could be to study it by a **discipline** within sport and exercise science. For example, you may decide to do a project involving the discipline of biomechanics. You could even combine the two areas to arrive at a project that incorporates the biomechanics of cycling. Similarly, you could involve the study discipline of physiology or psychology of your chosen sport.

> **Key term**
>
> **Study discipline** is a subject area in sports science that is often determined between biomechanics, physiology and psychology.

If you choose to study one discipline within your study, this is known as a **mono-disciplinary** study whereby the project focuses on just one discipline, ignoring the other disciplines as they are not measured. If you choose to create a study project that analyses the combination of performances such as psychology or physiology, then this is known as an **interdisciplinary** approach.

Rationale

The initial stages of your planning should consider the reasoning behind your study, known as the rationale. This should include a definition – an explanation of why your project is worth researching – as well as some or all of the following:

- The **applied reasons** why your project is of interest – i.e. what applications might your research project have for a sport and exercise scientist. Using existing literature, consider whether this study area is well understood. For example, the physiological responses to aerobic exercise may be more understood than when compared to the psychological responses.

- The **contextual reasons** why your project is of interest – i.e. if the topic is well understood you may want to consider looking at the same topic but applied to a different sport or activity.

- The **social reasons** why your project is of interest – i.e. focusing on a topic in relation to a particular and specific social group. For example, you could analyse sports provision for disabled people or ethnic minority participation in different activities. Again, while the topic itself may have been researched many times before, it may not have been looked at from this angle.

- **Methodological reasons** for your research – i.e. you are working on a familiar topic but have chosen to use a different research method from the normal approach. When reflecting on previous studies you could consider the methods that were used and how they could be changed or adapted to suit the needs of your own project. For example, you could use strength testing rather than power testing when measuring performance.

Another reason for your chosen project might be that there are gaps or flaws in the existing research. Perhaps the previous study didn't consider the social reasons for participation in sport for specific groups. Focusing on addressing these gaps or flaws is a sound reason for your research.

You don't always have to reinvent the wheel and make radical changes to find out something different in a project. All projects and research studies have their strengths and weaknesses. As sports scientists, it's important we identify these problems and try to refine ideas for future subject developments.

A2 Deciding on aims and research questions

Turning a research topic into a research question

Once you have considered your rationale you should begin to map out the question or questions as to what you are aiming to gain from your work. The project will need to be based around a research question that will eventually be proved or disproved. It is important that you have a clear idea as to what you want your project to prove or disprove. Not having a direction or appropriate achievement aim can make your project meaningless therefore it is a vital part of the planning.

The **aim** of the research must be clear along with the study title. The aim will provide you with what you want to achieve by the end of the project so again it must be clear. It will show the direction of your work and define what you are trying to investigate. You may have a general idea for a project, for example fitness in football players, but not a specific aim. Using this example (fitness in footballers), you need to consider: what do you want to test? Who would you test? As it currently stands the topic is too general, therefore it needs to be refined and focused on one particular aspect of fitness. In contrast, a study topic which examines a more defined study area could be an analysis of the anaerobic fitness performance of college male first-team and second-team football players. This has now become much clearer, with the project providing direction as to what it will be investigating. Exactly what the project is measuring is specific, i.e. anaerobic fitness, however you would still need to decide how to measure it and justify your chosen method. The people you are going to investigate would also need to be clearly stated, in this case it is the male first- and second-team players.

When you have decided the project aims you can begin to develop a defined research area. Referred to as the **research question,** it is a clear single sentence that summarises what you're trying to find out. The sentence will define the research area and identify whether the study will be quantitative or qualitative in research design. This is where our mind map becomes an important part of our planning as it can help to build your ideas and formulate the research question. When your mind map ideas pull together they can help to produce a subsequent research question. It is from the research question that we should set out a single statement as to what we think the project will show. This statement is known as the project hypothesis.

Hypothesis

From the research question we can prepare a clear hypothesis which is a single statement that implies a relationship between two or more variables

(Kent, 2006). In contrast, a **null hypothesis** is a prediction of there being no relationship between two or more variables, therefore the complete reverse to the hypothesis. For example, using our football study you might hypothesise that the first-team players will have a higher level of anaerobic fitness when compared to the second-team players. This would be easy to test by measuring both groups of players and comparing their results. By providing a well-defined hypothesis it can help you make the research clearer which can enable you to think about how you intend to collect the data.

> **Key terms**
>
> **Quantitative** is the use and collection of numerical data that may quantify a response of an action. For example, when measuring the height of an individual, this may be determined and gathered using a stadiometer which provides you with a numerical value, e.g. 183 cm.
>
> **Qualitative** is the use of descriptive information that may be analysed where numerical information is not a component. For example, 'Have you ever suffered from heart disease – Yes or No?'. The response is descriptive and requires no data for analogy.

A3 Deciding on an appropriate research methodology

The **research design** is key to the success of a project. It is important that we carefully plan how we will investigate a research problem. When designing our research project it is important to ensure we prepare a comprehensive testing method that is good enough to examine your project accurately. Therefore we should take time to design a project that gives us the greatest opportunity to gain the most accurate results and outcome. It is important to remember that the design will influence the overall project outcome, so take your time and examine all of the potential options. To improve our accuracy during the data gathering process, we should ensure that the method is correctly chosen and applied to meet our aims and objectives successfully. Similarly, our results collection should be appropriate in order to allow us to interpret our results clearly. The design

should be appropriate for what you're trying to examine, therefore it be should be both valid and reliable.

> **Key terms**
>
> **Validity** is the extent to which a test, measurement or investigation possesses the property of actually doing what it has been designed to do (Kent, 2007).
>
> **Reliability** is a characteristic of a measurement or experimental procedure which produces consistent results on two or more separate occasions (Kent, 2007).

The research design will depend on what you are hoping to examine. For example, if you aim to examine the effect of a training programme on a particular measure such as flexibility, you would need to record the value of this measurement (flexibility) before and after a training programme. The justification for this would be that it allows you to see if what you were measuring had changed and to infer that your training plan had caused the change. This is referred to as a pre-test, post-test research design as you reflect on your initial first pre-exercise measures. As a sports scientist, it's important that you can justify any decisions you make. Always be prepared to justify your research methodology so that it can be successfully tested within a project. Avoid selecting a method just as a guess, do your research.

When testing it is essential that you keep personal details and results **confidential**. Any information should be anonymously recorded with each individual being referred to as a 'subject' or 'participant'. By using these terms, the participating subject cannot be identified except by the managing sports scientist. This is in line with the Data Protection Act (1984). It is the responsibility of the sports scientist to ensure that the data is safely stored in a secure location. No information should be shared without the consent of the participant.

In sport and exercise research, special considerations are required as research involves testing on human subjects. As a sports scientist, any experiments that you design will need to be ethical. For example, asking people to undertake training without eating or drinking could have negative effects on the body therefore it is unethical. A great deal of thought needs to go into designing the project to avoid these problems. Even when you are happy that the research is ethical, the health and safety of your subject is vital. The American College of Sport Medicine suggests that researchers should adhere to the Declaration of Helsinki, which is a code of practice for conducting measurements on humans. If your research involves working with children or vulnerable adults you will need to have a CRB (criminal record bureau) or DBS (Disclosure & Barring Service) check completed to ensure you are suitable to work with these individuals.

Along with ethical testing it is important that **health and safety** considerations are pre-planned into the research design. It is the responsibility of the sports scientist to keep the subject safe throughout the testing. Once your subjects have agreed to participate, you should ensure that they all complete a health-screening questionnaire to ensure that they are fit and able to take part in your tests. A PAR-Q (Physical Activity Readiness Questionnaire) is more commonly used as it can help to determine if the participants are suitable to participate. Additionally you may wish to health screen your participants too, checking areas such as blood pressure and lung function. The depth of your screening will be dependent on the project that's being carried out.

More information on ethical testing and health and safety can also be found in Unit 4 – Field- and laboratory-based fitness testing, see page 160.

A4 Structure of the research proposal

A research proposal consists of a summary outline of a pre-planned project. It is not the complete project, it simply provides initial guidance on the 'proposed' research study in order to examine its purpose and suitability. The proposal is crucial as it can also help to identify any potential problems that may be encountered during the actual project report. At this early stage, the project remains open to change, allowing for further developments to be made if required.

A proposal should consist of:

1 Title
2 Introduction
3 Research methodology
4 Bibliography.

Here are more details on these different parts of a proposal:

1 **Title** – Your project title should always reflect the research question. At the proposal stage the study title can be flexible as it can be changed at a later stage. The main focus should be to show initial guidance as to what the study will be covering. Regardless of its flexibility it should relate to the aims and objectives.

2 **Introduction** – Within the proposal you should provide an initial broad overview of the subject area. For example, if your project will involve the testing of a particular fitness component, how may it be important to sports performance? What are the fitness demands of the sporting performance? The initial outline demonstrates your wider understanding before you direct your understanding to the project aims and objectives, e.g. how the component will affect your chosen outcome or performance.

You must then discuss the background to the topic. Using the reviewed literature from previous studies, you can identify any links their research has to your new proposed project. The reviewing process is important as it enables you to make predictions or develop additional ideas. It is extremely important you use varied resources including books, journals and the internet. Avoid relying on one single source of information, such as the internet. Books and journals are very good resources so don't be afraid to ask for them in the library. Regardless of how similar some of the information is to your study, **never** copy and paste the information into your introduction. Remember this is *your* introduction so *you* need to write it.

A key part of the proposal is to introduce technical terminology and that it is recorded correctly. For example, if analysing VO_2 max, what is it and how does it relate to the project? Remember to treat the reader as if they've never been taught the subject before. Consider this to be their first reading of sports science so try to be clear with the facts and terms you present. These terms should be defined so as to allow the reader to appreciate the full scope of the project. The rationale behind the study should be clear at this stage along with its aims. Linked to the aims, you should also state the project **hypothesis** and **null hypothesis** if conducting **quantitative** research.

3   **Research methodology** – The proposal should provide a clear outline of the methods that *will* be used to complete the study. It's important to remember that at the proposal stage the language should be written in the future tense. For example, the proposal should state – 'the cycle ergometer *will* be used to conduct the Wingate test', rather than it '*was* used' in the past tense. In addition the proposal should not be written in the first person – i.e. avoid terms such as me, I, our, my, I'm, and so on. Remember the project is not about you, it's about the subject of study so your personal thought or participation does not need to be reported.

The proposed research design should be clearly explained at this stage. You need to consider what you are going to do, how you are going to do it, where you are going to do it, who will be involved and what will be tested.

You should be clear on how you will gather the results, along with how you will analyse

them. You need to state the resources you will need to do this, both human and physical. You should also discuss the proposed participants in your research and the sampling methods you will employ.

This may include some form of data analysis within your project that should be explained as to how and why you will conduct it. If you are selecting a statistical analysis such as standard deviation, a t-test, Pearson product-moment correlation coefficient (Pearson's r), state the reasons why and what you hope you will find out using these analysis methods. For more information on data analysis see Unit 5 Section D.

You should also include significant detail on ethical standards which will be followed along with health and safety too. This information will be invaluable to show the steps you plan to prepare for when testing. This evidence may include the screening questionnaires to be used and information as to what you will do with them once collected. The ethical standards should follow the ethical guidelines as set out by the British Association of Sport and Exercise Sciences (BASES). Remember as stated before, special consideration must be taken when testing humans so plan this carefully.

As a part of the proposal methodology you should devise a timetable action plan of the stages you will follow for the completion of the project. Include deadlines for researching

Objectives (list of goals)	Tasks (what you need to do to achieve the goals)	Success criteria (how you will identify your success)	Time frame (when you need to complete the tasks by)	Resources (what or who can help you complete tasks)

Figure 9.1 An action plan

information, carrying out testing, analysing the results and when the individual sections of the research will be completed. The planning will enable you to develop goals which can help you stay on track for steady progress to competition in a timely manner.

4 **Bibliography** – Finally, you will need to provide details of the resources you have read and referred to throughout your proposal. This is where the information you read through in the introduction should be recorded. These should all be listed in alphabetical order using the Harvard system. For books and journals the basic principle is that they should be listed by, author; date; title; publisher.

Textbook example:

Thomas, J. R. and Nelson, J. K. (2005) *Research Methods in Physical Activity* (5th edition). Illinois: Human Kinetics.

Journal example:

Morris, T. (2000) Psychological characteristics and talent identification in soccer. *Journal of Sports Sciences*, 18, pp. 715–26.

Online (electronic) internet references are referenced differently due to the way they are published. Sometimes the date it was posted on the internet is given. Whether it is or not, the date you accessed the online resource should be given. Therefore, an online reference would appear as follows:

Sport England (2006). Equity and Inclusion [Online]. **www.sportengland.org/index/about_sport_england/equality_standard_for_sport.htm** [accessed 15th March 2016].

A Check your understanding

1 Use the internet to investigate a selected research study and analyse the structure of the study.

2 Justify whether you feel the methodology is appropriate to the study.

3 Discuss what you feel are its strengths and weaknesses.

4 If you were to repeat the test, explain what you could do to make it even better.

Meeting distinction criteria (A D1)

1 Research four journal articles online that have conducted research on a physiology-based subject, e.g. aerobic endurance, power, speed, strength, etc.

2 With the research you've found, summarise the research methods that were used.

3 Justify why you think the methodology may have been suitable for the project and analyse any other appropriate methods that you think could have been used instead.

B Carry out a sport or exercise science-based research project
(B P3 , B P4 , B M3 , B D2)

B1 Data collection

For the most accurate results to be gathered, it is important that the project is carefully planned using the appropriate resources. You need to consider a number of issues, all of which should be specific to your testing.

Resource availability: For example, do you need to book a room or a gym? Is it available at the time you wish to use it? Do you need to book a video camera and can you use it? When you pick it up will the battery be charged? Will it have a spare? Are the participants free and available at the same time as the physical resources? And so on. All of these factors should be built in and potential outcomes as best planned for as possible. Human and physical resources will both have a significant influence on the accuracy of a project outcome. For this reason it is essential that prior to any testing, resource availability is checked as there is nothing worse than preparing to test and being let down at the last minute. To overcome this problem the project researcher should try to book all facilities for testing and check all equipment rather than leave it all to the last minute. Always try to keep a detailed log or diary as to when your assessments will take place. This can help you be prepared for stages of data collection. Remember the phrase, 'fail to prepare, prepare to fail'.

Resource familiarity: Before testing, it is important that you become familiar with the method being used. This may involve a rehearsal of the testing procedure or practice using specific equipment. The practice can help you:

- make additional safety checks
- identify any additional risks for their assessment
- ensure all equipment is working correctly
- identify further ethical concerns
- identify areas that may require a specific skills set.

Research diary: When collecting the data, a diary can also help with the initial analysis or the recording of observational memos, i.e. observations during the testing that can be written down for future reference. During the testing you may notice some additional changes in performance or concerns with the working of equipment. For example, if you are measuring the heart rate of your subject and the results are not what you expected, are you sure the heart rate monitors were recording correctly? Was there any inconsistency in the measurement process? Were they erratic throughout the testing? The use of a research diary can allow you to record these observations which can help you with any further testing. The diary enables you to make an immediate reflection on the testing and observations shown.

From the observations, you can formulate new ideas or an action plan for when you retest your participants. You can use Gibbs' reflective cycle when considering your observations.

Other models that can help us when reflecting on our research include Johns' model of reflection and Kolb's learning cycle. Johns' model of reflection views learning as something we should describe, reflect upon, identify our response, and evaluate for future learning.

Kolb provides a more simplified learning style whereby we reflect on our testing, develop ideas for the future and apply them for future experiences. Regardless of the learning style you choose to follow, the key to the research diary is 'learn'. Nothing always goes right conducting research and we don't always have all the answers, therefore learning is a key part to developing our knowledge further.

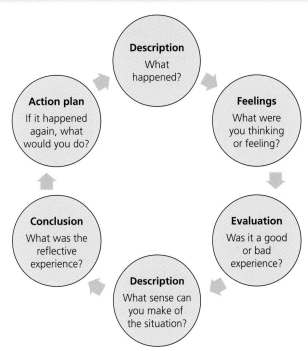

Figure 9.2 Gibbs' reflective cycle

Recording data: The recording of sensitive information may be required in many field and laboratory tests and it is very important that it is safely stored to protect confidentiality. The use of appropriate password protected ICT facilities are ideal for the storage of such information as it can be difficult to access and easy to transfer for future statistical analysis. It is important that any information is recorded anonymously with each individual being referred to as a 'subject' or 'participant'. By using these terms, the participant subject cannot be identified by any other individual involved within the testing except for the managing sports scientist. While there is legislation regarding the sharing of sensitive information, without the use of anonymity some subjects may be reluctant to provide sensitive information.

For example, subjects may feel reluctant to provide information on their body weight, body fat, heart rate and blood pressure, in fear of being ridiculed by their peers. By keeping all information anonymously, subjects will be confident in the confidentiality of their individual results.

For more information, see Confidentiality explained in A3 and in detail in Unit 4 – Field- and laboratory-based fitness testing (see page 160).

Subject	Resting Pulse (bpm)	Blood Pressure (mmHg)	Height (cm)	Weight (kg)	BMI (%)	Waist/Hip Ratio	Peak Flow (L.min^{-1})	Age (Yrs)
1	68	131/89	187	94	27	0.83	590	18
2	66	129/79	172	56	19	0.67	450	17
3	61	141/71	170	61	21	0.82	450	17
4	65	127/67	177	76	24	0.82	500	18

Figure 9.3 Data collection with 'subject anonymity'

B2 Data analysis

When you have completed your data collection, it is important you interpret what it means. We can use a number of methods from making comparisons to norms data, to performing various appropriate statistical calculations. The analysis of the data can enable us to identify study outcomes which can include:

- data accuracy
- examining the data reliability
- assessing data similarity
- making comparisons
- identifying trends
- enabling us to make predictions on sports performance.

In order to analyse data, you must first consider the **availability of resources** to help you do this. Typically this would include ICT resources, in order to run software with statistical analysis tools such as **Microsoft Excel** or **SPSS.** It might also include human resources, such as your tutor or participants in the research, in order that you repeat your data collection using a different research method. The process of using two or more methods when collecting data is called **qualitative triangulation.** This process helps to check the validity and accuracy of the data that has been collected. If the methods provide similar results then we can be confident that there is accuracy in the results.

In order to use data analysis resources you first must be familiar with their operation. The statistical tools within Microsoft Excel, for instance, can be intimidating if you have had no previous training in using them. However, with a little preparation you will be able to use these applications with confidence.

The storage of data that has been recorded is very important for two reasons: first, as mentioned several times, the data must be secure so that unauthorised people do not have access to it. Second, regardless of how you are collecting the data you must ensure that you have a backup. Otherwise, what would happen if the computer you were recording the data on broke down? Or got stolen? If you had spent weeks collecting data and then lost it all you would find it very difficult to complete the project on time.

When the data is being analysed, you should continue to use your research diary. It is useful to use some basic observations to see if anything stands out such as obvious differences. It may be simple but it can tell you a lot at the early stages of data analysis. You should try to identify any obvious discrepancies that could influence the outcome of your project. For example, are the responses to your questionnaires as expected? If all the answers are 'no' or 'disagree', maybe you need to redesign your questionnaire as it could be at fault. If you are measuring heart rate and the results are not what you expected, are you sure the heart rate monitors were recording correctly? A little bit of time early on spent looking at the results could save you time in the long run. You may even start to recognise a pattern in the results which could enable you to suggest some initial conclusions. Again, using the models of reflection described in section B1 will help you.

B Check your understanding

1 Explain why it is important that confidentiality is maintained at all times with personal information.

2 Perform a fitness-testing procedure and collect the results from a group of participants.

3 Using the data you have collected, analyse the outcome of the results and interpret their findings.

4 Evaluate the outcomes of the test: what does it show and why?

Meeting distinction criteria (B D1)

In small groups, collect data from four fitness tests and display them appropriately. Ensure appropriate tables are used, units are included, and that they are clear and concise. All tables must be boxed and data should not be free-floating.

Analyse the data collection procedure. On reflection, are there any changes you could have made to this process? Consider the methodology, people tested, time of day tested, numbers of participants, etc.

Prepare a presentation that evaluates the data you've collected and summarise the testing outcomes.

C Produce a sport or exercise science-based research report

(C P5 , C P6 , C M4 , C D3)

C1 Writing styles appropriate for research projects

When writing the project, it is important that it looks good and reads well. For it to look professional and make it easy to read you need to be familiar with word processing and spreadsheet software. Using ICT to record, report and present the results will go a long way towards making your work easier for the reader to understand. For it to read well, you should concentrate on your sentence structure, grammar and spellings. Remember you should consider that your reader is new to sports science so they need to gain a full understanding of what the project shows. There is no point in putting lots of hard work in developing an idea into a fantastic project only for it to not be understood due to poor reporting. It is important that the reader fully understands your outcome to get the most out of your project. Clear communication is key. Here are some tips:

1 Write the report itself in the **past tense**. Always explain what has happened, for example the heart rate *was* measured, or the average heart rate *was* 167 bpm. Remember the write up happens *after* the testing.

2 Write in the **third person**. This means do not use words such as 'I', 'we', 'me' and 'mine'. For example, 'the heart rate was recorded every 30 seconds' is better than 'I recorded heart rate every 30 seconds'. Don't forget, the project is not about you, it's about what was shown or happened in the project so try to reflect that.

3 Try and be **factual** rather than subjective. Only make important statements if you are able to back them up with facts. This is where your research information may be used. Your work should sound like a good professional newspaper article. The wording should be clear and easy to understand so try to keep it simple and direct. Try to avoid too much waffle. If you intend to use technical terms make sure they are well defined first. The definition should have a reference source which will come from your initial project research.

4 Write in **paragraphs**. A paragraph should be more than one sentence but avoid making them too long. The information in a paragraph should all relate to the point you're making. Take a look at the report once the first draft has been written and consider how it looks without reading it – would you would want to read it if you were presented with it for the first time? Big blocks of text are not appealing to read so try to break these up. When dividing your paragraphs, ensure they are spaced with a line between each one to show the divide.

5 **Headings** are useful to the reader as they provide structure and a clear direction as to what's being covered and where. The use of

sub-headings can also break up large chunks of text further. For example, if you are reporting on the method used in the project, you can insert a sub-heading that refers to the equipment used and another referring to the actual procedure used. If you are struggling to start the project you can use headings and sub-headings to brain-storm some initial ideas. These can be developed when typing up the project for presentation.

6   Make sure you write in **sentences** and check for spelling errors as these can put people off reading the work. Avoid sentences that are overly long. Always ensure that your sentences are correctly structured. Never use 'text-talk'. When describing the results, 'the results were gr8, my m8 got lvl 10 on bleep tst. Gonna tst tmrw and c if he gets same' (roughly translated as 'the results were great, my mate got to level 10 on the bleep test. I am going to test tomorrow to see if he gets the same result'). Clearly, the sentence fails to make sense and does not use the appropriate tense and tone. You must leave 'text-talk' on your mobile phone and use formal English language throughout your project. Remember it's important you treat the reader as if they have never been involved with sports science before. Everything should be clearly explained with an appropriate tone to help guide them through the topics involved.

7   The style of writing is probably the hardest thing to get right. The most common mistakes that learners make is for their writing to be too **informal** or too **dry**. Informal means that even though the spelling and grammar is fine, the work is too chatty and not technical enough. Dry means that the work is too technical, using too much jargon that the general reader will not understand, and with sentences that are overly long and complex. You need to write in a style that is between the two. Read some existing research papers at an appropriate level to get a clear idea as to the style you are aiming for.

8   Always **proofread** your project before submission. Sometimes it's helpful to read your work a couple of hours or even a day or more after you've finished writing it, as you are more likely to spot any basic problems spelling and grammar with fresh eyes. Alternatively, if you have time, ask friend or relative to read through your work. Remember, the marker will read it carefully so ensure you do too, as it will help you get the best grade possible.

9   Ensure you **number the pages** throughout your work. This can make it easy for the reader and also yourself. It also looks more professional.

10 You should not assume that people will automatically understand any **abbreviations** that you use. Spell them out the first time they are being used. For example, if I refer to 'the British Association of Sport and Exercise Sciences (BASES)', I firstly include their full name, after which I can simply state 'BASES'.

11 If you intend to use 'i.e.' or 'e.g.', make sure you know what they mean. The use of i.e. means 'that is', whereas e.g. is short for 'for example'.

12 You must ensure that you include references for any work, articles or data that you refer to anywhere in your report. Remember, the theories and research you use to explain your study do not belong to you. As a result, it is important that you always make sure you show where they have come from. If you fail to show where your resources originated from then this may be seen as plagiarism as you are passing the work off as your own. Always take time to ensure that your references are shown clearly and easy to find should the reader want to examine them further.

C2 Structure of the research report

The project will be reported in writing. The general structure of a written project is given below.

1   Title page
2   Preliminary pages
   i)   Abstract
   ii) Acknowledgements
   iii) General contents
   iv) Contents page for figures and tables
   v)   Contents page for Appendices.

3 Introduction

4 Literature review

5 Method

6 Results

7 Discussion

8 References

9 Appendices.

Here are more details on these different parts of a written project:

1 The **title page** should have on it the title of the study, the person who wrote it and the year. You may wish to include your institution (e.g. the name of your college).

2 The preliminary pages will contain the abstract, acknowledgements and contents. The **abstract** is a short summary of the entire report. It is normally in the region of 250 words, it will contain information on the aim, research questions, research plan, outcomes and overall conclusions. The abstract must be clear and separated from the main body of the report. The abstract should appear at the start of the report but it is usually written last as it is a summary of the entire report. The **acknowledgements** are where you can write something personal – normally a message of thanks for those who may have helped you during the project. It should include thanks to your supervisor for their support, and there might be others who you would like to mention. The **contents page** will list the chapters or the sections of the report, together with the number of the page on which it begins. A separate content section should be provided for figures and tables, complete with the title of each figure or table, and the appendices.

3 The purpose of the **introduction** is to give an outline of the research subject area. It should address the question, why have you completed this project? The introduction sets the tone of the project. It should:

● Provide a background to the topic area

● Identify key definitions

● Include your project rationale

● Include your research aims

● Include your research question

● Include your study hypothesis or null hypothesis as appropriate.

It should be interesting and make the reader want to continue reading to find out more. At the end of this section you should lead the reader to the overall aim of the project.

4 The **literature review** is an evaluation of the existing research on the topic you are tackling in your project. You should summarise what consensus there is from the existing work about the topic in question. If there is no consensus then you need to illustrate that. You should highlight the strengths of the existing research, as well as any limitations or gaps that you identify. You can use many sources of information for your literature review. The section should follow a funneled approach beginning with a broad description of the subject area before focusing on the aspects covered in your project.

5 The **methodology** is an explanation of what you did. It can be divided into subsections and you should use sub-headings. You need to discuss:

The **research design**, explaining how and why you decided to conduct the research in the way that you did. You should discuss your **data collection methods**, stating exactly how you collected your information. You need to list all of the equipment you used when gathering the data, and you should be specific with the brand name and model, as not all equipment works exactly the same. You also need to include some information on the participants – how many were used, were they chosen specifically or randomly, details of their average age, current fitness level, sampling methods and so on.

Finally, you will discuss the statistical method(s) you used to analyse the data and what equipment and software you used.

A properly written methodology would allow a reader to completely recreate the research you undertook and for this reason you must include enough detail to allow for that.

6   The **results** are the actual data you collected. The results should be presented in a clear format so that they can be easily interpreted. You do not need to include lists of numbers or piles of questionnaires unless you are specifically asked for this. Results can be summarised and the individual raw data be placed in the appendices. Patterns that you see in the data need to be described (e.g. heart rate increases with time). Tables and graphs are the best way of presenting lots of data but you need to write about what is in the table or graph. Ensure all tables are clear and concise. A title and table number should appear above each table, but a figure number can either appear above or below. You should ensure that each box of data is surrounded by a border to avoid any free-floating data which can be difficult to read clearly. The use of appropriate units for data is extremely important, otherwise the data becomes meaningless. Try to avoid excess information within a table, keeping it focused to the experimental data needed for your study.

Ensure all graphs and bar charts are clear and can be interpreted easily. They should have a title and a figure should be provided below the display. It is extremely important that appropriate units and a scale or label is provided for all the axes. Graphs and bar charts do not necessarily need to take up the whole page, however they should be large enough for them to be easily read. The scale does not necessarily need to start at zero but if not this must be clearly indicated on the graph. If a legend (an explanation of what different parts of the graph refer to) is required then remember that a black and white printer will print colours in shades of grey, which means that all colours will be similar and difficult to interpret the differences. It is important that graphs, tables and charts are not just added to the results section with little information provided to explain what they are. What was the average heart rate? What did heart rate go up to? What time did heart rate start to decrease? At this stage you are not trying to explain what the results mean, you are simply reporting the observations.

In this section you should also use statistical methods to analyse the results and allow you to draw conclusions from the testing. These are called inferential statistics. They allow you to make accurate statements about your results. Consider an investigation to see if a given training programme lowered the resting heart rate of a group of individuals. Your results might show that the average resting heart rate of the training group is 58 bpm (beats per minute), while that of a control group (a group of subjects who did no training) is 61 bpm. There is a difference of 3 bpm, but is this meaningful or is the difference just due to chance? A statistical difference test (e.g. t-test) would be able to establish if the difference in the values was significant, i.e. large enough to mean something. Where calculations are performed in analysing data, a sample calculation is helpful to explain the analysis. This can be included in the main text if it is relatively straightforward; however if the step-by-step details are rather complex such detail is better placed in an appendix.

7   The **discussion** is the most central part of your research as it tries to make sense of what the project has found out. This is your chance to explain what has happened and why. You should analyse the results in detail as this is your opportunity to try and prove or disprove your outcomes.

First, you must restate the aims of your project. You then go on to describe the results that you have outlined in the previous section. Try and give a summary of what you found. What do the results show? What do they mean? Are they valid and reliable based on the analysis? Are there any discrepancies in the results? If so, explain where and why. Make a detailed critical evaluation of the data collected. Always refer back to the aim of your project and to what you reported in the literature review. Did your idea of what was going to happen come true, if not why not?

You should consider the overall quality of your study. After gathering the data, analysing it and interpreting it, do you think there were any things you might change if you were to do it again? Explain what went wrong, and why and what you could have done better. Were there things beyond your control that might happen again if someone else were to repeat your approach? In this way you can explain how the study might be improved.

Given what you have said about the quality of your study, you need to discuss the implications of your findings. What use is the information you have found? Does it confirm or contradict the findings of previous research? Are there specific implications for the kind of participants in your research, or for the kind of activity you were considering?

Finally, give suggestions for future research. It may be that your findings require some further research to be sure they are valid, or they may have shown that a specific element of your investigation would benefit from a detailed study of its own. This is an important part of research as it could give you or others ideas for future studies.

8 The **conclusion** is part of the Discussion and should be made up of statements of fact. What are your main findings of your project? These should relate back to the aim of your research. The conclusion does not need to be too long or detailed; it should simply state the findings of the project. Any additional theories or reporting should be within the discussion – the conclusion simply outlines all that's been completed.

9 The **reference** section will list the references used in the report. In the text you will have quotes or citations referring to other people's work and then at the end of the report you will have a detailed list. You should always try to use a wide variety of resources including books, journals and the internet. The Harvard system of referencing is commonly used in sport and exercise science academic work.

In the **Harvard system** of referencing, you need to report the reference by giving the author of the work and also the year of publication. The full title of the work is given in the reference section. If work is transferred into your own words, this is called paraphrasing and quotation marks are not needed. Transferring

into your own words does not mean changing a word or two! It means completely rewriting a sentence of section in your own words. If a quote is included in the text, you should use single quotation marks.

In your report, the reference would appear like this: 'Recovery for athletes is essential (Child, 2004)'. If you are referencing more than one book for example, you can name them all: 'The stresses imposed by training can be harmful (Child, 1999; Tyzack, 2002; Watt, 2003)'. If more than two authors were involved in writing the work, you would not need to reference them all: (Ball, Brees, Chance and Stokes, 1989). To shorten this we can use an abbreviation which refers to the first author's surname followed by *et al.* This is only the case if there are more than two authors, for example, 'Ball *et al.* (1989) have shown that ...' You may come across two authors with the same surname; if this is the case use initials: 'A report (Barton, 2006) has indicated ...' If you need to reference more than one article for the same year add letters to the different references: 'Thomas (2000a, 2000b) showed that ...'

Sometimes it may be necessary to refer to letters, emails or conversations; these are called personal communications. They would be referenced as follows: 'In a telephone conversation on 15 January 2014, Mr J. A. Gilbert pointed out that ...' or 'Mr D. Goodchild's letter dated 2 November 2010 claimed that ...'

You may need to refer to work with no author's name, for example: 'A recent report by the American College of Sports Medicine (2001) states ...' or 'the Teesside Times (10 June 2014, p.4) reported that ...'

There are guidelines for entries in the list of references, depending on what you are referring to. Books are referenced:

● Thomas, J. R. and Nelson, J. K. (2005) *Research Methods in Physical Activity* (5th edition). Illinois: Human Kinetics.

Journals and periodicals are referenced:

● Morris, T. (2000) Psychological characteristics and talent identification in soccer. *Journal of Sports Sciences*, 18, pp. 715–26.

Online (electronic) material is a little different, as it has not been published in the traditional way. Sometimes the date it was posted on the internet is given. Whether it is or not, the date you accessed it should be given. Therefore, an online reference would appear as follows:

● Sport England (2006). Equity and Inclusion [Online]. **www.sportengland.org/index/about_sport_england/equality_standard_for_sport.htm** [accessed 15th March 2010].

10 After the reference section is the **appendix**. In here you can include any information that does not readily fit into the rest of your report. This is where you would put your raw data (which would just fill up the results section), and data collection sheets. You can refer to the any of the appendix in the main body of the report. The appendix should be labeled (example: Appendix A). If you do to refer to the appendix in your report you could do it like this: 'Appendix A shows that ...'or 'Crowd attendances are on the increase (see Appendix A)'.

Normally on completion of their research, people are asked to give a short presentation. Your presentation might include video footage, a poster presentation, handouts or a computer slideshow. It is not possible in a short presentation to cover the whole project so you will need to pick out the key parts of the study. You should start by introducing the area of research, explaining why you chose this area. You should give an overview of the main literature relating to your project such as theories and previous summaries in similar areas. After this you need to explain the method and list the main results, graphs and tables. The most important part of the presentation will be your detailed explanation of your research results. You should take time to discuss what they show and what they mean. Why did certain things happen or not? What went right and what went wrong? What are the implications of the study? Finish the presentation with your conclusions and remember to refer back to your original aims.

When giving a presentation from a computer, try not to include too much information on any one slide. Use the slides as prompt cards by bulleting the key facts which will be spoken about. Try and include some pictures or diagrams to make the work interesting. Make eye contact with those who you are presenting to and look confident; it is your research, you know what you did. Try to face your body posture 45 degrees to your audience as it can help you with the eye contact you need along with seeing the slides for your presentation. Finally, try to ensure you point to the presentation with your hand nearest the presentation so that you don't face in the opposite direction to the audience. You worked hard at this project so be proud of your efforts and show it off.

C Check your understanding

1 Complete the following reference correctly using the Harvard referencing system:
   Joe Bloggs and Ann Onymous, Introduction to Sports Project (5th ed). Hodda/Stowten. 2016

2 Why are search engines not a suitable reference when listing your search?

3 Using the internet, search for an article on sports nutritional supplements. Reference this website correctly.

4 Explain the differences when writing an introduction, discussion, and conclusion within a research project.

Meeting distinction criteria
(B D2 , C D3)

1 Create a project proposal and present it to your peers.

2 Create a project action plan with a timetabled outline of the progress review.

3 In groups of three, conduct a small-scale research experiment and summarise your report on one piece of flip chart paper:
   ○ You need to prepare a research title
   ○ Outline and apply the method you propose to use
   ○ Collect, summarise and analyse your results
   ○ Briefly evaluate its outcomes
   ○ Present your findings to the class.

Further reading

Coolican, H., (2014). *Research Methods and Statistics in Psychology (Sixth edition)*, Routledge.

George, D. and Mallery, P., (2013). *IBM SPSS Statistics 21 Step by Step: A Simple Guide and Reference (13th edition)*, Pearson.

Kent, M., (2007), *Oxford Dictionary of Sports Science and Medicine (Third edition)*, Oxford University Press.

Lynch, C. (2010), *Doing your Research Project in Sport: A Student Guide (Active Learning in Sport Series)*, Learning Matters.

Useful websites

BBC Bitesize

www.bbc.co.uk/education

Explorable – Think outside the box

https://explorable.com/

Maths is Fun

www.mathsisfun.com/

Social Research Methods

www.socialresearchmethods.net/kb/

Sports Science

http://sportsci.org/

References

Beam, W.C. and Adams, G.M., (1993), *Exercise Physiology Laboratory Manual (Seventh edition)*, McGraw-Hill Higher Education.

Coolican, H., (2014), *Research Methods and Statistics in Psychology (Sixth edition)*, Routledge.

George, D. and Mallery, P., (2013), *IBM SPSS Statistics 21 Step by Step: A Simple Guide and Reference (13th edition)*, Pearson.

Kent M., (2007), *Oxford Dictionary of Sports Science and Medicine (Third edition)*, Oxford University Press.

Lynch, C. (2010), *Doing your Research Project in Sport: A Student Guide (Active Learning in Sport Series)*, Learning Matters.

Price, M., (2013), *Lab Reports and Projects in Sport & Exercise Science: A Guide for Students*, Routledge.

10 Physical activity for individual and group-based exercise

About this unit

The health and fitness industry offers many opportunities for qualified instructors to lead exercise sessions for individuals and groups. However, as more and more people have come to understand the benefits of exercise the types of people that an instructor may encounter have increased significantly. To be an effective instructor you would be dealing with people from different age groups, from younger to older, who have specific needs. You may encounter people with different medical conditions who are training to manage these conditions.

Working with individuals and groups is dependent on you developing working relationships with your clients. This involves getting to know your clients as well as possible so that you can meet their training needs and deliver the results that they want.

This unit is practically based and to ensure that you learn about how to plan and deliver individual and group sessions you need to get as much experience of instructing these types of sessions. Leading a session can be hard initially but it becomes easier as you gain experience of leading more and more sessions. It is particularly important to spend some time after a session thinking about how the session went and what you did well, what problems arose and how they could be improved in the future.

Learning aims

The aims of this unit are to:

A Explore the processes of health screening prior to physical activity participation

B Examine different types of exercises for individual and group-based exercise sessions

C Undertake planning and instructing of individual and group-based exercise sessions.

How will I be assessed?

This unit will be assessed by assignments that have been designed internally by your tutors. It is likely that there will be three assignments for you to complete, where you will be able to apply the skills and knowledge you have learnt to a range of individual and group exercise sessions.

Learning aim A achievement

For distinction standard, learners will interpret the results of the lifestyle questionnaire and health screening tests for one participant and evaluate how the results can have an impact on that person's lifestyle and exercise choices. They will need to be able to provide suggestions as to what sorts of exercises would be suitable for that person, with reasoning and justification from evidence discovered in the screening processes.

Learning aims B and C achievement

For distinction standard, learners will evaluate how they planned and delivered the exercise session, making judgements and forming conclusions on their own performance. Their judgements will be based on the effectiveness and appropriateness of the exercise techniques and communication methods they planned and used for cardiovascular endurance training and resistance training, and the ways in which they adapted each exercise to make them more or less challenging, depending on the needs of the participant(s). Their judgements will be supported by evidence of observation and/or feedback from the participant(s) taking part in the session. From this evaluation they will justify their areas of strength, areas where improvement is needed and recommendations for how these improvements can be made.

How will I be graded?

The table below shows the assessment criteria for this unit. To achieve a pass grade you must meet all the P criteria; to achieve a merit grade you must achieve all the P and all the M criteria; to achieve a distinction grade you must achieve all the P, M and D criteria.

Pass	Merit	Distinction
Learning aim A: Explore the processes of health screening prior to physical activity participation		
A P1 Perform participant screening and interpret the results for one individual.	**A M1** Perform effective screening using methods that are appropriate to the needs of one individual.	**A D1** Evaluate the screening from one individual justifying suggestions for progression into exercising safely.
A P2 Explain factors that can affect safe exercise participation for three individuals in different specific groups.	**A M2** Assess the factors affecting the safe exercise participation of three specific individuals, making recommendations for their safe exercise participation.	
Learning aim B: Examine different types of exercise for individual and group-based exercise sessions		
B P3 Explain different methods of cardiovascular endurance training and resistance training for an individual exercise session.	**B M3** Compare different methods of cardiovascular and resistance training for individual and group exercise sessions justifying the use of each for participants with different needs.	
B P4 Explain different methods of cardiovascular endurance training and resistance training for a group exercise session.		
Learning aim C: Undertake planning and instructing of individual and group-based exercise sessions		
C P5 Plan and deliver a safe and effective individual or group-based exercise session that includes the performance of safe and effective cardiovascular and resistance-based exercises.	**C M4** Plan and deliver a comprehensive individual or group-based exercise session using effective communication and offering adapted and alternative exercises for different specific participants.	**B C D2** Evaluate own performance in the planning and delivery of an individual or group-based exercise session to specific participants, justifying choices of adapted and alternative exercises, session, strengths and recommendations on self-improvement.
C P6 Review own performance in the delivery of an individual or group-based exercise session, identifying strengths and areas for improvement.	**C M5** Review own performance in the delivery of an exercise session, explaining strengths and providing recommendations on self-improvement.	**C D3** Evaluate the impacts of participant assessment and choice of exercise on the planning and instructing of safe and effective exercise sessions.

Table 10.1 Assessment criteria

A Explore the processes of health screening prior to physical activity participation

(**A P1** , **A P2** , **A M1** , **A M2** , **A D1**)

A1 Participant screening

Health screening must be completed for all participants before they can take part in any exercise or be prescribed a programme of exercise. This can be difficult to do before a large group exercise session but it must be done to protect both the instructor and the participant. Screening will provide information about the participant's medical history, history of significant injuries and physical activity level. Screening is part of the legal 'duty of care' that an instructor must provide to participants in any exercise session that they conduct and without screening they would be guilty of negligence and at risk of being sued for resulting damages.

Selection of appropriate screening methods

There are several different methods that can be used for screening, such as a PAR-Q (physical activity readiness questionnaire), lifestyle questionnaires and informed consent.

Questionnaires

The PAR-Q form is the absolute minimum standard of screening that should be used. It will provide basic medical information for you and provide the information that you need to decide whether the participant needs to be referred to their GP before starting exercise. It acts as protection for both the instructor and the participant. An example of a PAR-Q form is provided (see Figure 10.1).

Another questionnaire that you should use is a lifestyle questionnaire and this will provide information about what an individual does on a daily basis and any factors that may affect their health and fitness. In particular you need to know about their current activity level and what their nutrition is like. It is also useful to find out about their job and the amount of stress that they face on a daily basis. This will give you an idea about factors that may influence their adherence to their exercise programme and any barriers there may be to achieving their goals.

An example of a lifestyle questionnaire is shown on page 324 (Figure 10.2).

Informed consent

An informed consent form makes the participant aware of what to expect during exercise and the risks associated with exercise. It also states that participation in exercise is voluntary and that

Key terms

A PAR-Q assesses whether a participant is healthy enough to take part in a programme of exercise.

A lifestyle questionnaire provides information about factors such as activity level, nutritional habits and stress levels which may affect the individual's health and fitness.

An informed consent form ensures that the participant knows what to expect from their exercise programme and any associated risks.

	Question	Yes	No
1	Do you have a bone or joint problem which could be made worse by exercise?	☐	☐
2	Has your doctor ever said that you have a heart condition?	☐	☐
3	Do you experience chest pains on physical exertion?	☐	☐
4	Do you experience light-headedness or dizziness on exertion?	☐	☐
5	Do you experience shortness of breath on light exertion?	☐	☐
6	Has your doctor ever said that you have a raised cholesterol level?	☐	☐
7	Are you currently taking any prescription medication?	☐	☐
8	Is there a history of coronary heart disease in your family?	☐	☐
9	Do you smoke, and if so, how many?	☐	☐
10	Do you drink more than 14 units of alcohol a week?	☐	☐
11	Are you diabetic?	☐	☐
12	Do you take physical activity less than three times a week?	☐	☐
13	Are you pregnant?	☐	☐
14	Are you asthmatic?	☐	☐
15	Do you know of any other reason why you should not exercise?	☐	☐

If you have answered yes to any questions please give more details:

_____

_____

_____

If you have answered yes to one or more questions you will have to consult with your doctor before taking part in a programme of physical exercise.

If you have answered no to all questions you are ready to start a suitable exercise programme.

I have read, understood and answered all questions honestly and confirm that I am willing to engage in a programme of exercise that has been prescribed to me.

Name _____ **Signature** _____

Instructor's name _____ **Instructor's signature** _____

Date _____

Figure 10.1 The PAR-Q form

Section 1: Personal details

Name _____

Address _____

_____

_____

Home telephone _____ Mobile telephone _____

Email _____

Occupation _____

Date of birth _____

Section 2: Goals

1 What are your long-term goals for the next year?

_____

_____

_____

2 What are your medium-term goals for the next three months?

_____

_____

_____

3 What are your short-term goals for the next four weeks?

_____

_____

_____

Section 3: Current training status

1 What type of training are currently engaged in?

☐ Muscular strength ☐ Muscular endurance ☐ Speed ☐ Flexibility ☐ Aerobic fitness

☐ Power ☐ Weight loss or gain ☐ Skill-related fitness ☐ Other (please state) _____

2 How would you describe your current fitness status?

_____

_____

3 How many times a week do you train?

_____

4 How long do you train for in each session?

_____

Section 4: Your nutritional status

1 On a scale of 1 to 10 (1 being very low quality and 10 being very high quality) how would you rate the quality of your diet?

_____

2 Do you follow any particular diet?

☐ Vegetarian ☐ Vegan ☐ Vegetarian and fish ☐ Gluten-free ☐ Dairy-free

3 How often do you eat? Note down a typical day's intake.

_____

_____

_____

_____

4 Do you take any supplements? If so, which ones?

_____

_____

Section 5: Your lifestyle

1 How many units of alcohol do you drink in a typical week? _____

2 Do you smoke? _____ If yes, how many a day? _____

3 Do you experience stress on a daily basis? _____

4 If yes, what causes you stress (if you know)?

_____

_____

5 What techniques do you use to deal with your stress?

_____

_____

Name _____ Signature _____

Trainer's name _____ Trainer's Signature _____

Date _____

Figure 10.2 A lifestyle questionnaire

they are free to stop exercising at any point. An example of an informed consent form is shown here (Figure 10.3).

Interviews

Questionnaires can be completed by participants on their own or as part of an interview. The benefit of asking the participant questions face-to-face is that they are more likely to give fuller answers rather than write down minimal amounts of information. Also, they may try to hide information from you and you may be able to pick up that something is being withheld by the way the question is answered. Interviews also allow you to ask follow-up questions to gain more information about an injury or medical condition. An interview will also enable to start developing rapport with the participant as you get to know and understand them better.

Observation

Observation is a less formal way of gaining information about a client. You can gain information about a person from the way they walk and their posture as to whether they are free from injury or have potential issues.

Health monitoring tests

Health monitoring tests will provide information about the functioning of a participant's cardiovascular and respiratory systems. Typical tests might be those that measure blood pressure, resting heart rate, body mass index (BMI), waist to hip ratio, or lung function. If you have any doubt about a participant's health, after interpretation of their results against normative data, they should be referred to their GP before they commence exercise. This is because exercise can exacerbate any medical conditions that they may have and put the participant at risk.

Table 10.2 provides an indication of when a participant should be referred to their GP prior to commencing any exercise programme.

---

1 Explanation of the exercises

You will perform a series of exercises which will vary in its demands on your body. Your progress will be observed during exercise and stopped if you show signs of undue fatigue. You may stop exercise at any time if you feel unduly uncomfortable.

2 Risks of exercise

During exercise certain changes can occur, such as raised blood pressure, fainting, raised heart rate, and in a very small number of cases heart attacks or even death. Every effort is made through screening to minimise the risk of these occurring. Emergency equipment and relevantly trained personnel are available to deal with any extreme situation which occurs.

3 Responsibility of the participant

You must disclose all information in your possession regarding the state of your health or previous experiences of exercise as this will affect the safety of exercise. If you experience any discomfort or unusual sensations it is your responsibility to inform your instructor.

4 Freedom of consent

Your participation in exercise is voluntary and you are free to deny consent or stop at any point.

I have read this form and understand what is expected of me and the exercise I will perform. I give my consent to participate.

Participant's signature: _____

Print name: _____

Date: _____

Instructor's signature: _____

Print name : _____

Date : _____

Figure 10.3 An informed consent form

Health test	GP referral
Resting heart rate	100+ bpm
Blood pressure (at rest)	160/100 mmHg and over
Body mass index	> 30 kg/m²
Waist: hip ratio	Males > 1.0
	Females > 0.85
Body fat	Males > 30%
	Females > 40%
Lung function	PEFR of 100 less than acceptable score

Table 10.2 Measures on health tests for GP referral

Reasons for temporary deferral of exercise for participants

It is always best to adopt a safety-first policy when it comes to a participant's health and rather than take any risks it is best to refer a participant to the GP if you have any doubts about their suitability for an exercise programme.

Concerns over health from screening process

Having completed a PAR-Q form, a lifestyle questionnaire and possibly interviewed the participant you will have gained sufficient information to make a judgement about their health. Any concerns about their health should result in a referral to their GP.

Contraindications

A contraindication is a condition or factor that would serve as a reason to prevent an individual taking part in an exercise programme. For example, medical conditions such as diabetes or coronary heart disease would act as contraindications to exercise. Participants with contraindications to exercise need GP clearance before taking part in exercise. Once they have provided the instructor with a letter they can then take part in exercise but they may have to adapt some exercises and train at an appropriate intensity.

Pregnancy is a contraindication to exercise and can be a complex condition for an instructor to manage. This is because pregnancy affects the mother's body in different ways depending on the stage, or trimester, that they are in. For example, a woman in the first trimester (0–12 weeks) will have low blood pressure and may feel dizzy, while in their third trimester (25 weeks to birth) they may have high blood and a lowered pulse rate.

Other contraindications, in addition to those identified in Table 10.2, include:

- Diabetes mellitus
- Lung disorders
- Blood pressure medications and blood thinners
- Coronary heart disease
- Angina pectoris
- Joint conditions.

> **Key term**
>
> A contraindication is any condition or factor that may prevent an individual participating in an exercise programme or in specific exercises.

Maintaining client confidentiality

As an instructor you will be dealing with information that the participant may be sensitive about. It is likely that they don't want their medical conditions or lifestyle factors to be made public. This means that any records that are kept on participants should not be shared with anyone else without the permission of the participant. For example, it may be necessary to share your findings with someone in the medical profession but it must be done with the permission of the participant.

All records must be held in a secure place with hard copies of questionnaires being secured in a locked place and soft copies being saved in an area accessible only with a confidential password.

Meeting distinction criteria

To meet the distinction criteria for learning aim A, you need to be able to show knowledge of the screening process and skills of evaluation to deal with the information that you have collected. You will need to be able to use the PAR-Q form, lifestyle questionnaire and informed consent forms and then use interviewing and questioning to gain as much information as you can about a person.

Once you have completed these screening methods you will need to evaluate the information by picking out the strengths of the individual and their weaknesses. It is best to make lists of each and then once you have the lists you can look at whether any of weaknesses would be a contraindication to exercise. You can check back on the contraindications to exercise to help you make this judgement and then you can make the decision as to whether they can progress safely into an exercise programme or if they need to be referred to the GP for clearance prior to exercise.

When you are explaining the decision that you have made you can use the lists of strengths and weaknesses to justify the decision that you have made. Remember that if you have any doubts then it is always best to refer a person to their GP.

Activity: Process of health screening prior to physical activity participation

Task 1

Work with a partner to complete participant screening by using the PAR-Q form and the lifestyle questionnaire. Once your partner has completed the questionnaires, check through them and then ask questions about any areas where you think you will need more information before allowing them to exercise. Once this process has been completed, decide whether they are healthy enough to participate in physical activity or whether they need to be referred to their GP.

Task 2

Taking all the information that you have gathered on the participant, evaluate the information by drawing up lists of strengths and weaknesses. In particular, examine the weaknesses and compare the information to the contraindications to exercise and then decide whether the participant is healthy to progress to exercise or whether they need to be referred to their GP. Using the strengths and weaknesses of the participant, provide reasons to justify the decision you have made.

A2 Factors affecting safe exercise participation

Exercising safely means that exercises chosen must be appropriate to the individual participant and not make any medical conditions or injuries worse. Particular attention should be paid to participants with back conditions or injuries as many exercises can worsen the pain they are experiencing.

Exercise intensity

Exercise intensity, or how hard the participant is exercising, is another area where particular attention must be paid. There needs to be a balance between working hard enough to gain a training effect but not too hard that the exercise intensity becomes dangerous to the participant's health.

Appropriate to health related level

When deciding on the appropriate intensity for a participant you need to examine lifestyle factors, such as age, activity level, amount of alcohol and cigarettes consumed; you need to consider any medical conditions or injuries and finally you need to look at the physical shape of the participant. Taking into account all these factors you then need to make a decision on how hard they are going to work; for example, are you going to stick to walking, brisk walking or would a gentle jog or run be appropriate?

Once you have made your decision about intensity you will need to carefully monitor the participant to assess whether your decision has been appropriate and be ready to make them work at a lower, or higher, intensity.

Methods of measuring exercise intensity

The intensity of aerobic or endurance exercise has traditionally be measured by monitoring an individual's heart rate because heart rate will increase in a linear fashion in response to increases in exercise intensity. Maximum heart rate (MHR) is assumed to be calculated by the following formula:

220 – age

It is worth being aware that this is an estimate and individuals' heart rates can vary drastically so it is worth observing the participant's response to exercise as well as monitoring their heart rate. In particular you are looking at the participant's breathing, colour and sweating. If there are significant changes and it looks like the participant is working too hard it is worth reducing the intensity.

Training zones for cardiovascular health and fitness are a useful way to monitor whether exercise is conducted at an appropriate intensity. Guidance on appropriate training differs between different authors but the general consensus is that to make aerobic gains exercise should be conducted at around 60–85% or 60–90% of maximum heart rate.

It should be said that a participant who has a low aerobic fitness level (e.g. a beginner) should exercise at the lower end of this zone (60–70% of MHR), a participant of moderate aerobic fitness level in the middle of this zone (70–80% of MHR) and a participant who is highly aerobically conditioned at the top end of the zone (80–90% of MHR). A training zone of 55–65% may be appropriate for a participant who has a very low fitness level (Hagerman, 2012).

Another method that can be used to monitor intensity of exercise is the rating of perceived exertion (RPE): this was developed by Gunnar Borg and is a scale which can be used by the participant to rate how hard they feel they are working. Rather

than monitoring heart rate the participant is introduced to the scale and then asked during the aerobic session where they feel they are on the scale of 1–15 (see Table 10.3).

1	Rest
2	Extremely light
3	
4	Very light
5	
6	Light
7	
8	Somewhat hard
9	
10	Hard
11	
12	Very hard
13	
14	Very, very hard
15	Exhaustion

Table 10.3 Borg's 15-point scale

Borg's scale has been modified to a ten-point scale (see Table 10.4) because some participants have found working between 1 and 15 difficult.

1	Extremely light
2	Very light
3	Moderate
4	
5	Somewhat hard
6	
7	Hard
8	Very hard
9	Extremely hard
10	Maximal exertion

Table 10.4 Borg's modified RPE scale

To achieve aerobic fitness gains the participant needs to be working around 12 to 15 on the 15-point scale and around 6 to 7 on the modified scale.

Factors affecting safe participation for specific groups

Children

Children are in a stage where their bodies are undergoing constant and significant change. In particular the skeletal and muscular systems are developing rapidly and thus careful consideration needs to be taken when deciding on resistance training.

Obviously the term 'children' covers a large age group and there will be significant differences between individual children so it is difficult to promote a 'one size fits all' approach to prescribing exercise. Each child needs to be considered in their own right.

The main considerations in training young people are their bone and muscle development. When a long bone develops the growth occurs at the end of a bone in the growth cartilage which is present predominantly at the epiphyseal plate. Once the epiphyseal plate has completely hardened (ossification) then the bone will stop growing. If this growth cartilage becomes damaged bone growth may be impaired.

The concern is that trauma to the bone can affect the supply of blood to the bone. The blood will deliver a steady supply of oxygen and nutrients to the bone, and without this supply the bone will not develop.

As the child grows their muscle mass will steadily increase. At birth muscle mass accounts for around 25% of the baby's body weight and once they have reached adulthood it makes up around 40%. As muscle mass increases strength will also increase. Strength will peak soon after their peak height has been reached.

Children under the age of 14 should not participate in resistance training and strength training should not be conducted with under 16s. It can take until an individual is in their early 20s before the skeletal system is fully developed so care must be paid to this age group. If children do participate in resistance training it should involve light weights with high repetitions (15–20 reps per exercise) and rest days in between sessions.

Pregnant women

Pregnancy is a time of rapid and significant change for a woman and only specially qualified instructors should consider instructing pregnant women in exercise. A pregnancy will go through three stages called 'trimesters' and there are different physiological changes that a woman's body will undergo during each trimester.

During the first trimester (0–3 months) the hormone progesterone will cause blood vessels to dilate (expand) and this will cause the following effects:

- lower blood pressure
- increased heart rate
- feelings of sickness, fatigue and dizziness.

In the first trimester the woman may experience symptoms of light-headedness and fatigue.

During the second trimester (4–6 months) the blood volume starts to increase and red blood cell count will start to rise causing the following effects:

- blood pressure returns to normal
- heart rate returns to normal
- mother starts to feel less nauseous and fatigued.

After about the fourth month of the pregnancy the hormone relaxin is released which has the effect of making the joints more mobile. Its role is to allow the pelvis greater movement for when the head of the baby passes through it. It will also affect every other joint in the body and cause the mother to become less stable.

During the third trimester the mother becomes much larger in weight and size and this becomes a problem. She will experience the following effects:

- rise in blood pressure
- lowered heart rate
- difficulty raising heart rate.

The mother will become even less stable and have difficulty balancing. She may also be fairly breathless and have back pain. She will experience difficulty getting up from and down to the floor.

The American College of Gynaecologists presented a set of guidelines that instructors should follow when dealing with pregnant participants, as follows:

- Choose regular, moderate-intensity exercise.
- Stationary cycling, swimming, walking and stretching are recommended.
- Avoid exercises which have jerky, bouncy movements and involve jumping or sudden changes in direction.
- Don't exercise lying on your back after the fourth month.
- Use longer periods of warming up and cooling down.
- Stop exercise when fatigued and consult a doctor if any unusual symptoms occur.

Older people

When instructing older people there are specific considerations that you need to make. Up to the age of 35 the structures of our body such as muscle and bone are building up. However, after this age we start to lose muscle and bone, and the tendons and ligaments become weaker. In particular, the ageing adult will lose their type 2 muscle fibres and as a result strength will be decreased.

In summary, older people will experience the following physiological changes:

- loss of muscle mass
- loss of bone density
- gains in body fat
- loss of muscular strength
- loss of muscular endurance
- decline in aerobic fitness
- lower ability to maintain balance.

When instructing older people it is essential that you have been through a thorough screening process and referred them to the GP if you had any doubts about their suitability to exercise. It is important to have longer warm-ups and cool-downs for older participants as their bodies' systems are not able to respond as quickly as a younger person's. They should last around 10 minutes and involve gradual increases and decreases in intensity. For resistance training the intensity should be relevant to their level of

strength and increases in intensity should be applied progressively. High impact exercises should be avoided and life-related movements incorporated into the routine. Importantly, all exercise should be pain free and if there is pain then the range of movement or exercise should be changed.

Distinction activity: Factors affecting safe participation in exercise for different groups (A P1 , A M2)

Explain what factors you would have to consider when instructing children, older adults and pregnant women in exercise sessions. Based on these factors make recommendations about the type of exercise that would be advisable for each group to ensure that exercise is conducted safely.

A Check your understanding

1. Explain what information will be gained from a PAR-Q form.
2. Identify the role of an informed consent form.
3. Identify five contraindications to exercise.
4. Explain what an appropriate intensity for endurance exercise is.
5. Explain the main considerations you need to take when instructing children.
6. Explain four guidelines you need to follow when instructing pregnant women.
7. Identify four physiological changes older people will experience.

B Examine different types of exercise for individual and group-based exercise sessions (B P3 , B P4 , B M3 , BC D2)

B1 Performing exercise safely

Ensuring participant safety should always be the prime consideration when instructing exercise sessions and to do this you need to take a range of factors into account. In particular, you need to ensure that participants and the environment are appropriately prepared for exercise. This means providing an appropriate warm-up/cool-down and exercises that are appropriate for the needs of the participant.

Warm-up

A warm-up is performed to make sure that the heart, lungs, muscles and joints are prepared for the activities which will follow. The warm-up also helps to activate the nervous system. A warm-up can be specific to the training session which is being performed or it can be more general.

A warm-up can be summarised as having three main objectives:

1 to raise the heart rate

2 to increase the temperature of the body

3 to mobilise the major joints of the body.

A typical warm-up will involve the following components:

- a pulse raiser
- a mobiliser (for joints)
- stretching for muscles.

Key term

A warm-up prepares the body for the exercise to follow and consists of a pulse raiser, mobility exercises and dynamic stretches.

Pulse raiser

The pulse raiser involves rhythmical movements of the large muscle groups in a continuous manner. This would involve cardiovascular (CV)-type activity such as running, rowing or cycling. The pulse raiser should gradually increase in intensity as time goes on. A pulse raiser would typically last for around five minutes but may go on for ten minutes. At the end of the warm-up the heart rate should be just below the rate that will be achieved during the main session. A person who is fitter is able to warm-up more quickly as their body is used to it, while an unfit person will take longer and needs to warm-up more gradually.

Mobiliser

The mobiliser is used to enable the joints to become lubricated by releasing more synovial fluid on to the joints and then warming them

up so they become more efficient. This means moving joints through their full range of movement. The movements will start off through a small range and slowly move through a larger range until the full range of movement is achieved. The joints that need to be mobilised are shoulders, elbows, spine, hips, knees and ankles. If a trainer is clever they can use the pulse-raising movements to also mobilise the joints. For example, rowing will have the effect of raising the pulse and mobilising all the joints.

Stretch

There are different types of stretching that be conducted. In a warm-up, dynamic stretching is preferable to static stretching. It is very important for the specific preparation of the muscles for the movements which are due to follow.

The benefits of dynamic stretching are that it:

- keeps the heart rate raised
- stretches muscles specifically through the range of movements they will be doing
- activates the nervous system and improves synchronisation between the nerves and muscles.

To perform dynamic stretching you need to copy the movements in the session you will perform. These movements are repeated in a steady and controlled fashion. In performing a set of ten repetitions you slowly speed up the movement as the set progresses. Figures 10.4, 10.5 and 10.6 show dynamic stretches.

Cool-down

The aim of a cool-down is to return the body to its pre-exercise state. If you consider that once you have finished training your heart rate is still high and the blood is still being pumped to your working muscles, you will need to slowly bring the heart rate back to normal.

Key term

A cool-down returns the body to its pre-exercise state and consists of an exercise to lower the pulse and stretching, both maintenance and developmental.

Figures 10.4, 10.5 and 10.6 Dynamic stretches: squat and press; rear lunge and arm swing; chest stretch

The cool-down has four main objectives:

1 to return the heart to normal
2 to get rid of any waste products built up during exercise
3 to return muscles to their original pre-exercise length
4 to prevent venous pooling.

The aim of the cool-down is opposite to that of the warm-up in that the pulse will lower slowly and waste products such as carbon dioxide and lactic acid are washed out of the muscles. Also, as the muscles work during the main session they continually shorten to produce force and they end up in a shortened position. Therefore, they need to be stretched out so they do not remain shortened. Also, as the heart pumps blood around the body, circulation is assisted by the action of skeletal muscles. The skeletal muscles act as a 'muscle pump' to help return the blood to the heart against gravity. If the participant stops suddenly the heart will keep pumping blood to the legs, but because the muscle pump has stopped the blood will pool in the legs. This causes the participant to become light-headed and they may pass out.

The cool-down consists of the following activities:

● a pulse lowerer
● stretches – maintenance and developmental.

Pulse lowerer

To lower the heart rate you need to do the reverse of the pulse raiser. First, choose a CV-type exercise involving rhythmical movements and the large muscle groups. This time the intensity starts high and slowly drops to cause a drop in heart rate. This part should last around five minutes and an exercise bike is a good choice because it enables the client to sit down and relax as well. The gradual lowering of the intensity allows the muscle pump to work and avoid venous pooling. You want to ensure the pulse rate is around 100 to 110 bpm at the end of the pulse lowerer.

Stretches

Two types of stretching can be used in the cool-down: maintenance and developmental. A maintenance stretch is used to return the muscles worked to their pre-exercise state. During training they will be continuously shortened and they need to be stretched out to prevent shortening. Stretching will also help eliminate waste products from the muscles and also prevent soreness the next day. A maintenance stretch is one where the muscle is stretched to the point of discomfort and then is held for around ten seconds or until the muscle relaxes and the stretch goes off. All muscles worked in the main session will need at least a maintenance stretch.

Developmental stretching is used on muscles which have become short and tight. They may be short because they have been over-trained or due to the positions adopted on a daily basis. If a person is sitting down all day, either in front of a computer or driving, they may develop shortened pectorals, hamstrings, hip flexors and adductors.

Developmental stretching involves stretching a muscle and then holding it for around ten seconds until it relaxes. Once it has relaxed the stretch is increased and held for ten seconds; this is repeated three times.

Safe alignment of exercise position

While there are specific points about alignment on all exercises there are two rules that apply for all exercising.

Firstly, the spine needs to be maintained in its 'neutral' position at all times. Neutral spine is described as a position where the natural curves of the spine are maintained and, in particular, the natural curve in the lumbar vertebrae. The opposite of neutral spine is where the spine moves into a position where there is only one curve. Loss of neutral spine places stress on the individual vertebrae and specifically the intervertebral discs which are fluid-filled structures which cushion the ends of bones between joints. Loss of neutral spine can lead to prolapsed intervertebral or 'slipped' disc where the fluid in the disc leaks out and creates pressure on the nerve. This results in extreme pain and loss of function.

Secondly, joints where there is a force passing through need to be kept 'soft'. This means that the joints are not fully extended but held in a position just short of full extension. It is particularly important that the knees are kept soft when the participant is standing up and that the elbows are kept soft when there is a force going through them, such as when weights are held above the body.

Health and environmental factors

Before you start instructing a group or individual session you will need to check the environment that you are operating within thoroughly. This means that before any exercise starts you need to check the following:

- All equipment is in working order.
- All cables are strong.
- Floor area is clear of equipment and cables.

- The area is at an appropriate temperature.
- There is adequate ventilation in the area.

Once you are happy the environment is safe your session can begin.

Developing client coordination

Exercises can either be complex or simple depending on the number of joints that are moving and the balance requirements of an exercise. For example, a bicep curl is a very simple exercise because it only involves movement at one joint and it does not challenge balance particularly. However, a lunge movement is complex as it involves movement at three joints, the hip, knee and ankle, and it challenges balance as it involves the body moving through a wide range of movement. A complex exercise should be made simpler by breaking down the exercise and then slowly building it back up again. Complex exercises could also be done by using just body weight and then progressing to weighted bars and barbells.

Intensity

Intensity relates to how hard a participant is working. Intensity can be modified by increasing the speed of movement during an activity or increasing the workload (weight) that is being moved. The intensity of walking can be changed by increasing speed, introducing a gradient or by the participant carrying weights. The intensity of an exercise such as a bench press can be changed by increasing weight or by moving from a resistance machine to a bench or even completing the exercise on a stability ball.

Impact

The terms high and low impact exercises relate to the amount of force that is being sent though the body. A high impact force occurs when feet or hands leave the ground and then return to the ground. For example, running is a high impact activity while walking is a low impact activity as there is always one foot in contact with the ground. High impact forces are dangerous when a person has a bone or joint injury or condition. The size of the high impact force is dependent on the weight of the body leaving the floor and thus they are more dangerous for heavier people.

Low impact exercises are preferable for older people as well as heavier people. They are also recommended for pregnant women who should avoid high impact exercise.

Alternative exercises for specific participants
It is very good practice in group exercise to offer at least three alternatives to each exercise. They can be referred to as level 1, level 2 and level 3 activities. For example, a press-up could have a box press-up as level 1, a press-up from the knees as level 2 and a full press-up as level 3. Walking, jogging and running could provide three levels for a cardiovascular exercise. This way the exercise session becomes accessible for participants of differing fitness levels.

B2 Types of cardiovascular exercise

Cardiovascular exercise aims to improve aerobic endurance by raising the heart rate into the aerobic training zone and then holding it there for a minimum of 20 minutes. There are a range of cardiovascular training methods that can be used. For gym-based exercise there are usually treadmills, stationary cycles and rowing machines. However, if you are in an environment without any equipment, such as a sports hall or a home training session, you will need to be more creative when designing cardiovascular exercise. You will need to use exercises that involve moderate intensity, whole body movements, such as skipping or jumping jacks.

Cardiovascular machines

The **treadmill** is a piece of equipment that can be used by everyone and it offers a range of intensities to work at. The least conditioned participants can walk at a normal pace and then this can be increased to a brisk walk, gentle jog, jog, run and up to sprinting for the fittest participants. Most treadmills will also be able to produce a gradient that can increase the intensity level. The treadmill is probably the most versatile piece of equipment because it can offer benefits for people of all fitness levels. While the treadmill focuses predominantly on muscles of the lower body (gluteus maximus, quadriceps, hamstrings and calves), the core muscles will also be working and there is a small amount of work produced by the muscles of the shoulder and arms.

By comparison the **cycle** offers only contractions in the muscles of the lower body (particularly the quadriceps and gluteus maximus) but it is still a very effective cardiovascular workout and can be useful for participants who find a seated position more comfortable. For example, pregnant women could find cycling to be more comfortable as it would support the additional weight created by the foetus. The intensity of cycling is easily increased by increasing the level on the cycle machine. The act of cycling focuses on a small number of muscles and if a participant is deconditioned they find that they tire very quickly and as a result it is not always the best exercise for beginners and less fit participants.

Figure 10.7 A treadmill

Figure 10.8 A cycling machine

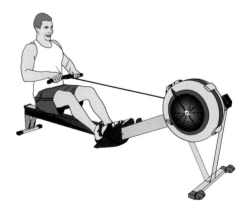

Figure 10.9 A rowing machine

The **rowing machine** offers an effective upper and lower body workout. In particular, the gluteus maximus, quadriceps, trapezius, latissimus dorsi and biceps muscles will be worked. Again, the intensity can easily be modified by increasing the resistance that is rowed against but also the amount of power put into each rowing stroke and the speed of each stroke. The rowing machine is not suitable for participants who have back injuries or back pain. The rowing machine is also the CV activity that relies most on using the correct technique. If the incorrect technique is used the exercise can seem very easy or it can lead to an increased risk of injury.

Cardiovascular exercises

These cardiovascular exercises can be used individually or as part of a group. Jogging requires a lot of space, such as a track or access to the outdoors; however, the other exercises can be done indoors in a much smaller space. You can produce a mini circuit for your participants by setting four of the cardiovascular exercises and then spending 60 seconds on each exercise before moving on to the next. This could be done continuously over 20 minutes or rest periods could be introduced. The intensity that each exercise can be performed at is always adaptable as well. For example, step-ups can be done by using differing heights of steps or by modifying the speed of the movements. Step-ups can be modified by changing the way the participant steps as well; for example, they may start to produce wide steps on the box so that they step to the far sides of the box. Also, they could step sideways on and off the box or perform a knee lift or heel flick once they stepped onto the box.

Figure 10.10 Jogging

Figure 10.11 Skipping

Figure 10.12 Jumping jacks

Figure 10.13 Step-ups

Figure 10.14 Shuttle runs

Using these types of exercise for cardiovascular training requires a bit more imagination and creativity on behalf of the trainer; however, they can still produce an effective cardiovascular session.

B3 Types of resistance-based exercises

Resistance-based exercises

Resistance-based exercises involve a range of methods where resistance can be applied to overload a muscle group. The traditional methods are dumbbells, barbells and resistance machines which are available in gyms; however, these methods may not be suitable for circuit training or training participants at home. However, there is equipment available that can be used outside the gym environment.

Dumbbells, barbells, resistance machines and bands offer the potential to work all the muscle groups of the body, particularly if they are used in conjunction with an exercise bench. Resistance-based exercise can be used to produce different training effects – strength, hypertrophy (muscular development), toning and muscular endurance. It may be difficult to produce strength gains and hypertrophy with resistance bands and body weight exercise but additional bands can be introduced to exercises and the complexity of body weight exercises can be increased as well. In comparison, producing strength gains and hypertrophy is relatively easy when using free weights (dumbbells and barbells) and resistance machines as the resistance can be adjusted by adding additional weights.

There is a debate about whether training with free weights or resistance machines are better.

Figure 10.15 Dumbbells

Figure 10.16 Barbells

Figure 10.17 A resistance machine

Figure 10.18 Bands

Figure 10.19 Body weight

Resistance machines are often favoured because they support the body weight and offer fewer health and safety risks, such as the risk of injury through dropping weights or poor technique. However, when you sit a participant down they will stop using many muscle groups in the body, such as the core muscles of the abdominals and the back that would be needed when standing up. Even a simple exercise like a bicep curl will be more beneficial if done with free weights rather than resistance machines because in addition to working the biceps there will be muscle contractions in the core muscles and the legs so more energy is used.

Weight training exercises

Free weights offer a whole range of exercises that will work all the muscles of the body. Examples of popular weight training exercises are shown here.

Figure 10.20 Front raise

Figure 10.21 Bent arm pullover

Figure 10.22 Shoulder press

Figure 10.23 Lateral raise

Figure 10.24 Flyes

Figure 10.25 Bicep curl

Figure 10.26 Lunge

Figure 10.27 Squat

All of these exercise can be adapted to make them more difficult and not just by increasing or decreasing the amount of weight used. For example, lunges are a complex exercise as they demand high levels of balance and body control as well as the movement of three joints; however, by decreasing the length of the lunge or the depth of movement they could be made simpler. For a beginner they may actually be holding onto something as they lunge. To make them harder you can introduce more weight or introduce walking lunges where they lunge and then, rather than returning to their start position, they take a step forwards. It is worth spending time with weight training exercises and finding how each exercise can be adapted to make it harder or easier.

Body weight exercises

If you are instructing participants in environments outside the gym, transporting equipment can be a problem. Many circuit training sessions are conducted in sports halls or even village halls and many one-to-one sessions are conducted in participants' homes. This is why body weight exercises can be very useful as they require no equipment at all. It can be difficult to continually apply overload with body weight exercises but it is possible with a little creativity. For example, press-ups can be done in different positions – box press-ups, press-ups from the knees and full press-ups. However, if you want to produce additional resistance you can add a resistance to the participant's back by pushing down gently as

Figure 10.28 Press-ups

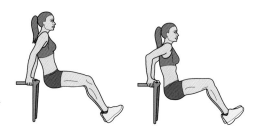

Figure 10.29 Tricep dips

Figure 10.30 Plank

Figure 10.31 Sit-ups

Figure 10.32 Lunge

Figure 10.33 Squat

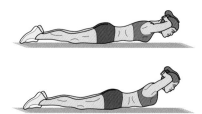

Figure 10.34 Prone back raise

they push up or you could introduce clap press-ups where they have to push themselves off the floor and clap between press-ups. Also, introducing press-ups on a stability ball can make them more difficult as well.

Applying manual resistance, where you push down on the participant, can be used in all the following exercises to increase the resistance level they are working at. It is important to be gentle and not push too hard so as to injure the participant.

B4 Activities for an individual exercise session

Gym-based exercise session

Instructing an exercise session in a gym environment is much easier than an exercise session in other environments as the equipment is all provided for you and is generally of good quality. In the gym environment you have access to areas for warm-ups, cool-downs and core exercises as well as for cardiovascular and resistance exercise.

Cardiovascular exercise

Gyms will usually contain the following equipment:

- Treadmills
- Cycles
- Rowing machines
- Cross trainers.

You can choose the equipment for your participant by assessing which would be safest and most effective to meet their needs. Remember that walking on a treadmill is likely to be an activity that all participants can perform. The aim is to get the participant to complete 20 minutes of cardiovascular exercise in a session. This can be done in one complete 20-minute session or it could be broken down into four bursts of 5 minutes using different equipment. For less conditioned participants it is preferable to break it down into smaller sessions and provide rest in between sessions.

Resistance exercise

In the gym you will usually be able to choose between free weights and resistance machine exercises. Some gyms will also have cable machines and other ways of applying resistance. In a gym session you should aim for between 8–10 resistance exercises that cover all the muscle groups at least once. It is important that the major muscles (pectorals, latissimus dorsi, trapezius, gluteus maximus, quadriceps and hamstrings) are worked first before the minor muscles are worked. It is also important to complete the more difficult exercises, such as lunges and squats, early in the session before muscle groups experience fatigue.

B5 Activities for a group-based exercise session

Circuit exercise session

A circuit exercise is an excellent way of instructing groups of people and ensure that they get an interesting and varied workout. A circuit can also be developed for an individual in their home or in a space such as a hall.

Circuit training sessions usually last 1 hour with 3–4 circuits being performed during that time. The warm-up and cool-down will last around 10 minutes each. Core training can either be done after the circuits or as a part of the circuit. A circuit will contain between 8–12 stations dependent on the amount of equipment and space that is available. The aim is to allocate 1 minute for each station and this would include rest. For example, you may spend 30 seconds working on a station and then 30 seconds resting until the next exercise begins. For this unit we will focus on circuits that contain 8 stations.

Stations to improve aerobic endurance

When choosing stations to improve aerobic endurance you need to choose exercises that use large muscle groups and can be performed in a steady and rhythmical manner. The aim of these stations is to raise the heart rate and keep it high. On these types of station you will either work for the full 60 seconds or you would work for 45 seconds and then rest for 15 seconds. The following exercises can be used to develop aerobic endurance (see figures 10.35–10.42).

Figure 10.35 Shuttle runs

Figure 10.36 Jogging on the spot

Figure 10.37 Jumping jacks

Figure 10.38 Spotty dogs

Figure 10.39 Squat thrusts

Figure 10.40 Knee lifts

Figure 10.41 Step-ups

Figure 10.42 Skipping

Stations to improve muscular strength and endurance

When choosing stations to improve muscular strength and endurance you will need to ensure that the exercises cover all the muscle groups in the body. If focusing on strength then the weights used would be slightly heavier than those used for muscular endurance and the work period would also be slightly shorter to allow more rest time between exercises. Exercise can utilise dumbbells and barbells but you should also consider using resistance bands and body weight to apply resistance. The following exercises can be used to develop strength and muscular endurance (see figures 10.43–10.56).

Figure 10.43 Shoulder press

Figure 10.44 Dumbbell flyes

Figure 10.45 Upright row

Figure 10.46 Lateral raise

Figure 10.47 Bicep curl

Figure 10.48 Tricep extensions

Figure 10.49 Dumbbell lunge

Figure 10.50 Barbell squat

Figure 10.51 Calf raise

Figure 10.52 Tricep dips

Figure 10.53 Press-ups

Figure 10.54 Lunge

Figure 10.55 Squats

Figure 10.56 Side bends

Circuit cards

When planning your circuit, you will need to produce cards that introduce each station to the participant. The cards should be as visual as possible and attractive to look at. They need to contain the following information:

1   **Name of exercise** – state the name of each station that the participant will be working at on each card.

2   **Diagram** – a diagram that shows the correct movement and technique that should be produced for each movement.

3   **Teaching points** – there should be a minimum of three teaching points for each exercise. They should be specific for each exercise rather than being generic in nature. For example, for a squat you might put in the following teaching points:

   ● Feet should be shoulder width apart.
   ● Squat down to a position where the thighs are parallel to the floor.
   ● Keep heels on the floor throughout the movement.

Generic teaching points would include:

   ● Keep the spine in its neutral position.
   ● Breathe out as you work against the resistance.

As the participants are exercising you should ensure that they are following the teaching points correctly.

Adaptations

Adaptations make the exercises suitable for all participants. Some exercises will be too difficult for a participant or potentially make an injury or medical condition worse. For example, you may be concerned that a step-up exercise may make a participant's knee injury worse so you would suggest that they step up and down on the spot.

Progressions

Progressions can be used to make exercises more difficult if a participant is finding that an exercise is becoming too easy.

Alternatives

When instructing a circuit session, the instructor must provide at least three alternatives for every exercise. These would represent three levels of difficulty so that the session is suitable for all fitness levels. For example, for squats the three levels may be:

Level 1: Body weight squat

Level 2: Squat with dumbbells

Level 3: Squat with barbell

Alternatively, the three levels could represent different weights being used.

Circuit training layouts

To keep circuit training sessions varied you can lay the session out in different ways. Different layouts will be suited to different spaces that are available to you.

The following five layouts (see figures 10.57–10.61) are samples of how you could present your circuits. You can also make up your own layouts to suit the exercises that you are including in your session.

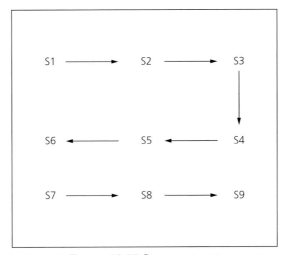

Figure 10.57 Square circuit

Figure 10.58 Lined circuit

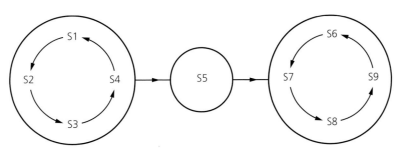

Figure 10.59 Bow tie circuit

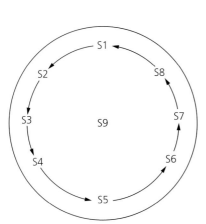

Figure 10.60 Circular circuit

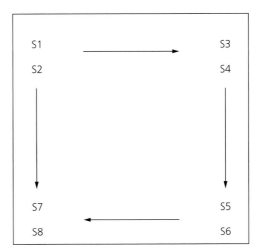

Figure 10.61 Corner circuit

B Check your understanding

1   Explain the benefits gained from a warm-up.
2   Identify three components of a warm-up.
3   Explain the benefits gained from a cool-down.
4   Identify when you would use developmental stretching in a cool-down.
5   Choose a resistance training exercise and identify three alternatives for that exercise.
6   Explain why a treadmill may be a better choice of cardiovascular exercise than a cycle for a deconditioned participant.
7   Explain whether free weights or resistance machines are preferable for muscular strength and endurance work.

Activity: Different types of exercise for individual and group-based sessions

Task 1

Imagine you are in the situation where you have instructed a participant in a health and fitness gym.

1   Explain four different types of equipment that you could use for improving a participant's cardiovascular fitness.
2   Explain different types of resistance equipment that could be used to improve a participant's strength and muscular endurance. For example, you may choose to look at resistance machines, dumbbells, barbells and cables.

Task 2

Imagine you are in the situation where you have to instruct participants in a group training session, such as circuit training.

1   Explain four different ways that you could use for improving the participants' cardiovascular fitness.
2   Explain different types of resistance equipment that could be used to improve the participants' strength and muscular endurance. For example, you may choose to look at resistance bands, body weight, dumbbells and barbells.

Task 3

Compare the different types or ways that you chose for training aerobic endurance and strength and muscular endurance. In particular, give reasons why different types of training would be most suited to specific participants.

Case study

Meet Joanna Howe

Joanna is a self-employed exercise instructor. She is involved helping people to achieve their health and fitness goals in a safe and effective manner. She is based in a gym where she works one on one with a variety of participants. In particular, her work involves her instructing training techniques to participants and providing motivation as well as support and encouragement to help participants achieve their goals.

When Joanna started working at this gym she got involved in delivering circuit training sessions three times a week. She loves this work because the sessions are upbeat and exciting and she gets to meet a lot of people. Some of the people have become one-to-one clients as they have asked for advice and guidance after the circuit session finishes.

She particularly enjoys the variety that circuit training offers and she prides herself that she has never instructed the same circuit session twice. She does find that she spends a lot of time planning exercise sessions for her participants and has had to keep going to workshops and training days to keep up to date with exercises and develop some new ideas.

1 Do you think that you would like to work as a self-employed instructor like Joanna?
2 What do you think are the benefits and drawbacks of her work?

C Undertake planning and instructing of individual and group-based exercise sessions

(P5 , P6 , M4 , M5 , D2 , D3)

C1 Aims and objectives of the exercise session

It is important to have a clear picture about what your session is aiming to achieve. The aims and objectives of your session will influence every decision you make about which exercises to include.

Individual or group-based session

The first decision to make is whether the session will be individual or group-based. This may be dictated by other people or the facilities that are made available to you.

Gathering information from the participants to determine aims and objectives of the exercise session

As part of the lifestyle questionnaire it is best to ask the potential participants about their current training status and then to find out what it is exactly that they would like to achieve from their training programme.

Training programmes can have several aims and objectives, particularly if the participant has a performance related goal to work towards. The following list shows the range of aims and objectives a participant may have:

- Improve aerobic endurance
- Improve muscular endurance
- Improve muscular strength
- Increase hypertrophy
- Improve flexibility
- Improve core strength
- Decrease percent body fat
- Improve body composition
- Improve sport-specific fitness.

If a participant has the aim of completing a specific event, such as a 10 km run, they may identify that they have several objectives that will all contribute to their running performance. For example, they would benefit from improving aerobic endurance, muscular endurance, flexibility and core strength.

C2 Individual exercise session planning

Appropriate exercises are identified

Once the aims and objectives have been established you can use the principles of training, particularly the principle of specificity, to plan a session to address the participant's aims. It is important to have a sound knowledge of a range of exercises so that you know what effect they will have on the participant and be able to select the ones most appropriate for the participant.

Appropriate sequence of exercises

The first decision to make is whether the aerobic endurance or resistance training components come first in the training programme. There is no straight answer to this as it depends on the needs of the participant. However, there are certain considerations that you need to make before deciding on this.

If the participant's main aim is aerobic endurance then it should make up the majority of the programme and should be done before the participant becomes fatigued, so at the start of the programme. However, resistance training exercises require more skill and they are best done when the participant is fresh as skill level decreases as fatigue increases. A good compromise is to split the resistance exercises into two groups – the more complex exercises and the more simple exercises. The more complex exercises, involving movement at more than one joint, can be done early in the programme while the simpler can be done later. The aerobic endurance component could be broken down into two or three smaller chunks.

For example, the programme may show the following structure:

1 Warm-up
2 First block of aerobic endurance training (10 minutes)
3 Complex resistance exercises (e.g. squats, lunges, bench press, bent over rows)
4 Second block of aerobic endurance training (10 minutes)
5 Simple resistance exercises (e.g. bicep curls, triceps extensions, lateral raises, calf raises)
6 Core exercises (e.g. plank and bridge)
7 Cool-down.

Alternately, you may decide to plan training so that aerobic endurance and resistance training are done on different days.

Appropriate timings of each exercise

Timing of aerobic endurance is again dependent on the aims of the participant. As a minimum you would aim for 20 minutes aerobic endurance exercise three to five times a week; however, if the participant is aiming to complete a half marathon or a marathon then this would be significantly higher.

Resistance training should account for between 30–45 minutes, again dependent on aims. After 45 minutes it is likely that the participant will have accumulated so many waste products that they won't be able to perform the exercises safely. Fatigue can seriously affect form on an exercise and increase the risk of injury.

Selection of correct equipment for the session

Once you have decided on the exercises that you will be instructing you will need to ensure that you have the correct equipment available.

Adapting a gym-based exercise programme to ensure appropriate progression and/or regression

When you are selecting exercises for your participant you need to offer exercises that would represent a progression from the current choice in terms of difficulty. For example, you may suggest that your participant starts working their pectorals on a chest press resistance machine. This can be adapted so that they move to a barbell bench press, then a bench press using dumbbells and even onto a dumbbell press lying on a stability ball. Each step represents an increasingly difficult method of training the pectorals. Alternatively, regression could be represented by taking these steps backwards.

It is worth spending some time considering how you can make exercises more challenging or making them simpler. This gives you a greater choice of exercises but also helps you to ensure that your participants will always be progressing.

C3 Group exercise session planning

Warm-up

Warming up a group of participants is more of a challenge than working with just one as you may have a group of mixed fitness levels. You can usually use a mixture of walking, brisk walking and running to raise the heart rate. The warm-up should steadily increase in intensity as it progresses. However, you also need to incorporate some mobility work and some dynamic stretching work which may allow the heart rate to drop. It is best to intersperse the mobility and stretching components between the heart rate raising activity and ensure that the last part of the warm-up raises the heart rate into the participants' heart rate training zones.

Main component

The main component may be aimed at improving cardiovascular fitness, strength or muscular endurance or even a mixture of the three. It is always good practice to have two to three cardiovascular (CV) endurance stations in a circuit to keep the heart rate high and if it is a CV endurance session then there may be four to five CV stations with the other stations focused on working the larger muscle groups as this acts to keep the heart rate high as well.

A session aimed at strength and muscular endurance is likely to have stations that cover all the muscle groups with a focus on exercises that produce movement in more than one joint.

Cool-down

The cool-down is opposite to the warm-up in that the aim is to progressively allow the heart rate to lower. You may start with running and then lower the intensity to brisk walking and then just steady walking. Once the heart rate has been lowered you can do some stretching. It is best to start with standing stretches for the upper body before sitting/lying on a mat to stretch the lower body. The participants will appreciate sitting on the mat for a while after the session.

Length of time for each component

An exercise session will last for an hour and it usually takes around 5 minutes to get everyone organised at the start of the session and about 5 minutes to tidy everything away at the end. The warm-up and cool-down will both last around 10 minutes leaving 30 minutes for the main component. There are usually three circuits leaving 10 minutes per circuit so it could be organised into a circuit of ten stations where participants work for 1 minute on each station, or you may only have eight stations and allow 2 minutes rest between circuits. It all depends on what the aims of your session are and how kind you want to be!

C4 Pre-exercise session preparation

Health and safety for all participants must always be a priority and you must never assume that just because someone else has been using a facility that it is actually safe. You must make checks yourself prior to any activity.

Checking equipment

Firstly, you need to check that all equipment is in good working order and not in need of maintenance. You will have to keep some alternatives in mind in the event of any equipment being broken.

You also need to make sure of the following:

- all cables are in good condition
- you have collars to secure all free weights
- the floor is clear of equipment
- all equipment is securely in place.

These checks can be made before the participants arrive.

Ensuring area is sufficient and safe for the session

When selecting appropriate exercises you need to keep in mind that there needs to be sufficient space for exercises and that some exercises can only be safely done is larger spaces. For example, shuttle runs need large amounts of space so that participants don't collide with each other. Some exercises such as squats and lunges need relatively large amounts of spaces as they involve large ranges of movement and it is important that the participant is not unbalanced by another participant.

Appropriate temperature and ventilation

The environment should have a temperature of 18°C which is around room temperature. A room that is too cold can lead to injuries as it can be difficult to warm up muscles enough, while a room that is too hot can lead to problems with heat related conditions.

There should be appropriate ventilation as well so that a steady supply of fresh air is introduced to the environment and that stale air can be dispersed.

C5 Preparing participants for exercise

Check participants' ability and any medical conditions

It is important that participants are checked prior to exercise. You need to check that all clothing is appropriate and is not likely to get caught in any equipment. Watches and jewellery should not be worn as they can get caught in equipment or they may injure another participant if they get hit by another participant's arm.

Before every session you must check for participants' medical conditions and any injuries, such as back problems, that may have developed since the previous session. If you are aware of any problems you can adapt exercises accordingly.

You must also check the participants' aims and objectives as then you can offer alternatives and adaptations to allow for these aims and objectives.

Inform the participant on the physical and technical demands of each exercise and the purpose and value of each exercise

Before a circuit training session you can spend some time introducing the stations to the participants. You would do this by covering the following:

- the name of the exercise
- the purpose of the exercise
- the muscle groups worked
- the correct technique for the exercise
- teaching points
- adaptations and alternatives.

This educates the participants so that they become aware of the value of each exercise and the session as a whole. This can also act to motivate the participants as they see that their aims/objectives are being catered for.

Confirm or revise plans with the participant as appropriate

Once you have introduced the exercises to the participants you can ask them whether they understand everything or need any clarification. If a participant is unsure what they should be doing you can clarify it with them before moving onto the next station.

Demonstrate any specific movements

Demonstrations on all exercises are essential so that the participants are able to model their technique on yours. Having said that it is vital that your technique is perfect. You need to give a silent demonstration as most people find it difficult to process images and words at the same time. Once you have performed three to four repetitions silently you can do another two to three accompanied by teaching points so that they are aware what the main points of technique are.

Advise participants of the facility's emergency procedures

As health and safety is so important, the session should be preceded by a health and safety briefing. In this briefing you will need to cover the following information:

- procedure if the fire alarm goes off
- location of fire exits
- emergency assembly point
- location of first aid kit and resuscitator
- name and location of the first aider
- location of the nearest telephone
- location of the water station.

Once this information has all been covered, it is safe for participants to start exercising.

C6 Instructing an individual or group-based exercise session

When you instruct an exercise session you need to be actively involved in the session and keep moving around the area and interacting with the participants. You should be involved in some or all of the following activities during the exercise session.

Explain and correctly demonstrate each exercise

This is done by using a silent demonstration followed by running through at least three teaching points per exercise.

Communicate as appropriate to the needs of the participant and the environment

Communication can be done through the use of language and by choosing the right words and speaking clearly to participants. You can also use your body language to motivate participants by looking energised and moving quickly around the area.

Change position to observe participant

Observation of participants is extremely important and you need to aim to observe every participant on every exercise of the session. When observing you need to move around the participant and in particular gain a front-on and side-on view as you will gain different information from each perspective about their technique.

Monitor the safety and intensity of each exercise

Observing the participant's technique will ensure that they are completing the technique safely but you also need to ensure that they are working at the appropriate intensity. As you become more and more skilled as an instructor you will be able to monitor the intensity that they are working at by observing the following signs:

- depth and speed of breathing
- colour of their skin
- amount of sweating
- facial expressions
- body language
- whether they talk easily or need to keep taking breaths
- exercise technique.

Provide timely clear instructions and feedback

Instructions are providing information on how to perform a technique and you should focus on telling them what to do rather than what not to do. For example, you should say 'keep your knees soft' rather than 'don't lock your knees'. This is because the brain finds it difficult to process negatives and it can lead to the participant being more likely to do what you tell them not to do.

Adapt exercise with suitable progressions and regressions according to participant needs

As you observe your participants you will be assessing whether the exercises are appropriate to their skill level and fitness level. If you think that an exercise is too hard or too easy you can suggest that the participant changes to an exercise that is easier or more difficult.

Safe and effective cool-down activities

Once the session has been completed it is important to slowly lower the heart rate by progressively decreasing intensity. This can avoid venous pooling where the blood pools in the lower body and leads to dizziness and possible fainting. Stretching after exercise also helps to eliminate muscle soreness and maintains the muscles length by avoiding adaptive shortening of muscles.

Feedback to the participant on how they have performed

It is very important to feed back to participants about their progress as it can be very motivational. If the participant truly believes that they are making progress and making training adaptations it can increase the possibility that they will keep exercising and adhere to their training programme. At times it may be necessary to give some negative feedback to the participant but you must also offer positive feedback at the same time to keep them motivated and positive.

Allow the participant to feed back to reflect on the session and ask questions

Once you have completed the exercise session it is useful to gain feedback from the participants about the session. This is not meant as an opportunity for them to tell you how wonderful you are but so that you can gain information about the effectiveness of the exercises you selected and how you planned the session. They can also feed back to you about your instructional skills, how well you communicated with them and how well they were motivated.

Follow correct procedures for checking and putting away equipment

Once the session is complete you need to be aware of any damage that has occurred to equipment and then report it to the appropriate person. You also need to check that the participants haven't sustained any injuries and that there were no incidents during the session. Any injuries or accidents need to be reported through the appropriate paperwork.

The equipment needs to be put away in its correct place. Participants must use correct lifting and carrying techniques when transporting equipment.

Ensure the area is left in an acceptable condition for future use

The area where exercise has been conducted must be left tidy and clear from any hazards. If there are any liquids, such as water or sweat, then these should be wiped up. The area should be left in the same condition to which it was found.

C7 Reviewing own performance in providing an individual or group-based exercise session

To improve as an instructor it is vital to regularly review your performance and identify any changes that need to be made. You can receive feedback from a range of sources and it is all useful.

Feedback is information about performance. It is neither good nor bad, it is just information. It allows us to improve our performance in the following ways:

- **Track progression:** we can assess whether exercise sessions are having the desired effect on the participant. This can be done by assessing whether they are meeting their aims and by getting feedback from them.
- **Adapt sessions:** if they are not achieving their aims or an exercise session has had a negative response you can adapt the programme to achieve a different response.
- **Improve your own performance:** you need to identify any weaknesses you may have as then you can improve how you work with your participants. Strengths will always be strengths but you will only improve if you address your weaknesses.

Evaluate how well the exercises met the participants' needs.

Once the session has finished it is valuable to ask the participants questions about the effectiveness of the session. The participants will be clear about their needs so you can ask how well the exercises and the session in general met their needs. It is worth asking questions about specific exercises as then you will gain more detailed information.

Relationship with participants – how effective and motivational it was and how well the instructing style matched participants' needs Assessing your relationship with the participants can be difficult as you may not have access to their thoughts and they may not give you totally honest answers. You can ask them questions, but you will also have to use self-reflection and consider whether the participants worked as hard as they should and whether your style of motivation was effective for all participants.

Ways to improve personal practice

Once you have identified where your strengths and weaknesses lie you need to develop an action plan to work on the weaknesses. You may find that attending other instructors' classes is a good way to get ideas about how you could develop your own practice. Also attending training events and conferences is a good way to get ideas.

Value of reflective practice

Reflective practice involves spending some time after each session to think back on the session that you conducted and break it down into the skills you were using. Reflecting on your own experiences can provide vital information for you to review your performance.

When reviewing your performance you can break down your performance into the following skills:

- **Communication** – Verbal and non-verbal aspects, questioning and listening.
- **Decision-making** – Speed, timing, consequences and options.
- **Observation** – What you observed, what you may have missed.
- **Judgement** – Accuracy and consequences of your judgements.

(Adapted from Ghaye and Lillyman, 2006)

As part of your reflection process you may work with a colleague and observe each other's training sessions. This may give another perspective on your instructional skills and highlight issues you would not have considered yourself.

Meeting distinction criteria

To meet the distinction criteria for this unit you need to be able to evaluate your own performance and to evaluate the impact that your choice of exercises had on the planning and instruction of your exercise sessions. When you are preparing and instructing your session you need to be fully aware of the impact of your session and what is working well and what could be improved.

Firstly, you need to evaluate your own performance in instructing a session and in choosing the exercises. To do this you need to honestly decide what your strengths and your weaknesses were. You can do this by gaining information from your participants, a colleague or friend who observed the session and by assessing your own thoughts and feelings. You can consider your skills in communication, motivation, decision-making and instruction. It may also be useful to have your session filmed to give you a second chance to reflect on your performance. You will also need to justify your choices of adapted exercises and alternative exercise that you provided by providing clear, well thought reasons why you chose these adapted/alternative exercises rather than other ones.

Once you have considered your own performance and choices of exercises you need to make some recommendations about how you will improve your performance. You may answer the following questions:

- What will you do and not do in the next session?
- What training needs do you think you have and how can you meet these?
- How can you improve your communication and motivational skills?

Secondly, you need to assess the impact that your session and the exercises within the session had on the participants. Again you can answer questions:

- Which exercises worked well?
- Which exercises did participants find difficult or struggle with?
- To what extent did the exercise session match the fitness level and skill level of the participants?
- Were the exercises chosen well and were they in an appropriate order within the session?

Once you have answered these questions you can write a reflective account of the impact of the session on the participants.

C Check your understanding

1 Identify four possible aims a participant may have.
2 Explain how you may design an exercise session for an individual.
3 Explain how you may design a group-based exercise session.
4 Identify four checks you would make to establish a safe environment prior to exercise.
5 Explain three ways you could ensure that the exercise session you are instructing is safe and effective.
6 Identify three sources from where you could obtain feedback on your performance.
7 Explain why it is important to review and evaluate your performance after every exercise session.

Distinction activity: Undertake planning and instructing of individual and group-based exercise sessions (C P5 , C P6 , C M4 , C M5 , B C D2 , C D3)

Task 1 – Planning and instructing a session

Choose to instruct either an individual or group-based exercise session.

Then gather information about the participants and plan an exercise session that will last 1 hour. You will need to screen participants and find out about their specific needs and aims/objectives.

The exercise session will consist of a warm-up, aerobic endurance work, resistance training and a cool-down. The exercise session must have clear aims and objectives and the selected exercises must meet the needs of the participants and offer adapted exercises and alternatives that could be used by them.

Task 2 – Reviewing own performance

Once you have planned and then instructed the exercise session you need to gain as much information about the session as possible. You can do this by asking the participants for feedback on the session, either face-to-face or in writing. You may ask a friend to observe the session and then give you feedback on your performance. Your teacher may also be able to offer you feedback. You can also gain feedback from yourself about how you felt during the session and what you thought went well or needed improvement.

When gathering feedback you need to gain information on the following:

- How effective were the exercises you chose?
- Were the alternatives and adaptations suitable for all participants?
- What impact did they have on the participants?
- Was the order of exercises safe and effective?
- How well did you communicate with and motivate your participants?
- How well did you lead the session and were you always in control?

Evaluation involves you looking at your performance critically and rather than taking any feedback personally, you need to use the feedback to provide a basis for planning how you will improve your performance. You need to ask yourself the question, 'What can I do to improve my performance?'

Further reading

Ansell, M. (2008). *Personal training.* Exeter, Learning Matters.

Coburn, W.C. and Malek, M.H. (2012). *NSCA's Essentials of Personal Training.* Champaign, Human Kinetics.

Coulson, M. (2013). *The Fitness Instructor's Handbook.* London, A&C Black.

Kennedy-Armbruster, C. and Yoke, M.M. (2014). *Methods of Group Exercise Instruction.* Champaign, Human Kinetics.

References

Ghaye, T. and Lillyman, S. (2006) *Reflection and Writing a Reflective Account.* UK, Maisemore.

Hagerman, P. in Coburn, J.W., and Malek, M.H. (Editors) (2012). *NSCA's Essentials of Personal Training, (Second edition)*, Champaign, Human Kinetics.

Useful websites

Netfit

www.netfit.co.uk/#

Sports Fitness Advisor

www.sport-fitness-advisor.com/circuit-training.html

Web MD

www.webmd.boots.com/women/guide/beginners-guide-to-exercise

Total Fitness

www.totalfitness.co.uk/facilities-classes/circuit-training

13 Nutrition for sport and exercise performancee

About this unit

As we seek to gain an extra edge in our sporting performances and to maximise the effects of our training so the spotlight has fallen on areas other than training. Nutrition has been shown to be an increasing area of interest. We know that training brings benefits to sporting and exercise performance and we know that eating properly brings benefits. However, if we combine the correct training with the correct nutritional benefits then the gains are multiplied. Nutrition is as important for people who are seeking to improve their performance as it is to people seeking their fitness gains or weight management objectives. It is important for all people involved in sport and exercise to know what a healthy balanced diet is and know how to adapt it for specific types of sport in order to maximise their performance.

How will I be assessed?

This unit will be **assessed externally** through a written task set and marked by the awarding organisation.

You will be provided with a pre-released case study two weeks prior to the supervised assessment period. The case study will focus on an individual that requires guidance on nutrition in response to their personal and training needs that are impacting on their performance. You should spend approximately 8 hours over the course of the two weeks that you have the pre-released case study carrying out research and making notes. You may take notes of up to four sides of A4 paper into the assessment with you.

In the assessment you will be given the set task which contains more information on the individual that you were given in the pre-release material and questions relating to assessing your ability to interpret, modify and adapt a nutritional programme for the given individual.

You will be given 2 hours to sit the assessment and the number of marks available is 50.

The assessment will be twice a year from 2018 – in January and the summer.

How will I be graded?

The assessment outcomes show the knowledge and the skills that you are expected to be able to demonstrate in the assessment. It is important when you are covering the unit content that you keep these objectives in mind as they show what you need to be able to do with the information you are learning about.

Assessment outcomes

The exam is split into four different assessment outcomes (AOs) and each will be covered in varying amounts within the paper. The command words that will be used for each assessment outcome are also provided, to help you to gain an understanding of the depth and breadth that you will need to include in your responses for each AO.

AO1 Demonstrate knowledge and understanding of nutritional principles, strategies and concepts

AO2 Apply knowledge and understanding of nutritional principles, strategies and concepts to sport and exercise performance in context

AO3 Analyse and evaluate information and data relating to an individual's needs in order to determine modifications and guidance to improve sport and exercise performance

AO4 Be able to develop and adapt a nutritional programme in context with appropriate justification

How will I be graded?

Grade Descriptors

Grade descriptors are provided by Pearson to give an idea of what sorts of skills and knowledge need to be shown to achieve a pass, merit or a distinction grade. However, further grades are available including:

U – Unclassified

Level 3 Pass

Learners are able to modify a programme for an individual that demonstrates knowledge and understanding of nutrition and fluid intake relevant to the requirements in the context. They will show an understanding of the health and well-being requirements of the individual, and are able to apply relevant nutritional principles and strategies to the scenario, evidencing the ability to conduct relevant research. They will identify the impact of factors affecting digestion and absorption of nutrients and fluids. Learners will be able to provide guidance and justify proposed adaptations/modifications to the nutritional programme which are appropriate to the individual, and realistic in the context of the specified sporting event and phase of activity.

Level 3 Distinction

Learners will be able to modify a programme for an individual that demonstrates a thorough knowledge and understanding of nutrition and fluid intake relevant to the requirements in the context, supported by justification and the application of relevant research. They will show a detailed understanding of the health and well-being requirements of the individual, and apply specific nutritional principles and strategies entirely relevant to the scenario. They will demonstrate an analytical approach to the identification of factors which will impact on digestion and absorption of nutrients and fluids and will justify actions to overcome these factors. Learners will provide guidance and recommendations which will contain sustained lines of argument leading to a cohesive nutritional programme that is entirely appropriate to the individual, and realistic in the context of the specified sporting event and phase of activity.

Command words meanings

In your external assessment, each question will start with one of the possible command words or terms, so it is important that you know what each means so that you know how to answer each question. Look at page 8 for a table of these.

A Principles of nutrition and hydration

You will need to be able to understand the basic nutritional principles and their effect on the body's ability to function in sport and exercise performance.

A1 Basic nutritional principles

Nutritional measurements and units

Calories and kilocalories

One calorie (cal) is defined as the amount of energy or heat needed to raise the temperature of 1 L of water by 1 °C. Therefore, the term kilocalorie or kcal is used, as one calorie would only raise the temperature of 1 ml of water by 1°C.

Joules and kilojoules

While in Britain we use calories, the international unit for energy is a joule (J) or more specifically, a kilojoule (kJ). To convert a kcalorie into a kjoule, you need to use the following calculation:

1 kcal = 4.2 kjoules

Recommended daily allowance (RDA)

The amounts of each nutrient we require have been worked out by a group of nutritional experts. They have worked out the nutritional needs of a number of different types of people, for example, children, adults, older people, etc. As you will see later on in this unit, each nutrient has a different function in the body and the amount we need will differ. There are a lot of different terms used to express the quantities of nutrients required in our diet, but the most commonly used term is the recommended daily allowance (RDA).

Metabolism

Metabolism is a term that refers to many different chemical processes occurring continuously inside the body that allow life and normal functioning. These processes require energy from food. The number of kcals your body burns at any given time is regulated by your metabolism.

Metabolism involves two complementary processes: catabolism and anabolism.

Catabolism is the breakdown of food components into their simpler forms which can then be used to provide energy. **Anabolism** is the combination of chemicals to create new substances.

Metabolism is controlled by hormones (chemical messages secreted by the glands of the endocrine system). The rates of catabolism and anabolism are monitored to ensure they stay in balance.

The amount of metabolism carried out in a person's body is called the metabolic rate. The body's metabolic rate is divided into two states: the number of kcals burned at rest (basal) and the number of kcals burned during physical activity.

Basal metabolic rate (BMR)

Basal metabolic rate is the minimal caloric requirement needed to sustain life in a resting individual. This is the amount of energy your body would burn if you slept all day or rested in bed (24 hours).

Energy is needed while a person is at rest for the brain and nervous system to produce and transmit nervous impulses, the digestive system to break down and transport nutrients, for repair of damaged tissues that occurs on a daily basis, for the heart to beat and the body to breathe. The brain will use between 500–600 kcals per day and the liver and digestive system around 300–400 kcals per day. These organs are dependent, under normal circumstances, predominantly on glucose and thus have a glucose requirement of around 1000 kcals per day between them. A variety of factors will affect your basal metabolic rate: some will speed it up so you burn more kilocalories per day just to stay alive, whereas other factors will slow your metabolic rate down so that you need to eat fewer kilocalories just to stay alive.

1   **Age** – As you get older you start to lose more muscle tissue and replace it with fat tissue. The more muscle tissue a person has, the greater their BMR, and vice versa. Hence, as you get older this increased fat mass will have the effect of slowing down your BMR.

2   **Body size** – Taller, heavier people have higher BMRs. There is more of them so they require more energy.

3   **Growth** – Children and pregnant women have higher BMRs. In both cases the body is growing and needs more energy.

4   **Body composition** – The more muscle tissue, the higher the BMR; the more fat tissue, the lower the BMR.

5   **Fever** – Fevers can raise the BMR. This is because when a person has a fever, their body temperature is increased, which speeds up the rate of metabolic reactions (which will help to fight off an infection) and will result in an increased BMR.

6   **Stress** – Stress hormones can raise the BMR.

7   **Environmental temperature** – Both heat and cold raise the BMR. When a person is too hot, their body tries to cool it down, which requires energy; when a person is too cold they will shiver, which again is a process that requires energy.

8 **Fasting** – When a person is fasting, as in dieting, hormones are released which act to lower the BMR.

9 **Thyroxin** – The thyroid hormone thyroxin is a key BMR regulator; the more thyroxin produced, the higher the BMR.

Harris-Benedict equation (to calculate BMR)

In order to get a better idea of a person's BMR, a calculation called the Harris-Benedict equation (named after the person who devised it) takes into account your gender, body weight, height and age, because body size (weight and height) and age both affect your BMR.

Men: BMR = 66.5 + (13.75 x weight in kg) + (5.003 x height in cm) – (6.755 x age in years)

Women: BMR = 655.1 + (9.563 x weight in kg) + (1.85 x height in cm) – (4.676 x age in years)

To add in the activity levels of a person, the BMR that is calculated from the equations above is then multiplied by the activity factor which is taken from the following options:

Sedentary (little or no exercise): BMR x 1.2

Lightly active (light exercise/sports 1–3 days/week): BMR x 1.375

Moderately active (moderate exercise/sports 3–5 days/week): BMR x 1.55

Very active (hard exercise/sports 6–7 days a week): BMR x 1.725

Extra active (very hard exercise/sports and physical job or 2 x training sessions in a day): BMR x 1.9

Activity

Use the Harris-Benedict equation to work out your BMR.

Effect of activity level on BMR

Energy balance

We get energy from the food we eat. The amount of energy that we get from each food is shown by the amount of kilocalories – the more kilocalories the food has the more energy it contains.

Energy expenditure

We use this energy to produce movement and for our body to function to keep us alive, such as breathing and digesting food – this is known as energy expenditure. When our body moves it uses energy produced from food to move our muscles and this also produces heat energy. This is why we get hot when we take part in physical activities.

Energy intake

The foods and kilocalories that we consume is our energy intake.

Energy intake versus energy expenditure

If we consume more energy than we need we will store this extra energy as fat. However, if we consume less energy than we need we will lose body fat. If we consume the same amount of energy that we use, our weight will stay the same.

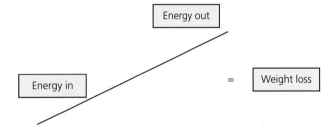

Figure 13.1 Energy taken in is less than given out, so weight is lost

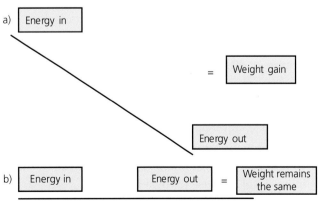

Figure 13.2a–b See-saw diagrams: a) Energy taken in is greater than given out, so weight is gained; b) Energy taken in is the same as given out, so weight remains the same

Usually, you will find that your energy in and energy out do not balance exactly every day – some days you may not feel very hungry and eat less than usual, other days you may eat more than usual.

Weight loss or weight gain occurs over a period of time when you are consistently eating less or more energy than you require.

For example, if you were to eat just 150 kilocalories (the equivalent of two slices of bread or a small packet of crisps) more than you required every day for 6 months, then you would gain almost half a stone in weight.

Physical activity

Calories used in different activities (intensity and length of time)

Different activities require differing amounts of energy. You are probably aware of these differences in some instances, for example, you may be able to walk at a steady rate over relatively long distances without feeling tired or out of breath; however, if you were to jog that distance you may well feel tired and you will be breathing much more quickly and your heart rate will be much higher.

Generally, activities that require you to move quickly will require more energy. Also, activities that use more muscle groups will require more energy. For example, swimming requires the use of both your upper body muscles and your lower body, which requires more energy than walking, which primarily uses your lower body muscles.

Table 13.1 shows average kcalories used per hour in a range of different activities.

The heavier a person is, the higher the intensity they will have to work for any exercises or sports that are weight-bearing, such as aerobics and badminton. Sports (such as cycling) that are not weight-bearing will not have such an effect on the intensity of exercise for heavier people.

Body composition

Tests can be carried out to assess the body composition of a person, to work out how much fat-free mass they have in comparison to fat mass.

Physical Activity	Average kcalories used per hour
Aerobics	480
Badminton	400
Basketball	745
Cleaning	312
Cricket	354
Cycling 9 mph	426
Hockey	570
Football	560
Gardening	420
Golf	360
Jogging	570
Rowing	510
Running	960
Skiing	500
Squash	900
Swimming	720
Table Tennis	288
Tennis	460
Volleyball	230
Walking	340
Yoga	264

Table 13.1 Activities and average kcalories used per hour (*Source:* adapted from *Medicine and Science in Sports and Exercise*)

Body mass index (BMI)

BMI is used to give us an idea about whether a person is underweight, normal weight or overweight; and if they are overweight, it gives an idea of the extent of the obesity.

This is worked out by using the following formula:

$$\text{Body mass index (BMI)} = \frac{\text{Weight (in kg)}}{\text{Height in m} \times \text{height in m}}$$

For example, a male who is 75 kg and 1.80 m tall:

$1.8 \times 1.8 = 3.24$

$75 \times 3.24 = 23.14$

Their body mass index will be 23.

The normative table then shows which class they fall into.

BMI classification	Obesity class	BMI (kg/m²)
Underweight		< 18.5
Normal		18.5–24.9
Overweight		25–29.9
Obesity	I	30–34.9
Obesity	II	35–39.9
Extreme obesity	III	> 40

Table 13.2 BMI classification

This test, however, is not appropriate for people who are very muscular, because muscle weighs more than body fat. A person with a very muscular build may well come out as obese from this test, which would be incorrect, as this test cannot differentiate between body fat and muscle content. The test is also not appropriate for use with older people, children or pregnant women as results are inaccurate.

Activity

Calculate your BMI, and from this, determine your BMI classification.

Bioelectrical impedance analysis (BIA)

This test gives a measure of body fat percentage and is therefore a more useful test of a person's body composition compared to the BMI test.

For the test, a Bioelectrical Impedance Analysis Analyzer will need to be used and electrodes attached to the person's right hand and right foot. A small electrical current is passed through the body which then provides a body fat percentage reading based on the fact that electrical current passes more easily through tissues that contain water compared to tissues that do not contain water. Fatty tissue does not contain water so this give a greater resistance for the electrical current to flow through which results in a higher body fat reading on the BIA.

The person taking the test will have to ensure that they are hydrated and have not consumed an alcoholic drink 48 hours prior to the test or taken part in high intensity exercise 12 hours prior to the test as this can affect hydration levels. If a person is dehydrated, the BIA test will overestimate their body fat percentage levels.

A person with a pacemaker or a pregnant woman should not be tested using this equipment.

A2 Macronutrients

For this topic you will need to be able to understand the different food groups, their function and how the body uses them.

The three macronutrients are:

- Carbohydrate
- Protein
- Fat.

The macronutrients are needed in large amounts in the diet and will all provide energy for the body. They are also used to build the structures of the body and produce functions needed to sustain life.

Carbohydrates

Almost every culture relies on carbohydrate as the major source of nutrients and calories, e.g. rice in Asia, wheat in Europe, the Middle East and North Africa, corn and potato in the Americas.

Carbohydrate should provide between 50–60% of calorie intake of the diet and its main role is to supply energy to allow the body to function. The energy content of carbohydrate is:

1 g provides 4 kcals

There are many sources of carbohydrates such as bread, rice, pasta, potatoes, fruit, vegetables, sweets and biscuits. They all differ in form slightly but will all be broken down into glucose because that is the only way the body can use carbohydrate.

Key term

Nutrients are chemical substances obtained from food and used in the body to provide energy, structural materials, and regulating agents to support growth, maintenance and repair of the body's tissues.

Functions of carbohydrate

1 Provides energy for the brain to function
2 Provides energy for the liver to perform its functions
3 Provides energy for muscular contractions at moderate to high intensities.

When carbohydrate foods are digested they are all broken down into glucose which is then absorbed in the small intestine and enters the blood stream. From the blood stream it can either be used immediately as energy or stored in the liver and muscles. When glucose is stored it is stored in the form of glycogen which is bound to water (1 g of glucose needs 2.7 g of water) for storage. However, the glycogen molecule is bulky and difficult to store in large amounts. The body can store around 1600 kcals of glycogen which would enable us to run for about two hours.

If you did not eat enough carbohydrates you would feel tired and lacking in energy. You would also find it difficult to take part in physical activities as you would not have enough energy for participation. Many people feel rather grumpy and find it hard to concentrate if they are not eating enough carbohydrates. This is because our brain needs a constant supply of carbohydrates for it to function properly.

Key terms

Glucose is the smallest unit of a carbohydrate. It is the main source of fuel for cells.

Glycogen is when the body does not need to use glucose for energy and it stores it in the liver and muscles. This stored form of glucose is made up of many connected glucose molecules and is called glycogen.

Types of carbohydrate

Carbohydrate comes in a variety of forms but they are all made up of molecules of sugar. These molecules of sugar are called saccharides and they come in different forms depending on the foods in which they are found. Eventually, through the process of digestion they will all become glucose. These saccharides will be found as one of the following:

● Monosaccharides
● Disaccharides
● Polysaccharides.

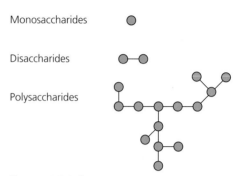

Figure 13.3 Structure of saccharides

Monosaccharides

These are one saccharide molecule on its own and there are three types of monosacharides:

● Glucose – occurs naturally in most carbohydrate foods
● Fructose – occurs in fruit and honey
● Galactose – does not occur freely but is a component of the sugars found in milk products.

Disaccharides

These are two saccharide molecules joined together by a bond and there are three types of disaccharides:

● Sucrose – glucose + fructose; it is most commonly found as table sugar
● Lactose – glucose + galactose; it is found in milk and milk products
● Maltose – glucose + glucose; it is found in malt products, beers and cereals.

Monosaccharides and disaccharides are commonly known as 'simple carbohydrates' because they are in short simple chains or exist as individual molecules.

Good sources of disaccharides

Activity

The following are sources of simple carbohydrates:

- Biscuits
- Tinned fruit
- Dried fruit
- Cakes
- Sweets
- Fresh fruit
- Jelly Babies
- Jaffa Cakes
- Fruit smoothies
- Fruit juice
- Sports energy drinks.

1 Put them in order of how healthy a choice you think each one would be.
2 Give three reasons why you have ranked the foods in this order.

Polysaccharides

Polysaccharides are long, complex chains of glucose molecules containing ten or more molecules. Due to their complicated structures they are called 'complex carbohydrates'.

To digest polysaccharides the bonds need to be broken down through the process of digestion so that they can become individual glucose molecules and be absorbed into the blood stream. However, if a complex carbohydrate is processed or cooked in any way then these bonds will start to be broken down before they enter the digestive system.

Polysaccharides or complex carbohydrates can come in either their natural or refined forms. Wheat and rice are naturally brown in colour due to their high levels of fibre, vitamins and minerals. Therefore, the brown varieties of bread, rice and pasta are of greater nutrient value than their white, refined varieties.

Good sources of polysaccharides

1 Wholemeal, wholegrain or granary breads
2 Wholemeal pasta
3 Wholegrain rice
4 Potatoes
5 Sweet potatoes
6 Vegetables
7 Pulses.

Figure 13.4 Carbohydrate-rich foods

Recommended daily amounts (RDA) of carbohydrates

Minimum recommended daily intake of at least 50% of total kilocalories consumed should come from complex carbohydrate sources.

The amount of carbohydrate a person should consume is based upon the activity level of the individual in terms of its length and intensity. If you only take part in low levels of activity you will need less energy and consequently need to consume lower levels of carbohydrates. This would place you in category A in Table 13.3. However, an endurance athlete would be training or competing for longer periods of time, would require greater amounts of carbohydrate and would therefore fall into category E.

Activity level	Recommended amount of carbohydrate in grams per kilogram of body weight
A Light (less than 1 hour a day/3–5 hours per week)	5g
B Light to moderate (1 hour a day)	6g
C Moderate (1–2 hours a day)	7g
D Moderate to heavy (2–3 hours a day)	8g
E Heavy (4 hours a day)	10g

Table 13.3 Activity levels and recommended amounts of carbohydrate

As with most nutrients, eating excess can lead to problems. Excessive consumption of sugar (e.g. sucrose) can lead to tooth decay and is linked to a number of major diseases (e.g. diabetes, obesity and coronary heart disease). Excess carbohydrate in the diet will be converted to and stored as fat. Thus it is possible to gain body fat even on a low fat diet if excess carbohydrates are eaten.

Glycaemic index (GI)

The rate at which carbohydrate foods are broken down and how quickly they raise blood glucose levels is measured via the glycaemic index. It is a ranking system which shows how quickly the carbohydrate is broken down and enters the blood as glucose in comparison to the speed glucose would enter the blood if consumed. Foods with a high glycaemic index break down quickly and rapidly increase blood glucose levels; table sugar is a good example of a food with a high glycaemic index. Pasta would have a lower glycaemic index, breaking down into glucose more slowly. It would also have less of an immediate effect on blood glucose levels, causing a slower increase over a longer period.

We deal best with foods of a low glycaemic index which release their energy slowly and over time. Foods of a high glycaemic index will cause a rapid release of glucose into the blood stream followed quickly by a rapid drop in blood glucose causing hunger and fatigue. The person who eats high glycaemic index foods will experience fluctuating blood glucose levels and be tempted to over eat the wrong type of food. High glycaemic index foods such as sweets, cakes, biscuits, fizzy drinks white breads and sugary cereals are linked to obesity and the development of type 2 diabetes. If a person eats low glycaemic index foods they will find that their stable blood glucose levels enable them to have energy and concentrate throughout the day.

Glycaemic index range
Foods will either be high, moderate or low glycaemic index.

Factors influencing glycaemic index
The speed a food is broken down and enters the blood stream is dependent on a range of factors.

High	Moderate	Low
Above 85	**60–84**	**Below 60**
Gluocose 100	Chips 75	Banana 52
Baked potato 85	White bread 70	White pasta 50
Parsnips	White rice 64	Porridge oats 49

Table 13.4 Glycaemic index range (*Source:* adapted from Bean, 2013, pp. 289–291)

The following will lower the speed glucose enters the blood stream:

1 The presence of fibre in the food
2 The presence of fat in the food
3 The presence of protein in the food
4 The type of saccharides present in the food*
5 Amount of carbohydrate eaten.

* fructose and galactose have to be converted into glucose before they can be used as energy; this process happens in the liver and takes a long time, so they enter the blood as glucose more slowly.

The following will increase the speed glucose enters the blood stream:

1 The length of the cooking process
2 The amount the food has been refined or processed
3 The riper the fruit has become.

Activity

Conduct an internet search using the key words 'glycaemic index' and print off a table showing the glycaemic of a range of food types.

Using your research notes, find out the glycaemic index of the following foods:

- Oranges
- French baguette
- Baked potatoes
- Muesli
- Ice-cream
- Baked beans
- Whole meal bread
- Bananas
- French Fries
- Wholemeal spaghetti.

Using the factors which affect glycaemic index explain why each food has their glycaemic index.

Fats

Fats are often perceived as being 'bad' or a part of the diet to be avoided. Contrary to this fats are vital to health and perform many important functions in the body. However, the intake of certain fats does need to be minimised and excess consumption of fats will lead to health problems.

Functions of fat

Fats and oils belong to a family called 'lipids' and they perform a variety of important roles in the body. Predominantly fats will supply energy for everyday activities and movement. They are described as being 'energy dense' because they contain a lot of energy per gram.

1 g of fat provides 9 kcals

The main functions of fat include:

- formation of the cell membrane
- formation of the myelin sheath which coats the nerves
- a component of the brain and nervous system
- protection of internal organs (brain, kidneys, liver)
- production of hormones (oestrogen and testosterone)
- transportation and storage of vitamins A, D, E, K
- constant source of energy
- store of energy
- heat production.

A fat deficiency in the diet is extremely rare in the western world. Most people are actually eating too much fat in their diet. However, people who are not eating enough fat in they would initially suffer from very dry and flaky skin and other deficiencies linked to reduced quantities of fat-soluble vitamins.

Types of fat

The difference between a fat and an oil is that a fat is solid at room temperature while an oil is liquid at room temperature.

The smallest unit of a fat is called a 'fatty acid' and there are different types of fatty acids present in the foods we eat. In particular, a fatty acid can be saturated or unsaturated and this is important because they will be shaped differently. In chemistry shape matters because it will influence the function performed. Therefore, different fatty acids will perform different functions in the body.

Triglycerides

Triglycerides are dietary fats in that they are how the fats we ingest are packaged. A triglyceride is defined as '3 fatty acids attached to a glycerol backbone'. Glycerol is actually a carbohydrate which the fatty acids attach to; during digestion the fatty acids will be broken off from the glycerol backbone to be used by the body as required. The glycerol will be used as all carbohydrates are used to produce energy.

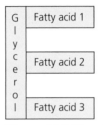

Figure 13.5 Structure of a triglyceride

Types of fatty acid

A fatty acid consists of long chains of carbon atoms with an acid group (COOH) at one end and a methyl group (CH_3) at the other. The structure of the chains of fatty acids attached to the glycerol molecule will determine whether the fat is classed as saturated, monounsaturated or polyunsaturated. If you think of different types of fats, such as butter, lard, sunflower oil or olive oil, you will notice that they differ in terms of their colour, texture and taste. This is because of the different types of fatty acids attached to the glycerol backbone.

Saturated fats

A saturated fat is one where all the carbon atoms are attached to hydrogen molecules; the chain is said to be saturated with hydrogen.

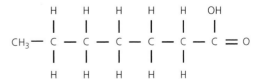

Figure 13.6 Saturated fatty acid

We can see that the carbon atoms each have single bonds between them and each carbon atom has four bonds. The hydrogen atoms possess a very slight charge and gently push away from each other. This has the effect of making the chain straight in shape. In chemistry shape matters as it affects function and it also makes the saturated fat solid at room temperature. This is because the fatty acids can pack tightly together with little space between each one. Saturated fats are also described as being stable or inert; this means that their structure will not change when they are heated. They will melt but the structure of the fatty acid chain stays the same. The majority of saturated fats come from animal sources.

Sources of saturated fats

Animal sources:

- Red meat
- Poultry
- Dairy products
- Eggs.

Plant sources:

- Coconut oil
- Palm oil.

Figure 13.7 Animal fats are sources of saturated fats

The Department of Health recommends a person should have a maximum of 11% of daily kilocalories coming from saturated fat; however, from recent research they found that the average saturated fat intake exceeded the recommended level and for people aged between 19 to 64 years was 12.6%.

Unsaturated fats

An unsaturated fat is one where there are hydrogen atoms missing from the carbon chain causing the carbon atoms to attach to each other with double bonds.

This is because carbon has to have four bonds and if there is no hydrogen present they will bond to each other. In this case the carbon chain is not saturated with hydrogen atoms and is therefore 'unsaturated'.

Monounsaturated fat

A monounsaturated fat is one where there is just one double bond in the carbon chain.

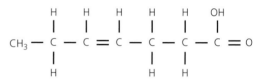

Figure 13.8 Monounsaturated fatty acid

Due to the slight charge the hydrogen atoms contain they will push each other away. Now that there are hydrogen atoms missing it will cause the chain to bend and become curved. The curved fatty acids cannot pack so tightly together so their appearance changes and they will be in liquid or oil form. They will also be less stable or more reactive. This is because of the double bonds between the carbon atoms. Carbon will only attach to itself if there is nothing else to be attached to and it will take the opportunity to break off and attach to something else if it can. If monounsaturated fats are heated they will change their structure.

Sources of monounsaturated fats
- Olive oil
- Peanut oil
- Avocados
- Rapeseed oil (Canola oil)
- Almond oil.

The Department of Health recommends a person should have a maximum of 12% of daily kilocalories coming from monounsaturated fat.

Polyunsaturated fat

A polyunsaturated fat is one where there are many double bonds in the carbon chain due to a shortage of hydrogen ions in the chain.

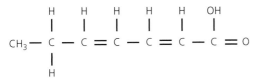

Figure 13.9 Polyunsaturated fatty acid

This has the effect of making the fatty acid even more curved and highly reactive in nature. They will also be in oil or liquid form. Polyunsaturated fats are highly unstable when heated to high temperatures and will change their structure.

Sources of polyunsaturated fats

- Sunflower oil
- Safflower oil
- Corn oil
- Fish oils
- Nuts
- Seeds.

The Department of Health recommends a person should have a maximum of 10% of daily kilocalories coming from these polyunsaturated fats.

Saturated versus unsaturated fats

Saturated fats have always received bad press until recently when people have realised they have an important role in the diet. Due to their stable nature they will always retain their structure. This is important because when they enter the fat cells the cells will recognise them and know what to do with them. Saturated fats are always stored as fat in the fat cells. Naturally occurring unsaturated fats, such as olive oil, will have very beneficial effects when they are stored in fat cells; for example, they will improve circulation, lower cholesterol levels and improve the health of hair, skin and nails.

Trans unsaturated fat

These occur when unsaturated fats are heated or processed in any way, because they then change their structure and start to look like saturated fats. They become altered structurally and when they enter the body they will be accepted into the fat cells because they look like saturated fats. Once inside the fat cells they start to cause damage to the cell and stop positive reactions occurring.

These have also been linked to heart disease and cancer and are present in some processed foods and deep fat fried foods.

Both butter and margarine contain fat, however, due to the margarine being an unsaturated fat (sunflower oil) it would appear to be beneficial to health. Sunflower oil is naturally a liquid and margarine is a solid product. This means it has been processed in some way and thus changed structurally. The butter will not be changed structurally because it is predominantly saturated fats. For these reasons the butter is a better health choice because it is a more naturally occurring product. In particular it is the cheap margarines which need to be avoided. If choosing a margarine check the contents for trans fats.

Essential fatty acids

The body can make all the fatty acids it needs except for two, the essential fatty acids (EFAs), which must be supplied in the diet. These fatty acids are omega 3 and omega 6.

Sources of omega 3 and 6
Omega 3 fatty acids:

- Oily fish (salmon, mackerel, herring)
- Flax oil
- Walnuts
- Soya beans.

Omega 6 fatty acids:

- Sunflower oil
- Pumpkin seeds
- Sesame seeds
- Safflower oil.

Research into omega 3 and in particular fish oils has shown that eating fish protects against heart disease. This is because the omega 3s may prevent the formation of blood clots on the artery walls and lower the levels of triglycerides circulating in the blood stream (Drexel *et al.*, 1994).

The essential fatty acids are also thought to improve the function of the brain and promote learning as well as being beneficial for arthritics because they reduce swelling in joints.

Cholesterol

Cholesterol is a substance that behaves like fat; however, it contains no fatty acid. Cholesterol can either be ingested or made in the body. It is only found in animal products, never in plants. It has some useful functions, including building cell membranes and helping the function of various hormones. There are two types of cholesterol: Low Density Lipoproteins (LDLs) and High Density Lipoproteins (HDLs). LDLs are responsible for the deposits lining the walls of arteries and lead to an increased risk of coronary heart disease. HDLs however, actually reduce this risk by transporting cholesterol away to the liver and so are beneficial to health.

Recommended daily amounts (RDA) of fat

Fat intake should make up no more than 30% of total kilocalories. Only 10% of kilocalories should come from saturated fat.

There are many health problems related to eating an excess of fat, especially saturated fats. These include obesity, high blood pressure and coronary heart disease, although it is important to distinguish between different types of fat eaten in a person's diet. Consumption of certain fatty acids (omega 3 fish oils found in tuna, for example) is linked to a decreased risk of coronary heart disease.

As fat provides just over twice as much energy per gram as carbohydrate, a diet high in fat can make over-consumption more likely. It is thought that excess dietary fat may be more easily converted to body fat than excess carbohydrate or protein. Research suggests that today, more people are obese than ever before. Obese people are more likely to suffer from a range of illnesses, including coronary heart disease, adult-onset diabetes, gallstones, arthritis, high blood pressure and some types of cancer. However, most of the health problems associated with obesity are removed once the extra weight is lost.

Protein

The word 'protein' is derived from Greek and means 'prime importance'. Protein is of prime importance because it consists of the building blocks which make up the structures of the body. For example, muscle, skin, bones, internal organs, cartilage and ligament all have a protein component. We gain our protein by eating protein rich foods such as red meat, fish, chicken, eggs and dairy products.

Functions of protein

When we eat protein it will be digested in the digestive system and then delivered to the liver as individual amino acids. The liver will then rebuild the amino acids into long chains to make up proteins. The proteins that the liver produces depend on the needs of the body at that time. For example, if we need to replace muscle then the liver will produce the relevant proteins to replace muscle tissue.

Proteins have three specific roles in the body:

1 To build structures (structural)
2 To perform functions (functional)
3 To provide fuel.

Protein deficiency is very rare in the Western world; however, vegetarians may be more susceptible to protein deficiency as they do not eat meat nor fish which are good sources of protein. If a person does not eat enough protein in the diet some of the things they may suffer from include delayed wound healing, muscle weakness and wasting and/or hair loss.

Structural

Protein forms part of the following structures:

1 Muscle (skeletal, smooth and cardiac)
2 Bone
3 Internal organs (heart, kidneys, liver)
4 Connective tissue (tendons and ligaments)
5 Hair
6 Nails.

Functional

Protein forms part of the following structures which perform specific functions in the body:

1 Hormones (which send messages to cells, e.g. insulin and adrenaline)

2 Enzymes (biological catalysts which speed up reactions in cells)

3 Part of the immune system (white blood cells are made partly of protein)

4 Formation of lipoproteins (these help to transport fats around the body).

Fuel

Protein is not the body's first choice of fuel but it can be used as energy. It is heavily used during endurance training and events or at times of starvation. 1 g of protein provides 4 kcals.

Types of protein

The smallest unit of a protein is an amino acid. Proteins are made up of long chains of amino acids which are formed into structures. Amino acids are the smallest unit of a protein and there are 20 amino acids in total. Amino acids can be seen to be like the alphabet. In the English language we have 26 letters from which we can make up millions of words; the protein alphabet has 20 amino acids from which can be produced approximately 50,000 different proteins present in the body. Just as different words are made up of different orders of letters so different structures are made up of different orders of amino acids.

There are 20 different amino acids to make up proteins. These can be split into essential and non-essential amino acids. An essential amino acid is one which must be gained through eating it in the diet; while a non-essential amino acid can be made in the liver if all essential amino acids are present. This means to produce all the structures of the body we must gain all essential amino acids on a daily basis.

Essential amino acids

There are eight essential amino acids to be gained from the diet. They are:

1 Isoleucine

2 Leucine

3 Lysine

4 Methionine

5 Phenylalanine

6 Threonine

7 Tryptophan

8 Valine.

Non-essential amino acids

There are 12 non-essential amino acids which will be synthesised in the liver if all eight essential amino acids are gained from the diet. They are:

1 Cystine

2 Tyrosine

3 Histidine

4 Glutamine

5 Glutamic acid

6 Glycine

7 Alanine

8 Serine

9 Praline

10 Aspartic acid

11 Asparagines

12 Arginine.

Sources of essential and non-essential amino acids

Foods which contains all eight essential amino acids are described as being complete, while a food which is missing one or more essential amino acid is described as being incomplete.

The following are sources of complete and incomplete proteins:

Sources of essential amino acids	Sources of non-essential amino acids
Chicken	Wheat
Eggs	Oats
Fish	Rice
Red meat	Pulses
Dairy products	Nuts
Soya bean	Vegetables

Table 13.5 Sources of complete and incomplete proteins

With the exception of the soya bean the sources of essential amino acids are from animals while

Figure 13.10a–b Complete and incomplete proteins

non-essential amino acids come from plant sources. However, to gain all 8 essential amino acids from incomplete protein sources you will need to eat a range of sources or combine protein sources. This is called 'complementary protein' and examples would be:

1   Wheat and pulses (beans on toast)
2   Nuts and vegetables (nut roast)
3   Rice and lentils (vegetarian chilli).

All protein sources will contain different amounts of amino acids. The greater the quantity of the essential amino acids in the food will give it a higher biological value. Eggs have the highest quality or biological value of all foods and are given a protein rating of 100; all other proteins are compared to them in terms of their quality and quantity of amino acids.

Quality of different sources of protein

Food	Protein rating
Eggs	100
Fish	70
Beef	69
Cow's milk	60
Brown rice	57
White rice	56
Soya beans	47
Wheat	44
Peanuts	43
Beans	34

Table 13.6 Quality of different sources of protein (*Source:* adapted from McArdle, Katch and Katch, 1999)

Recommended daily amount (RDA) of protein

The diet should consist of between 10–20% of protein depending on the specific needs of the individual and the amount and type of activity a person takes part in because the more exercise a person does, the more they break down muscle tissue and consequently the more protein they need in order to repair the muscle tissue.

The average daily intake of protein in the UK is 85 g for men and 62 g for women. The recommended daily amount of protein for healthy adults is 0.8 g per kilogram of body weight, or about 15% of total kilocalories. Protein needs are higher for children, infants and many athletes.

Table 13.7 below gives estimated recommended amounts of protein a person should eat based on their activity levels.

Activity Level	Recommended grams of protein per kg of body weight
A Sedentary adult	0.8 g
B Recreational exerciser	0.8–1.5 g
C Endurance athlete	1.2–1.6 g
D Speed/Power athlete	1.7–1.8 g
E Adult building muscle (hypertrophy)	2.0 g

Table 13.7 Activity levels and recommended amounts of protein (*Source:* adapted from ACSM, 2000)

Energy content of macronutrients

Each macronutrient can provide energy if broken down by the body as an energy source.

- 1 g protein provides 4 kcal or 17 kJ
- 1 g carbohydrate provides 4 kcal or 16 kJ
- 1 g fat provides 9 kcal or 37 kJ.

A3 Micronutrients

Vitamins

These are organic substances that the body requires in small amounts. The body is incapable of making vitamins for its overall needs, so they must be supplied regularly by the diet.

Vitamins are not related chemically and differ in their physiological actions. As vitamins were discovered, each was identified by a letter. Many of the vitamins consist of several closely related compounds of similar physiological properties.

Vitamins may be subdivided into:

- **Fat-soluble** – A, D, E and K
- **Water-soluble** – C and B (complex).

The water-soluble vitamins cannot be stored in the body, so they must be consumed on a regular basis. If excess quantities of these vitamins are consumed, the body will excrete them in the urine. Fat-soluble vitamins are stored in the body's fat, so it is not necessary to consume these on such a regular basis. It is also possible to overdose on fat-soluble vitamins, which can be detrimental to health.

Varying amounts of each vitamin are required – the amount needed is referred to as the recommended daily intake (RDI).

Fat-soluble vitamins

Vitamin A
- Function – Help maintain good vision, healthy skin, hair and mucous membranes and to serve as an antioxidant. It is also needed for proper bone and tooth development.
- Source – liver, mackerel, milk products.
- RDI – 1.5 mg.

Vitamin D (calciferol)
- Function – Essential to calcium and phosphorus utilisation. Promotes strong bones and teeth. Our main source of vitamin D is sunlight.
- Source – sunlight, egg yolk, fish, fish oils, fortified cereals.
- RDI – 0.01 mg.

Vitamin E
- Function – antioxidant helps prevent damage to cell membranes
- Source – wheat germ, nuts, whole grains, dark green leafy vegetables.
- RDI – 10 mg

Vitamin K
- Function – Used in the formation of blood clots
- Source – leafy green vegetables
- RDI – 70 mg.

Water-soluble vitamins

B vitamins
These vitamins are not chemically related, but often occur in the same foodstuff. Their main function is to aid in metabolism of food and in red blood cell production.

Vitamin B-1 (thiamine)
- Function – Helps convert food to energy and aids the nervous and cardiovascular systems.
- Source – rice bran, pork, beef, peas, beans, wheatgerm, oatmeal and soya beans.
- RDI – 1.5 mg.

Vitamin B-2 (riboflavin)
- Function – Aids growth and reproduction and helps to metabolise fats, carbohydrates and proteins. Promotes healthy skin and nails.
- Source – milk, liver, kidneys, yeast, cheese, leafy green vegetables, fish and eggs.
- RDI – 1.7 mg.

Vitamin B-3 (niacin)
- Function – Helps to keep the nervous system balanced and is also important for the synthesis of sex hormones, thyroxine, cortisone and insulin.
- Source – poultry, fish, peanuts, Marmite, rice bran and wheatgerm.
- RDI – 20 mg.

Vitamin B-5 (pantothenic acid)

- Function – Helps in cell building and maintaining normal growth and development of the central nervous system. Helps form hormones and antibodies. It is also necessary for the conversion of fat and sugar to energy.
- Source – wheatgerm, green vegetables, whole grains, mushrooms, fish, peanuts, Marmite.
- RDI – 10 mg.

Vitamin B-6 (pyridoxine)

- Function – Helps in the utilisation of proteins and the metabolism of fats. It is also needed for production of red blood cells and antibodies.
- Source – chicken, beef, bananas, Marmite, eggs, brown rice, soya beans, oats, whole wheat, peanuts and walnuts.
- RDI – 2 mg.

Vitamin C (ascorbic acid)

- Function – This vitamin is essential for the formation of collagen. It helps to strengthen tissues, acts as an antioxidant, helps in healing, production of red blood cells, fighting bacterial infections and regulating cholesterol. It also helps the body to absorb iron.
- Source – most fresh fruits and vegetables.
- RDI – 60 mg.

Vitamin summary

Vitamin	Food sources	Main function	Deficiency
A	Mackerel, liver, beef, carrots, liver, dark green vegetables, mackerel	Maintain good vision and ability to see in the dark, skin and hair	Night-blindness
D	Oily fish, sunlight, eggs	Helps to build strong bones and teeth	Rickets
E	Dark green leafy vegetables, whole grains, nuts, margarine	Help to protect our body cells from damage	Anaemia, eye damage
K	Leafy green vegetables	Helps blood to clot	Inability for blood to clot when wounded

Table 13.8 Fat-soluble vitamins

Vitamin	Food sources	Main function	Deficiency
B Group	Cereals, liver, yeast, eggs, beef, beans	Help to break down food to produce energy, help with blood production	Beriberi, anaemia
C	Most fresh fruits and vegetables, especially citrus fruits – oranges, lemons, etc.	Fights infection, maintains healthy skin and gums, helps with wound healing	Bleeding gums, slow wound healing

Table 13.9 Water-soluble vitamins

Minerals

There are several minerals required to maintain a healthy body. Some are needed in moderate amounts, others only in very small amounts and are referred to as trace minerals.

Calcium

- Function – It is needed to build strong bones and teeth, helps to calm nerves and plays a role in muscle contraction, blood clotting and cell membrane upkeep. Correct quantities of calcium consumption have been shown to significantly lower the risk of osteoporosis.

- Source – milk and milk products, whole grains and unrefined cereals, green vegetables, fish bones.
- RDI – adults 1200 mg.
- Deficiency – fragile bones, osteoporosis, rickets, tooth decay; irregular heartbeat and slowed nerve impulse response. Vitamin D is essential for proper calcium absorption and utilisation.

Iron

- Function – It is required for the production of haemoglobin.
- Source – liver, lean meats, eggs, baked potatoes, soybeans, kidney beans, whole grains and cereals, dried fruits.
- RDI – males 10 mg, females 18 mg.
- Deficiency – can lead to dizziness, iron deficiency anaemia, constipation, sore or inflamed tongue.

Sodium

- Function – This works in conjunction with potassium to maintain fluid and electrolyte balance within cells.
- Source – virtually all foods contain sodium: celery, cheese, eggs, meat, milk and milk products, processed foods, salt and seafood.
- RDI – 2500 mg.
- Deficiency – can lead to confusion, low blood sugar, dehydration, lethargy, heart palpitations and heart attack.

Salt

Salt is made up of sodium and chloride and adults should eat no more than 6 g per day, children should eat less, between 2 g to 5 g depending on age – up to the age of 11 and over where no more than 6 g should be consumed.

75% of salt eaten is found in sources where it is not expected such as bread, soup and breakfast cereals. Other foods such as processed food, crisps, bacon and olives contain high levels of salt. Also, many people add salt to food for flavour. Too much salt in the diet can lead to high blood pressure which increases the risk of a person suffering from a stroke or heart-related diseases.

Some manufacturers will just put the amount of sodium of the product on their packaging which is just less than half the salt content of the product which can be misleading, for example, 0.8 g of sodium equates to 2 g of salt.

Potassium

- Function – In conjunction with sodium, it helps to maintain fluid and electrolyte balance within cells. It is important for normal nerve and muscle function and aids proper maintenance of the blood's mineral balance. It also helps to lower blood pressure.
- Source – bananas, dried apricots, yoghurt, whole grains, sunflower seeds, potatoes, sweet potatoes and kidney beans.
- RDI – 2500 mg.
- Deficiency – decreased blood pressure, dry skin, salt retention, irregular heartbeat.

Mineral	Food sources	Main function	Deficiency
Calcium	Milk, fish bones, green leafy vegetables	Helps to build strong bones and teeth, helps to form blood clots	Osteoporosis, rickets
Potassium	Bananas, whole grains, dried apricots	Works with sodium to maintain fluid balance, aids muscle contraction, maintains blood pressure	
Sodium	Cheese, celery, dairy products, seafood, salt	Helps to maintain fluid and electrolyte balance in cells, helps in muscle contraction	
Iron	Liver, lean meats, eggs, dried fruits	Blood production	Anaemia

Table 13.10 Minerals and their sources and functions

A4 Fibre

Dietary fibre is the part of a plant that is resistant to the body's digestive enzymes. It is defined as 'indigestible plant material' and although it is a carbohydrate and contains calories the digestive system cannot unlock them from the plant.

Function of fibre

Fibre moves through the gastrointestinal tract and ends up in the stool. The main function of fibre is that when it is in the digestive system it retains water which results in softer and bulkier stools that prevent constipation and haemorrhoids. Research suggests that a high fibre diet also reduces the risk of colon cancer.

Source of fibre

All fruits, vegetables, and grains provide some fibre. There are two types of fibre, soluble and insoluble, that perform slightly different functions.

Soluble fibre dissolves into a gel in water and is found in the fleshy part of fruit and vegetables, oats, barley and rice. For example, when you make porridge the oats partly dissolve into a sticky gel and this is the soluble fibre. Soluble fibre has two main roles to play:

1 Slows down how quickly the stomach empties and slows down how quickly glucose enters the blood stream

2 Binds to fat and blood cholesterol thus decreasing the risk of heart disease.

Insoluble fibre will not dissolve in water and is found in the skins of fruit and vegetables, wheat, rye, seeds and pips of fruit. Insoluble fibre will pass through the digestive system without being altered in any way. Its main roles are:

1 Adds bulk to faeces and speeds its passage through the large intestine

2 Helps to keep the large intestine clean and prevent bowel disease

3 Stretches the stomach and makes you feel full for longer

4 Slows down the release of glucose into the blood stream.

Recommended daily intake (RDI)

It is recommended that we eat around 18 g of fibre a day and this can be done by eating foods in their natural form rather than in their processed or refined states.

A5 Fluid intake

One of the major chemicals essential to life is water; however, it has no nutritional value in terms of energy. About 2.5 litres a day is needed to maintain normal functions in adults. This amount depends heavily on environmental conditions and on the amount of energy expenditure. For example, in the heat a greater amount of water is needed and exercise requires an increased intake of water due to the loss of fluid via sweating.

Only half of the body's water requirement comes in the form of liquid. The other half will be supplied from food (especially fruit and vegetables) and metabolic reactions (the breakdown of food results in the formation of carbon dioxide and water).

Function of maintaining hydration levels

Thermoregulation

One of the main functions of water is to help to regulate body temperature. It does this by sweating. The sweat produced lies on the surface of the skin. The process of the sweat drying is called evaporation and when the sweat evaporates, you lose heat from your body.

You are probably familiar with this feeling. For example, if you go swimming, once changed and prior to entering the swimming pool you will probably feel the temperature of the surroundings to be quite comfortable. However, once you have finished swimming and come out of the water, you will probably feel quite cold. The coldness you are feeling is due to the water on your body evaporating. Once you have dried yourself off, you will no longer feel the same chill and the surrounding temperature will once again feel comfortable.

Exercise increases basal metabolic rate by around 20 to 25 times. This would result in an increase in core body of 1°C every six minutes if heat loss did not take place. This increase in body temperature would eventually result in death from over-heating if exercise continued. However, the process of sweating is the main method by which we lose this excess body heat. The maximum volume of sweat an average person can produce is around one litre per hour. However, athletes who train and compete in hot climates are able to produce around two to three litres of sweat per hour. With this excessive fluid loss, athletes must be sure to consume high levels of fluids to replace this loss.

Water plays a major role in maintaining the body at a constant temperature. When the body is hot it produces sweat to help it to cool down through evaporation of the sweat.

Maintaining optimal sports performance

Dehydration causes a significant loss of performance. This is because dehydration, also called hypo hydration, will cause a loss of blood plasma affecting blood flow and the ability to sweat. Thus temperature starts to increase steadily. When we sweat it is predominantly blood plasma that is lost and thus cardiac output (the amount of the blood leaving the heart per minute) is reduced. Therefore, dehydration affects the circulation of the blood and the body's ability to control temperature.

Types of fluid

While plain water is a good drink for athletes to consume there are now a huge array of sports drinks available that help to quench thirst, supply the body with carbohydrates and some supply the body with electrolytes lost in sweat such as sodium.

Sports drinks have been rumoured to originate from a coach to an American Football team called the Gators. As the athletes lost sweat and other substances in their sweat while playing American Football, the coach thought the players would recover more quickly if they were able to replace these lost substances. The coach took the athletes socks and clothes at the end of the game and collected all the sweat from these articles in a bucket. He then added more fluid (probably water) and some flavouring and then shared it out between the players after the game!

Figure 13.11 An athlete consuming a sports drink

Isotonic

These drinks are the most popular type of sports drink. They are used to help the body rehydrate and also contain some carbohydrates. The drink is termed 'isotonic' because it has a similar concentration of dissolved solids as our blood, this results in the drink being absorbed very quickly into the body so that we rehydrate at a much faster rate than if we were to drink water alone. The drinks contain 6 mg of carbohydrate per 100 ml of fluid which provides energy which is beneficial to endurance athletes.

Hypotonic

The main aim of these sports drinks it to hydrate the athlete after exercising. These types of sports drinks are low calorie drinks and have a lower concentration of dissolved solids than blood. They are absorbed by the body at a faster rate than isotonic drinks. They contain no more than 2 g of carbohydrate per 100 ml of fluid so they provide little energy to the athlete during exercise. They are therefore a relatively poor source of energy.

Hypertonic

The main purpose of these drinks is to supply the body with energy after exercise or during endurance events that last longer than 90 minutes. These drinks have a higher concentration of dissolved solids than blood and are absorbed relatively slowly. They contain 10 g of carbohydrate per 100 ml of water and are a very good source of energy but relatively poor for hydration. They are mostly used in endurance events of over an hour and a half.

These drinks will also contain the correct amounts of the electrolytes which ensure optimum speed

Activity: Sports drinks

Name as many different sports drinks as you can. Look through magazines, the internet or sports shops to help you. Write down the prices of these drinks and any claimed benefits of consuming this drink.

Designing a sports drink

Aim

The aim of this practical is to make a sports drink. You need to decide which athletes you are making the drink for and when it should be consumed (i.e. if you want to make an isotonic, hypertonic or hypotonic drink).

Equipment

(For this experiment, if you are using equipment taken from the science lab, it must have been thoroughly sterilised.)

- measuring cylinders
- beakers
- weighing scales
- glucose
- sweeteners
- flavourings – your choice
- colourings – your choice
- tasting cups
- drinking water
- salt.

Method

Isotonic drink

1. If you are designing an isotonic drink, you need to ensure that the carbohydrate content of your drink is between 6% and 8%. To do this, for every 100 ml of water, you need to add between 6 g to 8 g of glucose.
2. You can then add other flavourings to your drink to make it taste better – however, these flavourings should not contain any carbohydrates, so use things that contain sweeteners, such as reduced sugar squash.

Hypertonic drink

1. If you are designing a hypertonic drink, it should contain at least 9% carbohydrates. This means for every 100 ml of water, you need to add at least 9 g of glucose.
2. You can then add other flavourings, which can contain carbohydrates.

Hypotonic drink

1. If you are designing a hypotonic drink, it should contain 5% or less carbohydrates. To do this, to every 100 ml of water add 5 g of glucose or less.
2. You can then add other flavourings, but these should not contain any carbohydrates, so you could use things that contain sweeteners.

→

of absorption. However, on the negative side they often contain additives such as sweeteners and colourings which have a negative effect on health. They are also relatively expensive when compared with water.

Effects of temperature of fluid on speed of rehydration

Research suggests that the temperature of fluids can have an effect on how quickly the fluid is absorbed into the blood stream in order to hydrate a person. Remember, it is only when the fluid enters the blood stream from the stomach that a person starts to become hydrated. The process of consuming a drink takes fluid into the stomach, how quickly it leaves the stomach and enters the blood stream is very important in the process of hydration. Some research suggests that very cold drinks take longer for the body to absorb the fluids compared to drinks that are not so cold. However, research has also shown that drinks that are quite cold are more palatable so people are more likely to drink more of the fluid if they are cold rather than at room temperature.

Effects of carbonated fluid on time to rehydrate

Some research suggests that carbonated drinks (fizzy drinks) take longer for the body to absorb the fluid compared to non-carbonated drinks. It is not clear how carbonation may affect the absorption of the fluid and research is ongoing in this area. Aside from rehydration, it is interesting to note from a nutritional point of view that cola-based carbonated drinks have been linked to reducing bone density which could lead to osteoporosis if large quantities (three or more cans a day) over prolonged periods of time.

Recommended daily intake (RDI)

Our body is sensitive to hunger pangs, however, we have a much lower sensitivity to hydration levels. In fact, if you actually feel thirsty then you are more than likely to already be slightly dehydrated. Another method of determining if you are dehydrated is to take a look at the colour of your urine! If it is a light yellow straw colour then it means that you are sufficiently hydrated. However, if your urine is a darker yellow or orangey colour then you are dehydrated. The quantity of urine is also a good indicator, the more you produce the more hydrated you are.

A person who does not take part in sports should consume around 2 litres of fluids per day. This fluid can be sourced from drinks and also from solid foods.

A sports person should consume around 2.5–3 litres of fluids at regular intervals throughout the day. If they are training or competing in hot environments, they should drink around 0.3 litres of fluids every 20 minutes. After exercise, a sports person should drink enough fluids to quench their thirst plus a little more. A good method of judging whether you are fully hydrated after exercise is to weigh yourself in your underwear prior to exercise. After exercise, weigh yourself again; any weight loss will be due to fluid loss. Therefore, consume enough liquids until you weigh the same amount as you did prior to exercise.

- Thirst
- Dizziness
- Headaches
- Dry mouth
- Poor concentration
- Sticky oral mucus
- Flushed red skin
- Rapid heart rate.

Effects of dehydration (hypernatremia)

Dehydration is a condition which occurs when fluid loss exceeds fluid intake. The signs and symptoms of dehydration are:

Effects of hyperhydration (hyponatremia)

Hyperhydration is when an athlete drinks extra water before exercising. This is done when they are exercising in a hot environment to prevent

A Check your understanding

1 Define the following terms:
   a) Kcal
   b) kJ
   c) RDI
   d) Metabolism.
2 Explain why a sports person could have a high BMI and also a low BIA.
3 Complete the table below with the missing information.

Nutrient	Food Sources	Functions	Kcals per 1 g	% kcal recommended intake
Carbohydrates	Bread Rice Pasta Fruit	Provide energy to the brain and nervous system, liver, heart and muscles	4 kcals	50–60% of kcals
Proteins				
Fats				30% of kcals
Vitamins	Fruits Vegetables	Energy production, immunity		
Minerals			0	0% of kcals

Table 13.11 A summary of nutrients

4 Explain what is meant by an essential protein.
5 Describe what is meant when a food has a high glycaemic index (GI).
6 Identify which nutrient has the highest energy content per gram.
7 Identify which nutrients are required for healthy strong bones.
8 Describe where fibre is found and its function in the body.
9 Explain what type of sports drink would be most suited to a long distance runner during a race.
10 Explain how dehydration can affect an endurance athlete's sporting performance.

the negative effects of dehydration and it will minimise the rise in body temperature. The advice is to increase fluid intake over the preceding 24 hours and then drink around 500 ml of water 20 minutes before the event starts. This does not replace the need to continually top up water levels during the competition.

B Factors affecting digestion and absorption of nutrients and fluids

B1 Basic principles of digestion

Functions of digestion

The digestive system is where foods are broken down into their individual nutrients, absorbed into the blood stream and the waste excreted. It works through processes of mechanical and chemical digestion. Mechanical digestion starts before the food enters the mouth as we cook the food and then cut it up or mash it to make it more palatable. In the mouth we chew the food to tear it apart further, then digestive juices continue this process. The chemical digestion of foods occurs through the presence of digestive enzymes which are present in the mouth and the other organs the food passes through. Enzymes are defined as biological catalysts which will break down the large molecules of the nutrients into smaller molecules which can be absorbed.

The aim of the digestive system is to break the nutrients down into their smallest units. These are:

Nutrient	Smallest unit
Carbohydrate	Glucose
Protein	Amino acid
Fats	Fatty acid

Table 13.12 The smallest units of nutrients

The digestion, absorption and elimination of nutrients takes place in the gastrointestinal tract which is a long tube running from the mouth to the anus. It includes the mouth, oesophagus, stomach, small intestine and large intestine.

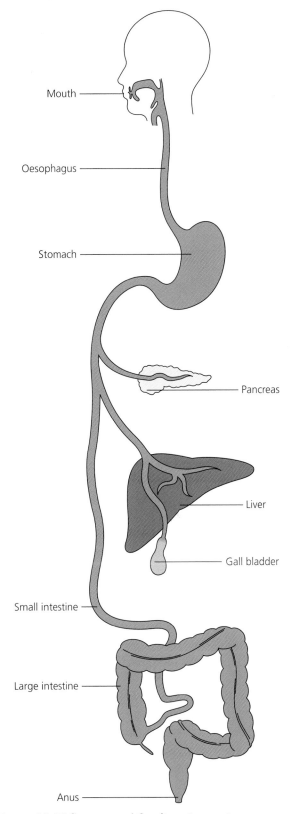

Mouth

Oesophagus

Stomach

Pancreas

Liver

Gall bladder

Small intestine

Large intestine

Anus

Figure 13.12 Structure of the digestive system

Mouth

The technical term for the mouth is the buccal cavity and this is where the journey of the food begins. The teeth and jaw will produce mechanical digestion through a process of grinding and mashing up the food. The jaw can produce forces of up to 90 kg on the food. Saliva will act to soften and moisten the food making it easier to swallow and more like the internal environment. Saliva contains the digestive enzyme, amylase which starts the breakdown of carbohydrates. The tongue is also involved in helping to mix the food and then produce the swallowing action.

Oesophagus

When the food has been swallowed it enters the oesophagus which delivers the food to the stomach through a process of gravity and peristalsis. Amylase will continue to break down the carbohydrates.

Stomach

The stomach is situated in the upper left of the abdominal cavity and is behind the lower ribs. The stomach continues the process of chemical digestion. However, no absorption of nutrients occurs in the stomach because the pieces are still too large. The only substance absorbed in the stomach is alcohol which can enter the blood stream here. The stomach is made up of three layers of smooth muscle which help to mix up the food. The parietal cells that line the inside of the stomach will release hydrochloric acid which helps to dissolve the food and kill off the bacteria present. These cells also release another digestive enzyme 'pepsinogen' which produces protein breakdown. The stomach takes around 1–4 hours to empty fully depending upon the size of the meal. Carbohydrates will leave the stomach most quickly, followed by proteins and then fats.

Small intestine

Around 90% of digestion will occur in the upper two thirds of the small intestine with help from the pancreas, liver and gall bladder. The large intestine is between 5–6 metres long and consists of three areas: the duodenum, which is the first 25 cm; the jejunum which is the next 2 m and the ileum which is around 3–4 m long. The partly digested foods move through the small intestine partly by gravity and mainly through the peristaltic action of the smooth muscle present in the intestine walls. The peristaltic action is also aided by the action of the villi and microvilli, which push the food along. These structures line the walls of the intestine and absorption of nutrients occurs between the villi.

Pancreas

The pancreas is an important organ in digestion because it secretes around 1.5 litres of a juice which contains three digestive enzymes. They are amylase to digest carbohydrates, lipase to digest fats and trypsin to digest protein.

Liver

The liver is by-passed by the food but it does secrete bile which helps to emulsify and digest fats. Bile is synthesised in the liver and is stored in the gall bladder which sits just below the liver.

The small intestine

The small intestine is where the nutrients will become the smallest units and then be absorbed into blood stream through the villi. Any waste is passed into the large intestine.

Large intestine

The large intestine or colon will perform the following functions:

- Storage of waste before elimination
- Absorption of any remaining water
- Production of vitamins B and K
- Break down of any toxins which will damage the colon.

The colon contains many millions of bacteria which work to keep the colon healthy through detoxifying the waste and producing vitamins. They are intestinal micro flora and there are as many of these present in the colon as there are cells in the body. These can be supplemented by yoghurt drinks that promote and increase the number of friendly bacteria.

Anus

The anus is the end of the gastrointestinal tract and is the opening to allow the elimination of waste products of digestion.

Timing of digestion of different macronutrients

Different types of food will take different lengths of time to be digested depending on the chemical composition of the food. Liquids will take much less time to be digested as they do not need to be broken down in the same way as solid foods.

Table 13.13 Types of food and digestion times

Type of food	Digestion time
Water and sports drinks	20–30 mins
Fruit, soups, smoothies	30–45 mins
Vegetables	30–45 mins
Sea food (fish, prawns etc.)	30–60 mins
Egg	45 mins
Starch (potatoes) Grains (brown rice, oat flakes) Beans (lentils, chick peas)	2–3 hours
Dairy products (milk, cheese)	1.5 milk 4 hours cheese
Chicken	1.5–2 hours
Beef and lamb	3–4 hours
Pork	4.5–5 hours

Foods that contain high levels of protein and fats will take longer to break down compared to foods that contain simple carbohydrates.

Timing of absorption of different types of fluids

Fluids that contain low levels of sugar and fruit will be absorbed by the body quickly; the more sugar, fruit or other substances in the fluid, the longer the fluid will take to be absorbed by the body.

Redistribution of blood flow during digestion

The process of digestion is to break down foods into their smallest sizes and then for these nutrients to pass into the blood stream. This means, blood flow is directed to the stomach and small intestine to help with the process of digestion. However, if a person is exercising, the blood flow is directed to the working muscles to supply them with the oxygen and nutrients required to allow them to continue to contract. If a person has eaten a heavy meal and then takes part in exercise straight away, this presents competition for the additional blood flow as it is required in two different places. The muscles' requirement

will take priority which means the food will stay in the stomach and not be digested while the person is exercising which can lead to stomach cramps or sickness as the body is not able to supply the blood required to digest the food.

B2 Hormonal control of blood sugar and water balance

Glands from the endocrine system release hormones. These hormones allow the glands to send signals to parts of the body to inform it how to respond in order to regulate blood sugar and water balance. The glands that release the hormones have target organs that respond in specific ways when they are in contact with the hormone. This system is similar in some ways to the nervous system; however, rather than sending electric nerve impulses which allow for very quick messages to be sent in the nervous system, the endocrine system is much slower at producing reactions in comparison as the hormones are released into the blood stream and carried to the target organ via the blood which takes longer than nervous impulses.

Hormonal control of blood sugar levels

Carbohydrates are all broken down in the following way:

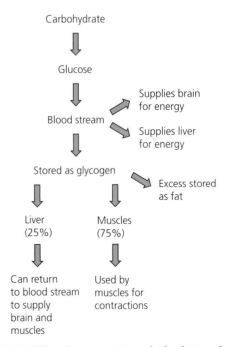

Figure 13.13 What happens to carbohydrate when it is digested

Blood sugar levels are the amount of glucose in the blood. The average accepted levels are 4.0–5.9 mmol/L before meals and less than 7.8 mmol/L 90 minutes after a meal. People with diabetes are not able to control their blood sugar levels and have to take regular medication in the form of synthetic hormones to control their blood sugar levels. People with diabetes can control their blood sugar levels with a hormone called insulin.

Low levels of blood sugar

When a person experiences hypoglycaemia they can become light-headed, dizzy, start to not make sense and eventually fall into a coma and in the worst case they can die. For most people, receptors in the pancreas detect the low levels and responds by releasing a hormone called glucagon. Glucagon is released from the alpha cells in the islets of Langerhans in the pancreas. This hormone has the effect of acting on the liver to stimulate it to break down its stores of glycogen into glucose which is then released into the blood stream and returns blood sugar levels to normal.

Key term

Hypoglycaemia means low levels of blood sugar.

High levels of blood sugar

Hyperglycaemia does harm the blood vessels and if left untreated over time can lead to heart disease, eye sight problems, kidney and nerve damage. When there is excess sugar in the blood, the beta cells in the islets of Langerhans release insulin. This stimulates the liver to convert the excess sugar into glycogen so that it can be stored in the body. If the glycogen stores are full, then the excess sugar will be converted into fat and stored in the fat cells of the body.

Key term

Hyperglycaemia means excess glucose in the blood.

Hormonal control of water balance

Seventy per cent of our body is made up of water, so it is important that we maintain a balance of fluids in the body for optimal performance and health. 70% of our body is made up of water, so it is important that we maintain this 70% balance of water in the body in order to maintain health and allow for optimal sports performance.

Dehydration

The effects of dehydration have already been covered in this unit (see A5, page 372). When the body detects that there are low levels of fluid in the body it acts to try to conserve as much water as possible by releasing antidiuretic hormone (ADH) from the pituitary gland. This hormone acts on the kidneys by making them reabsorb more water into the blood than usual during the filtration process. This has the effect of the person producing less urine. The decreased quantity of urine means that it is more concentrated and therefore is a darker colour.

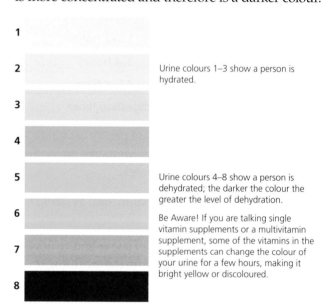

Urine colours 1–3 show a person is hydrated.

Urine colours 4–8 show a person is dehydrated; the darker the colour the greater the level of dehydration.

Be Aware! If you are talking single vitamin supplements or a multivitamin supplement, some of the vitamins in the supplements can change the colour of your urine for a few hours, making it bright yellow or discoloured.

Figure 13.14 Urine colour chart

Hyperhydration

When a person has sufficient water in their blood stream the pituitary gland no longer releases ADH which results in less water being reabsorbed by the kidneys and more water excreted in the urine by the body. This results in more dilute urine which has a pale colour.

B3 Control of glycogen synthesis

Types and timing of food to maximise glycogen synthesis

During the first two hours immediately after exercise or competition, your body is able to convert carbohydrates into glycogen at a very fast rate. Conversion of glucose to glycogen is at its fastest during the first two hours after exercise – a time frame which is described by athletes as a 'golden window'. 50–75 g of high or moderate GI carbohydrates which works out at 1–1.2 g of carbohydrates per kg of your body weight should be consumed in the first 15 minutes after exercise and then another dose of 50–75 g in the next two hours.

B Check your understanding

1 Describe the process of digestion.
2 Identify which foods are digested:
   a) very quickly (30–60 mins)
   b) very slowly (4–5 hours).
3 Explain the hormonal control of blood glucose.
4 Describe why a person with diabetes is not able to control their blood sugar levels.
5 Explain the hormonal control of fluids in the body.

C Nutritional intake for health and well-being

C1 Balanced diet for health and well-being

If a person eats a balanced and nutritious diet then they are much more likely to be in good health. A balanced diet means that the person is eating the right amount of foods from all of the five food groups.

Balance of food groups

Food can be divided into five groups; we should eat differing amounts from each group in order to have a healthy diet. The amount we eat depends on many things, for example age, gender, level of activity, state of health and many more. The five food groups are:

1 Grains
2 Fruits and vegetables
3 Protein – meat and fish and pulses
4 Milk and dairy foods
5 Foods containing fat and sugar.

Grains (bread, cereals and potatoes)

Examples of these types of foods are bread, pasta, rice, noodles, oats and breakfast cereals. The majority of the food you eat should be from this group of foods; in fact, every meal should include at least one food from this group. You should aim to eat between 6 to 11 portions of foods per day from this food group. A portion size would be: 1 slice of bread; 3 tablespoons of cereal; 2 small boiled potatoes; 3 heaped tablespoons of noodles or pasta.

The best types of foods to eat from this food group are the whole grains such as wholemeal bread, brown rice and oatmeal as these contain more vitamins, minerals and fibre compared to processed foods such as white bread and white rice.

Fruits and vegetables

This group includes all fruit and vegetables, such as apples, oranges, onions, carrots, etc. except for potatoes. You should aim to eat at least five portions of fruit and vegetables per day. A portion would be one apple, one orange or a handful of grapes, etc. You can choose to eat fresh, frozen, canned or juiced fruit and vegetables. If you choose to eat canned fruit you should be careful to choose fruit in fruit juice rather than syrup as the syrup contains high levels of sugar. When looking to buy canned vegetables you should try to avoid vegetables canned in brine as this contains salt and too much salt is not good for you.

Protein (meat, fish and alternatives)

This food group includes all kinds of meat and meat products (e.g. hamburgers), poultry, eggs, and fish. For vegetarians, this group would incorporate foods such as soya products, lentils, pulses and tofu products. Around two portions of food from this food group should be eaten each day. A portion would be two medium eggs, lean meat about the size of a deck of cards, fish the size of a cheque book, one small tin of beans or five tablespoons of lentils.

Dairy (milk, cheese and yogurt)

You should eat servings from this food group around two to three times per day. Foods in this group include milk and any products made from milk such as cheese, yogurt and cream. A portion would be would be one yogurt, cheese the size of a match box or a glass of milk (200 ml).

Fats and sweets

This food group includes all foods containing high quantities of fats and sugars. Examples of fatty foods are butter, margarine, olive oil, cakes, biscuits, pastries, ice-cream, cream and fried foods (e.g. chips). Examples of sugary foods include sweets, jam and fizzy drinks (not the diet drinks though). We should only eat small quantities of foods from this group.

Food pyramid

A food pyramid is a good way of showing how much of each food group you should eat. The bottom layer of the food pyramid is the largest and contains foods that we should eat in large amounts. As the pyramid gets higher, each layer gets progressively smaller to show the reduced quantities of food we should eat from each food group.

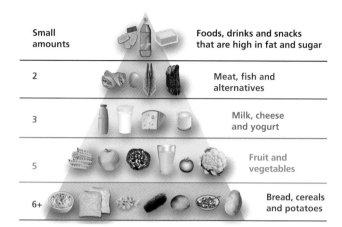

Figure 13.15 The food pyramid

Eatwell guide

The Eatwell guide helps to provide us with a picture of how a plate should be filled in line with the food pyramid to help to provide us with an idea of how much of each type of food we should be eating in order to have a balanced diet.

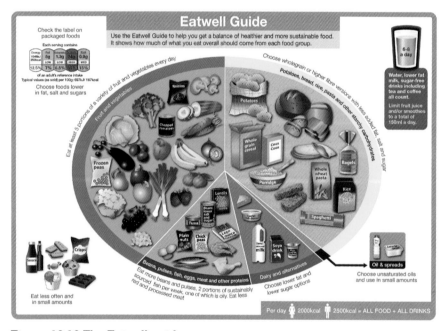

Figure 13.16 The Eatwell guide

Impact of food preparation on the nutritional composition of food

How food is prepared can have a significant impact on the nutritional composition of food and can result in some foods that are deemed healthy becoming unhealthy due to the nature of how it has been cooked.

Raw

On the whole, most fruits and vegetables are best eaten raw because raw food retains all of its

Activity

Copy and complete the table below with your food intake over the next three days:

Day	Breakfast	Lunch	Dinner	Fluids throughout the day	Snacks throughout the day	Calories	Macronutrients (g)	
							Carbs	
							Fats	
							Protein	
							Carbs	
							Fats	
							Protein	
							Carbs	
							Fats	
							Protein	

Table 13.14 Recording food intake

Where possible, try to weigh the food so you know how much you are eating.

When you have eaten any pre-prepared foods, look at the food label and include the calories and grams of each macronutrient in your table.

Work out if you are eating the right quantities of each macronutrient.

Where possible, explain how you can improve your diet.

nutritional value and does not add any additional calories to that food. However, it is best not to peel fruit and vegetables where possible as the majority of nutrients in vegetables, such as vitamins, are usually located close to the skin surface. Therefore, it is best to either wash fruit and vegetables thoroughly rather than peel them or to 'scrape' vegetables as this will reduce the amount of nutrients lost from the vegetable or fruit.

Boiled
Boiling foods can mean that some of the water-soluble vitamins can be lost as these can dissolve in the water. If foods do need to be boiled they should be boiled quickly to reduce nutrient loss and also the nutrient-laden water that they have been cooked should be used to make soup, stock or gravy.

Steamed
Steaming food does help to retain most of the nutritional benefits of foods as no water-soluble

vitamins are removed in this process. The process also does not add any kcalories to the food.

Grilled
The method of grilling food can be beneficial if foods such as meats that contain fat, for example sausages or beef burgers, are placed on a grilling tray. Some of the fat from the meat will drip out of the meat product, which means the food contains less fat, which on the whole is beneficial for a person wishing to reduce their kcalorie or fat intake.

Fried/roasted
In order to fry or roast food, there has to be the addition of some form of fat to the food so that it can cook in this manner. This means that the food contains a higher fat content after having been cooked in this way and can actually make healthy foods much less healthy when they are fried or roasted. For example, a boiled potato contains no fat, however, if the potato is cut up and fried to make chips, it then

has a very high fat content and is therefore much higher in kcalories than a boiled potato.

Baked

This method of cooking does not add any additional fat and as there is no water involved in the process, water-soluble vitamins will not be lost in the process.

Cured

Food that is cured has been through a process to preserve the food and add flavour. This usually means the addition of salt, sugar and sometimes nitrates or nitrites and can involve smoking the food. Examples of cured food include bacon, smoked salmon and pepperoni. Some of the processes involved in curing foods have been deemed unhealthy for a variety of reasons including some links to increasing the risk of certain types of cancer. Excess sugar and salt in the diet is also not good for a person so adding these to cured foods may mean a person ends up eating too much salt and sugar in their diet.

Processed foods

Processed foods are foods that have been physically or chemically changed so that they can be easily prepared and eaten, such as ready meals. Processed foods will often have additional ingredients added for flavour and to preserve them so that they will last longer on the shop shelf or in a person's fridge. They will often contain more salt than foods that have not been processed and can have other colours and flavour added to them to help them to look and taste better. We have come to accept foods to look a certain colour in order to match their flavour. Flavourings are added to improve the taste of the food. Monosodium glutamate is a popular type of flavouring found in many 'ready' meals. It is another source of salt and is commonly added to enhance the flavour of foods.

Juicing

This has become popular over the last few years and involves passing raw fruits and vegetables through a juicer which removes all of the pith and skin, etc. from the fruit or vegetable to leave just the juice. The juice will still retain a lot of the vitamins and minerals from the original fruit but all of the fibre from the fruit or vegetable is removed in this process.

C2 Benefits of a balanced diet

Weight maintenance

By eating a balanced diet, a person is more likely to be able to maintain a healthy weight which means that they have appropriate amounts of body fat for their age, gender and height. If a person eats too much of foods that are deemed unhealthy, the fats and sugars, then they will put on excess body fat which has been linked to a number of chronic diseases.

Reduced risk of chronic disease

Certain diseases have been linked to not eating a balanced diet. These diseases include:

- type II diabetes
- osteoporosis
- coronary heart disease
- cancer.

Type II diabetes

This condition occurs when a person's body does not react to insulin in the same way that it used to which means it is not able to remove glucose from the blood stream as efficiently as people without this condition. It can occur from eating too many sugary foods over time – each time a sugary food is eaten, insulin is released to remove this excess glucose to control the blood sugar level. Over time either less insulin is produced by the pancreas or the body becomes less sensitive to the effects of insulin so more has to be produced in order to remove glucose from the blood stream which is type II diabetes.

Osteoporosis

This is sometimes referred to as a 'thinning' of the bones which means the bones are become more fragile and less able to withstand impact so a person with osteoporosis is more likely to suffer a fracture if they fall over compared to a person without this condition.

It can occur for a number of reasons that are not related to a balanced diet; however, if a person does not consume appropriate intakes of vitamin D and calcium they may suffer from this condition.

Coronary heart disease (CHD)

This occurs when the coronary blood vessels that feed the heart with oxygen and nutrients become blocked. A diet high in saturated fat has been linked to increasing the risk of CHD.

Cancer

Eating an unhealthy diet which is low in fresh fruit and vegetables and high in fatty and sweet foods has been linked to an increased risk of cancer.

C3 Eating disorders

Definition of eating disorders and effect on health

Eating disorders are classed as psychological conditions and are treated through psychological intervention. Usually a combination of factors are responsible for eating disorders, these can include low self-esteem, problems with family or friends, lack of confidence or abuse. An eating disorder is often thought to give sufferers a form of control in their life.

The Eating Disorders Association estimates that around 165,000 people in the UK are suffering from anorexia nervosa or bulimia nervosa, with females aged between 15–25 being the most common age to be affected. However, the incidence of these eating disorders in males of a similar age is increasing.

Anorexia nervosa

This eating disorder is characterised by a form of self-starvation which may start out as a crash diet but then is continued for a prolonged period of time.

The signs and symptoms of anorexia nervosa are:

- extreme weight loss
- dehydration
- dizziness/fainting
- in females, loss of periods
- downy hair on body called lanugo
- distorted perception of body image
- mood swings
- a yellowish skin tone

- weakened immune system
- tooth decay
- lethargy
- low blood pressure
- heart failure
- kidney failure
- depression.

As the body needs energy to survive, it will start to break down its own body tissue in order to attain this energy. The heart muscle and other muscles are broken down which leads to heart damage and could lead to heart failure.

Bones are also affected by anorexia nervosa in that they will become more brittle as insufficient minerals are consumed. This means they are more likely to break – this bone condition is called osteoporosis. Osteoporosis is a condition that cannot be reversed even when the person has recovered from anorexia.

If a person suffering from anorexia is not treated, this disease will eventually result in their death.

Bulimia nervosa

This type of eating disorder is characterised by a person consuming large quantities of food (binge eating) followed by the use of laxatives, self-induced vomiting and/or excessive exercising in order to try to rid this body of the excessive calorie intake.

A person suffering from bulimia may well have a normal body weight and this condition can go unnoticed for prolonged periods of time. However, there are serious health problems associated with bulimia, these include:

- kidney and bowl problems from excessive use of laxatives
- tooth decay
- mouth ulcers
- sore throats
- frequent fluctuations in weight
- anxiety and/or depression
- heart failure
- choking
- lethargy

- in females, a loss of or irregular periods
- skin problems
- low blood pressure.

People suffering from bulimia will suffer from severe health problems including heart failure if left untreated.

Over eating

Most people enjoy the occasional indulgence in food that they know is not very good for them – chocolate and crisps are a popular choice for many. The occasional treat is fine, however, when it becomes a regular fixture in a person's diet and these treats are eaten in addition to regular meals then there is an issue of an eating disorder which is classed as over eating. Over eating is typically eating more calories per day than the body requires, the excess calories are then stored in the body as fat. Fat is stored both internally around body organs which is something that we cannot see and just underneath the skin which can be seen and felt. The majority of people who over eat do not have any hormone imbalances which make them eat excessively. One of the causes of over eating is 'comfort eating' and people do this because some foods increase the release of endorphins which are our feel good hormone and make us feel happy and content and/or eating distracts us from negative thoughts.

C Check your understanding

1 Describe the foods and quantity of each food on the Eatwell plate.
2 Identify what food groups should make up most of a person's diet in order for them to be eating a balanced diet.
3 Explain how the following methods of food preparation can negatively affect the nutritional content of food:
   a) Boiling
   b) Frying
   c) Curing.
4 Identify two methods of preparing food that can positively affect the nutritional content.
5 Describe the difference between anorexia nervosa and bulimia nervosa.

D Nutritional strategies for sports performance

D1 Nutritional strategies based on the demands of different sports

Nutritional strategies and the application of nutritional strategies for different sports event

Training, especially weight training to increase strength, is catabolic in nature because it causes damage to the muscles being trained. We know this has occurred because we tend to feel sore and stiff the next day until the body has repaired itself. The process of catabolism releases energy.

Key term

Catabolism refers to the breaking down of the structures of the body.

Anabolism refers to the building up of the structures of the body. When the body is resting and recovering it will be in an anabolic state and eating also promotes anabolism. While training is the stimulus to improving our fitness and strength of the body's structures, it is actually when we rest that the body builds up and becomes stronger. The process of anabolism requires energy.

When looking at different athletes' diets we need to give advice on two of the nutrients specifically. They are carbohydrate to replace the energy used and protein to replace the damage which has occurred to the body structures, primarily the skeletal muscle. Each sports performer will still require around 30% of kcals to come from fats with 10% from saturated fats, 10% from monounsaturated and 10% from polyunsaturated. They will still require at least five to nine portions of fruit and vegetables a day and enough water to replace their fluid loss.

Carbohydrate/glycogen loading

The store of carbohydrates in the body is relatively small, there is only enough stored to supply energy for around 90 minutes to 2 hours of moderate to high intensity exercise. Any athlete who is planning to compete in an endurance event which will last longer than 90 minutes, a marathon for example, would be able to exercise for longer and at a higher intensity if they were able to increase their body's store of carbohydrate. A strategy called 'carbohydrate loading' or 'glycogen loading' has been developed that allows an athlete to maximise their carbohydrate stores prior to competition. The strategy involves both training and nutritional changes over a four-day period immediately prior to competition. The athlete would taper his or her training over four days, for example a marathon runner would run 15 miles on day 1, 10 miles on day 2, 5 miles on day 3 and may then have a day of complete rest on day 4. On each of these days they would also consume higher than normal quantities of carbohydrates, around 10–12 g per kg of body weight.

Increased protein intake

People that take part in strength training or power related sports such as sprinting, shot put throwing, javelin throwing will need to increase their muscle size as larger muscles are able to produce more force which makes the athlete stronger and therefore more powerful.

The main role of protein in the diet is to provide the building material to help the body grow and repair itself. In order to increase the size of muscle tissue, a person must overload the tissue by lifting heavy weights. The process of lifting these weights will actually result in tiny microscopic tears in the muscle tissue. If you have taken part in weight training you may well feel sore and stiff afterwards and this feeling will last until the body has repaired itself. This muscle damage acts as the stimulus for the body to repair the muscle tissue and actually makes it larger than before training. In order for the muscle tissue to heal and grow, the athlete must rest and supply the body with sufficient quantities of protein and energy in the form of carbohydrates.

The amount of protein recommended depends on how much activity a person takes part in. The more exercise a person does, the more they break down muscle tissue and consequently the more protein they need in order to repair the muscle tissue. Research has found that protein is best utilised if it is taken in amounts of 30–35 g at a time. If a person was to eat more than this then the excess would be excreted or converted to fat and stored in the body. Therefore, increased protein intake should be spread out into a number of different meals and snacks, for example a power athlete that needs to eat 180 g of protein should consume six snacks and meals with 30 g of protein as opposed to three large protein meals.

Protein supplements

Some athletes may find it difficult to consume all their protein requirements from their daily food. Therefore, a range of protein supplements have been devised that deliver high concentrations of protein. These supplements are usually made out of powdered milk, eggs and/or Soya. Protein shakes are a popular choice with many power athletes as they contain plentiful supplies of amino acids and are quick and convenient to use. Protein bars are also available which deliver high concentrations of protein and low levels of carbohydrates with very little fat.

Weight loss

Some sports require the athlete to maintain a low body weight, for example a jockey or a gymnast. Other sports may require the athlete to lose weight prior to competition so that they may compete in lower weight category, for example boxing or judo. For these athletes, they will need to consume a diet that allows them to maintain their training levels but will also produce weight loss in the form of excess fat.

If the amount of energy taken in (via food) equals the amount expended (physical activity and BMR) then a person will remain at the weight they are. To lose weight energy intake must be less than energy expenditure and to gain weight energy intake must exceed expenditure. Therefore, in order to lose weight a person needs to reduce intake (eat less) and increase expenditure (do more physical activity).

To lose one pound in body weight (approximately 0.45 kg) the energy deficit needs to be around 3500 kcal. For example, if you expended 350 kcal more energy per day than you consumed you would have a daily deficit of 350 kcal. In ten days (10 x 350 = 3500) you would have a deficit of 3500 kcal and hence would have lost one pound in body weight.

To lose body weight, the athlete will need to burn up more calories than they consume. For many athletes a low fat diet would reduce their calorie intake yet still supply them with sufficient carbohydrates to maintain their energy requirements.

A typical low fat diet would incorporate consuming low fat alternatives, especially for dairy foods, for example, skimmed milk, low fat cheese, low fat yogurts, low fat cooking oils. Foods would also be cooked in such a way as to reduce the fat

Athlete group	Carbohydrate %	Protein %	Fat %	Kcals per kg of body weight
Triathlete				
M	66.2	11.6	21.2	62.0
F	59.2	11.8	29	57.4
Cyclists				
M	54.3	13.5	31.7	46.2
F	56.5	14.0	29.5	59.1
Swimmers				
M	50.3	15.0	34.7	45.3
F	49.3	14.2	36.5	55.6
Runners				
M	48.0	14.0	38.0	42.2
F	49.0	14.0	36.0	42.9
Basketball players				
M	49.0	15.0	36.0	32.0
F	45.3	16.0	34.7	45.6
Gymnasts				
M	49.8	15.3	34.9	37.8
F	44.0	15.0	39.0	53.3
Dancers				
M	50.2	15.4	34.4	34.0
F	38.4	16.5	45.1	51.7
Rowers				
M	54.2	13.4	23.7	46
F	55.8	15.3	30.3	58
Soccer players				
M	47	14	39	48
Weightlifters				
M	40.3	20.0	39.7	46.5
Marathon runners				
M	52	15	32	51

Table 13.15 A summary of the studies done into male and female athletes and the quantities of each macronutrient that should be consumed for optimal performance

content or certainly not add to it. For example, the athlete would eat baked potatoes with no additional butter as opposed to chips which are slices of deep fried potatoes. They should also have regular consumption of complex carbohydrates like potatoes and brown bread. Low-fat diets are usually quite filling because they involve eating large amounts of complex carbohydrates, which include fibre. Weight loss is steady at about 1.5 to 2 pounds per week. Most experts agree that faster weight loss is not sustainable as the weight lost is from the glycogen stores and not from the fat stores of the body.

Weight gain

In a minority of events it is necessary for an athlete to gain weight to increase their body fat percentage. A swimmer wishing to swim the English Channel, for example, will be advised to gain body fat for it to act as an insulator against the cold water so that the person is less likely to suffer from hypothermia while attempting their swim.

To gain weight, the person should maintain the percentage of each macro nutrient, however, they should just eat more of them so that they have a higher energy intake than expenditure which will then result in weight gain.

Daily intakes of energy, protein, fat and carbohydrate

Table 13.15 is a summary of the studies done into male and female athletes and the quantities of each macronutrient that should be consumed for optimal performance.

D2 Supplements to support nutritional strategies

A number of supplements have been produced to help to enhance sport and exercise performance which are legal for sports people to take in completion, but some do have specific levels of how much can be consumed prior to or during competition. Research indicates that most of these supplements can enhance performance but the supplement has to be specific to certain types of sport or exercise in order to be beneficial to performance.

Supplements and their effect on the body and health and benefits to sporting performance

Caffeine

Caffeine is found in coffee (100–150 mg) and tea (30–60 mg) and depending on the strength of the drink will determine how much caffeine each contains. Chocolate bars and cola drinks also contain caffeine at around 50 mg. Caffeine is also often added to sports and energy drinks.

Caffeine enhances endurance performance by increasing the alertness of a person as well as improving the mobilisation of fatty acids. This allows for the more efficient use of fat as an energy source during endurance exercise which has the effect of sparing glycogen reserves. It has also been shown to lower a sports person's perception of effort at a given work rate. For sports performers that need to be alert and have high reaction times, caffeine has been shown to improve reaction time and alertness.

Caffeine doses of 210–1050 mg, which is 3–15 mg per kg body weight, has been shown to have an ergogenic effect, the less sensitive a person is to caffeine the less they will need to have an ergogenic effect. The following side effects may be experienced by a person with a single intake of caffeine or after chronic use: diuretic, insomnia, anxiety, diarrhoea and hypertension.

Low to moderate caffeine consumption is permitted by the International Olympic Committee at a level in the urine of less than 12 mg per ml; any amount higher than this is considered doping and is not permitted.

Creatine

Creatine is a substance that can be eaten as a supplement or is found in meat and fish and research suggests that it can help to increase muscle mass and enhance sporting performance in sports that involve high intensify work periods such as interval sprints or weight lifting. This is a relatively new supplement so the long-term side effects are still not clear, however, short-term side effects can include weight gain, anxiety, diarrhoea, fatigue, stomach upset. Using creatine with other supplements such as caffeine has been shown to increase the risk of a person experiencing these side effects.

Creatine is a banned substance in France and cannot be sold in that country, however, it is currently permitted to be on sale in all other countries and is not on the banned substance list for WADA (see page 391).

Energy gels/glucose tablets

These supplements can be used by aerobic endurance athletes to try to spare muscle glycogen stores. When taking part in long distance events, the body will use glycogen as its main energy supply in order to supply energy at a moderate to high intensity. These stores are limited so by taking on glucose in the form of energy gels or tablets, the body will use this ingested source of glucose and spare the muscle glycogen stores while it is utilising these supplements.

An energy gel is a mixture between a sports drink and an energy bar, sort of like a runny jelly. They contain high levels of carbohydrate and very little protein and fat. Many athletes choose to consume these during exercise as they deliver higher levels of carbohydrate than sports drinks, are easy and quick to consume and cause little or no stomach discomfort. Most energy gel manufactures advise that athletes should drink some water with every energy gel consumed in order to help digestion and maintain hydration levels. The general recommended amount is to consume 30–60 g per hour. Some people prefer to consume the gel where as others prefer the tablets.

Protein shakes/powders/branched-chain amino acids (BCAA)

These supplements are used by athletes who want to lay down more muscle and need to gain more protein on a daily basis. Protein shakes are usually high in whey protein because it contains high levels of three essential amino acids which are branched-chain amino acids: leucine, isoleucine and valine. These are important because they are the amino acids which are broken down most during training.

Protein shakes will contain plentiful supplies of amino acids and are quick and convenient to use. However, there are several issues to consider:

- The human body has evolved to gain its protein from natural rather than processed sources (meats rather than powders).

- They often contain additives such as sweeteners, sugars, colourings.
- The process of drying the proteins into powder form damages the structure of amino acids making them unusable by the body.
- They are often very expensive.

Activity: Make your own protein shake

It is possible to make your own protein shake. This will supply you with 35 g of protein and cost much less than the commercial protein shakes.

Equipment

50 g dried skimmed milk powder

500 ml fresh milk

Flavoured milk shake powder (these come in a range of flavours including strawberry, banana and chocolate – choose the flavour that appeals to your taste).

Method

1. Mix the dried skimmed milk powder in a bowl with some of the milk.
2. Place the dried skimmed milk paste, the rest of the milk and the milk shake powder into a blender, or use a hand blender until thoroughly mixed and frothy.

You may like to add further flavours to your protein shake by including honey and/or fresh fruit such as bananas or strawberries.

Beetroot juice

This is a relatively new supplement on the market and has been shown to help to improve some aerobic endurance performances. Beetroot juice contains nitrous oxide which has the effect of vasodilating blood vessels leading in the skeletal muscles which helps to increase blood flow to that area. This in turn will help to increase the delivery of oxygen and nutrients to the working muscles and remove the waste products, all of which will improve sporting performance. 300–500 ml of beetroot juice is the recommended amount to show an increase in sports performance. The supplement is legal to be used in sports competitions and currently there is no set limit for how much an athlete can consume prior to or during completion (where drinks are permitted).

Diuretics

Diuretics act to help increase the excretion of fluids from body tissues and to help reduce high blood pressure and these are banned in sports related competitions in accordance with World Anti-Doping Agency (WADA).

One of the main reasons diuretics are misused by athletes is to reduce their body weight quickly in sports where weight categories are involved. Hence, boxers, weightlifters or judo competitors may take this drug in order to remain in their weight category. If their body weight is only slightly above the category lower limit, they will be competing against athletes who are larger than them and, therefore, also presumably have a greater muscle mass, which would leave the athlete at a disadvantage. Athletes may also take diuretics in order to reduce the concentration of other banned substances by diluting the urine, or to attempt to eliminate the banned substance from their body in order to escape detection of the drug through testing. The possible side effects of taking diuretics include dehydration, which could then lead to dizziness and fainting, vomiting and muscle cramps. If the athlete becomes severely dehydrated through taking the diuretics, the effect on the kidneys and the heart could lead to death.

Vitamin supplements

There is some debate as to whether it is beneficial to supplement athletes' diets with vitamin and mineral supplement. The general consensus is that it is better for an athletes to gain their vitamins and minerals from the usual food sources and if the diet is balanced and varied then vitamin and mineral supplementation is unnecessary.

Some vitamins though act as anti-oxidants which limit the damage caused by free radicals. Free radicals are molecules with an unpaired electron. Most molecules have paired electrons and an unpaired electron makes them unstable so they will try to steal an electron from other molecules. This causes damage to cells and is linked to heart disease and cancer. Oxygen produces free radicals that will attack cells, nerves and joints and damage them. The more oxygen that is taken on then the more damage that will be produced. This is why athletes that take part in aerobic endurance events are at a greater risk of free radical damage due to the extra oxygen taken in during exercise. The body is able to neutralise most free radicals, as long as we have plenty of fruit and vegetables in the diet. Vitamins A, C, E and the minerals zinc and selenium are referred to as the antioxidants as they provide the greatest defence against free radical damage. Some nutritionists will advise endurance aerobic athletes to take these antioxidant vitamin and mineral supplements as additional protection against free radicals.

Nutritional supplements and competition regulations according to World Anti-Doping Agency (WADA)

The practice of using banned substances to enhance athletic performance is called doping. The first drug tests on athletes were conducted at the Olympic Games in Mexico, in 1968. Since then, drug testing has become a major part of sporting competition. WADA was established in 1999 and in 2004 created a World Anti-Doping Code which covers anti-doping policies and rules and regulations within sport on anti-doping. This code is reviewed and updated in line with new research into doping. The majority of all sporting events and organisations have accepted this code and all athletes taking part in sporting events run by these organisations much follow the requirements of the code in order to compete. In accordance with the code, athletes are tested for doping while they are training as well as during competition.

Quantities permitted in training and competition

Some substances are only permitted in set amounts when a person is training and competing such as caffeine, where as other substances have no set limit and athletes are free to use as much as they would like, such as energy gels and protein shakes. The main concern is that athletes are not gaining an unfair advantage over athletes from taking a particular supplement. The code set by WADA, including the banned substances and set limits, helps to try to ensure athletes when they are training and competing are not cheating.

Banned substances

There is a long list of banned substances which is updated regularly as new research and new products arrive on the market.

The majority of banned ergogenic aids used by athletes today were initially designed by the medical profession in order to treat patients with various illnesses or disorders. Many types of drugs are available to the athlete, and what they take is determined by the sport in which they compete. The main effects of the different groups of drugs are to:

- build muscle mass
- increase the oxygen carrying capacity of blood
- provide pain relief
- stimulate the body
- relax.

Building muscle mass

Athletes competing in sports that require a high muscle mass, such as weightlifting, throwing events, sprinting, or boxing, may take muscle building drugs. There are a variety of drugs available that will increase the muscle mass of an athlete, including anabolic steroids, human growth hormone (hGH) and insulin.

Anabolic steroids

Anabolic steroids are man-made substances. They were developed in the late 1930s primarily to treat hypogonadism, which is a condition in which the testes do not produce enough testosterone. This reduction in testosterone production resulted in impaired growth, development and sexual functioning. It was later discovered that anabolic steroids could not only treat males with hypogonadism, but could also increase the growth of skeletal muscle in humans.

Athletes and others abuse anabolic steroids to enhance performance and improve physical appearance. However, just taking anabolic steroids will not increase muscle bulk; the athlete must still train hard in order to achieve an increase in muscle mass. The main advantage in taking these drugs is that the muscles recover more quickly from training. This will allow the athlete to train at a higher level and for longer than if they were not taking these drugs.

The main disadvantages of taking anabolic steroids are:

- liver and kidney tumours
- jaundice
- high blood pressure
- severe acne
- trembling.

There are also some sex-specific side effects.

Males:

- shrinking of the testicles
- reduced sperm count
- infertility, baldness
- development of breasts
- increased risk for prostate cancer.

Females:

- growth of facial hair
- male-pattern baldness
- changes in or cessation of the menstrual cycle
- enlargement of the clitoris
- deepened voice.

Scientific research also shows that aggression and other psychiatric side effects may result from abuse of anabolic steroids. Depression can be experienced when the person stops taking the drugs and may contribute to them becoming dependent on anabolic steroids.

Human growth hormone (hGH)

Human growth hormone (also known as human chorionic gonadotropin, hCG) is a naturally occurring protein hormone produced by the pituitary gland and is important for normal human growth and development, especially in children and teenagers. Low hGH levels in children and teenagers result in dwarfism. Growth hormone stimulates the development of natural male and female sex hormones.

Growth hormone is not banned for female athletes because it would not lead to muscle development and might naturally occur in high levels if the athlete is pregnant. In males, growth hormone acts to increase testosterone levels and results in increased muscle development, as with anabolic steroids. Excessive growth hormone levels increase muscle mass by stimulating protein synthesis, strengthen bones by stimulating bone growth and reduce body fat by stimulating the breakdown of fat cells. The side effects of growth hormone in males are the same as those of anabolic steroids together with enlarged internal organs. The athlete taking the drug may also develop acromegaly, which results in the person's hands, feet and lower jaw growing much larger than normal. If a person's lower jaw grows faster than the rest of the bones of the face, their teeth will become misaligned and they will often need to wear braces.

Insulin

Insulin is produced naturally in the body by the pancreas. Its main function is to help to control the concentration of sugar within the blood stream. If there is too much sugar, insulin acts to remove this sugar by stimulating the synthesis of glycogen or fat. Athletes may take insulin in combination with anabolic steroids or growth hormone as it also helps to increase muscle mass by stimulating protein synthesis. The main side effects of abusing insulin are hypoglycaemic responses such as shaking, nausea and weakness. If too much insulin is taken this may lead to severe hypoglycaemia, which could lead to coma and death.

Increasing oxygen carrying capacity of blood

Athletes competing in endurance sports are the principal abusers of drugs that increase the oxygen supply to their muscle tissues. There are two main methods of increasing the oxgyen supply to the tissue, these are by taking erythropoietin (rhEPO) or by blood doping.

Erythropoietin

rhEPO is a naturally occurring protein hormone that is secreted by the kidneys. After being released into the blood stream it acts on the bone marrow, where it stimulates the production of red blood cells (erythrocytes). Medically, EPO is used to treat certain forms of anaemia.

Since EPO increases a person's red blood cell count, it will result in increased blood haemoglobin concentrations. Therefore, after taking EPO, a person's blood will have an increased oxygen-carrying capacity which potentially has the effect of increasing an athlete's performance. Endurance

athletes, such as those who compete in marathons, the Tour de France, cross-country skiing, and so on can use EPO to increase their oxygen supply by as much as 10%.

EPO is difficult to detect because it is identical to the naturally occurring form produced by the body. As there is no established normal concentration range of EPO it is very difficult to determine if an athlete has been using EPO.

The main side effect of taking EPO is an increase in the 'thickness' of the blood. This thickened blood will not flow through the blood vessels very well because it has a greater resistance. As a result, the heart must work harder to pump blood around the body, which will increase the chances of the athlete suffering from a heart attack.

Pain relief

At some point in their career, most athletes will probably suffer from a sport injury. If this injury occurs during competition, athletes may try to mask their injury pain with drugs, such as narcotics, cortisone and local anaesthetics. Narcotics are taken in order to reduce the amount of pain felt from injury or can be used as recreational drugs. The main narcotics used are morphine, methadone and heroin. They act to give the person a 'high', which helps to mask the pain of the injury. Narcotics will affect a person's mental abilities, such as balance and co-ordination, which may have a detrimental effect on performance. In addition, athletes who continue to compete with a sport injury run the risk of further damage or complications to the injured area.

Stimulants

The main stimulants used by athletes are amphetamines. Stimulants act to mimic the action of the sympathetic nervous system.

Stimulates have the effect of constricting the blood vessels supplying blood to skin, dilating the blood vessels supplying the heart and skeletal muscles, dilating the bronchioles to increase ventilation and increasing the release of glucose from the liver. They have the effect of increasing a person's mental alertness and also help to conceal feelings of exhaustion. As a result, athletes competing in endurance events, contact sports, or those demanding fast reactions may take stimulants in order to enhance their performance.

As stimulants hide feelings of fatigue, it is possible for athletes to over-exert themselves to the point where they can suffer heat stroke and cardiac failure. Other side effects include increased blood pressure and body temperature, increased and irregular heartbeat, aggression, anxiety and loss of appetite. If an athlete requires medication to treat asthma or other common respiratory disorders they are at risk of inadvertently taking stimulants as these commonly prescribed substances often contain powerful stimulants.

Beta blockers

Beta blockers are medically used to treat heart disease, to lower heart rate and blood pressure and reduce anxiety. These drugs act to interfere with actions of the sympathetic nervous system, which controls involuntary muscle movement.

Beta blockers slow the heart rate, relax muscle in blood vessel walls, and decrease the force of heart contractions. Athletes may use these drugs in sport in order to reduce anxiety levels and to prevent their body from shaking. As a result, athletes who take part in sports that require steady nerves and hands (e.g. snooker, archery, shooting and darts) may abuse this type of drug.

The side effects of taking this drug include lowered blood pressure, slow heart rate and tiredness. In extreme cases, the heart may actually stop because it has been slowed down too much.

D3 Nutritional intake during different phases of event

Phases of event

For most sporting athletes there are three main phases of an event that they need to consider when and what they are going to consume in order to gain the optimal nutritional benefits.

These phases are:

1 **pre-event** – the first 2–3 hours before the event starts

2 **during event** – while the athlete is exercising as in during a marathon, or when they are

on a break during the event (e.g. a football tournament between games)

3 **post-event** – what the athlete consumes for the first 2 hours after the event.

The types of food and fluid to be consumed during each phase, the timings of the intake, and the appropriate supplements are covered below.

Pre-event

There are three aims of the food consumed before the event which include:

- To ensure the glycogen stores are well stocked
- To ensure blood glucose levels are stable
- To ensure the body is well hydrated.

This will ensure that the athlete feels energised and motivated for their training session or performance. It is best to avoid fats and proteins pre-exercise because they take a long time to be digested.

On the day of the competition an athlete should eat a high carbohydrate meal 3 to 4 hours prior to the event. This will give the body time to digest the meal and top up carbohydrate stores. The meal should be carbohydrate rich at around 150–300 g so that it provides the athlete with 3–4 g carbohydrate per kg of their body weight. Therefore, for an athlete weighing 70 kg, they would need to consume a meal with around 210 g of carbohydrate. It is also important to ensure that there are enough vitamins and minerals in the meal to allow glucose to be converted into energy. There is some controversy as to whether carbohydrate should be high or low GI and based on the available evidence, low GI meals appear to be better as they produce a sustained source of glucose for the exercise to come.

Some athletes benefit from consuming a high carbohydrate snack 60 to 30 minutes prior to competition. The snack should provide around 70 g of carbohydrate such as a carbohydrate energy bar. Some athletes suffer from abdominal cramps if they eat so close to an event; if this is the case, it is best not to consume a high carbohydrate snack.

Athletes that take part in sports that require strength or power may include some protein in their pre-exercise meal so that they have available amino acids to replace those damaged during the event. It is also important to ensure optimal hydration by continually sipping water in the two hours before exercise.

Pre-exercise meals need to be experimented with as foods will have different impacts on different people. Some foods will make you energised and some will make you feel fatigued. If you arrive at the event feeling fatigued or unmotivated it may be that the pre-exercise meal is not appropriate. Some athletes find that fructose from fruit can cause stomach disturbances and are best avoided.

During the event

Aerobic endurance exercise at a high intensity will reduce glycogen stores by around 55% an hour and after 2 hours they will be fully depleted. Therefore any athlete training or competing for more than an hour and a half is recommended to take on carbohydrates during performance. By eating carbohydrates during exercise, the body will use this as a fuel and this will therefore help to conserve their glycogen stores. In order to help to prevent nausea and stomach cramps, athletes should consume simple carbohydrates; many prefer sports drinks as these will not only serve to supply the body with carbohydrates but will also help to keep them hydrated during the event. Some athletes do use sweets like jelly beans to provide glucose quickly. Adding small amounts of protein can also help to reduce time to fatigue at a ratio of roughly 3:1 in favour of carbohydrates. Whatever the preferred source of carbohydrates, athletes should aim to consume around 30–60 g of carbohydrates per hour of exercise in order to delay the depletion of their body's store of carbohydrate stores.

During event eating needs to be practised because if something new is tried out during a competitive event it may have negative consequences for the athlete.

Post event

The priority post event is to replace the depleted glycogen stores and replace fluids lost through sweating. During the first two hours immediately after exercise or competition, your body is able to convert carbohydrates into glycogen at a very fast rate. Glycogen storage is at its fastest in the first two hours after exercise – a time frame which is

described by athletes as a 'golden window'. 50–75 g of high or moderate GI carbohydrates, which works out at 1–1.2 g of carbohydrates per kg of your body weight, should be consumed in the first 15 minutes after exercise and then another dose of 50–75 g in the next two hours. If glycogen stores have been completely depleted it may be necessary to keep refuelling by eating additional doses of 50–75 g of carbohydrates every two hours. Most people do not feel like eating a large carbohydrate meal after exercise; many prefer to eat a series of carbohydrate snacks and sports drinks, for example isotonic sports drinks and a currant bun or carbohydrate bar. Carbohydrate bars and energy gels are also popular choices. Some athletes eat fresh fruit and yogurt after exercise as these provide additional vitamins and minerals as well as protein in the yogurt.

Strength and power event athletes will often take on a protein shake as it provides them with amino acids that can be taken on very quickly. Protein shakes tend to made of whey protein that has high levels of branch chain amino acids (BCAAs) as these are heavily catabolised during exercise and need to be replaced.

D Check your understanding

1 Describe a suitable nutritional strategy for an athlete who is due to take part in a long distance cycle race.

2 Explain a suitable nutritional strategy for a weightlifter.

3 Explain a suitable nutritional strategy for a boxer trying to reduce their weight to be able to enter into a specific weight category event.

4 Describe a sport where performers may benefit from taking creatine.

5 Explain how caffeine could improve the performance of a marathon runner.

6 Describe three banned substances and which sports athletes may try to use them to cheat and gain an advantage.

7 Explain what foods a tri-athlete should consume:

   a) before the event

   b) during the event

   c) after the event.

Further reading

Burke, L., and Cox, G. (2007). *The Complete Guide to Food and Sports Performance*. Crows Nest, Australia, Allen and Unwin.

Jeukendrup, A., and Gleeson, M. (2010). *Sports Nutrition: an introduction to energy production and performance (Second edition)*, Champaign, IL. Human Kinetics.

McArdle, W.D., Katch, F.I. and Katch, V.L. (2013). *Sports and Exercise Nutrition (Fourth edition)*, Baltimore, Lippincott, Williams and Wilkins.

Williams, M.H. (2007). *Nutrition for Health, Fitness, & Sport*. New York, McGraw-Hill.

References

American College of Sports Medicine: www.acsm.org/

Bean, A. (2013). *The complete guide to sports nutrition (Seventh edition)*, London, Bloomsbury.

McArdle, W.D., Katch, F.I. and Katch, V.L. (2013). *Sports and Exercise Nutrition (Fourth edition)*, Baltimore, Lippincott, Williams and Wilkins.

WADA prohibited list: www.usada.org/wp-content/uploads/wada-2016-prohibited-list-en.pdf

Useful websites

British Nutrition Foundation
www.nutrition.org.uk/

Canadian Centre for Ethics in Sport
www.cces.ca/en/nutrition

Real Meal Revolution
http://realmealrevolution.com/

Science in Sport
www.scienceinsport.com/sports-nutrition/

Australian Institute of Sport (Nutrition)
www.ausport.gov.au/ais/nutrition

Index

Photo credits

Figures:

1.18 © wareham.nl (sport)/Alamy Stock Photo; 1.19 © PHILIPPE PSAILA/SCIENCE PHOTO LIBRARY; 1.23 © Errol Brown/Alamy Stock Photo; 1.24 © Simon Balson/Alamy Stock Photo; 1.25 © Mediscan/Alamy Stock Photo; 2.49 © Mike Powell/Allsport Concepts/Getty Images; 4.12 © David Madison/Photographer's Choice/Getty Images; 4.19 © Bill Wippert/National Hockey League/Getty Images; 4.23 © BanksPhotos/E+/Getty Images; 4.25 © michael Gray/123RF; 4.27 © Dennis MacDonald/Alamy Stock Photo; 4.28 © Roman Milert/123RF; 4.32 © Javier Larrea/age fotostock/Getty Images; 4.33 © Science Photo Library/Getty Images; 6.1a © Trinity Mirror/Mirrorpix/Alamy Stock Photo; 6.1b © epa european pressphoto agency b.v./Alamy Stock Photo; 6.3 © VI Images/Getty Images; 6.4 © GUSTOIMAGES/Science Photo Library/Getty Images; 7.1 © Cosmo Condina/Alamy Stock Photo; 7.6 © Simon McIntyre/Alamy Stock Photo; 7.12a © technotr/iStockphoto.com; 7.12b © Action Plus Sports Images/Alamy Stock Photo; 7.13 © speedpix/Alamy Stock Photo; 7.17 © Oleksandr Lysenko/123 RF; 7.18 © kho/123RF; 8.1 © Action Plus/The Image Bank/Getty Images; 8.3 © Wavebreak Media Ltd/123RF; 8.4 © joSon/The Image Bank/Getty Images; 8.5 © Jozef Polc/123RF; 8.6 © AFP/Getty Images; 8.7 © Cultura Creative (RF)/Alamy Stock Photo; 8.9a © Dmytro Panchenko/123RF; 8.9b © dolgachov/123RF; 8.9c © Michael Stuparyk/Toronto Star/Getty Images; 10.15 © Alex Maxim/123RF; 10.16 © ljupco/123RF; 10.18 © Mark Herreid/123RF; 12.1 © Courtesy of This Girl Can; 13.4 © Art Directors & TRIP/Alamy Stock Photo; 13.7 © Africa Studio - Fotolia; 13.10a © alex9500/123RF; 13.10b © TATUYOSHI TORIU/123RF; 13.11 © Image Source/Alamy Stock Photo; 13.16 © Crown copyright. Public Health England in association with the Welsh government, the Scottish government and the Food Standards Agency in Northern Ireland; 14.1 © Linda Steward/Getty Images; 14.2 © JACK GUEZ/Getty Images; 14.3 © Homer W Sykes/Alamy Stock Photo; 14.4 © technotr/Vetta/Getty Images; 14.5a-c © Runnersneed.com; 14.6a © Corbis Super RF/Alamy Stock Photo; 14.6b © Vladimir Galkin/Alamy Stock Photo; 14.7 © Gennadiy Poznyakov/123RF; 14.8a © Courtesy of Bioflow Ltd.; 14.8b © Courtesy of Bioflow Ltd.; 14.9 © John Leyba/The Denver Post/Getty Images; 14.10a © Jordan Mansfield/Getty Images; 14.10b © SpecialistStock/REX/Shutterstock; 14.11a © Bicipici/Alamy Stock Photo; 14.11b © Popperfoto/Getty Images; 14.12a © GP Library Limited/Alamy Stock Photo; 14.12b © National Motor Museum/Heritage Images/Getty Images; 14.13 © Sport Picture Library/Alamy Stock Photo; 14.14a © Peter Werner/Alamy Stock Photo; 14.14b © Julian Rovagnati/123RF; 14.15 © CandyBox Images/Alamy Stock Photo; 14.16 © Lars Baron/FIFA/Getty Images; 14.17 © Quintic; 14.18 © www.kinovea.org; 14.19 © Yoon S. Byun/The Boston Globe via Getty Images; 14.20 © Stuart Franklin/Getty Images; 14.21a © Handout/Omega via Getty Images; 14.21b © Ian Walton/Getty Images; 14.22a © ZUMA Press Inc/Alamy Stock Photo; 14.22b © Yaacov Dagan/Alamy Stock Photo; 15.7 © ocskaymark/123RF; 15.14 ©Jozef Polc/123RF; 15.25 © ullstein bild/Getty Images; 15.26 © JOHN THYS/REPORTERS/SCIENCE PHOTO LIBRARY.